卢福波

　　1954年12月出生于大连。博士学位。现任南开大学汉语言文化学院教授，对外汉语系主任，研究生导师。主要研究兴趣有：对外汉语教学语法研究、汉语语法、语义、语用研究。研究成果获得过多种奖项，2002年曾获国家汉办颁发的"全国对外汉语教学优秀教师奖"。曾赴韩国、日本、德国讲学并参加国际学术会议。

　　主要研究成果有：《对外汉语教学语法研究》《对外汉语教学实用语法》《〈对外汉语教学实用语法〉练习参考答案及要解》《HSK精解活页题选》等多部著作；在《世界汉语教学》《语言教学与研究》《语言文字应用》等学术刊物发表论文30余篇；主持过多项国家、学校重点教学研究项目。

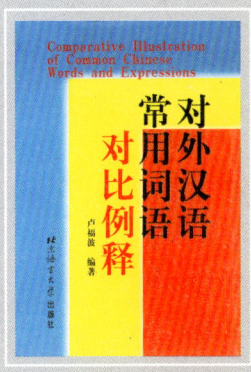

本书2000年首次印刷时所用封面

对外汉语常用词语对比例释

Comparative Illustrations of Common Chinese Words and Expressions

卢福波　　编　著
洪惠玲　刘　萍　英文翻译

北京语言大学出版社
BEIJING LANGUAGE AND CULTURE
UNIVERSITY PRESS

图书在版编目（CIP）数据

对外汉语常用词语对比例释/卢福波编著.
－北京：北京语言大学出版社，2008重印
ISBN 978-7-5619-0879-2

Ⅰ．对…
Ⅱ．卢…
Ⅲ．对外汉语教学－词汇－教学参考资料
Ⅳ．H195.3
中国版本图书馆CIP数据核字（2000）第39543号

书　　名：	对外汉语常用词语对比例释
责任印制：	汪学发

出版发行：北京语言大学出版社

社　　址：	北京市海淀区学院路15号　邮政编码100083
网　　址：	http://www.blcup.com
电　　话：	发行部　82303650/3591/3651
	编辑部　82303647
	读者服务部　82303653/3908
印　　刷：	北京画中画印刷有限公司
经　　销：	全国新华书店
版　　次：	2000年12月第1版　2008年1月第4次印刷
开　　本：	787毫米×1092毫米　1/32　印张：24.5
字　　数：	617千字　印数：8501-10500册
书　　号：	ISBN 978-7-5619-0879-2/H·0064
定　　价：	49.00元

凡有印装质量问题，本社负责调换。电话：82303590

序

凡是参与过对外汉语教学工作的人,都一定曾体会到对外国学生讲解汉语词语的困难。尤其是词义和用法相近的词语,要说清楚它们的区别,有时费尽九牛二虎之力,效果却不见得好。这是从教师角度说的。从学生的角度说,由于他们的汉语语感还比较薄弱,对词语的理解和运用往往会出问题;尤其对意义和用法相近的词更不容易分辨其间的区别,因此使用起来往往出错。以上情况说明,无论从教或学的角度看,都很需要对意义和用法相近的词语进行对比分析、解说的工具书性质的著作。不错,国内已经出版了几种同义词词典,但正如卢福波女士所说,这些词典都是为中国人写的,即为对汉语有丰富语感的人写的,所以其分析、解释都很难为外国学生所理解。他们使用这种词典会遇到很大困难。所以从对外汉语教学的角度来看,急需一种以外国人学汉语为对象的词语对比分析的工具书。卢福波女士的这部《对外汉语常用词语对比例释》正适应了这种需要,因而我相信这部书一定会受到对外汉语教师和外国学生的欢迎。

我有幸读了这部书的部分样稿,感到此书有以下几个特色:

1. 从实用出发,把相关的词语编成组,进行对比分析,特别在如何使用上下功夫,因而显得分外实用。一般同义词词典进行分组时都有严格的理论标准,比如词性要同一。这样做在该种词典中是必要的,但对于对外汉语教学来说,就显得拘泥了,因为外国学生发生的问题并不限于同一词性的范围之内。因此

I

本书打破这个框框,按照实际需要进行分组,只要是容易相混、容易出问题的,都收在一起进行比较分析,因此其实用性就大大增强了。

2. 从分布上讲解词语用法,而不限于单纯对词义解释。这样使解说更准确,又使学生容易掌握。例如"才、都、就",这组词是带有主观评价性质的词,用法比较复杂。如按词典义项的分法去讲,将会很烦琐,读者也不易记。本书作者将它分成几种格式:

"时间、数量词语等+才……""时间、数量词语等+就……"

"才+时间、数量词语等……就……"

"都+时间、数量词语等……了,才……"

然后对每种形式所表示的意义进行对比分析,说明其意义的区别,效果就好多了。

3. 对比分析十分详细、周到,对组内各词在词义、用法上的细微差别都详加解说;同时进行正误对比,很容易为读者理解。

本书的优点还很多,这里就不一一赘述。细心的读者一定还会发现更多的优点。

从上述可以看出,作者写作此书是花了大量心血的。有过编工具书经验的人都知道,如果是创造性地进行工作,而不是陈陈相因地抄袭,此项工作是既烦琐又艰难的。没有足够耐心和相当的积累,是做不好这项工作的,何况本书又是面向对外汉语的开创之作呢?卢福波女士积多年的教学工作经验,积累了正反两方面的大量材料,又经过细心的对比分析,终于完成了这部辞书性质的著作。她的努力和贡献是应该得到充分的肯定的。我认为这部书对对外汉语教学将会产生较大的积极的影响。

从事语言研究的朋友们也会从此书中得到一定的启发。所以此书也具有一定的学术价值。

　　大作完成后,作者嘱我写几句话以为序。我就就我所见写了如上的一些话,不见得准确,尚希读者诸君批评指正。

宋 玉 柱

1997年酷暑中写于南开园

Preface

Those who have engaged in teaching Chinese as a foreign language must have experienced the difficulty in explaining Chinese words and expressions to foreign students. It is especially difficult to explain the distinction among words and expressions with similar meanings and usages. Sometimes teachers have to spend a great deal of efforts in explaining the distinction but may not achieve good results. That is from the point of view of teachers. From the angle of students, since their language sense in Chinese is rather weak, they often have difficulties in understanding and using words and expressions, and it is especially hard for them to make a distinction among those with similar meanings and usages, which may often cause mistakes in using the language. The above shows that from the perspective of both teaching and learning, there is a great need of reference books that can give comparative analyses and explanations of words and expressions with similar meanings and usages. Several synonym dictionaries have been published in China, nevertheless, just as Ms. Lu Fubo has said, these dictionaries are written for Chinese, namely those who have strong language sense in Chinese, thus its analyses and explanations are difficult for foreign students to understand. Therefore, from the perspective of teaching Chinese as a foreign language, reference books intended for foreigners which offer comparative analyses of words are badly needed. *Comparative Illustrations of Common Chinese Words and Expressions* by Ms. Lu Fubo meets this need, and I believe that this book will surely be welcomed by both teachers who teach Chinese as a foreign language and foreign students.

Having read part of this book, I feel this book possesses the following characteristics:

Ⅰ. Based on practical use, the author puts related words into groups and gives comparative analyses, with a special emphasis on how to use them, which proves to be very practical. Common synonym dictionaries follow strict theoretical standards when putting words into groups. For example, words in the same group should have the same part of speech. This method is necessary in this kind of dictionaries, but it seems too rigid in the field of teaching Chinese as a foreign language, as foreign students' problems may not necessarily exist among words of the same part of speech. Thus, this book gets rid of the stereotype and puts the words into groups according to practical need. Words that may be easily confused or may cause problems are put together for comparative analyses, thus its practicality is greatly improved.

Ⅱ. The author gives explanations of word usages in terms of distribution, not limited to simple explanations of word meanings, which makes the explanation more precise and also easier for students to master. For instance, the words "才,都,就" as a group have subjective and evaluative sense and are rather complicated in usage. If explanations are given according to the semantic items as listed in dictionary entries, they will be rather complex and difficult to remember. The author of this book has divided this group into several patterns:

"Time or numeral-classifier compound + 才…"

"Time or numeral-classifier compound + 就…"

"才 + time or numeral-classifier compound…就…"

"都 + time or numeral-classifier compound…了, 才…"

Then comparative analyses are made on the meanings conveyed by each pattern, with explanations of the differences among the meanings, thus achieving much better results.

Ⅲ. Comparative analysis is very detailed and comprehensive, with detailed explanation of the minute differences among each word in the group in terms of their meanings and usages. Meanwhile, right and wrong usages are offered, which makes it easy for readers to understand.

The book has many more advantages, which will not be elaborated here. And it is my belief that readers will certainly find more merits.

From the above, it can be seen that the author has spent great efforts writing this book. Anyone who has compiled reference books knows that this kind of work is complicated and tough if one works creatively rather than copy, and that one cannot do this job well without enough patience and accumulation. Ms. Lu Fubo, who has many years of teaching experience and has accumulated rich materials, has finished this work, only after much careful comparative analyses. Her efforts and contribution should be acknowledged. I believe that this book will exert significant influences on teaching Chinese as a foreign language. Scholars who are engaged in language research will surely get certain enlightenment from this book, so this book is also of scholastic value.

Having completed this book, the author asked me to write a few words as the preface. I have written the above sentences, which may not be precise. It is open to your comment.

Song Yuzhu
Nankai University, summer,1997

前　言

《对外汉语常用词语对比例释》是一部具有学习和参考价值的辞书性著作，它的主要使用对象是把汉语作为外语或第二语言的学习者、从事对外汉语教学与研究的教师和研究生等。它是将现代汉语中一部分最常用的、意义相近的或有相似点的词语分组进行对比分析，指出意义上、色彩上、搭配上、使用上的异同，以便学生正确理解、掌握与使用，为教师教学与研究提供参考。

到目前为止，词语辨析类工具书国内已出版了几部，最有代表性的要算刘叔新先生主编的《现代汉语同义词词典》，此外汉语综合性工具书中由冯志纯、周行健先生主编的《新编汉语多功能词典》也对大量词语进行了辨析，那么为什么还要写这部书呢？这主要是因为使用对象的不同。现有的此类书主要是以操汉语的中国人为对象编写的，因此无论是选词范围、分析角度，还是例句选用都以汉语语感丰富的中国人的理解、体味及存在的问题为切入点和研究点，这往往解决不了外国留学生存在的问题。外国留学生遇到的词与词的对比，常常并不局限在同一词性上，如："怕"、"害怕"与"可怕"，"全体"、"全部"与"整个"，"希望"与"愿望"，"友好"与"友谊"等；有些词意义上似乎不那么相近，如："想"与"要"、"还是"与"或者"、"知道"与"了解"、"问"与"打听"、"教"与"请教"、"信心"与"决心"等；有些词用法上完全混为一谈，如："见"与"见面"、"看"与"看见"、"帮"与"帮忙"、"送"与"送行"；还有很多弄不清的意义虚的或较虚的词，如："再"、"又"、"也"等，"很"、"真"、"太"等，"对"、"对于"、"跟"、"朝"、"向"、"往"等，"的"、"了"等等。外国学生对于这些词不是理解了就会用，因为语感达不到，往往需要有具体规则帮助他们把握可用或不可用的情况，用具体例子告诉他们可取与不可取的用法,这些是一般的辨析词典几乎不涉及的问题,也是编写这部书的难点、重点所在。外国留学生遇到的难题,常常也是教师的难题。因为一般的工具书很难解决学生的问题,这些问题常常自然地被摆在老师面前。这些在中国人眼中十分熟悉、习焉不察的词,对比起来往往相当困难。老师们常常为解决几个词的对比绞尽脑汁、查遍所有的工具书,既费时又费力。为此,学习汉语的外国人、从事对外汉语教学的教师等都迫切需要一部适应对外汉语教学的词语对比类的工具书和参考书。

《对外汉语常用词语对比例释》是以外国人学习汉语遇到的问题为主要切入点、研究点。它以外国学生学习汉语中最常用的、意义或用法易混淆的词语为对比对象和选词范围,所对比的一组词语中不管词性是否一致、实虚是否统一,也不管是词还是词组;对比的角度不仅限于词义,还更多地注意结构、语用等方面;分析论述及例句的选择基本照顾到外国学生一般的接受水平,部分内容与例句还作了英语翻译,分析对比中为帮助学生具体理解意义和规则,还进行了正误用例的对照。在词与词对比的义项上,既不是所有的义项都对比,也不一定局限在一个义项上,学生出现的错误常常并不局限在一个义项里,有时是两个、三个义项的混用,因此只能根据学生最常出现的问题决定义项的选择。总之,从实际需要和实际问题出发,切实地解决汉语学习和教学中的问题,使之成为方便、实用的工具书或参考书,是写这部书的宗旨。

这部书的意义主要在于它对于教与学的实用价值,从对外汉语的角度,也算填补了一种对比类工具书的空白。此外从研究的角度看,它对汉语词汇、语法、语用等的研究也具有一定的学术价值。书中很多对比分析与研究对于语义对结构、语用的制约作用、搭配规则和语用环境对结构的影响等有一些新的揭示和见解,对于某些词语的搭配组合有较深入的理据分析,这对于从事汉语词汇与语法研究的研究生、教师、学者来说,会有一定的参考价值。

书稿完成后,我请求我的老师宋玉柱先生为本书作序,宋先生欣然允诺。宋先生本是从日本回国度暑假的,然而却顶着炎炎酷暑,认真地阅读书稿并作序,其精神实在令人感动。我在此谨向宋玉柱先生表示深深的敬意和谢意。此外,洪惠玲女士、刘萍女士承担了本书的英文翻译工作(洪惠玲女士承担了从 A 到 H 还有 Z 部分的翻译;刘萍女士承担了从 J 到 Y 部分的翻译),我对于二位女士的积极配合和协助致以真诚的感谢。本书得到北京语言大学出版社及王建勤先生、周建民先生和陈华兰女士的积极支持和帮助,得以问世,在此一并表示由衷的感谢。由于本人水平有限,工作繁忙,时间紧促,尽管参阅了大量文献资料,得到了不少同行的帮助指点,依然难免有疏漏、问题乃至错误,恳请各位同仁多予包涵并批评指正。

作　者
1997 年 9 月于南开园

Introduction

Comparative Illustration of Common Chinese Words and Expressions is a lexicographical work of learning and reference value. It is mainly intended for learners who learn Chinese as a foreign language or a second language, teachers and postgraduates who are engaged in teaching and research of Chinese as a foreign language. The book, which may serve as a reference book for teaching and research, puts into groups and makes comparative analyses of some of the most common words with similar meanings or usages, pointing out the differences and similarities in their meanings, colours, collocations and usages, so that students can understand and use them correctly.

Up to now, several reference books on word discrimination have been published in China, among which *Modern Chinese Synonym Dictionary* compiled by Mr. Liu Shuxin is the most representative. In addition, *New Chinese Multi-functional Dictionary* compiled by Feng Zhichun and Zhou Xingjian, as a general Chinese reference book, also offers discrimination on a great many words. Then why should this book be written? This is mainly because it is intended for different users. At present, this kind of books are mainly written for native Chinese speakers. Thus, the selection of words, the angle of analyses and the selection of illustrative sentences are based on the understanding, perception and the problems of Chinese who have rich language sense in Chinese. Often, this can not solve the problems facing foreign students who often make comparisons among words of different syntactical functions, for example: "怕","害怕" and "可怕";"全体","全部" and "整个";"希望" and "愿望";"友好" and "友谊",etc. In some cases, they are often confused by words that do not have very similar meanings, such as: "想" and "要"; "还是" and "或者"; "知道" and "了解"; "问" and "打听"; "教" and "请教"; "信心" and "决心". In other cases, they can not tell the differences of words with different usages, for example, "见" and "见面"; "看" and "看见"; "帮" and "帮忙"; "送" and "送行", etc. Also, they do not know how to use words with abstract or relatively abstract meanings, such as "再", "又", "也", "很", "真", "太", "对", "对于", "跟", "朝", "向", "往", "的", "了", and many others. As foreign students do not have strong language sense in Chinese, it is likely that they are unable to use these words although they can understand them. So specific rules are needed to help them familiarize with actual usage of these words and specific examples are required to tell them the accepted and unaccepted use of the words. This area is rarely covered by ordinary discrimination dictionaries and is also where the difficulties and key points in compiling this book lie. The difficulties foreign students often meet with are usually also the problems encountered by teachers. As ordinary reference books usually cannot solve them, these problems remain for the teachers. It is often rather difficult to compare these words, which are very familiar to native Chinese speakers. In order to make comparisons on several words, the teachers often have to rack their brains and consult all the reference books, which consumes a lot of time and efforts. Thus, foreigners who study Chinese and teachers who are engaged in teaching Chinese as a foreign language are in urgent need of a reference book which contains comparisons of words, aimed at teaching Chinese as a foreign language.

Comparative Illustration of Common Chinese Words and Expressions takes the problems foreigners often have in learning Chinese as the starting point and the focus. It chooses the most common words in foreign students' Chinese learning and words whose meanings and usages are difficult to distinguish as objects of comparison. Within the groups of words selected, comparisons are made no matter whether they have the same syntactical functions, they are notional words or function words, or they are words or phrases. The comparison is made not only in the light of meanings, but also in terms of structures and pragmatics. The analyses and the selection of illustrative sentences are made with consideration of foreign students' acceptance level, and there is English translation for all explanation and some of the example sentences. In order to help students understand the meanings and rules, comparisons of right and wrong uses are offered. In comparison of words, not all their semantic items are compared. The mistakes students make are not confined to one item either. Sometimes the mistakes involve the confusing of two or three items. Thus the selection can be only made in accordance with the most common problems students have. In conclusion, the aim of this book is to solve the problems in Chinese learning and teaching and to meet the practical need, so as to make it a practical reference book.

The significance of this book lies in its practical value in the field of teaching and learning. From the perspective of teaching Chinese as a foreign language, it somewhat fills a gap in comparative reference books. From the viewpoint of research, it is of certain scholastic value in terms of the research on Chinese words, grammar and pragmatics. A lot of comparative analyses and research in this book shed new light on the restrictive functions of semantics on structures and pragmatics and the influences of collocation rules and pragmatic environments on structures, and the book offers comparatively thorough analyses of the collocation of certain words, which is of reference value to postgraduates, teachers and scholars who conduct research on Chinese words and grammar.

Having completed the manuscript, I invited my teacher Mr. Song Yuzhu to write the preface. Mr. Song, who returned from Japan to spend the summer vacation, read the manuscript and wrote the preface in spite of the hot weather, which was really moving. I hereby express my deep gratitude to him. Ms. Hong Huiling undertakes the translation of the book from A to H and Z, and Ms. Liu Ping from J to Y. I hereby too give my sincere gratitude to these two ladies who have offered active cooperation and help. The book is published with the support and help from Mr. Wang Jianqin and Mr. Zhou Jianmin and Ms. Chen Hualan at Beijing Language and Culture University Press, to whom I also express my sincere appreciation. Although I have read a lot of materials and received the help and advice of many scholars in this field, there still might be slips, problems and even mistakes in this book. Comments and criticisms from readers are welcome.

The Author
Nankai University, September, 1997

总 目

Contents

凡例　Guide to the Use of the Book …………………（1）

对比词组音序索引　Pinyin Index of Words in Comparative Groups ……………………（3）

正文　The Text ………………………………（1—738）

词目音序索引　Pinyin Index …………………（739—746）

词目笔画索引　Stroke Index …………………（747—754）

主要参考文献　Main References ………………（755—756）

凡 例
Guide to the Use of the Book

（一）本书以把汉语作为外语或第二语言的学习者在学习汉语中最常用的、意义或用法易混淆的词语为对比对象和选词范围。

This book, which is mainly intended for learners who learn Chinese as a foreign language or second language, selects, puts into groups and makes comparative analyses of some of the most common words with similar meanings or usages that are easily confused.

（二）本书对比的词语组例为 254 例,涉及 630 多个词。

The book contains two hundred and fifty-four groups of examples of comparative analyses, involving over six hundred and thirty words.

（三）全书按汉语拼音字母顺序排列,以对比词语组例中第一个词的首字进行音序排列。书后另附词目音序索引和词目笔画索引。

The entries are done according to the alphabetical order in Chinese Pinyin of the first character of each group. And at the end of the book are attached both pinyin index and stroke index of word groups.

（四）词目的声调及轻声的标示方法,依据《汉语拼音方案》,即阴平 ˉ 阳平 ˊ 上声 ˇ 去声 ˋ,轻声不标声调符号。

The phonetic symbols of the Four Tones and Light Tone are cited according to the Chinese Phonetic Scheme, namely the first tone ˉ, the second tone ˊ, the third tone ˇ, and the fourth tone ˋ. The light tone is not marked.

（五）对比组中属于词的都标有词类,词类用"〈　〉"表示。标有一种词类的,说明对比主要在该词类范围内进行;标有两种甚至三种词类的,说明对比在两种或三种词类内进行。

The parts of speech in a group are marked by " < > ". If a single kind of part of speech is marked, it indicates that the comparison is mainly made in

1

the range of the marked one, and if two or even three kinds of parts of speech are marked, that indicates the comparisons are made among them all.

(六) 词目例释中有一定数量的正误用例。不标有符号的为正确用例；标有"＊"的为不恰当或错误用例。

Certain numbers of correct and wrong examples are provided in the entries. Those unmarked are the correct examples and those marked with ＊ are the improper or erroneous uses.

(七) 重点符号的使用：强调单个词，用"．"或"△"；强调一个成分用"＿＿"。

Symbols for emphasis are used. "．" or "△" is used to emphasize a single word and "＿＿" is used to emphasize a composition.

(八) 同一例句中，相对比的词语同时出现时，其间用"／"分隔，表示它们的用法或意义在此相同。例如：

When the words being compared appear in the same sentence, "／" is used in between, indicating their usages or meanings are the same. e.g.

我几乎／差点儿没赶上飞机。("几乎／差点儿"都可用并都是正确的。)(both are correct)

＊你路上没有吃的，这些食品给予／给以你。("给予／给以"都不可用并都是错误的。)(both are incorrect)

(九) 用"……＋……＋……"表示多项成分的组合顺序。

"……＋……＋……" is used to indicate the constituent order of the multiplex compositions.

(十) 对于"词组"、"短语"、"结构"等不同名称，本书统用"词组"。

As for such terms as "word group", "phrase", "structure", etc., they are generally called "word group" in the book.

(十一) 正文中部分内容有英文翻译，其选定翻译内容的原则是：释义部分全部翻译，较难的例句给以一定的翻译。

All the explanation in the book and part of the examples have been translated into English.

对比词组音序索引

Pinyin Index of Words in Comparative Groups

A

啊 吧 呢 吗 ································ 1
安静 宁静 平静 ······················ 10
按 依照 按照 依照 ·················· 14

B

把 被 ·· 18
把 将 ·· 21
把 拿 ·· 22
白 白白 ···································· 23
帮 帮助 帮忙 ·························· 25
被 叫 让 ·································· 29
被 由 ·· 31
～边 ～旁 ································ 36
别的 其他(的) 另外(的) ······· 38
别人 别的 ································ 42
别人 人家 大家 ······················ 44
冰凉 冰冷 ································ 47
不 没(有) ································ 50
不比 没有 ································ 53
不如 没有 ································ 56
不同 不一样 ···························· 58
不再 再不 再也不 ·················· 61

C

才 都 就 ·································· 64
参观 访问 看 ·························· 66
差(一)点儿 差不多 ················ 69

常常 通常 ································ 74
常常 往往 ································ 79
朝(着) 沿(着) ························ 82
迟 迟到 ···································· 85
充分 充足 充沛 ······················ 87
充满 充实 ································ 91
初 开始 当初 ·························· 93
除 除了 ···································· 97
处处 到处 ································ 99
次 遍 趟 ································ 101
从 自 由 打 ·························· 104
从 自 自从 ···························· 108
从来 历来 向来 ···················· 109
村子 村庄 乡村 农村 ·········· 112

D

大概 大约 大体 ···················· 115
大概 也许 恐怕 ···················· 118
大量 大批 ······························ 119
耽搁 耽误 ······························ 122
当 当时 ·································· 124
当 在 ······································ 127
到达 达到 ······························ 132
到 到达 达 ···························· 133
倒 却 ······································ 138
倒(倒是) 可是 ······················ 139
的 地 得 ································ 142
等 等待 等候 ························ 144
等 等等 什么的 ···················· 147

3

低 矮 浅	150	感到 觉得	237
的确 确实	154	感觉 感受	239
地 地方 地点 地区	155	感谢 谢谢 谢	242
点儿 些	159	赶紧 赶快 赶忙	247
对 朝 向	162	刚 才	249
对 对于 对/对于…来说	165	刚才 刚 刚刚	250
对(对于)…来说 在…看来	168	告诉 通知 说	256
对 跟 给	171	各自 各个 个个	259
对 双	174	根 条 支	262
对 是 行 好	176	根据 依据 据	265
对于 关于 至于	179	更 还	269
对比 对照	181	更加 更	273
对比 比较	183	更加 越发	274
短 短暂 短促	186	关心 关怀 关切 关照	276
顿时 一时 暂时	188		

E

二 两 第二 俩	193

F

发生 产生	198
发现 发明	201
法子 点子	202
反应 反映 反响	204
方便 便利	208
方法 办法	209
房子 屋子 房间 房屋 楼房	213
吩咐 嘱咐	217
丰富 富裕 富有	219
风景 景象 情景	222

G

改 改变	224
改变 改进 改善	227
感动 感激	230
感动 激动	234

H

忽然 突然 忽而	282
花 花费 费	285
坏 差	288
会 见面 见 会见	291
或者 还是	293

J

几乎 差点儿	295
几乎 简直	297
急 着急	299
急忙 匆忙	302
急忙 连忙 赶忙	303
给予 给以 给	305
记 记忆	307
记得 记住	310
继续 持续	313
简单 简便 简易	315
见解 看法 意见	317
将 将要 就要	322
讲 说 谈	324
讲话 说话 谈话	328

教 教导 指教 请教	330
进行 加以	334
进行 举行	339
精神 精力	341
究竟 到底	345
举行 举办	348
觉得 认为	350

K

看 看见	355
考 考试 测验	359
口 嘴	363
宽阔 宽敞 宽广 广大 广阔	368
困难 艰难 难	371

L

~来/去 ~到	376
了 的	378
粒 枚 颗 棵	380
冷 凉	382
里 上	384
里 中 内	388
聊 聊天儿	391

M

满意 满足	394
满意 中意	397
每 各	398

N

那时 这时 当时	402
能 会	404
能 可以	406
你 您	408
暖和 温暖	410

P

| 怕 害怕 可怕 | 413 |

Q

其他 其余	417
起 起来	419
起 上	422
起来 出来	423
起来 上来	425
起来 下去	427
气 生气	428
千万 万万	431
前 前面	433
前 以前	435
亲切 亲热	437
亲自 亲身	439
全 都	440
全 全部 所有	442
全 完全	446
全体 全部 整个(儿)	448
群 帮 伙 批	450

R

| 然而 反而 | 456 |
| 热情 热烈 | 457 |

S

身体 身材 身子 个子	460
时代 年代	463
时代 时期	464
时候 时	467
时候 时间 时刻	469
时机 机会	472
事 事情 事件 事故	475
送 送行 送别	478
随便 顺便	481

5

T

谈　谈话　交谈 …… 484
特意　专门 …………… 487
天天　每天 …………… 489
听　听见 ……………… 490
通过　经过 …………… 493

W

往　向　朝 …………… 496
为　为了　因为 ……… 498
未必　不必 …………… 502
问　打听 ……………… 504
问　询问　质问　提问　疑问 …… 506

X

希望　愿望 …………… 511
下来　下去 …………… 513
想　要 ………………… 515
像　好像 ……………… 519
小时　钟头 …………… 522
信心　决心 …………… 523
兴趣　乐趣　爱好 …… 525
兴趣　兴致 …………… 529
兴趣　有趣(儿) ……… 532

Y

沿着　顺着 …………… 534
要不　不然 …………… 536
要不是　要不然 ……… 539
要么　或者 …………… 541
要是　如果　假如　倘若 …… 542
也　都 ………………… 544
也　又 ………………… 546
一边…一边…　又…又… …… 549
一般　普通 …………… 553
一点儿　有点儿 ……… 556

一点儿　一会儿 ……… 560
一定　肯定 …………… 563
一会儿　不一会儿 …… 564
一起　一齐 …………… 566
一向　一直 …………… 567
已经　曾经 …………… 570
以后　后来　然后 …… 575
以前　从前 …………… 579
以来　后来　从来 …… 581
以为　认为 …………… 586
意见　成见 …………… 590
永远　永久 …………… 593
由　由于 ……………… 595
友好　友爱　友谊 …… 597
有名　著名　闻名 …… 601
又　再　还 …………… 605
原来　本来 …………… 609
原来　起初 …………… 612
愿意　情愿 …………… 614
愿意　希望 …………… 616
越…越…　越来越 …… 618

Z

在　到　于 …………… 621
在…上　在…中　在…下 …… 627
再三　反复　屡次 …… 630
咱　咱们 ……………… 634
咱们　我们 …………… 634
暂时　临时 …………… 635
怎么　为什么 ………… 637
怎么　怎样　怎么样 … 641
怎么样　什么样 ……… 647
这么/那么　太 ……… 651
真　太　很　更 ……… 657
整洁　整齐 …………… 661
正在　正在 …………… 663
正好　正巧　凑巧 …… 666

知道　了解	669	重要　重点	701
只好　只有	675	重要　主要	704
只要　只有　除非	677	逐渐　逐步	706
只是　不过　可是		自己　本人　本身	708
但是　然而	680	自己　自我	713
中　中间	683	总(是)　一直	715
中间　当中　之间	685	最　更　极	720
中间　中央　中心	689	左右　前后　上下	723
终于　到底　毕竟	692	做　干　搞	725
重　重量　分量	696	做　造　制造	732
重点　要点	699	座　家　所	736

7

A

啊 a   吧 ba   呢 ne   吗 ma

〈语气助词〉用于句中、句末,表示各种不同的语气。
(<modal particle> indicating various moods and used in the middle or at the end of the sentences.)

"啊"受前一音节尾音的影响,常发生几种音变现象。具体规则如下("啊", affected by the ending sound of the preceding syllable, has the following sound variations):

1. 前一音节尾音是 a、e、i、u 的,读作"ia",写作"呀"。(When the ending sound of the preceding syllables are a, e, i, or u, it is pronounced as "ia" and written as "呀".)

   爬呀   唱歌呀   来呀   真累呀   吃鱼呀

2. 前一音节尾音是 u、ou、ao 的,读作"ua",写作"哇"。(When the ending sound of the preceding syllables are u, ou or ao, it is pronounced as "ua" and written as "哇".)

   哭哇   快修哇   游哇   多好哇   要哇

3. 前一音节尾音是 n 的,读作"na",写作"哪"。(When the ending sound of the preceding syllable is "n", it is pronounced as "na" and written as "哪".)

   干哪   喊哪   戒烟哪   真热心哪

4. 有时,还会出现与前一音节合音的现象,即前一音节的声母与"a"合为一个音节。(Sometimes it is co-pronounced with the former syllable, that is, the initial consonant of the former syllable is co-pronounced with "a".)

   (1)前一个词是"了"的,"了+啊"读作"la",写作"啦"。(If the preceding word is "了","了" and "啊" are co-pronounced as "la", and written as "啦".)

   长这么高啦   不走啦   学会啦   住了五年啦

1

(2) 前一个词是"呢"的,"呢+啊"读作"na",写作"哪"。(If the preceding word is "呢", "呢" and "啊" are co-pronounced as "na" and written as "哪".)

  时间还早着哪 天热着哪 自尊心强着哪

(一)"啊"、"吧"、"呢"、"吗"表示疑问语气的区别。("啊","吧","呢" and "吗" indicating different interrogative moods.)

  "啊"、"吧"、"呢"、"吗"都可以用在疑问句末尾,表示疑问语气,但是用于哪种类型的疑问句和所表达的疑问语气是有差别的。("啊","吧""呢" and "吗" all can be used at the end of an interrogative sentence to express the interrogative mood, but there are differences when being used in different types of interrogative sentences and being used to express different interrogative moods.)

  1. "啊"和"呢"都可以用于特指问句(包括特指反问句)、选择问句、正反问句句末,但是语气轻重不同。"啊"语气轻,"呢"语气重。〔"啊" and "呢" can both be used in special questions(including special rhetorical questions), alternative questions, affirmative-negative questions, but the degree of the mood is different. "啊" indicates a lower degree but "呢" indicates a higher degree.〕例如:

  我们怎么去啊/呢?(特指问句)
  光看怎么行啊/呢?得动手做呀。(特指反问句)
  (How could you only look at it? Do it yourself.)
  我的这些意见你倒是同意啊/呢,还是不同意啊/呢?
              (选择问句)
  (Do you agree with me or not?)
  你有没有时间啊/呢?(正反问句)

  "呢"不能用于是非问句,包括反问句中的是非问句。("呢" is not used in general questions, including those in rhetorical sense.)例如:

  * 你是新来的留学生呢?
  * 你将来当记者呢?(是非问句)

＊这件事是你经手办的,你会不知道呢?

　　　　　　　　　　　　(反问句中的是非问句)

　2."吧"和"吗"主要用于是非问句。是非问句中没有表示疑问的词语或方式,通过疑问语气词"吗"、"吧"表示疑问。"吧"主要用于含有测度语气的疑问句中。通常是问话人已经有了初步想法,但是不能十分肯定,于是用自己的推测来试探相问,以求得到证实。句中多用"大概"、"大约"、"也许"等副词与之呼应,句末用降调。"吗"也可以用于反问句中的是非疑问句中。("吧" and "吗" are mainly used in general questions. There are no definite words or ways to show interrogative mood, and the interrogative mood is expressed by the interrogative words "吗" and "吧". "吧" is mainly used in the questions of suppositional mood. Usually when a speaker has got an idea in mind but feels uncertain, he may ask exploratorily to confirm his own inference. Adverbs such as "大概","大约" and "也许" are usually used in combination with "吧" and the falling tone is used at the end of the sentence. "吗" can also be used in general questions in rhetorical sense.)例如:

　　　　你了解中国历史吗?

　　　　图书馆里有外国杂志吗?

　　　　难道他连这么简单的道理都不懂吗?

　　　(How could he know nothing about such a simple principle?)

　　　　你大概记错了吧?

　　　　车上没有座位了吧?

　　　　李力今天没来,也许是病了吧?

　"吧"和"吗"一般不用于特指问句、选择问句、正反问句;"吧"表示的主要是不定,所以不能用于反问句中。("吧" and "吗" are not used for special questions, alternative questions or affirmative-negative questions. Since "吧" indicates a sense of uncertainty, it cannot be used in rhetorical questions.)例如:

　　＊你能不能帮帮他吗/吧?

* 你去哪儿找他吗/吧?
* 咱们就此打住吗/吧,还是往下看看再说吗/吧?
* 你怎么能这么说吗/吧?
* 这不正是你所需要的吧?

3."啊"和"吧"有时都可以用于具有商量意味的问句中,语气相差不大。但是侧重建议的,最好用"啊";侧重请求的最好用"吧"。("啊" and "吧" can be used in questions for the purpose of discussion and there is a slight difference between them in the moods. "啊" is best used to emphasize the suggestive tone; "吧" is best used to make a request.)试比较:

太累了,咱们在这儿坐一会儿啊?(侧重建议)
太累了,咱们在这儿坐一会儿吧?(侧重请求)

(二)"啊"、"吧"表示祈使语气的区别。("啊" and "吧" indicate different meanings in imperative mood.)

"啊"和"吧"都可以用在祈使句末尾,表示请求、催促、命令等语气,但是所表达的语气和使用的语言环境稍有不同。用"啊"时,多用于客观原因引起的催促、命令等,有时含有指责、挑衅、不耐烦等口气;用"吧"时,多用于说话人主观上对听话人的请求、催促、命令等。(Both "啊" and "吧" are used at the end of imperative sentences, expressing the mood to request, to urge and to command, etc., but there is difference in the mood and in the context. "啊" is mostly used for urging and command caused by objective reasons, and sometimes implying the meaning of blaming, provoking and impatience, etc.; while "吧" is used for the speaker's subjunctive request, urging and command to the listener.)例如:

帮我拿拿呀!(怎么就站在那儿看?)
快说呀!(你怎么哑巴啦?)
(How could you keep silent?)

帮我拿拿吧！（我实在拿不动了。）
　　　快说吧！（别犹豫啦！）
　　　（Don't hesitate.）
　前两例用于由于对方的某种表现而引起说话人的催促的语境；后两例用于说话人主观意愿的催促、请求的语境。(The first two examples are used in the situation when certain behavior of the person spoken to makes the speaker urge; while the last two are used in the situation when the speaker urges or requests by his own wishes.)

　"啊"用在祈使句里，还可以表示提醒、警告、禁止的语气；"吧"一般不用来表示这种语气。(In imperative sentences, "啊" is used for reminding, warning or prohibiting, while "吧" is not used in this way.) 例如：
　　　过马路时要注意安全哪！
　　　这儿什么人都有，小心，可别上当啊！
　　　这是公共场所，不许抽烟哪！
　句中有"要"、"应该"、"该"、"应当"等表示理应如此的词，有"一定"、"必须"等表示肯定语气的词，有"别"、"不要"、"不准"、"不许"、"禁止"等表示制止、禁止的词的祈使句，句末一般都不能用"吧"。(When such words as "要", "应该", "该" and "应当" which mean "something ought to be like this", or such words as "一定", "必须" which indicate an affirmative mood or, such words as "别", "不要", "不准", "不许" and "禁止" indicating prevention or prohibition are used, "吧" is not needed at the end of the sentence.) 例如：
　　* 值班时可要负起责任吧！
　　* 你应该努力学习吧！
　　* 不准大声讲话吧！
　　* 明天一定不要迟到吧！
(三) "啊"和"呢"、"吧"表示陈述语气的区别。("啊", "呢" and "吧" can all be used in declarative sentences but each shows a different tone.)

　1. "啊"和"呢"都可以用于陈述句末尾。"啊"用以表示肯

5

定、强调、解释等语气;"呢"主要用于表示夸张的语气或带有某种感情色彩。句中常用"才"、"还"、"着"等配合。("啊"and "呢" both can be used at the end of the declarative sentences. "啊" expresses moods of affirmation, emphasis and explanation, etc.; while "呢" expresses moods of exaggeration or emotion. The words "才", "还" or "着" are usually used coordinately in the sentences.)例如:

小王是个好同志呀。

他们是在小礼堂听的报告呀。

时间还早呢,再坐一会儿吧。

商店里的人多着呢。

自己有自己的活法,管别人怎么说呢。

要我看,他才不会不来呢。

(In my opinion, he will not be absent for sure.)

"呢"还用于表示动作或情况正在进行的语气。句中常有"正"、"正在"、"在"和"着"等词配合。("呢" also expresses that activities or matters are in procession and usually is supported by "正","正在","在" or "着" in sentences.)例如:

我正忙呢,你别总打搅我。

孩子们正在院子里玩着呢。

妹妹在哭呢,快去劝劝她吧。

我在看书呢。

2. "吧"主要用于表示不定语气的句子中,句中常用"可能"、"大概"、"也许"、"或许"等表示不定或推测语气的副词相配合。("吧" is generally used to express an uncertain mood in sentences. Words with indefinite or suppositional moods such as "可能","大概","也许" or "或许" are usually used together.)例如:

这几天怎么没看到山本啊?——可能去北京了吧。

大力怎么没来参加活动?——也许不知道吧。

我想来想去还是不去吧,万一人家不欢迎我怎么办?

(I thought about it again and again, and I had better not

6

to go in case they receive me with cold face.)

3. "啊"和"吧"都可以表示同意的语气,但是感情色彩有所不同。"啊"表示赞同或欣然同意的语气,常用在"好"、"行"后边;"吧"表示一般或勉强同意的语气,常用在"好"、"就这样"后边。("啊"and "吧" express mood of agreement, but the emotional flavour is not the same. "啊" expresses approvals or joyful agreement and usually is used after "好" or "行"; "吧" expresses plain or reluctant agreement and is used after "好" or "就这样".)例如:

这个周末我们去郊外踏青啊?(What about going for a trip to the suburbs this weekend?)——好哇。

明天时间不够了,今晚咱们打通宵吧?——行啊。

我没有时间,你带他们去看看吧。——好吧。

看来我们的计划很难十全十美了。——算了,就这样吧。

(It seems that it is very hard for our plan to become perfect.)

(四)"啊"用于表示感叹语气。("啊" is used to express exclamatory mood.)

"啊"多用于感叹句末尾,句中常用"多"、"多么"、"真"一类程度副词,表示赞美、兴奋、遗憾、惊奇等语气。("啊" is mainly used at the end of exclamatory sentences and the adverbs of degree like "多", "多么" or "真" are usually used to express the moods of praise, excitement, regret or surprise, etc.)例如:

今天天气多好哇!

孩子们玩得多么开心哪!

这么多粮食都糟蹋了,真可惜呀!

真怪呀!这草怎么还会害羞哇?

(How strange! How could the grass be shy?)

"呢"、"吧"一般不用于感叹句。("呢" and "吧" are usually not used in exclamatory sentences.)例如:

* 这儿的树木真茂密呢!

* 多么灵巧的一双手呢!
* 他们的精神真令人感动吧!
* 他的态度多么诚恳吧!

(五)"啊"、"吧"、"呢"用于句中表示停顿的区别。(The distinction of "啊", "吧" and "呢" when used in sentences to indicate pauses.)

1. "啊"和"吧"都可以用在句中例举项后,表示语气停顿,但是语言环境有所不同。"啊"一般只用于并列关系中的每一个例举项后边(这时一般不考虑"啊"的音变条件,都写作"啊");"吧"一般用在一个例举项后边。〔"啊" and "呢" both can be used after the cited examples to indicate a pause of the speech, but they are used in different contexts. "啊" is generally used after every single coordinate instance (Here there is no sound variation for "啊" and is written as "啊"); while "吧" is usually used when there is only one instance cited.〕例如:

这下可热闹了,猪啊、鸡啊、鸭啊,跑得满院子都是。

(This was really a sight to see: the pigs, chicken and ducks were scattering all over the yard.)

房间里,电视啊、电话啊、冰箱啊、空调啊,设备齐全极了!
就拿交通问题来说吧,这已经是几年来的老问题了。
就说你吧,一个人寂寞的时候,不也哭过鼻子吗?

* 房间里,电视吧、电话吧、冰箱吧、空调吧,设备齐全极了!
* 就拿交通问题来说啊,这已经是几年来的老问题了。

2. "啊"和"呢"都可以用于句中表示语气停顿,但是作用不同。"啊"在于引人注意,"呢"在于引出另一话题,常用于转折关系的句子中,含对比的意味。("啊" and "呢" both can be used to indicate a pause of the speech in sentences, but they have different functions. "啊" is used to arouse other's attention. "呢" is used to

8

lead to another topic, usually used in the sentences of transition, implying contrast.) 例如:

老王啊,人心都是肉长的呀!
(Lao Wang, everyone has his fellow feeling.)
这个周末呀,我想出去玩玩。
* 老王呢,人心都是肉长的呀!
那时候有多难哪!如今呢,生活富得都流油。
(How difficult those days were! But today, the life is so rich and abundant.)
伤是痊愈了,可是容貌呢,完全毁了。
(The wound has healed, but as to the appearance, it is totally destroyed.)
她说她不会做,实际上呢,是她根本就不想做。
(She said she couldn't do, but in fact, she wouldn't like to do it at all.)
* 伤是痊愈了,可是容貌啊,完全毁了。

3. "呢"和"吧"都可以用于含假设意味的正反对举的句子,用"吧"时常常含有不定或左右为难的意味。"呢"没有这种意味。("呢" and "吧" can both be used in the sentences implying positive and negative assumption. "吧" indicates the meaning of uncertainty or in a dilemma, but "呢" doesn't.) 例如:

这是我的一点儿建议,你同意呢,咱就落实下去;你不同意呢,就算我没说。
(This is only my suggestion. If you agree, we'll carry it out; if you don't, just count my words as being unsaid.)
若有呢,就拿出来;若没有呢,就去买。
* 这是我的一点儿建议,你同意吧,咱就落实下去;你不同意吧,就算我没说。
你说我没有朋友吧,我还有七八个;你说我有朋友吧,却没有一个知心的。

9

不吃吧,人家请的我;吃吧,实在不喜欢。

去吧,家里放心不下;不去吧,又舍不得放弃这次机会。

(If I'm going, my family would worry about me, if not, I am reluctant to give up this opportunity.)

* 你说我没有朋友呢,我还有七八个;你说我有朋友呢,却没有一个知心的。

安静 ānjìng   宁静 níngjìng   平静 píngjìng

〈形容词〉< adjective >

"安静"、"宁静"、"平静"都有静而不动、没有动荡的意思,但是词义侧重的角度和用法有所不同。("安静","宁静"and "平静"all mean silent and still, without motion, but they emphasize different angles and they are different in usage.)

(一) 意义上(In meaning)

1. "安静"和"宁静"都可以表示周围环境没有声响。("安静" and "宁静" both indicate the surroundings are quiet, soundless.)例如:

安静的屋子里,只有张敏在看书。

宁静的教室里,只听到考生们唰唰的写字声。

比较起来,"宁静"的"静"比"安静"的"静"要更静一些。"安静"着重指没有吵闹、没有喧哗,多用于具体的环境;"宁静"着重指安宁、特别地静,没有一丁点儿声音,多用于大的环境。(Comparatively speaking, "宁静" is quieter than "安静"。"安静" emphasizes there is no din, "noiseless", and it is mainly used in a particular environment. "宁静" emphasizes "tranquil and peaceful", "particularly quiet", "soundless", and it is used for a larger environment.)例如:

资料室里很安静,同学们都在认真地读书。

消息传来,安静的校园里立刻沸腾起来。

载重汽车重重的喘息声打破了凌晨的宁静。

(The loud sounds of the lorry broke the peacefulness of the early morning.)

宁静的夜空中,只有三三两两的星星在眨着眼。

* 安静的夜空中,只有三三两两的星星在眨着眼。

"平静"着重指"平稳"的意思,通常指水波不翻滚,时局、环境安定、不动荡等。("平静" emphasizes "smooth and steady", usually refers to still water, situation or environment, without turbulence.)例如:

湖面上平静得很,一只小船浮在上面一动也不动。

(The surface of the lake is so smooth that a boat on it does not move at all.)

外面很平静,不像有敌人打进来的样子。

* 湖面上安静/宁静得很,一只小船浮在上面一动也不动。

表示没有声响一般不能用"平静"。("平静" can not be used to indicate "soundless".)例如:

* 平静的教室里,只听到考生们唰唰的写字声。
* 资料室里很平静,同学们都在认真地读书。

2."安静"、"宁静"和"平静"都可以用于表示人的心情、人的生活没有不安和动荡,都可以表示安稳的意思,有时可以换用,只是表义角度稍有不同。"平静"侧重没有不安和动荡;"安静"侧重安定;"宁静"侧重特别地平和,没有一点儿骚扰。但是用于表示人的心情时,一般多用"平静","安静"次之,"宁静"用得很少。("安静","宁静"and"平静" can all be used to indicate the steadiness of people's life and tranquility of people's mind which have no ups and downs. They are sometimes exchangeable with only slight difference in meaning. "平静" stresses having no ups and downs; "安静" stresses being settled, while "宁静" stresses being particularly peaceful, without any harassment. But usually when indicating people's state of mind, "平静"is most frequently used and "安静" takes the second place, "宁静" is rarely used.)例如：

听了英雄们的事迹,同学们激动的心情久久不能平静。

大家好不容易有了这样一个环境,可以平平静静／安安静静地生活了,千万不要让战争把它破坏掉。

过了好长时间,她的心情才平静／安静／宁静下来。

这位不速之客的到来,打破了我们家几年来平静／安静／宁静的生活。

(The coming of this unexpected guest breaks the quiet / peaceful / tranquil life we have had for years.)

表示人的心情从动荡不安到安定平和一般只用"平静",不用"安静"、"宁静"。(When indicating the state of mind changes from being disturbed to peaceful, generally "平静" is used, "安静" or "宁静" is not.)例如：

读了丈夫的信,茹琳的心怎么也平静不下来了。

* 读了丈夫的信,茹琳的心怎么也安静／宁静不下来了。

* 听了英雄们的事迹,同学们激动的心情久久不能安静／宁静。

"安静"、"宁静"有时还可以用以描写人"静"的性格；"平静"不能这样用。("安静" and "宁静" sometimes are used to describe the silent nature of a person; but "平静" can't.)例如：

她是一个那么美丽、那么安静／宁静的女孩儿。

* 她是一个那么美丽、那么平静的女孩儿。

"平静"还可以表示人的态度不紧张、不慌乱、不激动等；"宁静"不能用于这种情况。("平静" is also used to indicate a person being not nervous, flustered or excited, while "宁静" can't be used in these cases.)例如：

她平静地看着考官们,一点儿也不紧张。

"我同意离婚。"他异常平静地说。

* 她宁静地看着考官们，一点儿也不紧张。

* "我同意离婚。"他异常宁静地说。

(二) 用法上(In use)

1. "安静"、"平静"可以构成"AABB"的重叠式；"宁静"一般不能。("安静" and "平静" can form the reduplicated pattern as AABB; but "宁静" can not.)例如：

孩子们安安静静地坐在屋子里等着阿姨。

他平平静静地处理着文件，好像根本就没听到那剧烈的敲门声。

(He was dealing with the documents quietly as if not hearing the fierce knocking at the door.)

* 外面宁宁静静的。

2. "安静"、"平静"可以在句中用作状语、补语，"宁静"一般不能。("安静" and "平静" can be used as an adverbial or complement in sentences, while "宁静" can not.)例如：

孩子总算安静地睡着了。

不知为什么，教室里显得异常安静。

他平静地注视着那几个气势汹汹的敌人。

(He gazed at those fierce enemies calmly.)

虽然刚刚遭受了巨大的打击，可是她在大家面前表现得很平静。

(She appeared very calm in front of everyone present though she had had suffered a huge strike.)

* 孩子总算宁静地睡着了。

* 虽然刚刚遭受了巨大的打击，可是她在大家面前表现得很宁静。

3. "安静"还可以用作动词，可以重叠为"ABAB"式；"平静"、"宁静"没有这种用法。("安静" can also be used as a verb in the reduplicated pattern ABAB; while "平静" and "宁静" can not.)例如：

请大家安静一下,林主任有话要对大家说。
你安静一会儿,好吗?
　*请大家平静/宁静一下,林主任有话要对大家说。
你们安静安静好吗?我们要休息了。
　*你们平静平静/宁静宁静好吗?我们要休息了。

(三) 色彩上(On the aspect of color)

"安静"、"平静"一般通用于口语、书面语;"宁静"书面语色彩很重,一般只限于书面语。("安静" and "平静" are generally used in both spoken and written languages; while "宁静" has a strong flavour of written language and generally confined to written language.)

按 àn　　依 yī　　照 zhào
按照 ànzhào　　依照 yīzhào

〈介词〉介绍出做事凭借的某种标准、意见或根据。

(< preposition > introducing certain standards, ideas or grounds on which something is done.)

(一)"按"与"依"、"照"

1. "依"与"按"比,含有"严格地依顺"的意思,书面语色彩较浓;"照"与"按"比,含有"模仿某样子"的意思,口语色彩较浓;而"按"不含有"依顺"和"模仿某样子"的意思,语体色彩上属中性。因此,"依"常与较抽象的名词或书面语色彩较重的词语结合在一起。"照"常与表示具体标准、样子、意见等的词语结合在一起。"按"这两种情况都可以。但是表示以时间、地区或某种度量衡单位为规定时,用"按",不用"依"或"照"。(When compared with "按", "依" means "strictly obey", and it has a strong flavour of written language; while compared with "按", "照" means "imitating some way or pattern" and has a strong flavour of spoken language; but "按" doesn't mean obedience and imitation. It is neutral. Therefore, "依" is generally used together with these abstract nouns or phrases of written language. "照" is usually used together

with these concrete nouns and phrases indicating standards, patterns, or opinions, etc. "按" can be used in both ways. But when expressing sticking to some stipulations in terms of time, region or units of measurement, "按" will be used instead of "依" or "照".)例如:

依次就座(to be seated according to order)
依法惩处(to be punished according to the laws)
依样画葫芦(to paint according to the sample)
照他的意思做　照这个样子写　照猫画虎　按时起床　按期交货　按区进行　按斤计量
* 依时起床　* 依区进行
* 照期交货　* 照斤计量
* 战士们毫无声息地按次前进。("按"换作"依"。)
* 到村里去,我们就依这个计划进行。("依"换作"照"或"按"。)
* 电影一定要依时开演。("依"换作"按"。)

"依"和"照"还可以构成"依/照……看"、"依/照……说"的固定格式;"按"常常构成"按……说"、"按……讲"这种格式。("依" and "照" can form the fixed patterns like "依/照…看", "依/照…说;" "按" usually forms the patterns as "按…说," "按…讲".)例如:

依你看,这件事该怎么办?
照我说,就不应该让他去。
(In my opinion, he shouldn't be allowed to go.)
按条件讲,咱可比人家差多了。
(As far as the advantages are concerned, we fall far behind them.)

在表示依照具体样态的意思时,一般用"照",不用"依"。
(When indicating doing things according to the concrete sample or

15

pattern,"照"is generally used, but"依"is not.)例如:

照这样看,任务很难按时完成。

照这么说,他不会来了?

* 依这样看,任务很难按时完成。

* 依这么说,他不会来了?

"按"构成的格式中,一般不用人称代词,它表示的一般不是主观意志,而是客观标准或常理。(In the pattern composed of "按", personal pronouns will not be used. Generally "按" doesn't indicate subjective will, but objective standard or general truth.)例如:

按理说(reasonably speaking)

按节气讲(to speak according to solar terms)

按规律办事(to work according to laws)

* 按我看,该管的还是要管。("按"换作"依"或"照"。"按"should be replaced by "依" or "照".)

(二)"按照"与"依照"

"按照"强调以某种标准为依据做,使用范围较宽;"依照"强调严格地以某事物为样子或完全顺从某种意见等,使用范围较窄,多用于书面语。("按照"emphasizes doing something according to certain standard and it is used in a fairly broad range; "依照"emphasizes strictly taking something as the example or obeying a certain opinion completely, and it is used in a fairly narrow range and mostly in written language.)例如:

我们应该按照实际情况来制定施工方案。

按照惯例,你应该选修四门课。

(Convention dictates that you ought to take four courses.)

依照学会的规定,入会者须由本人申请,不可由他人代为申请。

(According to the stipulation of the Institute, the applicants must apply personally and application can not be done by others.)

我是依照先生的嘱托来处理这件事的。

(I am dealing with the matter just in accordance with the teacher's entrust.)

(三)"按照"与"按","依照"与"依"、"照"

"按照"与"按","依照"与"依"、"照"的区别主要在于选择后面词语音节多寡的问题。"按照"、"依照"后面只能接两个音节以上的词语,不能接单音节词。(The difference between "按照" and "按", and that between "依照" and "依","照", actually lie in the number of the syllables of the words following. "按照" and "依照" can only be followed by nouns or phrases of more than two syllables other than those of monosyllables.)例如:

按照考试成绩(录取)　按照原则(办事)　按照法律程序(处理)

按区(进行)　依法(处理)　照样(画葫芦)　按时期(分段)

依他的意思(去办)　照我说的(做)

＊ 我们一定按照期完成。(改作:"按期"或"按照预定期限"。)

＊ 依照法办事,不徇私情。(改作:"依法"或"依照法律"。)

构成"照……说"、"依……看"这种格式,介绍出对事物的看法或采取某种说法的主体时,一般只用"照"或"依",不用"按照"、"依照"。(The patterns of "照…说" and "依…看" introduce the views on a matter or the subject holding a certain opinion. Usually "照" or "依" can not be replaced by "按照" or "依照"。)例如:

＊ 按照这样看,我也很难说服他了。("按照"改作"照"。)

＊ 依照你看来,谁有资格参加这次比赛?("依照"改作"依"。)

B

把 bǎ　　被 bèi

〈介词〉< preposition >

(一)"把"和"被"构成的句式在意义上和用法上有相同之处。(The sentence patterns made up by "把" and "被" are sometimes identical in meaning and use.)

1. 由"把"和"被"构成的句式都是把动词连带的已知的名词性成分移到谓语动词前,谓语动词大都含有处置意义,通常不能由单个动词担当谓语,动词前后应该有一些相关的附加成分。(In sentence patterns made up by "把" and "被", the noun compositions are put in the front of the predicate verbs, which often mean disposal and which are not used alone and usually are supported by some related elements before or after the verb.) 例如:

　　他又带回来(一位)客人。——他又把客人带回来了。
　　我办完了今天该办的事。——我把今天该办的事都办完了。
　　* 他又把客人带。
　　* 我把今天该办的事都办。
　　老师批评了小张一顿。——小张被老师批评了一顿。
　　弟弟的事搅得我心神不定的。——我被弟弟的事搅得心神不定的。
　　(My brother's trouble makes me distracted. — I was distracted by my brother's trouble.)
　　* 小张被老师批评。
　　* 我被弟弟的事搅。

2. "把"字句、"被"字句被否定时,否定词应放在"把"、"被"的前面,一般不能放在"把"字词组、"被"字词组后面。(When the sentence with "把" or "被" is a negative sentence, the negative

18

word should be used before "把" and "被" and generally can't be used after the phrase led by "把" or "被".)例如：

他没把作业交给老师。

不把这些题做完，我就不走了。

从小到大，他从来没被妈妈打过。

(From his childhood on, he has never been beaten by his mother.)

他第一次尝到不被他人信任的苦头。

* 他把作业没交给老师。
* 把这些题不做完，我就不走了。
* 他从来被妈妈没打过。
* 他第一次尝到被他人不信任的苦头。

(二)"把"、"被"构成的是两种完全不同的句式。(The sentences made up by "把" or "被" are two kinds of totally different patterns.)

1. "把"和"被"所引进的成分不同。由"把"引到动词前的一般是句中的受事；由"被"引到动词前的一般是句中的施事。(The sentence element introduced by "把" is different from that by "被". The one led by "把" is usually the patient in the sentence; and the one led by "被" is the agent.)例如：

大家把会议室打扫干净了。(打扫会议室)
　　(受事)
会议室被大家打扫干净了。(大家打扫)
　　(施事)

"把"字句的主语一般是施事，"被"字句的主语一般是受事。因此，"把"字句一般是主动句；"被"字句一般是被动句。(The subject in the "把" sentences is the agent, while the subject in the "被" sentence is the patient. Therefore, "把" sentences are active ones; and "被" sentences are passive ones.)例如：

19

狂风把桥边的大柳树刮倒了。(狂风刮)
(施事)　　　(受事)
桥边的大柳树被狂风刮倒了。(刮大柳树)
　(受事)　　(施事)

2. 从语义上看,"把"字句多表示施事如何处置或影响受事;"被"字句多表示受事不如意或不期望的遭遇。(From the viewpoint of semantics, "把" sentences mainly indicate how the agent deals with or influences the patient, while "被" sentences mainly indicate the unpleasant or unexpected happenings to the patient.)例如:

　　大雨把石子小路冲刷得干干净净。
　　你快去把他找回来吧!
　　战斗中,他不幸被一颗子弹射中了。
　　(Unfortunately, he was hit by a bullet in the battle.)
　　这件事使他一直被别人瞧不起。
　　(This made him looked down upon all along.)

3. 从结构形式上看,"把"字词组中,"把"引进的受事不能省略;"被"字词组中,当"被"引进的施事是不明确的或不需要说明的时候,可以不说,即可以省略。(From the perspective of structure, the object introduced by "把" can't be omitted in the word group led by "把", while in the word group led by "被", when the object introduced by "被" is not clear or is unnecessary to be identified, it can be omitted.)例如:

　　我把饭做好了。
　　他把这篇报告文学又读了一遍。
　　* 我把做好了。
　　* 他把又读了一遍。
　　他被公司开除了。
　　钱包被他弄丢了。
　　他被开除了。
　　钱包被弄丢了。

把 bǎ　　将 jiāng

〈介词〉< preposition >

由"把"或"将"构成的动词结构都有表示对人或事物处置的意思，但是，意义和用法不完全相同。(Both verbal structures made up by "把" or "将" express the meaning of dealing with someone or something, but they are different in meaning and usage.)

(一)"把"和"将"的语体色彩不同。(The register of "把" is different from that of "将".)

"把"通用于口语和书面语，"将"只用于书面语。("把" is generally used in both spoken language and written language, while "将" is only used in written language.)例如：

只用了一个月的时间就把小楼建起来了。

我上午就把传真发出去了。

她已经把床铺收拾好了。

现将物品与信件一并送上，请查收。

(Please check the articles and letters which are sent together.)

我们会将理想变为现实的。

(二) 意义和用法有所不同。(There are differences in meaning and usage.)

1."将"还有"拿"、"用"的意思，"把"有"拿"、"对"的意思。但是"将"引进的是动作、行为凭借的工具或事物，"把"没有这种用法。"把"引进的是动作的对象，"将"一般不用于这种情况。("将" also means "with" or "by way of", while "把" means "with" or "to". "将" introduces tools or things by which some action or behavior is done, while "把" doesn't. "把" introduces the object of the action and "将" is not usually used in this way.)例如：

将心比心(put oneself in another's place or shoes)

将错就错(leave a mistake uncorrected and make the best of it)

恩将仇报(requite kindness with enmity)

将功折罪(expiate one's crime by good deeds)

孔乙己显出极高兴的样子,将<u>两个指头的长指甲</u>敲着柜台。("用"的意思。)(Kong Yiji looked quite happy, knocking at the counter with his two long-nailed fingers.)

这个淘气鬼,奶奶把<u>他</u>一点办法也没有。("拿"的意思。)
(He is an imp, with whom his grandma can't do anything.)

他们从不把<u>我</u>当外人。

* 把鸡蛋碰石头,哪有不碎的?("把"换作"将"。)

* 她把手搭个凉棚,向村口望去。("把"换作"将"。)

2. "把"后有时可加量词"个",显得语气轻松、随便,口语色彩较浓。"将"没有这种用法。(Sometimes the measure word "个" is put after "把", indicating easy and casual mood. It is of strong flavour of spoken language. "将" is not used in this way.)例如:

偏偏把个老爷子病了。

(How could the old chap be made sick?)

这一玩可好,把个孩子丢了。

(We have such fun as to have not found the kid missing.)

李大爷的评书讲得好极了,把个小高听得入了迷。

* 我几年没回家了,将个老娘也想病了。("将"换作"把"。)

把 bǎ 拿 ná

〈介词〉< preposition >

(一)"把"和"拿"在引进动作对象上,可以通用,"拿"有"对"的意思;"把"侧重处置意义。比较起来,"拿"的口语色彩更浓一些。(When introducing the target of the action, both "把" and "拿" can be used, while "拿" has the same meaning of "对"; and "把" puts more emphasis on "handling something". Comparatively, "拿" is of stronger flavour of spoken language.)例如:

> 你能把/拿他怎么样?
>
> 他脸皮也太厚了,我们拿/把他一点办法也没有。
> (He is too thick-skinned. We can do nothing to him.)
>
> 我们都不把/拿张大爷当做五十岁的人。

(二)"拿"通常用来介绍出动作、行为凭借的工具或事物,表示这种意思时,"拿"有"用"的意思。"把"没有这种用法。("拿" usually introduces the tools and things by which an action or behavior is done. In this case, "拿" means "用", while "把" does not have such a usage.)例如:

> 拿笔写字　　拿碗盛饭　　拿礼物送人
>
> 拿鸡毛当令箭(take a chicken feather for a warrant to give commands)
>
> * 把笔写字　　* 把碗盛饭
>
> * 我进来的时候,他正把水果刀削苹果呢。("把"换作"拿"。)
>
> * 你们别把老实人开心了。("把"换作"拿"。)

白 bái　　白白 báibái

〈副词〉< adverb >

(一)"白"、"白白"都可以表示所做的事情没有达到预期的目的或取得应有的效果的意思,但是表示的语气和句子结构上有差别。("白" and "白白" both indicate one's effort has not reached the goal or produced the proper effect, but there is difference in the mood and the structure of the sentence construction.)

1."白白"比"白"语气更重。("白白" is stronger than "白" in the tone.)试比较:

> 白白费了半天嘴皮子。
>
> 白费了半天嘴皮子。

(waste my breath for nothing)

白白跑了几十里路。

白跑了几十里路。

2."白白"后边可以加"地",构成"白白地";"白"后边不能加"地"。("地"can be put after "白白" to form the expression "白白地", but that can't be done after "白".)

这场灾害使他白白地辛苦了一年。

(The calamity made his whole year's labour gone in vain.)

＊ 这场灾害使他白地辛苦了一年。

我不能白白地做出牺牲。

(I can't make the sacrifice for nothing.)

＊ 我不能白地做出牺牲。

3."白"可以修饰单个动词和单音动词;"白白"不能修饰单个动词,尤其是单个单音动词。"白白"所修饰的动词前或后应该有其他修饰语或补充语。("白" can modify a single verb and monosyllabic verb while "白白" can't do that, particularly with a single monosyllabic verb. There should be other modifiers or supplementary phrases before or after the verbs which "白白" modifies.)例如：

刚才那些道理算是白讲了,他半点儿也不懂。

(That talking with him has gone in vain, for he can't understand that at all.)

你托他帮忙,一定白托,他不会帮助你的。

客人没有来,害得他白白忙了一下午。

(His bustling the whole afternoon went in vain, for the guests didn't show up.)

咱们不能就这么白白地花了钱,一定得让他们赔偿经济损失。

＊ 你托他帮忙,一定白白托,他不会帮助你的。(白托)

＊ "功到自然成",功夫不会白白下。(功夫不会白下)

＊ 书店今天没开门,我白白跑。(我白白地跑了一趟)

24

4. "白"前可以用"不"、"没"等否定副词否定;"白白"前一般不可以用。(Negative adverbs like "不" and "没" can be used before "白" to indicate negative sense but that generally doesn't work before "白白".)例如:

不白下工夫　　没白费时间

这些东西没白押给他。(These things are not mortgaged to him for nothing.)

* 不白白下工夫　　* 没白白费时间
* 这些东西没白白押给他。

(二)"白"还可以表示不付出代价而得到好处的意思;"白白"不表示这种意思。("白" also indicates that one gets benefit for nothing, while "白白" does not have this meaning.)例如:

我们这是小本生意,你这样白吃白住我们可受不了。

(Ours is small business, so we can't endure your eating and staying here for nothing.)

走吧,白看的电影还不去呀。(Come on. How could you refuse to see the movie free of charge?)——白看的电影我也不去。

* 我们这是小本生意,你这样白白吃白白住我们可受不了。

* 走吧,白白看的电影还不去呀。——白白看的电影我也不去。

帮 bāng　　帮助 bāngzhù　　帮忙 bāngmáng

〈动词〉给以援助,使摆脱困难。

(<verb> give aids; help somebody get rid of difficulties.)

(一)"帮"、"帮助"、"帮忙"使用范围上稍有差别。(There is some difference among "帮","帮助"and "帮忙"in the scope of their use.)

"帮"多用于物质上的或具体的帮助;"帮助"可用于物质上、精神上的援助及非具体的帮助;"帮忙"则只用于别人有困难时具体地帮助做事。此外,"帮"口语色彩较浓,多用于口语;"帮助"则通用于口语和书面语。("帮" mainly means to help somebody materially or specifically, while "帮助" means to help somebody materially, spiritually and non-specifically, and "帮忙" means to help someone in straits with specific aid. Besides, "帮" has more flavour of the spoken language while "帮助" is commonly used in both spoken and written languages.)例如:

这行李太重了,你帮我拿一些吧。
你在这儿照看一下,我去帮他取药。
他现在很困难,我们应该帮助他渡过难关。
郝师傅不仅从精神上帮助了他,还从物质上帮助了他。
(Master Hao not only gave him spiritual help, but helped him materially.)
听说谢力星期天搬家,你去帮忙吗?
他结婚的时候,还是我帮忙做的家具呢。
* 郝师傅不仅从精神上帮了他,还从物质上帮了他。
* 郝师傅不仅从精神上帮了他的忙,还从物质上帮了他的忙。
* 听说谢力星期天搬家,你去帮 / 帮助吗?

"帮助"一词中含有"协助"这种对于非具体事情的帮助的意思,因此表示笼统的帮助的意义时,要用"帮助"。"帮"则多用于相对具体的帮助,语境中或句中有表示具体做的事情时,用"帮"较合适。(The word "帮助" implies giving assistance in non-specific cases. Therefore when indicating help in the general sense, "帮助" is used. "帮" is just mainly used for the specific help, so in the context or sentences where something specific will be done, "帮" is more proper.)例如:

她主动帮助孤寡老人。

(She helps the old widowed people without support on her own accord.)

　　* 她主动帮孤寡老人。
　　老师经常帮助同学们。
　　* 老师经常帮同学们。
　　她主动帮孤寡老人<u>洗衣服</u>。
　　老师经常利用课余时间帮同学们<u>练听力</u>。
　　我帮他<u>收拾完了</u>再走。

另外,音节数的协调有时也制约了对"帮"与"帮助"的选择。(Besides, the metric coordination requirements sometimes also restrict the selection of "帮" or "帮助".)例如:

　　你们要互相帮助。
　　* 你们要互相帮。
　　请您多加帮助。
　　* 请您多加帮。
　　请给以帮助。
　　* 请给以帮。

前面谈到具体意义的"帮"和笼统意义的"帮助",不是绝对的,而是相对用哪一个更好的问题。如这里只能用"帮助",不能用"帮",除了具体、笼统和语体色彩的区别外,主要是音节上的协调问题。(The uses of "帮" with its specific sense and "帮助" with its general sense as we talked before are not absolute. The point is which functions comparatively more properly in the sentences. Here it is only proper to use "帮助" but not "帮". Besides the differences of their registers, the main problem is how to coordinate the syllables.)

(二)具体用法上的区别。(The differences in specific use.)

1."帮"和"帮助"后边都可以接助词"过"或"了","帮"后边可以接"着",表示动作的一种方式,"帮助"后边一般不能接"着"。(Particles "过" or "了" can be used after "帮" and "帮助". While "着" can be used after "帮", indicating the way of the act;"着" can't be used after "帮助".)例如:

我帮过他。

他帮了我一次。

战士们帮着老乡抗洪救灾。

(The soldiers helped the villagers combat the flood and helped them tide over the natural disaster.)

他帮助过这个孩子。

她帮助了那位老人三年多。

* 她帮助着邻居打扫卫生。(她帮着邻居打扫卫生。)

* 我帮助着你提行李吧。(我帮着你提行李吧。)

"帮忙"是支配式离合词,后边不能接"了"、"着"、"过",但是可以把"了"、"着"、"过"插到"帮忙"之间。("帮忙" is a separable word. And "了","着","过" can't be used after it, but "了", "着","过" can be put between these two characters.)例如:

* 帮忙了一次 * 给我帮忙过 * 正帮忙着呢

　帮了一次忙　　给我帮过忙　　正帮着忙呢

2. "帮助"可以做某些具有抽象意义的动词的后续成分,"帮"和"帮忙"不可以。("帮助" can be used after some verbs of abstract meaning, but "帮" and "帮忙" can not be used that way.)例如:

进行帮助　给以帮助　感谢你们的真诚帮助

* 进行帮　* 给以帮　* 感谢你们的真诚帮

* 进行帮忙　* 给以帮忙　* 感谢你们的真诚帮忙

3. "帮"、"帮助"可以带宾语,"帮忙"的"忙"具有被支配的性质,在结构上它是"帮"的宾语,所以不能再带宾语。("帮" and "帮助" can be followed by objects. "忙" in "帮忙" is something like the object of the action and it constitutes the object of "帮" in structure, so the word can not be followed by other objects.)例如:

同学们正帮李大爷收麦子呢。

你们应该想办法帮助他。

＊ 你放心,我们可以帮忙你。(你放心,我们可以帮助你。)
　　＊ 他们会帮忙孩子们摆脱困境的。(他们会帮孩子们摆脱困境的。)

4. "帮助"一词中间不能插入其他成分,重叠使用时为 ABAB 式,即"帮助帮助";"帮忙"是离合词,其间可以插入别的成分(助词、代词、数量词等要放到"忙"前,做"忙"的修饰、限制语),甚至"忙"也可以用在"帮"的前边。重叠使用时为 AAB,即"帮帮忙"。〔Other compositions cannot be put between "帮" and "助". "帮助" can be reduplicated as ABAB, that is "帮助帮助". "帮忙" is a separable word, other compositions (such as particle, pronoun, and numeral-classifier compound can be put before "忙" as a modifier, or qualifier) and even "忙" can also be used before "帮". The reduplicated pattern is AAB, namely "帮帮忙"。〕例如:

　　　帮了一次忙　　帮我的忙　　帮了很大的忙　　帮这个忙
　　＊ 帮忙了一次　＊ 帮忙我　＊ 帮忙很大
　　＊ 帮忙这个

　　忙倒能帮,不知能否帮到点子上。
　　(It is all right to give you help, but I am not sure whether I could help you to the point.)
　　忙是帮了不少,只是一件事也没办成。
　　(I did help a lot but without even a simple result.)
　　＊ 帮忙帮忙,可以吗?(帮帮忙,可以吗?)
　　＊ 我帮了他一次助。
　　＊ 老师帮过我的助。

被 bèi　　叫 jiào　　让 ràng

〈介词〉< preposition >

"被"、"叫"、"让"都可以在被动句中引进动作的施事,这种句式中的主语一般是动作的受事。("被","叫" and "让" all introduce the agent of the action in a passive sentence. The subject in this sentence pattern is usually the object of the action.)例如：

困难终于被克服了。(克服困难。)

自行车叫小王借去了。(小王借自行车。)

那件事让他知道了。(他知道了那件事。)

(一)"被"、"叫"、"让"在语体色彩和构句上稍有不同。(For "被","叫" and "让", there are some differences in registers and sentence constitution.)

"被"书面语色彩较浓，口语中用的较少；"叫"、"让"口语色彩较浓，多用于口语。("被" has a fairly strong flavour of written language and is not very often used in spoken language. "叫" and "让" have a fairly strong flavour of spoken language and is generally used in spoken language.)例如：

从即日起，杨中已被公司开除。

(From today on, Yang Zhong is dismissed by the company.)

小三子叫人打了。

我的雨伞不知让谁拿去了。

在"被"字结构中，当说话人不想、不需要或不能说明动作的施事时，"被"字后面可以不必引进施事，此时"被"可以单用；"叫"、"让"结构中，"叫"、"让"后面的施事不可省掉，必须构成"叫/让＋动作施事"的结构。(In the "被" pattern, when the speaker doesn't need or can't explain the agent of the action, the agent can be omitted after the word "被". Here "被" can be used singly. In the "叫" and "让" patterns, the agent behind "叫" and "让" can not be omitted, and they must constitute the "叫/让＋agent of the action" pattern.)例如：

敌人被我们彻底消灭了。

敌人被彻底消灭了。

敌人叫／让我们彻底消灭了。

＊敌人叫／让彻底消灭了。

(二)"被"、"叫"、"让"构成的句式在结构上有一个共同特点:往往不能用一个光杆动词结束句子。因为这种句子主要用于"被(谁／什么)把(谁／什么)怎么样了"的语言环境中,因此,动词后一般要有动作形成的结果或某种情况、影响等的内容。(The sentence patterns of "被","叫" and "让" have one point in common, that is usually the sentence can't be ended with a single verb. The reason is this kind of sentence is mainly used in the context of "被(谁／什么)把(谁／什么)怎么样了". Generally there should be elements expressing the results or some circumstances and effect, etc. made by an action after verbs.)例如:

雨伞让我弄丢了。
房子被拆掉了。
衣服叫树枝刮破了。
石级小路被雨水洗刷得干干净净。
(The stone path was washed thoroughly clean by the rain.)
* 雨伞让我弄　　　* 衣服叫树枝刮
* 石级小路被雨水洗刷

此外,从意义上说,"被"、"叫"、"让"所构成的被动句多用于不如意的事情或没有明显好恶倾向的事情,用于如意的事情比较少(见上述例句)。[In addition, the passive voice which is made up by "被"、"叫" and "让" is mostly used for things going on not as one wishes or for those without obvious likes or dislikes and they are rarely used for pleasant things (take the examples above for your reference).]

被 bèi　　由 yóu

〈介词〉< preposition >

"被"、"由"都可以在句中引进动作的施事,这种句式中的主语通常是动作的受事。("被" and "由" in the sentences can both introduce the action doers and the subjects in the sentence patterns are usually the action receivers.)例如：

掉在湖里的<u>孩子</u>被解放军同志救了出来。(解放军同志救<u>孩子</u>。)

图纸被他弄丢了。(他弄丢了<u>图纸</u>。)

<u>队长</u>由小王担任。(小王担任<u>队长</u>。)

<u>铁的队伍</u>是由钢的班子带出来的。(钢的班子带出<u>铁的队伍</u>。)

(The iron troops is led by the steel leader group.)

但是,"被"、"由"在大多情况下不能通用。(But, in most cases, "被" and "由" are not exchangeable.)区别在于(Their differences are as follows):

(一) 结构关系上(In structure)

1."被"字句中的动词通常带有处置意义,大多使用具有具体动作性的动词,强调动作给受动者带来的结果或影响,所以大多情况下,不能以光杆动词结束句子,动词后常常有其他成分;"由"字句没有这种句义特征,句中动词可以用具体动作的动词,也可以用抽象意义的动词,常常用光杆动词结束句子。(In "被" sentences, the verbs usually mean acting on something and the verbs with the specific acting sense are often used to emphasize the result and influence brought to the action bearer. So generally, a single verb can not be used to finish the sentence, and there should be other elements after verbs. "由" sentences don't have this kind of feature. Both specific and abstract verbs can be used. Usually a single verb is used to finish the sentence.)例如:

花瓶被我打碎了。

雨伞被风刮走了。

下午的会议由陈主任主持。

这门课由李教授担任。

会标被张新写坏了。

＊会标被张新写。
　　会标由张新写。
　2."被"字句的受事只能出现在主语位置上,句中不再有宾语;"由"字句的受事可以出现在主语位置上,也可以出现在宾语的位置上。(The receiver of "被" structure can only be put in the position of the subject and there should be no other objects in the sentence; the receiver of the "由" sentence can be put either at the subject's place or at the objective's place.)例如:

　　敌人被我们打败了。
　　＊被我们打败了敌人。
　　这个计划由你来做。
　　总结报告由老刘做。
　　由你来做这个计划。
　　由老刘做总结报告。

　3."被"字引进的施事,当不想或无需说出或不知是谁不能说出时可以不说;"由"则必须构成"由"字词组出现在动词前。(The agent introduced by "被" may not be mentioned if unable, unnecessary or unwilling. A "由" word group has to be constituted in front of the verb.)例如:

　　他被大家批评了一顿。
　　他被批评了一顿。
　　钱由我来分配。
　　(The money must be distributed by me.)
　　＊钱由来分配。

　4."被"只能带表示人、组织、机构等意义的施动者;"由"除能带表示人、组织、机构等意义的施动者外,还可以带表示原因或来源、组成成分、方式等意义的词语。("被" will only be followed by the action-makers that represent people, organizations or institutions, etc. Besides being followed by people, organizations, and institutions, it can also be followed by words and phrases representing reasons or origin, component parts and methods.)例如：

　　这个案件的主犯已经<u>被公安局</u>抓获了。
　　方案被<u>有关部门</u>批准了。
　　他由<u>感冒</u>引起了肺炎。
　　(His flu caused pneumonia.)
　　琥珀是由<u>远古时代的松胶</u>变成的。
　　(Amber was transformed from pine gum of remote antiquity.)
　　我们这个侦破小组由<u>三个成员</u>组成。
　　主席由<u>民主选举</u>形成。
　　* 他被感冒引起了肺炎。
　　* 琥珀是被远古时代的松胶变成的。
　　* 我们这个侦破小组被三个成员组成。
　　* 主席被民主选举形成。

(二)语体色彩上(In flavour of style)

"被"构成的句式带有一定的消极色彩，多用于不情愿、不愉快或不如意的状态或行为。"由"构成的句式则具有一定的积极色彩，大多表示施事积极、愿意或主动承担的事情。(The sentence pattern of "被" is of certain negative flavour and mostly used in the unwilling, unpleasant or unfavourable states or behaviour. The sentence pattern of "由" is just of positive flavour and mostly indicates things that the action doers would undertake actively, willingly or initiatively.)例如：

　　他家的房子被洪水冲垮了。
　　我的心被这些事搅得七上八下的。
　　由我负责承担这项工程。
　　由连长带头向敌人的碉堡冲去。
　　由你用计算机来处理这份文件。

(三)语用环境上(In pragmatic context)

1. 句中强调的点不同。(There are differences in emphatic points.)

"被"字句强调受事,不强调施事。所以受事不能省,施事可以省(特定的语言环境例外);"由"字句恰好相反,强调施事,不强调受事。所以施事不能省,它可以在句首出现并支使宾语。(In "被" sentences, the object is emphasized, but the doer is not. That's to say the object can't be omitted except in particular contexts. In "由" sentences, there is totally different situation, that is, the doer is emphasized. So the doer can't be omitted and it can be placed at the beginning of the sentence to introduce the action to the object.)例如:

花瓶被我打碎了。

花瓶被打碎了。

* 被我打碎了。(没有受事。)

由你请他较为合适。

由你请较为合适。

由老张当头儿,怎么样?

(What if Lao Zhang be the head?)

2. 使用环境不同。(They are used in different contexts.)

"被"字句主要用于叙述,同时强调动作对后果的影响。所以句中动词通常为表示具体动作的动词,动词后也通常有其他成分,以表现对动作后果的影响。"由"字句则主要用于说明,说明的点主要在于施事的责任。所以,动词可以用具有抽象意义的动词,动词后不强调有表现对动作后果影响的成分。("被" sentences are used to narrate and emphasize the effect of the action. So, the verbs used generally are those that mean specific action and there are generally other compositions after the verbs in order to show the influence on the consequence of the action. The "由" sentence is mainly used for explanation, particularly on the responsibility of the agent. So the verbs of abstract meaning can be used and after such verbs, there aren't necessarily compositions emphasizing the consequence of the action.)例如:

衣服被雨淋湿了。
她被海洛因毒死了。
* 衣服被雨淋。
* 她被海洛因毒。
有关的目录由我整理汇编。
(The concerning catalogue will be arranged and compiled by me.)
由我来做他的工作。

~边 biān　　~旁 páng

〈方位词〉表示在相关事物的附近。
(<noun of locality> indicating being close to related things.)
(一)意义上的差别。(Differences in meaning.)

1."~边"所指的附近,几乎是贴近那个相关的事物,甚至是进入那个相关事物的边缘;"~旁"所指的附近,一般与那个相关的事物不连接,更不能进入那个相关事物的边缘。可以离那个相关事物稍有距离甚至稍远一点儿。("~边" means being close to something or even getting into the scope of something. "~旁" means being near to something but not closely linked to it and not in its scope — there usually leaves a certain distance between the related parts.)例如:

把桌子边上那本词典递给我。(进入桌子的边缘。)
他沿着游泳池边游着。(进入游泳池内,是游泳池的边缘。)
他靠着我身边坐了下来。(他的身体与我的身体相连接。)
湖边有一棵很大的垂柳。(接近湖。)
小明就是那个在车旁玩的孩子。(车的附近。)
楼旁有一个很大的停车场。(楼左右的附近,离楼有距离。)

* 他沿着游泳池旁游着。
* 楼边有一个很大的停车场。

2."~旁"所指的附近,多指那个相关事物的左右两侧;"~边"所指的附近,则不限于那个相关事物的左右两边,只要是那个相关事物的边缘或周围附近都可以。("~旁" usually refers to either left or right side of the concerning object, while "~边" is not restricted to this but means any place surrounding the concerning object.)例如:

我站在他身旁。(他左右的某一侧。)
门旁挂着一个牌子。(门的左右的某一侧。)
墙边有一个洞。(墙的任何一边。)
她坐在床边,一句话也不说。(床的任何一边。)

有时"~边"、"~旁"可以换用,这是因为它们都表示离相关的事物很近的意思。(Sometimes "~边" and "~旁" are exchangeable when they express the meaning of being near to the related parts.)例如:

路边/旁有很多人。
她身边/旁没有什么人了。

有时"~边"、"~旁"虽然可以换用,但是表示的意思不一样。(Although "~边" and "~旁" sometimes are exchangeable, the meanings they express are different.)例如:

井边垂着一根绳子。(绳子可能垂在井的内侧边缘。)
井旁放着一根绳子。(绳子一定是在井的外侧附近。)
她坐在沙发边跟我说话。(没有离开沙发,在沙发的边缘。)
她坐在沙发旁跟我说话。(离开了沙发,在沙发附近。)

(二)"边"与"旁"跟名词搭配上的差别。(The differences between "边" and "旁" when they collocate with nouns.)

1."边"、"旁"常常可以跟长形、方形及边儿突出的事物的名词、有阻隔作用的事物的名词或跟水、火等有关的名词搭配。

("边" and "旁" can be used together with nouns describing long-shaped, square-shaped and protruding edged things and nouns which mean blocking or with nouns related to water, fire, etc.)例如：

马路边/旁 操场边/旁 桥边/旁 桌子边/旁 枕头边/旁
主席台边/旁 窗户边/旁 帘子边/旁 门边/旁 柱子边/旁
池边/旁 河边/旁 井边/旁 桶边/旁 火边/旁

2. 很广阔的、在视线范围内很难控制住的事物，或者位于事物边缘的事物名词，一般与"边"搭配不与"旁"搭配。(Nouns denoting things which are broad and hard to control within eyesight or those on the edge of something else generally collocate with "边" but not "旁".)例如：

水边　海边　岸边　天边　云边　田边
地边　墙边　床边　手边　腮边　嘴边
＊海旁　＊岸旁　＊天旁　＊田旁　＊地旁
＊腮旁

3. 某些跟楼房类建筑物、跟食品、植物类或跟工具、人体部位等有关的名词与"旁"搭配，不与"边"搭配。(Some nouns related to buildings, food, plants or tools and parts of human body, etc., can collocate with "旁", but not with "边".)例如：

楼旁 车站旁 饭店旁 学校旁 商店旁 银行旁 庙旁
＊楼边　＊车站边　＊饭店边　＊学校边　＊商店边
豆腐旁 馒头旁 西瓜旁 橘子旁 白菜旁 柳树旁
＊西瓜边　＊橘子边　＊白菜边　＊柳树边
汽车旁 拖拉机旁 被子旁 钢笔旁 口袋旁 扁担旁
鼻子旁　眉毛旁　舌头旁　眼旁　尾巴旁
＊口袋边　＊头发边　＊眼边　＊尾巴边

别的 biéde　其他(的) qítā(de)　另外(的) lìngwài(de)
别的、其他(的)〈代词〉< pron. >

另外(的)〈代词〉〈副词〉〈连词〉< pron. > < adv. > < conj. >

"别的"、"另外(的)"、"其他(的)"作代词用时,都可以用来指示或指代某范围以外的人或事物,但是意义和用法有一定差别。〔When used as pronouns, "别的", "另外(的)" and "其他(的)" all can indicate or refer to sb. or sth. beyond certain limits, but there is certain difference in meaning and in use.〕

(一) 意义上(In meaning)

"别的"指示或指代某范围以外的人或事物通常具有泛指性,即不是确定的;"另外(的)"则通常具有确指性,即确定的,只是不明说罢了;"其他(的)"通常有两种情况:一是泛指的(不确定的),一是确指的(确定的)。〔"别的" indicates or refers to people or things beyond certain scope and usually in general sense; "另外(的)" usually makes a particular reference. It just does not mention it clearly. "其他(的)" is used in both ways: one is in general sense (being indefinite) and the other definite.〕例如:

我只要一碗米饭、一个汤就行了,别的都不要。(泛指)
你还想买点儿别的吗?(泛指)
我只要这一本就够了,另外那几本你们分了吧。

(确指)

你稍等一下,我还要告诉你另外一件事情。(确指)
从桂林分手后我们就回来了,他们又去其他地方旅游去了。(泛指)
小王、小李由我带,其他三个人由你带。(确指)

当"别的"和"其他(的)"都具有泛指意义时,有时可以互换使用;当"另外(的)"和"其他(的)"都具有确指意义时,有时也可以互换使用。〔"别的" and "其他(的)" are exchangeable when in general reference sense, "另外(的)" and "其他的" are exchangeable when in definite sense.〕例如:

39

你还想买点儿其他的吗?(泛指)

我只要这一本就够了,其他几本你们分了吧。(确指)

从桂林分手后我们就回来了,他们又去别的地方旅游去了。(泛指)

小王、小李由我带,另外三个人由你带。(确指)

(二) 搭配上(In collocation)

因为"别的"只具有泛指意义,所以不能与有确定范围的数量词语结合;"另外(的)"、"其他(的)"有确指性,可以跟数量词语结合。但是,与"另外(的)"结合的数量短语可以是表示单数意义的,也可以是表示复数意义的;与"其他(的)"结合的数量短语则只能是表示复数意义的。〔Because "别的" only makes a general reference, it can not be used together with numeral-classifier compounds. "另外的" and "其他的" have their definite reference, so they can be used together with numeral-classifier compounds. The numeral-classifier phrases used together with "另外(的)" can either be singular or plural, while the numeral-classifier phrases used together with "其他(的)" can only be plural.〕例如:

可惜的是我只记住了诗的这两句,别的都忘了。

(It is a pity I only remember these two lines in the poem and forget all the others.)

* 可惜的是我只记住了诗的这两句,别的那些句都忘了。

这几份是日文资料,另外那几份是英文资料。

这几份是日文资料,其他几份是英文资料。

你先走吧,我还有另外一件事要办。

* 你先走吧,我还有其他一件事要办。

"另外(的)"确指性比较强,它常常跟指量词组结合;"其他(的)"虽然可以用于确指,但是指示性没有那么强,因此通常不跟指量词组结合。〔"另外(的)" has a fairly strong flavour of the definite reference and usually is used together with measure word group. Although "其他(的)" can be used to express definite reference, its reference meaning is not that strong and usually is not put together with measuring word group.〕例如：

我们住这一间,另外那几间你们住。

就剩这三辆车了,另外那几辆都叫别人买走了。

我们住这一间,其他几间你们住。

就剩这三辆车了,其他几辆都叫别人买走了。

(三) 功能上(In function)

1."别的"、"其他(的)"都可以单独在句子中作主语、宾语、定语；"另外(的)"可以单独作定语,但是一般情况下,不能单独作主语、宾语,与指量、数量等词组结合后,可以作主语、宾语。〔"别的"and "其他(的)"can be independently used as a subject, object or attribute in the sentence; "别的" can be independently used as an attribute, but generally it can not be independently used as a subject or object, but when collocated with measuring word group and numeral-classifier compounds, "另外(的)" can be subject as well as object.〕例如：

别的都卖了,就剩下这一点儿破烂了。(主语)

(The others are sold out except these little worthless stuff here.)〔subject〕

先说说大家最关心的房子问题,有时间的话再说点儿别的。(宾语)

除了广州,你们还去别的地方了吗？(定语)

除了环境卫生合格了,其他都不合格。(主语)

(All the other items failed except the environmental sanitation.)〔subject〕

别只关心吃的了,我们聊点儿其他的吧。(宾语)

不光东北下了大雪,其他地区也下了大雪。(定语)

除了百货大楼,你顺便再到另外几家商店看看。(定语)

那天来了两个人,一个是男的,另外那个是女的。(与

指量词组结合后作主语)

我拿这三捆,你拿另外三捆。(与数量词组结合后作宾语)

* 那天来了两个人,一个是男的,另外是女的。

* 我拿这三捆,你拿另外的。

2."别的"、"其他(的)"都只有代词用法;"另外"还有副词用法和连词用法。作副词用时,它可以作状语;作连词用时,它可以连接句子。"别的"、"其他"都不能这样用。〔"别的" and "其他(的)" are used only as pronouns. "另外" can also be used as an adverb and conjunction. While used as an adverb, it functions as an adverbial; while used as a conjunction, it can join the sentences. "别的" and "其他" cannot be used this way.〕例如:

今天实在是没有时间,我们另外再找时间谈吧。(副词——状语)

除了三个日本朋友,另外还请了几个中国朋友。(副词——状语)

上午我们把这几件事情处理一下,另外,你还得去通知一下小李,明天务必到会。(连词——连接句子)

* 今天实在是没有时间,我们别的/其他再找时间谈吧。

* 除了三个日本朋友,别的/其他还请了几个中国朋友。

* 上午我们把这几件事情处理一下,别的/其他,你还得去通知一下小李,明天务必到会。

别人 biéren　　别的 biéde

〈代词〉 < pron. >

"别人"跟"别的"虽然都有另外的意思,但是意义差别很大,使用范围不同。"别人"只指人,它指另外的人、其他的人或指自己以外的某个人、某些人,甚至个别对话环境中,还可以指说话人自己。(Both "别人" and "别的" have the meaning of "another" but there is a big difference in their meanings and usage. "别人" refers to other persons, the other person or somebody else, and in specific conversational context, it may even refer to the speaker himself.) 例如：

我觉得他哪个方面都比别人好。

(In my opinion he is superior in every aspect to the others.)

家里只剩下我一个人了,没有别人了。

你只关心自己,从来不关心别人。

别人都说了,该你说了。

她不太愿意说话,别人问了才回答。

(She is unwilling to speak and would give answers only when being asked by others.)

你们笑什么？少拿别人开心好不好！(指说话人自己)

(What do you laugh at? You'd better not make fun of others.)

"别的"却不同,它主要指另外的、其他的事物、事情等。("别的" is different. It mainly refers to something else or other things.) 例如：

这个饭店不太干净,我们去别的饭店看看。

别的节目都没有意思,只有这个节目还行。

(The other performances are not interesting except this.)

风衣除了这种样子的以外,还有别的样式的吗？

"别的"单独作句子的主语、宾语时,只能指代事物,不能指代人或处所。指代人或处所时,应该用"别人"或"别处"。(When independently used as a subject or object in a sentence, it only refers to things, but not people or places. When referring to people or places, "别人" or "别处" is used.) 例如：

我只负责这一项工作,别的都交给别人做了。

(I am only in charge of this job and the others have been

consigned to other people.)

这个电视剧太没有意思了,我们看点儿别的吧。

你们看看这些菜够不够,是不是再要点儿别的?

* 宿舍里只剩下我们俩了,别的都出去玩了。(改作"别人"。)

* 我觉得他哪个方面都比别的好。(改作"别人"。)

* 我们去别的看看吧。(改作"别处"。)

别人 biéren　　人家 rénjia　　大家 dàjiā

〈代词〉代指人。

(< pron. > referring to people.)

(一)"别人"与"人家"

1."别人"与"人家"都可以代指自己或某人以外的人,即都可以泛指第三人称。(Both "别人" and "人家" refer to someone else or other people except oneself or a certain person. They all indefinitely refer to the third person.)例如:

别人/人家躲都来不及呢,你却主动往上凑。

(Others are hurrying to avoid, but you take the initiative to step forward.)

要学习别人/人家的长处,克服自己的短处。

(One must learn other's strong points and overcome one's own shortcomings.)

小声说话,别妨碍别人/人家学习。

(Lower your voice. You oughtn't to disturb others from studying.)

别人/人家都走了,只有小王还在继续看书。

但是,"人家"还有确指第三人称的用法,指前面提到的某人或某些人,相当于"他"、"他们";"别人"没有这一用法。(But "人家" can definitely refer to the third person, that is, somebody or some people mentioned formerly and has the same meaning as "他" or "他们", but "别人" is not used this way.）例如：

让我去做工作,人家会听我的吗?（确指某部分人。）

这些东西我们不能要,还给人家吧。（确指某人或某些人。）

人家不想见你,你就别去惹人烦了。（确指某人或某些人。）

(You'd better not bother others since he/she/they doesn't/don't want to see you.)

* 这些东西我们不能要,还给别人吧。
* 别人不想见你,你就别去惹人烦了。

2. "人家"在对话环境中还可以称代说话人自己,相当于第一人称"我"。这种句子通常含有亲昵味道的埋怨和不满,多用于关系亲近的人之中。"别人"个别情况下也有这种用法,但是很少。(In dialogues, "人家" may refer to the speaker himself just as the first person "我". This kind of sentence usually implies intimate complaint and discontent, mainly used among people with close relationship. Occasionally "别人" also means the same but only in rare cases.）例如：

人家都快急死了,你却在这儿看人家的笑话。

(I am worried to death, but you are just here to laugh at me.)

人家都忙死了,你也不来帮帮忙。

你们笑什么? 少拿人家开心好不好!

(What do you laugh at? Don't make fool of me.)

你们笑什么? 少拿别人开心好不好!

"人家"还可以用于人名前,具有复指作用。"别人"不能用于这种情况。("人家" can also be used before a person's name, referring to the same person. While "别人" cannot be used in this case.）例如：

你看人家王师傅,多谦虚呀!

人家王力才是真正的男子汉呢。

＊你看别人王师傅，多谦虚呀！

＊别人王力才是真正的男子汉呢。

(二)"大家"与"别人"、"人家"

1."别人"、"人家"都可以代指自己或某人以外的人,而"大家"则指一定范围内所有的人。("别人" and "人家" can both refer to someone else or some other people while "大家" refers to all the people within a certain range.)例如：

大家都到齐了,我们开始吧。

这个话题大家都感兴趣。

这种句子如果用"别人"、"人家"的话,就会含有其他意义。(If "别人" or "人家" is used in these two sentences, they mean something else.)例如：

别人都到齐了。(王主任却还没来。)

(The others are all here.)〔The Dean, Mr. Wang, hasn't shown up.〕

这个话题别人都感兴趣。(只有我不感兴趣。)

(All the others are interested in this topic.)〔Except me.〕

有时"大家"也可以不包括在场的所有的人,但一定用于跟某人或某些人对举的环境,在这种环境中,"大家"不包括用来对举的某人或某些人。(Sometimes "大家" doesn't necessarily include all the people present, especially when enumerating contrastingly, and here the scope of "大家" doesn't include the person or persons enumerated.)例如：

王师傅,大家看你来了。("大家"不包括王师傅。)

大家都在为你们俩担心,你们俩怎么用这种态度对待大家？("大家"不包括"你们俩"。)

(The others are worrying about you two. How could you treat us all with such an attitude?)

2."大家"还可以用在"你们"、"我们"、"咱们"后面,具有

46

复指作用。"别人"、"人家"没有这一用法。("大家" can also be used after "你们","我们"and "咱们" to refer to the same people. "别人" and "人家" cannot be used in this way.)例如:

　　这是<u>你们大家</u>的事,<u>你们大家</u>应该坐下来好好商量商量。
　　他是<u>咱们大家</u>的孩子,咱们一定要把他抚养成人。
　　* 他是咱们别人/人家的孩子,咱们一定要把他抚养成人。

冰凉 bīngliáng　　冰冷 bīnglěng

〈形容词〉表示很凉、很冷。

(<adjective> very cool, very cold.)

(一)"冰凉"、"冰冷"的相同之处:(Similarities between "冰凉" and "冰冷":)

　1. 意义上都有"很冷"的意思。(Both can mean "very cold".)

　2. 结构上,"冰"都带有程度意义,是"像冰那样(凉/冷)"的意思,所以不再接受程度副词的修饰。〔In terms of structure, "冰" has the meaning of degree (as cool / cold as ice), therefore it does not need to be modified by adverbs of degree.〕例如:

　　* 很冰凉/冰冷　　　* 十分冰凉/冰冷
　　* 不太冰凉/冰冷

　3. "冰凉"、"冰冷"的重叠方式都是 ABAB 式,不能重叠成 AABB 式。(The reduplicated patterns of "冰凉"and "冰冷"are ABAB, not AABB.)例如:

　　海水冰凉冰凉的,不能游泳。

　　(The sea water is cold and chilly. It is impossible to swim in it.)

　　天是太冷了,稍站一会儿,浑身上下就冰冷冰冷的。
　　* 海水冰冰凉凉的,不能游泳。
　　* 天是太冷了,稍站一会儿,浑身上下就冰冰冷冷的。

(二)"冰凉"、"冰冷"的不同之处主要是意义上的差别。(The

differences between "冰凉" and "冰冷" are mainly in meaning.)

1. "冰凉"的"凉"主要是触觉上可以触及得到的"冷";"冰冷"的"冷"则主要是一种感觉,不一定非要触及到。(In the word "冰凉","凉" means the tactile sensation of "cool"; while in "冰冷","冷" is a kind of feeling, it isn't necessarily tactile.)例如:

桔子汁冰凉冰凉的,喝着真舒服。(口触及到的)

她用手捧着孩子冰凉的小脸,心疼极了。(手触及到的)

(She cupped the kid's cold face and felt a great sorrow.) [by hands]

冰冷的月光倾撒在湖面上。(只是一种感觉)

(The cold moonlight spread over the surface of the lake.) [a feeling]

随着他的到来,一股冰冷的寒气也涌了进来。(只是一种感觉)

(A puff of cold air got into the room with his entrance.) [a feeling]

所以"冰凉"常常用来形容"~的雨点"、"~的泉水"、"~的石头"、"~的板凳"、"~的铁板"、"~的手脚"、"~的脊背"等等;"冰冷"常常用来形容"~的寒气"、"~的海风"等等。(So "冰凉" is usually used in the following expressions like "cool raindrops", "cool spring water", "cool stones", "a cool bench", "a cool iron plate", "cool hands and feet", "cool back", etc.; and "冰冷" is used in "cold air", "cold sea wind", etc.)

2. 因为"冰冷"一般不用于具体的触及到的"冷",而多是一种感觉,所以具有一定的抽象性,常常被用来形容神态、心情、心肠、环境、气氛等等;而"冰凉"一般不能用于这些方面。(Because "冰冷" does not express the coldness felt by touch, but a

kind of feeling, it is an abstract word and is generally used to describe expression, state of mind, heart, circumstance and atmosphere, etc.; but "冰凉" cannot be used in those senses.)例如：

她看她丈夫时,那双美丽的眼睛是冰冷冰冷的。

(Her beautiful eyes were cold while she was looking at her husband.)

他冰冷的脸上没有一丝笑意。

(There is no smile on his cold face.)

她不是那种心肠冰冷的人。

她像一只扑灯蛾似的到处乱闯,遇到的只是冰冷的现实。

(She rushed herself here and there like a moth flapping to lights, with the result of having to be faced with only the cold reality.)

大姐忍受不了家中冰冷的空气,很快地嫁人了。

* 她看她丈夫时,那双美丽的眼睛是冰凉冰凉的。
* 他冰凉的脸上没有一丝笑意。
* 她不是那种心肠冰凉的人。
* 她像一只扑灯蛾似的到处乱闯,遇到的只是冰凉的现实。
* 大姐忍受不了家中冰凉的空气,很快地嫁人了。

3. 色彩上也稍有不同。"冰凉"可以用于中性义,也可以用于褒义。用于褒义时,它可以表示清凉可口、凉爽舒适的感觉；"冰冷"可以用于中性义,也可以用于贬义。用于贬义时,它可以表示冷淡、冷漠甚至冷酷的意思。(There is some difference in their tints. "冰凉" can be used in neutral sense as well as in commendatory sense. When used in commendatory sense, "冰凉" may indicate the feeling of cool taste and cool comfort. "冰冷" can be used in neutral sense as well as in derogatory sense. While used for derogatory sense, it may indicate the meaning of being cheerless,

indifferent and even cold-blooded.)例如:

夏日里,喝一口冰凉的山泉水,真是从里凉到外,舒服极了。
(In summer days, drinking a mouthful of the cool spring water makes one feel extremely comfortable from the inside to the outside.)

冰凉的晚风拂去一身的燥热,孩子们终于甜甜地睡了。
(The cool night wind brought away the hot and dry, and the children finally fell into a sweet sleep.)

* 夏日里,喝一口冰冷的山泉水,真是从里凉到外,舒服极了。
* 冰冷的晚风拂去一身的燥热,孩子们终于甜甜地睡了。

我已经从他那冰冷的眼神里读懂了一切。
(I have read all the meaning in his cold eyes.)

面对这冰冷的现实,他更加清醒了。
(Facing the cold reality, he is much clear-minded.)

* 我已经从他那冰凉的眼神里读懂了一切。
* 面对这冰凉的现实,他更加清醒了。

不 bù　　没(有) méi(yǒu)

〈副词〉表示否定。

(<adverb> negative in meaning.)

"不"、"没有"都有否定的意义,都可以放在动词、形容词前,对动作、性状进行否定。但是它们的意义和用法不同。(Both "不" and "没有" mean negation and can be used in front of verbs or adjectives to negate the actions, characters and states. But they are different in meaning and use.)

(一)"不"多用于主观意愿,否定现在、将来的动作行为,也可以用于过去;"没(有)"主要用于客观叙述,否定动作、状态的发生或完成,因此只限于指过去和现在,不能指将来。("不" is mainly used to express subjective desire and negate the present or future actions, and it is also used for past actions; "没有" is mainly used in objective description to negate the happening or accomplishment of the action and state and is restricted to the past time and the present period, and can not be used for the future.)例如:

上次、这次他都没参加,听说下次还不想参加。
（客观、过去）　　　　（主观、将来）
* 上次、这次他都没参加,听说下次还没想参加。
我不吃早饭了。（主观、现在）
我没吃早饭呢。（客观、现在）

(二)否定经常性、习惯性动作或非动作性动词(是、认识、知道、像等),要用"不",不能用"没(有)";否定"有"要用"没"。〔When negating regular, habitual actions or non-action verbs (like "是","认识","知道","像"), "不" is used instead of "没(有)"。 The negation of "有" is "没有".〕例如:

他从来不迟到、不早退。
他既不抽烟,又不喝酒。(是指他没有抽烟、喝酒的行为。)
(He neither smokes nor drinks.)
这不是我的房间。
我不认识他。
我不知道选什么专业好。
这儿没有你要的资料。
* 他从来没迟到、没早退。
* 我没知道选什么专业好。
* 我没认识他。
* 这儿不有你要的资料。

(三)用在形容词前表示对性质的否定,要用"不";表示对状态

51

变化发生的否定,可以用"没(有)"。("不" is used in front of adjectives to negate the nature; "没有" can be used to negate the change of the states.)例如:

近来他身体不好,让他休息吧。
这种材料不结实,换别的吧。
* 近来他身体没好,让他休息吧。
* 这种材料没结实,换别的吧。
天还没亮,再睡一会儿吧。
苹果还没红,过些日子再摘吧。

(四)"不"可以用在所有的能愿动词前;"没"只能用于"能"、"能够"、"敢"等少数几个能愿动词前。("不" can be used in front of all the modal verbs, while "没" can only be used in front of a few modal verbs such as "能","能够" and "敢".)例如:

不能说　不要讲　不敢看　不会写　不该做　不愿走
没能听完　没能够说服他　没敢看
* 没会写　* 没该做　* 没愿走　* 没可以告诉他

(五)"不"可以放在动词和结果补语中间,表示不可能;"没"没有这一用法。("不" can be used between the verb and the complement of result to mean impossibility, while "没" cannot be used this way.)例如:

捆不住　看不完　记不住　听不清楚　扫不干净
* 捆没住　* 看没完　* 记没住　* 听没清楚
* 扫没干净

(六)"不"只有副词功能,只能出现在谓词性词语前;"没(有)"除了副词功能外,还有动词功能,所以它可以对具有、存在、比较、数量等进行否定。("不" only functions as an adverb and is only used in front of predicative words and phrases. Besides functioning as an adverb, "没有" can also function as a verb. It may negate the concepts like possession, existence, comparison and quantity.)例如:

副词:这个课题暂时不研究了。
　　　　这个课题还没研究。
　　副词:衣服不干。
　　　　衣服没干。
　　动词:他是个没有头脑的人。
　　　　屋里怎么没有人呢?
　　　　这件行李没有二十公斤重。
　　　　他汉语说得没有我好。
　* 他是个不头脑的人。
　* 屋里怎么不人呢?
　* 他汉语说得不我好。
　* 这件行李不二十公斤重。

不比 bùbǐ　　没有 méiyǒu

这两个词语都可以用于比较句,都可以构成"不比/没有 + 名 + 形"的句式,但是意义和结构形式有一定差别。(These two words can both be used in comparative sentences and can make up the pattern of "不比/没有 + n. + adj.", but there are some differences in meaning and structure.)

(一) 意义上(In meaning)

"不比"是"比"形式上的否定,但是不一定是意义上的否定。它实际上常常是对话语语用上的否定、预设条件上的否定或者客观常理、常识上的否定。("不比" is the negation of "比" in form, but it is not necessarily its negation in sense. It is actually quite often the pragmatical negation, prefixed condition, or the objective rules or knowledge.)例如:

　　他的学问不比你高,要相信自己。(他低你高。)
　　他的学问不比你高多少。(他、你接近。)
　　他的学问不比你高,我看你们俩差不多。(他、你几乎一样。)

他的学问不比你高,我甚至觉得你比他还要好些。(可能被认为他高你低,实际上有可能你高他低。)

〔He is not superior to you in learning and I even think you are much better than him. (Maybe you are considered inferior to him in learning but actually you are likely to be superior.)〕

别看他是教授,可是他的学问并不比你高,他只是比较喜欢显示罢了。(应该他高你低,实际上他低你高。)

(Don't regard him as a professor for he is no more learned than you. It is just because he is fond of showing off.)

这些句子形式上是 A 低 B 高,但是说话人实际上表达的并不是这个意思,而是括号中的意思,括号中的意思实际上是从语用上的预设条件中来的。(In these sentences A is inferior to B in form, but actually that is not what is meant by the speaker. The expressions in brackets are actually what the speaker really means, and that meaning is only got from the pre-arranged pragmatic conditions.)

"没有"用于比较句的否定倒可以看成是对"比"字句意义上的否定,因为它是对 A 项真正地否定。("没有"used in the comparative sentence can be taken as the negation of "比" sentence, for actually it is the negation to "A".)例如:

他没有我高。(他跟我比,否定他高。)

我读的书没有他多。(我跟他比,否定我读的书多。)

这个售货员没有那个售货员热情。(这个售货员跟那个售货员比,否定这个售货员热情。)

(二) 结构上(In structure)

1."没有"对句中形容词的色彩有所限制,它一般要求形容词含有人们对人与事物的性质状态抱有希望或喜欢的积极色彩,例如:漂亮、美、干净、聪明、灵巧、舒服、细致、热情、潇洒等。大多情况下,不选择具有消极意义的形容词,例如:丑、坏、脏、笨、死板、难受、马虎、庸俗等。"不比"句没有这种限制。(By "没有", certain restrictions are placed on the adjectives which usually express one's hopes and aspirations, such as beautiful, pretty, clean, intelligent, smart, comfortable, careful, enthusiastic, natural and unrestrained. In most cases, adjectives with negative sense, such as ugly, bad, dirty, stupid, rigid, miserable, careless, vulgar, etc. are not used. The sentence of "不比" doesn't have these restrictions.)例如：

他处理问题可没有你那么灵活。

(In respect of handling problems he is by far less flexible than you.)

* 他处理问题可没有你那么死板。

张力写作业没有李明认真。

* 张力写作业没有李明马虎。

这条河没有那条河长。

* 这条河没有那条河短。

他不比你笨，你就放心大胆地让他去吧。

(He is as clever as you. Just set your mind at rest to let him go.)

他不比你聪明，你要相信自己的能力。

(He is not brighter than you. Just believe in your own ability.)

这间屋子不比那间屋子小，就用这间吧。

这间屋子不比那间屋子大，却显得那么宽敞。

2. "不比"句可以含有比较的双方相差不大的意思，所以形容词后可以接"几"、"多少"、"哪"等疑问词构成的非疑问方式，表示差不多的虚指数量。"没有"句没有这种意思，所以不能接这种词语。(There is a little difference between the two comparative parts in the sentence of "不比", so adjectives can be followed by non interrogative pattern made up of "几", "多少" or "哪", indicating the approximate number or amount. The sentence of "没有" doesn't function like this and cannot be followed by these word groups.)例如：

他不比你高多少。
(He is not much taller than you.)
我不比他早来多长时间。
(I didn't arrive much earlier than him.)
老刘的情况不比老马好到哪儿去。
(Lao Liu's condition is no better than Lao Ma's.)
* 他没有你高多少。
* 我没有他早来多长时间。
* 老刘的情况没有老马好到哪儿去。

不如 bùrú   没有 méiyǒu

〈动词〉< verb >

"不如"、"没有"都可以用于比较句,表示 A 项达不到或赶不上 B 项的意思,有时可以互换使用。这两个词对句中比较点——形容词或动词性词语都有共同的要求,要求形容词或动词性词语含有人们对人与事物的性质、状态抱有希望、喜欢的积极色彩。(Both "不如" and "没有" are used in comparative sentences, indicating A is worse than B or A falls behind B. Sometimes they are exchangeable in use. These two words require that the adjectives or verbal phrases have positive flavour like qualities of men and things and condition that people hope for and like very much.)例如:

那个沙发看上去没有/不如这个沙发舒服。
今年夏天没有/不如去年夏天凉快。
他还没有/不如你聪明呢。
那本词典不如/没有这本词典好。
坐汽车还不如骑自行车方便呢。
* 去年夏天没有 / 不如今年夏天闷热。
* 你没有 / 不如他笨。
* 骑自行车不如 / 没有坐汽车麻烦。

但是,这两个词有时有一定的差别,并且不能互换使用。

(But sometimes there is some difference between these two words and they are not changeable.)主要差别有:

(一)意义上(In meaning)

1."不如"、"没有"就一般的使用来说,意义稍有偏颇。"不如"句稍微侧重肯定 B 项;"没有"句稍微侧重否定 A 项。这与"不如"的 A 项赶不上 B 项好、"没有"的 A 项达不到 B 项的标准的意义有关。(Generally, "不如" and "没有" lay emphasis on different points. The sentences of "不如" lay particular emphasis on B; while the sentence of "没有" lay particular emphasis on A. This relates to the meaning that A is not as good as B in "不如" sentence and A can't reach the standard in B in "没有" sentence.)例如:

那个沙发看上去不如这个沙发舒服。(重在肯定这个沙发。)

那个沙发看上去没有这个沙发舒服。(重在否定那个沙发。)

2."不如"句只有比较的意义,"没有"句除了比较的意义外,还有比拟的意义,即说话人不是真的要将 A 项与 B 项进行比较,而是表示比拟。表示比拟时,要用"没有"。(The sentence of "不如" only has its comparative meaning. Besides its comparative meaning, the sentence of "没有" also has its metaphorical meaning, namely the speaker does not really make the comparison between A and B, but use metaphor. When making a metaphor, "没有" has to be used.)例如:

你刚生下来那会儿,脑袋还没有拳头大。

(At the time you were born, your head was not bigger than a fist.)

个子没有枪高,倒想扛枪啦。

(You are not taller than a gun, how could you think about being a soldier?)

(二)结构上(In structure)

1. "不如"句可以构成"A 项 + 不如 + B 项 + 形容词"的格式,也可以构成"A 项 + 不如 + B 项"的格式;"没有"句只能构成"A 项 + 没有 + B 项 + 形容词"的格式,不能构成"A 项 + 没有 + B 项"的格式。(The sentence of "不如" can form the pattern "A + 不如 + B + adj.", or "A + 不如 + B"; while the sentence of "没有" can only form the pattern "A + 不如 + B + adj.", not the pattern "A + 没有 + B".) 例如:

要说方便的话,坐汽车还不如骑自行车呢。

(As far as convenience is concerned, riding in a bus is no better than cycling.)

他写字不如我。

这个方案不如那个方案,那个方案更实际些。

* 要说方便的话,坐汽车还没有骑自行车呢。

* 他写字没有我。

* 这个方案没有那个方案,那个方案更实际些。

2. "不如"可以跟"与其"搭配,构成"与其……不如……"的格式,用于对比两件事的利害得失以决定取舍;"没有"没有这一用法。("不如" is used together with "与其" to make the pattern "与其…不如…", which can be used to compare the advantages and disadvantages, gains and losses of the two things and then make a decision; but "没有" can not be used so.) 例如:

与其在家里坐着,不如出去走走。

与其空想,不如实干。

(It is better to do some practical jobs than daydreaming.)

* 与其在家里坐着,没有出去走走。

* 与其空想,没有实干。

不同 bùtóng   不一样 bù yíyàng

"不同"、"不一样"都表示两者没有相同之处,作谓语用时,有时可以通用。(Both "不同" and "不一样" indicate that there isn't similarity between two things; but when used as predicates, they may be exchangeable sometimes.)例如：

我们俩的想法完全不同/不一样。

他跟我不同/不一样,他总喜欢自由自在。

但是,"不同"、"不一样"在意义上和用法上还有一定的差别。(But "不同" and "不一样" are different in meaning and use.)它们的主要差别有：

(一) 意义上(In meaning)

"不同"书面语色彩稍重些,意义上有时侧重非同一种、非同一个的意思,这时不能跟"不一样"通用。("不同" has a stronger written language flavour, and it lays particular emphasis on the other kind and the other one and here "不同" and "不一样" are not exchangeable.)例如：

我们生活在不同的年代,思想不一致,没什么可奇怪的。

(We live in the different times so there is nothing strange about it when we disagree with each other ideologically.)

* 我们生活在不一样的年代,思想不一致,没什么可奇怪的。

"不一样"多用于两者不相同。("不一样" is mainly used to show the difference between the two.)例如：

他们虽说是父子俩,长得却一点儿也不一样。

(Although they are father and son, there is nothing similar in appearance.)

(二) 用法上(In use)

1."不一样"多用来作谓语,很少作定语;"不同"除作谓语外,还较多地用来作定语。("不一样" is mostly used as a predicate and occasionally as an attributive. Besides being used as a predicate, "不同" is usually used as an attributive.)例如：

我现在想的可跟那时不一样/不同了,那时净做些不现

59

实的梦。

(What I am thinking now is not the same as / is different from what I did then. At that time I had nothing but unrealistic dreams.)

不同的思想方法,不同的分析角度,会得出完全不同的结论。

(Thinking by different ways and analysing from defferent angles, you will come to a totally different conclusion.)

2."不一样"和"不同"相对的词语不同。"不一样"相对的词语是"一样";"不同"相对的词语是"相同"。(The opposites of "不一样" and "不同" are different. The opposite of "不一样" is "一样", and the opposite of "不同" is "相同".)例如:

女儿长得像母亲一样漂亮,而跟父亲却一点儿也不一样。

这对双胞胎姐妹外貌相同,可是脾气却不同。

3."不一样"作谓语时,后面还可以接形容词,表示比较点;"不同"后面不可以接形容词。(When used as a predicate, "不一样" will be followed by adjectives to emphasize the comparative points; but "不同" can not be followed by adjectives.)例如:

这两个尺子不一样长。

南屋跟北屋不一样大。

两口井不一样深。

* 这两个尺子不同长。
* 南屋跟北屋不同大。
* 两口井不同深。

4."有"字后边可以接"不同",一般不接"不一样"。("有" can be followed by "不同", but "不一样" can not.)例如:

这两篇论文的观点有所不同。

(The viewpoints of these two theses are somewhat different.)

两者之间有很大的不同。

他的意见跟我稍有不同。

* 这两篇论文的观点有所不一样。
* 两者之间有很大的不一样。
* 他的意见跟我稍有不一样。

不再 bú zài　　再不 zài bù　　再也不 zài yě bù

这几个词语都是副词"再"和"不"的连用形式,"再也不"可以看做"再不"的扩展式——"再不"中间又加进去副词"也"。(These phrases are the conjunctive forms of adverbs "再" and "不"。"再也不" can be taken as the expanding form of "再不", that is, to put the adverb "也" in the mid of "再不".)

(一)这几个词语都可以表示否定重复或否定继续进行前边已经进行过的某种活动的意思,但是否定程度的轻重有所不同。(These words and phrases can be used to stop the repetition or stop the certain continuing activity which had been done before, but the degree of being negative is different.)

1."不再"的否定比较和缓;"再不"的否定比较坚决;"再也不"的否定更坚决、更强硬,有"永远不"的意思。("不再" indicates rather mitigating negation; the negative meaning of "再不" is fairly firm; and that of "再也不" is firmer and stronger, with the meaning of "never".)试比较:

既然张先生已经出国了,我就不再来了。

(Since Mr. Zhang has gone abroad, I would no longer come.)

我想这些道理你都懂,我就不再说什么了。

(I think you know all of these principles, so I wouldn't say any more.)

那家饭店脏极了,我再不去那家饭店了。

他们不太守信用,剩下的两个项目再不跟他们合作了。

(They didn't do so well as to keep their promise, so we

61

will no longer cooperate on the two left projects with them.)

我再也不提这种无理的要求了。

(I will not raise this kind of unreasonable request any more.)

他说那个地方又穷又乱,他再也不去那个鬼地方了。

(He said it was poor and dirty there and he would never go back to that evil place.)

2."不再"否定的程度比较和缓,所以常常可以用在试探性疑问句中,作试探性的疑问。句中常常有"一"、"几"等构成的数量词组,句末常常有"了"。"再不"、"再也不"一般不这么用。(The negative degree of "不再" is not so strong and is usually used in the interrogative sentence with exploring sense to make an exploring question. There are generally numeral-classifier compounds made up of "一" or "几" and has "了" at the end of the sentences. "再不" and "再也不" are not used in this way.)例如:

你不再打一遍电话试试了?

你不再走几步试试?

你不再说几句?

* 你再不打一遍电话试试了?
* 你再不走几步试试?
* 你再不说几句?
* 你再也不打一遍电话试试了?
* 你再也不走几步试试?
* 你再也不说几句?

(二)"不再"和"再不"还可以用于假设条件的句子中,"不再"或"再不"用于前一分句,后面不加"了",表示的意思不同,所以不能换用。("不再" and "再不" are also used in conditional clauses of assumption; both are used in the former clause and without "了" at the back. Since "不再" and "再不" have different meanings, they are not exchangeable.)

"不再"的句子是指前面已经做过的事情不重复或不继续的话,会出现什么样的结果;"再不"的句子是指所说的事情一直没出现、没做,如果不出现、不做的这种情况继续下去的话,会出现什么样的结果。(The sentence with "不再" shows what might be the result if the things had been accomplished before stopping repeating or continuing; and the sentence with "再不" shows what might be the result if the matter being talked about hasn't occurred or hasn't been done, and if these conditions continue to be like that.)例如:

你不再去见大家一面,大家会怪你的。

(All the others will blame you if you still keep yourself away from them.)

你不再进一步论证论证的话,恐怕不行。

老李快过来吃啊! 再不吃,就没有了。

她的病已经很危险了,再不去医院,恐怕就没救了。

(She has got seriously ill, so she might not get saved if not going to the hospital.)

* 老李快过来吃啊! 不再吃,就没有了。

* 她的病已经很危险了,不再去医院,恐怕就没救了。

C

才 cái　　都 dōu　　就 jiù

〈副词〉< adverb >

"才"跟"都"、"就"在表示时间早晚长短、年龄大小、数量多少的意义上,都含有主观评价性,有相对立的意义。("才","都" and "就" imply the meaning of subjective evaluation and the opposite meaning in respect of time, ages and amounts.)

(一)"才"与"就"

当时间、数量词语等与"才"、"就"构成下列格式时:(When "才" and "就" make up of the patterns with time, numeral-classifier compounds as in the following:)

时间、数量词语等+才……

(time, numeral-classifier compound +才…)

时间、数量词语等+就……

(time, numeral-classifier compound +就…)

"才"表示说话人认为时间晚、时间长、年龄大、数量多等。("才" indicates that the speaker thinks it is late, it takes a long time, one is old, the number or amount is great, etc.)

"就"表示说话人认为时间早、时间短、年龄小、数量少等。("就" indicates that the speaker thinks it is early, something does not cost time, one is young, the number or amount is small, etc.)

搭配形式常常为:(The collocative patterns usually are:)

"时间、数量词语等+才……,时间、数量词语等+就……"

(time, numeral-classifier compound + 才…, time, numeral-classifier compound + 就…)例如:

八点才上课,你怎么七点就来了?
　　（时间晚）　　　　　（时间早）
我排了半天队才买到,你这么一会儿就买到了?
　　　　（时间长）　　　　　（时间短）
(I had been queuing up for a long time to get it while you got it so soon.)
呦,真不得了! 这孩子不到一岁就会说话了,我那闺女
　　　　　　　　　　（年龄小）
五岁才会说话呢!
（年龄大）
我跑了好几趟,才找到他。
　　　　（数量多）
这么多单词,他背了两遍就记住了。
　　　　　　　　（数量少）

(二)"才"与"都"

当"才"、"都"与时间、数量词语等构成下列格式时:(When "才" and "都" form these patterns with temporal words, numeral-classifier compound as following:)

才 + 时间、数量词语等
(才 + time or numeral-classifier compound …)
都 + 时间、数量词语等
(都 + time or numeral-classifier compound …)

"才"表示说话人认为时间早、时间短、年龄小、数量少等。("才" indicates that the speaker thinks it is early or something takes short time, one is young, the quantity is small, etc.)
"都"表示说话人认为时间晚、时间长、年龄大、数量多等。("都" indicates that the speaker thinks it is late, is takes long time, one is old, the quantity is large, etc.)
其搭配形式常常为:(The collocable patterns are:)

"才 + 时间、数量词语……,就……"
("才 + time, numeral-classifier compound…,就…")
"都 + 时间、数量词语……了,才……"
("都 + time, numeral-classifier compound…了,才…")

例如:

才五点,你怎么就起床了?
(时间早)

都下半夜两点了,才睡觉。
(时间晚)

你看人家孩子,才十四岁就上了大学,你都十八了,还
　　　　　　　(年龄小)　　　　　　　　(年龄大)
在上初二。

才两件毛衣,不够穿的,再买两件吧!
(数量少)

都三十五万字了,太多了,最好在三十万字以内。
(数量多)

都三十八岁了,才结婚。

都十二点多了,才下课。

* 都三十八岁,才结婚。
* 都十二点多了,就下课。
* 都十二岁,就承担起家庭重担了。(改作:才十二岁。)
* 通知我们八点发车,现在都七点半,车怎么才走了?
(改作:才七点半,车怎么就走了?)

参观 cānguān　　　访问 fǎngwèn　　　看 kàn

〈动词〉< verb >

(一)"参观"与"访问"

"参观"表示实地观察的意思,因此句中总要有与"参观"动作有关的具体场所。("参观" indicates to observe on the spot, so there will generally be specific places concerning the action of visiting

66

in sentences.)例如:
>　　许多外国朋友参观了这里的幼儿园、学校、工厂。
>　　留学生们去西安参观了四天。
>　　学者们非常仔细地参观了半坡遗址。
>　　孩子们兴致勃勃地参观了自然博物馆。
>　　(The children visited the Natural Museum with zest.)

"参观"主要跟具体场所相联系,不能带表人的宾语。而"访问"则主要用于跟人有关的活动。"访问"连带的宾语主要是表人或国家、地区的。尽管有时是国家或地区的,也必须有与那里的人进行交谈的活动,只是观察不能用"访问";只是可看的场所,也不能用"访问"。("参观" is mainly connected with specific places, and can not take objects representing people. While "访问" is used for the activities concerning people. The objects of "访问" mainly represent people, countries and regions. Although sometimes the objects represent countries or regions, there ought to be conversational activities with the people there, but if only to observe, "访问" cannot be used. When there are only places for people to visit, "访问" cannot be used either.)例如:
>　　师生们访问了敬老院的老人们。
>　　总理正在法国访问。
>　　我们怀着敬仰的心情,访问了这位英雄的母亲。
>　　(With respect, we visited this hero's mother.)
>　* 师生们参观了敬老院的老人们。
>　* 我们怀着敬仰的心情,参观了这位英雄的母亲。
>　* 学者们非常仔细地访问了半坡遗址。
>　* 留学生们访问了八达岭长城。

(二)"看"与"参观"、"访问"

"看"与"参观"、"访问"相关的意义有两个。("看" has two meanings interrelated to "参观" and "访问".)

一是"看望"的意思。这时"看"一定与人有关,它所连带的

67

宾语都是表人的受事宾语。"访问"也是与人有关的动作,它与"看"的区别在于:"访问"是一种有一定礼仪的正规的活动;"看"则是非正规的、一般性的活动。(Firstly it means "看望". Here "看" necessarily is an action concerning people and the objects are all people. "访问" is also an action concerning people, and the difference between "访问" and "看" is that "访问" is a formal activity with a certain etiquette; while "看" is an informal, general activity.)例如:

我明天去北京看一位老朋友。

逢年过节,他总要去看看那些退了休的老同志。

(Whenever any festival or holiday comes, he would always go to visit the retired old people.)

奶奶住院了,我们去医院看看她吧。

* 我今天去访问我的朋友。

* 春节的时候,我访问了不少亲戚朋友。

不是表人的宾语,不是表某个具体事物的宾语,不能用这种意义的"看"。("看" cannot be used if the objects do not represent people, or specific things.)例如:

* 代表团看了非洲四国。

* 我们去北京看了颐和园。

* 外宾们看了这儿的乡镇企业。

二是"观察"的意思。它与"参观"的观察不同在:"参观"是与具体场所相联系的;"看"则是与人、事物、现象相联系的。"参观"通常只是"观察",它连带的宾语通常只是表示具体场所的宾语;"看"常含有"观察并分析"的意思,"看"连带的宾语可以是具体的,也可以是抽象的。(Secondly it means "观察". But it is different from that of "参观": "参观" relates to specific places; while "看" relates to people, things and phenomena. "参观" generally means "observe", and its objects usually indicate specific places; "看" implies "observing and analyzing". The objects can

68

be either specific or abstract.)例如：

我们要学会全面地看问题。

(We should learn to observe problems all-sidedly.)

再等一等,看看事态的发展再说。

(Leave it alone. We will wait to see how the matter develops.)

你帮我看看这个化验结果。

有经验的老农都很会看天气。

(The experienced farmers are all good at observing weather.)

我看了他好长时间了,他的举止很可疑。

日本朋友想参观一下这里的学校。

参观完这个小区,大家感触很深。

(All felt deeply impressed after visiting this small community.)

* 再等一等,参观参观事态的发展再说。
* 有经验的老农都很会参观天气。
* 我参观了他好长时间了,他的举止很可疑。

差(一)点儿 chà(yi)diǎnr　　差不多 chàbuduō

〈副词〉表示距离某种情况、程度等差距小。

(<adverb> indicating a little distance to a certain condition or degree.)

(一) 意义上(In meaning)

"差(一)点儿"和"差不多"都可以表示距离某种情况、程度等差距小的意义。〔"差(一)点儿" and "差不多" both indicate a little distance to a certain condition, degree.〕例如：

差(一)点儿晚了。〔距离晚(某一限定时间)很近。〕

这篇课文我差不多背下来了。(距离背下来的程度极近。)

但是"差(一)点儿"和"差不多"却根本不能互换使用,这是因为它们使用的主客观因素及意义上的差别造成的。(But they simply cannot be exchanged in use and this is caused by the difference of using the subjective and objective factors and meaning.）

"差不多"通常用于一种客观的叙述和说明,几乎没有说话者主观的某种倾向性。它主要用于客观地表示与某种限度、性状、数量相差无几的情况,也可以用于对数量的估计。("差不多" is usually used for objective narration and explanation, nearly without the certain subjective tendency of the speaker. It is mainly used to indicate objectively the conditions of few differences in certain restrictions, characters and amount, and it can be used to estimate quantity.）例如:

剩下的活儿再有半天差不多就能干完。(客观地估测活儿的量。)

(The tasks left can be accomplished in nearly half of a day.）〔objectively estimate the amount〕

天差不多全黑下来了。(对天黑的状态的客观描写。)

人们差不多都进入了梦乡。(对人们入睡情况的客观叙述。)

(People are about to fall asleep.）

我觉得他们俩差不多一般大。(对他们俩的年龄情况作客观估测。)

与会代表差不多有上千人。(对数量的估计。)

(The representatives present are nearly more than one thousand.）

"差(一)点儿"则总是伴有说话者的某种主观心理倾向,不是完全客观性的叙述说明。它表示庆幸不希望发生的事情接近发生而终于没发生或希望发生的事情几乎不能实现而实现了;它还可以表示遗憾、惋惜希望发生的事情几乎要实现而终于没实现;有时也可以对其原因表示不满。〔"差(一)点儿" usually implies certain subjective psychological tendency but does not recount objectively. It indicates the rejoicing at things which is expected not

70

to happen but just about to occur or things seem hopeless to happen but do come true. It also indicates having regret or feeling sorry for things expected to happen are just about to achieve but fail in the end, and sometimes indicates dissatisfaction with the causes.]例如：

1. 带有庆幸的主观心理倾向。(With subjective psychological tendency of rejoicing.)

(1) 庆幸不希望发生的事情终于没发生。(To rejoice at things wished not to happen finally fail to happen.)例如：

  今天真危险,差点儿撞到人。
  我差点儿把这件事说出来了。
  这场球赛差点儿没输给他们。
  (The team was just about to lose the game.)

(2) 庆幸希望发生的事情几乎不能实现而终于实现了。(To rejoice at things hoped to happen seem hopeless but do come true.)例如：

  我差点儿没买到卧铺,幸亏小李帮了我。
  (I nearly failed to get the train ticket for sleeper, and rejoice to have Xiao Li's help.)
  他去年考大学,差点儿没考上。
  路上总塞车,差点儿没赶上火车。
  (There was traffic jam all the way and I was almost late for the train.)

2. 带有遗憾、惋惜的主观心理倾向。(With subjective psychological tendency of regretting and feeling sorrow.)

表示为希望实现的事情几乎实现而终于没有实现而遗憾、惋惜。(Having regret or feeling sorrow for the things expected to happen are almost achieved but are not achieved in the end.)例如：

  实验差点儿就成功了,结果突然停电,全给破坏了。
  (There was suddenly a power cut when the experiment was just about to accomplish, it was ruined.)

你看,我差点儿就做出来了,没想到一不小心就成了这个样子了。

(Look, I was about to make it done, but nobody could expect we have it like this due to carelessness.)

"我差不多做出来了。"和"我差点儿就做出来了。"两句的情况是不同的。前者距离"做出来"很近是客观事实,说话人只在于客观地叙述这一种情况。后者距离"做出来"很近也是客观事实,但是最终的结果是没有做出来,说话人用这种表达方式在于对没做出来的结果表示遗憾、惋惜的心情。因此,这两句在具体的语言环境中,不能互换使用。(The sentence "我差不多做出来了" and the sentence "我差点儿就做出来了" are different. The fact is that the former is very close to "做出来", and the speaker only objectively recounts it. The latter is also close to "做出来", but the final result hasn't been attained and the speaker used this way to express his pity. So they can not be exchanged in the specific language environment.)

3. 表示不满的心理倾向。(Indicating psychological tendency of dissatisfaction.)

听了这句话,差点儿把我气死了。

(Hearing this, I was almost enraged to death.)

这孩子太顽皮了,差点儿把我折腾死。

(The kid is too naughty and I am almost worn out.)

(二) 用法上(In use)

1. "差不多"主要用于从正面表示距离某种程度、数量等的最高限度极近,因此一般不用否定形式,除非否定形式也是为了表示一种最高限度;而"差点儿"则不受这种限制,这是因为它主要不在于表示达到某最高限度,而在于表示预设中的某种心理倾向。("差不多" is mainly used to indicate positively that something is extremely close to some degree and amount, etc., so the negative form is generally not used, except the negative form indicating an

extreme limit. While "差点儿" is not restricted by this, for it doesn't mainly indicate to reach a certain extreme limit, just indicates a certain psychological trend which has been pre-designed.)例如：

火车差不多进站了，快进去吧。

＊火车差不多没进站，再等一会儿吧。

他在国外呆了差不多十年了，时间不短了。

＊他在国外呆了差不多不到十年，时间不短了。

半夜了，路上差不多没人了。（没人了——一种程度的最高限度。）

那道题我差点儿就做上来了。（事实上没做上来，因此而遗憾。）

那道题我差点儿没做上来。（事实上做上来了，为此而庆幸。）

2. "差(一)点儿"作状语时，有时句子的肯定形式与否定形式意思一样。(When "差(一)点儿" is used as an adverbial, the positive and negative forms of the sentence sometimes mean the same.)例如：

我差点儿没忘了告诉他这件事。（没忘。）

他差点儿把暖瓶打碎了。（没打碎。）

他差点儿没把暖瓶打碎。（没打碎。）

但是，有时句子的肯定形式与否定形式意思并不一样。(But sometimes the positive and negative forms in sentences may be different in meaning.)例如：

球票我差点儿就买到了。（没买到。）

球票我差点儿没买到。（买到了。）

那么，什么情况下句子的肯定形式与否定形式意思一样，什么情况下句子的肯定形式与否定形式意思不一样呢？大致规律如下：(Then, when will positive and negative forms mean the same in sentence, and when do they not mean the same? Here are the general rules：)

"差点儿"用于不好的事情或不希望实现的事情时，句子的肯定形式与否定形式意思一样,都表示否定的意思;用于好的事情或希望实现的事情时,句子的肯定形式与否定形式意思不一样,否定形式表示肯定的意思,肯定形式表示否定的意思。〔When "差(一)点儿" indicates no good things or things desired not to realize, the positive and negative forms of the sentence mean the same, with the same meaning of negative. When indicating good things or things desired to realize, the positive and negative forms of the sentence do not mean the same, the negative form means positive, and the positive form means negative.〕例如:

句子的肯定形式与否定形式意思一样:(Positive and negative mean the same in sentences:)

他差点儿误了时间。(肯定形式——表示没误时间。)

他差点儿没误了时间。(否定形式——表示没误时间。)

句子的肯定形式与否定形式意思不一样:(Positive and negative do not mean the same in sentences:)

我差点儿没借到这本书。(否定形式——表示借到了。)

我差点儿借到那本书了。(肯定形式——表示没借到。)

常常 chángcháng 通常 tōngcháng

常常、通常〈副词〉< adverb >

通常〈形容词〉< adjective >

"常常"、"通常"用作副词时,都可以出现在谓词性词语前,对后面的成分进行修饰限制,意义和用法看上去好像有相似之处。(When "常常" and "通常" are used as adverbs, they can be put before the predicative words or phrases to restrict the compositions followed. "常常" and "通常" seem to have some common points in meaning and use.)例如:

他早上常常七点以前到办公室。
他早上通常七点以前到办公室。
星期天他常常不吃早饭。
星期天他通常不吃早饭。

但是实际上,这两个词意义差别较大,因而也制约了构句的条件。(Actually, these two words differ from each other, thus restrict the sentence constructing condition.)

(一)意义上的差别(Differences in meaning)

"常常"侧重于表示动作、行为或事件发生的频率,即不是三次、五次发生,而是屡次发生。("常常" stresses the frequency of an action, a behavior or an incident, and the frequency is high.)例如:

星期二她有课,有课的时候她常常来我这儿吃饭。
她睡觉前常常要写日记。

"通常"则侧重于表示动作、行为或事件发生的一般性或规律性,即按照一般规律会发生某一动作、行为或事件,不是在一般规律的条件下,就不会发生某一动作、行为或事件。(While "通常" stresses the generality or regularity of an action, a behavior or an incident, that is an action, a behavior, or an incident will take place according to the general rules.)例如:

他早上通常五点起床。
他写完信,通常连一遍也不看就发出去。

(After writing the letter, usually he would send it without reading it over again.)

"通常"表示动作、行为、事件的发生带有一贯性,当然发生的频率要高,在这一点上,它跟"常常"相似,但是,"通常"意义所侧重的点不是它的频率,而是它产生这一动作、事件频率的前提条件——一般的条件下或一般的情况下。("通常" also indicates that the occurrence of actions, behaviors or incidents is consistent and certainly of high occurring frequencies. In this point "通常" is similar to "常常", but "通常" doesn't stress the frequency, but the premise, under general condition or circumstance which causes this frequency of action or incident.)

(二) 构句上的差别(Differences in construction)

由于上述意义上的差别,形成"常常"、"通常"构句条件上的差别。(Because "常常" and "通常" are different in meaning, they are different in construction.)

1. "常常"是对动作、事件等发生的频率而言的,所以它可以用于没有别的条件的单个动词前。("常常" emphasizes the frequency that actions or incidents take place, so it can be used before single verbs which have no other relevant conditions.)例如:

他常常喝酒,而且一喝就喝个酩酊大醉。

(He drinks quite often, and every time would get dead drunk.)

他常常感冒,不知怎么回事。

他常常发脾气,心情很少有好的时候。

(He often gets angry and is always in a bad mood.)

"通常"是就动作、事件等在一般条件下一贯性或规律性地发生而言的,所以句中动词前后要有一定的条件,这个条件一般指时间、地点、方式、条件等,没有一定条件的单个动词,一般不能用在"通常"后面。("通常" emphasizes actions or incidents consistently or regularly occur under general conditions. Therefore, there needs certain conditions, which generally refer to time, places, ways or conditions, etc. before or after the verb in the sentence. As for the single verbs without certain conditions, they generally can not be used after "通常".)例如:

他通常晚饭后散步。(时间——晚饭后。)

他常常散步。

＊他通常散步。
　　她通常在书房里写作。(地点——在书房里。)
　　她常常写作。
　　＊她通常写作。
　　她通常骑自行车去商店。(方式——骑自行车。)
　　她常常去商店。
　　＊她通常去商店。

2."通常"指按照一般规律会发生某一动作、行为或事件,不是在一般规律的条件下,就不会发生某一动作、行为或事件,因此,当说话人强调它的一贯性而只在特殊情况下不出现这一情况时,常常需要对照句。("通常" indicates a certain action, behavior or matter will occur by the general rules, and those will not occur if not under regular conditions. So when the speaker emphasizes the consistency of the condition and this condition will not occur in a special circumstance, the contrasting sentences are needed.)例如:

　　他通常洗冷水澡,只有身体不舒服的时候才洗热水澡。
　　(He usually takes cold shower and only when he doesn't feel well he will take a hot bath.)
　　在公共场合下,他通常说普通话,只有回到家里的时候才说方言。
　　(He usually speaks mandarin on public occasions, but speaks dialect only at home.)

有时,虽然对照句没出现,但是暗含这种意思,听话人可以理解出这一意思。(Sometimes, although the contrasting meaning is not expressed, it is implied and the listeners can learn it themselves.)例如:

　　一般的头疼脑热,他通常不吃药。
　　(He usually wouldn't take medicine if it is slight illness.)
这里暗含着"只有得了大病的时候才吃药",虽然这句话没说出来,但是可以理解出来。(Here the meaning "he will take medicine

if it is serious problem" is not mentioned, but it can be learnt.)

"常常"侧重于频率,所以不强调一般与特殊的对照。("常常" emphasizes frequency, not contrast between generality and specialty.)

3."通常"表示的是动作的一贯性,所以一般不能用于某一限界的时间里;"常常"不受这一限制。(Since "通常" indicates the consistency of actions, it can't be used within a certain limited time; while "常常" is not restricted by this.)例如:

* <u>上个月</u>,他通常加班两个小时,这个月不加了。
* <u>去年</u>,他早上通常散步。
* <u>两年前</u>,他通常步行上班。
* <u>你住院期间</u>,我通常会来看你的。

上个月,他常常加班两个小时,这个月不加了。

去年,他早上常常散步。

两年前,他常常步行上班。

你住院期间,我会常常来看你的。

4."常常"表示动作、事件等发生得频繁,所以时间的间隔应该短,当时间词所表示的时段比较长时,"常常"的使用就要受到限制;"通常"表示动作、事件等有规律地发生,跟时间长短没有直接关系,所以不会受到限制。("常常" indicates actions or incidents happening frequently, so the interval between times should be short and when temporal words indicating quite long period of time, the use of "常常" will be restricted; "通常" indicates actions or incidents happening regularly and has not direct relation to the length of the time, so it will not be restricted in use.)例如:

他常常隔一天给我来一次电话。

他通常隔一天给我来一次电话。

* 他常常两年回老家看一次奶奶。

他通常两年回老家看一次奶奶。

(Usually he goes back to his hometown to visit his

grandmother every two years.)

＊这种病常常一年犯一次。

这种病通常一年犯一次。

(This illness usually attacks again once every year.)

此外,"通常"还可以修饰限制名词性成分,在句中作定语,具有非谓形容词的性质与功能,表示"一般"、"平常"的意思。"常常"没有这种用法。(Besides, "通常" can be used as an attributive modifying and restricting the noun compositions in the sentence. It has the character and function of the non-predicative adjectives, which means being general or ordinary. "常常" does not have this sense.)例如:

A:明天星期天,他该在家休息吧。

B:按理应该在家休息,可是他总是很忙,按通常的情况,他恐怕又不可能在家休息了。

(Normally he ought to stay at home, but he is always busy and maybe he is unable to rest at home according to the usual cases.)

＊按理应该在家休息,可是他总是很忙,按常常的情况,他恐怕又不可能在家休息了。

把两个事物放在一起对照比较是最通常的研究事物的方法。

(The most usual method of studying things is to put the two things together to contrast and to compare.)

＊把两个事物放在一起对照比较是最常常的研究事物的方法。

常常 chángcháng　　往往 wǎngwǎng
〈副词〉< adverb >
(一)意义上的差别(Differences in meaning)

"常常"侧重于表示动作、行为或事件发生的频率,即不是三

79

次、五次发生,而是屡次发生。("常常" stresses the frequency of the action, behavior and incident, which is not an occassional occurrence, but a frequent occurrence.)例如:

晚饭后她常常一个人去外面散步。

她睡觉前常常要听一段古典音乐。

"往往"则侧重于表示动作、行为或事件发生的一般性或规律性,即按照一般的规律、一般的推理而发生某一动作、行为或事件。("往往" indicates the generality or regularity of actions, behaviour or incidents, namely a certain action, behaviour or incident will happen according to general rules and inference.)例如:

他晚上往往半夜以后才睡觉。

(He often goes to bed after midnight.)

他对事情的评论非常多,而且往往很独特。

(He has done a lot of talks about something and they often show uniqueness.)

他是个聪明人,许多事情往往不等你张嘴,他就已经明白了。

(He is a bright man. He often gets to know your intention before you speak it out.)

在表示有很强的规律性的动作、事件或由某情况推理出来的常理性的情况时,用"往往"更加贴切。(When indicating actions or incidents of strong regularity or condition of common practice reasoned by certain condition, "往往" will express the meaning more properly.)例如:

他的病每到阴天下雨往往会加重。

(His illness often becomes heavier whenever it is cloudy or raining.)

那里没有汽车,又是山路,往往需要步行。

精神太紧张,往往会影响水平的发挥。

(Nerves often influence the full playing.)

(二) 构句上的差别(Differences in construction)

1."常常"是对动作、事件等发生的频率而言的,所以它可以用于没有别的条件的单个动词前。("常常" refers to the frequent occurrence of an action or an incident so it is used in front of a single verb without other determiners.)例如:

不知怎么回事,他常常走神儿。

(Nobody knows why he is so often absent-minded.)

妈妈常常说:"人要学会知足,不然会永远痛苦的。"

(Mother often says that man must learn to be content with his lot or will suffer the whole life.)

他常常发脾气,我们大家都躲着他。

(He often gets angry and we all just avoid being seen by him.)

"往往"是就动作、事件等在一般条件下有规律性地发生或按常理可能发生而言的,所以句中动词前后要有一定的条件,这个条件通常指时间、地点、方式、条件等,没有一定条件的单个动词一般不能用在"往往"后面。("往往" indicates that an action or an incident will happen regularly under the general conditions or is likely to happen according to usual rules. There should be a certain conditions in front or after verbs. And here the condition generally refers to time, places, ways or condition, etc. and a single verb without a certain condition generally can't be used after "往往".)例如:

她往往写作到深夜。(时间——到深夜。)

她常常写作。

* 她往往写作。

为了不让老板发现,小柱子往往躲在地窖里看书。(地点——地窖里。)

(In order not to be seen by the boss, Xiao Zhuzi often hid in the cellar to read.)

小柱子常常看书。

81

* 小柱子往往看书。
* 他往往走神儿,不知怎么回事。
* 妈妈往往说:"人要学会知足,不然会永远痛苦的。"
* 他往往发脾气,我们大家都躲着他。

2. "往往"句只用于过去的情况或一般规律、一般常理,不能用在限定将来时间的句子里;"常常"句不受这种时间的制约。(The sentence of "往往" is only used for the past condition or general rules and routines, but not for the sentence restricted by the future condition; "常常" will not be restricted by this time condition.) 例如:

那时他很喜欢玩水,往往在水里一泡就是四五个小时。
(He liked swimming very much at that time and once he got into the water, he would often steep for four or five hours.)

听不进去别人的批评,往往会栽跟头的。
(If one refuses to listen to others' criticism, he will often come a cropper.)

那时他很喜欢玩水,常常在水里一泡就是四五个小时。
你读书期间,我会常常寄钱给你的。
下班以后,你应该常常去看看她。
* 你读书期间,我会往往寄钱给你的。
* 下班以后,你应该往往去看看她。

朝(着) cháo(zhe)   沿(着) yán(zhe)

〈介词〉 < preposition >

"朝"、"沿"都可以与后面的名词组成介词词组,用在谓语动词前作状语。("朝" and "沿" can both compose prepositional word group with the nouns followed and is used as an adverbial in front of predicate verbs.)

(一) "朝"表示的是动作的方向,它后面可以带方位词,也可以

82

带场所意义的名词或代词。("朝"indicates the direction that the actions go towards and it can either be followed by nouns of locality or nouns or pronouns of places.)例如：

朝前跑　朝左看　朝后使劲儿　朝里望了一眼　朝东飞去
朝马路跑去　朝河边走去　朝飞机场开去　朝这儿走来

"沿"表示的是动作经过的路线。它后面只能接表示场所意义的名词,常常跟"路"有关系。("沿" indicates the route that an act passes through. There can only be nouns of places followed, and usually concerning "路".)例如：

沿街叫卖(calling and selling along streets)
沿池边游
沿河西岸奔去(along the west bank of the river)
沿山路走
沿墙根种(to plant along the foot of the wall)

"沿"表示的是路线,所以不能带只表示方向意义的词或由代词所表示的某一个点的场所意义的词。("沿" can't be followed only by words of direction or pronouns made up of words of certain location.)例如：

﹡沿前跑　﹡沿左看　﹡沿后使劲儿　﹡沿东飞去
﹡沿里望了一眼　﹡沿这儿走来　﹡沿那儿飞去

"朝/沿马路跑去"、"朝/沿河边走去"虽然都可以说,但是表示的意义不同,"朝~"表示的是方向;"沿~"表示的是路线。〔The two expressions "朝/沿马路跑去"(running away towards/along the street) and "朝/沿河边走去"(walking towards or along the river side) are different in meaning, "朝~" indicates the direction, while "沿~"indicates the route.〕

"沿~"表示经过的路线,不一定必须是走过的,也可以是视线等经过的。("沿~"indicates the passing route but not necessarily the route one passes by or one just sweeps over.)例如：

田地好大呀！沿着田埂一直望去,好像没有尽头。

(What a vast field! It seems endless while looking straight along the ridges.)

(二)"朝"、"沿"也可以说成"朝着"、"沿着",基本意思和用法跟"朝"、"沿"相似。有两点稍需注意:("朝" and "沿" are also addressed as "朝着" and "沿着" and they have the similar meanings and usages. Attention has to be paid to the following points:)

1. 说话人强调持续状态时,最好用"(朝／沿)着"。〔When the speaker stresses continuous state, it's better to use "(朝/沿)着".〕例如:

他们朝着广大观众热情地高歌着。

(They are singing enthusiastically towards the numerous audience in a high voice.)

我们正沿着社会主义的康庄大道前进着。

(We are just marching forward along the broad road of socialism.)

2. 有时也需考虑音节数问题,用"(朝／沿)着"时,后边多宜用多音节词语。(Sometimes the amount of the syllables are taken into account. It is better to use multi-syllabic words after it when "(朝／沿)着" is used.)例如:

形势继续朝着有利于经济发展的方向发展。

(The situation is continuing to develop in the direction of benefiting the economy.)

人们沿着弯弯曲曲的道路,从四面八方朝这儿涌来。

(People were pouring from everywhere towards here along the crooked roads and paths.)

* 他朝着东走去。(改作"朝东走去"才好。)

* 她不得不提着篮子沿着街叫卖。(改作"沿街叫卖"更好些。)

迟 chí   迟到 chídào

迟〈形容词〉表示比规定的时间或比合适的时间晚。(< adjective > indicating later than the fixed time or the appropriate time.)

迟到〈动词〉表示比规定的时间到得晚。(< verb > indicating to arrive later than the fixed time.)

(一)词义、用法不同(Differences in meaning and use)

1."迟"、"迟到"都可以表示比规定的时间晚的意思,但是,"迟"是形容词,表示比规定的时间或比合适的时间晚的意思,常用来作状语、补语;"迟到"是动词,表示"到得晚"的意思,只能用于比规定的时间到得晚这一种特指的意思,常用来作谓语。("迟" and "迟到" both mean being late after the fixed time, but "迟" is an adjective, indicating to be late after the fixed time or the proper time, and is used as an adverbial or complement; "迟到" is a verb, indicating to arrive late. It is only used specifically for arriving late after the fixed time and used as a predicate.)例如:

她迟迟不肯给我答复。

(Tardily she is unwilling to give me the answer.)

对不起,我来迟了。

昨天晚上我睡迟了。

* 她迟到不肯给我答复。

* 昨天晚上我睡迟到了。

对不起,我迟到了。

希望你今后不要迟到。

2."迟"是形容词,可以接受程度副词的修饰;"迟到"是动词,不能接受程度副词的修饰。("迟" is an adjective and can be modified by adverbs of degree; while "迟到" is a verb and can't be modified by adverbs of degree.)例如:

那天晚上我睡得太迟了。

* 今天开会连李主任都太迟到了。

3. "迟"是形容词,不能带宾语;"迟到"虽是动词,但是是不及物动词,所以也不能带宾语。(Since "迟" is an adjective, it can't be followed by objects. Although "迟到" is a verb, it is an intransitive verb and can't be followed by objects.)例如:

小王起床晚了,上课迟到了。
* 小王起床晚了,迟课了。(或 * "迟上课了"。)
* 小王起床晚了,迟到课了。(或 * "迟到上课了"。)

4. "迟"、"迟到"都可以带补语,尤其是时段补语。("迟" and "迟到" can both be followed by complements, especially by the complement of duration of time.)例如:

今天我去迟了一会儿。
你迟了五分钟。
今天我迟到了一会儿。
你迟到了五分钟。

个别程度补语只能用在"迟"后,不能用在"迟到"后。(Some individual complements of degree can only be used after "迟", not after "迟到".)例如:

你不光是送迟了,而且还迟得很呢。
* 你不光是迟到了,而且还迟到得很呢。

(二)"迟到"只限于人到得晚,不能用于来晚的火车、飞机、轮船等,也不能用于其他晚做的事情;"迟"则不受这种限制。("迟到" is restrictedly used only for people arriving late, not for trains, planes or ships, etc. as well as for things being done late. "迟" is not restricted by this.)例如:

* 这趟火车迟到了。
* 班机怎么迟到了?
不知怎么回事,今天的船来迟了。
老师今天下课下迟了。
* 老师今天下课下迟到了。

表示火车、飞机、轮船等比规定的时间到得晚的意思,应该用"晚点"。〔When indicating trains, flights and steamers that arrive late after the fixed time, the term "晚点"(behind schedule) is used.〕例如:

312次列车晚点两个小时。

飞机晚点了。

充分 chōngfèn　　充足 chōngzú　　充沛 chōngpèi

〈形容词〉都可以表示足够多的意思。(< adjective > indicating being sufficient.)

"充分"、"充足"、"充沛"都可以表示足够多的意思,在句中都可以作定语和谓语,但是通常不能互换使用,这是因为它们在意义上、使用范围上、句法功能上有一定差别。("充分","充足" and "充沛" all mean sufficiency and are used as attributives or predicates. Since there are some differences in meaning, applying scope and sentence function, they are not exchangeable.)

(一) 意义上、使用范围上(In meaning and in range of use)

1. "充分"多用于抽象事物,表义上侧重于富足的程度高。("充分" is usually used for abstract things. It lays emphasis on the high degree of richness.)例如:

充分的说服力(strong powers of persuasion)

充分的民主(full democracy)

充分的信心(full confidence)

充分的准备　　理由很充分

证据很充分(the evidence are fairly abundant)

列举的事实很充分(the facts given are quite powerful)

他们享受着充分的民主与自由。

(They are enjoying the full freedom and democracy.)

你们对困难的估计太不充分了。

"充足"多用于具体事物,表义上侧重于量多,足够用,能满足需要。(Being used for particular things, "充足" stresses large quantity, being enough for use, and able to meet the need.)例如：

充足的水源(have rich water resource)

充足的阳光

充足的时间

充足的资金(have ample funds)

电力充足

经费充足(have sufficient funds)

财力充足(sufficient financial resources)

理由很充足

你们放心,我们会给你们提供充足的人力、物力。

(You may rest assured we will provide you with enough manpower and material resources.)

这些水果味道甘甜、水分充足,很好吃。

"充分"、"充足"都可以用于"理由",使用时稍须注意意义上的侧重点就可以。(Both "充分" and "充足" can be used to modify "理由" and a little attention has to be paid to the particular emphasis in meaning.)例如：

我有充分的理由这样做。

他的理由很充足、很有说服力,无可辩驳。

(His argument is adequate and rather convincing, beyond all dispute.)

"充沛"含褒义色彩,多用于精力、感情等抽象事物,也可用于水量等具体事物,但较少。表义上侧重于丰足而旺盛。("充沛" is of commendatory flavour and is mostly used for abstract things as energy and emotion and for specific things like water amount as well, but this is of rare use. In meaning it emphasizes abundance and exuberance.)例如：

充沛的热情(full of enthusiasm)

充沛的生命力(vigorous vitality)

充沛的水量

感情充沛

精力很充沛(energetic)

雨水充沛

他那强壮的体魄里蕴藏着充沛的生命力。

(In his strong body there holds in store the vigorous vitality.)

这些年轻人个个朝气蓬勃、精力充沛,一定能完成任务。

2."充足"一般不用于特别抽象的事物。("充足"is not used for particularly abstract things.)例如:

* 他们享受着充足的民主与自由。
* 你们对困难的估计太不充足了。

3."充分"和"充沛"虽然都可以用于抽象的事物,但是搭配对象不同。表示精力、生命力、感情等,只能用"充沛",不能用"充分";表示说服力、民主、信心等抽象事物,只能用"充分",不能用"充沛"。(Though both "充分" and "充沛" are used to modify abstract things, their collocations are different. "充沛" modifies energy, vitality or emotion, etc.; while "充分" is used instead of "充沛" when modifying the abstract nouns as persuasion, democracy or confidence, etc.)例如:

* 充沛的说服力　　* 充沛的民主
* 充沛的信心　　　* 充沛的准备
* 他那强壮的体魄里蕴藏着充分的生命力。
* 这些年轻人个个朝气蓬勃、精力充分,一定能完成任务。

"充分/充沛"不能用于"人力、物力、财力"等,也不能用于水分。〔But "充分" and "充沛" neither modify manpower, material resources or financial resources nor moisture content.〕例如:

* 你们放心,我们会给你们提供充分/充沛的人力、物力。
* 这些水果味道甘甜、水分充分/充沛,很好吃。

(二)语法功能上(In aspect of grammatical function)

1. "充分"、"充足"、"充沛"在句中都可以作定语和谓语（见上例），"充分"还可以作补语。"充足"、"充沛"一般不用作补语。〔"充分","充足" and "充沛" can all be used as attributives or predicates in the sentences (as in the examples above), and "充分" can also be used as a complement, while "充足" and "充分" cannot.〕例如：

　　他说得很充分。
　　演员们表演得很充分。
　　(The actors and actresses acted properly.)
　　论证得很充分。

2. "充分"也常常用作状语，作状语时，它表示"尽量"的意思，被修饰的动词多用"利用"、"发挥"、"调动"、"展示"、"证明"、"显示"等。"充足"、"充沛"一般没有这种意义和用法。〔"充分" is used as an adverbial, indicating "to the best" and the usual verbs it modifies are "利用"(make use of), "发挥"(give play to), "调动"(mobilize), "展示"(display), "证明"(prove) and "显示"(show), etc., while "充足" and "充沛" can not.〕例如：

　　我们要充分利用现有的条件，扭转生产不景气的局面。
　　(We must make full use of the present factors to reverse the depression of our production.)
　　这幅作品充分显示了王辉的想象力。
　　你们应该充分调动广大群众的积极性，这样才有利于事业的发展。
　　* 我们要充足／充沛利用现有的条件，扭转生产不景气的局面。
　　* 这幅作品充足／充沛显示了王辉的想象力。
　　* 你们应该充足／充沛调动广大群众的积极性，这样才有利于事业的发展。

充满 chōngmǎn　　充实 chōngshí

"充满"〈动词〉< verb >

"充实"〈动词〉〈形容词〉< verb > < adjective >

"充满"、"充实"都可以用作动词,但是在意义上、用法上有差别。("充满" and "充实" both can be used as verbs, but they are different in meaning and in use.)

(一) 意义上(In meaning)

"充满"表示填满或者表示充分具有、普遍存在的意思;"充实"则表示使增加、使加强的意思,而且多用于内容、人员物力的配备等方面。("充满" indicates filling in or full possessing or universal existing; "充实" just indicates to increase something or strengthen something and is mainly used for content, provision of manpower or material resources, etc.) 例如:

她的眼眶里充满了泪水。

生活中充满了阳光。

(There is abundant sunlight in life.)

她的歌声中充满了忧伤之情。

(Her songs are full of grief.)

这篇文章还是有点儿空,想办法再充实一点儿内容。

(This article is still deficient. Just try to replenish a little to it.)

调你去车间是为了充实一下基层的力量。

(The purpose to transfer you to the workshop is to strengthen the power of the grass-roots unit.)

* 生活中充实了阳光。

* 她的歌声中充实了忧伤之情。

* 这篇文章还是有点儿空,想办法再充满一点儿内容。

* 调你去车间是为了充满一下基层的力量。

(二) 用法上(In use)

1."充满"、"充实"都作带宾谓语(见上例),但是由于"充满"的"满"可以直接表示"充"的结果,所以它不能再带补语;"充实"词义凝固得很紧,后边还可以再带补语。〔"充满" and "充实"can be followed by objects (as in the examples above). Because "满" in the word "充满" can directly show the result of "充", it cannot be followed by complements; while the meaning of the word "充实" is condensed and a complement may follow.〕例如:

三年的学习,使这个小伙子充实了很多。

(Three years' study has enriched this young man's mind.)

我们要用最现代化的装备把军队充实得更加具有战斗力。

(We will enrich our army with the most modernized equipment to have stronger fighting capacity.)

2. "充实"有重叠式和否定式的用法,"充满"没有。("充实"can be reduplicated and negated, but "充满" cannot.)例如:

你应该从各个方面好好充实充实自己。

不充实自己的话,你就没有什么前途了。

3. "充实"还有形容词用法,作谓语、定语、补语;"充满"没有形容词用法。("充实" is also used as an adjective, functioning as a predicate, an attributive or a complement, while "充满" is not.)例如:

库存很充实,完全可以满足需要。

(The sufficient stock will surely meet the need.)

这是一篇内容十分充实的文章。

他们娘俩日子虽然苦点儿,但是却过得很充实。

(The life of the mother and her son is a bit hard but they feel their life meaningful.)

* 库存很充满,完全可以满足需要。

* 这是一篇内容十分充满的文章。

* 他们娘俩日子虽然苦点儿,但是却过得很充满。

初 chū　　开始 kāishǐ　　当初 dāngchū

初〈形容词〉〈副词〉< adjective > < adverb >
开始〈动词〉< verb >
当初〈名词〉< noun >

(一)"初"与"开始"

"初"与"开始"都有表示开始的阶段的意思,但是意义、功能、用法相差较大。(Both "初" and "开始" mean the beginning period, but they are quite different in meaning, function and usage.)

1."初"在表示开始的时间或阶段的意思上有三种意义和用法:(There are three meanings and usages when "初" indicates the beginning time or the beginning period:)

(1)用在表示时间的名词前面,表示某一初始的时间。("初" indicates a certain beginning period when used before nouns of time.)例如:

初春　初夏　初秋　初冬　建国初年　初伏　初旬

(2)表示时间、季节的开始阶段,只限于用在时间词"年"、"月"、"春"、"夏"、"秋"、"冬"后面。〔When used restrictedly after words of time as "年"(year), "月"(month), "春"(spring), "夏"(summer), "秋"(autumn) and "冬"(winter), it indicates the beginning period.〕例如:

年初　月初　1992年初　十二月初　秋初
他是夏初来到这儿的。

①"周"、"日"等表示时间的词不能这样用。(The words of time like "周"(week) and "日"(day) can not be modified by "初".)例如:

＊周初　　　＊日初

② 只限于"春"、"夏"、"秋"、"冬"的单音节词,"春天"、"夏天"、"秋天"、"冬天"这样的双音节词也不能这样用。〔"初" is only used after "春"(spring), "夏"(summer), "秋"(autumn) and "冬"(winter), which are monosyllabic words. It can't be used after

93

"春天","夏天","秋天"and"冬天",which are disyllabic words.〕例如:

* 春天初　* 夏天初　* 秋天初　* 冬天初

③不能用在动词性词语后。(It cannot be used after verbal phrases.)例如:

* 到中国初　* 学汉语初　* 上课初　* 开会初
* 讲话初

(3)表示"刚"、"刚开始"的意思,是副词,要用在动词前,而且主要是单音节动词前。(When indicating "just", "just begin", it functions as an adverb and is used before verbs, especially monosyllabic verbs.)例如:

初到中国时,他一句汉语也不会说。

(When he just arrived in China, he couldn't speak even a single Chinese word.)

这里的建设已初具规模。

(The construction here has begun to take shape.)

站在山顶,望着初升的太阳,呼吸着清新的空气,感觉好极了。

用在双音节动词前,通常用"初次",动作一般是可用"次"计量的动作,通常表示"第一次"的意思,有时也可以表示"刚开始"的意思。〔Before a disyllabic verb,"初次"is usually used and the action can be measured by"次"(time). Therefore, it usually means "for the first time" or something just begins.〕例如:

初次见面,请多关照。

初次拜见王先生,心里不免有些紧张。

(At the first time visiting Mr. Wang, I unavoidably felt a bit nervous.)

初次见到他,觉得他有些怕人,时间长了,才知道他是个很随和的人。

(The first time meeting him, I thought he was fearsome,

but with time going I get to know he is an easy-going man.)

2. "开始"只有动词用法,它一般构成"开始的时候"或者"刚开始(的时候)"。有时也可以直接用"开始",但是表示的仍然是"开始的时候"的意思。〔"开始" is only used as a verb. It composes word groups as "开始的时候"(at the beginning) or "刚刚开始的时候(just at the beginning)" and sometimes only the word "开始" is used but it still means "开始的时候"。〕例如：

开始的时候,我一点儿也不习惯这里的生活,现在都习惯了。

刚开始的时候,他们说的汉语我一句也听不懂。

到一个陌生的环境里,开始一定会觉得很别扭,时间长了就好了。

(When you get to a strange environment, you will surely feel awkward at the beginning and will feel at ease after some time.)

3. 以上讲到的"初"和"开始"几种表示时间的意义,在用法上一般不能互换。(The expressions of time "初" and "开始" presented above are generally not inchangeable in use.)例如：

* 开始春 * 开始冬 * 开始年 * 开始月

* 年开始 * 月开始 * 秋开始 * 1992年开始

* 九月开始

* 开始到中国时,他一句汉语也不会说。

* 这里的建设已开始具规模。

* 初(初次)的时候,我一点儿也不习惯这里的生活,现在都习惯了。

* 初(初次)的时候,他们说的汉语我一句也听不懂。

4. "刚开始+动词+的时候"的用法有时可以跟"初(初次)+动词+的时候"互换使用。(The pattern "刚开始 + v. + 的时候" sometimes can be substituted by the pattern "初(初次) + v. + 的时候"。)例如：

刚开始学汉语的时候——初学汉语的时候

刚开始写作的时候——初次写作的时候

5."开始"还可以直接用作谓语,表示从头起或从某一点起。("开始" is also used as a predicate, indicating to start from the beginning or from a certain point.)例如:

  开始工作　　就从这里开始　　新学期开始了
  开始了全新的生活

(二)"当初"与"初"、"开始"

"当初"与"初"、"开始"意义完全不同。"当初"是时间名词,只表示过去的时间。它表示的时间意义是"泛指从前或特指过去发生某件事情的时候,"当初"的时间通常跟事件相联系,是某事件在原先的某时间里的一种情况。("当初" is completely different from"初" and "开始"."当初" is a noun of time, indicating the past time. It generally refers to the past or particularly refers to the past time during which a certain thing happened. The time of "当初" usually concerns incidents. It was the situation some incident used to be at the former time.)例如:

  当初我妈怎么都不同意,可我偏要嫁给他。

  (Originally my mother insisted on her disagreement, but I would just marry him.)

  都怪你当初不听我的劝告,才把事情搞成这样。

  当初的情景至今记忆犹新。

  (Even today the situation at that time still remains fresh in my memory.)

"初"、"开始"所指的开头的时间或阶段一般都是跟动作有紧密关系的,是做该动作的最初阶段,而且也不限于从前、过去,还可以指将来时间或一般规律。(The beginning time or period that "初" and "开始" indicate has close relation with the action. It is the initial phase of the action being done and is not confined to the time long ago or the past time, it may also refer to the future time or the general rules.)例如:

初学时都会感到很难,学一段时间就好了。

手术开始的时候,你一定要告诉我一声。

* 当初学的时候都会感到很难,学一段时间就好了。

* 手术当初的时候,你一定要告诉我一声。

除 chú　　除了 chúle

〈介词〉表示不计算在内。

(< preposition > indicating not including.)

(一)"除"、"除了"都可以表示不计算在内的意思,都可以组成介词词组在句中作状语。通常有以下几种用法。(Both "除" and "除了" mean not including and can compose prepositional phrases which are used as adverbials in sentences. Generally there are following usages):

1. 排除特殊的,强调一般的。后面常用"都"、"全"等词配合。(Eliminating the particular parts and emphasizing the general and usually used together with "都" or "全".)例如:

这次会议除少数著名的老专家以外,都是新成长起来的青年学者。

(Except for a few famous old experts, the ones present at this meeting are the newly grown young learners.)

除了工具书外,这里只卖文学类书。

他每天除了看书学习,不做别的事。

除了他,别人都不知道这件事。

2. 排除已知,补充其他。后面常用"还"、"也"、"又"等词配合。(Eliminating the known parts and adding others and usually used together with "还","也" or "又".)例如:

我们班懂日语的除王莉外,还有孙勇和赵强。

这个月,除产量有所增加外,质量也有所提高。

冬天,他除了喜欢滑冰以外,还喜欢冬泳。

他除了搞技术革新以外,又搞了几项发明创造。

(Besides doing technical innovations, he has made several inventions.)

3. 跟"就是"、"便是"等配合,表示二者必居其一或包括了已说出的两者,排除第三者。(Indicating one of the two or both the two mentioned, excluding the third one when used together with "就是" or "便是".)例如:

> 在全国,人口最多的省,除四川之外,便是河南。
> 这几天除了刮风,就是下雨,一直没个好天气。
> 你每天除了吃饭就是睡觉,这样活着,有什么意义?
> 跟他有往来的同学,除了你,就是我了。

(二)"除"、"除了"表示的意思相同,但是用法上有时有区别。"除"通常要与"外"、"以外"、"之外"等词配合用,不配合的情况少,而且有一定的条件。"除了"不受这种限制。("除" and "除了" have similar meaning but they are different in use sometimes. "除" is usually used together with "外","以外" or "之外", and rarely used separatedly, only in a certain condition. "除了" is not restricted by this.)例如:

a. 这件事,除他以外,谁都不知道。
   这件事,除了他,谁都不知道。
   * 这件事,除他,谁都不知道。

b. 今天天气太不好了,除刮风外,还下了一阵雨。
   今天天气太不好了,除了刮风,还下了一阵雨。
   * 今天天气太不好了,除刮风,还下了一阵雨。

c. 他没什么别的爱好了,除喝酒外,就只有睡觉了。
   他没什么别的爱好了,除了喝酒,就只有睡觉了。
   * 他没什么别的爱好了,除喝酒,就只有睡觉了。

也就是说,当"除"不与"外"、"以外"、"之外"等配合使用时,"除"后面不能接一般的单个词(见 a 例),通常也不能接简单的谓词性词组。一般来说,当"除"后面所接的成分是复杂的谓词性词组或复杂的非谓词性词组时,有时是可以不与"外"、

"以外"、"之外"等配合使用的。在意义上,它也多用于表示"排除特殊的,强调一般的"意义的句子。["除" can't be followed by a single word if not used together with "外","以外" or "之外"(see e.g. a). The word "除" can neither be followed by a single verb nor a simple predicative word group. Generally, when "除" is followed by a complicated predicative word group or complicated non-predicative word group, it can be used without "外","以外" or "之外" in the sentences. In meaning, "除" is mainly used to indicate eliminating the specific and emphasizing the general.]例如:

除九楼不查,别的楼都查。

除小林去过桂林,我们都没去过。

全连除指导员年龄最大,其余都不过十七八岁的小伙子。

(Except that the political instructor is the senior, the others in the company are young men of seventeen or eighteen.)

在我们村,除我祖父会银匠这种手艺,别人都不会。

(In my village, except that my grandfather masters the silversmith craftsmanship, nobody else can.)

除十个小时的工作、八个小时的睡觉,就没有多少时间了。

此外,"除"还可以单独与单音代词"此"结合用,"除了"不行。(In addition, "除" can also be used together with the monosyllabic pronoun "此", but "除了" can't.)例如:

除此,我别无所求了。

(I have no other requests except this.)

* 除了此,我别无所求了。

处处 chùchù   到处 dàochù

〈副词〉都可以指全部范围。

(<adverb> to or in every place.)

(一) 意义上 (In meaning)

99

"处处"、"到处"都可以表示各个地方。"处处"更加强调所有的地方无一例外;"到处"表示所有的地方都包括在内,所以多与表示范围的"都"配合使用。("处处" and "到处" refer to every place. "处处" strongly emphasizes all the places without exception. "到处" indicates that all the places included so it is usually used together with "都".)例如:

这里处处是春天。

祖国处处有亲人。

草原上,牛群、羊群、马群处处可见。

(There are herds of cattle, flocks of sheep and droves of horses everywhere on the grassland.)

车站内外到处都是人。

春天,公园里到处飘着花香。

浑身上下到处都是土。

(There is mud all over the body.)

(二) 用法上(In use)

1. "处处"、"到处"在句中主要作状语,不能作宾语、定语。("处处" and "到处" are mainly used as adverbials, but they can't be used as objects and attributives in the sentence.)例如:

植物园里,处处是鲜花,美丽极了!

参与竞选活动的人处处可见。

现在人的确太多了,到街上一看,到处都是人。

今天是"六一"儿童节,公园里到处是孩子们兴致勃勃的笑脸。

* 这里很美,我要去处处/到处看看。

* 在法国时,他游遍了法国的处处/到处。

* 今天不知怎么了,处处/到处的商店都不开门。

2. "处处"还可以表示各个方面的意思,在句中作状语。"到处"没有这一意义和用法。("处处" may indicate every aspect and is used as an adverbial in the sentence, while "到处" can not.)例如:

队长时时处处严格要求自己。

他处处为别人着想。

(He thinks about all the interests of others.)

他总是处处走在前面。

(He is found in all aspects at the leading position.)

* 队长时时到处严格要求自己。

* 他到处为别人着想。

* 他总是到处走在前面。

次 cì　　遍 biàn　　趟 tàng

〈量词〉< measure word >

(一)"次"、"遍"、"趟"都可以用来计量动作的量,但是表示的意义不同。("次","遍"and"趟" can be used to measure the amount, but they indicate different meanings.)

1."次"、"遍"、"趟"不同的意义(Different meanings of"次","遍"and"趟".)

"次"用来计量反复出现的动作或者可能反复出现的动作。("次"indicates actions occur repeatedly or actions might occur repeatedly.)例如:

去了一次北京　给他送了两次文件　试了三次　穿了一次

"遍"用来计量从开始到结束的整个过程的动作。("遍" indicates the action which takes place from the beginning to the end.)例如:

看三遍　写了一遍　翻了好几遍　检查两遍了　洗三遍了

"趟"用来计量来回走动的动作。("趟"indicates the actions moving back and forth.)例如:

去了一趟广州　往医院跑了三趟　来了两趟　回趟家

2.从使用上看,"次"和"遍","次"和"趟"都可能出现交叉现象,但是一定要注意它们不相同的意义。("次"and"遍","次"

and "趟" can be used inchangeably ways, but attention has to be paid to their different meanings.)

(1) "次"和"遍"交叉使用时意义的分辨。(The distinction between "次" and "遍" when used exchangeably.) 例如:

这部电影我看了三次。

这部电影我看了三遍。

"三次"只在说明"看"动作重复的数量,不管完整不完整;"三遍"则在说明"看"的动作每次都是从开始到结束的整个过程,是完整的三次。下个例子可以清楚地表现出"次"和"遍"的差别。(Here "三次" only illustrates the number of times the action of "看" is repeated, regardless of the fact if the action is completely repeated or not; "三遍" indicates the whole process from the beginning to the end is done three times, meaning complete three times. The next example will show this clearly.)

这部电影我看了三次才看完一遍。

"遍"由于强调动作从开始到结束的整个过程,所以句中如果有强调"从头到尾"、"全部经过"、"整个"、"全套"这样的内容,动作的量应该选用"遍",不要选用"次"。("遍" emphasizes the complete process, as from the beginning to the end, of the action. So if the content needs to emphasize "from the beginning to the end", "the whole process", "the whole" or "the complete set", the measure of the verb is "遍", but not "次".) 例如:

她把信从头到尾读了两遍。

(She read the letter from the beginning to the end twice.)

* 她把信从头到尾读了两次。

我把事情的全部经过叙述了一遍。

* 我把事情的全部经过叙述了一次。

你把全套动作做一遍,好吗?

(Would you please do the whole movements once more?)

他帮我把整个机器认真地检查了一遍。

(2) "次"和"趟"在使用上交叉现象更严重,有时在表示走动的动作的次数时，不需要刻意区分。(It is very common to use "次" and "趟" exchangeably. When indicating the frequency of trips, there isn't considerable difference.)例如：

这个月，我去了三次北京了。

这个月，我去了三趟北京了。

但是，如果说话人特意强调来往走动的动作次数时，就应该选用"趟"，而不要选用"次"。还要注意的是说话人特意强调来往走动的动作时，一般要选择表示来往走动的动词，这类动词很有限，常用的只有"来"、"去"、"跑"、"走"、"回"和其他少数趋向动词等。(But if the speaker puts emphasis on the frequency of going back and forth, "趟" is used instead of "次" and when this kind of action is stressed, verbs indicating going back and forth are chosen. The verbs indicating coming and going are limited in number. The commonly used ones are "来","去","跑","走","回" and a few directional verbs.)例如：

下午你去哪儿了？——我去了趟邮电局。

她妈妈住院了，情况挺危险，她每天都要往医院跑好几趟。

(Her mother is in the hospital and in a serious condition so that she goes to the hospital several times a day.)

我往书店跑了三趟了，才买到这本书。

当动作不表示来往走动的动作时，当然不能用"趟"了。(When the action doesn't indicate moving back and forth, "趟" can't be used.)例如：

他来了三次信了，我一次也没回过。

这个动作做了好几次了，总也做不好。

＊他来了三趟信了，我一趟也没回过。

＊这个动作做了好几趟了，总也做不好。

(二)"次"和"趟"除了直接表示动作的量以外，还可以表示跟动作相关的事物的量。(Besides directly showing the amount of action,"次" and "趟" can be followed by the amount of things related with the action.)

1."次"可以用于重复出现的事物。("次" is used for things repeatedly happen.)例如:

这次机会很难得,你一定要争取过来。
(This is a rare occasion, you must strive to get it.)
两次会议都没有把这个问题解决好。
你们跟他们两次大战的结果怎么样?
(What are the results of your two wars with them ?)

2."趟"可以用于来往开行的列车。("趟" can be used to modify travelling trains.)例如:

一趟列车　这趟车开往天津　那趟车该进站了

(三)"趟"还有名量词的用法,用于成行的东西,相当于量词"行(háng)"。("趟" also functions as a nominal measure word, used to indicate things in rows, similar to the measure word "行".)例如:

这趟街　几趟大字　两趟桌椅　一趟脚印

从 cóng　　自 zì　　由 yóu　　打 dǎ

〈介词〉< preposition >

(一)"从"、"自"、"由"、"打"都可以表示起点意义,尤其是时间、处所的起点。("从","自","由" and "打" mean beginning point, especially that of time and place.)例如:

1. 表示时间:(Indicating time:)

从上一周我们就开始上课了。
由明年一月开始执行新方案。
(From January next year, the new project will be carried out.)
自古以来,泰山一直为游人所喜欢。
(From ancient times Mount Tai has been a beloved place of the tourists.)

打明天起,不用你来照顾我了。

2. 表示处所:(Indicating places:)

人们从四面八方涌进广场。

(People crowded into the square from all directions.)

下午两点,由公司乘车出发。

本次列车自北京开往上海。

小明打屋子里跑了出来。

(二)"从"、"自"、"由"、"打"在表示时间、处所起点意义时的不同之处。(Differences of "从","自","由" and "打" when indicating the starting points of time and places.)

1. 色彩不同(Difference in flavour)

比较起来,"自"、"由"多用于书面语,"打"只用于口语。(Comparatively speaking, "自" and "由" are generally used in written language and "打" is only used in spoken language.)例如:

此公告自发布之日起执行。

(The announcement will come into effect from the day it is issued.)

队伍由此向西排列。

(The contingent ranged from here to the west.)

俺打山东老家来。

(I come from my hometown Shandong.)

2. 功能不同(Difference in function)

"自"可以组成介词词组放在动词后,作表示处所意义的补语;"从"、"由"、"打"不可以。("自" can compose prepositional phrase which is put after the verb to be the complement of places. "从","由" and "打" cannot.)例如:

他的朋友来自世界各国。

她一声声的道谢完全发自内心深处。

(All her thanks are sincerely coming from the bottom of her heart.)

* 他的朋友来从／由世界各国。
* 她一声声的道谢完全发从／由内心深处。
* 这篇小说选从／由／打《鲁迅全集》。

(三)"从"、"自"、"由"、"打"其他不相同的意义和用法。(The different meanings and usages of "从","自","由" and "打".)

1. 除时间、处所起点外,"从"、"由"还可以表示发展、变化、范围的起点;"自"可以表示空间范围的起点;"打"一般不表示这种意义。(Besides introducing the starting point of time and place, "从" and "由" can also indicate the starting points of development, change and scope. "自" indicates the starting point of space scope, but "打" generally can't express this meaning.)例如:

由／从不懂到懂,需要经过一段艰苦的学习过程。

(From being unknowledgeable to being knowledgeable, one needs spending a period of time studying hard.)

他从／由一个农家孩子成长为一名优秀的大学生。

(From a country boy he has become an excellent college student.)

从学习、工作到生活问题,我们都应该解决好。

从教学到科研他都很出色。

(From teaching to researching he has done excellently.)

自下而上地进行民主评议。

(From bottom to top the democratic discussion is being done.)

2."从"、"由"除表示"起点"意义外,还可以表示经过的路线、场所。("从" and "由" can also indicate the routes and places somebody or something passes by.)例如:

阳光从／由树缝中射了进来。

请观众由／从东西两门出场。

3."从"、"由"还可以表示根据。"自"、"打"不可以。("从" and "由" can indicate taking something as the base, but

"自" and "打" can't.)例如：

  计划要从实际出发，不能想当然。

  (A plan must be in accordance with the reality and can't be taken for granted.)

  由此可见，原来的方案脱离实际。

  (By this, we come to the conclusion that the former project is just divorced from reality.)

  * 计划要自/打实际出发，不能想当然。

  * 自/打此可见，原来的方案脱离实际。

4."由"可以表示方式、原因或来源，"从"等不可以。("由" can indicate styles, causes or origins, but "从" can't.)例如：

  由民主协商解决这一问题。

  (This problem will be solved by democratic consultation.)

  孩子由感冒引起了肺炎。

  (The kid's pneumonia was caused by flu.)

  由一个小小的失误造成了重大的经济损失。

  (The heavy economical loss was caused by a small fault.)

  * 从民主协商解决这一问题。

5."由"还有引进动作施动者的作用。"从"等不可以。("由" can also be used to introduce the action maker, but "从" can't.)例如：

  这项工作由他负责。

  会议由你主持。

  参观团由张小姐陪同参观。

  (This visiting group is accompanied by Miss Zhang.)

  * 这项工作从他负责。

  * 会议自你主持。

  * 参观团从张小姐陪同参观。

从 cóng   自 zì   自从 zìcóng

〈介词〉表示起点。

(< preposition > starting from.)

(一)"从"、"自"、"自从"都可以表示时间的起点。"从"、"自"表示时间起点时,不受过去、现在、将来时间的限制,但是"自"含有书面语色彩;"自从"表示时间起点则只能表示过去的时间。("从","自" and "自从"all mean the starting point of time."从"and "自"are not restricted by the past, the present, or future, but"自"has the flavour of written language,"自从"is only used for the past time.)例如:

从现在起,我们谁也不要说话,自己思考自己的问题。

自明天起,实验就进入下一个阶段了。

自从来中国以后,我才真正地了解了中国。

* 自从现在起,我们谁也不要说话,自己思考自己的问题。

* 自从明天起,实验就进入下一个阶段了。

(二)"从"、"自"还可以表示地点、范围等起点,"自从"则只表示时间的起点。("从" and "自" can also indicate the starting points of place and scope, but"自从"only indicates the starting of the time.)例如:

我们从学校一毕业就来到这儿。

这封信自上海寄来。

从学习到生活,学校对我们照顾得很好。

* 这封信自从上海寄来。

* 自从学习到生活学校照顾得很好。

(三)"自"在构成介词词组表示地点、来源等意义时,还可以放在动词后作补语;"从"、"自从"没有这种用法。(When indicating places and origins,"自" can compose prepositional word groups after the verbs as complements, but"从" and "自从"can't.)例如:

我们都是来自五湖四海。
(We all come from all corners of the country.)
这段话引自昨天的《人民日报》。
她的感谢是发自内心的。
* 我们都是来从五湖四海。
* 这段话引从昨天的《人民日报》。
* 她的感谢是发自从内心的。

从来 cónglái　　历来 lìlái　　向来 xiànglái

从来、历来、向来〈副词〉表示从过去到现在一直是这样。
(从来,历来,向来(<adverb> from the past till now; all the same)

历来〈形容词〉 <adjective>

"从来"、"历来"或"向来"虽然都可以表示某种情况或状态从过去到现在一直是这样的意思,但是意义和用法还有一定的差别。(Though "从来", "历来" or "向来" indicates that it has been the same like this from the past, but there are differences in meaning and usage.)

(一) 意义上、色彩上的差别(Differences in meaning and in flavour)

"从来"对"某种情况或状态从过去到现在一直是这样"有强调意味,语气稍重;"历来"、"向来"这种强调意味较轻,所以主要用来叙述,而不是强调。"历来"跟"从来"、"向来"比,语义较侧重于"早已如此"。此外,"历来"的书面语色彩较重,多用于书面语;"从来"、"向来"没有这种倾向,口语、书面语都常见。("从来" emphasizes a certain situation or state has been the same from the past to the present time. Compared with "从来", "历来" and "向来" express a lighter emphatic tone and are mainly used to recount but not to emphasize. Besides, "历来" indicates a bit stronger written language flavour and is generally used in written

109

language. "从来"and "向来" lay no emphasis on that, they are generally used either in oral or in written language.)例如:

一定是搞错了,这种话我从来没说过。

(There must be something wrong for I have never said this before.)

他历来如此,现在仍然这样。

(He hes always been like this and is still the same now.)

他是个谨慎的人,向来不说这种话。

(He is always a careful man and has never talked like this.)

(二)用法上的差别(Differences in use)

"从来"大多用于否定句,用于肯定句的情况较少。用于肯定句时通常有一定的条件——一般不能用来修饰单个动词或形容词,而要修饰动词性词组或形容词性词组,并且常跟"都"、"就"搭配。("从来" is mostly used in negative sentences, rarely in positive sentence. When used in positive sentences, a certain condition has to be provided, usually it is not used to modify a single verb or adjective, but to modify verbal word group or adjective word group, they are usually used together with "都" or "就".)例如:

他只顾自己,从来不关心别人。

(He only cares about himself and never does that to others.)

这样的话他从来不说。

林先生是个严于律己的人,他对自己的要求从来都没放松过。

(Mr Lin is very strict with himself. He has never relaxed himself from his own strict demands.)

对待这种事情,他从来就是这种态度。

(He has ever held this kind of attitude while treating things like this.)

你放心吧,他做事情从来都很认真。

* 这样的话他从来说。

* 他对自己的要求从来放松。

* 你放心吧,他做事情从来认真。

"历来"则基本上相反,通常用于肯定句,而不用于否定句。此外,"历来"对于句中的谓词性成分也有限制——多选用表示主张、观点、态度等抽象性动词或"有"、"是"等动词,还可以选用形容词,一般不选用非常具体的动作性动词。("历来" is basically opposite. It is usually used in positive sentences, not in negative sentences. Besides, there is a certain restriction to the predicative composition in the sentence—the abstract verbs indicating propositions, viewpoints and attitudes and verbs like "there be" or "be", etc. are used and so are adjectives. Generally, verbs of specific actions are not used.)例如:

我们历来主张在法律面前人人平等。

(We always advocate that everybody is treated equal in front of law.)

马克思主义历来认为历史是人民创造的。

中国人民历来勤劳、勇敢、有智慧和善于创造。

这个人历来忠诚老实,完全可以信赖。

(This person has always been honest and can be fully trusted.)

* 这个人历来负责任。

* 他历来抽烟、喝酒。

* 我历来学习汉语。

"向来"不受肯定句、否定句的限制,也不受句子成分简单、复杂的限制,用起来比较自由。("向来" is neither restricted by positive nor negative sentences. It is not restricted by the simplicity or complication of the sentence compositions either, and is quite flexible in use.)例如:

王成向来说话算数。

她向来不喜欢看电影。

刘师傅对工作向来负责。

在这种场合,他向来不肯表态。

(三) 功能上的差别(Differences in function)

"历来"除作副词用作状语外,还可以作形容词用作定语;"从来"、"向来"没有作定语的用法。(Besides being used as an adverbial in sentence, "历来" also functions as an attributive since it can be an adjective in the sentence. "从来" and "向来" can't be attributives.)例如:

提倡顾全大局是我们历来的原则。

(It is our consistent principle to promote taking the interests of the whole into consideration.)

这是我们历来的规定,不能因为你而改变。

(This is our usual rule so it can't be changed just because of you.)

* 提倡顾全大局是我们向来的原则。

* 这是我们从来的规定,不能因为你而改变。

村子 cūnzi　　村庄 cūnzhuāng
乡村 xiāngcūn　　农村 nóngcūn

〈名词〉都指以从事农业为主的人聚集居住的地方。

(< noun > referring to the places where the farming people reside.)

"村子"、"村庄"、"乡村"、"农村"这几个词虽然都可以指以从事农业为主的人聚集居住的地方,但是意义还是稍有差别,所以使用上也稍有不同。(Although the four nouns all refer to the places for people taking up farming to live in a compact community, there are differences among them both in meaning and use.)

(一)意义上的差别(Differences in meaning)

"村子"、"村庄"跟"乡村"、"农村"比起来,不属于有具体明确界域的地方,它们属于"乡村"、"农村"中一些具体的、大小不等的自然区划的地方。"乡村"、"农村"则是属于有较明确的界域的地方,它指跟城市相对的地方,也就是说非城市的、以从事农业为主的人聚集居住的地方就是"乡村"或"农村"。

(Compared with "乡村"and "农村","村子"and "村庄" indicate places not belonging to the specific and definite boundary, they belong to some specific places of some specific and naturally divided districts. "乡村"and "农村"are places with rather clear boundary. They refer to the places opposite to cities, namely the places away from cities and where residents are mainly engaged in farming.)

"村子"和"村庄"比起来,"村庄"的书面语色彩浓一些,口语多用"村子"。"乡村"和"农村"比起来,"乡村"属于集合名词,即它是农村的"乡"的基本单位和"村"的基本单位相加而得的名词,泛指农村,但不是界域清楚的"农村"本身;"农村"则是城市界域以外的、从事农业为主的人居住的广大地域。〔Compared with "村子","村庄"has stronger written language flavour, and "村子"is often used in spoken language. Compared with "农村","乡村"is a collective noun, which is compounded of the basic administrative unit "乡"(rural area)and "村"(village)。"乡村"generally refers to rural areas, but it doesn't mean "农村"。"农村"means the broad area away from city boundary and for people taking up farming to reside at.〕

(二) 使用上的差别(Differences in use)

1."乡村"、"农村"因为是属于有较明确界域的地方,所以它属于可以表示场所意义的名词,它可以直接用在"在"、"到"、"自"等介词后构成场所意义的词组,跟动词结合。"村子"、"村庄"只从词本身看不到明确的界域,不具有场所意义,因此一般不能用在"在"、"自"等介词后跟动词结合。("乡村"and "农村"refer to places of clear boundary, they are nouns of places, which can be used directly after a preposition such as "在","到" or "自"to make word groups of places and join together with verbs. "村子"and "村庄"by words themselves don't show clear boundary so they can't be used after the preposition "在"or "自"to join with verbs.)例如:

我来自乡村/农村,对那儿的生活很熟悉。

他生活在农村/乡村,对农民有深厚的感情。
你在哪儿读的小学?——在农村读的小学。
你在哪儿读的小学?——＊在村子/村庄/乡村读的小学。

＊我来自村子/村庄,对那儿的生活很熟悉。
＊他生活在村子/村庄,对农民有深厚的感情。

2."村子"和"村庄"是农村基本的自然区划单位,所以它们可以跟数量词结合;"乡村"和"农村"不是某个基本单位,所以不能跟数量词结合。(Because "村子" and "村庄" are basic administrative units in the countryside, they can be used together with numeral-classifier compounds. But "乡村" and "农村" are not. Therefore, they can't be used together with numeral-classifier compounds.)例如:

一个村子　几个村庄　有个村子　某个村庄
＊一个农村　＊几个乡村　＊有个农村　＊某个乡村

3."乡村"还可以用来表示某种有别于城市的风格、特点等,"村子"、"村庄"、"农村"一般没有这种用法。("乡村" is also used to indicate style or character which differs from that in cities. "村子","村庄" and "农村" can't be used in this way.)例如:

饭店这样一布置,充满了浓郁的乡村气息。
(Being decorated this way the restaurant is filled with a strong rural life flavour.)
这种服饰倒满有乡村的风格。
(The dress is quite of a rural style.)
＊饭店这样一布置,充满了浓郁的村子/村庄/农村气息。
＊这种服饰倒满有村子/村庄/农村的风格。

D

大概 dàgài　　大约 dàyuē　　大体 dàtǐ

大概、大体〈副词〉〈名词〉〈形容词〉

大概、大体 < adverb > < noun > < adjective >

大约〈副词〉 < adverb >

(一)"大概"、"大约"、"大体"都有副词的意义和用法,都可以用作状语,但是意义有差别。("大概","大约" and "大体" are all adverbs and used as adverbials but there are differences in meaning.)

1."大概"、"大约"用作对数量、时间作不很精确的估计时,意思大体相当,结构上都要求后边带数量词或时间词,有时可以通用。"大体"没有这种用法。(When used to make unclear measurement of amount and time, "大概" and "大约", meaning nearly the same, are structurally followed by numeral-classifier compounds or words of time. They are interchangeable, but "大体" can't be used this way.)例如:

现在大概/大约<u>三点半</u>了。

他大概/大约<u>年底</u>回国。

这里离张庄大概/大约有<u>五十多里地</u>。

* 现在大体三点半了。

* 他大体年底回国。

* 这里离张庄大体有五十多里路。

2."大概"作为副词,主要表示对某种有很大可能性的情况的推测、估计;"大约"基本上不表示这种意义。"大体"没有这种意思和用法。(As an adverb, "大概" mainly indicates inference and estimation of a certain condition with good possibility. "大约" is essentially not used in this situation and "大体" doesn't mean this and can't be used this way.)例如:

115

他大概是日本人,那天我听见他用日语打电话。

你看他浑身是伤,大概吃了不少苦头。

(Look, he is injured all over. Maybe he has suffered a lot.)

看他美滋滋的,大概有什么好事吧。

(He looks very pleased. Maybe there is good news for him.)

* 你看他浑身是伤,大约吃了不少苦头。
* 看他美滋滋的,大约有什么好事吧。
* 他大体是日本人,那天我听见他用日语打电话。
* 你看他浑身是伤,大体吃了不少苦头。
* 看他美滋滋的,大体有什么好事吧。

3."大体"表示的是"就大多数情形来说"或"就主要方面来说"的意思,它强调的重点是"基本上来说"的意思,所以它有时候可跟"上"连用,构成"大体上"的形式,在句中充当状语。("大体"indicates "according to most cases" or "in the principal aspects." It emphasizes "basically speaking", so sometimes it is used with "上" to make the word group "大体上" which will be adverbial in the sentence.)例如:

会议日程大体安排就绪。

最近的生活大体过得去。

我们的看法大体相同。

这本书的内容我大体看懂了。

(二)"大概"还有名词用法,表示大致的内容或情况;"大约"、"大体"没有这种用法。("大概" can also be used as a noun, indicating approximate content or information."大约"and "大体" can't.)例如:

这件事我已经了解了个大概。

(I have approximately got to know the matter.)

知道个大概就行了,没必要查那么细。

(To know approximately is OK. It is unnecessary to examine

it that carefully.)

看来我的汉语水平还不行,只能听懂个大概。

* 这件事我已经了解了个大约／大体。

* 知道个大约／大体就行了,没必要查那么细。

(三)"大体"也有名词的用法,但是它表示是的"重要的义理"或"有关大局的道理"的意思,跟"大概"的意思完全不同。而且能跟它搭配的动词有很大的局限,通常只有"识"、"知"、"关"等个别单音节动词,跟"大概"的搭配组合完全不同。("大体"can also be used as a noun, but it indicates principal argumentation or principle concerning the overall situation. It is different from"大概". The verbs that could be used together with"大体"are limited, usually only monosyllabic verbs as "识","知"and "关"and their collocations are completely different from those of"大概".)例如:

这孩子识大体、顾大局,真是好样的。

这些都是细小而无关大体的事。

* 这孩子识大概、顾大局,真是好样的。

* 这些都是细小而无关大概的事。

(四)"大概"、"大体"还有形容词用法,在句中都可以充当定语。"大概"表示不十分精确或不十分详尽的意思;"大体"表示多数情况的或主要方面的意思;"大约"没有这种意思和用法。("大概"and"大体"are also used as adjectives and serves as attributives in sentence."大概"indicates something which is not exactly accurate or exhaustive,"大体"indicates in most cases or the principal aspects."大约"doesn't indicate this and can't be used in this way.)例如:

他的话虽然我没有全听懂,大概的意思还明白。

你们把大概的情况了解一下就行了。

这个数字我不敢说精确,只能说是一个大概的数字。

(I can't say this figure is accurate, but only say it is a general figure.)

有个大概的印象就行了。

(It is all right to have a general impression.)

* 他的话虽然我没有全听懂,但大约的意思还明白。
* 你们把大约的情况了解一下就行了。
* 有个大约的印象就行了。

大概 dàgài   也许 yěxǔ   恐怕 kǒngpà

〈副词〉表示推测、估计。

(<adverb> indicating inference and estimation.)

"大概"、"也许"、"恐怕"在句中都用作状语,意思很接近。常常可以互换使用。但是意思的侧重点仍有细小差别。("大概","也许"and"恐怕"are used as adverbials in sentence and they are close in meaning, and often exchangeable in use, but there are some slight differences in the way they emphasize.)

"大概"在表示推测、估计时,带有较强的客观判断性,肯定意味较重;"也许"则侧重于猜测,不定的意味较重;"恐怕"则商量的意味较重。此外,"恐怕"还兼有担心、忧虑的意味,这是"大概"、"也许"所没有的。(When used for inference or estimating, "大概" has a fairly strong characteristic of objective judgement and the meaning of affirmation is expressed strongly. "也许" lays stress on guessing and expresses strongly the indefiniteness. "恐怕" lays stress on discussion. Besides, "恐怕" has simultaneously the meaning of worry and anxiety, "大概" and "也许" haven't.)例如:

他大概有什么事,不然不会迟到的。

(Maybe he got something to do or he wouldn't be late.)

看他的眼神,大概是个很聪明的孩子。

(By the expression in his eyes, maybe he is a fairly bright boy.)

他最近很忙,也许今晚不来了。

也许情况不像你想像的那么糟。
(Maybe the situation isn't as terrible as you have imagined.)

这样不注意身体,时间长了,恐怕要出大问题呀。

天又变了,恐怕又要下了。

恐怕这样不好吧。

此外,"也许"有时还可以表示委婉的肯定。(In addition, "也许" also sometimes indicates tactful affirmation.)例如:

青年人学点儿历史也许是十分必要的。

对你的饮食严格控制一下也许是有益的。
(Maybe the strict restriction of your diet is useful.)

大量 dàliàng   大批 dàpī

〈形容词〉都有数量很多的意思。

< adjective > large quantities.

(一) 意义上的异同(Similarities and differences in meaning)

"大量"、"大批"都有数量很多的意思,但是表示多的角度稍有不同。("大量" and "大批" both indicate large quantities but the amount they emphasize is slightly different.)

1."大量"是指一个个的个体很多;"大批"是指一次的或每一次的数量很大。("大量" indicates many individuals;"大批" indicates the large amount one time or every time.)例如:

储存了大量的外汇

培养了大量的人才(have trained a lot of qualified personnel)

购进了大批的货物 (purchased large quantities of goods)

输送了大批的优秀人才(have provided ... with a great many excellent qualified personnel)

2."大量"、"大批"都可以用于货物和人,但是"大量"使用范围大,它既可以用于具有相对动态意义的词语结构中,也可以用于具有相对静态意义的词语结构中;"大批"使用范围小,通常只

119

用于具有相对动态意义的词语结构中,句中动词常常跟"进"、"出"的意义有关。(Both "大量" and "大批" can be used for goods or people, but "大量" is used extensively and can be used in the sentence structure with dynamic meaning and may also be used in the sentence structure with static meaning. "大批" is not used extensively and usually used in the phrasal structures with comparatively dynamic meaning. The verbs in these structures often concern "进" or "出".) 例如:

化工厂打算大量地生产化肥。

高等院校为社会输送了大量的有用人才。

(Institutions and universities have provided the society with a great many qualified personnel.)

可以大量地投入生产了。

(It can be put into production by great amount.)

化工厂打算大批地生产化肥。

高等院校为社会输送了大批的有用人才。

可以大批地投入生产了。

这种影响还大量地存在着。

(The influence is still hugely existing.)

大量地占有资料是搞好科研的前提。

(To extensively gather data is just the premise of scientific research.)

* 这种影响还大批地存在着。

* 大批地占有资料是搞好科研的前提。

从今天开始,我们要大量储备这种货。

你们要大量安置待业人员。

从上月开始,仓库里就大批地储备了这种货。

今年我校毕业了大批的本科生、研究生。

图书馆购进了大批的图书。

3. "大量"既可以用于具体事物,又可以用于抽象事物;"大

120

批"则一般只用于具体事物,通常只用于大宗货物和人。("大量"can either be used for specific objects or abstract objects. "大批" is generally used for specific objects and especially for a large amount of goods and a great many people.)例如:

大量的财产	大量的资金	大量的人力
大量的科技人员		大批的货物
大批的图书	大批的人材	大批的学生

做了大量的思想工作(have done a lot of ideological work)
占用了大量的时间
搜集到大量的信息(have gathered a lot of information)
采取了大量的保护措施(have taken a lot of protective measures)
摆出了大量的事实
* 做了大批的思想工作　* 占用了大批的时间
* 搜集到大批的信息　* 采取了大批的保护措施
* 摆出了大批的事实

(二) 功能用法上的异同(Similarities and differences in function)

1."大量"、"大批"都是非谓形容词,都不能用作谓语,也不能接受程度副词的修饰。("大量"and "大批"are non-predicative adjectives and can neither be used as predicates nor be modified by adverbs of degree.)例如:

* 货物大量　　　　* 人才大量
* 货物大批　　　　* 人才大批
* 骑自行车的人很大量　* 图书馆有很大量的图书
* 骑自行车的人很大批　* 图书馆有很大批的图书

2."批"本身又是一个量词,构成"大批"后,还具有一些量词的组合功能;"大量"只有形容词的用法,所以没有量词的组合功能。("批"itself is also a measure word and after the words "大批", it has the composing function of measure words. "大量"can only be used as an adjective and hasn't the composing function of measure words.)例如：

(1)"大批"前可以加数词"一",表示的数量更大。"大量"没有这种用法。(Numeral "一" can be put before "大批" to indicate a larger number. "大量" can not be used in this way.)例如：

一大批知识分子志愿奔赴落后地区为知识的传播做贡献。

(A great many intellectuals have willingly hurried to the less developed areas to dedicate themselves to the knowledge spreading.)

我给你搞到了一大批货。

* 一大量知识分子志愿奔赴落后地区为知识的传播做贡献。

* 我给你搞到了一大量货。

(2)"大批"可以重叠为"大批大批",表示批数多的意思。"大量"没有这种用法。(The expression "大批" can be reduplicated as "大批大批". "大量" can't.)例如：

大批大批的优秀大学生走上了社会。

大批大批的劣质商品流入市场,除了管理不当的因素外,还有法制不健全的因素。

(Besides the factors of improper management, the reasons why a great amount of low quality commodities have flowed into the markets are that of imperfect legal system.)

* 大量大量的优秀大学生走上了社会。

* 大量大量的劣质商品流入市场,除了管理不当的因素外,还有法制不健全的因素。

耽搁 dānge   耽误 dānwu

〈动词〉 <verb>

(一)"耽搁"、"耽误"都是动词,都有表示拖延的意思。在表示"拖延时间"的意思上,可以互换使用,但是表义的侧重点仍有不同。"耽搁"是指在时间上多占用了,只指时间上的拖延;"耽误"不只是时间上拖延了的问题,还有由此而误了事情的意思。(Both "耽搁" and "耽误" are verbs, they indicate the meaning of "拖延时间"(delay) and they are exchangeable in this sense, but lay stresses on different aspects. "耽搁" refers to "take up much time", the delay of time, while "耽误" means not only taking up much time but holding up the matter.)例如:

实在对不起,为了我的事,耽误/耽搁了你的工作。

他为了工作,连婚期都耽搁/耽误了。

种子不及时运到,耽误/耽搁了农时,损失可就大了。

(If the seeds can't be sent in time, the farming season will be held up and there would be great damage.)

事情没办完,他只好又在北京耽搁一天。

这件事不急,耽搁一天没事儿。

* 事情没办完,他只好又在北京耽误一天。

* 这件事不急,耽误一天没事儿。

(二) 在使用上,"耽误"总要跟"误"的对象、"误"的情况发生联系——各种事情、时间或者时段等,没有宾语、补语一般不能用"耽误";"耽误"后边没有任何其他成分一般不能使用。"耽搁"的对象应该更加具体些;"耽搁"还有"停留"的意思,所以没有宾语、补语或没有其他成分也能成立。〔"耽误" should establish contact with the object of "误"(delayed) or the matter which is delayed, such as different things, times or periods of time. Without objects or complements "耽误"(delay) can't be used. "耽误" can't be used if there isn't any element after it. The objects of "耽搁" have to be more specific. "耽搁" also means "停留"(stay). It remains meaningful without objects, complements or other compositions.〕例如:

耽误了学习	耽误了前途	耽误了事业
耽误了治病	耽误了时间	耽误了半天
耽误了好几个小时	耽误了一次	耽误不得
耽搁了学习	耽搁了工作	耽搁了吃饭
耽搁了治病	耽搁了时间	耽搁了半天
耽搁了好几个小时	耽搁了一次	耽搁不得

时间很紧,路上千万不要耽搁。

(Time is limited, be sure not to delay on the way.)

你别在这儿耽搁了,有什么事我们替你办好了。

(Don't hold up here. We will take care of everything for you.)

* 时间很紧,路上千万不要耽误。

* 你别在这儿耽误了,有什么事我们替你办好了。

当 dāng　　当时 dāngshí

当〈介词〉< preposition >
当时〈名词〉< noun >

(一)"当"和"当时"结构特点和语法功能不同。(The structural characteristics and grammatical functions of "当" and "当时" are different.)

1. "当"是介词,不能单独使用,它一般要用在动词性词组前,后面通常要跟"时"、"……的时候"、"时节"或"以前"、"以后"等词配合,构成表示时间的词组才能充当句子成分。"当时"是名词,可以单独作句子成分,表示时间。("当" is a preposition and can't be used separately. Generally it is used before the verbal phrase, and it is often used together with "时", "…的时候", "时节" or "以前", "以后". "当时" is a noun and can be separately used as a component to indicate time.) 例如:

当飞机平稳降落时,我心里才感到一阵轻松。

(Only when the plane was smoothly descending did I relaxed in the mind.)

当她听到儿子被北京大学录取的消息时,激动得热泪滚滚。

* 当飞机平稳降落,我心里才感到一阵轻松。

* 当她听到儿子被北京大学录取的消息,激动得热泪滚滚。

当时,她激动得一句话也说不出来。

我当时并没有想到问题会那么严重。

2."当"构成的介词词组,在句子中只作状语,一般用在句子前面。"当时"常常用作时间状语,作状语时,位置比较活,可以出现在主语前,也可以出现在主语后。此外它还可以作定语,甚至主语、宾语。(Prepositional word group composed of "当" is only used as an adverbial in the sentence, and generally is used in front of the sentence. "当时" is often used as an adverbial of time. Being an adverbial, its position is flexible. It may appear before subjects and after subjects. Besides, "当时" may also be used as attributives and even subjects or objects.)例如:

当春暖花开的时节,同学们来到了山清水秀的桂林。

(When spring came and flowers were blooming, the fellow students got to Guilin, a place with green hills and clear waters.)

每当我心情不好的时候,她总是耐心地劝说我。

他听到这件事,当时脸就变了颜色。(状语)

(At the moment he heard the news, his face changed.)

当时的情况谁都难以预料。(定语)

(It was difficult for everyone to anticipate the situation at that time.)

当时是当时,现在是现在。(主语、宾语)

3."当"前面还可以与"正"或"每",后面还可以与"着"等词配合使用;"当时"不能这样用。("正"or "每"can be used before

"当"and "着"can be used after "当"."当时"can't be used this way.)例如：

正当人们欢庆胜利的时候,这几个坏人又搞起了新的阴谋。

每当我想家的时候,她总是来陪我、安慰我。

当着革命形势已经改变的时候,革命的策略也必须跟着改变。

(While the revolutionary situation has been changing, the revolutionary tactics must follow to change.)

(二) 由"当"构成的介词词组跟"当时"都可以表示时间,但是它们所表示的时间有不同的意义,所以一般不能互换使用。(The prepositional phrases composed of "当"and "当时"both indicate time, but they are not exchangeable for the time they indicate doesn't mean the same.)

由"当"构成的介词词组,表示事情发生的那个时间、那个时候,所以它事实上是要有两件事情出现,第一件事情的出现只表示时间,在第一件事情出现的时候发生第二件事情。"当时"只表示时间,没有相互联系的两件事的情况。此外,"当"所表示的时间,没有过去、现在、将来的限制,有时也可以表示某一有规律的时间;"当时"则只能表示过去发生某件事时,只指一个具体的时点,不能表示某一有规律的时间,也不能表示将来的时间。(The prepositional word group composed of "当"indicates the time and the moment that the cases happen, so actually it needs two cases to be involved, the happening of the first thing just indicates the time, when the first case occurs the second follows. "当时"indicates only time, having nothing to do with two connecting matters. Besides, time indicated by "当" has no limits of the past, the present and the future, but sometimes it can indicate some regular time. "当时", otherwise, merely refers to a particular point of time, can't indicate some regular time and time in future.)例如：

那天上午,当我提着行李要出门的时候,她来了。

〔我提着行李要出门——第一件事(时间);她来了——第二件事。〕

〔I carried the luggage and was going to leave—the first thing (time); she came—the second thing.〕

当时,我简直不知道说什么才好。(只有一件事。)

当她急需别人帮助的时候,你怎么不帮助她?

(Why didn't you give her a hand when she was in need of help?)

(这里是指过去,但不一定是一个时间,也可能是多个这样的时间。)

(Here it refers to the past, not necessarily at one time in the past, but maybe at many such moments.)

当时她十分需要别人的帮助,那时你怎么不帮助她呢?(指过去,但是只指一个具体的时点。)

(At the moment she was badly in need of help, why didn't you help her then?)(Refers to one specific time in the past.)

明年,当毕业论文答辩完以后,我一定陪你好好去玩玩。(将来。)

* 明年,毕业论文答辩完,当时我一定陪你好好去玩玩。(将来。)

当 dāng　　在 zài

〈介词〉都可以表示事情发生的时间、处所。

(< preposition > both indicate the time when or place where things happen.)

(一) 由"当"和"在"构成的介词词组都可以表示时间,但是多数情况下不能互换使用,这是因为它们表示的时间意义和语法结构功能不完全相同。(Prepositional word groups composed of "当" and "在" can indicate time, but in most cases they are not exchangeable, because they indicate the incomplete similarities in the significance of time and the structural function of grammar.)

1."当"所表示的时间是以某件事的发生为背景的,所以由"当"构成介词词组表示时间的句子里,事实上应该有两件事情发生,第一件事情的出现只表示时间,第一件事情出现的时候是发生第二件事情的时间。(The time indicated by "当" usually takes some occurrence as its background, therefore, in the sentence with the prepositional word group composed of "当", actually there should be two cases occurring. The first case's occurrence only indicates the time and it is also the time that the second case takes place.)例如:

当他走过来用手抚摸着我的脸时,我再也控制不住自己了。

(When he came over to me stroking my face with his hand, I could no longer control my emotions.)

〔他走过来用手抚摸着我的脸——第一件事(时间);我再也控制不住自己了——第二件事。〕

(He came over to me stroking my face with his hand—the first case(time); I could no longer control my emotion—the second.)

当你走过这里时,你会发现这里的草是那样的柔软。

〔你走过这里——第一件事(时间);你会发现……——第二件事。〕

所以,与"当"组成介词词组的词语必须是动词性的词组或小句,而不能只是一个名词性词语。"在"构成的介词词组没有这种意义和结构的限制,所以动词性的、名词性的词语都可以跟它结合。但是当句子的时间以强调某件事的发生为背景或强调时间背景的事情跟发生的事情几乎是同时发生时,用"当……"更为贴切。(So the words or phrases composed with "当" must be verbal phrases or small sentences and can't only be a noun term. The prepositional phrase composed by "在" is not restricted by this significance and structure, so verbal or noun phrases can be used together with it. It is apter to use "当" when the adverbial of time of the sentence emphasizes the happening of something as the background or the thing that takes place as the background occurs almost at the same time as the action in the main clause does.)例如：

当明年春暖花开时,我想去南方一趟。(春暖花开;去南方)

* 当明年春天时,我想去南方一趟。

当我走进房间的时候,他已经睡着了。(走进房间;睡着了)

* 当这时,他已经睡着了。

* 当晚上时,他总是要工作。

他在节假日也总是不休息。

客轮在晚上八点钟才抵达港口。

* 客轮当晚上八点钟才抵达港口。

2. 由"当"构成的表示时间的介词词组在句子中只能作状语,而且通常出现在句首;"当"跟动词性词组结合后,后面还要配合上"时"、"……的时候"等词语才能使用。由"在"构成的表示时间的介词词组在句子中不只作状语,还能作补语。作状语时,既可以出现在主语前,也可以出现在主语后。需要时词组后也可以跟上"时"、"……的时候"等词语,但不是必须的。(The prepositional phrase composed of "当" can only be used as an adverbial in sentence and usually appears at the beginning of the sentence. When "当" is used together with verbal phrases, it has to be followed by "时" or "…的时候". The prepositional phrase composed of "在" is not only used as an adverbial, but also as a complement. As an adverbial, it can be put either before or after the subject. Sometimes "时" or "…的时候" is used after the phrases, but not necessarily.)例如：

当月亮升起时,我们一起唱起了歌,跳起了舞。
当她不喜欢你的时候,你就离她远一点。
* 当月亮升起,我们一起唱起了歌,跳起了舞。
* 当她不喜欢你,你就离她远一点。
我在夜深人静时,工作起来会更投入。(状语)
(When it is in the dead of night, I would throw myself into what I am doing thoroughly.)
这件事发生在一年以前。(补语)
* 这件事发生当一年以前。

3. 由"当"构成的表示时间的介词词组在句子中只能表示时点;由"在"构成的表示时间的介词词组在句子中不光可以表示时点,还可以表示时段。(The prepositional phrase made up of "当" can only indicate point of time, while the prepositional phrase made up of "在" may either indicate the point of time or the period of time.)例如:

每当看到这张照片时,我就想起和他在一起的那些日子。(时点)
当看到女儿高兴得流下眼泪时,妈妈的眼泪也止不住了。(时点)
在/当我过生日的时候,他总是要给我寄来精致的生日礼物。(时点)
在这些日子里,我反反复复地想了很多很多。(时段)
在五年多的时间里,他完成了两部颇有分量的学术著作。(时段)
(During the period of over five years, he accomplished two academic works which are of considerable weight.)
* 当这些日子里,我反反复复地想了很多很多。
* 当五年多的时间里,他完成了两部颇有分量的学术著作。

(二)由"当"和"在"构成的介词词组都可以表示场所,但是意义和用法有所不同。(All the prepositional phrases made up of "当" or "在" can indicate places, but they are different in significance and use.)

1. "当"表示处所时,通常只能跟少数单音节一般名词结合,不能跟方位词组组合;"在"一般不能跟一般名词组合,可以跟方位词组、场所名词组合。(When "当" indicates places, it can only combine with few general monosyllable nouns and can't combine with nouns of locality. "在" generally can not be used together with common nouns, but it can combine with phrases of locality and terms of place.)例如:

  当面点清(to count in somebody's face)
  当场逮住(be caught on the spot)
  当众出丑(make an exhibition of oneself)
  当头一棒(hit on the head)
  当胸一拳(a punch on the chest)
 *在面点清 *在场逮住 *在众出丑
 *在头一棒 *在胸一拳
 在学校   在天安门广场 在屋里
 在前边   在同学当中
 *当学校   *当天安门广场 *当屋里
 *当前边   *当同学当中

2. "当"有时后边常带"着",表示的意思是"对着"、"朝着"的意思,这时它后面只能带表示人的名词,而且常常跟"面"配合用。"在"没有这种意思和用法。("当" is usually followed by "着", indicating "对着" or "朝着". It can only be followed by personal nouns and often combines with "面". "在" can't be used in this way.)例如:

  今天非要你当着大伙的面把这件事情讲清楚不可。
  (Today you must explain the matter clearly in front of all the people here.)

你对我有什么看法就请你当着我的面说出来。
你怎么当着同学们的面就发起火来了。
(How could you flare up in front of the students?)
* 今天非要你在大伙的面把这件事情讲清楚不可。
* 你对我有什么看法就请你在我的面说出来。
* 你怎么在同学们的面就发起火来了。

到达 dàodá　　达到 dádào

〈动词〉< verb >

"到达"、"达到"都有"到"的意思,但是它们在使用上几乎不能换用。(Both "到达" and "达到" mean "to arrive", but they are almost unexchangeable in use.)

(一) 意义不同,搭配对象、适用范围也不同。(Differences in meanings require different collocation of targets and scope of application.)

"到达"是指"到了某一点或某一阶段",强调"进入到"的意思,所以后边多接具体的场所意义、某一阶段意义的词语。"达到"除有"到"的意义外,还有"实现"的意义,主要用于表示到了某种目标或某种程度,所以它后边多接抽象意义的词语或多用于抽象的事物。〔"到达" refers to getting to certain point or certain period, emphasizing on "进入到(getting into)", therefore, there are words and phrases of specific place or a certain period followed. Besides the meaning of arriving, "达到" also has the meaning of realizing, it mainly indicates to reach some goal or a certain degree, so words of abstract meaning are used after it or it is used for abstract objects.〕例如:

到达上海 到达机场 到达旅馆 到达终点 到达目的地
到达了美好的境界(have reached a wonderful state)
到达了高级阶段　　达到国际水平　　达到最高的标准
达到一定程度　　　达到目的

达到了相当的规模(have reached a considerable scale)
气氛达到了高潮(The atmosphere has reached high tide)
烦躁达到了极点(The agitation has reached the extreme point)

＊ 达到上海 ＊ 达到目的地 ＊ 达到终点
＊ 到达国际水平 ＊ 到达一定程度 ＊ 到达目的
＊ 气氛到达了高潮　＊ 烦躁到达了极点

(二) 结构上的差异:(Differences in structure:)

1."达到"后边可以接数量补语;"到达"一般不能接。("达到" can be followed by complement of quantity, and "到达"can't.)例如:

达到过一次目标
这种水平我也达到过一回
＊ 到达过好几次这里 ＊ 到达过三次西安

2. 构词方式不同:"到达"是联合式合成词,中间不能插入别的词;"达到"是补充式合成词,中间可以插入别的词。(The way of construction is different, "到达"is a combined compound word and no other words can be put in the middle. "达到"is a complementary compound word, and can have other word put in between.)例如:

＊ 到不达长城顶端,决不罢休。
＊ 到不达标准不行。
达不到目的,决不罢休。
(We'll never give up until the goal is reached.)
达不到标准不行。
(It is no good if the criterion is not reached.)

到 dào　　到达 dàodá　　达 dá

〈动词〉< verb >

"到"、"到达"、"达"都有"到"的意思,但是大多不能换用。(All mean "get to", but generally not exchangeable with one another.)

133

(一)"到"和"到达"

1."到"和"到达"都有"进入到某场所或某阶段"的意思,但是色彩有所不同。"到"口语色彩较浓,多用于口语;"到达"书面语色彩较浓,多用于书面语。(Both indicate to get to a certain place or a certain stage. But there is some difference in flavour. "到" has strong spoken language flavour, mainly used in oral language. "到达" has strong written language flavour, and mainly used in written language.)试比较:

已经到边境了　到学校了　已经到达边境　到达学校

2."到"和"到达"跟单音节词和多音节词组合的情况也有所不同。"到"可以跟单音节词组合,也可以跟多音节词组合;"到达"只能跟多音节词组合。(There are differences between "到" and "到达" when combined with monosyllables and polysyllables. "到" can be used either with a monosyllabic word or with a polysyllabic word. "到达" can only be used with a polysyllabic word.)例如:

到家了　　到站了　　到点了　　到期了　　迟到
到车站了　到宾馆了　到目的地了　到现阶段
*到达家　*到达站　*到达点　*到达期　*迟到达
到达车站　到达宾馆　到达目的地　到达现阶段

3."到"和"到达"意义有同有异。(Similarities and differences of "到" and "到达" in meaning.)

(1)"到"和"到达"只有在表示"进入到某处所或某阶段"的意思时才是相同的,表示这种意思时,两词大多可以换用。〔"到"and "到达" are similar only when the meaning of "进入某处所(get into a certain place)" or "进入某阶段(get to a certain stage)" is indicated. In this sense, they are exchangeable.〕例如:

到终点　　　到工地　　　到司令部
到汽车站　　到现阶段　　到达终点
到达工地　　到达司令部　到达汽车站
到达现阶段

134

但是,"到达"往往更加强调经过一段历程,所以多用于长途旅行等,这样它后面连带的场所应该是相对大的场所,从起点到终点没有什么距离的小的具体的场所不应该用"到达";"到"不强调这种意思,所以跟它相联系的场所可大可小。("到达"usually means to arrive after a period of course, but usually the stress being laid on undergoing a course, so it mostly refers to a long-distance journey, etc. The places followed should be the relatively large, and the small particular places that have not much distance from the starting point to the terminal point shouldn't be indicated by"到达"。"到"will not lay emphasis on this, so the places concerned can either be big or small.)例如:

  他们明天乘专机到达上海。
  我们已经到达目的地了。
  他们明天乘专机到上海。
  我们已经到目的地了。
  他到资料室了。
  妈妈到里屋了。
  * 他到达资料室了。
  * 妈妈到达里屋了。

(2)"到"还可以表示"去"的意思;"到达"没有这种意思。〔"到"also means "去(to go)", while "到达"doesn't.〕例如:

  今天晚上到我家住吧。
  我到过广州,但是没到过桂林。
  * 今天晚上到达我家住吧。
  * 我到达过广州,但是没到达过桂林。

(3)"到"还可以表示"来到"的意思;"到达"没有这种意思。("到"means "come to...", and "到达"doesn't.)例如:

  你的汇款已经到了。
  你去看看到了多少人了?
  * 你的汇款已经到达了。

* 你去看看到达了多少人了。

(4)"到"还可以表示时间或年龄达于某一点;"到达"一般不用来表示时间或年龄。("到" may indicate time or age that reaches a certain point, while "到达" is not used for time or ages.)例如:

不知不觉又到了开学的日子了。
(Unconsciously it is the date of school opening.)
到五点,我们就走。
他牺牲的时候,还不到二十岁。
你快到十八岁了,该懂事了。
* 不知不觉又到达了开学的日子了。
* 到达五点,我们就走。
* 他牺牲的时候,还没到达二十岁。
* 你快到达十八岁了,该懂事了。

4."到"和"到达"在结构上也有出入。("到" and "到达" are different in structure.)

(1)"到"后面可以直接接"了",表示已经达于某地;"到达"后面一般不能只接"了",通常要加场所词。("到" can be followed directly by "了", indicating having got to some place. "到达" can't be simply followed by "了", generally words of place have to be added as well.)例如:

我们已经到了,请首长们放心!
我们已经到达阵地,请首长们放心!
* 我们已经到达了,请首长们放心!

(2)"到"后面可以接表示来到某地时间早晚程度的补语;"到达"后面一般不能接这种补语。("到" can be followed by the complement indicating how early or late one arrives at a place, "到达" can't.)例如:

今天王师傅到得很晚,不知道为什么。
大家到得都很早,所以我们提前出发了。
* 今天王师傅到达得很晚,不知道为什么。

＊大家到达得都很早,所以我们提前出发了。

(二)"达"和"到"、"到达"

"达"和"到"、"到达"一样,也有"进入到某处所或某阶段"的意思,但是"达"是文言词,文言色彩很重,使用起来跟"到"、"到达"差别较大。"达"表示"进入到某处所"的意思时,常常须接受"直"、"即"等单音词的修饰;"到"口语色彩较重,一般情况下不这样用;"到达"则一般不能跟这样的单音节词组合。(Same as "到" and "到达", "达" also means getting into some place or getting to some stage. "达" is a word of classical Chinese, so it is of strong flavour of classical Chinese and it is used fairly differently compared with "到" and "到达". When "达" indicates getting into some place, it usually has to be modified by monosyllabic words like "直","即";"到" has a strong flavour of spoken language and it can not be used this way. "到达" usually can't combine with such monosyllable words.)例如:

孙先生乘飞机直达美国。

明晨我们即达广州。

＊孙先生乘飞机直到/到达美国。

此外,"达"还有"实现"、"达到"的意思;"到"、"到达"没有这种意思。(Besides, "达" also means "实现", "达到", while "到" and "到达" don't.)例如:

我们目的已达,部队可暂时休整一下。

来这儿观看礼花的达几万人。

他连续工作长达二十八小时。

这所房子,价钱高达三百万。

＊我们目的已到/到达,部队可暂时休整一下。

＊来这儿观看礼花的到/到达几万人。

＊他连续工作长到/到达二十八小时。

＊这所房子,价钱高到 / 到达三百万。

倒 dào   却 què

〈副词〉表示转折语气。

(<adverb> indicating the mood of transition.)

(一)"倒"、"却"都可以表示转折语气,在表示转折语气时,意义、用法大体相同,只是"倒"的口语色彩更重一些。(Both can indicate a turning in the tone and similar in meaning and use. But, "倒" has a stronger flavour of spoken language.)例如:

> 别看这间屋子不大,布置得却/倒挺漂亮。
> 他虽然汉语说得不太流利,却/倒挺感人。
> 这儿虽然有些嘈杂,交通却/倒挺方便。

但是,当句子表示很重的转折关系时,后一分句用"但是"、"可是"、"然而"表示转折关系时,句子一般多用"却"来加重转折的语气。(But, when the sentence shows a fairly strong sense-turning relation, and the second clause indicates the transitional relations with "但是","可是" or "然而","却" is used to emphasize the mood.)例如:

> 文章虽然不长,但是却很有分量。

(The article is not long, but it is of considerable weight.)

> 他年龄虽然不大,然而却有一肚子鬼心眼儿。

(He is quite young, but is full of wicked ideas.)

用"倒"表示转折语气的句子,"倒"后一般要用表示积极意义的词语;用"却"表示转折语气的句子,"却"后面的词语不限制。(The sentence using "倒" to indicate transitional mood generally has words of positive meaning after "倒". And in the sentence with "却" indicating transitional mood, the words after "却" will not be restricted.)例如:

> 他的手粗糙得很,却/倒巧得出奇。

(He has got a pair of rough hands, but they are strangely

deft.)

  小说篇幅不长,却/倒很有趣儿。
  太阳虽然明晃晃的,气温却很低。
  人长得还可以,干起活来却那么笨。
  * 太阳虽然明晃晃的,气温倒很低。
  * 人长得还可以,干起活来倒那么笨。

(二)"倒"还可以表示让步语气和其他一些语气——祈使、追究、舒缓等语气。"却"没有这些用法。("倒" can also indicate compromise, imperative, enquiry or alleviation, etc. "却" can't.)例如:

  扔几个烟头倒是小事,万一酿成火灾,可就不得了了。
  (Throwing several cigarette ends is indeed nothing serious, but it might be disastrous if that leads to fire.)
  这儿方便倒方便,就是贵了点儿。
  你倒是快点儿呀! 车快要开了!
  你说得倒容易! 既然这么容易,你倒去办呀!
  (What you said is easy. Since it is so easy why don't you do that?)
  你倒是答不答应呀? 人家还急着等你的回话呢。
  他倒的确不是故意的,咱们就原谅他这一次吧。
  (He didn't do it intentionally. Let's forgive him this time.)
  * 这儿方便却方便,就是贵了点儿。
  * 你却快点儿呀! 车快要开了!
  * 你说得却容易,既然这么容易,你却去办呀!

倒(倒是) dào(dàoshi)　　可是 kěshì

  倒(倒是)〈副词〉< adverb >
  可是〈连词〉< conjunction >

(一)"倒"、"倒是"意义、用法大体相同。"倒(倒是)"和"可是"都可以表示转折,但是"倒(倒是)"主要表示转折语气;"可

139

是"主要表示转折关系。所以,既有转折语气,又表示转折关系的句子,"倒"和"可是"可以通用,只是侧重点不同。"倒"侧重于语气,"可是"侧重于上下句的关系。但是,用"倒"表示转折语气的句子,"倒"后一般要用表示积极意义的词语;用"可是"表示转折关系的句子,后面的词语不限制。〔"倒" and "倒是" are basically the same in both meaning and use. "倒(倒是)" and "可是" can indicate transition, but "倒(倒是)" mainly indicates transition in the tone, while "可是" indicates transition in the relation between the two clauses. So in sentences indicating transition both in tone and in relation, "倒" and "可是" are inchangeable in use, but with different emphasis. "倒" stresses the tone, while "可是" stresses the relation between the clauses. When "倒" indicates transition in the terms with positive meaning should be used after "倒". When "可是" indicates transition in relation, the words after it are not restricted.〕例如:

这个公园不大,人倒不少。

这个公园不大,可是人却不少。

现在虽然已经四月份了,可是气温还很低。

* 现在虽然已经四月份了,气温倒还很低。

有些句子前面常用"虽然"、"尽管"等表示让步关系的连词,后面再用"可是"、"倒"等词语配合,表示一种让步转折关系或语气。(At the beginning of some sentences, concessive conjunctions "虽然","尽管", etc. are used, and "可是","倒", etc. are used after, indicating a kind of concessive transitional relation or mood.)例如:

虽然人不大,可是/倒满机灵的。

(He is quite young , but is very smart.)

文章语句虽然欠佳,可是观点却很鲜明。

(The sentences in the essay are not good enough, but the viewpoints are quite clear.)

文章语句虽然欠佳,观点倒是很鲜明。

但是,当上下句的关系只有转折的连接关系时,通常只能用"可是",不能用"倒"。(But when there is only a transitional relationship between the clauses, usually "可是" can be used, but not "倒".)例如:

为了休息方便,大家在总理办公桌旁安放了一张沙发。可是带病坚持工作的总理从未在这张沙发上休息过片刻。

部队已经进入草地,可是当走到草地中心地带时,突然停止北上,又掉头南下了。

(The troops had already got to the grasslands, but while walking onto the central part, they suddenly stopped marching up to the north and headed southwards.)

老年人头发白是自然现象,可是为什么一些年轻人头发也白了呢?

* 为了休息方便,大家在总理办公桌旁安放了一张沙发。倒是带病坚持工作的总理从未在这张沙发上休息过片刻。

* 部队已经进入草地,倒是当走到草地中心地带时,突然停止北上,又掉头南下了。

(二)"倒(倒是)"是副词,只能用在主语之后;"可是"是连词,通常用在主语之前。〔"倒(倒是)" is an adverb and can only be used after the subject. "可是" is a conjunction and is usually used before the subject.〕例如:

电影的内容很一般,语言倒挺生动。

电影的内容很一般,可是语言却挺生动。

* 电影的内容很一般,倒语言挺生动。

她身体不太好,意志倒挺坚强。

她身体不太好,可是意志倒挺坚强。

* 她身体不太好,倒意志挺坚强。

的 de　　地 de　　得 de

〈结构助词〉< structural particle >

(一)"的"、"地"、"得"都是结构助词,都读作"de",区别在于使用上。(All are structural particles and all are pronounced as "de". Their differences are in use.)

"的"通常被看做定语的标志,即"的"用在定语后边,表示它前边的词或词语是定语,定语修饰、限制的中心语通常是名词性的。("的" is usually regarded as the symbol for attributives, namely, "的" is used after attributives, indicating words or phrases before it are attributives. The central word which is modified and restricted by the attributive is generally nominal.)例如:

　　明天的会　李老师的课　美丽的风景 晴朗的天空 吃的菜
　　买回来的书 一脸的汗 谁的钥匙 我的朋友

"地"通常被看做状语的标志,即"地"用在状语后边,表示它前边的词或词语是状语,状语修饰、限制的中心语通常是谓词性的。("地" is generally taken as the symbol for adverbials, namely "地" is used after adverbials, indicating the words or phrases before it are adverbials. The central word modified and restricted by adverbials is generally predicative.)例如:

　　慢慢地亮了　　　　认真地想　　　　亲切地抚摸着
　　哗哗地下着

"得"通常被看做补语的标志,即"得"用在补语前边,表示它后边的词或词语是补语,补语前边的成分通常是谓词性的,"得"连接的补语通常是表示程度或情态的。"得"也可以单独用在动词后边或动词和补语中间,表示可能(否定式把"得"换成"不")。〔"得" is generally regarded as the symbol for complements, namely, "得" is used before complement, indicating words or phrases after it are complements. The element in front of the complement is generally predicative. The complement which is linked by "得" generally indicates the degree or tone. "得" can

142

also be used alone after a verb or between a verb and a complement, indicating possibility (in its negative pattern "得" is replaced by "不").]例如:

好得很　厉害得不得了　打得不错　打扫得干干净净
做得不太好　忙得他连饭都顾不上吃了

气得她浑身直发抖(She was so angry that she was shaking all over.)

这些东西吃得吃不得?　　听得懂　看不清楚(否定式)

(二)以上是三个"de"的基本分工,但是有时还是会出现三个"de"混淆不清的现象,下面简单介绍两点。(The above is the basic division of their functions, but sometimes the confusing phenomena of the three "de" are likely to occur. Here is a brief explanation:)

1."形容词+的/地+动词"("adj. + 的/地 + verb")

这种结构可能有时用"的",有时用"地"。用哪个"de"主要要看这个结构在句子中的作用。如果作主语或者宾语,就要用"的";如果作谓语,就要用"地"。(In this pattern sometimes either "的" or "地" is used. The function of the structure in the sentence has to be considered. If it functions as the subject or the object, "的" is used; if it functions as the predicate, "地" is used.)例如:

他科学地论证了这一原理。("论证"作谓语。)

*他科学的论证了这一原理。

他对这一原理进行了科学的论证。("论证"作宾语。)

*他对这一原理进行了科学地论证。

2."动词+的/得+谓词性词或词语"("verb + 的/得 + predicative words or phrases)

这种结构可能有时用"的",有时用"得"。用哪个"de"也要根据在句子中的作用来决定。如果"动+de"作主语,就要用"的";如果整个结构作谓语,就要用"得",不能用"地"。(In this pattern either "的" or "得" is used, it depends on its function in sentence. "的" will be used if "v + 的" is the subject. If the whole structure is used as predicate, "得" had to be used, but not "地".)例如：

> 她唱<u>的</u>很动听。("唱的"作主语。)
> 她唱<u>得很动听</u>。("唱得很动听"作谓语部分。)
> 老师说<u>的</u>很有道理。("说的"作主语。)
> 老师说<u>得很有道理</u>。("说得很有道理"作谓语部分。)
> * 她唱地很动听。
> * 老师说地很有道理。

（三）作为结构助词，"的"还有一种用法。"的"可以用在名词、代词、动词、形容词或词组后面，构成没有中心语的"的字词组"，表示人或者事物，作用相当于名词。"的字词组"有时需要借助于上下文才能明确它的含义。〔As structural particle, "的" is also used after nouns, pronouns, verbs, adjectives or phrases, forming phrase with "的", in which there is no central term to form "word group of '的'" to indicate people or things and functions equal to noun. In "word group of 的", sometimes the implication can't be defined until you draw support from the context.〕例如：

> 至于筷子，虽说不锈钢的很值钱，但我还是喜欢竹子的。
> 装东西最多的那个书包是我的。
> 学校里骑自行车的特别多。
> 你检查一下这些零件，好的放这儿，坏的扔筐里。

等 děng   等待 děngdài   等候 děnghòu

〈动词〉表示不采取行动，直到所期望的人、事物或情况出现。(< verb > indicating not taking action until the expected people, things or situations appear or occur.)

（一）色彩不同。(Difference in flavour.)

"等"口语色彩较重，多用于口语，使用频率较高。"等待"、"等候"含有不同程度的书面语色彩和庄重色彩，使用上受到一定限制。("等" has a strong flavour of spoken language and is used in high frequency in oral language. "等待" and "等候" have strong flavour of written language and seriousness at various degrees and are restricted in certain aspect in use.)

有时音节数量也有一定影响。只有一个音节的宾语,常用"等";两个或两个以上音节的宾语可以酌情选择。(Sometimes the number of syllables makes certain influence. When there is an object with only one syllable, "等" is generally used, and objects with two or more than two syllables are used flexibly.)例如:

   等车 等人 等米下锅
  * 他正在等待／等候车。
  * 我站在门前等待/等候人。
  他正在等待/等候汽车。
  我站在门前等待/等候客人。

(二)"等"可以重叠使用;"等待"很少用重叠形式,"等候"一般不能重叠使用。("等" can be reduplicated. "等待" is rarely reduplicated, and "等候" can't.)例如:

  我们等等他们,他们一会儿就来。
  * 我们等待等待/等候等候他们,他们一会儿就来。

(三)"等"在时间上没有长短的问题;"等候"在时间上相对长些。所以"等"可以用重叠式表示短时,也可以接表示短时或长时的补语;而"等候"后边一般只接表示长时的补语。("等" is not limited by the length of the time, "等候" needs comparatively longer time. So "等" can indicate short period of time by reduplication, and can be followed by the complements indicating short period or long period of time. "等候" only link with the complement indicating longer period of time.)例如:

   等一下,马上就好   稍微等一会儿
   等你好长时间了 等了半天 等了好几年

＊等候一下,马上就好　　　　＊稍微等候一会儿
　　等候你好长时间了　等候了半天　等候了好几年
(四)"等"后边可以接结果、情态、可能等补语;"等待"、"等候"后边一般不能接这几种补语。("等" can be followed by the complements of result, modal condition or possibility, etc. "等待"and "等候"can't be followed by these complements.)例如:

我终于等着他了。
小李都等急了,你快点儿吧!
这班车还等得上吗?
快点儿! 司机都等得不耐烦了!
(Be quick! The driver is waiting impatiently!)
＊ 我终于等待/等候着他了。
＊ 小李都等待/等候急了,你快点儿吧!
＊ 快点儿! 司机都等待/等候得不耐烦了!
＊ 这班车还等待/等候得上吗?

(五)"等待"除用于具体、确定的人、事物外,还常用于抽象的、不确定的人与事物。"等候"则多用于具体、确定的人与事物。(Besides being used with particular and definite people and things, "等待"is also used for abstract and indefinite people and things. "等候"is generally used for specific or definite people or things.)例如:

她在等待中度过了艰难的四个月。
(The four difficult months passed while she was waiting.)
他们正在等待胜利的最后时刻。
他犯了错误,正在等待处分。
＊ 他们正在等候胜利的最后时刻。
她站在门口等候客人的到来。
大家排好了队,等候出发的命令。
我一直在电话机旁等候你的电话。

等 děng   等等 děngděng   什么的 shénmede

等、等等〈助词〉< particle >

什么的〈"的"字词组〉< word group of "的" >

(一)"等"、"等等"、"什么的"都可以表示列举未尽的意思,但是用法上有差别。("等","等等"and "什么的"all indicate the act of enumerating is unfinished, but their usages are different.)

1."等"、"等等"通用于口语和书面语;"什么的"只用于口语。("等"and "等等" usually are used in spoken and written language;"什么的" is only used in spoken language.)

2."等"后面可以直接出现包容前边各列举项的概括性词语;"等等"一般不接包容前边各列举项的概括性词语;"什么的"一般用于句尾,后边不接其他词语。(The summarizing terms which include every enumeration in front can directly be used after "等"; but not after "等等". Usually "什么的"is used at the end of the sentence and with no other terms following.)例如:

这个地区今年虽然遭受了洪水、台风、冰雹等<u>自然灾害</u>,但是仍然确保了粮食的丰收。

水、电、暖气、煤气等<u>设备</u>的检修工作均已完毕。

* 这个地区今年虽然遭受了洪水、台风、冰雹等等自然灾害,但是仍然确保了粮食的丰收。

* 水、电、暖气、煤气等等设备的检修工作均已完毕。

毒蛇的种类很多,著名的有五步蛇、眼镜蛇、蝮蛇等等。

青年人积极、热情、有朝气、肯于学习、接受新事物快等等,这些都是难能可贵的优点。

(Young people are active, enthusiastic, full of vigor, eager to learn and quick at accepting new things, etc. These are their commendable advantages.)

她买了许多糖、水果、点心什么的,准备招待她的小伙伴。

桌子上摆满了书、本、词典什么的,可是他连一个字也

147

看不进去。

3. "等"可以用在专有名词后;"等等"一般不用于专有名词后;"什么的"口语色彩很重,多用于普通的事物或动作、行为等,一般不用于专有名词后,尤其不用于地名、人名后。("等" can be used after proper nouns; and usually "等等" is not used after these terms; "什么的" is of strong spoken flavour, used more after common things or actions, behaviour, etc., especially it is not used after names of places and people.)例如:

学习结束后,我们将去<u>西安</u>、<u>上海</u>等地旅游。
唐代著名的诗人有<u>李白</u>、<u>杜甫</u>、<u>白居易</u>等。
<u>市长</u>、工业局局长等市里领导人也参加了剪彩仪式。
思想、意识等等是主观的东西,做或行动是主观见于客观的东西。
花呀、草呀、鸟呀、鱼呀、猫呀、狗的,等等,等等,都是她所喜欢的。
我刚买了些啤酒、火腿、面包什么的,咱们一起吃吧。
她不喜欢唱歌、跳舞什么的,却很喜欢摄影。

* 学习结束后,我们将去西安、上海等等。
* 北京、西安什么的,名胜古迹很多。
* 唐代著名的诗人有李白、杜甫、白居易什么的。
* 市长、工业局局长什么的也参加了剪彩仪式。

4. "等"、"什么的"可以用于一项列举后;"等等"只能用于两个或两个以上的列举项后。("等" and "什么的" can be used after one enumerated item; "等等" can only be used after two or more items enumerated.)例如:

<u>雅典</u>等城市输出的精美的手工艺品,都是奴隶血汗的结晶。

(The elegant handicrafts which are exported from Athens and other cities are the crystallization of the sweat and toil of the slaves.)

妻子在家做饭什么的,丈夫在外打工什么的,日子过得倒也满好。

* 思想等等是主观的东西,做或行动是主观见于客观的东西。

* 他假期在家看书等等,过得很充实。

5. "等等"还可以重复使用,之间常用逗号隔开。有时除表示列举未尽的意义外,还含有"很多"的意思;有时还直接用在"如此"后面。("等等" can also be used repeatedly and usually there is a comma between them. Besides indicating the act of unfinished enumeration it sometimes implies the meaning of "many"; sometimes it is used directly after "如此".)例如:

除了这些正在受罪的人以外,长廊两侧还摆着压杠、老虎凳、皮鞭、竹钎、手铐、脚镣,等等,等等。

这个说"离铁矿太远了",那个说"附近没有水源",还有的说"交通也很不方便",如此等等。这都说明了这个建厂方案存在着许多问题。

(二)"等"还有全数列举后煞尾的作用,后面常常带有前边列出的各项的总计数字。"等等"、"什么的"没有这一用法。("等" has the function of winding up after all the things enumerated, and are often followed by a total figure which summarizes all the items in front.)例如:

中国古代有造纸、印刷术、指南针、火药等四大发明。

这学期开设了语法、精读、翻译、报刊、中国文学史、中国文化讲座等六门课程。

中国有北京、上海、天津、重庆等四个中央直辖市。

* 这学期开设了语法、精读、翻译、报刊、中国文学史、中国文化讲座等等六门课程。

* 中国有北京、上海、天津、重庆等等四个中央直辖市。

* 中国古代有造纸、印刷术、指南针、火药什么的四大发明。

低 dī　　矮 ǎi　　浅 qiǎn

〈形容词〉< adjective >

(一) "低"和"矮"

"低"和"矮"都可以表示不高的意思,都可以跟"高"相对。但是它们适用的范围或表示不高的角度不同。〔Both can be used to indicate not high, and opposite to "高"(high). There is difference in the scope they apply and in the angle of height they indicate.〕

1. 表示离地面近的,用"低",这时"低"跟"高"相对。(When expressing the close distance to the earth, "低" is used and here "低" is opposite to "高".)例如:

飞机绕广场低空飞行一圈。

＊ 飞机绕广场矮空飞行一圈。

要变天了,你看,燕子飞得很低。

(Look, the weather is coming bad, the swallows are flying very low.)

＊ 要变天了,你看,燕子飞得很矮。

这里地势太低,经常闹水灾。

(The terrain is too low here and often suffers from drought.)

＊ 这里地势太矮,经常闹水灾。

院墙很低,可以跨过去。

2. 表示高度小的,用"矮","矮"跟"高"相对。通常用于人的身材短、树、建筑物等高度小。(When showing one is short in height, "矮" is used, "矮" is the opposite to "高". "矮" usually is used to indicate shortness of man's stature, trees and buildings, etc.)例如:

排队的时候请注意,个子高的在后边,个子矮的在前边。

我觉得他的个子并不比你矮。

不知怎么回事,这两棵树是一起种的,可是这棵树比那棵树矮多了。

院墙很矮,可以跨过去。(这一句可以用"低",也可以用"矮",但是角度不同。用"低"是说从上向下距离小,离地面近;用"矮"是说从下向上高度小。)

* 排队的时候请注意,个子高的在后边,个子低的在前边。

* 我觉得他的个子并不比你低。

* 不知怎么回事,这两棵树是一起种的,可是这棵树比那棵树低多了。

3. 表示在一般标准或平均程度之下的,用"低",不用"矮"。(When indicating things below general standard or average degree, use "低" instead of "矮".)例如:

听说,他的外语水平不低,让他跟我们一起翻译这些资料吧。

声音太低了,听不见。

价钱压得那么低,我们会赔的。

(We will sustain losses in business since they demand such a low price.)

* 听说,他的外语水平不矮,让他跟我们一起翻译这些资料吧。

* 声音太矮了,听不见。

* 价钱压得那么矮,我们会赔的。

4. "低"和"矮"都可以表示地位、级别不高,有时可以通用,有时不能通用。表示地位、级别小于某一基准的,用"低"和"矮"都可以;表示地位、级别属于不高的程度的,只能用"低",不能用"矮"。(To indicate lowness in position and rank, sometimes "低" and "矮" are interchangeable and sometimes not. When indicating position or rank is lower than some standard, both "低"and "矮"can be used. And when indicating position or rank is high, "低" is used, but "矮" can not be used.)例如:

我们俩不是一个班的,他比我低/矮一班。

他俩都是厨师,但是级别不同。王师傅比李师傅低/矮两级呢。

我是低年级的学生,他是高年级的学生。

告诉小孙,不要联系低档次的饭店。

(Just tell Xiao Sun that he shouldn't contact with low-grade restaurants.)

这是通俗读物,更适合低层次的读者。

* 我是矮年级的学生,他是高年级的学生。
* 告诉小孙,不要联系矮档次的饭店。
* 这是通俗读物,更适合矮层次的读者。

(二)"低"和"浅"

1. "低"和"浅"都可以表示跟水有关的上下距离小,但是所指内容不同。用"低"只能指水位,它是指水的位置的高度距离小,在一般标准之下,这时"低"跟"高"相对;用"浅"是指水的厚度距离小,这时"浅"跟"深"相对。(Both "低" and "浅" indicate a short distance which relates to water, but there is difference in the content that they refer to. "低" can only be used to indicate water level, the level of the water is below the normal standard. At this time, "低" is opposite to "高". "浅" indicates small depth of water, at this time, "浅" is opposite to "深".)例如:

水库的水位太低了,各村务必做好抗旱准备。(跟"水位低"相对的是"水位高"。)

(The water level of the reservoir is too low. Every village must get well prepared for fighting drought.)

* 水库的水位太浅了,各村务必做好抗旱准备。

河水很浅,可以趟过去。(跟"河水很浅"相对的是"河水很深"。)

(The water in the river is quite shallow and we can wade across it.)

这么浅的水,怎么能游泳?(跟"这么浅的水"相对的是"这么深的水"。)

* 河水很低,可以趟过去。

* 这么低的水,怎么能游泳?

2."低"和"浅"都可以用于跟程度不深有关的情况,但是情况不同。"低"只能用于水平、标准等,是指在一般标准或程度之下的意思,这时"低"跟"高"相对。"浅"则用于程度不深的具体情况怎么样,如:内容浅显;资历、功夫浅薄等等。(Both can be used in the condition relating to degree which is not deep, but in different cases. "低" is used to indicate being lower than general standard or degree. "浅" is used for how the non-profound specific condition is, as for plain content, being of meager qualifications and record of service, inadequate skill.)例如:

今天是低水平应战,打得很不好。(相对的——高水平。)

(Today we didn't do ourselves justice in the game, and we played poorly.)〔contrary—high level〕

对自己的要求不能太松,不能低标准要求自己。(相对的——高标准。)

* 今天是浅水平应战,打得很不好。

* 对自己的要求不能太松,不能浅标准要求自己。

教材的内容太浅了,不适合你们的水平。

你的功夫还太浅,还不能给别人看病。

(Your level of diagnosing skill is still low, so you are unable to treat patients.)

* 教材的内容太低了,不适合你们的水平。

* 你的功夫还太低,还不能给别人看病。

3."浅"还可以用于颜色淡。"低"没有这种用法。("浅" is used to indicate the lightness of color. "低" does not have this meaning.)例如:

浅蓝　浅黄　浅绿　浅紫色　浅灰色　颜色浅
* 低蓝　* 低黄　* 低绿　* 低紫色　* 低灰色
* 颜色低

的确 díquè　　确实 quèshí

的确〈副词〉< adverb >
确实〈副词〉〈形容词〉< adverb > < adjective >

(一)"的确"、"确实"都可以用作副词,都可以表示所说的客观情况完全符合实际,其真实性肯定无疑的意思。在句子里都可以作状语,可以换用。(Both can be used as adverbs and both mean the objective conditions being mentioned conform to the reality and they are of undoubted affirmation. In sentences both can be used as adverbials and can be interchanged.)例如:

这件事的确/确实不是他干的。
这部电影的确/确实对我触动很大,使我想了很多很多。
这个问题我的确/确实还没弄明白,你再给我讲讲吧。
电脑的发展速度的确/确实很快。

(二)"确实"还有形容词用法,表示真实可靠的意思,在句子里可以作定语、谓语、补语等;"的确"没有这种用法。("确实" functions as an adjective to indicate something true and trustworthy. It can be used as an attribute, predicate, complement, etc.;"的确" hasn't this usage.)例如:

我已经得到了确实的消息。
你必须想办法搞到确实的证据来证明这一点。
(You must try every means to get hold of the conclusive evidence to prove this.)
* 我已经得到了的确的消息。
* 你必须想办法搞到的确的证据来证明这一点。
情况是否确实,还需要作进一步的调查。
(Whether the information is reliable we need to make further

investigation.)
>你说的情况确实吗?——确实。
>＊情况是否的确,还需要作进一步的调查。
>＊你说的情况的确吗?——的确。
>他就是这样说的,我听得确确实实的。
>(He just said like this. I really heard it.)
>＊他就是这样说的,我听得的的确确的。

(三)"的确"和"确实"都可以重叠为"AABB"式,用以表示强调或加强语气。(Both of them can be reduplicated as AABB, used for emphasis or enhancing mood.)例如:
>我的的确确那样想过。
>这的的确确是汉代的文物。
>我当时也在场,他确确实实说过这句话。
>这是确确实实的事情,没有一点儿虚假。

地 dì　　地方 dìfāng
地点 dìdiǎn　　地区 dìqū

〈名词〉< noun >

(一)"地"和"地方"

1. "地"和"地方"都可以指一定的区域,但是色彩和用法有很大差别。"地"是文言词,多用于书面语;"地方"则通用于口语和书面语。"地"是单音节词,与其他词配合时,通常也限于单音词;"地方"是双音节词,多用于与多音节词的组合。("地" and "地方" indicate certain region, but there are big differences in flavour and in usage. "地" is a word of classical Chinese, mostly used in written language; "地方" is commonly used in both spoken language and written language; "地" is a monosyllable and usually collocates only with other monosyllabic words; "地方" is a disyllable which usually collocates with polysyllabic words.)例如:
>他生于西北某地。

此地不能久留(We can't stay long in this place.)
无地自容(can't find place to hide for shame)
上海、西安等地
前边有一块空地,我们就在那儿搭帐篷吧。
* 前边有一块空地方,我们就在那儿搭帐篷吧。
那个地方人很少。　　我去过许多地方。
这么大的地方还不够住呀。
* 那个地人很少。　　* 我去过许多地。
* 这么大的地还不够住呀。

2."地方"除了有一定区域的意思外,还可以指空间范围的某一部分或某一部位。"地"没有这种用法。(Besides indicating a certain region, "地方" also refers to a certain part or a certain position of the space scope. "地" does not.)例如:
包里还有地方,再买一点儿吧。
这个地方画得不太好,再改一改。
这部小说有几个地方写得挺精彩的。
(Several parts in this novel were described in excellent writing.)
* 包里还有地,再买一点儿吧。
* 这个地画得不太好,再改一改。
* 这部小说有几个地写得挺精彩的。

3."地"除了有"地方"的意思外,还有"地点"和"地区"的意思。(Besides indicating "area", "地" means "place" and "district" as well.)例如:
地点:目的地　　所在地
地区:省地县各级领导　　地县两级会议

(二)"地方"和"地点"

"地方"所指的一定的区域,可大可小,可确定可泛指。"地点"却不同,它指的是人或事物活动或存在的具体的、确定的地方,不会是特别小或者十分广大的地方。(The specified region

"地方" refers to may be big or small, specific or general. "地点" refers to the specific, definite places where people or things can hold activities or exist, so they can not be very small or quite broad places.) 例如：

这么大的地方，举办百人的舞会没问题。

(In such a big place, it is no problem to hold a party for a hundred people.)

江南许多地方都遭了水灾。

(Many places in the southern part of the Yangtze are hit by the floods.)

我们就在这个地方坐一坐，歇一会儿，好吗？

* 这么大的地点，举办百人的舞会没问题。
* 江南许多地点都遭了水灾。
* 我们就在这个地点坐一坐，歇一会儿，好吗？

把你们学校的地点写在这儿。

大华宾馆的地点在哪儿？

人们纷纷奔向出事地点。

(People rushed to the spot of the accident in succession.)

* 把你们学校的地方写在这儿。
* 大华宾馆的地方在哪儿？
* 人们纷纷奔向出事地方。

"地方"除有一定区域的意思外，还有一定的空间范围或部分的意思；"地点"没有这种用法。(Besides indicating the meaning of certain region, "地方" also means certain space or parts, but "地点" doesn't.) 例如：

屋子里没有地方了，我们去外面坐吧。

厂房设计图纸我们已经看了，有几个地方还需要斟酌一下。

(We have already studied the design of the factory building and several parts of it still need careful consideration.)

* 屋子里没有地点了,我们去外面坐吧。
* 厂房设计图纸我们已经看了,有几个地点还需要斟酌一下。

(三)"地方"和"地区"

"地方"可以指一定的区域,"地区"也可以指一定的区域,但是所指不同。"地区"所指的区域应该是范围较大的、面积较大的区域,此外,更重要的是,"地区"属于具有一定界线的地方,它能够跟相邻的其他地区划分开来。"地方"没有这种确定的界线,"地方"所指的区域可大可小,可确指可泛指。因此"地区"在使用时,常常可以接在双音节地名之后;"地方"没有这种用法。("地方" refers to certain region, "地区" does the same, but there is difference. "地区" means the region with large scope and area, and in addition, it belongs to the places with certain boundary and it can be divided from with the other places nearby. "地方" has no such limits, the region which it refers to may be big or small, specific or general. So "地区" is often used after a place with a disyllable name. "地方" has no such use.)例如:

流行病在这个地区迅速蔓延开来。

(The epidemic is spreading rapidly in the area.)

这个地区的绿化工作做得很好。

东北地区下了一场四十年来罕见的大雪。

(There is a rare heavy snow in forty years in the northeast part of China.)

沿海地区近些年来经济发展得很快。

* 东北地方下了四十年来罕见的大雪。
* 沿海地方近些年来经济发展得很快。

这个地方扫得不干净,再扫一扫。

很多人都说大连是个很美的地方,有时间一定去看看。

* 这个地区扫得不干净,再扫一扫。

点儿 diǎnr   些 xiē

〈量词〉< measure word >

"点儿"、"些"都是表示不定量的量词,在意义上和用法上都存在着一定的差别。("点儿" and "些" indicate the indefinite quantity, but there are certain differences between them in meaning and in use.)

(一) 从表示具体事物的数量上看,"点儿"比"些"表示的数量相对要少。(For indicating specific things, "点儿"refers to amount that is a bit less than "些".)试比较:

去商店买了点儿吃的。
去商店买了些吃的。
假期看了点儿书,写了点儿东西。
假期看了些书,写了些东西。
我还有点儿事要跟您商量呢。
我还有些事要跟您商量呢。

(二) "点儿"、"些"跟"这/那"、"这么/那么"等指示代词组合后意义上的差别较大。(There are bigger differences in meaning when "点儿","些" are combined with demonstrative pronouns such as "这/那" and "这么/那么".)

1. "些"放在"这/那"后,构成"这些/那些"时,就只有复数意义,而没有数量多与少的意义了。"这/那"后加"点儿",构成"这点儿/那点儿"就不同了,它不仅表示数量少,还有强调数量"很少"的意义。("些"is added after "这/那"to form "这些/那些", so there is only plural meaning left, but not any more or less in amount. "点儿"is added after "这/那"to form "这点儿/那点儿". It doesn't only indicate "less in amount"; but emphasize the meaning "awfully less in amount".)例如:

这些礼物是送给谁的?
把那些书发给大家。
这点儿饭够谁吃的呀?再做点儿吧。

159

(How can such little rice be enough for all of us? Cook a little more, please.)

您放心,那点儿活儿一会儿就干完了。

2."这么/那么"后也可以加"点儿/些",构成"这么点儿/那么点儿"、"这么些/那么些",但是表示的数量完全相反。("这么/那么" can be added by "点儿/些" to form "这么点儿/那么点儿","这么些/那么些", but the quantity indicated is opposite.)

"这么点儿/那么点儿"强调数量极少,有故意把数量往少处说的意味;"这么些/那么些"强调数量很多,有故意把数量往多处说的意味。("这么点儿/那么点儿" emphasizes extremely small amount with exaggeration;"这么些/那么些" emphasizes big amount with exaggeration.)例如:

怎么就来了那么点儿人啊?不是说有十几个人吗?
这么点儿作业也嫌多,还想不想学习了?
这么小的屋子哪儿能坐下这么些人啊?
洗那么些衣服啊,不嫌累吗?

(三)"点儿"和"些"都可以用在形容词或少数动词后,作补充成分,都表示程度、数量略有增加或减少的意思,可以换用。比较起来,"些"显得稍俗点儿。("点儿" and "些" can be used after adjectives or a few verbs as the complement, indicating a little increase or decrease in degree or amount, and they are exchangeable in use. Comparatively, "些" appears a little vulgar.)例如:

贵了点儿	再亮点儿	放松点儿
再高兴点儿	注意点儿	
贵了些	再亮些	放松些
再高兴些	注意些	

(四)"点儿"和"些"一些具体用法上的差别。(Differences between "点儿" and "些".)

1. "点儿"前可以加"一"、"半",构成"一点儿"、"半点儿",用在否定句中表示全部否定,对全部否定有强调作用。"些"没有这一用法。("一" and "半" can be added before "点儿" to form "一点儿","半点儿", indicating total negation and emphasizing that in the negative sentence. "些" has no such usage.)例如:

你最好别去打扰他,他一点儿时间也没有。

屋里闷得一点儿气也不透。

(The room is so stuffy that even a thread of air couldn't get in.)

这次比赛,我半点儿信心也没有。

(I haven't any confidence in winning the match.)

一星半点儿的错,谁也难免。

(It is understandable that nobody can avoid making no mistake.)

* 你最好别去打扰他,他一些时间也没有。

* 屋里闷得一些气也不透。

* 这次比赛,我半些信心也没有。

2. "点儿"还可以重叠使用,前面加"一"构成"一点点儿",表示数量极少的意思。"些"没有这种用法。("点儿" can be reduplicated and "一" is added before it to form "一点点儿", indicating only few in amount. "些" has no such usage.)例如:

就这么一点点儿困难就把你吓倒了?

(Will such a little difficulty frighten you?)

这种染料特别好,只用一点点儿就行了。

* 就这么一些些困难就把你吓倒了?

* 这种染料特别好,只用一些些就行了。

3. "些"前可以加"好"、"老"等词,构成"好些"、"老些",表示数量相当多。"点儿"没有这种用法。("好","老" can be added before "些" to form "好些","老些", indicating a lot in amount. "点儿" has no such usage.)例如:

外面来了好些人,不知道为什么。

吃了老些的药,也不见病好。

(I have taken a lot of medicine, but haven't got better.)

* 外面来了好点儿人,不知道为什么。

* 吃了老点儿的药,也不见病好。

4. "些"还可以用在"某"后面,作定语,表示不确定的意义。"点儿"没有这一用法。("些" can be used after "某" as an attribute, indicating the indefiniteness. "点儿" has no such usage.)例如:

某些司机总是酒后开车,造成很大的危险性。

(Some drivers always drive after drinking and that will bring out a great danger.)

这种现象已经在某些地区蔓延开。

(This phenomenon has been spreading in some areas.)

* 某点儿司机总是酒后开车,造成很大的危险性。

* 这种现象已经在某点儿地区蔓延开。

对 duì   朝 cháo   向 xiàng

〈介词〉< preposition >

在指示动作对象的意义上,"对"、"朝"、"向"有时可以互换使用。(To indicate the object of an action, "对", "朝" and "向" can be used exchangeably.)例如:

他对/朝/向我挥了挥手。

小柱子对/朝/向李大叔做了个鬼脸。

(Xiao Zhuzi made a wry face towards Uncle Li.)

"对"、"朝"、"向"的主要区别在于:(The main differences among "对"、"朝" and "向":)

(一)"对"还表示可以人对人或人对事物的"对待"的意义,句中谓语通常用一些表示人的情感或态度等的词语。"朝"、"向"

没有这种意义和用法。("对" indicates treatment of people to people or people to things. The predicates in the sentence are generally those terms of emotion and attitude, etc. "朝" and "向" have no such meaning and usage.)例如:

她对我非常热情。

孙老师对这个决定很有意见。

他们夫妇俩对孩子太溺爱了。

(The couple have terribly spoiled the child.)

* 她朝我非常热情。
* 孙老师朝这个决定很有意见。
* 他们夫妇俩朝孩子太溺爱了。
* 她向我非常热情。
* 孙老师向这个决定很有意见。
* 他们夫妇俩向孩子太溺爱了。

(二)"朝"、"向"有表示动作方向的意义,"对"没有这种意义。"朝"、"向"用于表示动作方向的意义时,后边引进的一般是表示方向或场所的词语,此时"朝"、"向"可以互换使用。("朝" and "向" indicate the direction of an action, "对" has no such sense. When "朝" or "向" is used to indicate the direction of an action, the terms following it generally refers to direction or places and "朝" and "向" are interchangeable in use.)例如:

火车朝/向北京开去。

他边脱衣服,边朝/向河边跑去。

* 火车对北京开去。
* 他边脱衣服,边对河边跑去。

(三)"朝"、"向"的区别:(Differences between "朝" and "向":)

1.用法上的区别:(Differences in use:)

(1)在指示动作对象的意义上,"朝"的使用范围比"向"小,

163

一般只用于跟身体有关的动作,并且要有较强的动作性,此时也可以换用"向"。(When indicating object of an action, the applied range of "朝" is narrower than "向" and usually only modifies the action relating to the body, and have the strong character of acting, for this case, "朝" can be replaced by "向".)例如:

　　王厂长走上台来,朝/向大家挥了挥手,大家立刻静了下来。

　　她只是朝/向我点点头,一句话也没说。

　　他滑稽地朝/向大家鞠了一躬,把大家逗得前仰后合。

　　(He bowed amusingly towards everybody and this made them rock with laughter.)

(2)"向"可以为抽象的动作、行为引进对象、事物、方向等;"朝"不可以。("向" introduces targets, things and directions, etc. for the abstract action or behaviour. "朝" can not be used in such a way.)例如:

　　他们正在游行示威,向政府争取公民应有的权利。

　　(They are just holding a demonstration to the government in order to strive for the due rights as citizens.)

　　我们一定要向困难作斗争。

　　向英雄们学习! 向英雄们致敬!

　　* 他们正在游行示威,朝政府争取公民应有的权利。

　　* 我们一定要朝困难作斗争。

　　* 朝英雄们学习! 朝英雄们致敬!

(3)"向"还可以用于语言性活动的动作;"朝"一般不可以。("向" can also be used for actions of conversational activity; usually "朝" can not be used this way.)例如:

　　她向我道出了实情。

　　(She told the truth to me.)

　　向法院表示抗议。

　　(lodging a protest to the court)

164

　　　　同学们再三向老乡们致谢。
　　　＊她朝我道出了实情。
　　　＊朝法院表示抗议。
　　　＊同学们再三朝老乡们致谢。
　2. 结构上的区别：(Difference in the structure：)
　　"向"表示动作方向的意义时,可以构成介词词组用在动词后；"朝"不能。("向" can be used to indicate the direction of an action, composing a prepositional phrase placed after the verb; "朝" has no such a way.)例如：
　　　　河水欢快地流向远方。
　　　　一群大雁飞向天空。
　　　　走向光明,走向胜利!
　　　＊河水欢快地流朝远方。
　　　＊一群大雁飞朝天空。
　　　＊走朝光明,走朝胜利!

对 duì　　　　对于 duìyú
对/对于……来说 duì/duìyú……láishuō

　　对、对于〈介词〉＜preposition＞
　　对/对于……来说〈词组〉＜word group＞
　　"对"、"对于"、"对/对于……来说"都有引进动作、行为对象的作用,尤其是"对"和"对于",在很多场合可以通用。就一般情况来说,能用"对于"的地方,大多都可以用"对"。("对"、"对于" and "对/对于…来说" act on introducing the targets of action and behavior, especially, "对" and "对于" can be used interchangeably in many occasions. Generally speaking, "对" can also be used where "对于" is used．)例如：

　　　　这种做法对/对于解决问题没有任何益处。
　　　　(This course of action will not do any good to solving the problem.)

165

现实生活的体验对于/对我们文艺工作者十分重要。

(To experience the reality is very important to us literary and art workers.)

对我们文艺工作者来说,现实生活的体验十分重要。

它们的主要区别在于:(Main differences are:)

(一)"对"有指示动作、行为对象的作用,意义大体跟"朝"、"向"相当。"对于"和"对/对于……来说"没有这一用法。("对" functions as the target of action and behavior, it is about equal to "朝"or "向"in meaning. There is no such a usage for "对于"and "对/对于…来说".)例如:

她对我妩媚地一笑。
老师拉着她的手对她说:"不要怕!"
老刘对我使了一个眼色,暗示我快走。

(Lao Liu winked at me to leave.)

* 她对于我妩媚地一笑。
* 老师拉着她的手对于她说:"不要怕!"
* 老刘对我来说使了一个眼色,暗示我快走。

(二)"对"、"对于"都有表示"对待"的意义,但是适用范围不尽相同。表示人与人之间相互对待的关系,一般用"对",不用"对于"。("对"and "对于"both can be used to indicate "对待", but the application of the range is not the same. When acting on the mutual treatment between people, "对" is usually used, but not "对于".)例如:

他对部下很和蔼。

(He is very kind to his subordinates.)

她对孩子从不放松要求。
我们对外国朋友一定要热情。

* 他对于部下很和蔼。
* 她对于孩子从不放松要求。
* 我们对于外国朋友一定要热情。

"对于"表示对待的意义时,最好用于表示做某事的某种人、所做的某类事、表现的某方面等,所以较复杂的结构,尤其是谓词性结构,最好用"对于"。(When "对于" indicates "treat", it is better to be used for someone doing something, for some kind of thing being done or for some aspect being shown. Therefore, it is used in the fairly complicated structure, especially in the structure of predicative character.)例如:

对于学成归来的学子,我们热烈欢迎。

(To the students who have just finished their study abroad, we should give our warm welcome.)

对于这些鸡毛蒜皮的小事,最好不要放在心上。

(To these trivial matters, you'd better not keep in mind.)

多听、多说对于学习外语十分重要。

晨练对于身心健康很有益处。

(Doing morning exercises is very good to one's body and mind.)

(三)"对/对于……来说"跟"对"、"对于"使用的角度不同。"对/对于……来说"表示从某人、某事的角度来谈论问题,有强调的意味,强调提出的论断、观点与相关的人或事物的关系。"对"、"对于"不适合用于这种环境。〔"对/对于…来说" and "对","对于" are used from different angles. The former is to talk about the problem from the angles of a certain person or a certain thing, with emphasis, emphasizing the relationship between the proposed inference or viewpoints and the interrelated people or things, the latter is improper in this case.〕例如:

有没有孩子,对我来说,太重要了。

春节对中国人来说,是十分重要的节日。

对于我们的战士来说,没有克服不了的困难。

对于我这个日本女孩子来说,中国已成为我的第二个故乡。

* 春节对中国人,是十分重要的节日。
* 对于我这个日本女孩子,中国已成为我的第二个故乡。

对(对于)……来说 duì(duìyú)……láishuō
在……看来 zài……kànlái

"对(对于)……来说"和"在……看来"在句子中是两种插说成分,形式上虽然很接近,但是几乎不能换用,这主要是由于它们意义上的差别造成的。("对(对于)…来说"and"在…看来"are two parentheses interspersed with flashbacks in sentence. Although similar in forms, they are almost unexchangeable in use due to their different meanings.)

(一) 意义上(In meaning)

"对(对于)……来说"的"对"主要作用在于介引出对象,其对象可以是人,也可以是事物。"说"主要是评价的意义,即对介引出的对象,从某方面给予评价。一般来说,评价多限于实力、影响、性质等等,而且相对来说,评价是客观的、真实的或符合常理的。〔The "对" in "对(对于)…来说" mainly functions to introduce the target, which may either be people or things. "说" is to evaluate the introduced target at certain aspect. Generally the aspects of evaluation are limited to the actual strength, influence and character, etc., and relatively, the evaluations are objective, real or tallying with the common rules.〕例如:

对于他来说,下棋是生活中不可缺少的部分。

(To him, playing chess is the indispensable part to his life.)

对长跑运动员来说,跑个千八百米的不成问题。

(To the long-distance-race athletes, it is not a problem to run the distance of a thousand or slightly less.)

对于讲课来说,我还是个新手。

对于学习游泳来说,胆量是至关重要的。

(Courage is extremely important to the beginners of swimming.)

"在……看来"的"在"主要在于限定方面,因为"看"是表示某人或某一类人看法、想法的,所以"在"所限定的方面只能是人,不能是事物。此外,因为限定的是某个人、某些人或某一集团、某一组织、某一阶层的人的看法,所以看法不一定是客观的、真实的或符合常理的,也许是主观的、片面的、甚至是错误的。(The word "在" in the phrase "在…看来" refers to the part being restricted. Since "看" indicates someone's or some group of people's opinion or thought, the part restricted can only be people, not things. Besides, "在" is restricted to only the opinions of someone, some people or the opinion of the people from some group, some organization, some class, so these opinions are not certainly objective, real or tallying with the common rules, or maybe they are subjective, unilateral and even incorrect.)例如:

在我看来,他简直是个流氓。

(In my opinion he is purely a hoodlum.)

在某些人看来,计划生育政策一无是处。

(In some people's opinion, the birth-control policy is devoid of any merit.)

在外国人看来,中国厨师做菜像变魔术似的。

(In foreigners' eyes, the Chinese chefs are like magicians when they are cooking.)

"对(对于)……来说"构成的句子是一种评价性的意义;"在……看来"构成的句子则表示某人对事物的一种看法,所以这两种句式不能换用。(The sentence composed of "对(对于)…来说" indicates evaluation, while the sentence composed of "在…看来" expresses a kind of opinion that one has about things, so the two sentence patterns are not interchangeable.)例如:

在他们看来,张总经理是个打不垮的人。

(In their opinion, General Manager Zhang is an unyielding man.)

在学校看来,学生的天职就是学习。

* 对他们来说,张总经理是个打不垮的人。
* 对于学校来说,学生的天职就是学习。

有时"对(对于)……来说"和"在……看来"在一个同样的句子里可以换用,但是表示意思的角度不同。(Sometimes "对(对于)…来说" and "在…看来" can be exchanged in the same sentence, but their meanings are expressed from different angles.)例如:

对于他来说,买下这所房子不成问题。(客观评价他的实力。)

在他看来,买下这所房子不成问题。(他对自己实力的看法。)

对于我来说,中国已经成了我的第二个故乡了。(客观评说中国对我的影响。)

在我看来,中国就是我的第二个故乡。(我对中国的看法。)

(二) 搭配上(In collocation)

"对(对于)……来说"中间可以插入表示事物的有关词语;"在……看来"中间只能插入人或者跟人有关的单位、集团等词语。(Terms concerning things can be embedded in the midst of "对(对于)…来说", while terms concerning only people or administrative units and groups can be embedded in the midst of "在…看来".)例如:

对于电脑来说,我还是个外行。

对于爱情来说,金钱不应该是决定的因素。

(Money oughtn't to be the decisive factor in love.)

* 在电脑看来,我还是个外行。
* 在爱情看来,金钱不应该是决定的因素。

对 duì　　跟 gēn　　给 gěi

〈介词〉引进动作的对象。

(<preposition> introducing the target of the action.)

"对"、"跟"、"给"都可以引进动作的对象,在指示与动作有关的对象时,有时可以互换使用。(All of the three can introduce the target of the action. When they refer to the targets relating to the action, occasionally they can be exchanged.)例如:

他对/跟/给我使了一个眼色。

把你的想法对/跟/给大家说一说。

即使在通用时,它们意义的角度仍稍有差别。"对"侧重于面对的对象,"跟"侧重于与动作相关的对象,"给"侧重于承受动作的对象。因此,说话时,角度不同,还是应作不同的选择的。(Though they are exchangeable, the meanings they express are still different. "对" emphasizes the target faced, "跟" emphasizes the target interrelated to the action and "给" otherwise emphasizes the target of the action.)

但是在更多的情况下,"对"、"跟"、"给"是有区别的,不能互换使用。它们的主要区别在于:(But in most cases, "对", "跟" and "给" are different and are not exchangeable. The essential differences are:)

(一) 意义上(In meaning)

"对"指示动作对象或予以动作对象某种态度;"跟"指示协同动作者或与动作有关的人或事物;"给"引进动作接受者或受益、受害者。("对" indicates the target of the action or grants the target of the action some manner; "跟" indicates the action cooperator or people or things relating to the action, and "给" introduces the action receiver, beneficiary or victim.)例如:

这段时间的学习对我很有帮助。

我对你抱有很大的希望。

(I place great hopes on you.)

171

她不想跟我见面。

这份计划还需要跟老师商量商量。

你给小李去个电话吧。

他要把自己的全部知识才能献给科学事业。

(He wants to contribute all his knowledge and talent to the caues of science.)

1. 在表示人、事物间的对待关系时,只能用"对",不能用"跟"、"给"。这时"对"所强调的通常是单方面的行为。(When showing the treating relation between people and things,"对"will be used instead of"跟"and"给". Here"对"emphasizes usually the unilateral act.)例如:

你是什么人我不管,我只知道我是医生,我要对病人负责。

听说他对你很有意思,你呢?

(It is said he is interested in you. What's your opinion?)

＊ 你是什么人我不管,我只知道我是医生,我要跟/给病人负责。

＊ 听说他跟/给你很有意思,你呢?

2. 强调动作有某种协作关系或共同的相互关系时,要用"跟",不能用"对"、"给"。(When emphasizing the action having a certain cooperating relation or other mutual relations,"跟"is used, instead of"对"or"给".)

"跟"用在引进动作的协作者时,句中表示动作的动词有时也具有相互动作的特点。(When"跟"introduces the cooperator of the action, the verb which indicates action in sentence sometimes indicates interaction.)例如:

商量 讨论 谈话 见面 聊天儿(chat) 联系(contact)
交涉(make representations) 纠缠(get entangled)

有时句中也配合其他表示协作意义或共同动作意义的词语。(Sometimes the words indicating cooperation or action in concert are used to support in the sentences.)例如：

　　一起　　一块儿　　一同　　一道

　　我去跟他们交涉，你们在这儿等着。

　　这是我跟他一起完成的课题。

　　＊ 我去对/给他们交涉，你们在这儿等着。

　　＊ 这是我对/给他一起完成的课题。

3. 表示动作的承受者，只能用"给"，不能用"对"、"跟"。(When indicating the object of the action, "给" is used instead of "对" or "跟".)例如：

　　听说前不久她还给你写了一封信。(你——动作的承受者。)

　　我们的责任就是给老人们送温暖、送关怀。(老人们——动作的受益者。)

　　(Our responsibility is to give warmth and great care to the old people.)

　　我要给他一点儿颜色看看。(他——动作的受害者。)

　　(I'll teach him a lesson.)

　　＊ 听说前不久她还对/跟你写了一封信。

　　＊ 我们的责任就是对/跟老人们送温暖、送关怀。

　　＊ 我要对/跟他一点儿颜色看看。

(二) 结构上(In structure)

"给"构成的介词词组根据表达的需要，在句中可以有两个位置：动词前、动词后；"跟"、"对"构成的介词词组一般只有一个位置——只能出现在动词前。(The prepositional phrase composed of "给", according to the need of expression, could be placed both before or after the verbs. The prepositional phrases, composed of "跟" or "对", usually have only one position——before verbs.)例如：

　　我给他送一封信。

　　王师傅亲自给他做示范。

173

(Master Wang demonstrated personally to him.)
我送给他一封信。
战士们把自己的青春年华献给了革命事业。
他对我有意见。
老师们对工作很负责任。
* 他有意见对我。
* 老师们很负责任对工作。
他跟这件事没关系。
我跟他很要好。
* 他没关系跟这件事。
* 我很要好跟他。

对 duì   双 shuāng

〈量词〉用于在一起的两个东西。

(< measure word > two things usu. used together.)

"对"与"双"虽然都用于在一起的两个东西,但大多不能通用。最根本的区别在于:(Although "对" and "双" both indicate two things used together, generally they are not exchangeable. Their basic differences are:)

(一)"对"主要用于非天然的或人为形成的两个在一起的东西。它通常用于按性别、左右、正反等配合的成双的人、动物、事物等,有时也可以用于两个在一起的同类的人或物。("对" means something that is unnatural and composed of two parts artificially. Generally it referrs to people, animals and things coordinated and is composed of two parts according to sexual distinction, the left and right sides, positive and negative and so on, and sometimes "对" can also be used for two people or things of the same type.)例如:

一对恋人 (lover)　　　一对夫妇
一对男女　　　　　　一对鸽子(pigeon)

一对金鱼(goldfish)　　　一对鸳鸯(mandarin duck)
一对古瓶(antique vase)　两对枕头(pillow)
一对耳环(earring)　　　一对矛盾(contradiction)
一对电池(battery)　　　一对活宝 (funny fellow)
一对草包 (block-head)

(二)"双"主要用于原本两个在一起的东西。它通常用于左右对称的人与动物的器官或与人体器官有关系的物品,跟"对"比,"双"更侧重于两个的数。("双" refers to things originally two parts used together, and generally refers to the organs of human or animal which are left and right symmetrically or things relating to human organs. Compared with "对", "双" lays stronger emphasis on the number of two.)例如:

一双眼睛　　　一双长腿
一双长满茧子的手(hands with thick callus)
一双翅膀(wings)
两双皮鞋　三双袜子(three pairs of socks)
一双筷子(one pair of chopsticks)

只有极个别的东西,"对"、"双"才可以换用。(Only for some specific things, "对" and "双" can be exchanged.)例如:

一对/双翅膀　一对/双眼睛　一对/双儿女

但是即使可以换用,也仍稍有差别。应该说,用"对"时,仍倾向于性别、左右等的相配;用"双"时,更侧重于两个的数。(Though they are exchangeable, there is still some difference. "对" inclines to mean mutual match in gender, left-and-right, etc. "双" emphasizes the number of two.)

适应于量词"对"或"双"范围内的大多名词一般是不能随意换用"对"或"双"的。(Most of the nouns that are suitable to be used together with "对" or "双" usually can't be exchanged.)例如:

* 一双恋人　* 一双鸽子　* 一双鸳鸯　* 两双枕头
* 一对腿　　* 一对手　　* 两对鞋　　* 三对袜子
* 一对筷子

对 duì   是 shì   行 xíng   好 hǎo

"对"、"是"、"行"、"好"都可以直接地、单独地表示简单的应答,但是意义不完全相同,有时可以换用,但是表义角度有差别;有时根本不能换用。(The four can all directly and independently make a simple reply, but they don't mean completely the same, and sometimes can be exchangeable. But there is difference from the angle of expression. And sometimes they can not exchange with one another.)

(一) 意义上 (In meaning)

"对"主要表示意见、说话内容是正确的;"是"主要表示肯定,也可以表示"遵命";"行"主要表示可以、许可,某一建议、计划可行、承担某事没问题等;"好"主要表示同意的意思。("对" mainly expresses the content of the opinions and talks are correct; "是" expresses affirmation and obedience; "行" indicates possibility and permission, or a certain suggestion, or a plan is feasible or it is no problem to undertake, etc.; "好" expresses agreement.) 比较以下例句:

你过来看看,这个电话号码对吗? ——对。
——不对,应该是3501618。
她的名字应该这样写吧? ——对,完全正确。
你是新来的留学生吗? ——是。
昨天(是)你在这儿修车吗? ——是啊。
你现在就打电话通知他。——是。
张经理您看看这个计划怎么样? ——行,可以印发。
您帮我一下,行吗? ——行。有什么要帮的,您就说吧。
老师让你去一下办公室。——好,我这就去。
星期天咱们去海边玩玩吧。——好。好久没出去玩了。

(二) 适用范围上 (In range of application)

1.一般来说,用"对吗"提出的问题,或者用跟是否正确有关的测度疑问句提出的问题,多可以用"对"或"不对"回答。用"对吗"提出的问题,一般不能用"是"回答,更不能用"行"、"好"回答。(Generally speaking, the question advanced with "对吗" or advanced by the measuring interrogative, mostly are replied by "对" or "不对". The answers to the question advanced with "对吗" can't be "是", nor "行" or "好".)例如:

  你过来看看,这个电话号码对吗? ——＊ 是。
            ——＊ 行/＊ 好。

用与是否正确有关的测度疑问句提出的问题,可以用"对"回答,也可以用"是"回答,但是不能用"行"、"好"回答。(Towards the question advanced by the measuring interrogative, "对" is used as well as "是", but "行" and "好" can't be used.)例如:

  去北京的火车八点开吧? ——对/是。
         ——＊ 行/＊ 好。

  你来中国一年多了吧? ——是的/对。

2.用是非问句提出的问题,一般可以用"是"、"不"回答,因为是非问句是对是否肯定提出问题,回答也应该是对是否肯定予以回答。一般不用"对"回答,更不能用"行"、"好"回答。(The yes-or-no question is to question whether a statement is affirmative or not, so the answer should be "是" or "不", generally "对" is not used, nor "行" or "好".)例如:

  那个女孩子是你的女朋友吗? ——是的。
         ——＊ 行/＊ 好。
  你想见见他们吗? ——是的,我很想见见他们。
       ——＊ 行/＊ 好,我很想见见他们。
  你不喜欢这部电视剧吗? ——是的,我不喜欢。
         ——＊ 行/＊ 好,我不喜欢。

3.对于表示商量、请求的问题,一般都可以用"行"、"好"回答,不能用"是"、"对"回答。(To the questions about discussion or require-

ment,"行"or"好"are the answers, but not"是"or"对".)例如：
　　我们一起搭车走吧。——行/好。
　　　　　　　　　——＊对/＊是。
　　你去邮局时,顺便帮我把信发了好吗？——好/行。
　　　　　　　　　　　　　　　　　——＊对/＊是。
　但是,有时用"行"还是用"好",感觉不同。(To reply with "行" shows different implication from that with "好".)例如：
　　你帮她找找吧！——行。（建议可行,帮她做没问题）
　　　　　　　　——好。（同意,接受对方的请求）
　　她心里不痛快,你在这儿陪陪她吧。——行。（同上"行"）
　　(She feels bad and you stay to accompany her.)
　　　　　　　　　　　　　　——好。（同上"好"）
　下级请示上级,上级对于请示的内容表示准许、可行的意思时,一般多用"行"。(When it expresses the meaning that a junior asks his higher authorities for instruction and his higher authorities give the permission or think feasibly about the content, "行" is generally used.)例如：
　　刘主任,您看我们的日程安排怎么样？——行,就这样吧。
　　我们把原料这样调配一下,您看怎么样？——行。
　4.因为"是"有"遵命"的意思,所以对于表示命令的句子,尤其是上级对下级、长辈对晚辈简短的、严肃的命令句,最好用"是"（特定环境下,如：军队,只能用"是"回答,显得干脆、利落、表示服从）或"好"回答。因为命令主要是是否接受的问题,不是"准许"的问题,所以一般不能用"行"回答。〔Since "是" expresses "遵命"(obedience), the sentences indicating orders, especially the short and formal imperative sentence given by the higher authorities to the junior or that given by the senior to the junior. It's better to use "是"(in particular

condition, e. g. in army, "是" is the only answer indicating being straightforward, brief and showing obedience.) As for an order, the point is whether it is to be accepted, but not if it is to be permitted. Therefore, "行" can't be used.]例如：

把通知立刻传达下去！——是/好！
——＊行！
把处境危险的老百姓马上转移到安全地带！——是/好！
——＊行！
就地休息五分钟！——是/好！
——＊行！

对于 duìyú　　关于 guānyú　　至于 zhìyú

〈介词〉(也有将"至于"划入连词的。)

[<preposition> ("至于" is sometimes taken as an conjunction.)]

"对于"、"关于"、"至于"都可以构成介词词组作状语，表示与动作有关的人、事物、情况等。(All the three can compose prepositional phrases as adverbial to indicate people, things and situation relating to action, etc.)

(一)"对于"与"关于"

1. 从意义上看，"对于"、"关于"有时可以通用，有时不能通用。(In meaning, "对于"and"关于"are sometimes interchangeable, but sometimes not.)

(1)可以通用的情况。(Cases when they are interchangeable.)例如：

对于/关于你们的建议，领导会认真考虑的。

对于/关于这个湖，还有一段美丽的传说呢。

但是，即使在通用的情况下，它们的表义角度仍有不同。用"对于"时，侧重于与动作有关的对象，用"关于"时，侧重于与动作有关的人、事的范围。(Though being interchangeable, there is still difference in meaning between "对于" and "关于". "对于" lays emphasis on the target which relates to the action, while "关于"

lays emphasis on the range of people or the scope of things that relates to the action.)

(2)不能通用的情况。(Cases when they are not interchangeable.)例如：

①只侧重表示动作的对象,句子内容突出对动作有关对象对待的态度时,用"对于",不能用"关于"。(When the content of the sentence stresses the attitude towards the target of the action, "对于" is used instead of "关于".)例如：

对于你们的批评,他不会不接受的。

对于您的治学态度,我是很钦佩的。

(As for your attitude in doing scholarly research, I really admire.)

* 关于你们的批评,他不会不接受的。

* 关于您的治学态度,我是很钦佩的。

②只侧重表示动作涉及的范围,句子内容突出采取的措施、做法时,用"关于",不能用"对于"。(When emphasizing only the scope the action involving, or the measures and practice given to prominence, "关于" is used but "对于" can't be used.)例如：

关于出国的有关手续问题,还得请你帮帮忙。

关于精神文明建设问题,是今后思想政治工作的中心问题。

* 对于出国的有关手续问题,还得请你帮帮忙。

* 对于精神文明建设问题,是今后思想政治工作的中心问题。

2.在句子形式上,"关于"构成的词组,只能出现在句子前；"对于"构成的词组在句子前、句子中(谓语动词前)都可以。〔About its sentence pattern, the word group composed of "关于" can only be used at the beginning of the sentence, while the word group composed of "对于" can either be used before or in the middle of (before the predicate verb) the sentence.〕例如：

关于今年的工作安排,我们下次讨论。

* 我们关于今年的工作安排下次讨论。
　　对于这里的风俗,我还不很熟悉。
　　我对于这里的风俗还不很熟悉。
(二)"至于"与"对于"、"关于"

　　"对于"、"关于"是就一个话题来说的,"至于"是在原话题之外,引进与这一话题有关的另一话题。用来引进另一话题时,只能用"至于",不能用"对于"、"关于"。用"至于"构成的介词词组可以用在小句或句子的开头,后面是话题。("对于"and "关于"concerns a topic,"至于"means besides the original topic of conversation, another topic is being introduced. When introducing another topic,"至于"can be used but"对于"and"关于"can't. The prepositional phrase composed of"至于"can be put at the beginning of the clause or the sentence, and the topic of conversation follows.)例如:

　　这只是我个人的想法,至于行不行,还得看大家的意见。
　　活动就这样定了,至于具体计划,你们再研究吧。
　　人是接受了,至于具体安排,还得等一段时间。

对比 duìbǐ　　对照 duìzhào

　　〈动词〉把相互有联系的人或事物放在一起比较。
　　(<verb> compare people or things relating to one another.)
(一)意义上的差别(Difference in meaning)

　　"对比"和"对照"除了都有把相互有联系的人或事物放在一起比较的意思外,在意义上,还有不同之处。"对比"强调两种事物或人进行相互比较,没有以哪一方为基准的问题;"对照"则不同,它或者突出了以哪一方为基准进行相互比较,或者突出以哪一方为原型进行参考比较。(Besides putting the mutually associated people or things together to compare,"对比"and "对照"are still different."对比"emphasizes two things or people are compared with neither part being taken as the criterion, while "对照" is different. It may stress one part as the base or prototype when making comparison.)例如:

跟先进人物一对比,才感到自己的差距实在是太大了。
(Compared with the excellent ones, I just realize I really have a long way to go.)
把两个队的实力对比一下,看看哪个队的力量更强。
通过汉日语法现象的对比,我们发现了很多十分有趣的语法特点。
* 把两个队的实力对照一下,看看哪个队的力量更强。
* 通过汉日语法现象的对照,我们发现了很多十分有趣的语法特点。
你应该对照这些条例好好检查检查自己。
我们应该不时地对照先进人物找找差距。
(We should contrast the advanced figures now and then with us to see where we lag behind.)
大家对照这张表格,看看你的表格中有没有漏掉的内容。
对照一下原文,看看引用的是否准确。
王师傅对照着图纸把机器安装了起来。
* 我们应该不时地对比先进人物找找差距。
* 大家对比这张表格,看看你的表格中有没有漏掉的内容。
* 对比一下原文,看看引用的是否准确。

(二) 用法上的差别(Difference in use)

"对比"所比较的两种情况,不能构成"A 对比 B"的格式;"对照"所比较的两种情况,可以构成"A 对照 B"的格式。(The two conditions compared by "对比" can't compose the pattern "A 对比 B", but they can compose the pattern as "A 对照 B".)例如:

把这两张图纸进行了认真的对比。

两种款式对比一下,好像还是这种款式更好一些。

(Comparing the two styles, it seems that this style is much better.)

把这两个地区三年来的产值对比一下,就知道哪个地区经济发展得更快一些了。

* 这种款式对比那种款式,好像还是这种款式更好一些。
* 把这个地区三年来的产值对比一下那个地区,就知道哪个地区经济发展得更快一些了。

他正在对照着《守则》进行反省呢。

(He is checking against the *Regulations* to do self-examination.)

你好好地对照着小李找一找差距吧。

* 他正在对比着《守则》进行反省呢。
* 你好好地对比着小李找一找差距。

对比 duìbǐ　　比较 bǐjiào

〈动词〉把相互有联系的人或事物放在一起比较。

(<verb> put the mutual connected people or things together to make a comparison.)

(一)"对比"和"比较"的方式不完全相同。(The way of "对比" and "比较" is not completely the same.)

"对比"主要是两种情况、两个事物、双方的相互比较,以显示出两者之间的差距。句中"对比"的前后总有"两"、"双"或摆出相对比的两个人、两个事物、两种情况等。("对比" means the mutual comparison between two conditions, two things, in order to show the disparity between the two. In the sentence, before or after "对比", there are always "两", "双" or two people, two things and two conditions being compared.)例如:

今昔对比(contrast the present with the past)

新旧对比　　中外对比　　　男女对比

优劣对比(contrast the good with the bad)

两种方法对比一下,看看哪一种更好。

两种情况前后一对比,就可以看出问题来。

有时虽然"对比"的比较项中也会出现"几"或多个比较对象,但是它的比要理解成是一对一的比,如果有多个,就是某个与其他的一对一地比较多次。(Though sometimes there are more comparing objects, it should be comprehended as the "contrast" by one to one, and if there are more objects, then someone will repeatedly compare with the others in one to one pattern.)例如:

把小李跟另外三个青年对比一下,就会发现小李的优点是很突出的。

对比一下这几套邮票,选一套最好的。

"比较"的比较项可以是两个,但是不限于两个,也可以是多个人、多个事物、多种情况的放在一起相互比较,以辨别高低、优劣。(The items being compared by "比较" can be two, but not restricted to two. It might be many people, many things and several conditions put together to compare one another, in order to differentiate height or qualities.)例如:

比较一下这两个词,看看用法上有什么不同。

比较一下全班同学,王彬的身体素质最好。

这几个方案我们反复比较了几次,难以分出高下来。

(We have repeatedly compared these projects but feel difficult to tell which is better.)

(二)构句情况不完全相同。(Conditions are not completely the same.)

1."对比"作谓语,后边可以不跟任何其他成分,前边也可以没有状语;"比较"一般不能这样用。(Being used as a predicate, "对比" may not be followed by any other compositions, and it is possible that there is no adverb in front. "比较" usually can't.)例如:

两相对比,就可以分出高下来。

新旧对比教育了很多年青人。
* 两相比较,就可以分出高下来。
* 新旧比较教育了很多年青人。

2."对比"可以单独作主语;"比较"一般不能这样用。"对比"通过比,表示两者反差大时,后边可以接表示反差大的形容词补语;"比较"不表示这种意思,不能这样用。"比较"后面也可以接补语,表示的是动作的情态、状态等。("对比"can function as a subject independently, while "比较"can't. Through comparison, when there is big difference, the adjective complement expressing big contrast can be used after. "比较"doesn't have this meaning nor could be used in this way. "比较"can also be followed by complement which indicate mood or state of the action.)例如:

对比强烈(strong)　　对比鲜明(distinct)
对比明显(obvious)　　对比显著(notable)
* 比较强烈　　* 比较鲜明
* 比较明显　　* 比较显著
对比得强烈　　对比得鲜明
对比得很明显
* 比较得强烈
* 比较得鲜明　　* 比较得很明显
比较得仔细　　比较得认真
比较得很清楚　　比较得很具体

3."比较"可以接上"起来"用在句子前面;"对比"不能这样用。("比较"can be followed by "起来" to be used in front of the sentence, "对比"can't.)例如:

比较起来,还是红队的身材更高一些。
* 对比起来,还是红队的身材更高一些。

(三)"对比"和"比较"的功能还有所不同。(Functions are different.)

1."对比"还有名词用法,表示"比例";"比较"没有这种用法。("对比"can also be used as a noun, indicating percentage,

185

while "比较"can't.)例如：
> 学生和教师的对比是十比一。
> 与会代表男女对比是二比一。
> * 学生和教师的比较是十比一。
> * 与会代表男女比较是二比一。

2."比较"还有介词用法；"对比"没有这种用法。("比较" can also be used as a preposition; but"对比"can't.)例如：
> 他的汉语水平比较刚来的时候提高了不少。
> 全民的素质比较十年前，有明显的提高。
> * 他的汉语水平对比刚来的时候提高了不少。
> * 全民的素质对比十年前，有明显的提高。

3."比较"还有副词用法，表示达到一定的程度；"对比"没有这种用法。("比较"can also be used as an adverb, indicating to reach certain degree; but"对比"can't.)例如：
> 孙老师的课讲得比较清楚。
> 小说的这一部分写得比较精彩。
> * 孙老师的课讲得对比清楚。
> * 小说的这一部分写得对比精彩。

短 duǎn　　短暂 duǎnzàn　　短促 duǎncù
〈形容词〉< adjective >

(一)"短"和"短暂"

"短"表示两端之间的距离小，可以用于时间，也可以用于空间，跟"长"相对。"短暂"则只能用于时间，表示时间的量少，并带有一定的书面语色彩。("短"refers to the small distance between the two ends and it can be used for time as well as for space, to be opposite of "长"."短暂"is only used for time, indicating little amount of time and has the flavour of written language.)例如：
> 这支铅笔太短了，不能用了。
> 冬天剪这么短的头发会冷的。

今天是冬至,是一年之中白天最短的一天。

＊ 这支铅笔太短暂了,不能用了。

＊ 冬天剪这么短暂的头发会冷的。

＊ 今天是冬至,是一年之中白天最短暂的一天。

我们只在那儿做了短暂的停留,就又出发了。

我们的谈话虽然十分短暂,但是对我的震撼却不小。

(Although our talk was very short, it is really a shock to me.)

＊ 我们只在那儿做了短的停留,就又出发了。

＊ 我们的谈话虽然十分短,但是对我的震撼却不小。

(二)"短暂"和"短促"

"短暂"和"短促"都可以用于表示时间短,但是时间的长度不同。"短促"表示的时间极短,同时还有急促的意思,一般多用于时间、声音、生命等。"短暂"的时间是相对的短,没有急促的意思。(Both are used to indicate the shortness of time, but their length is different. "短促" indicates very short time and also means being hurried. It is generally used for time, voice and life, etc. The time indicated by "短暂" is relatively short and with the meaning of not being hurried. It doesn't mean hurry.)例如:

我听到一声短促的叫声。

由于时间短促,我们只说了几句话。

＊ 我听到一声短暂的叫声。

四年的时间在历史的长河中只是短暂的一瞬。

(Four years time is just a twinkling in the long process of history.)

我们在一起的时间只有短暂的十天。

＊ 四年的时间在历史的长河中只是短促的一瞬。

＊ 我们在一起的时间只有短促的十天。

187

顿时 dùnshí　　一时 yìshí　　暂时 zànshí
〈副词〉< adverb >

(一)"顿时"和"一时"

1."顿时"和"一时"都有短时间的意思,也都有后边不加"地"的用法。(Both mean short time and both can be used without "地".)例如:

他顿时/一时紧张得喘不过气来。

(He was immediately / for a little while too nervous to breathe.)

看到这种情况,我顿时/一时傻了眼。

(Seeing this, immediately / for a little while I stunned.)

主席的话音刚落,全场顿时/一时掌声雷动。

* 看到这种情况,我顿时地/一时地傻了眼。

* 主席的话音刚落,全场顿时地/一时地掌声雷动。

2."顿时"和"一时"在意义上稍有差别。"顿时"只侧重于强调某种情况突然发生、某种现象一下子出现,而不管它的持续性;"一时"也可以用于某种情况突然发生、某种现象一下子出现的情况,但是它或者还有短时间持续的意思或者它还有再现的可能。(They have a little difference in meaning. "顿时" lays particular emphasis on something suddenly taking place or some phenomenon appearing all of a sudden, but without concerning its continuity; "一时" can be used for something suddenly taking place or some phenomenon appearing all of a sudden, but it also means a short period the thing or phenomenon may last for or it is likely to reappear.)例如:

首长突然提出这样的问题,我一时紧张得不知怎么回答才好。

听到这个不幸的消息,笑声顿时消失了。

(When hearing the sad news, all the laughter disappeared all of a sudden.)

* 听到这个不幸的消息,笑声一时消失了。("一时"

意味着笑声可能再现。)

听了他的话,我顿时勇气倍增。

* 听了他的话,我一时勇气倍增。("一时"意味着勇气只是短时间的持续。)

以上两例之所以用"一时"不贴切,是因为"一时"只管短时间,短时间过去了,前面的情况还有出现的可能;"顿时"只强调一下子出现的情况,不管以后,所以用在这里更贴切些。(The two examples above show the improper use of "一时", that is because "一时" only refers to short time. When this passes, the same thing as occurred before might reoccur. "顿时" emphasizes something happens all of a sudden and has nothing to do with the future.)

此外,"一时"还可以只表示"短时间"或"突然间"的意思,这时不能用"顿时"换用。(Besides, "一时" can also just refer to short time, all of a sudden and here "顿时" can't replace it.)例如:

他叫什么名字来着?我怎么一时想不起来了?

* 他叫什么名字来着?我怎么顿时想不起来了?

你可不能一时高兴就忘乎所以了。

(You oughtn't to forget yourself just because you suddenly feel happy.)

* 你可不能顿时高兴就忘乎所以了。

这几个人只是一时得势,没有什么了不起的。

(Several of these are just in power for a little while and it's nothing to be proud of.)

* 这几个人只是顿时得势,没有什么了不起的。

(二)"暂时"和"一时"

1. "暂时"和"一时"都可以表示"短时间"的意思,但是意义上稍有差别。"暂时"的时间常常属于人为控制的短时间或短时期以内;"一时"常常不是人为控制的短时间,而是临时的,是事情发生后的短时间。所以它们大多不能互换使用。(Both indicate short time. but there is little difference in meaning. "暂时" means

a limited short time or within the short time; the time indicated by "一时" is not a limited time but temporary time usually the short time after something happened. Therefore they are not exchangeable.)例如：

这件事挺麻烦，你不要急着走，暂时住下来，我们再想想办法。

今天暂时写到这儿，明天再接着写。

你放心，我只是暂时拖欠，不久就还给他。

(Don't worry. I am just temporarily in arrears and will pay him soon.)

* 这件事挺麻烦，你不要急着走，一时住下来，我们再想想办法。

* 今天一时写到这儿，明天再接着写。

* 你放心，我只是一时拖欠，不久就还给他。

她感动得一时不知道说什么好了。

我一时高兴，把话说得过了头。

(I was happy for the moment and overdid it.)

* 她感动得暂时不知道说什么好了。

* 我暂时高兴，把话说得过了头。

2. 在使用上(In use)

(1)"暂时"后边可以加"地"，"一时"不能加。("暂时" can be followed by "地" and "一时" can't.)例如：

我们暂时地接济接济他，有什么不可以的？

(What is wrong if we give him financial help temporarily?)

* 我一时地高兴，把话说得过头了。

(2)"暂时"可以用于祈使句，"一时"不能用于祈使句。("暂时" can be used in imperative sentence and "一时" can't.)例如：

你暂时把行李放在这儿吧，办完事，再来取。

这里正在修马路，各种车辆暂时禁止通行。

* 你一时把行李放在这儿吧，办完事，再来取。

* 这里正在修马路，各种车辆一时禁止通行。

(3)"一时"多用于否定句或具有否定意义的句子,"暂时"没有这种限制。(Mostly "一时" is used in the negative sentence or in the sentence with negative meaning. "暂时" doesn't have such restriction.)例如:

遇到这种情况,一时竟不知道怎么办好了。

他一时没了主意。

(He was at a loss for the moment.)

他们之间的矛盾暂时得到了缓解。

(The contradiction between them has got temporarily lessened.)

护照暂时不办了。

(三)"顿时"、"一时"和"暂时"在功能上的差别。("顿时"、"一时" and "暂时" are different in function.)

1. "暂时"还有形容词用法,只作定语或用在"是……的"格式中。"顿时"没有这种用法。("暂时" can be used as an adjective and is only used as an attributive or in the pattern "是…的". "顿时" doesn't have this function.)例如:

大家不要急,公司不景气只是暂时的现象。

(All of you be quiet. The depression of the company is only a temporary phenomenon.)

困难只是暂时的,我们会渡过难关的。

* 大家不要急,公司不景气只是顿时的现象。

* 困难只是顿时的,我们会渡过难关的。

2. "一时"还有名词用法,表示一个时期的意思,可以作宾语、补语;"暂时"没有这种用法。"顿时"只有副词用法,也没有这些用法。("一时" can also be used as a noun, indicating a period. It can be object or complement. "暂时" doesn't have this function. "顿时" can only be used as an adverb and doesn't have this function either.)例如:

你不能只顾一时啊,要从长远考虑。

191

你真是聪明一世,糊涂一时啊!
(You are really smart as a rule, but this time a fool!)
呼啦圈运动风行一时。
(For a moment Hula Ring became popular.)
* 你不能只顾暂时／顿时啊,要从长远考虑。
* 你真是聪明一世,糊涂暂时／顿时啊!
* 呼啦圈运动风行暂时／顿时。

E

二 èr　　两 liǎng　　第二 dì'èr　　俩 liǎ

"二"、"两"、"第二"、"俩"都是表示数目的词,代表的数字一样,都可以表示与"1+1"相等的数目,但是用法和意义有所不同。(They are all numeral words, representing the same figure which equals the sum of "1+1". But there are some differences in their use and meaning.)

(一)"二"和"两"

1."二"和"两"意义相同,只是用法有区别。("二" and "两" are the same in meaning, but different in use.)

(1)在数字排列、分数、小数及序数的表示中,用"二"不用"两"。(While referring to numeral sequence, a fraction, a decimal or an ordinal "二" is used instead of "两".)例如:

　　1234　＊1两34　2657　＊两657
　　二分之一　＊两分之一　三分之二　＊三分之两
　　零点二　＊零点两　二点一　＊两点一
　　第二　初二　二月　二等　二级　二班
　　二叔　二哥　二楼
　　＊第两　＊初两　＊两月　＊两等
　　＊两叔　＊两哥　＊两楼

(2)读数时,"二"在"十"、"百"位前,读作"二";在以"千"、"万"、"亿"开头的数字前多读作"两";在"半"前读作"两"、写作"两"。〔Before the numbers of "十"(ten) and "百"(hundred), the figure "二" is read as "二"; when the figure precedes the figures of "千"(thousand), "万"(ten thousand) and "亿"(hundred million), it is read as "两"; when the figure precedes "半"(half), it is often read and written as "两", too.〕例如:

　　20/200　　　读作:二十/二百

2000/22222　　读作：两千/两万二千二百二十二
两半　　　　读作：两半
　　　　　　写作：两半

(3)单个数出现于一般量词前用"两",不用"二"。("两"is used when a single number appears in front of general measure words. "二" can't be used.)例如：

两本书　两个人　两张桌子　两间屋子
两棵树　两只耳朵
两种　两头猪　两夜　两天　两趟　两遍　两次
＊二本书　＊二个人　＊二张桌子　＊二间屋子
＊二只耳朵　＊二头猪　＊二种　＊二夜
＊二天　＊二趟　＊二遍　＊二次

(4)出现在度量衡单位前比较活,有时"二"、"两"都可以用。一般来说,在传统的度量衡单位前,多用"二";新度量衡单位前多用"两";但是在度量衡单位"两"前只能用"二"。(Sometimes both "二" and "两" can be used. Generally speaking, "二" is used often before traditional capacity and weight units; "两" is often in front of the new capacity and weight units; but only "二" is used before "两" when the latter is employed as capacity and weight unit.)例如：

二尺/两尺　二亩/两亩　二升/两升
二斤　二里
两米　两公斤　两公里　二两
＊两两

2.除了表示与1+1相等的数目外,"两"还可以表示概数。它所表示的概数一般为少量的数目。"二"没有这种意思。(In addition to representing the same amount of that "1+1", "两" is often employed to indicate approximate number of a small amount, whereas "二" does not have such a kind of indication.)例如：

这两天太忙了,过两天我再去找你。
我来说两句。

怎么就来了这么两个人?

(How have come so fewer people?)

* 这二天太忙了,过二天我再去找你。
* 我来说二句。
* 怎么就来了这么二个人?

3. "两"还可以表示双方的意思,"二"没有这种意思。("两" often suggests "both sides", "two sides", or "mutually" while "二" does not.)例如:

两相情愿(two-sided wish)
势不两立(mutually exclusive)
两败俱伤(both sides lose)
两全齐美(satisfy both sides)
* 二相情愿　* 势不二立　* 二败俱伤
* 二全齐美

(二)"第二"与"二"、"两"

"第二"也表示"二"的数目,只是它表示的是序数。它通常在句中作状语,也可作主语、宾语。但是不能用来表示时段,也不表示动量。只表示与 1+1 相等的数目,没有次序的意思,可以用"二"或"两",不能用"第二"。(Like "二", "第二" is also a number, but an ordinal number, which is often employed as an adverbial, and subject and object as well. However, it cannot be utilized to indicate the duration of time or quantity of motion. When one wants to express the idea of the number of two but not number 2 or the ordinal number in Chinese, one uses "二" or "两", but not "第二".)例如:

我第二次见到他掉眼泪。

第二天他就倒下了,从此再也没有站起来。

(On the second day he fell down and could never stand up.)

第二名不是我所期望的。

他到北京来学习已经是第二次了。

去了两次车站都没走成。

故宫我已经去了两次了。

* 李立在这儿住了第二年了。(李立在这儿住了两年了。)

* 山本来中国第二次了。(山本来中国两次了。)或(山本是第二次来中国。)

* 这个电影我已经看了第二遍了。(这个电影我已经看了两遍了。)

* 第二本词典都不错。(两本词典都不错。)

* 去了第二次车站都没走成。

(三)"俩"与"二"、"两"

"俩"与"二"、"两"的词义不完全相同,"俩"是"两个"的意思,因为它已含有"个"这个量的意义,所以后边不能再加任何量词,而"二"和"两"后边是可以加量词的;"二"和"两"使用范围很广、频率很高,"俩"则较少使用,而且有很多限制。"俩"多用于某些人称代词和某些成对的称谓名词后,少数情况下也可用于一些普通名词前。("俩" and "二","两" differ from each other in meaning, "俩" suggests the meaning of "two", for it has the meaning of the measure word "个". There should be no measure words following it while measure words can be used after "二"and "两". "二"and "两" are used more widely and more frequently than "俩". For in terms of the usage of "俩" it usually has more restrictions. And "俩" is generally used after certain personal pronouns or appellative nouns in pairs, it can also be used before some common nouns.)例如:

我们俩一起去吧。

苹果只有俩了,不够怎么办?

哥俩一点儿也不像。

* 我们俩个一起去吧。

* 苹果只有俩个了,不够怎么办?

* 哥俩个一点儿也不像。

拿俩走吧　　吃了俩

＊拿两走吧　　＊吃了两
＊拿二走吧　　＊吃了二
我们俩　你们俩　他俩　咱俩
＊我们两　＊你们两　＊他两　＊咱两
父子俩　母女俩　兄弟俩　姐妹俩
爷俩　　娘俩
＊父子两　＊母女两　＊兄弟两
＊姐妹两　＊爷两　＊娘两
俩人　　俩战士　　俩馒头
＊人俩　＊战士俩　＊馒头俩
＊两战士　＊两馒头
＊二战士　＊二馒头

197

F

发生 fāshēng　　产生 chǎnshēng

〈动词〉 < verb >

"发生"和"产生"都可以表示某事情、事物等出现了,但是基本上不能换用,主要在于意义上和搭配上的差别。(Both "发生" and "产生" can be used to indicate the idea of "take place" or "into being" or "arise", but in terms of their meanings and collocations, they are not exchangeable.)

(一) 意义上(In meaning)

"发生"不需要生出的条件,只要出现了就可以了;"产生"则要求生出的条件,它必须依赖原有的人、事物等,由此生出新的人、事物、态度等。("发生" doesn't require any condition. "产生" needs condition for its occurance and it has to depend on the original people and things to create new people, things or attitudes, etc.)试比较:

这里发生了翻天覆地的变化。

今天怎么发生了那么多事儿?

近期内物价不会发生什么变化。

就因为你的一句话,使他们产生了矛盾。

(It is just because of your words that there is contradiction between them.)

最近他对观察小昆虫产生了浓厚的兴趣。

(Recently he has become densely interested in observing the small insects.)

(二) 搭配上(In collocation)

1. 表示某处所出现某种原来没有的变化、情况时,用"发生",不用"产生"。(Instead of using "产生","发生" is used while indicating that in a certain place, certain change or condition which

did not happen before now occurs.)例如：

中国农村正发生着喜人的变化。(The countryside of China)

他们国家又发生了一次地震。(Their country)

这里发生了一起重大抢劫案。(Here)

＊ 中国农村正产生着喜人的变化。

＊ 他们国家又产生了一次军事政变。

＊ 这里产生了一起重大抢劫案。

2.表示某方面或某事物出现某种原来没有的变化、关系等时,用"发生",不用"产生"。(Instead of "产生", "发生" is used when certain change or relation which didn't happen before now occurs.)例如：

没想到,她的命运竟发生了历史性的转变。

(It is unexpected that a historical change has happened to her fate.)

我跟这些人没有发生过任何关系。

(I have never done any business with these people.)

＊ 没想到,她的命运竟产生了历史性的转变。

＊ 我跟这些人没有产生过任何关系。

3.表示人与人之间生出的某种情感、想法等,用"产生",不用"发生"。(When indicating certain emotion and opinion, etc. between people, "产生" is used instead of "发生".)例如：

他们俩在互助合作中产生了爱情。

我对他产生了一种莫名其妙的依赖感。

(In my mind, an inexplicable dependent feeling to him comes into being.)

他对刘力表现出的过分殷勤产生了想法。

(The excessive hospitality Liu Li offered has made him think more.)

＊ 他们俩在互助合作中发生了爱情。

199

* 我对他发生了一种莫名其妙的依赖感。

* 他对刘力表现出的过分殷勤发生了想法。

4. 表示由某事物、事件、思想等生出的作用、结果、影响等，用"产生"，不用"发生"。(When indicating the function, result and influence, etc. happen because of certain thing, event and thinking, "产生" is used instead of "发生".)例如：

这一思想对经济的发展产生了不可估量的作用。

(This thinking has played an unmeasurable role in the economical development.)

我担心这件事会产生不良后果。

这次演讲产生了很好的效果。

他的思想对过去和现在已经产生了巨大的影响，对将来也必将会产生相当深远的影响。

(His thought has made huge influence on the past and the present, and will surely make considerable influence on the future.)

* 这一思想对经济的发展发生了不可估量的作用。

* 我担心这件事会发生不良后果。

* 这次演讲发生了很好的效果。

* 他的思想对过去和现在已经发生了巨大的影响，对将来也必将会发生相当深远的影响。

5. 人或作品等具体事物的生出，只能用"产生"，不能用"发生"。("产生" not "发生" is used when expressing the idea of coming into being.)例如：

我校最新的领导班子已经产生了。

(The newest leading body of our university has come into being.)

有能力的技术人才，只有在实践中才能产生。

好的文学作品只能产生于火热的生活之中。

(The fine works of literature can only come into being in the

fervent life.)
  * 我校最新的领导班子已经发生了。
  * 有能力的技术人才,只有在实践中才能发生。
  * 好的文学作品只能发生于火热的生活之中。

发现 fāxiàn　　发明 fāmíng
〈名词〉＜noun＞
〈动词〉＜verb＞
(一)"发现"和"发明"都可以用作名词和动词,都具有寻求并得到以前不知道的事物的意思,但是"发现"所指的不知道的事物或规律原本是存在的,人们经过研究、探索把原本存在的事物、规律揭示出来;"发明"所指的不知道的事物则原本是不存在的,人们通过创造活动,使原本不存在的事物、方法出现了。(Both "发现" and "发明" can be used as noun and verbs and both have the meaning of seeking and gaining things which are unknown before. The word "发现" refers to the unknown things or laws that had been existing, and after people's study and exploration the original existing things and laws are brought to light. The word "发明" refers to the unknown things which originally didn't exist, but by creating, the originally non-existing things and laws come into being.)例如:

　　两个农民在打井的时候,发现了这块价值连城的古物。
　　勘探队在这一带发现了大量的石油。
　　人们在长期的生产劳动中,发现了气候变化的规律和农作物生长的规律。
  * 两个农民在打井的时候,发明了这块价值连城的古物。
  * 勘探队在这一带发明了大量的石油。
  * 人们在长期的生产劳动中,发明了气候变化的规律和农作物生长的规律。

　　东汉科学家张衡发明了浑天仪和地动仪。
　　造纸的方法相传是由东汉蔡伦发明的。

(The method of paper-making is said to be invented by Cai Lun of the Eastern Han Dynasty.)

指南针是中国的四大发明之一。

* 东汉科学家张衡发现了浑天仪和地动仪。
* 造纸的方法相传是由东汉蔡伦发现的。
* 指南针是中国的四大发现之一。

(二)寻求到以前原本存在的然而寻求者不知道的东西也同样是"发现","发现"可以随时随地发生。因此,"发现"的东西可大可小、可具体也可抽象;"发明"则不同,"发明"的特点在于"新",在于以前没有,所以它一般用于具有一定意义和价值的事物,日常生活中一些没有什么意义的小事一般不用"发明"。("发现" is also used to indicate "discover something that used to exist but was unknown to the finder at first"; "发现" can take place anywhere at any time. Things that can be the object of "发现" can be big or small, concrete or abstract; whereas the characteristics of "发明" is to invent something "new" that did not exist before, so generally it is used for things of significance value, and "发明" is usually not employed to form collocations with things without much meaning.)例如:

我收拾屋子的时候,在桌子底下发现了这本书。

我才发现他是一个那么有意思的人。

* 我收拾屋子的时候,在桌子底下发明了这本书。
* 我才发明他是一个那么有意思的人。

法子 fǎzi   点子 diǎnzi

〈名词〉表示方法、办法的意思。

(<noun> means or methods.)

"法子"、"点子"都有方法、办法的意思,跟"方法"、"办法"比起来,都具有很强的口语色彩,多用于口语之中,有时可以换用。("法子","点子"all mean methods or ways. In comparison with "方法" and "办法", they are colloquial, and are used very often in informal situations, and they are all exchangeable.) 例如：

我发生"经济危机"了,没钱吃饭了,帮忙想个法子/点子吧。

(The "economical crisis" happens to me and I have no money for a meal. Help me think of a way.)

对付这种事,小王有法子/点子,你找他去。

但是这两个词又有一定的区别,主要是意义上和搭配上的差别。(Yet the two words differ from each other mainly in meaning and collocations.)

(一) 意义上(In meaning)

"法子"只有方法、办法的意思,指的是一些具体的手段,带有操作性的特点;"点子"不同,它除了方法的意思外,还有主意的意思,而且主要是主意的意思,所以操作性不是它的特点,主要是理性的东西。("法子" refers to methods or ways, which involves concrete means and is operational, whereas "点子", besides the concept of method, mainly and particularly something abstract or rational, indicates ideas without the characteristics of operation.) 例如：

你有法子找到他吗?

外面商店都关门了,你有没有法子弄点儿吃的来。

(The shops outside are all closed. Could you find a way as to get something to eat.)

* 你有点子找到他吗?

* 外面商店都关门了,你有没有点子弄点儿吃的来。

他现在遇到麻烦了,你给他出个点子帮帮他吧。

(He has got into trouble. Just help him think of a way.)

不用你帮我做,只要给我出个点子就行了。

(二) 搭配上(In collocation)

"法子"常跟"想"、"没"、"有"搭配,构成"想法子"、"没法子"、"有法子"等较为固定的用法;"点子"主要跟"出"搭配,构成

203

"出点子"这样较为固定的搭配用法。"法子"不能跟"出"搭配。("法子" often forms collocations with "想","没","有", such as "想法子","没法子" and "有法子" which are set expressions; while "点子" mainly forms collocation with "出" as "出点子",which is also a set expression. "法子" can not collocate with "出".)例如：

没法子呀，不干不行啊！

有法子了，刘先生会针灸，让刘先生用针给你止疼吧。

* 没点子呀，不干不行啊！

* 有点子了，刘先生会针灸，让刘先生用针给你止疼吧。

你去求求老王，他会给你出点子的。

* 你去求求老王，他会给你出法子的。

反应 fǎnyìng　　反映 fǎnyìng　　反响 fǎnxiǎng

反应、反映〈动词〉〈名词〉 < verb > < noun >

反响〈名词〉 < noun >

(一)"反应"和"反映"

1."反应"和"反映"都可以用作动词。("反应" and "反映" both are verbs.)

(1)"反应"和"反映"都可以用作动词，但是意义不同，所以不能换用。"反应"主要用于表示有机体受到外界刺激后而引起相应的活动；也可以指物质发生化学或物理的变化。(Both "反应" and "反映" are verbs with different meanings, they are not interchangeable in use. "反应" indicates that the organism is stimulated by the external world and arouses corresponding activity. It may also refer to the chemical change or physical change of materials.)例如：

他走了半天了，你怎么才反应过来？

(He had been away for quite a while. How come you've just realized it?)

他这是讽刺你呀，你反应得也太慢了。

(He was satirizing you and you are so slow in reaction.)

吃了药以后，她反应得挺厉害。

(After taking the medicine she reacted strongly.)

酸和碱在试管里反应得很剧烈。

(Acid and alkali react fiercely in the test tube.)

"反映"则指通过某事物把客观事物的实质表现出来。("反映" shows the substance of the reality through certain things.)例如：

这部电视连续剧反映了经济建设中尖锐复杂的矛盾斗争。

(The TV series mirrored the sharp and complicated conflicts in the economic construction.)

代表们的提案反映了人民的心声。

(The motion of the representatives reflects the voice of the people.)

这个问题已经在报告中反映出来了。

"反映"还可以表示把客观情况或别人的意见告诉上级。("反映" also indicates to report objective circumstances or the opinion of others to the higher level.)例如：

我一定会把你的意见反映上去的。

(I will surely report your opinion to the higher level.)

他已经把你的意见反映给老师了。

(2)"反应"和"反映"在用法上也有一定的区别。"反应"一般不带宾语；"反映"可以带宾语。"反应"一般不能重叠使用；"反映"则可以重叠使用。("反应" and "反映" vary in usage, "反应" can not be followed by objects while "反映" can. "反应" can not be used repeatedly whereas "反映" can.)例如：

("反应"见上面例句。)

(For the usage of "反应", see the examples above.)

他的介绍反映了我们厂的实际情况。

如何处理这件事恰恰反映了我们对改革开放的认识和态度。

(How to deal with the matter merely shows our knowledge

and attitude towards the improvement and the open policy.)
> 谁能把这里的情况向上级领导反映反映?

2."反应"和"反映"都可以用作名词,但意义有差别,不能换用。"反应"表示由于受到某些刺激而引起的症状、现象;由某种情况而引起的意见、态度、行动等。("反应"and"反映"both can be used as nouns whereas they are different from each other in meaning, therefore they are not exchangeable."反应"refers to the symptoms and phenomena caused by certain stimulation, or the opinions, attitudes and actions caused by certain situation.)例如:
> 她怀孕五个月了,妊娠反应还那么厉害。
> 你的反应太迟钝了。
> 对这个报告大家的反应还不错。
> 厂长贪污受贿的事在群众中引起了不小的反应。
> (The case of the factory director's corruption has caused rather strong response.)

"反映"主要表示对人或事物的批评性意见。("反映"expresses the critical opinions to the people or things.)例如:
> 多听听群众的反映,是可以促进我们的工作的。
> (Listening to the masses' opinions more often may promote our work.)
> 你听到工人们对你的反映没有?

(二)"反应"和"反响"

1."反应"和"反响"都可以用作名词,都可以表示事情发生后所引起的意见、态度、行动,但是意义上还有一定的差别。"反响"侧重于引起人们热烈的议论、普遍的称赞、强烈的意见等,有以声音作为回响的特征。由于这种回响是大的,所以常受"强烈"、"热烈"、"极大"等词的修饰,词义较重。"反应"不一定是众多的、普遍的、强烈的或以声音作为回响的特征的情况,它可以是个人的意见、态度等,也可以是微小的态度、行动的变化等,词义较轻。("反应"and"反响"both are nouns, both can be used to indicate the opinion, attitude, action caused by an event, but are different from each other in meaning. "反响" lays emphasis on the hot discussions, widespreading appraisings and strong opinions. Sometimes it is with the characteristic of echoes. As so the sense of the word is often expressed in a heavy way. "反应" is not necessarily characterized by the condition of being multitudinous, widespread or echoing with sound. It may be the individual's opinion and attitude, etc., and may be delicate attitude or change of the action as well. It is a mild word.)例如：

消息一传开,立刻引起全校师生强烈的反响。

他的科学报告在大会上引起极大的反响。

观众对这部电影反响如此强烈,是我们所没有想到的。

(It is unexpected to us that the audience's response to this movie is so strong.)

对这个规划,大家的反应不错。

他听到这个消息后反应怎么样？

布告贴出去后,注意一下大家的反应。

(Pay attention to the people's response after the notice is put up.)

* 他听到这个消息后反响怎么样？

* 布告贴出去后,注意一下他的反响。

2. 一般来说,"反响"常受"引起"、"激起"、"有"、"没有"等动词的支配；"反应"常受"有"、"没有"、"注意"、"发生"、"听到"等动词的支配。"反响"不用于气氛温和的场景。〔Generally speaking, "反响" often forms collocations with verbs like "引起"(cause),"激起"(arouse),"有"(have),"没有"(have not) whereas "反应" often forms collocations with verbs like "有"(have),"没有(have not),"注意"(pay attention to),"发生"(cause; give rise to),"听到"(hear of). "反响" cannot be used in a kind of gentle situation.〕

3."反应"还可以用于人或事物由某因素、某刺激引起的情况状态,"反响"不能用于这种情况。("反应" may express the condition of people or things caused by some factor or by some stimulation. "反响" can't be used in this situation.)例如:

人老了,反应就会很慢。

这孩子虽小,反应却很快。

你把这两种东西放在一起会发生化学反应的。

停药以后,好像没有出现什么不良反应。

(It seems that there isn't any bad reaction after stopping using the medicine.)

* 人老了,反响就会很慢。
* 这孩子虽小,反响却很快。
* 你把这两种东西放在一起会发生化学反响的。
* 停药以后,好像没有出现什么不良反响。

方便 fāngbiàn　　便利 biànlì

〈形容词〉表示做事情或行动不费事、没有麻烦。

(<adjective> indicating to do things or to act without any trouble.)

1."方便"和"便利"都可以表示做事情或行动不费事、没有麻烦,但是意义上还是稍有差别的。"方便"主要强调不麻烦、不费事。(Although "方便" and "便利" both indicate to do things or to act without any trouble, they have some slight difference in meaning. "方便" mainly indicates taking no trouble or without any trouble.)例如:

这里的交通很方便,想去哪儿就去哪儿。

(The traffic here is very convenient and you can get to anywhere as you wish.)

你住在学校里买东西方便吗?——方便。

我这儿有传真机,传递文件方便极了。

208

"便利"则主要强调具有某种有利的条件,从而有利于达到目的。("便利" emphasizes having certain advantageous condition that helps reach the goal.)例如:

有了这趟车,我们往来就便利多了。
把开关安装在这儿,操作起来会很便利的。
有了这么便利的条件,你的工作应该更出色才对呀。
(Since you have got such good condition you ought to have done a remarkable job.)

比较起来,"方便"的使用更平常些,使用频率更高些;"便利"使用得比较少。
(Comparatively speaking, "方便" is more commonly used, "便利" is used less commonly.)

2. "方便"作为形容词还有"适宜"的意思。"便利"没有这种意思。["方便" as an adjective, has the meaning of "适宜" (suitable) while "便利" does not.]例如:

方便的时候,常来我这儿坐坐。
我们在这儿谈话有点儿不太方便。
(It is really inconvenient to talk here.)
你那儿方便吗?我现在过去行吗?
* 便利的时候,常来我这儿坐坐。
* 我们在这儿谈话有点儿不太便利。
* 你那儿便利吗?我现在过去行吗?

方法 fāngfǎ　　办法 bànfǎ

〈名词〉表示进行工作、处理事情所采取的手段、措施等。
(<noun> indicating the means, measures, etc. taken in doing work or in dealing with matters.)

"方法"、"办法"虽然都可以表示进行工作、处理事情所采取的手段、措施等,但是由于它们具体所指有出入,所以大多数情况下,不能通用。主要区别有:(Though "方法" and "办法" indicate the means or measures in the beginning of work or in the dealing of matters, yet they vary and in most cases, they are not exchangeable. The major differences are as in the following.)

(一) 意义上(In meaning)

"方法"通常用于进行某种工作、处理某类事情的完整的、系统的手段、措施等,带有理性的特点。"办法"则仅是针对具体的事情所采取的手段、措施等,具有直接操作的特点。("方法" means the complete, systematic means and measures to do certain work or to deal with certain matter, and is of rational character. "办法" means the means or measures taken to be directed against the certain matter, and is of the directly operating character.)例如:

学习方法→解决学习问题的一系列手段、措施等。

我有办法记这个单词了。→针对这个单词不好记的问题所采取的具体的手段、措施等。

管理方法→指在管理中的一系列的成套的措施、制度等。〔(It) refers to the whole series of measures and systems, etc. in the management.〕

管理办法→指针对一些具体的问题所采取的手段、措施等。〔(It) refers to the means and measures taken to be directed against some specific problems.〕

另外,可以说"方法体系",不能说"办法体系",也是由以上意义上的差别形成的。〔In addition, the expression "方法体系(method system)" is tenable, but the expression "办法体系(way system)" is not, for the difference of the meaning forms the distinction.〕

(二) 用法上(In usage)

1.由于"方法"通常用于进行某种工作、处理某类事情的完整的、系统的手段、措施等,所以单独一个"方法"很少直接被动词支配或作主语,"方法"前面常常有表示某方面、某门类的修饰、限制语;"办法"则常常不需要这种修饰限制语,单独一个"办法"常作主语、宾语。尤其是"有"、"是"、"想"等动词,可以只单独带一个"办法"或只单独陈述一个"办法",一般的情况下却不能只单独带一个"方法"。(Because "方法" usually refers to complete, systematic means or measurement for carrying out certain tasks or dealing with certain things, it seldom follows a verb or acts as the subject by itself. A modifier or determiner indicating a certain aspect or discipline is usually required in front of it. "办法" usually does not require this kind of modifiers. "方法" is usually used as a subject, or an object. Especially "有","是"and"想", each can be followed by "办法"alone. Generally speaking, we cannot use "方法" alone.)例如:

思想方法　治学方法　看书方法
教学方法　研究方法　科学方法
* 思想办法　* 治学办法　* 看书办法
* 研究办法　* 科学办法
办法有了。
这不是个办法。
我们有办法解决这个问题了。
他急得一点儿办法也没有了。
帮他想想办法吧!
* 方法有了。
* 这不是个方法。
* 我们有方法解决这个问题了。
* 他急得没有方法了。
* 帮他想想方法吧!

2. 由于"方法"带有一定的理性意义,常用于相对郑重的场合,与动词的搭配也有一定的选择。常选择那些有郑重色彩的、有一定抽象性的动词。(As "方法" often has some rational meaning, it often appears in some relatively solemn occasions. It is selective to certain verb collocations. It often goes with verbs with a flavour of seriousness or abstractness.)例如:

注意工作方法,做好思想工作。
我们提倡理论与实践相结合的学习方法。
(We encourage the learning method of combining theory with practice.)
改进教学方法,提高教学水平。
* 注意工作办法,做好思想工作。
* 我们提倡理论与实践相结合的学习办法。
* 改进教学办法,提高教学水平。

3. "办法"是具体的手段、措施,它对于数量词的修饰不受限制。"方法"主要是指解决某门类问题的系统性的措施,所以通常表示某门类的限制语不可少,而在某门类的限制语前再接受数量限制的情况较少,尤其是表示不定量的"一点"、"点"等,一般不用来表示"方法"的数量。("办法" refers to specific means and measures, the modifying of the numeral-classifier compound will not be restricted. "方法" mainly refers to the systematic measures of solving problems of a certain category, so a qualifier indicating the category is essential, but a word indicating quantity is seldom used in front of this qualifier, especially words indicating indefinite quantity like "一点" and "点" are not used to modify "方法".)例如:

我这儿有几个办法,供你选择。
拿他一点儿办法也没有。
(To him I could do nothing.)
给他想点办法。
面对这一大堆困难,我毫无办法。
(Facing this big pile of difficulties I can't do anything at all.)
* 我这儿有几个方法,供你选择。
* 拿他一点儿方法也没有。
* 给他想点方法。
* 面对这一大堆困难,我毫无方法。

房子 fángzi　　屋子 wūzi　　房间 fángjiān
房屋 fángwū　　楼房 lóufáng

〈名词〉指供人居住或做其他用途的建筑物。

(< noun > referring to a building for people to live or for other purposes.)

这些词都可以指供人居住或做其他用途的建筑物,但是词义范围的大小有一定差别,因此使用上也有所不同。(These words can be used to refer to buildings for people to live or for other purposes, but their denotation varies, and they are used differently.)

(一) "房子"和"屋子"

"房子"和"屋子"有领属关系,"房子"指有墙、顶、门、窗等的完整的建筑物;"屋子"只属于房子的一部分,是房子内分隔成多个部分的部分,即房子内可以分隔成多个屋子。所以,可以说"一所房子",却不能说"一所屋子",因为"所"是一个完整的建筑物的量词;可以说"一间屋子",却不能说"一间房子",因为"间"是房子分隔后的一个部分的量词。("房子"and "屋子"belong to the same category. "房子"refers to an integral building, while "屋子"are the parts among several partitioned sections of the house, namely, a "房子" can be divided into many "屋子". We can say "一所房子", but not "一所屋子"for "所" is a measure word modifying an integral building. We can say "一间屋子"but not "一间房子"for "间"is a measure word modifying a part after the house partitioned.)

此外,"房子"可以从外观上描述评价;"屋子"只能从内部描述评价。(In addition,"房子" can be described from appearance; "屋子"can only be described internally.)例如:

这所房子真漂亮。(指外观——质料、颜色、形状、样式等。)

这间屋子真漂亮。(指内部——装饰、陈设、布置等。)

谈到与其他建筑物或物体的关系时,用"房子",还是用"屋子",方位关系上有差别。(Concerning the relation with other buildings or objects, whether we use "房子"or "屋子"there is a difference in positional relation.)例如:

> <u>房子</u>前面有一棵高大的银杏树。(指建筑物前。)
>
> <u>屋子</u>外面有一棵高大的银杏树。(用"屋子前面"不合适,"屋子"是建筑物内部的一部分,跟树是内外的关系。)

现在,人们有时也将一个建筑物内其中的一套住房称为"房子"。(An apartment inside the building is also called "房子".)例如:

> 我最近在宏光大厦新买了一套房子,是三楼,三室两厅。
>
> (I bought an apartment in Hongguang Building recently. It is on the third floor and with three bedrooms and two living rooms.)

(二)"屋子"和"房间"

"屋子"和"房间"都指房子内分隔成多个部分的部分,都可以用"间"作量词,但是色彩稍有不同,所以使用环境有差别。"屋子"稍俗点儿,多用于口语;"房间"稍雅点儿,多用于书面语或正式场合。所以宾馆、饭店、旅馆等行业部门、楼房设计、租售房屋等部门、订住房间等,都要用"房间",不用"屋子";具体谈论述说某一房间时,可以用"屋子"。("屋子" and "房间" both refer to the partitioned sections inside the house, both can use "间" as the measure words, but are different in flavour and in use. "屋子" is more popular, and mainly used in spoken language. "房间" is more refined and mostly in written language or on formal occasions. Therefore, when referring to guest houses and hotels, building design, renting and selling of houses and room reservation, the word "房间", not "屋子", is used. But when some room is specially mentioned, "屋子" can be used.)例如:

> 这里房间设施齐备,服务优良。
>
> 每个房间都装有电话,很方便。
>
> 她住在友谊宾馆,房间号码是314。

* 这里屋子设施齐备,服务优良。
* 她住在友谊宾馆,屋子号码是314。

你的屋子/房间有多大?

你的屋子/房间收拾得可真干净呀!

此外,"房间"在宾馆、饭店、旅馆等地方有时可以不止一间屋子,而指几个有联系的成套的屋子。"屋子"不能这样用。("房间"can refer to more than one room which form complete set of rooms in hotels and guest houses. While "屋子"can not be used this way.)例如:

我在南山宾馆订了一套高级房间,有里外两个卧室,外加一个客厅。

(I've booked a first-class apartment in Nanshan Guesthouse. There are two bedrooms, one is out and another is inner, and a living room in addition.)

* 我在南山宾馆订了一套高级屋子,有里外两个卧室,外加一个客厅。

(三)"房子"和"房屋"

"房子"可以指一所房子,也可以指多所房子;"房屋"不能指一所房子,只能指两所或两所以上的房子,因为"房屋"是房子的统称。所以,可以说"一所房子",也可以说"这片房子";而"房屋"可以说成"这些房屋"、"这片房屋"、"这里,房屋的设计都很讲究",却不能说成"这所房屋"、"一所房屋"。("房子"can refer to one house, or more houses. "房屋"can not refer to only one house, but two or more houses, as "房屋"is a general designation for house. We can say "一所房子" or "这片房子", but we cannot say "这所房屋","一所房屋". We can say "这些房屋","这片房屋"or"这里,房屋的设计都很讲究"。)

(四)"房子"、"房屋"、"楼房"

1."房子"、"楼房"可以指个体,即一所房子,也可以作统称,即指两所或两所以上的房子。"房屋"只作统称,不指个体。所以,"房子"、"楼房"都可以用个体量词限定,也可以用非个体量词限定;"房屋"则只能用非个体量词限定,不能用个体量词限定。(Both "房子" and "楼房" can be used to refer to a specific house, or two or more than two houses, but "房屋" can only be used for general reference. "房子" and "楼房" can be qualified by measure words both indicating one or more than one, but "房屋" can't be modified by measure words indicating one.)例如:

　　一所房子　　一座楼房
　　* 一所房屋　* 一座房屋
　　这些房子(these houses)
　　这些楼房(these buildings)
　　这些房屋(these houses)

2. "房子"和"楼房"也有差别。"房子"可以指只有一层的房子,即平房,也可以指两层以上的房子;"楼房"则只能指两层或两层以上的房子。"楼房"相对以高大为特点,所以它的量词用"座";"房子"的量词一般可以用"所"。(Differences exist between "楼房" and "房子". "房子" can refer to house with only one floor, i. e. single-story house. or refer to building of more than two floors; "楼房" can only refer to house with two or more floors; "楼房" is comparatively higher so we use the measure word "座"; for "房子" we use "所" as the measure word.)例如:

　　这所房子真漂亮,环境、地点也很理想。

　　(This house is very beautiful and its surroundings and site are quite ideal.)

　　我住的是一座楼房。

　　广场周围有十几座不同风格的楼房,漂亮极了!

　　(Around the square there are ten odd buildings of different styles. They look very beautiful!)

吩咐 fēnfù　　嘱咐 zhǔfù

〈动词〉表示把自己的主张、愿望告诉给别人,并要求、希望他照着做。

(<verb> Indicates to tell others one's proposition, desire, and ask or hope him to do accordingly.)

"吩咐"和"嘱咐"都有把自己的主张、愿望告诉给别人,并要求、希望他照着做的意思,但是意义、使用场合、语气都有一定的差别,所以一般情况下不能换用。("吩咐" and "嘱咐" mean to tell one's proposition or desire to others, and ask or hope that he could meet the requirement. However, there are differences in meaning, occasion, and tone, so they are uninterchangeable.)

(一) 意义上(In meaning)

"吩咐"、"嘱咐"都多用于长辈对晚辈、上级对下级口头上提出要求或希望,但是"吩咐"词义着重于要求别人做什么,有指派或命令的意味,带有一定的强制性;"嘱咐"词义着重于告诉对方记住应该怎样、不应该怎样。(Both "吩咐" and "嘱咐" mainly indicate the demand or hope of the elder to the young, or the senior to the junior. "吩咐" emphasizes on orally requiring people to do things with the meaning of appointing or ordering, which is coercive. "嘱咐" emphasizes telling people to remember what should be done or what shouldn't be done.)例如:

王大夫吩咐护士立即将病人推进手术室。

还有什么要做的,请吩咐!

(Anything else need be done? I am at your service.)

* 王大夫嘱咐护士立即将病人推进手术室。

* 还有什么要做的,请嘱咐!

奶奶再三嘱咐我,一定要听妈妈的话。

老师嘱咐我,好好复习,考出好成绩来。

* 奶奶再三吩咐我,一定要听妈妈的话。

* 老师吩咐我,好好复习,考出好成绩来。

(二) 使用场合上(In use)

"吩咐"多用于对方听到提出的要求后能马上照做的场合，所以指派对方做的事情，通常是一些非常具体的事情。"嘱咐"则不同，它一般不是马上就做的事情，例如临别的嘱咐，常常要过一段时间再做；或者做的话，也不是很快就能做完的事情；有时嘱咐的内容可能就是一些原则或精神，不是具体的事情。("吩咐" is mostly used on the occasion when the opposite side hears the requirement he will follow immediately. The requirement are usually specific. "嘱咐" is different. It is not necessarily to bring into action at once. Take the enjoining at parting for example, it usually will be accomplished after a period of time, Sometimes the content of enjoining may be some principles or spirit, but not specific things.)例如：

老师吩咐班长把通知传达下去。
老爷吩咐司机把汽车开到门前。
妈妈嘱咐我路上一定要好好照顾爷爷。
老县长嘱咐我们十年内一定要让这个穷山村彻底变个样。
(The old county magistrate enjoins that we change this poor mountain village with a new appearance thoroughly within ten years.)
我嘱咐孩子听老师的话，不要辜负老师的期望。
(I told my child to listen to the teacher's teaching and not to let the teacher down.)

* 老县长吩咐我们十年内一定要让这个穷山村彻底变个样。

* 我吩咐孩子听老师的话，不要辜负老师的期望。

(三) 语气和用法(Tone and usage)

"吩咐"带有一定命令的意味，所以语气显得稍重些；使用时，为了体现命令意味，"吩咐"前一般不带状态性的修饰语。"嘱咐"则带有明显的恳切、温和的语气，含有语重心长的意味；使用时，前面常用"再三"、"一再"、"反复"等词修饰，突出它的语重心长。(In usage, the mood of "吩咐" appears a bit strong. Before "吩咐" there is no modifier of condition. "嘱咐" bears the mood of obvious sincerity and mildness, implying sincere words and earnest wishes; often used with modifiers like "再三", "再" and "反复".)例如：

经理吩咐我来锁门，我怎么能不照办呢？

(The manager instructs me to lock the door. How could I disobey?)

爸爸吩咐我到客厅里陪陪张叔叔。
姐姐一再嘱咐我，一定要把这封信交到大山哥哥手里。
他再三嘱咐我好好养病，爱惜自己的身体。
妈妈反复嘱咐孩子千万不要触摸电源。

(Mother told the kid again and again never to touch the power supply.)

丰富 fēngfù　　富裕 fùyù　　富有 fùyǒu

〈形容词〉表示财富很多。

(< adjective > meaning rich in property.)

(一)"丰富"、"富裕"、"富有"虽然都可以表示财富很多的意思，但是意义上的差别很大，一般不能换用。(Although "丰富", "富裕" and "富有" all indicate being rich in property, the discrepancy in meaning is great, they can not be used exchangeably.)

1."丰富"表示的财富很多主要在于数量上和种类上；"富裕"、"富有"主要不是这个意思。("丰富" mainly indicates being rich in the aspect of quantity and variety, "富裕" and "富有" don't mean this.)例如：

我们的祖国地域辽阔，资源十分丰富。(数量、种类都多)

他们的业余文化生活丰富极了。(种类多)

＊我们的祖国地域辽阔，资源十分富裕/富有。

219

＊他们的业余文化生活富裕/富有极了。

2."富裕"表示的财富很多主要是充足,一般用来形容生活水平高。"丰富"、"富有"主要不是这个意思。("富裕" generally is used to describe higher living standard,"丰富","富有"do not mean that way.)例如:

眼下农民的日子过得越来越富裕了。

(The farmers' life of these days is becoming more and more prosperous.)

我们这里再也不是过去那个穷山村了,现在生活已经很富裕了。

＊眼下农民的日子过得越来越丰富/富有了。

＊我们这里再也不是过去那个穷山村了,现在生活已经很丰富/富有了。

3."富有"主要强调大量的拥有或具有。除了用于财产方面外,还可以用来比喻精神方面。此外,"富有"有较强的书面语色彩,多用于书面语。"丰富"、"富裕"主要不是这种意思。("富有" mainly emphasizes large ownership or possession. Besides being used in the aspect of property, it is also used in the aspect of spirit and is often used in written language,"丰富" and "富裕" do not have such meaning.)例如:

他生于一个十分富有的家庭,不太了解劳动人民的生活。

这里的族长一般是最富有的和最有威望的人。

(The clan elder here is generally the richest and the most authoritative man.)

我们在物质上虽然是贫穷的,但是我们在精神上却是富有的。

(Although we are poor in materials, we are rich in spirits.)

＊这里的族长一般是最丰富的和最有威望的人。

＊我们在物质上虽然是贫穷的,但是我们在精神上却是丰富/富裕的。

（二）"丰富"除了用于财富以外,还可以形容学识、经验、想象力多,思想感情强烈复杂等。"富裕"、"富有"不能这么用。(Besides describing property, "丰富" also describes richness in knowledge, experience, imaginative power and strong and complicated thinking and emotion. "富裕" and "富有" can not be used that way.)例如：

张老师的知识丰富极了。

这位老师傅,虽然没上多少学,但是经验却很丰富。

他是一位想象力十分丰富的画家。

她是一个感情十分丰富却羞于表达的人。

(She is a person of rich feelings but is shy to express herself.)

* 张老师的知识富裕/富有极了。

* 这位老师傅,虽然没上多少学,但是经验却很富裕/富有。

* 他是一位想象力十分富裕/富有的画家。

* 她是一个感情十分富裕/富有却羞于表达的人。

（三）功能上(In function)

"丰富"还可以用作动词,表示"使丰富"的意思,使用时后面要带宾语。"富裕"、"富有"没有"使富裕"、"使富有"的意思,也没有带宾语的用法。("丰富"can also be used as a verb meaning "使丰富" and it has to be followed by an object. "富裕" and "富有" do not mean "使富裕" or "使富有" and usually will not be followed by an object.)例如：

这个老年活动中心极大地丰富了老年人的<u>文化生活</u>。

(This seniors' club has greatly enriched the cultural life of the old people.)

除了工作,还应该想办法丰富自己的<u>业余生活</u>。

这些游戏有助于丰富孩子们的<u>想象力</u>。

(These games are conducive to enrich the children's imagination.)

* 经济的发展极大地富裕／富有了人们的物质生活。

221

* 除了工作,还应该想办法富有自己的生活。
* 这些游戏有助于富有孩子们的想象力。

风景 fēngjǐng　　景象 jǐngxiàng　　情景 qíngjǐng
〈名词〉 <noun>

"风景"、"景象"、"情景"都可以指某一现象,但是由于所指对象、范围不同,一般的情况下不能换用。(Although "风景","景象","情景" can refer to a sight. They refer to different objects, range, usually they can not be used exchangeably.)

(一)"风景"主要指可供观赏的山水、花草、树木、楼台等景色、景物及雨雪等自然现象。它最突出的特点:一是大自然中的,一是从观赏的角度看的,一是相对静的现象。(Mainly "风景" refers to the scenery like mountains and rivers, flowers and plants, trees and high buildings, and the natural phenomena like rain and snow for people to enjoy. Its main characteristics are: it refers to nature, is seen from the point of view of appreciation, and is a relatively still phenomenon.)例如:

　　这里的风景可真美啊!
　　几个外宾正在欣赏西湖的风景。
　　从沿路的风景可以看出这是一个十分美丽的海滨城市。
* 这里的景象/情景可真美啊!
* 几个外宾正在欣赏西湖的景象/情景。
* 从沿路的情景可以看出这是一个十分美丽的海滨城市。

(二)"景象"则不限于大自然中的,它可以指工厂、农村、集体、社会等一些较大场面中呈现出来的现象。它的特点:一是大的场面,一是带有"呈现出来"的这样一种动态的现象。("景象" indicates the phenomena appearing in some vast scenes like in factories, countryside, collectives and society, etc. Its characteristics: it refers to a vast scene, and is a dynamic state of phenomenon coming into sight.)例如:

农田里一派丰收的景象。

城市不大,但是到处充满着生机,到处是欣欣向荣的景象。

(The city is not very big, but everywhere is full of life and prosperity.)

草原上这种万马奔腾的景象真壮观啊!

(What a magnificent scenery it is with ten thousand horses galloping ahead on the grasslands.)

* 农田里一派丰收的风景/情景。
* 城市不大,但是到处充满着生机,到处是欣欣向荣的风景/情景。
* 草原上这种万马奔腾的风景真壮观啊!

(三)"情景"不光可以指某些景象,还可以指某些情况。它的特点是要有具体的时间、地点等,指在这种具体的条件下出现的某种情况或现象。("情景" can not only refers to some scenes, but also some situations. It is characterized by providing specific time or places, referring to certain case or phenomenon that presents in the specific condition.)例如:

他在机场为我送行的情景又浮现在我的眼前。

(The scene that he saw me off at the airport appears before my eyes again.)

我戴着博士帽到台上领取学位证书的情景,至今还记忆犹新。

(The scene that I ran onto the stage wearing the doctoral cap to receive my certificate of the degree remains fresh in my memory till today.)

地震发生时的情景,我还清楚地记得。

你把当时的情景向大家描述一下。

* 他在机场为我送行的风景/景象又浮现在我的眼前。
* 地震发生时的风景/景象,我还清楚地记得。
* 你把事情发生时的风景/景象向大家描述一下。

223

G

改 gǎi   改变 gǎibiàn

〈动词〉表示更改、变更的意思。

(< verb > indicating to correct, to change.)

"改"、"改变"都有更改、变更的意思,但是由于还有其他意义上的差别,单音节、双音节的差别,结构上的差别,所以在许多情况下不能换用。("改" and "改变" both have the connotation of correction or change. Because of their differences in meaning, in syllables as well as in structure, they can not be used interchangeably in many cases.)

(一)"改"在表示更改、变动具体时间、地点、路线、方式等时,只要不受单、双音节的影响,就可以跟"改变"换用。(When "改" indicates changing of specific time, place, route, way, etc., it can be substituted by "改变" as long as there is no restriction of single syllable or double syllable.)例如:

开会地点改了　　上车时间改了
开会地点改变了　上车时间改变了
改航线了　　　　改一下方式
改变航线了　　　改变一下方式

但是,表示使抽象事物发生变化时,一般多用"改变",少用或不用"改"。(While indicating the abstract things are made to change, "改变" is generally used. "改" is seldom used, or not used.)例如:

想办法把这种不利的情况改变一下。
你需要改变一下对他的看法。
他的态度明显地改变了。
* 想办法把这种不利的情况改一下。
* 你需要改一下对他的看法。

(二)"改"还有一些"改变"没有的意义。("改" has more

meanings beyond "改变".)

1. "改"有修改的意思,"改变"没有。("改" means to revise, while "改变" doesn't.)例如:

老师正在改作文,别去打扰老师。

小王现在正在制图车间改图纸呢,一会儿才能来。

作业不多,可改起来挺麻烦的。

(The homework is not much but it is really troublesome to do the correction.)

* 老师正在改变作文,别去打扰老师。

* 小王现在正在制图车间改变图纸呢,一会儿才能来。

* 作业不多,可改变起来挺麻烦的。

2. "改"还有改正的意思,"改变"没有这种意思。("改" also means to correct, while "改变" doesn't.)例如:

有错就改,改了就好。

(Just amend if you make mistakes, and everything would be OK.)

这里还有几处错误,你给改一改。

你得好好地改一改你的坏脾气。

(You ought to amend your nasty temper thoroughly.)

* 有错就改变,改变了就好。

* 这里还有几处错误,你给改变改变。

3. "改"还有改换成的意思,"改变"没有这种意思。例如:

("改" means to change into, while "改变" doesn't.)

本来是小张值班,他身体不舒服,临时改我了。

(Xiao Zhang should have been on duty. Because he didn't feel well, I have taken his place temporarily.)

星期三的参观改星期天了,大家互相通知一下。

* 本来是小张值班,他身体不舒服,临时改变我了。

* 星期三的参观改变星期天了,大家互相通知一下。

(三)"改"和"改变"在意义相同的情况下,有时受到单、双音节的影响,也会出现不能换用的情况。(In case "改"和"改变" have the same meaning, occasionally affected by single syllable or double syllable, they can not be used exchangeably.)例如:

"改"是单音节词,可以跟单音节词结合;"改变"是双音节词,要跟双音节词结合。("改" is a single syllable word, can be combined with a single syllable word; "改变" is a double syllable word, it should be used together with other double syllable words.)例如:

才几天的工夫,她就瘦得改了样。

(Just in several days' time she becomes so thin that she has changed her appearance.)

原来计划明天走,因为车有问题,又改期了。

* 才几天的工夫,她就瘦得改变了样。
* 原来计划明天走,因为车有问题,又改变期了。

才几天的工夫,她就瘦得改变了模样。

原来计划明天走,因为车有问题,又改变日期了。

(四)由于意义上的差别,也形成结构上的不同。(Discrepancy in meaning leads to different structures.)

结构上最突出的是关于带补语的问题。"改"可以带结果补语、情状补语、介词词组补语等;"改变"一般不能带这几种补语。(The remarkable thing in structure is the requiring of complements. "改" can have a resultative complement, situational complement, prepositional complement, while "改变" does not usually require such complements.)例如:

那件衣服让她改好了。

这个时间改得不错。

这几个地方改得很有意思。

今天的报告改在大会议室了。

226

* 那件衣服让她改变好了。
　　* 这个时间改变得不错。
　　* 这几个地方改变得很有意思。
　　* 今天的报告改变在大会议室了。
(五)功能上的差别。(Discrepancy in function.)
　　"改变"可以活用为名词,并具有相应的功能;"改"没有这种用法。("改变"can be used as a noun with corresponding functions, "改"does not.)例如:
　　她的服务态度有了显著的改变。
　　法律就是法律,不能因为领导的改变而改变。
　　(Law is just law. It can't be changed with the change of the leader.)
　　形势的突然改变是我们没有预料到的。
　　(The sudden change of the situation is what we didn't expect.)
　　* 她的服务态度有了显著的改。
　　* 法律就是法律,不能因为领导的改而改变。
　　* 形势的突然改是我们没有预料到的。

改变 gǎibiàn　　改进 gǎijìn　　改善 gǎishàn

〈动词〉使原有的情况发生变化。

(<verb> cause the existing situation to change.)

(一)"改变"、"改进"、"改善"都有使原有的情况发生变化的意思,但是变化以后的情况有所不同。("改变","改进"and"改善"all have the meaning to cause the existing situation to change, but with different results.)

　　"改变"不管变化的发展方向,而侧重于有较大的或根本性的变化,所以"改变"的情况有可能跟原来完全不同。"改进"和"改善"则不同,它们不会是把原有的完全地改变了,而是改变一部分,改变时都要突出变化的方向,即在原有的基础上向好的方向发展,使之有好的变化。(Regardless of the direction to which the change develops, "改变" emphasizes the bigger or fundamental changes, therefore the result of "改变" is possible to be totally different with what the situation was before. "改进" and "改善" both indicate a partial change, not a complete change of the original state. And they emphasize the changing direction, that is to say, they refer to a change of the original state for the better.)例如:

展览的地点已经改变了,你知道吗?

我们一定要改变这种不利的被动局面。

(We must change this unfavourable passive situation.)

老师们听取了学生们的意见,正在研究改进教学方法。

你们俩负责把这个工艺流程再改进改进,使它既能保证质量,又能加快速度。

(You two are resspossible for the improvement of this technological process to enssure its quality as well as increase of the speed.)

想办法改善一下劳动条件,使工人们的劳动有安全保障。

(Try to find a way out to improve the work conditions so that the workers can get their safety guarantee.)

星期天食堂总要给大家改善一下伙食。

(二)"改变"、"改进"、"改善"使用的范围也有所不同。("改变","改进" and "改善" can be used in different range.)

1."改变"可以用于具体的时间、地点、路线、计划等,也可以用于抽象一些的看法、观念、态度、作风、方式等。"改进"、"改善"不能用于具体的时间、地点、路线等,也不能用于观念、看法等这种眼睛看不到的抽象事物。("改变" can be used for the specific time, places, routes and plans, etc. and also for a bit abstract things as views, ideas, attitudes, style and pattern. "改进" and "改善" can neither be used for the specific time, places, routes, etc. nor be used for ideas, views, etc. these abstract things that can't be seen by eyes.)例如：

从去年起,我们的作息时间就改变了。

不知为什么飞机改变了航线。

得把你的观念彻底改变一下了,否则你是不可能领导好这个工厂的。

(You ought to change your ideas thoroughly, or it is impossible for you to exercise leadership properly in this factory.)

我们要改变工作作风,深入到基层去,不能总坐在办公室里。

(We have to change our style of work to go down to the grass-roots units. It is not right sitting in the office all the time.)

* 从去年起,我们的作息时间就改进/改善了。

* 不知为什么飞机改进/改善了航线。

* 得把你的观念彻底改进/改善一下了,否则你是不可能领导好这个工厂的。

2."改进"一般多用于跟做法有关的工作、作风、方法、措施等。"改善"一般不用于这些方面。("改进" is generally used with work, style, method and measure, etc. that relate to course of action.)例如：

我们需要认真地改进一下我们的工作。

希望领导能改进工作作风,到基层去了解一些真实的情况。

改进工作方法,以适应新时期工作的需要。

(Improve the method of working in order to suit the needs of the work in the new period.)

* 我们需要认真地改善一下我们的工作。

* 希望领导能改善工作作风,到基层去了解一些真实的情况。

* 改善工作方法,以适应新时期工作的需要。

3."改善"一般多用于生活、条件、环境、待遇、关系等;"改进"一般不用于这些方面。("改善" is generally used for life, condition, environment, treatment and relationship, etc.)例如:

要想尽一切办法改善人民的生活。
我厂的生产条件已有很大的改善。
知识分子的待遇有了明显的改善。
为了改善两国关系,两国首脑都做出了一定的让步。
(For the sake of improving the relationship of the two countries, the heads of both sides have made certain concessions.)

* 要想尽一切办法改进人民的生活。
* 我厂的生产条件已有很大的改进。
* 知识分子的待遇有了明显的改进。
* 为了改进两国关系,两国首脑都做出了一定的让步。

感动 gǎndòng   感激 gǎnjī

〈动词〉 < verb >

"感动"、"感激"都可以表示内心所引起的强烈的感情,但是这两个词所表示的主动、被动关系完全不同,意义上也有很大差别,从而形成结构上较大的差别,所以一般情况下不能换用。("感动" and "感激" both mean an expression of strong feelings, but they have differences in active and passive relations, in meaning and structure. So, in most cases, they can not be exchangeable.)

(一)"感动"和"感激"表示的主动、被动关系完全不同。("感动" and "感激" are different in active and passive relations.)

1."感动"表示的实际上是一种被动关系,产生"感动"这种感情的人是受感动的,即人一定要受到外界的刺激、影响,由此而产生某种强烈感情。因此用"感动"作句子成分的句子,句中常常可以用"受"、"被"等词。(Sentences with "感动" often use the words actually describing a passive relation. People are stimulated or affected by the external world and from this some strong emotion comes into being. Therefore, in a sentence with "感动",

"受"or"被"is often used.)例如：

她感动地连声说："谢谢你！谢谢你！"（她被某事感动。）

听了这番话，我深受感动。（我被话感动。）

战士们都被感动得流下了热泪。（战士们被某事感动。）

当感动者作句子宾语时，即"感动"带宾语时，表示的是"使……感动"（本质上还是"被感动"）的意思。(When the person who is moved becomes the object of a sentence, i.e."感动"is followed by an object, it means"使…感动".)例如：

他的英雄事迹感动了孩子们。

（他的事迹使孩子们感动。）

（孩子们被他的事迹感动。）

他的真诚感动了我。（他的真诚使我感动。）

（我被他的真诚感动。）

2."感激"则不同，它表示的不是受动关系，而是主动关系。它是由于某种原因而自发产生对他人的感情。因此，在用"感激"的句子中，不能用"受"、"被"等这种表示被动关系的词。(What"感激"indicates is not the passive relation, but active relation. It is a feeling that spontaneously comes into being due to some reason. Therefore, in the sentence with"感激", words indicating passive relations like"受"and"被"can't be used.)例如：

在我困难的时候，是他帮助了我，所以我很感激他。（我感激他。）

民警帮她找到走失的儿子，她对民警感激不尽。（她感激民警。）

(The police helped her find her lost son so she felt deeply grateful to them.)

＊在我困难的时候，是他帮助了我，所以我被感激他。（＊我被他感激。）

＊民警帮她找到走失的儿子,她对民警受感激。(＊她受民警感激。)

(二)"感动"和"感激"意义上的差别。(Discrepancy between "感动" and "感激" in meaning.)

"感动"是指由于外界事物的刺激或影响使人在内心里产生感情的震荡,这种震荡可能是敬慕的,也可能是钦佩的等等,总之是人的一种自身感受。"感激"不同,它一定是得到别人某种帮助、关怀、教育等益处,由此而对帮助、关怀他的人产生一种带有谢意的好感,是对他人的一种情感。("感动" indicates a kind of emotional vibration grows in the heart owing to the external stimulation or influence. This kind of vibration might be respecting and admiring and might be esteeming, etc. In a word, it is a self-experience of people. "感激" indicates when a person receives benefits from another person such as help, care, education, etc., he has a favourable impression with gratefulness on the person he gets benefits from. It is a feeling towards others.)例如:

　　他的诚恳感动了我。(我←——感动)
　　他的这种高尚情操感动了每一个人。(人←——感动)
　　(His lofty sentiment moved everyone.)
　　他帮小李找到了丢失的钱包,小李十分感激他。(感激——→他)
　　她很感激政府对她的关怀。(感激——→政府)
　　(She is deeply grateful to the government for its concern.)

(三)结构上、用法上的差别。(Differences in structure and in use.)

1. "感动"的主语可以是人,也可以是事迹、话语、精神、行为等跟人有关的事物;"感激"的主语只能是人,不能是事物。("感动"'s subject can be people, can also be things, remarks, spirit, act and something relative to people; "感激"'s subject can only be

people, but not things.)例如：

他的这种无私无畏的精神感动了在场的每一个群众。
(His selfless and fearless spirit moved everyone present.)
这部影片感动了多少少男少女的心。
* 他的这种无私无畏的精神感激了在场的每一个群众。
* 这部影片感激了多少少男少女的心。

"感动"的主语可以是不表示人的主语,但是如果带宾语的话,宾语却一定是表示人的宾语,因为事实上,"敬慕"、"钦佩"等情感是宾语的情感。〔The subject of "感动" does not have to be people. But if it is followed by an object, it must be an object referring to people. In fact, verbs like "敬慕(admire)" and "钦佩(esteem)", etc. indicate the feeling of the object.〕例如：

雄伟的长城感动了他。(他 —— 感动)
战士们的精神感动了我。(我 —— 感动)
* 他感动了雄伟的长城。
* 我感动了战士们的精神。

2. "感动"可以用于"被"字句、"把"字句；"感激"一般不可以。("感动" is used in the "被" sentence or the "把" sentence; but "感激" can't.)例如：

孩子们都被感动了。
大娘被感动得不知道说什么好。
把她感动哭了。
* 孩子们都被感激了。
* 把大娘感激得不知道说什么好。
* 把她感激哭了。

3. "感激"可以用在用"对"引进对象的句子里；"感动"一般不可以。("感激" can be used in the sentence in which the object is introduced by "对"; and "感动" can't be used in this way.)例如：

老师如此关照他的孩子,他对老师感激不尽。
政府及时运来救灾物资,灾民们对政府十分感激。

233

* 老师如此关照他的孩子,他对老师很感动。
* 政府及时运来救灾物资,灾民们对政府十分感动。

4."感动"可以作"受"的宾语,"感激"不可以;"感激"可以作"表示"的宾语,"感动"不可以。("感动" can be the object of "受", and "感激" cannot. While "感激" can be the object of "表示", "感动" cannot.)例如:

在场的群众深受感动。

* 在场的群众深受激动。

她对含辛茹苦把她抚养成人的母亲表示感激。

(She feels grateful to her mother who has endured all kinds of hardship to bring her daughter up.)

* 她对含辛茹苦把她抚养成人的母亲表示感动。

感动 gǎndòng　　激动 jīdòng

〈动词〉表示受到外界的影响而产生感情的震荡。

(< verb > indicating an emotional shock caused by the external influence.)

"感动"、"激动"都是表示心理活动的动词,都可以表示受到外界的影响而产生感情的震荡的意思。但是,"感动"、"激动"所表示的成分间的关系不完全相同,意义也有差别,词语的配合关系也有不同。("感动"and "激动" are verbs indicating one's activity in mind. Both can indicate the meaning of growing emotional vibration by the influence from the external world. But the relations between the compositions which "感动"and "激动" indicate are not completely the same as well as in meaning, and sometimes the coordinating relations of the words and phrases are also different.)

(一) 表示不同的关系。(When indicating different relations.)

"感动"在本质上表示的是一种被动关系,即人受到外界的影响、刺激而感情震荡;"激动"在本质上是一种使动关系,即外界的影响使人产生感情的震荡。从下面的转换中,我们可以看到这一点。(Essentially "感动" refers to a passive relationship, indicating being emotionally shocked by the influence or stimulation of the external world, while "激动" emphasizes a causative relationship, namely the external influence makes people feel emotionally shocked. We will see this point in the following transformations.)

  他的话感动了我。—— 他的话使我感动。
       —— 我被他的话感动了。
  听了他这番温暖人心的话,我很激动。—— 他的话使我激动。
(Having heard his warm speaking, I feel deeply moved.)
       —— * 我被他的话激动了。

  可见,用"感动"的句子,可以转换成使动关系,也可以转换成被动关系;用"激动"的句子则只能转换成使动关系。所以,用"感动"的句子,句子里常常可以用"被"、"受"等词;用"激动"的句子,一般不这么用。(A sentence with "感动" can be changed into a causative relationship and a passive relationship, but the sentence with "激动" can only be changed into a causative relationship. Therefore, in this kind of sentence, "被" or "受" is generally used; while "被" or "受" is not used in the sentence with "激动".) 例如:

  乡亲们的热情,使战士们深受感动。
  她被这激动人心的场面感动得流下了热泪。
  * 乡亲们的热情,使战士们深受激动。
  * 她被这个场面激动得流下了热泪。

(二) 意义不完全相同。(Not completely the same in meaning.)

  "感动"所说的感情震荡,含有对使之感情震荡的人、事物等敬慕、钦佩、崇敬等情感;"激动"只是内心强烈的震荡、冲动,不含有敬慕、钦佩、崇敬等情感。("感动" implies the feelings of respect, admiration, esteem and reverence towards the people and things that have made feelings vibrated; "激动" merely describes strong innermost vibration and impulse and doesn't imply the feelings of admiration, esteem and reverence, etc.)

(三) 词语的配合关系也不同。(Being different in coordinating relation.)

1.用"感动"的句子,受感动的一定是人,表示人的词或者在主语的位置上,或者在宾语的位置上。用"激动"的句子,使激动的不一定是人,可以是跟人有关的心情、感情、人心等。(In the sentence with "感动", definitely the ones who are moved are people, and the words for people are usually in position of subject or object. While in the sentence of "激动", the ones who cause people excited are not necessarily people, and those can be mood, emotion or the will of the people.)例如:

听了他的事迹,大家感动得热泪盈眶。(大家感动。)
他舍己为人的精神感动了我。(我感动。)
(His spirit sacrificing his own interests for the sake of others moved me.) [I am moved.]
今天大家的心情格外激动。(心情激动。)
(Today everyone feels especially excited.) [Exciting mood.]
同学们的情绪都特别激动。(情绪激动。)
* 今天大家的心情格外感动。
* 同学们的情绪都特别感动。

2."感动"可以带表示人的宾语;"激动"一般不这么用,或者说极少这么用,它连带的宾语除了表示任指的"什么"以外,一般情况下,只有"人心"这个比较固定的用法。["感动"can be followed by objects of people, while "激动" is not generally used in this way or is rarely used. The object of "激动", under general condition, is only "人心"(the will of the people), a set phrase, besides "什么"(what), which is an indefinite reference.]例如:

老师的话感动了小王。(感动了小王。)
* 老师的话激动了小王。
这真是一个激动人心的好消息。(激动人心。)

* 这真是一个感动人心的好消息。

你激动什么？这有什么好激动的？

(Why are you so excited? Is there anything worth exciting?)

感到 gǎndào　　觉得 juéde

〈动词〉< verb >

"感到"、"觉得"都可以表示人对外界某种具体或抽象的事物有所感觉、有所认识。有时可以通用，但是由于意义上有一定差别，通用时，侧重点稍有差别；有时则不能通用。("感到"and "觉得"both indicate people's feeling or knowledge that is attained or learnt from some specific or abstract objects in the external world. Sometimes they are exchangeable, but since there is certain difference in meaning, when being exchanged, the parts stressed are slightly different, and sometimes even unexchangeable in use.)

(一) 意义上(In meaning)

表示通过身体器官得到某种感受时，"感到"、"觉得"常常可以通用，但是"感到"更加突出来自器官的感受。(When indicating some feeling attained through physical organs, "感到" and "觉得" are exchangeable, but "感到" lays strong emphasis on the organic feeling.)例如：

她感到/觉得春天很温暖。

我感到/觉得身体不舒服。

我感到/觉得这样活着才有意义。

但是，如果强调由于某种客观因素、条件等使人有身体的、心理的感觉时，应该用"感到"。(But "感到" should be used if emphasizing the physical and psychological feelings caused by some objective factor and condition, etc.)例如：

父亲也能流泪？这使我感到很吃惊。

(How could father shed tears? This makes me greatly surprised.)

237

孩子上了名牌大学,这使她感到很体面。

(Her child has been enrolled by the famous university and this makes her feel honorable.)

我当上了保卫人民的警察,感到很光荣。

如果不强调从某种客观因素、条件等中得到感受,而只侧重于个人对客观事物的一种看法、想法,应该用"觉得"。(If the emphasis is not laid on the feeling attained from some objective factors or conditions, but laid on the individual's view or idea of the objective things, "觉得" should be used.)例如:

我觉得生活对我很不公平。

(I think life is unfair to me.)

我觉得你不应该这么草率行事。

她觉得妈妈还是在把她当做孩子。

(二) 用法上(In use)

1."感到"有"感觉到"的意思,所以在特殊的语言环境中,"感到"后面不带宾语可以说得通,"觉得"一般不能这样用。("感到"also means "感觉到", so in the special language environment, it is possible if there is no object follows. "觉得" cannot be used like this.)例如:

他们好像不太欢迎我们,你感到了吗?

她好像有什么心事,你感到了吗?

* 他们好像不太欢迎我们,你觉得了吗?
* 她好像有什么心事,你觉得了吗?

2."感到"有一定的感受的意思,所以可以用"深深"作状语修饰语;"觉得"主要表示以为、认为等这种个人认识,所以不能用"深深"作状语。(When "感到"means having experienced in certain way, "深深"can be used as an adverbial modifier. While "觉得" mainly indicates personal thinking such as "take something as" or "in one's opinion", "深深"cannot be used as an adverbial.)例如:

这几年的发展使他们深深感到实干才是唯一的出路。

(These years' development makes them profoundly feel that doing solid work is their only way out.)

* 这几年的发展使他们深深觉得实干才是唯一的出路。

3."感到"有一定的感受、感觉的意思,它前面可以用"应该"表示合乎情理;"觉得"尤其在表示以为、认为等这种个人认识时,一般不用"应该"来突出个人的一种认识。("感到" also means having certain experience of feeling and "应该" can be used before it to show something that is reasonable. Especially when "觉得" is to indicate personal thinking such as "take something as" or "in one's opinion", "应该" is not used to emphasize the personal thinking.)例如:

你应该感到这样做对你很不利。

生活条件这么好,你应该感到满足了。

* 你应该觉得这样做对你很不利。

* 生活条件这么好,你应该觉得满足了。

感觉 gǎnjué   感受 gǎnshòu

〈动词〉< verb >
〈名词〉< noun >

(一)"感觉"和"感受"都可以作动词用,都可以表示外界事物引起人的一种反应的意思,不同的是:(Both "感觉" and "感受" can be used as verbs to indicate a kind of reaction of people caused by the things of the external world. The differences between the two words are:)

1."感觉"既可以是具体的,也可以是抽象的。无论具体还是抽象,都是人的感官对客观事物的一种直接的反应。("感觉" is either concrete or abstract. No matter being concrete or abstract, they all mean a direct reaction that man's sensory organs feel about the objective things.)例如:

你感觉怎么样? 好一点儿了吗? —— 我感觉好多了。

239

你冷吗？我怎么感觉那么冷啊？

这间屋子你感觉怎么样？——我感觉很舒服。

以上都是人的感官具体感受到的，"感受"不能用于这种感官的具体感受。(The above feelings are attained by people, while "感受"can't be used for this specific sensory experience.)例如：

* 你感受怎么样？好一点儿了吗？——我感受好多了。
* 你冷吗？我怎么感受那么冷啊？
* 这间屋子你感受怎么样？——我感受很舒服。

下面"感觉"表示的是抽象的感受，通过人的感官使人产生某种认识、看法等。"感受"不能用于这种认识、看法类的地方。(The following indicates the abstract feelings, that is, some understanding or idea, etc. grows through people's sensory organs. "感受" cannot be used in this way.)例如：

你感觉长城怎么样？——我感觉长城很雄伟。

我感觉李彬是一个很不错的小伙子。

我感觉这件事不是那么简单的。

(I feel that the case is not that simple.)

* 你感受长城怎么样？——我感受长城很雄伟。
* 我感受李彬是一个很不错的小伙子。
* 我感受这件事不是那么简单的。

2."感受"主要不是强调感官的感受，而是侧重于人内心深处的体会、感触等，它一般是指人处身于某个环境中，在这当中的体会和感触，所以所"感受"的一般多是抽象的事物。这种侧重于体会、感触的事物，不能用"感觉"表示。(Essentially, "感觉"doesn't emphasize organic feeling, but people's innermost experience and feeling, etc. It generally indicates that one is in certain condition and his experience and feeling there, therefore the things being felt generally are abstract. The things that emphasize on experience or feeling can't be expressed by "感觉".)例如：

大家多给他一些关怀,让他好好感受一下集体的温暖。
　　(We will give more care to him and let him just feel the warmth of the collective.)
　　我们去南方走一走,感受感受南方的春天怎么样?
　　半年多国外的生活使我感受到很多很多。
　　* 大家多给他一些关怀,让他好好感觉一下集体的温暖。
　　* 我们去南方走一走,感觉感觉南方的春天怎么样?
　　* 半年多国外的生活使我感觉到很多很多。

(二)"感觉"和"感受"都可以用作名词,意义的本质跟上面是一样的,只是转换成名词的功能而已。("感觉" and "感受" both are used as nouns and the meanings are the same as in the above cases, but their parts of speech have to be transformed into nouns.)例如:
　　长城给人一种雄伟的感觉。
　　李彬这个人给你的感觉怎么样?
　　* 长城给人一种雄伟的感受。
　　* 李彬这个人给你的感受怎么样?
　　同样去了五台山,可是大家的感受完全不同。
　　该看的都看了,下面大家谈谈感受吧。
　　虽然到乡下生活才一个来月,可是我的感受却不少。
　　* 虽然到乡下生活才一个来月,可是我的感觉却不少。

　　有时,"感觉"、"感受"可以出现在结构形式完全相同的句子里,这时一定要注意它们不同的意义。(Sometimes "感觉" or "感受" is used in the sentences which are completely the same in construction or in pattern, and here attention has to be paid to their different meanings.)例如:
　　你有什么感觉? —— 问的是感官的具体感受或者认识、看法等。
　　(The specific feelings or understanding and views from the sensory organs are being asked.)
　　回答可能是:——(感觉)胸闷。

————(感觉)一阵阵发冷。

————(感觉)这个计划有点儿太空了。

你有什么感受？———— 问的是内心的体会、感触等。

(The innermost experiences and feelings, etc. are being asked.)

回答可能是:————(我感受到)大自然是那么的美。

———— 感受多了,不过最突出的感受是:山里人真朴实啊！朴实得让人感动。

〔The answers might be:

————(I feel that)The nature is so beautiful.

———— I was impressed greatly. But the thing impressed me most is that the mountain people are really plain! Their plainness moved me.〕

感谢 gǎnxiè　　谢谢 xièxie　　谢 xiè

〈动词〉表示对别人的好意或帮助表示谢意。

(< verb > indicating the gratefulness one feels to other's kindness or help.)

(一)"感谢"和"谢谢"

1.表示方式有所不同:(Differences in the ways of expression:)

"感谢"可以用口头表示,但是不限于口头,还可以用物质的赠送或行动等来表示。"谢谢"一般限于口头的表示,有时仅仅是一种礼貌的表示。("感谢"can be expressed orally, but it is not limited to this, for gift presenting or action means the same, "谢谢" otherwise is generally limited to the oral expression and sometimes it is merely an expression of politeness.)例如:

感谢领导支持我们的工作。

人家帮了你那么大的忙,你应该准备一份厚礼感谢一下人家。

(Since they have given a lot of help, you should prepare

generous gifts to show your gratitude.)

  最好的感谢父母的方式是好好学习,成为一个有用的人材。

  谢谢大家为我送行。

  往前一直走就到百货大楼了。——谢谢。

  * 最好的谢谢父母的方式是好好学习,成为一个有用的人材。

2.色彩不同:(Differences in flavour:)

"感谢"有郑重的色彩,多用于正式的场合,口语、书面语都可以用;"谢谢"没有郑重色彩,使用起来随意性较强,多用于口语,尤其是一些临时的表示谢意的场合。("感谢"is of serious flavour and mainly used on formal occasions and in either oral or written language. "谢谢"is more casual in use, mainly used in the oral language, especially on the temporary occasion to express gratitude.)例如:

  我们非常感谢贵饭店的热情款待!(正式的场合,郑重地表示。)

  对于你们的援助,我们深表感谢!(正式的场合,郑重地表示。)

  我去取报,顺便把你的报也取来呀?——好,谢谢!(这里随意性较强,又多出于礼貌,一般不能用"感谢"。)

3.用法上的差别:(Differences in use:)

(1)"感谢"可以用于口头直接表示,也可以用于客观叙述;"谢谢"多用于口头直接表示,一般不用于客观叙述。("感谢"is either used directly in oral language or in objective recounting. "谢谢"is essentially used directly in oral language, but generally not used in the objective narration.)例如:

  他站在医院门口,一再感谢张医生。

  乡亲们正在感谢救援他们的解放军战士。

  * 他站在医院门口,一再谢谢张医生。

＊乡亲们正在谢谢救援他们的解放军战士。

(2)"感谢"可以接受程度副词的修饰;"谢谢"不能。("感谢" can be modified by adverbs of degree, but "谢谢"can't.)例如:

　　我们非常感谢你们。

　　他很感谢李老师。

　　乡亲们十分感谢战士们。

　　＊我们非常谢谢你们。

　　＊他很谢谢李老师。

　　＊乡亲们十分谢谢战士们。

(3)"感谢"可以带补语;"谢谢"不能带补语。("感谢" can be followed by complements, and 谢谢 can't.)例如:

　　我只帮了他一点儿忙,可是他却对我感谢得<u>不得了</u>。

　　(I have just given him a little help, but he feels extremely grateful to me.)

　　你怎么感谢<u>起</u>我<u>来了</u>,是他帮的你。

　　(How could you thank me? It is him that gave you the help.)

　　是他救了孩子的命啊!我一定要好好感谢<u>一下</u>他。

　　＊我只帮了他一点儿忙,可是他却对我谢谢得不得了。

　　＊你怎么谢谢起我来了,是他帮的你。

　　＊是他救了孩子的命啊!我一定要好好谢谢一下他。

(4)"感谢"后面可以接助词"过";"谢谢"不可以。("感谢" can be followed by the particle "过", but "谢谢" can't.)例如:

　　我已经代你感谢过他们了。

　　＊我已经代你谢谢过他们了。

(5)"感谢"可以直接加以否定;"谢谢"除了疑问、反问、假设等特殊的句式外,一般不能直接加以否定。("感谢" can be negated directly. Except in the special sentence patterns as interrogative sentence, rhetorical question and presuming sentence, etc., "谢谢" can't be directly negated.)例如:

不必感谢我们,这是我们应该做的。
我代表公司感谢你们! —— 不用感谢。
* 不必谢谢我们,这是我们应该做的。
我代表公司谢谢你们! —— * 不用谢谢。
(I will say thank you on behalf of our company.)

(二)"谢谢"和"谢"

"谢谢"和"谢"意义上基本上是相同的。用法上,都不能接受程度副词的修饰。(Basically "谢谢" and "谢" have the same meaning. Neither can be modified by adverbs of degree.)例如:

* 我们十分谢谢/谢你们。
* 我在这里非常谢谢大家的帮助。
* 他很谢医生救了他的命。

除以上相同的用法外,它们在用法上还有不少差别。(Except being used in the same way as mentioned above, "谢谢" and "谢" also have quite many differences in use.)

1."谢谢"多用于口头直接表示,一般不用于客观叙述;"谢"则一般只用于客观叙述,不用来直接向对方说。("谢谢" is mainly used directly in the oral way and not the objective narration, but "谢" is generally used in the objective narration, but not used directly with the opposite side.)例如:

谢谢你   谢谢大家
谢谢各位捧场(Thank everyone for the company.)
谢谢你的关照
* 谢你 * 谢大家 * 谢各位捧场 * 谢你的关照
他又在谢师母呢。
老伯谢了谢帮他的民警,拉着孙子走了。
* 他又在谢谢师母呢。
* 老伯谢谢了帮他的民警,拉着孙子走了。

2."谢"可以带补语;"谢谢"不能带补语。("谢" can be followed by a complement, but "谢谢" can't.)例如:

你们怎么谢<u>起</u>他来了,他不是张师傅。

谢<u>错</u>了? 咳! 谢了<u>半天</u>白谢了。

(Did I express my thankfulness to the wrong person? Damn it! I said so many thanks for nothing.)

* 你们怎么谢谢起他来了,他不是张师傅。
* 谢谢错了? 咳! 谢了半天白谢了。

3."谢"后面可以接助词"了"、"过";"谢谢"不可以。("谢" can be followed by particles "了"and "过", but "谢谢"can't.)例如:

他谢了王大夫,又去谢司机。

我已经谢过他们了。

* 他谢谢了王大夫,又去谢司机。
* 我已经谢谢过他们了。

4."谢"前面可以加表示方式的状语或其他单音节状语;"谢谢"不可以。(The adverbial of means or other monosyllable adverbials can be added before "谢", and "谢谢"can't.)例如:

你这样谢我们,叫我们很难为情。

你们这样关照我们,叫我们怎么谢你们才好?

我们敬谢各位先生!

白谢了一顿,一点儿好处也没得到。

(We have expressed our gratefulness for nothing. There isn't any benefit at all.)

* 你这样谢谢我们,叫我们很难为情。
* 你们这样关照我们,叫我们怎么谢谢你们才好?
* 我们敬谢谢各位先生!
* 白谢谢了一顿,一点儿好处也没得到。

"谢"有时还可以单独用在"道"前;"谢谢"不可以。(Sometimes, "谢" can also be used separately before "道", and "谢谢" can't.)例如:

他连忙谢道:"亏了你们帮忙,谢谢! 谢谢!"

* 他连忙谢谢道:"亏了你们帮忙,谢谢! 谢谢!"

5."谢"可以直接加以否定;"谢谢"除了疑问、反问、假设等特殊的句式外,一般不能直接加以否定。("谢"can be negated directly. Except in the special sentence patterns as interrogative sentence, rhetorical question and presuming sentence, etc., "谢谢" can't be directly negated.)例如:

你别谢我,不是我帮的你。
谢谢你的照顾! ——别客气,不用谢!
甭谢了,那么客气干什么?
谢谢了! ——不谢!
* 你别谢谢我,不是我帮的你。
* 谢谢你的照顾! ——别客气,不用谢谢!
* 甭谢谢了,那么客气干什么? / * 谢谢了! ——不谢谢!

赶紧 gǎnjǐn　　赶快 gǎnkuài　　赶忙 gǎnmáng

〈副词〉表示迅速做出某一动作行为。

(< adverb > indicating to act immediately.)

"赶紧"、"赶快"、"赶忙"意义、用法很相似,都表示迅速、紧张地做出动作行为,毫不拖延;在句中都用来作状语。(The meanings and usages of "赶紧","赶快"and "赶忙"are quite similar, all mean to act rapidly and intensely, without any delay. And they are used as adverbials in the sentences.)例如:

听到我的喊声,母亲赶紧打开门让我进去。
她红着脸刚要道歉,我赶快止住她,告诉她没什么。
(She flushed and was about to apologize and I hastened to stop her to tell her there was nothing serious.)
孩子的头就要溺到水里了,我赶忙游过去,把孩子救起来。

但是它们在不同的语用环境中,使用上有差别。(But there is still some difference between them in various context.)

(一)"赶忙"在意义上与"赶紧"、"赶快"比,不光有时间上的迅速、紧张,还有"忙"的样子。所以它通常用于叙述自己或他人已完成的事情,不用于将来时或祈使句。"赶紧"、"赶快"侧重在时间上迅速、紧张,不拖延,所以可以用于叙述已发生的事情,也可以用于将来时或祈使句。(Compared with "赶紧" and "赶快" in meaning, "赶忙" doesn't simply mean rapidity and intensity in terms of time, and it also means bustle. Therefore, it is generally used for accomplished things done by oneself or others. It is not used in future tense or in imperative sentences, "赶紧" and "赶快" lay emphasis on being prompt, intense and without delay as fast as time is concerned. So they can be used for the things already happened as well as in future tense or imperative sentences.)例如:

听到我的声音,她赶忙迎出屋来。
看到老师,他赶忙摘下帽子,行了一个大礼。
你赶快吃吧,饭都凉了。
要撞到人了,赶快刹车!
你赶紧去看看她吧,她病得很厉害。
明天赶紧去交电话费吧,再不交,人家要切断电话了。
(Hurry up to pay your telephone dues tomorrow. If you don't, they will cut off the line.)

* 你赶忙吃吧,饭都凉了。
* 要撞到人了,赶忙刹车!
* 你赶忙去看看她吧,她病得很厉害。
* 明天赶忙去交电话费吧,再不交,人家要切断电话了。

(二)"赶紧"跟"赶快"比,差别很小。"赶紧"侧重时间抓紧,不拖延;"赶快"侧重紧张而迅速。所以表示马上、迅速要做的事情,最好用"赶快";表示抓紧、不拖延的意思,最好用"赶紧"。(There is slight difference between "赶紧" and "赶快". "赶紧" stresses making the best use of one's time, without any delay, while "赶快" stresses being intense or promptly. It is better to use "赶

快" to describe things need doing immediately and quickly. And it is better to use "赶紧" to indicate the meaning of losing no time.)
例如：

> 时间不多了,赶快做吧!
> 不好了! 火着起来了! 赶快拉闸!
> 计划得赶紧实施了,不能再拖了。
> 明天你赶紧去工地看看,催催他们。

刚 gāng　　才 cái

〈副词〉表示事情发生在不久以前。
(< adverb > Indicating things happened not long ago.)
(一)"才"有强调意味,强调事情的发生离说话时很近,一般重读;"刚"没有强调意味,只表示事情的发生离说话时很近。试比较:("才" is used for emphasizing that the occurrence of the matter is close to the time of speaking. Generally stress is laid on "才". "刚" is not used for emphasis, but for indicating the occurrence of the matter is quite close to the time of speaking. Compare：)

> 会议才结束。　　　会议刚结束。
> 我才从国外回来不久。
> 我刚从国外回来不久。
> 她身体才恢复,不能太劳累。
> 她身体刚恢复,不能太劳累。

(二)"刚"和"才"都可以与"就"搭配使用,表示一件事情紧挨着另一件事情发生。用"刚"时,侧重于在时间上紧接着发生;用"才"时,侧重于两件事情紧凑地相继发生。试比较:(Both "刚" and "才" can be used together with "就", indicating one matter occurs on the heels of the other. When "刚" is used, the emphasis is the time something takes place, which is immediately after the former occurrence. When "才" is used, it emphasizes the occurrence of two things in rapid succession. Compare：)

刚买来一辆新车子,就给弄丢了。
才买来一辆新车子,就给弄丢了。
他刚回来就下车间去了。
他才回来就下车间去了。
我刚把屋子收拾干净,你们就给弄脏了。
我才把屋子收拾干净,你们就给弄脏了。
你的病刚好怎么就去上班了。
你的病才好怎么就去上班了。

刚才 gāngcái　　刚 gāng　　刚刚 gānggāng

刚才〈名词〉表示行动或情况发生在说话前不久的时间。

刚才（ <noun> indicating the time when an action or a matter took place not long before speaking.）

刚、刚刚〈副词〉表示行动或情况发生在不久前。

刚、刚刚（ <adverb> indicating an action or a matter took place not long ago.）

(一)"刚才"与"刚"、"刚刚"

1."刚才"是名词,"刚"、"刚刚"是副词,词性不同,功能也就不同。("刚才" and "刚"、"刚刚" are different in their parts of speech, so their functions are different as well.)。

(1)"刚才"可以用在主语前;"刚"、"刚刚"不可以。("刚才" can be used before the subject, but "刚" and "刚刚" can't.)。例如:

刚才,李大夫来找过你。
刚才,我看了一会儿电视。
* 刚刚/刚,我洗了几件衣服。
* 刚,我打了一个电话。

(2)"刚才"可以用在"比"、"跟"、"在"等介词后,构成介词词组;"刚"、"刚刚"不可以。("刚才" can be used after prepositions like "比","跟","在" to make prepositional phrases. "刚" and "刚刚" can't.)例如:

我的肚子比刚才好多了,不那么疼了。

(My stomach feels much better than a moment ago. It doesn't ache so much.)

跟刚才比,他显得不那么紧张了。

我说的这件事就发生在刚才。

* 他跟刚刚/刚一样,烧一点儿也没退下。
* 我说的这件事就发生在刚刚。

(3)"刚才"可以作名词性词语的限制语;"刚"、"刚刚"不可以。("刚才" can be a determiner modifying noun terms, but "刚" and "刚刚" can't.)例如:

刚才的事你都看见了吧?

他把刚才的想法跟经理说了一遍。

* 刚刚/刚的话你记住了吗?
* 刚刚／刚的事你都看见了吧?

2."刚才"与"刚"、"刚刚"都可以用在动词前,表示动作或情况发生在不久前的时间,但是所表示的时间意义有差别。"刚才"只表示距离说话前不久的时间;"刚刚"、"刚"则表示距离动作发生时时间不长,所以"刚才"只能用于现在的时间里,"刚"、"刚刚"可以用于现在以前的某一时间里。"刚才"表示的是一个具体时间,句中不再有别的具体的时间词语;"刚"、"刚刚"不是具体时间,句中还可以有别的具体的时间词语。("刚才" and "刚","刚刚" can all be used before verbs, indicating an action or things happened not long ago, but the time they indicate is different. "刚才" merely indicates it is not long from the point of speaking, "刚刚" and "刚" just indicate it is not long since the action's occurrence. So "刚才" can merely be used to describe the present time; "刚" and "刚刚" can be used to describe a certain period of time before the present time. "刚才" indicates a specific time and there aren't any other specific words of time in the sentence. "刚" and "刚刚" aren't specific time, so there may be other specific words of time in the sentence.)例如:

我刚才去操场打了一会儿球。
我刚刚/刚从学校回来。
那时他才刚刚/刚懂事。
昨天,天刚刚亮,他就进城了。
现在刚刚/刚上课。
最近他刚刚/刚开始写论文。
刚来的时候,我谁也不认识。
* 那时他刚才懂事。
* 昨天,天刚才亮,他就进城了。
* 现在刚才上课。
* 最近他刚才开始写论文。
* 刚才来的时候,我谁也不认识。

3."刚才"与"刚"、"刚刚"都可以出现在句中谓词性词语前,但是对句子的构句要求有所不同。("刚才" and "刚","刚刚" can be used before the predicative words in sentence, but they require different ways of construction.)

(1)"刚"、"刚刚"直接用于谓词性词语前,谓词性词语后边直接加上趋向、时段、结果等补语,可以成立;"刚才"一般不可以,常常需要加进别的词。(It is tenable when "刚" and "刚刚" are directly used before the predicate terms, and the predicate terms are directly followed by the complement of direction, complement of duration or complement of result, etc. But "刚才" usually can't. It needs to add other words.)例如:

刚站起来　　刚坐一会儿　　刚记住
刚平静下来　刚刚站起来　　刚刚坐一会儿
刚刚记住　　刚刚平静下来
* 刚才站起来　* 刚才坐一会儿　* 刚才记住
* 刚才平静下来　刚才才站起来
刚才已经坐了一会儿了　刚才才平静下来

(2)"刚"、"刚刚"可以用于复句或紧缩复句中,表示一动作紧挨另一动作之前发生,后面常用"就"呼应。"刚才"不可以。("刚" and "刚刚" can be used in the compound sentences or the tightened compound sentences, indicating one action occurs closely before the other. In this case "刚" or "刚刚" is often followed by "就"."刚才"can not be used in this way.)例如:

你怎么刚刚坐了这么一会儿就要走哇?

(How could you want to leave since you have just stayed here such a little while?)

他刚放下筷子就跑出去了。

王新刚要走,就被刘厂长发现了。

* 你怎么刚才坐了这么一会儿就要走哇?
* 王新刚才要走,就被刘厂长发现了。

(3)"刚"、"刚刚"可以用于表示有能力、有条件做某事的"能"、"会"前;"刚才"不能。("刚" and "刚刚" can also be used before "能","会",which indicate being able or qualified to do something, "刚才" can't.)例如:

学了这么长时间,他刚/刚刚能读懂这种小文章。

这孩子刚/刚刚会走路。

* 学了这么长时间,他刚才能读懂这种小文章。
* 这孩子刚才会走路。

(4)用"刚才"的句子,如果否定的话,否定副词"不"、"没"要放在"刚才"后边;用"刚"的句子,在"刚"的前后不能用"不"、"没"否定。(If the sentence of "刚才" is in the negative, the negative adverb "不"or "没"will be put after "刚才", while in sentence with "刚", the negative adverb "不" or "没" can neither be put before nor after "刚".)例如:

你刚才怎么不说　　刚才没告诉他
刚才我还不知道这件事　刚才没做

* 你刚怎么不说　　* 刚没告诉他

253

* 我刚还不知道这件事　　* 刚没做
　　* 我不刚知道这件事　　　* 没刚做

(5)"刚才"可以独立地用在问句中的动词前,询问在这一时间所做的事情;"刚"不可以这样用。("刚才" can be used alone before verbs in the sentence intending to ask things being done during this period of time; while "刚" can't be used in this way.)例如:

　　你刚才去哪儿了?
　　刚才谁来了?
　　他刚才坐在那儿看什么?
　　* 你刚去哪儿了?
　　* 刚谁来了?
　　* 他刚坐在那儿看什么?

4. "刚"、"刚刚"还可以表示时间、空间、数量恰好在那一点上和勉强达到某种程度,有"仅仅","只"的意思。"刚才"没有这两种意思。("刚","刚刚" can also indicate that the time, space or quantity has just reached a point or only reaches some degree with difficulty, meaning "仅仅" or "只"."刚才" doesn't have such meanings.)例如:

　　我们赶到时刚/刚刚两点。
　　这双鞋,我穿刚/刚刚合适。
　　(This pair of shoes just suits my feet.)
　　这些材料刚/刚刚够我们班用。
　　(These materials are just enough for our class.)
　　她说话声音太小,大家刚/刚刚能听到。
　　* 我们赶到时刚才两点。
　　* 这双鞋,我穿刚才合适。
　　* 这些材料刚才够我们班用。
　　* 她说话声音太小,大家刚才能听到。

(二)"刚"与"刚刚"

1. "刚刚"比"刚"所表示的距离动作的时间间隔更短。(Compared with "刚", the time interval from the action occurrence

indicated by "刚刚" is much shorter.)试比较:

我刚回来。 我刚刚回来。 电影刚开始。
电影刚刚开始。

2. "刚"能与副词"一"连用,后一动作常用"就"呼应,表示两种动作或状态紧挨着发生;"刚刚"不可以这样用。("刚" can be used together with the adverb "一", and the other act following usually works in combination with "就", indicating the two acts or states happen closely. "刚刚" can't.)例如:

他刚一张嘴就被老叔制止住了。

(He was stopped by his youngest uncle when he just started to speak.)

他刚一露面,就被公安人员逮住了。

(Just after his showing up he was caught by the police.)

嫩芽刚一出土,就被厚厚的白雪盖上了。

(The tender buds are covered by the thick snow just after their coming up.)

* 他刚刚一露面,就被公安人员逮住了。

* 嫩芽刚刚一出土,就被厚厚的白雪盖上了。

3. "刚刚"有时用法同"刚才",只是表示的时间间隔比"刚才"更短。"刚"在这一点上,不同于"刚刚"。(Occasionally "刚刚" is used in the same way as "刚才", but the interval of time is much shorter than "刚才", "刚" does not do the same as "刚才" in this point.)例如:

(1)当连动句中后一动作是前一动作的目的、前一动作是后一动作的方式时,前一动作前可以用"刚刚"。(When the latter action in a sentence with successive verbs is the purpose of the former, or the former action is the means of the latter, "刚刚" is used before the former verb.)例如:

小王刚刚去资料室查资料去了。(目的)
经理刚刚坐车去工地了。(方式)

255

* 小王刚去资料室查资料去了。

* 经理刚坐车去工地了。

(2)复句中,表示距离说话时很近的某一存在、持续着的动作或状态突然发生变化时,前一分句动作、状态前可以用"刚刚",其后常接"还",后一分句常用"就"呼应。"刚"一般不这样用。(In the compound sentences, when indicating a certain existing and continuing action or state suddenly changes, "刚刚" can be used before the action or state of the preceding clause and "还" follows, the latter clause usually uses "就" to work in combination. "刚" is not used in this way.)例如:

这孩子<u>刚刚</u>还喜笑颜开的,一转眼<u>就</u>哭了起来。

(Just now the kid was wreathed in smiles, but in a flash she burst into tears.)

他<u>刚刚</u>还躺在床上看书呢(,怎么转眼<u>就</u>不见了)。

天<u>刚刚</u>还晴着,转眼之间便大雨瓢泼了。

(Just a moment ago it was sunny, but in the twinkling of an eye there is the heavy rain.)

* 这孩子刚还喜笑颜开的,一转眼就哭了起来。

* 他刚还躺在床上看书呢(,怎么转眼就不见了)。

* 天刚还晴着,转眼之间便大雨瓢泼了。

告诉 gàosu   通知 tōngzhī   说 shuō
〈动词〉 < verb >

(一)"告诉"和"通知"

1."告诉"和"通知"都有把某事说给别人听,使人知道的意思。有时可以通用,但是色彩和使用场合有一定差别。(Both mean to say something to others and make them known. Sometimes they are interchangeable, but there is difference in the flavour and the occasions they can be used.)

"告诉"侧重于述说,常用,随意性很强;"通知"则侧重于传达,常用,但是更多地用于公事,用于一些正式的场合或重要的事情。("告诉"emphasizes recounting, used widely and flexibly. "通知"merely emphasizes transmitting and is mainly used for public affairs and for some formal occasions or important cases.)例如:

你告诉小王明天下午来开会。

你通知小王明天下午来开会。(比较正式地。)

"告诉"只有把某事说给别人听,使人知道的意思;"通知"除了有把某事说给别人听,使人知道的意思外,还有让人按照所说的去做的意思。只有把某事说给别人听,使人知道的意思不能用"通知"。("告诉"only means to say something to others and make it known. But besides saying something to others and making it known, "通知"also means to ask others to do according to what is said. If one only wants to say something to others and make it known, "通知"is not used.)例如:

这件事千万不要告诉我爱人。

晚上来我家,我告诉你一个特大新闻。

＊这件事千万不要通知我爱人。

＊晚上来我家,我通知你一个特大新闻。

2.结构上,"告诉"和"通知"也有所不同。"告诉"和"通知"都是可以带双宾语的动词。"告诉"除了可以带双宾语外,也可以只带一个表人宾语,但是一般不能只带一个表事宾语;"通知"不受这种限制,只带一个表人宾语或者只带一个表事宾语都可以。(In structure, "告诉" is also different from "通知". "告诉" and "通知" are all verbs being followed by double objects. Besides being followed by double objects, "告诉"can also be followed by one object of people, but not by one object of things. "通知"will not restricted by this. It can be followed either by one object of people or one object of things.)例如:

这件事你别告诉小王。(表人宾语——小王)

我告诉你一个好消息。(表人宾语——你;表事宾语——消息)

* 我告诉一个好消息。(表事宾语——消息)

下午开会的事,你通知一下张先生好吗?(表人宾语——张先生)

办公室通知我们下午两点乘车去参观。(表人宾语——我们;表事宾语——下午两点乘车去参观)

办公室通知下午两点乘车去参观。(表事宾语——下午两点乘车去参观)

(二)"告诉"和"说"

1."告诉"和"说"最大的区别是动作的方向性问题,"告诉"的动作具有方向性,即把某事说出来的目的在于传给对方;"说"不具有这种方向性,它只是用话表达思想、意思的方式。所以,"告诉"可以带双宾语,"说"不可以;"告诉"用在"把"字句里,后边可以只用一个表人宾语,"说"不可以。(The principal difference between "告诉" and "说" is the direction of the acts. The purpose of speaking out is to transmit the words to the opposite side. "说" doesn't imply this meaning, it is only a way by words to express ideas and opinions. Therefore, "告诉" can be followed by double objects, and "说" can't. "告诉" can also be used in the sentence with "把" and followed by one object of people, while "说" can't.)例如:

你去告诉小王来听电话。

* 你去说小王来听电话。

我们把这件事的真相告诉他吧。

(Let's tell him the truth of the matter.)

* 我们把这件事的真相说他吧。

2."说"还有"解释"、"批评"等意思,"告诉"没有这种意思。("说" also means explaining and criticizing, but "告诉" doesn't.)例如:

老师,您能说一说这个词是什么意思吗?("解释"义)

＊老师,您能告诉这个词是什么意思吗?

张力好几天没来上课,老师正说他呢。("批评"义)

(Zhang Li hasn't been to school for several days so the teacher is criticizing him.)

＊张力好几天没来上课,老师正告诉他呢。

各自 gèzì   各个 gègè   个个 gègè

各自、各个〈代词〉 < pronoun >

个个〈量词重叠〉 < reduplication of measure words >

"各自"、"各个"、"个个"在意思上都含有"每一个"的意思,但是由于词的构成不同,侧重的角度和用法也不同,所以大多不能换用。("各自","各个"and "个个" all imply everyone. Since their constructions, angles being emphasized and usages are different, generally they are not exchangeable.)

(一) 词的构成不同,意义上有一定差别。(Because of the difference in construction, they mean differently.)

"各自"是代词"各"加"自"构成的;"各个"是代词"各"加量词"个"构成的,它们都含有"各"的"每"的意思,除了这个意思以外,"各自"侧重于"自己","各个"侧重于"一个"。"各个"、"个个"没有"自己"的意义,但是都有"一个"的意义,不同在"各个"所指的每一个实际上本意在指所有的、全体等,"个个"只是量词的重叠,所以只指全体中一个个的个体。〔"各自" is composed of the pronoun "各" and "自"; "各个" is composed of the pronoun "各" and "个", they all imply the meaning of "每 (every)" in "各 (each)". Besides these, "各自" emphasizes "自己 (oneself)" and "各个" emphasizes "一个 (single one)". "各个" and "个个" don't have the meaning of "自己 (oneself)", but they both have the meaning of "一个" (one). The difference lies in that "各个" actually refers to the whole, while "个个" is only a reduplicated form of the measure word and refers to each individual.〕例如:

培训班结束后,他们各自回到自己的工作岗位上。

(After the training class was over, each of them has been back to his own working post.)

代表们各自介绍了本单位的情况。

* 培训班结束后,他们各个回到自己的工作岗位上。

* 代表们各个介绍了本单位的情况。

我了解他,他各个方面都很出色。

各个房间都找遍了,也没有找到他。

(We have been to every room but haven't found him.)

* 我了解他,他各自方面都很出色。

* 各自房间都找遍了,也没有找到他。

这些小伙子个个都是好样的。

(Every young fellow here is a fine example.)

孩子们被你们调教得真好,个个懂礼貌、讲卫生。

* 这些小伙子各自/各个都是好样的。

* 孩子们被你们调教得真好,各自/各个懂礼貌、讲卫生。

(二) 用法上(In use)

1."各自"和"个个"在句子里主要作主语,而且要求称代的对象在前文出现过,也就是说它们所指的对象应该是在一定范围内的。所以"各自"和"个个"常常与所指的对象一起构成复指词组作主语。所不同的是,"各自"多用于叙述性强的句子,"个个"多用于描写性强的句子。("各自"and"个个"are mainly used as subjects in sentence and require the substituted object to appear in the preceding content, that is the object indicated should be within the certain limits. So generally together with the indicated objects "各自" and "个个" make up compound indicating clauses to be subjects. The differences are:"各自"is generally used in the sentence of strong account and "个个" is in the sentence of strong description.)例如:

<u>它们</u>(一种鸟)一起生活一段时间后就分开了,后来,各自又找了新伙伴。

<u>他们</u>各自动手,自己做自己负责的那一部分。

(Each one of them got to work and each just did the portion that one was responsible for.)

* 它们一起生活一段时间后就分开了,后来,个个又找了新伙伴。
* 他们个个动手,自己做自己负责的那一部分。

孩子们在公园里玩着、笑着、闹着,个个兴高采烈。
(The children are playing, laughing and making fun. Everyone is in high spirits.)

姑娘们个个漂亮可爱。
* 孩子们在公园里玩着、笑着、闹着,各自兴高采烈。
* 姑娘们各自漂亮可爱。

2. "各自"在句子里还可以作定语,"个个"一般没有这种用法。("各自" is also used as an attributive in sentence, and "个个" is not.)例如:

同学们根据各自的爱好参加了兴趣小组。
开完会,他们回到各自的房间。
* 同学们根据个个的爱好参加了兴趣小组。
* 开完会,他们回到个个的房间。

3. "各个"在句子里主要作定语,一般不能用来作主语。因为它意在全体,所以句子里常用副词"都"加以配合。("各个" is mainly used as attributive, but not subject in sentence. Since it implies "the whole", it is usually supported by adverb "都" in the sentence.)例如:

各个方面的情况都了解清楚了再下结论。
(Don't come to conclusion until you find out every situation.)

各个单位都派了代表来。
这张表上记录了她各个学科的成绩。
* 所有的情况,各个都了解清楚了再下结论。
* 每个单位各个都派了代表来。

261

4."各个"有时也可以作状语,表示"逐个"的意思。〔"各个" sometimes is used as an adverbial, indicating "逐个"(one by one).〕例如:

集中优势兵力,各个击破敌人。

(To concentrate the armed forces to destroy the enemy one by one.)

根 gēn   条 tiáo   支 zhī

〈量词〉表示长条物的量。

(＜measure word＞ quantities of long-size.)

"根"、"条"、"支"都可以用于长条物,但是大多不能互换使用,这是因为它们表示不同事物的量。(The three can all be used for long-sized things. Since they represent quantities of different things, they are not exchangeable.)主要区别如下:

(一)"根"与"条"

1.所计量的事物形状上的差别:(The differences among the shapes of the things being measured:)

"根"所计量的东西大多是柱形或近似柱形的细长的东西。(The things measured by"根"mostly are pillar-shaped or approximately pillar-shaped and long-and-thin things.)例如:

一根线　一根绳子　一根火柴

三根针　两根筷子

粗长的东西有时也可以用,但仍必须是长柱体、长方体或近似长柱体、长方体的东西。("根"is also used for thick things, which must be long columned, rectangular or things similar to those.)例如:

俩人抬一根木头　由十二根柱子支撑着

两根电线杆

"条"所计量的东西大多是平面的或有表面的长形的东西。(The things measured by"条"are mostly plane or long things with surface.)例如：

　　自然界的：两条河　三条沟　一条路
　　　　　　　这条胡同　那条山脉
　　物品
　　（大多是织物）：两条毛巾　一条毛毯
　　　　　　　　　围了条围巾　买两条裤子
　　　　　　　　　用了五条麻袋　系了条漂亮的领带
　　　　　　　　　舞动着两条彩绸
　　动物：九条龙飞舞着　一条蛇　买了三条鱼
　　　　　捉了五条毛虫
　　* 一条火柴　* 三条针　* 两条筷子
　　* 俩人抬一条木头
　　* 两根毛巾　* 一根毛毯　* 围了根围巾
　　* 买两根裤子

2.物类上的差别：(Difference in categories：)
(1)"根"除了形状上的条件外,它常常还用来计量细长的原本有根部的植物性的东西或有根部的东西。"条"大多不用于这种情况。(Except for the requirement of shapes, "根" is also used to measure long and thin plant-like things that originally had roots or things with roots.)例如：

　　两根竹竿　一根木棍　无数根柳条
　　一根藤条　买了几根葱
　　三根胡萝卜　两根黄瓜　几根草
　　掉了十几根头发　三根漂亮的羽毛
　　* 几条草　* 掉了十几条头发　* 三条漂亮的羽毛

(2)"条"所计量的物品大多与织物有关系(见上)；它还可以用来计量动物(见上),"根"一般不能用来计量动物。〔Things measured by "条" are mainly concerning fabric(seeing above). It is also used for measuring animals (seeing above) "根" can't be used for measuring animals.〕例如：

263

＊九根龙飞舞着　　＊一根蛇
＊买了三根鱼　　＊捉了五根毛虫

3."条"只能用于可弯曲的东西;"根"不受这种限制,虽然它大多用于不可弯曲的东西,但是少数弯曲的东西也可以用。("条" can only be used for the things possibly to be crooked. "根" is not restricted in this way for it can be used for some crooked things, though it can't be used mainly for those crooked things.)例如:

两条河　一条路　一条毛毯
围了条围巾　一条蛇　买了三条鱼
一根线　一根绳子　一根火柴
一根木头　十二根柱子

4."条"还可以计量较抽象的或抽象的事物。("条" can also be used to measure things comparatively abstract or abstract things.)例如:

(1)与人体或人有关的(Concerning human body or people):

三条人命　众人一条心　他是一条好汉

(2)与抽象事物有关的(主要用于可以分项的事物):(Concerning abstract things—mainly used for the things that could be itemized:)

两条计策　　一条经验　　定了五条规则
给你提两条意见　　列出十条罪状
措施要一条一条地落实下去
这是唯一的一条出路
＊众人一根心　＊他是一根好汉　＊两根计策
＊一根经验　　＊一根出路

(二)"支"与"根"、"条"

1."支"用于计量物品时,与"根"、"条"的差别主要不是形状上的,从形状上来说,它与"根"接近,属于接近细长而具有柱形的东西,但是,它们最大的差别在于,"根"可用于能弯曲的事物;"条"只用于可弯曲的事物,而"支"则只用于直而不可弯曲的物品。(When "支" is used for measuring things, the differences between "支"and "根","条" are not mainly in shape. As far as its shape is concerned, "支" resembles "根", belonging to the things nearly long and thin but pillar-shaped, "根" is used for the things possible to crook. "条" can merely be used for things that can be crooked. But "支" is only used for the articles straight but not crooked.)例如：

　　　　三支铅笔　　两支毛笔　　一支粉笔
　　　　一支烟　　　买了支笛子　十支蜡烛

2.物类上也有不同。"支"还可计量歌曲、队伍等。("支"is also used for measuring other categories as songs, troops, etc.)例如：

　　　　唱了三支民歌　　听了一支小夜曲
　　　　她演奏了许多支大家爱听的曲子
　　　　这是一支年轻的队伍
　　　　一支战斗力很强的生力军
　　　　前面有一支船队
　　＊ 三根铅笔　　＊ 两根毛笔　　＊ 一根粉笔
　　＊ 一根烟　　　　买了根笛子
　　＊ 三条铅笔　　＊ 两条毛笔　　＊ 一条粉笔
　　＊ 买了条笛子
　　＊ 唱了三根民歌　＊ 听了一根小夜曲
　　＊ 一根年轻的队伍　＊ 前面有一根船队
　　＊ 唱了三条民歌　＊ 听了一条小夜曲
　　＊ 一条年轻的队伍　＊ 前面有一条船队

根据 gēnjù　　依据 yījù　　据 jù

〈介词〉引进行为的凭据或结论的前提。

(< preposition > introducing the evidence of the action or the prerequisite of the conclusion.)

(一)"根据"和"依据"

　　"根据"和"依据"都可以构成介词词组用在句首或谓语动词

之前。"根据"和"依据"意义上很接近,稍有侧重在于:"根据"更加强调根本的来源;"依据"强调的是凭据。此外,"根据"和"依据"的色彩也有所不同。"根据"通用于口语和书面语;"依据"则有较强的书面语色彩,所以多用于书面语。("根据"and "依据" both can compose prepositional phrases which are put at the beginning of the sentence or before predicative verbs. Both are close in meaning. "根据" lays more emphasis on the cardinal source, and "依据" emphasizes the evidence. In addition, "根据" is generally used in either spoken or written languages, but "依据" has comparatively strong flavour of written language and mainly used in written language.)

由于意义侧重角度不同,色彩也有不同,虽然有时可以通用,但是有些情况下还是不能通用的。(Because of particular emphases laid on meaning and being in different flavours, the two sometimes are exchangeable and sometimes not.)

1. 当"根据"和"依据"的东西是可以看到的,并且是意见、精神、情况、原理、文件、法令等时,动作凭此而形成新的文件、材料、结论或出现某一局面、结果等时,"根据"和"依据"基本上是可以通用的。当然使用哪一个,说话人凭据的侧重角度是不同的。(The things indicated by "根据" and "依据" are visible. When they are opinions, spirits, circumstances, principles, documents and degrees, and when the action depends on those to form new documents, materials, conclusions or reveals a certain aspect and result, etc., "根据" and "依据" are basically interchangeable. Which one is chosen to use depends on the points the speaker intends to emphasize.)例如:

根据/依据总经理的意见,我们起草了这份文件。

根据/依据大家的要求,我们把某些规定又改了一下。

2. 当凭据的东西是看不到的、无形的东西时,以用"根据"为好,这是因为"依据"的"依"重在强调有直接依凭的东西。(When the things taken as evidence are invisible, it is better to use

"根据", for the character "依" in the word "依据" mainly emphasizes the things with direct evidence.)例如:

根据生活创造人物,人物才会更加有生命力。

(The persons in literature will just have more great vitality when the creating work is done on the basis of reality.)

根据十几年的生活经验,我才有了这么一点儿体会。

* 依据生活创造人物,人物才会更加有生命力。

* 依据十几年的生活经验,我才有了这么一点儿体会。

我依据制度的规定来处理这件事情。

(I have just dealt with the matter according to the rules and regulations.)

我是依据这份材料介绍的情况。

但是,当句中的内容正是"根据"的内容时,即内容的来源时,应当用"根据",不要用"依据"。(But, when the content in the sentence is just that of "根据" — the source of the content, it is "根据" but not "依据" that should be used.)例如:

根据老师的意见,今天交作业的,算作按时完成作业,明天交作业的,不能算作按时完成作业。("今天交作业的……"是"老师的意见"的内容。)

根据我们的调查,这个案子跟你有关。("这个案子跟你有关"是我们的调查的内容。)

* 依据我们的调查,这个案子跟你有关。

此外,"根据"还可以构成"根据……来看/来判断"等形式,"依据"一般不这么用。(Besides, "根据" can also compose the pattern as "根据…来看/来判断", etc. but "依据" can't.)例如:

根据查访的情况来看,这件事好像挺复杂。

根据预测图来判断,这里近期内不会有雨。

(二)"据"和"根据"、"依据"

"据"的意思虽然跟"根据"、"依据"比较接近,但是由于单音节、双音节的差别,形成它们完全不同的用法。(Though "据" is close in meaning with "根据"and "依据", there are differences between monosyllable and disyllable and this causes their completely different uses.)

1."据"既可以与单音节词搭配,又可以与双音节词搭配;"根据"、"依据"一般只能跟双音及双音以上的词语搭配。("据" can either collocate with monosyllabic word or disyllabic words. "根据"and "依据"are generally collocated only with disyllabic words and above.)例如:

> 据说　据我看
> 据实招来(to confess on the basis of truth)
> 据理力争(to argue strongly on just grounds)
> 据调查　据了解　据材料介绍　据预测图分析
> ＊根据实招来　＊根据理力争
> ＊依据实招来　＊依据理力争
> 根据了解的情况　根据预测图分析
> 依据调查的资料　依据材料介绍情况

2."据"后边的词语是动词或者小句;"根据"、"依据"后边的词语一般是名词性的,尤其不能接小句。(The words after"据"are verbs or clauses and those after "根据"and "依据" generally are words that function as nouns, especially, clauses are forbidden.)例如:

> 据调查　据他说　据天气预报报道
> 据小道消息说(according to the hearsay)
> ＊根据他说　＊根据天气预报报道
> ＊根据小道消息说
> ＊依据他说　＊依据天气预报报道
> ＊依据小道消息说
> 根据他的说法　根据天气预报的报道
> 根据小道消息　依据他的说法
> 依据天气预报的报道　依据小道消息

3."据"构成的介词词组一般用在句首,尤其是"据"后接小句的类型;"根据"、"依据"构成的介词词组多用在句首,但也可以用在谓语动词前。(The prepositional phrases made up of "据" is generally used at the beginning of the sentence, especially the type which has a short sentence used after "据". The prepositional phrases composed of "根据"or "依据"are generally used at the beginning of the sentence and used before predicative verbs.)例如:

据群众反映,他有不少违法乱纪的行为。

(According to the masses' report he has been engaged in many illegal activities.)

据气象云图分析,明天有暴风雨。

* 他据群众反映,有不少违法乱纪的行为。

* 明天据气象云图分析,有暴风雨。

根据你的意见,我们修改了方案。

我们根据你的意见修改了方案。

依据刑法的具体规定,法院做出了这个裁决。

(The court gave this ruling in accordance with the specific regulations of the penal code.)

法院依据刑法的具体规定做出了这个裁决。

更 gèng　　还 hái

〈副词〉表示程度增加。

(< adverb > increase the degree.)

"更"、"还"都可以表示程度增加,意义比较接近。它们的区别主要在于用法上。(Both words indicate to increase degree and they are close in meaning. Their difference shows in usage.)

(一)"更"、"还"都可以用于比较句中,表示程度加深。("更" and "还" are both used in comparative sentences, indicating degree is increasing.)例如:

今天比昨天更/还冷。

小刘比李科长更/还有能力。

但是,"还"在不是突出夸张语气的前提下,一般只能用于"……比……还……"的格式中,即相比较的两项,在句式中都应出现。"更"不受这种限制,它可以用于"比"字句,也可以不用于"比"字句,而表示比较。(But if not on the presupposition of exaggeration, "还" is only used in the pattern as "…比…还", namely the two items being compared should both appear in the sentence pattern. "更" is not restricted by this pattern. "更" can be used in a sentence either with "比" or without "比" to indicate comparison.)例如:

这件衣服比那件还贵,不买了。
* 这件衣服还贵,不买了。
这件衣服更贵,不买了。
* 我们要做出还优异、还突出的成绩来。
我们要做出更优异、更突出的成绩来。
(We will achieve more excellent and remarkable success.)
比较起来,我更愿意到山区去工作。
* 比较起来,我还愿意到山区去工作。
这样做,更能使他信服。
* 这样做,还能使他信服。

(二)"还"用于"比"字句中,除表示程度进一层外,还有夸张意味,所以句末可用具有夸张意味的语气词"呢"。"更"没有这种意味,句末一般不用"呢"。("还" is also used in the sentence with "比". Besides indicating a further degree, it also has the meaning of exaggeration. So at the end of the sentence the particle "呢" is used for exaggeration. "更" doesn't mean this and there is no "呢" at the end of the sentence.)例如:

今天的风比昨天还大呢。
他写得比你还好呢。
我看,你比他还高兴呢。

(三)"还"字句的谓词性成分后还可以有比较的数量,包括不定数量和准确数量。"更"字句则只能用表示不定数量的"一些"、"一点"等,不能用准确数量。〔In the sentence with "还" there can be comparable quantities including the indefinite and the exact quantities after the predicate composition, but only words that indicate indefinite quantity, such as "一些"(some), "一点"(a little), etc. can be used in the "更" sentence, not the words indicating definite quantity.〕例如:

　　他比我还聪明<u>些</u>。
　　这儿的房租比原来的地方还要贵<u>点儿</u>。
　　他比我更聪明<u>些</u>。
　　他介绍得更详细<u>一点儿</u>。
　　这本书显得更容易<u>一些</u>。
　　这件行李比那件行李还重<u>十公斤</u>。
　　我比他还高<u>两公分</u>呢。
　　* 这件行李比那件行李更重十公斤。
　　* 我比他更高两公分。

(四)"更"还可以用于三项比较之中,"还"不能用于三项比较之中。("更" can also be used in the comparison among three things, but "还" can't.)例如:

　　<u>他</u>比<u>你</u>稳重,比<u>我</u>更稳重。(他、你、我)
　　这个<u>阶梯教室</u>比旁边的<u>小会议室</u>大,比一般<u>教室</u>更大。
(阶梯教室、会议室、一般教室)

　　(This lecture theatre is bigger than the small meeting room nearby and it is much bigger than the common classrooms.)

　　* 他比你稳重,比我还稳重。
　　* 这个阶梯教室比旁边的小会议室大,比一般教室还大。

(五)"还"和"更"有时都可以用于递进关系的复句中,但是表示的意义有差异。"还"主要表示另有增补的意义,"更"则表示程度加深一步。因此,只表示程度加深一步的递进关系句中,不能用"还"。("还" and "更" sometimes can both be used in the compound sentence of progressive advance but their meanings are different. "还" mainly indicates that there is other supplement, "更" indicates to deepen in the degree. Therefore, we draw the conclusion that "还" can't be used in the sentence of progressive advance.)例如:

我不但佩服他的才学,还敬重他的为人。(另有增补。)

(I admire not only his scholarship but also his behaviour.)

评价一个人不光要看他怎么说,还要看他怎么做。(另有增补。)

我不但佩服他的才学,更敬重他的为人。(程度加深一步。)

评价一个人不光要看他怎么说,更要看他怎么做。(程度加深一步。)

这里山美,水美,人更美。

他没有经济条件读大学,更不可能去国外读大学。

* 这里山美,水美,人还美。

* 他没有经济条件读大学,还不可能去国外读大学。

(六) 在"比"字句中,"还"、"更"有时也有意义差异。(In the sentence with "比","还"and "更"indicate different meanings.)例如:

现在,他车开得比老王还好。(以前不如老王,现在超过老王。)

现在,他车开得比老王更好了。(以前就比老王好,现在好的程度又有增加。)

(七)"还"还可以表示比拟,即把被比项作为一种衡量标准,来比拟、衬托前一项,并不是要做真正的对比。"更"一般不用于这种情况。("还"is also used in metaphor, namely taking the compared item as a measuring standard to match and contrast with the preceding item, but doesn't mean to do the real comparison. "更"generally is not used in this way.)例如:

你看,孩子的小脸蛋儿比苹果还红。

那个微型相机比火柴盒还小。

(That mini-camera is smaller than a matchbox.)

她的腿比我的腰还粗。

(Her leg is thicker than my waist.)

粮食堆得比山还高。

从语用的角度说,说话人比较的目的并不是要将"脸蛋"跟"苹果"比颜色深浅、将"相机"跟"火柴盒"比大小、将"腿"跟"腰"比粗细、将"粮堆"跟"山"比高低,而只是以被比项作为一种衡量标准,来衬托、描写脸蛋红、相机小、腿粗、粮堆高。所以,"还"不能换成"更"。(In terms of pragmatic use, the purpose of the speaker is not to compare the child's cheeks with the color of apple, to compare the camera with the matchbox, to compare leg with waist or to compare the piled grain with hills, but to take the reference item as a measuring standard, in order to set off or to describe that the cheeks are red, the camera is tiny, the leg is strong and the grain piles are tall. So "还" can't be replaced by "更".)

更加 gèngjiā   更 gèng

〈副词〉表示程度加深一步。

(<adverb> expressing further increase of the degree.)

"更加"和"更"意义十分接近,但是由于它们语体色彩上、用法上有一定差别,所以有时不能换用。("更加" and "更" are very close in meaning. Because there is certain difference between the two words in the flavour or in use, they are sometimes unexchangeable.)

(一)"更加"书面语色彩较浓,多用于书面语;"更"则多用于口语。("更加" is stronger in the flavour of the written language, mostly used in written language. "更" is more often used in spoken language.)

(二)"更加"多用于修饰双音节或多音节词语,修饰单音节词有一定局限;"更"一般不受局限。("更加" is mostly used to modify disyllable or polysyllable phrases and there are certain limits in modifying the monosyllable words. Generally "更" is beyond limits.)例如：

　　* 我们要更加快、更加好地建设我们的祖国。
　　我们要更快、更好地建设我们的祖国。
　　* 他问我的问题更加难。
　　他问我的问题更难。
　　这儿的生活更加丰富、更加多彩。
　　在做学问上，他比我更加严谨。
　　(In the aspect of doing research, he is more rigorous than me.)
　　这儿的生活更丰富、更多彩。
　　在做学问上，他比我更严谨。

(三)"更"还可以单纯表示递进关系，"更加"则不适用这种关系的复句。(The word "更" can plainly indicate the relation of increase by degrees. While "更加" is not suited to the compound sentence like this.)例如：

　　我爱这里的山水，爱这里的土地，更爱这里的人们。
　　王先生欣赏你的灵气儿，更欣赏你的勤奋。
　　(Mr. Wang admires your intelligence and your diligence even more.)
　　* 我爱这里的山水，爱这里的土地，更加爱这里的人们。
　　* 王先生欣赏你的灵气儿，更加欣赏你的勤奋。

更加 gèngjiā　　越发 yuèfā

〈副词〉表示程度进一步加深。

(<adverb> indicating further increase of the degree.)

"更加"和"越发"都可以表示程度进一步加深，但是由于它们的构句条件有一定差别，所以有时不能换用。(Both "更加" and "越发" can indicate further increase of the degree. Since there is difference between the conditions of composing sentence, sometimes they are not exchangeable.)

(一) 在表示程度加深的意义上,"更加"和"越发"有时可以通用。(In the sense of increasing degree, "更加" and "越发" sometimes can be interchangeable.)例如:

这几天,旱情更加/越发严重了。

(These days the ravage of the drought has been more and more serious.)

现在,约翰的汉语说得更加/越发好了。

但是,"越发"总是与时间因素相联系,即它总是表示在不同时间平面上程度加深的情况。因此,用"越发"的句子,句中总能看到或隐含着与之相比的以前的时间。由于它所表示的是随时间推移的程度加深,所以句末一般要用"了"。(Yet, the word "越发" always has something to do with the factor of time. It always indicates the degree gets higher at different times. In the sentence with "越发", a former time compared with the present is always found or implied. Because it indicates the degree gets higher with the elapse of time, generally "了" is used at the end of the sentence.)例如:

王丽比我上次看到她时越发瘦弱了。

她长得比小时候越发秀气了。

(She becomes much more elegant than what she was like as a child.)

你怎么越发不听话了?

* 我发现他最近越发不愿意说话。

* 你怎么越发不听话?

"更加"可以表示随时间推移的程度加深,也可以表示同一时间平面上同其他人、事物相比的程度加深。在表示后一种的程度加深时,句末不用"了"。"越发"不能用于后一种情况。("更加" can indicate both the degree gets higher with the elapse of time and the degree is higher when compared with other people or other things at the same time. In the latter case, "了" is not be used at the end of the

sentence and "越发" can't be used either.)例如：
> 这儿比我上次来时显得更加美丽了。
> 她好像更加漂亮了。
> 他在学业上比你更加有成就。
> (He has achieved much more success in studies than you.)
> 比较起来，我更加喜欢游泳。
> * 他在学业上比你越发有成就。
> * 比较起来，我越发喜欢游泳。

(二)"更加"可以用于两项比较，也可以用于多项比较；"越发"只用于两项比较。("更加" can be used to make comparison between two things or among several things, while "越发" can only be used for two things.)例如：
> 坐船去比坐火车麻烦，比坐汽车更加麻烦。
> 她的汉语(现在)比上学期流利，比刚来的时候更加流利。
> * 坐船去比坐火车麻烦，比坐汽车越发麻烦。
> * 她的汉语比上学期流利，比刚来的时候越发流利。

关心 guānxīn　　关怀 guānhuái　　关切 guānqiè 关照 guānzhào

〈动词〉表示重视、爱护并放在心上。

(< verb > indicating attaching importance to, taking good care of and keeping in mind.)

"关心"、"关怀"、"关切"、"关照"都是表示心理活动的动词，都可以接受程度副词的修饰。(All the four are verbs indicating psychological activities and all can be modified by adverbs of degree.)例如：
> 很关心　很关怀　很关切　很关照
> 十分关心　十分关怀　十分关切　十分关照

但是，它们在意义上有一定的差别，在使用上不同点更多一些，所以大多不能换用。(But since there is certain difference in

meaning and more difference in use, they are mostly unexchangeable.)
(一) 意义上(In meaning)

1.比较起来,"关切"比"关心"程度更深一些,它表示非常关心的意思。此外,它还含有"亲切"的意义,所以可以用来描写人的表情、感情、语气等,其他几个词一般没有这种用法。(By comparison, the degree of "关怀" is deeper than "关心", it means to care very much. Besides, it also implies the meaning of "亲切 (cordial)", can be used to describe people's expressions, emotions and moods, etc. The other words generally can't be used in this way.)例如:

她用关切的目光注视着我。
(She looked attentively at me with concerns in her eyes.)
他的话里充满了关切之情。
(What he said is full of concerns.)
妈妈关切地嘱咐道:"路上一定要小心。"
(Mother told me with concerns, "Be careful on the way.")
* 她用关心/关怀/关照的目光注视着我。
* 他的话里充满了关心/关照之情。
* 妈妈关怀/关照地嘱咐道:"路上一定要小心。"

2."关怀"则含有一定的庄重色彩,使用时,须注意一定的场合。"关照"除了表示重视、爱护并放在心上的意思外,还含有其他几个词所没有的几层意思:一是全面安排、照应的意思;一是口头通知、提醒等意思。("关怀" has the solemn flavour. So attention has to be paid to the proper occasion of using it. Besides the meaning of paying attention to, cherishing and caring, it also implies some other meanings that the other words don't have: one means the overall arrangement, and one means to inform orally and to remind, etc.)例如:

李主任住院了,暂时不工作,你关照一下他那里的工作。
(Director Li is in the hospital and temporarily can't work. You have to look after his work there.)

他把这里的工作一一关照完才离去。

你去关照一下食堂,给我们再加两个菜。

(Go to the canteen to remind them to add two other dishes for us.)

你关照一下小王,下午有课,别忘了。

* 李主任住院了,暂时不能工作,你关心/关怀/关切一下他那里的工作。

* 他把这里的工作一一关心/关怀/关切完才离去。

* 你去关心/关怀/关切一下食堂,给我们再加两个菜。

* 你关心/关怀/关切一下小王,下午有课,别忘了。

(二) 用法上(In use)

1. 关于适用的对象(The suitable objects)

(1)"关心"、"关照"的对象可以是人,也可以是事情;"关怀"的对象则通常是人,如果是事物的话,须跟人有直接关系。(When using "关心","关照", the object being cared or taken care of can be people or things, but the objects of "关怀" usually are people and if they are things, then it must be directly concerned with people.) 例如:

我的朋友很关心我。

他很关心这件事,已经问过我好几次了。

他刚来,你多关照关照他。

今天我外出办点儿事,你关照一下公司。

(I will be out to do some business today. You have to take care of the affairs of the company.)

老首长这样关怀我们,我们怎么能辜负他的期望呢?

(Since the old senior officer has showed the utmost solicitude for us, how can we let him down?)

领导应该多多关怀群众。

* 他很关怀这件事,已经问过我好几次了。

* 今天我外出办点儿事,你关怀一下公司。

老校长十分关怀孩子们的成长。
政府十分关怀残疾人的生活。
(The government shows deep solicitude for the life of the disabled people.)

(2)"关心"的对象还可以是施动者自身;"关怀"、"关照"不可以。(The object of "关心" can also be the agent himself, but "关怀" and "关照" can't be used this way.)例如:

他比谁都关心他自己。
我很关心我的考试结果。
谁不关心自己的前途和命运啊?
(Who will not care for one's own future and destiny?)
* 他比谁都关怀/关照他自己。
* 我很关怀/关照我的考试结果。
* 谁不关怀/关照自己的前途和命运啊?

(3)"关怀"一般用于上级对下级、长辈对晚辈的关系;"关心"、"关照"不受这种关系的限制。("关怀" is generally used for the relationship between the senior and the junior or between the elder and the younger generation, while "关心", "关照" are not restricted in these bearings.)例如:

政府非常关怀灾区人民的生活,调拨了大量的救灾物资。
(The government greatly cares for the living of the people in the disaster area and has allotted a large number of goods and materials to help the people to tide over the disaster.)
领导对我们这样关怀,我们也应该多关心关心领导。
(Since the leaders have showed so much care for us we should show more care for them as well.)
* 领导对我们这样关怀,我们也应该多关怀关怀领导。
领导关心我们,我们也应该关心领导。
最近,总经理太忙了,你在生活上多关照关照他。

(4)"关怀"有时可以作"体现"、"表示"等具有抽象意义的动词的宾语。(Sometimes "关怀" can be the objects of "体现","表示", etc;—verbs of the abstract meaning.)例如:

菜篮子工程的实施体现了矿领导对矿工生活的亲切关怀。

(The implementation of the Vegetable-basket Project merely embodies the kind attention to the miners from the mine leaders.)

政府以迅速调来的大量物资表示对灾区人民的深切关怀。

(The government expresses the deep solicitude to the people in the disaster area by quickly allocating and transferring a large quantity of goods and materials.)

2.结构形式上(In structure)

(1)"关心"、"关怀"、"关照"都可以重叠,"关切"不能重叠。("关心","关怀" and "关照" can be reduplicated, but "关切" can't.)例如:

你应该多关心关心/关怀关怀/关照关照他。

* 你应该多关切关切他。/ * 你应该对他多关切关切。

(2)"关心"、"关怀"、"关照"都可以带宾语;"关切"一般不直接带宾语,它的对象通常用"对"引进,放到动词前边。("关心","关怀" and "关照" can be followed by objects. "关切" usually will not be followed directly by an object and its object is usually introduced by "对" and is to be used before verbs.)例如:

张老师非常关心/关怀/关照实验小组的孩子们。

* 张老师非常关切实验小组的孩子们。

张老师对实验小组的孩子们非常关切。

(Teacher Zhang shows deep concern over the children in the experiment group.)

(3)"关心"、"关照"可以带补语;"关怀"有时也可以带,但是比较少;"关切"不能带补语。("关心" and "关照" can be followed by complements, "关怀"can occasionally be followed by a complement and "关切"can't.)例如：

大家对我关心极了。

你这个做父亲的,对孩子关心得很不够。

(You are a father but you have showed too little concern to the child.)

他们对小李关照得很好。

咱们对他关照得还不够。

(We haven't taken good care of him.)

他对孩子们关怀得不得了。

你对群众的生活关怀得太少。

* 大家对我关切极了。

* 你这个做父亲的,对孩子关切得很不够。

* 咱们对他关切得还不够。

(4)"关怀"、"关照"可以构成"在……下"的介宾词组作状语；"关心"、"关切"一般不可以。("关怀"and "关照" can compose preposition-object phrases to be used as adverbials, and "关心" and "关切"usually can't.)例如：

在政府的关怀下,灾区人民的生活很快得到了改善。

(Thanks to the deep solicitude of the government, the life of the people in the disaster area has rapidly got improved.)

在山民的关照下,他很顺利地完成了勘察任务。

(Thanks to the mountainous people's concern he successfully fulfilled the prospecting task.)

* 在政府的关心/关切下,灾区人民的生活很快得到了改善。

* 在山民的关心/关切下,他很顺利地完成了勘察任务。

H

忽然 hūrán   突然 tūrán   忽而 hū'ér

忽然、忽而〈副词〉< adverb >
突然〈形容词〉< adjective >

"忽然"、"突然"、"忽而"都有事情发生得迅速而又出乎意料的意思,但是"忽然"、"突然"有词性上的差别,"忽然"、"忽而"有意义上的差别,所以有时不能通用。("忽然","突然" and "忽而" indicate the matters happen quickly and unexpectedly, but there is different in part of speech between "忽然" and "突然" and there is difference in meaning between "忽然" and "忽而". Therefore, they are unexchangeable sometimes.)

(一)"忽然"和"突然"

1."忽然"和"突然"都可以作句子的状语,因为意义很接近,所以有时可以换用。(Both can be used as an adverbial in sentence. Since they are close in meaning, sometimes they are exchangeable.)例如:

门忽然/突然开了,走进来一个陌生人(a stranger)。

忽然/突然狂风大作,豆大的雨点从天而降。

(Suddenly / Unexpectedly the fierce wind blew and the raindrops of the pea size came from the sky.)

如果说"忽然"、"突然"意义上还有区别的话,那就是"忽然"较侧重于事情来得迅速,"突然"较侧重于事情来得出乎意料。(If there is difference in meaning between "忽然" and "突然", that is, "忽然" comparatively emphasizes the rapid occurrence of things "突然" otherwise emphasizes the unexpected occurrence of things.)

2."忽然"和"突然"主要的差别是词性不同,所以具有不同的功能,在一些情况下是不能换用的。(The essential differences between "忽然" and "突然" lie in their parts of speech so they function differently and in some circumstances they are not exchangeable.)

(1)"忽然"是副词,不能接受程度副词的修饰;"突然"是形容词,可以接受程度副词的修饰。("忽然"is an adverb and can't be modified by adverbs of degree. "突然"is an adjective and can be modified by adverbs of degree.)例如:

这件事来得太突然了,我一点儿思想准备也没有。

(The matter happened too unexpectedly I was not mentally prepared at all.)

这个结果使我感到很突然。

* 这件事来得太忽然了,我一点儿思想准备也没有。

* 这个结果使我感到很忽然。

(2)"突然"可以作谓语、定语、补语,"忽然"没有这一功能。("突然"can be used as a predicate, attributive and complement, but "忽然"doesn't function like that.)例如:

你得的这个结论太突然了,我看不出为什么会得出这样一个结论来。(作谓语)

突然的情况随时都会发生,要做好充分的准备。(作定语)

(Sudden matters can happen at any time. We have to get well prepared.)

你走得太突然了,怎么不早点儿告诉我呢?(作补语)

* 你得的这个结论太忽然了,我看不出为什么会得出这样一个结论来。

* 忽然的情况随时都会发生,要做好充分的准备。

* 你走得太忽然了,怎么不早点儿告诉我呢?

(二)"忽然"和"忽而"

1."忽然"和"忽而"都是副词,都可以作状语。在表示事情发生得迅速而又出乎意料的意思上,两词相当,但是"忽然"用得更普遍、更经常。(Both are adverbs and can be used as adverbials. When indicating that something happens promptly and unexpectedly,

they mean the same, but "忽然" is used more common and often.)
例如：

美丽的梦境忽然/忽而消失得无影无踪。

(The beautiful dream world suddenly disappeared for nothing.)

满是笑容的脸忽然/忽而变得异常严肃起来。

(The smiling face suddenly turned into unusual seriousness.)

2."忽而"还有一种用法：同时用在两个或两个以上意义相对或相近的动词或形容词性词语前,意义大体相当于"一会儿"。表示这种意义的时候,一般不能用"忽然"。〔"忽而" has another usage. It can be used before two or more verbs or adjectives which are opposite or similar in meaning at the same time, approximately meaning "一会儿 (a while)". "忽然" can't be used in this sense generally.〕例如：

他忽而放声大笑,忽而失声痛哭,简直疯了。

(He burst into laughter for a while then burst into tears for a while. He has really gone mad.)

你怎么忽而站起来,忽而坐下去的,到底发生了什么事,叫你这样心神不定的？

(How come you stand up and sit down by turns? What on earth happens? You look so distracted.)

天是怎么啦？怎么忽而晴,忽而阴的？

敌人忽而软,忽而硬,施尽了各种手段。

(The enemy used both hard and soft tactics by turns. They had tried every means.)

* 你怎么忽然站起来,忽然坐下去的,到底发生了什么事,叫你这样心神不定的。

* 敌人忽然软,忽然硬,施尽了各种手段。

花 huā　　花费 huāfèi　　费 fèi

〈动词〉表示用去了、消耗掉了的意思。

(<verb> indicating having expended or used up.)

(一)"花"和"花费"

"花"和"花费"都有"用掉~"的意思,都可以带宾语,都可以跟时间、精力、心血、力气、工夫等词搭配,有时可以换用。(Both mean to expend something and can be followed by objects or collocated with words like time, energy, effort, strength, labour. etc. Sometimes "花" and "花费" are exchangeable.)例如:

老师为培养你花/花费了多少心血啊!

(In order to foster you the teacher has expended so much of his energy!)

为了这个课题的研究,他的确花/花费了不少工夫。

为值得做的事花/花费点儿时间是值得的。

(Spending time on the things worth doing is meaningful.)

但是由于它们词义轻重不同,色彩不同,使用范围也不同,使用起来有一定差别。(But there is still difference in use since they are different in meaning, in flavour and in range of application as well.)

1. 词义轻重不同(Difference in meaning)

"花费"比"花"多了"费"的意思,所以它比"花"多了一点儿"过多"的意思,这样"花费"的词义比"花"就要重一些。(Compared with "花", "花费" adds the meaning of "费". It means a little excess, therefore "花费" expresses stronger meaning than "花".)

2. 词义色彩不同(Difference in flavour)

"花"是口语色彩较浓的一个词,主要用于口语。"花费"则含有更多的书面语色彩,多用于书面语。(The word "花" has stronger flavour of spoken language and is mainly used orally. "花费", on the other hand, expresses stronger flavour of written language and is generally used in written language.)

3. 使用范围不同(Difference in range of application)

(1)"花费"一般用在一些较抽象的对象上——精力、心血、力气、工夫、钱财、口舌等。表示多用了口舌,只能用"花费",不能用"花"。("花费" is generally used in some abstract objects such as energy, effort, strength, labour, wealth, dispute, etc. But when expressing "it takes a lot of talking", "花费" is the only choice, and "花" can never be used in this sense.)。例如:

他花费了不少的口舌,才办成了这件事。

(It took him a lot of talking to settle the matter.)

* 他花了不少口舌,才办成了这件事。

(2)具体的用钱,只能用"花",不能用"花费"。(When indicating the concrete spending of the money, "花" is merely used, "花费" can't be used.)例如:

这些钱你先拿去花吧。

花了十几块钱买了一件衣服。

这套邮票花了多少钱?

* 这些钱你先拿去花费吧。

* 花费了十几块钱买了一件衣服。

* 这套邮票花费了多少钱?

(二)"费"和"花"

"费"和"花"在意义上有一定的区别,"费"有过多地用、过多地消耗的意思,所以它的词义比"花"要重得多。它们在使用范围上、用法上差别很大。(There is certain difference in meaning between the two words. Since "费" means the excessive spending or expending, it is much stronger in meaning than "花". They are considerably different in the range of application and in use.)

1."费"不能用于一般地用钱,一般地用钱,只能用"花",过多地用和消耗,才能用"费"。("花" but not "费" is used in the general sense of spending money. "费" can only be used when the spending or consumption is excessive.)例如:

这些钱你先拿去花吧。

这套邮票花了多少钱?

* 这些钱你先拿去费吧。

* 这套邮票费了多少钱?

为了搞到这个花瓶,他费了不少的钱。

(He has spent a lot of money for obtaining this flower vase.)

在这里玩,太费钱了。

(It costs me dearly to have fun here.)

2."费"可以直接带"脑子"、"心思"、"口舌"等词的宾语,"花"一般不可以。〔"费"can be followed directly by "脑子"(brain), "心思"(thinking) and "口舌"(talking), etc. as objects, but "花" can't.〕例如:

费脑子(be drained of brains)

费心思(mind-exhausted)

费口舌(take a lot of talking)

* 花脑子　* 花心思　* 花口舌

3."费"还可以与许多单音词结合,"花"不可以。例如:

费时(be time-consuming)

费力(need great effort)

费劲(be strenuous)

费神(be drained of brains)

费心(take a lot of trouble)

费事(take a lot of trouble)

费水(be water-consuming)

费电(be power-consuming)

* 花时　* 花力　* 花神　* 花心

* 花事　* 花水　* 花电

4."费"有"过多"的意思,所以它可以接受程度副词的修饰,接受程度副词的修饰后,还可以带宾语,这一点与一般动词不同;"花"是一般动词,没有这一特点,不能接受程度副词的修饰。〔Since "费" means "过多" (excessive), it can be modified by adverbs of degree and objects after, so "费" is different from other verbs in this point. "花" is a common verb which can't be modified by adverbs of degree.〕例如:

你这个破车真费油。
(Your damn car is really gas-consuming.)
这个年龄的孩子穿衣服、穿鞋最费了。
(The children at this age will expend dearly on clothes and shoes.)
不行,不能再这样干了,这样干太费时间了。
这个工作太费脑子了。
(This work drained my brains.)
* 不行,不能再这样干了,这样干太花时间了。
* 这个工作太花脑子了。

"费"因为有这个特点,所以有时也能带表示程度的补语,"花"同样不可以。("费" is also used together with some monosyllabic words, and "花" can't.)。例如:

这个冰箱费电费得<u>不得了</u>。
这孩子穿衣服费<u>极了</u>。
(This child expends exceedingly on clothes.)
* 这个冰箱花电花得不得了。

坏 huài 差 chà

〈形容词〉 < adjective >

"坏"、"差"都可以接受程度副词的修饰,都可以表示不好的、不满意的意思,但是它们所指的"不好",在本质上有很大不同,所以一般是不能换用的。(Both can be modified by adverbs of degree and both indicate not good, dissatisfactory, but here the meaning they refer to is greatly different in nature, therefore they are generally unexchangeable.)

（一）"坏"跟"好"是相对的,它的"不好"主要指缺点多、品质恶劣等;"差"的"不好"主要指不够某一标准。因此在使用上,"坏"常常跟具体的人、事、话、主意、心眼、脾气等结合,也可以跟人的品质有关的抽象一点儿的名声、影响、毛病等结合。("坏" and "好" are opposite in meaning. "不好" refers to being full of shortcomings or unprincipled, "差" refers to being inadequate to reach a certain standard. So practically, "坏" is often used together with particular people, things, words, ideas, mind, temper, etc. as well as with reputation, effect, defect, etc. which are a bit abstract and relating to moral character of people.)例如:

坏人　坏事　坏主意
坏心眼　坏天气　脾气很坏
他说了你不少坏话。
这个家伙做了很多坏事,在我们这里名声极坏。
他借钱不还,造成很坏的影响。
(He wouldn't pay back the money he borrowed and this creates an extremely bad impression.)
他又酗酒、又赌博、又打架,坏毛病真不少。
(He drinks excessively and gambles and fights as well.)

（二）"差"主要用于可以用某一标准衡量的有一定概括性的事物。("差" is mainly used to indicate things of certain generality and can be measured by some standard.)例如:

质量很差(of poor-quality)
条件差极了(in extremely poor condition)
环境卫生很差(the environmental sanitation is too bad)
他的学习成绩是我们班最差的一个。
这部机器性能很差。
(The machine performs poorly.)

"差"一般不用于人的品质或很具体的事物;"坏"一般不用于跟人的品质无关的概括性的事物。("差" is not used for people's moral qualities or particular things; "坏" is not used for generalized things which have nothing to do with people's moral qualities.)例如:

* 差人　* 差事　* 差主意　* 差心眼
* 差天气　* 脾气很差
* 他借钱不还,造成很差的影响。
* 质量很坏　* 条件坏极了　* 环境卫生很坏
* 他的学习成绩是我们班最坏的一个。
* 这部机器性能很坏。

(三)"坏"可以单独用在名词前作定语,"差"不能。("坏" can be used separately before nouns as attributive, and "差" can't.)例如:

坏天气　坏习惯　坏书　坏思想
坏毛病　坏心眼
* 差质量　* 差条件　* 差卫生
* 差性能　* 差成绩

(四)"差"还可以指"错误"或"出入","坏"没有这种意思。("差" can also indicate "错误(incorrect)" or "出入(discrepancy)", and "坏"can't.)例如:

他的话一点儿也不差。

(What he said is completely correct.)

你说得不差,是这样的。

(You are right. Things are just like this.)

* 他的话一点儿也不坏。
* 你说得不坏,是这样的。

(五)"差"和"坏"可能出现在同一种类型的句子中,这时要注意,它们的意思是完全不同的。(Both "差" and "坏" may appear in the sentence of the same pattern, but attention has to be paid for they indicate totally different meanings.)例如:

你说得不坏。——是指说得好。
你说得不差。——是指说话的内容没有错误、没有出入。

把差的都卖了。——是指不够某一质量标准的,但不一定是坏的。

把坏的都卖了。——是指该东西有残或变质的等。

会 huì　　见面 jiànmiàn　　见 jiàn　　会见 huìjiàn

〈动词〉一方跟另一方面对面地相见。

(<verb> meeting face to face between one party and the other.)

"会"、"见面"、"见"、"会见"虽然都有一方跟另一方面对面地相见的意思,但是由于它们的色彩、使用场合、用法有所不同,所以大多不能换用。(Although the four all have the meaning of meeting face to face between the two sides, they are different in flavour, on occasion, and in use, therefore they are usually not exchangeable.)

(一)"会"和"见面"

"会"和"见面"的意思基本相同,但是用法上有差别。(Essentially the two mean the same things but are different in use.)

1."会"后面可以带宾语,"见面"是动宾结构,后面不能再带宾语。("会"can be followed by an object,"见面"is a verb-object structure so can't be followed by an object.)例如:

晚上我要去会一个朋友。

我想会他一次。

* 晚上我要去见面一个朋友。

* 我想见面他一次。

2."见面"的对象一般用介词"跟"引进,放在谓语动词前作状语,"见面"后面不需要其他成分,可以直接结句;"会"的对象也可以用介词"跟"引进,但是单个"会"不能结句,后面要有其他成分。(The object of "见面" is generally introduced by preposition "跟" and is used as an adverbial before the predicate verbs. And there needs no other compositions after "见面", the clauses can be connected directly. While the object of "会" can also be introduced by preposition "跟" but a separated "会" can't make clauses and it needs other compositions.)例如：

  我今天跟他见面。
  你知道他要跟谁见面吗？
  他跟女朋友会过三次了。
  * 我今天跟他会。
  * 你知道他要跟谁会吗？

  3. "会"可以重叠使用；"见面"作为一个词不能重叠，但是分离后，"见"可以重叠，构成"见见面"的形式。("会" can be reduplicated. "见面" can't, but if "见面" is separated, "见" can be reduplicated to compose "见见面".)例如：

  他说他想会会你。
  什么时候咱们会一会他吧。
  * 我想见面见面你的朋友。
  我想跟你的朋友见见面。

(二)"会"和"见"

  1. "会"多用于随意性较强、没有很强的目的性、较亲近关系的相见；"见"比"会"使用的场合要严肃多了，而且通常有一定的目的性。("会" is mainly used to describe the meeting which is rather casual, without clear purposes and among the people of close relationship. The situation where "见" is used is much more solemn than the situation where "会" is used, and the action "见" usually has certain purposes.)例如：

  听说咱们的老同学王力来了，十几年没见了，我想会会他。
  今天晚上我一定去会会他。
  我去见见你们老师，跟她谈谈这个问题。
  事不宜迟，明天我一定去见你们经理。

  (The matter oughtn't to be delayed. I will go to meet your manager tomorrow for sure.)

  2. 表示跟朋友、跟客人会面，一般用"会"，一般不用"见"，尤其不能直接用。(If going to meet friends or guests, "会" is used instead of "见", especially "见" can't be used directly.) 例如：

我去会朋友。　　　　　　他正在会客。
* 我去见朋友。　　　　　　* 他正在见客。

(三)"会"、"见"和"会见"

1."会"和"见"、"会见"比，比较轻松、随意性较强；"见"、"会见"要严肃一些，尤其是目的性比较强。(Compared with "见" and "会见", "会" means comparatively relaxed and with the character of bit strong casualness. "见" and "会见" are used on rather formal occasions, especially, with strong purpose.) 例如：

找个时间我们会一会，聊一聊，好吗？
我想见见你们领导，反映一下这个情况。

2."会见"含有庄重的色彩，"会见"的活动通常都是有意安排的，所以它多用于外交场合或者庄重的场合，普通的、一般的相见，不能用"会见"。("会见" expresses formal flavour and the activities of "会见" are all intentionally arranged, so "会见" is mainly used on the occasion of foreign affairs or the occasion of solemnness. "会见" can't be used for usual meetings.) 例如：

外交部长会见了来我国访问的美国朋友。
中央有关领导会见了前来我国投资的几位商人。
(The leaders of the Central Committee concerned met with a few businessmen who came to China to invest.)

* 外交部长会/见了来我国访问的美国朋友。
* 中央有关领导会/见了前来我国投资的几位商人。
* 今天晚上我去会见女朋友。
* 我妈妈昨天到中国了，晚上我去会见她了。

或者 huòzhě　　还是 háishì

〈连词〉表示选择。
(<conj. > indicating to select.)

(一)"或者"、"还是"都可以表示选择，但是不能通用，它们适用于不同的句式。"或者"只适用于叙述、说明具有两项以上可供选择的情况或条件的叙述句;而"还是"则主要适用于问句,让对方在两个或两个以上的选择项中选择一项。(Both mean to select, but they are not exchangeable for they are used in different patterns. "或者" is applicable to the declarative sentences of stating or illustrating the situations or conditions with more than two items provided to be selected, "还是" is mainly applicable to the interrogative questions which provide the opposite side to select one from the two or more than two items.)例如:

大学毕业以后,我或者参加工作,或者继续读书。
这次会你去参加,或者他去参加,都行。
你们骑自行车去,还是坐汽车去?
咱们先学习后讨论,还是先讨论后学习?
(Shall we study first and then discuss or discuss first and then study?)

* 星期六下午,我们常常去外边玩,<u>还是</u>去商店买东西。(改:或者)
* 晚上,我们常常聊天儿<u>还是</u>唱歌。(改:或者)
* 这样说对,<u>或者</u>那样说对?(改:还是)
* 他问:"打完电话我付钱<u>或者</u>对方付钱?"(改:还是)

(二)"还是"有时也可以用在叙述句中,但是只能构成词组作句子的某一成分,而且这一成分本身要含有疑问的意思。这种时候不能用"或者"。("还是" is sometimes used in declarative sentences, but it is only used to form an element of the sentence, and this element itself should imply the meaning of making enquiry, and "或者" can't be used.)例如:

我也不知道先去西安好,还是先去上海好。
他说他也不清楚在学校集合,还是在车站集合。
(He said he is not sure where everyone is supposed to gather, at the school or at the station.)

* 我也不知道先去西安好,或者先去上海好。
* 他说他也不清楚在学校集合,或者在车站集合。

J

几乎 jīhū   差点儿 chàdiǎnr
〈副词〉 < adverb >

(一)"几乎"、"差点儿"的相同之处:(The similarity between "几乎" and "差点儿":)

"几乎"、"差点儿"都可以用于表示所说的事情是说话人不希望发生的事情。它们在使用上都有一个共同的特点:使用肯定式或使用否定式,表达效果是一样的。在这种情况下,两词可以换用。(Both "几乎" and "差点儿" can be used to express something happened against the speaker's wish or hope. They have a common feature in use. They can express the same meaning either in a positive or a negative form. They are interchangeable in such a case.)例如:

两人眼睛里都冒了火,几乎打起来。(结果没打。)
(Both of them flared up, and almost came to blows.)
两人眼睛里都冒了火,几乎没打起来。(结果没打。)
一阵大风刮来,几乎把我掀倒。(结果没倒。)
(A sudden blast almost blew me down.)
一阵大风刮来,几乎没把我掀倒。(结果没倒。)
两人眼睛里都冒了火,差点儿打起来。(结果没打。)
两人眼睛里都冒了火,差点儿没打起来。(结果没打。)
一阵大风刮来,差点儿把我掀倒。(结果没倒。)
一阵大风刮来,差点儿没把我掀倒。(结果没倒。)

(二)"几乎"、"差点儿"的不同之处:(The differences between "几乎" and "差点儿":)

1. 当所说的事情或现象是说话人希望发生的而没有发生时,并且后面多为肯定式时,一般不用"几乎",多用"差点儿"。(When what the speaker says is what he wishes to happen, but

does not happen, and it's usually followed by a positive sentence, use "差点儿" rather than "几乎".)例如：

* 排了好几个小时的队,几乎就买到球票了。
* 花瓶掉下来时,我几乎就给接住了。
* 我几乎就赶上火车了,就怨小李动作那么慢。

排了好几个小时的队,差点儿就买到球票了。

花瓶掉下来时,我差点儿就给接住了。

我差点儿就赶上火车了,就怨小李动作那么慢。

(Had Xiao Li not been so slow, I would have caught the train.)

但是,当所说的事情或现象是说话人希望发生的而终于发生了,句中含有庆幸的意思,后面为否定式时,可以用"几乎",也可以用"差点儿"。(But, when what the speaker says is what he wishes to happen and really happens, and a happy feeling is implied, it is followed by a negative sentence and either "几乎" or "差点儿" can be used.)例如：

那天,车在路上"抛锚"了,我几乎/差点儿没赶上飞机。

(That day, my car broke down on the way, and I almost missed the plane.)

在中国旅游时,他把护照给丢了,几乎/差点儿没走成。

也就是说,"差点儿"不受说话人希望或不希望发生的限制,"几乎"受到一定的限制。(That is, "差点儿" is not restricted by the speaker's subjective wish; while "几乎" has some restriction.)

2. "几乎"、"差点儿"在色彩上有一定差别。"几乎"书面语色彩较强,多用于书面语。"差点儿"口语色彩较强,多用于口语。("几乎" and "差点儿" are different to a certain degree in flavour. "几乎"can be used in written language to express emphasis while "差点儿" can be widely used in spoken language.)

几乎 jīhū　　简直 jiǎnzhí

〈副词〉表示非常接近某种情况、度或状态等。

(< adverb > expressing something being close to a certain condition, degree or state, etc.)

"几乎"、"简直"词义很接近,但是仍有一定差别。("几乎" and "简直" are quite similar in meaning, but different to a certain degree.)

(一) 词义轻重、表达语气有所不同:(Difference in degree of meaning and tone in expressing:)

"几乎"跟"简直"比,词义要轻一些,它只是表示接近于某种情况、程度、状态等,有"差不多"的意思。"简直"则表示更接近于所说的某种情况、程度、状态等,相差无几,甚至于有的已经完全达到所说的情况。"简直"含有夸张的语气,"几乎"基本上没有这种语气。"简直"表示的意思比较肯定,"几乎"没有"简直"那么肯定。(Compared with "简直", "几乎" is weaker in meaning. It just expresses being close to a certain condition, degree or state, etc, and implies "差不多"."简直" means almost the same in condition, degree, or state as what is said, or with little difference, or sometimes completely the same as what is said. "简直" is somewhat exaggerative. "几乎" basically does not possess such tone. The meaning expressed by "简直" is a little positive, while "几乎" is not as positive as "简直".) 试比较:

他几乎不敢想像事情的结局。

(He could hardly imagine the result of this matter.)

他简直不敢想像事情的结局。

(He simply couldn't imagine the result of the matter.)

连续半年不给雨的老天,终于给雨了,人们几乎乐疯了。

连续半年不给雨的老天,终于给雨了,人们简直乐疯了。

一场灾害,使得农民们一年来的辛苦几乎等于零。

(A disaster made the farmer's whole year's hard work almost

in vain.)

一场灾害,使得农民们一年来的辛苦简直等于零。

(A disaster made the farmer's whole year's hard work simply in vain.)

(二) 使用范围有所不同:(Differences in the scope of use:)

1."简直"后面可以带有比喻或比较;"几乎"一般不用于这种情况。"几乎"只用于如实叙述的情况,它所修饰的一般是客观存在着的事物。("简直" could be followed by a metaphor or comparison, "几乎" generally can not be used this way. "几乎" is only applied to express the actual fact. It is generally used to modify the objective things in existence.)例如:

雪大得简直像鹅毛一样。

(The flakes of snow are simply as big as goose feather.)

你简直连畜牲都不如。

(You are simply a beast.)

＊ 雪大得几乎像鹅毛。

＊ 你几乎连畜牲都不如。

火辣辣的太阳烤着后背,后背光亮光亮的,几乎要流油了。

(The bare back is almost scorched to ooze oil by the burning sun.)

惊马奔来时,他几乎给吓傻了。

2."简直"有时用于表达简短的、含有强烈不满语气的话;"几乎"不能用于这种情况。("简直" is sometimes used to express short or brief words with dissatisfying tone. "几乎" can not be used in such a case.)例如:

简直不像话!(It's simply shocking.)

简直没人性!(It's simply inhuman.)

简直是个畜牲!(He's simply a beast.)

简直太小气了!(He's simply too mean.)

简直没家教!(He's simply ill-bred.)

* 几乎不像话！　* 几乎没人性！　* 几乎是个畜牲！
　　* 几乎太小气了！　　* 几乎没家教！

(三) 意义上的不同：(Differences in meaning：)

　　1."几乎"还有"差点儿"的意思,表示某事眼看就要发生,而结果没有发生的意思;"简直"没有这种意义。("几乎" possesses the meaning of being on the verge of something. It expresses that something is about to happen, but does not happen as a result."简直" does not possess such meaning.)

　　　脚下一滑,几乎摔倒了。
　　　(He slipped and almost fell down.)
　　　毕业考试,他几乎不及格。
　　* 脚下一滑,简直摔倒了。
　　* 毕业考试,他简直不及格。

　　2."几乎"还有接近于某数量、范围的意思;"简直"没有这一意义。("几乎" also implies the meaning of being close to a certain number, amount or scope."简直" doesn't have such meaning.) 例如：

　　　一篇毕业论文,他几乎写了三年。
　　　两个多月的假期,他几乎走遍了半个中国。
　　　(He almost toured half of China during the two months' vacation.)
　　* 一篇毕业论文,他简直写了三年。

急 jí　　着急 zháojí

〈形容词〉< adjective >
〈动词〉< verb >

"急"、"着急"词义有差别,用法也不同。("急" and "着急" are different in meaning and in usage.)

(一)"急"、"着急"都可以用作形容词。(Both "急" and "着急" can be used as adjectives.)

　　1."急"、"着急"都可以用作谓语、补语。(Both "急" and "着

急" can be used as predicates and complements.)例如:

他的性子特别急。

(He is of impatient disposition.)

一个多小时过去了,大家都等急了。

别着急,他一定会来的。

孩子还没找到,妈妈十分着急,生怕出什么问题。

他终于控制不住自己了,变得着急起来。

(Finally he lost control of himself, and got anxious.)

在同一种功能下,有时也有区别。"急"主要用于一种情形、状态、性质;"着急"则主要用于表示人的一种情态。所以,"急"可以用于人,也可以用于事物;"着急"则只能用于人,不能用于事物。(In this case, "急" and "着急" are sometimes different even when performing the same grammatical function. "急" is mainly used to express a certain condition, state, nature or quality, "着急" is mainly used for people but not for things.)例如:

任务很急,不能再拖了。

雨下得很急,还是等一等再走吧。

(It's raining hard, you'd better wait a while.)

* 任务很着急,不能再拖了。

* 雨下得很着急,还是等一等再走吧。

* 他的性子特别着急。

2."着急"还可以用作状语,表示动作的方式、情态;"急"没有这种用法。("着急" can also be used as an adverbial to express manner and mood of action; "急" can not be used this way.)例如:

临上车前,他着急地收拾着行李。

他着急地催促道:"快点儿吧,晚了!"

* 临上车前,他急地收拾着行李。

* 他急地催促道:"快点儿吧,晚了!"

3."急"、"着急"都可以带补语,但是所带补语类型不完全一样。"急"后接补语较自由。(Both "急" and "着急" can be followed by a complement, but not always by the same type of complement. A wider range of complements can be added to "急".)例如:

急死了　　　急得很　　　急得不得了
急得不像样(to be worried to death)　　急得直哭
急得坐立不安(to be too worried to feel at ease whether sitting or standing)
急得话都说不出来了

"着急"带补语的情况很少,一般可带的只有很少的程度意义的补语,描写性补语几乎不带。(There are few cases that "着急" is followed by a complement. If possible, it can be only used with a complement of degree, seldom with a descriptive complement.)例如:

着急得很　　　　　　着急得不得了
* 着急得坐立不安　　* 着急得直哭

(二)"急"、"着急"还可以用作动词,可以带宾语,但是宾语形式和宾语与动词之间的关系并不相同。"急"可以带代词宾语,表示的是"使人急"的意思;"着急"带宾语的现象很少,带的一般是词组或非名词性词组,通常表示"着急"的原因。(Both "急" and "着急" can be used as verbs and followed by objects. But the types of objects and the relations between the object and the verb are different. "急" can be followed by an object of pronoun which means to make somebody worry; "着急" is seldom followed by an object, and is often used with a word group or non-noun phrase, which indicates the cause of "着急".)例如:

真急人!(I'm so worried.)
急死我了!(I'm worried to death.)
* 真着急人!　　* 着急死我了!
我不着急别的,我着急他找不到工作怎么办。

(I am worried about nothing but what he'll do if he can't find a job.)

"着急"所带宾语的性质,与"着急"的构词方式有关。"着急"构词语素间的关系属于支配关系,具有离合的特点,所以后面一般不再带支配关系的宾语,结构上有离合词的特点。例如:可以说"急什么"、"急了半天",用"着急"时,一般要说"着什么急"、"着了半天急"。(The feature of the object of "着急" has something to do with the structure of "着急". The word formation of "着急" belongs to subordination with the feature of coordination and separation. So it is generally used without objects whose word formation belongs to subordination or which has the feature of coordination and separation.)

急忙 jímáng   匆忙 cōngmáng

〈形容词〉< adjective >

(一)"急忙"、"匆忙"在意义上稍有差别,"急忙"侧重于由于心急而使行动加快;"匆忙"侧重于加紧地忙。(There is a slight distinction in meaning between "急忙" and "匆忙". "急忙" emphasizes the hurriedness of action because of impatience, while "匆忙" mainly means to speed up the hurriedness.)

(二)"急忙"、"匆忙"在用法上差别较大:(There is a large distinction in usage between "急忙" and "匆忙":)

1."急忙"只充当状语,不用"地";"急忙"前不用程度副词。("急忙" can only be used as an adverb; take neither "地" after it, nor adverbs of degree before it.)例如:

听到敲门声,她急忙把门打开。

看到爸爸走下车,我急忙迎了上去。

听了我的话,老张竟误会了,我急忙解释,可是怎么也说不清楚了。

(Hearing my words, Lao Zhang actually misunderstood. However I explained, I couldn't make it clear.)

* 听到敲门声,她很急忙把门打开。

＊ 看到爸爸走下车,我很急忙迎了上去。

2."匆忙"则可充当状语、谓语、补语、定语;可以用"地";"匆忙"前可以用程度副词。("匆忙"can be used as an adverbial, predicate, complement and attribute; it can take either "地"after it, or adverbs of degree before it.)例如:

时间不多了,她匆忙地收拾着。(状语)

这次出门太匆忙了,哪儿也没去。(谓语)

(I left home for so short a time that I didn't go anywhere else.)

走得很匆忙,什么也没带。(补语)

你看她那匆忙的样子,一定遇到了麻烦。(定语)

＊ 这次出门太急忙了,哪儿也没去。

＊ 走得很急忙,什么也没带。

＊ 你看她那急忙的样子,一定遇到了麻烦。

3."急忙"、"匆忙"都可以构成 AABB 的重叠式,后边都可以加"地"作状语,都可以加"的"作谓语、定语、补语。("急忙" and "匆忙" both can be attributes used to form the overlapping pattern AABB. And both of them can be used as adverbials when followed with "地", and used as predicates, attributes and complements when followed by "的".)例如:

放下电话,他就急急忙忙地/匆匆忙忙地跑了出去。(状语)

你怎么总是急急忙忙的/匆匆忙忙的?(谓语)

看他那急急忙忙的/匆匆忙忙的样子,一定有什么事。(定语)

他走得急急忙忙的/匆匆忙忙的。(补语)

急忙 jímáng   连忙 liánmáng   赶忙 gǎnmáng

急忙〈形容词〉< adjective >

连忙、赶忙〈副词〉< adverb >

(一)"急忙"与"连忙"、"赶忙"意义稍有不同。"急忙"侧重于心

303

急而忙,"连忙"、"赶忙"侧重于动作行为的紧张而迅速。(There is a slight distinction in meaning among "急忙","连忙" and "赶忙". "急忙" emphasizes the impatience of mind; "连忙" and "赶忙" emphasize the swiftness and tensity of actions.)

(二)"急忙"与"连忙"、"赶忙"都可以用于动词前作状语,除意义差别外,用法相同。(All of them can be used before the verb as adverbial and the usage is the same except the slight difference in meaning.)例如:

他急忙走上前拦住我,试图说服我。

(He hastened to stop me, trying to talk me over.)

看到老队长走进来,王平连忙招呼大家让出一个座位,请老队长坐下。

看到一位大嫂手拎着包裹,怀抱着孩子,雷锋赶忙走上前帮忙。

(三)"急忙"与"连忙"、"赶忙"词性不同,所以功能、用法也不相同。"急忙"是形容词,它可以构成 AABB 的重叠式,构成重叠式以后可以在后边加"地"作状语,加"的"作谓语、定语、补语。"连忙"、"赶忙"没有这一用法。("急忙" and "连忙","赶忙" are different in part of speech, grammatical function and the usage. "急忙" is an adjective and can be used to form the reduplicated pattern AABB. In the pattern AABB, it can be used as adverbial with "地" after it and as predicate, attribute and complement with "的" after it. "连忙" and "赶忙" can not be used this way.)例如:

张嫂急急忙忙跑下楼来,喊道:"不好了,老爷出事了!"

(Sister Zhang hurried downstairs, crying: "Our lord had an accident.")

你怎么总是急急忙忙的?

看他那急急忙忙的样子,一定有什么事。

你看他,走得急急忙忙的。

* 张嫂连连忙忙跑下楼来,喊道:"不好了,老爷出事了!"

* 你怎么总是赶赶忙忙的？

给予 jǐyǔ　　给以 gěiyǐ　　给 gěi

〈动词〉表示使对方得到某东西或某种待遇等。

(< verb > expressing making somebody get something or a certain treatment.)

(一) 色彩不同(Differences in flavour)

"给予"、"给以"都含有较强的书面语色彩,一般多用于书面语;"给"口语色彩很强,多用于口语,而且使用频率很高。(Both "给予"and"给以"imply strong flavour of written language, generally used in written language; while "给"implies strong oral flavour, mostly used in spoken language and frequently used.)

(二) 使用上有所不同(Differences in use)

1."给予"、"给以"、"给"都可以带双宾语。(All of them can be followed with direct object and indirect object at the same time.)例如：

他给了<u>你许多礼物</u>。(你、礼物)
老师给予<u>他很多鼓励</u>。(他、鼓励)
贵公司给以<u>我们不少帮助</u>。(我们、帮助)

但是,"给予"、"给以"必须带宾语;"给"在一定的语言环境中可以省略宾语。(But, both"给予"and "给以"must be followed by objects, while in a certain language circumstance, the object following "给" can be omitted.)例如：

(这本书)是谁给的？

*(这本书)是谁给予/给以的？

2."给予"、"给以"连带的宾语一定是抽象的事物,不能是具体的事物,宾语多为动词宾语;"给"连带的宾语可以是具体的事物,也可以是抽象的事物。(The object following "给予"or "给以" must be something abstract, but not something specific and must be verb object; the object following "给"can be something either abstract or specific.)例如：

他的这种精神给予孩子们巨大的精神力量。

(Such spirit of his gives the children a great strength spiritually.)

贵厂给以我们许多无私的援助。

你路上没有吃的,这些食品给你。

她的信给了我不少的温暖。

* 你路上没有吃的,这些食品给予/给以你。

"给予"、"给以"可连带的宾语类型几乎相同,但是属于更加抽象的情感的事物,最好用"给予"。("给予"and"给以"could be followed by the same type of objects, but "给予"had better be used when object refers to abstract emotions or feelings.)例如：

对于她的遭遇,很多人都给予了同情。

(Many people show sympathies for her misfortune.)

3."给予"、"给以"连带的表事宾语一般要求是双音节或双音节以上的;"给"没有限制。(Generally speaking, the object following "给予"or "给以"should have double syllables or more; "给"is not restricted by this.)例如：

几年来,王先生精心地照顾我,给予我父亲般的慈爱。

(For years Mr. Wang has taken best care of me, giving me fatherly love.)

读书的这几年,他给予我许多关怀和照顾。

政府给以这个地区许多物质上的援助。

他给了我不少机会,可是我一个也没有把握住。

小王给了我一封信。

4."给予"、"给以"由于词的构成不同,与其他词语结合时,有时有一定差别。"给予"是"给"和"予"两个同义动语素结合的词;"给以"严格讲不是一个词,为了学习方便,我们暂且把它看成一个词。"给以"实际上是动语素"给",加上引进所凭借的事物的虚语素"以"构成的。因此,使用时,"给予"后边还可以接用

"以"引进所凭借的事物的介宾词组;"给以"则不能这样用了。("给予"and "给以"are different in word formation, so sometimes they differ to a certain degree when combined with other words. "给予"is a word formed by combining "给"and "予"; Strictly speaking, "给予" is not a single word. For the sake of convenience, we regard it as a single word for the moment. In fact, "给以"comprises of the morphemes "给"and "以"which are used to introduce something. "给予" can be followed by a prepositional phrase introduced by "以". "给以" can't be used like that.)例如:

我们给予敌人以沉重的打击。

(We gave the enemy a heavy blow.)

雷锋精神给予广大青少年以巨大的精神力量。

对于在工作中做出显著成绩的人,应该给以表扬和鼓励。

* 我们给以敌人以沉重的打击。

* 雷锋精神给以广大青少年以巨大的精神力量。

"给"是单语素动词,所以它后面可以接用"以"引进所凭借的事物的介宾词组。("给"is a single verb, so it can be followed by "以"to introduce a prepositional phrase.)例如:

给敌人以沉重的打击　　给他以关怀和照顾

给别人以说话的机会(to give others a chance to speak)

记 jì　　记忆 jìyì

〈动词〉< verb >

〈名词〉< noun >

"记"和"记忆"都有把对某事的印象保留在脑子里,使之不忘掉,或者想起的意思,有时可以互换使用。(Both "记"and "记忆" have the meaning of keeping the impression of something in mind in order not to forget or mean recalling. Sometimes they are interchangeable.)例如：

> 他记/记忆单词的能力很强。
> 小时候的事,我还记得清清楚楚的。
> 过去的事,有的他还能记忆起来。

但是由于这两个词色彩、意义、用法上的差别,使得它们在很多情况下不能互换使用。(But because of the differences in flavour, meaning and usage, they are not interchangeable in most cases.)

(一) 词义的语体色彩不同(Differences in flavour)

"记"多用于口语;"记忆"多用于书面语。("记" is mainly used in spoken language;"记忆", otherwise, is mainly used in written language.)

(二) 词义不完全相同(Not quite the same in meaning)

1."记忆"可以表示保留在脑子里某印象的一种功能性行为。"记"一般不能用于这种情况。("记忆"can express a kind of functional behavior of keeping some impressions in mind."记" generally cannot be used in this case.) 例如：

> 我脑子里一片混乱,已经无法记忆了。
> 〔My mind is in a turmoil, and I can't remember anything. (or I am too confused to remember anything.)〕
> 他现在能够记忆了。
> 这台电脑能够记忆。
> 这个仪器有很好的记忆功能。
> * 我脑子里一片混乱,已经无法记了。
> * 他现在能够记了。
> * 这台电脑能够记。
> * 这个仪器有很好的记的功能。

2."记"则多用于把一些具体的东西通过脑力活动保留在脑子里的行为。("记" emphasizes the action of maintaining some specific things within one's mind through mental activities.)例如：

记数字　记单词　记歌词　记电话号码

3.临时记着某事,只能用"记",不能用"记忆"。(When expressing remembering something for the moment, only "记" can be used and "记忆" can not.)例如:

你记着告诉他,明天早上六点集合。

(Remember to tell him that we will gather together at six tomorrow morning.)

* 你记忆着告诉他,明天早上六点集合。

4."记"还有"记录"的意思,"记忆"没有这种意思。〔"记" implies the meaning of "记录"(recording), "记忆" doesn't possess such meaning.〕例如:

大家把这些练习题记下去。

〔Please record (copy) these exercises.〕

我帮你把歌谱记下来了。

(I recorded the music of the song for you.)

你上课记笔记了吗?

(Did you take a note in class?)

* 我帮你把歌谱记忆下来了。

(三)用法上、功能上有差别(Differences in usage and function)

1."记"后面可以接结果补语等,"记忆"不可以。("记"can be followed by a complement of result. "记忆"can not be used like that.)例如:

请你记住你刚才说的话。

我总也记不住身份证的号码。

* 请你记忆住你刚才说的话。

* 我总也记忆不住身份证的号码。

2."记"后面接动态助词"了"、"着"、"过"比较自由;"记忆"有时可以接"了",但是"着"、"过"几乎不接。("记"can be followed by aspect particles "了","着" or "过" freely; sometimes "记忆" can be followed by "了", but hardly by "着"or"过".)例如:

309

我正记着单词呢。
我记得我记过这个单词。
* 我正记忆着单词呢。
* 我记得我记忆过这个单词。

3."记忆"和"记"还有名词性功能,但意义完全不同。"记忆"是指把过去的事物保留在脑子里的印象。"记"是指记载或者描写事物的书或文章。两词不能换用。(Both "记忆" and "记" can function as nouns, but they are completely different in meaning. "记忆" refers to the impressions which bear something in the past in mind. "记" refers to books or articles recording and describing things. They can not be exchanged.)例如:

美好的记忆(happy memories)
儿时的记忆(childhood memories)
他失去了记忆(He lost his memory.)
留在我的记忆里(remain in my memory)
* 美好的记　　　　* 儿时的记
* 留在我的记里　　* 他失去了记
《史记》　　　　　《岳阳楼记》
日记　笔记　　　　传记

记得 jìde　　记住 jì zhù

"记得"和"记住"虽然都有把某事记在脑子里的意思,但是基本上不能换用,它们结构不同,意义不同,使用的环境和用法也不同。(Although both "记得" and "记住" imply keeping something in mind, basically they can not be used interchangeablely, because they are different in both structure and meaning and they are used in different circumstances and different ways.)

(一) 意义上(In meaning)

"记得"是作为一个词用的;"记住"应该看成"记"和"住"两个词,"住"是"记"的结果。因此,"记得"不强调"记得怎么样了"

这种结果,而"记住"则是强调的。所以从意义上看,"记得"主要表示所记的事情还清楚、还没有忘;"记住"主要表示通过记的活动,把要记的事物牢固地保留到脑子里。("记得"is used as a single word, "记住" should be regarded as two words, "记"and "住", and "住"is the result of "记". Therefore "记得"does not emphasize the result of "记得怎么样了" but "记住"does stress its result. "记得" usually means something learnt is still remembered; while "记住" generally means to keep what you are going to learn firmly in mind.)
例如:

你还记得我的朋友张欣吗？她上个月结婚了。
你小时候刚刚学走步的情景我还记得。
* 你还记住我的朋友张欣吗？她上个月结婚了。
* 你小时候刚刚学走步的情景我还记住。
把我的电话号码记住,别再忘了。
今天学的二十个单词我都记住了。
* 把我的电话号码记得,别再忘了。
* 今天学的二十个单词我都记得了。

(二) 使用环境上(In applying circumstances)

"记得"所指的事情一定是过去的事情或者过去获知的事情,它强调某事情至今还保留在脑海里,所以使用"记得"时,常常配合副词"还"。"记住"没有事情过去、现在、将来的限制,它只是一种记忆的活动,并有"住"的结果。("记得"must refer to something that happened or acquired in the past and it emphasizes that something still remains in mind by now. Therefore when "记得"is used, it's usually supported by "还"while "记住"is not restricted by the time of things, the past, the present or the future. It is just a kind of activity of remembering and with the result of "住".)例如:

我还记得那一年的事。
我们下乡那天的情景,至今我还清清楚楚地记得。
(I still remember clearly the day when we went to the coun-

tryside.)
   你不记得了？他姓王，去年我带他见过你。
   这些单词我都记住了，不信，你考考我。
   那天老师跟我说的话，我都记住了。
   明天我要记住下面这些单词。
   ＊明天我要记得下面这些单词。

(三) 用法上(In use)

1. 否定形式："记得"的否定形式是"不"，不能用"没"；"记住"的否定形式主要是"没"，在假设的条件句中，可以用"不"。(Negative form: In the negative sentence, "记得" is preceded by "不" not "没"; while "记住" is preceded by "没" in the negative sentence. In supposed conditional clause, "不" can be used.) 例如：
   他住在哪儿，我不记得了。
   我不记得那件事了。
   ＊他住在哪儿，我没记得了。
   ＊我没记得那件事了。
   游戏的规则你怎么还没记住呀？
   你记住他的地址了吗？——没记住。
   ＊游戏的规则你怎么还不记住呀？
   ＊你记住他的地址了吗？——不记住。
   不记住这几条规则，你就别想离开这间屋子。
   (You are not allowed to leave the room if you can't remember the rules.)

2. "记得"后面不能用动态助词，尤其是"着"、"过"，"了"在"记得"后面带宾语的时候也不能用；"记住"不能用"着"、"过"，但可以用"了"。(Aspect particles, especially "着", "过" can not be used after "记得", and "了" can not be used when "记得" is followed by object; while "着" and "过" can not be used after "记住", and "了" can follow it.) 例如：
   我记得那件事。

* 我记得了那件事　　* 我正记得着那件事
* 我记得过那件事
我记住了那件事。
* 我正记住着那件事　　* 我记住过那件事

继续 jìxù　　持续 chíxù

〈动词〉< verb >

"继续"和"持续"都有延续不断的意思,但是大多不能换用,这是因为它们意义的侧重角度不同,由此也形成用法上的差别。(Both "继续" and "持续" mean continuing without stop, but in most cases, they are not interchangeable, because they emphasize different points in meaning, which leads to the difference in usage.)

(一) 意义上(In meaning)

"继续"和"持续"最大的差别在于:"继续"可以中断,然后接着进行,也可以不中断;"持续"不能中断,必须是一直保持着某种动作、状态等。(The greatest difference is that "继续" implies going on after suspending while "持续" expresses going on in a specified course of action or condition without interruption.) 例如:

由于病重,他不得不放下研究课题养病,可是病情稍有好转,他就又继续研究起来。

(Because of his serious illness, he had to lay down his research and rest. However, he continued his work as soon as he was better.)

大家休息好了吧? 好,继续干吧!

* 由于病重,他不得不放下研究的课题养病,可是病情稍有好转,他就又持续研究起来。

* 大家休息好了吧? 好,持续干吧!

我跟他的书信往来持续了二十多年。

(I have kept correspondence with him for more than twenty years.)

年利润持续增长。

(Annual profits keep increasing.)

(二) 用法上(In use)

1."持续"后面除了接发展、变化等动词外,一般要接表示持续状态的助词"着",或者趋向动词、延续的时段、延续到某时刻的时点等;"继续"在表示不中断的意义时,也可以这样用,但是表示中断后接着进行的意思时,就不能这么用了。"持续"则不能用于中断后接着进行的情况。(Besides being followed by verbs expressing changes or developments, "持续" should be followed by the aspect particle "着" which indicates the continuing state, or a verb of direction, or words indicating duration or moment, etc.; when "继续" indicates no interruption, it can be used the same way. However when "继续" means going on after an interruption, it can not be used this way. "持续" can not be used in case of going on after interruption.)例如:

经济形势持续良性发展。
他们的斗争还在持续着。
地震竟持续了十几秒钟。
我们的友谊一直持续到现在。
经济形势继续良性发展。

(The economic situation keeps improving steadily.)

他们的斗争还在继续着。
地震竟继续了十几秒钟。
我们的友谊一直继续到现在。
你继续说吧。
他们又继续前进了。
咱们继续写吧。

* 你持续说吧。
* 他们又持续前进了。
* 咱们持续写吧。

2."继续"后面可以带名词性宾语;"持续"不能。("继续"

can be followed by a nominal object; while "持续" cannot.) 例如：
　　一年以后,他又继续了父亲未竟的<u>事业</u>。
　　(One year later, he carried on his father's unfinished career.)
　　谁继续他的<u>话题</u>说一说?
　　* 一年以后,他又持续了父亲未竟的事业。
　　* 谁持续他的话题说一说?
　3."继续"可以用作名词;"持续"不能。("继续"can be used as a noun; while "持续" can not.) 例如：
　　到农村去了解农村和农民是课堂学习的继续。
　　* 到农村去了解农村和农民是课堂学习的持续。

简单 jiǎndān　　简便 jiǎnbiàn　　简易 jiǎnyì

〈形容词〉表示单纯、不复杂的意思。

(< adjective > expressing simplicity.)

"简单"、"简便"、"简易"都有单纯、不复杂的意思,但是由于意义侧重的角度不同,用法不同,所以大多情况下不能互换使用。(All of these three words imply simplicity, but because of the differences in both point of emphasis and usage, in most cases, they are not exchangeable.)

(一) 意义有所不同(Differences in meaning)

"简单"主要指结构单纯,内容不复杂,容易理解和使用;"简便"则还有方便的意思;"简易"还有容易的意思。("简单" mainly refers to being simple in structure, uncomplicated in content, and easy to understand and use; while "简便" implies convenience; "简易" implies easiness.)

1.表示结构、式样等单纯、不复杂,一般用"简单";如果跟一般的比起来还含有部件、设备不是那么完备、齐全,容易携带或组装的特点的话,一般用"简易"。(When indicating the simplicity of structure or style, usually use "简单"; while expressing something easy to carry or construct, not complete in spare parts or equipment, usually use "简易".)试比较：

这种沙发太简单了，没有富贵感。
因为这是简易沙发，所以构造很简单。
鞋的样子简单大方，我很喜欢。
这是防震时盖的简易房。

表示上述句子的意思时，不能用"简便"。(When indicating the meanings in sentences above, "简便" can not be used.)例如：

* 因为这是简便沙发，所以构造很简便。
* 这是防震时盖的简便房。

2.表示内容不复杂，容易理解等，用"简单"，不用"简易"和"简便"。(When indicating something uncomplicated in content and easy to understand, usually use "简单" other than "简易" and "简便".)例如：

故事的情节很简单。
你说得太简单了。
这么简单的道理你都不懂。
* 故事的情节很简易。
* 你说得太简易了。
* 这么简易的道理你都不懂。
* 故事的情节很简便。
* 你说得太简便了。
* 这么简便的道理你都不懂。

3.表示跟做事有关的方法、操作等的不复杂，方便地实现目的的意思，用"简便"，一般不用"简单"，更不能用"简易"。(When indicating the uncomplicated methods and operations which can help achieve purposes, use "简便" rather than "简单" and "简易".)例如：

最简便的方法是打电话通知他。
用这种方法操作很简便。
* 最简易的方法是打电话通知他。

＊用这种方法操作很简易。
(二) 用法上的差别(Differences in use)

"简单"、"简便"、"简易"虽然都是形容词,但是"简易"属于非谓形容词,即它不能单独作谓语,只作定语,而且作定语时一般不用"的"。(Although all of them are adjectives, "简易" is a non-predicate adjective. That is, it can only be used as an attribute without "的" but not as predicate alone.)

"简单"、"简便"不同,它们的主要功能是作谓语和定语,作定语时,大多用"的"。("简单"and "简便"principally function as predicates or attributes, when used as attributes, they should be followed by "的".)例如：

　　这儿有个简易房屋,可以作临时车库。
　　按照书上写的做,太复杂、太难了,你有什么简易方法吗?
　　＊这个房屋太简易了。
　　＊这儿有个简单/简便房屋,可以作临时车库。
　　他的行李很简单。
　　他提了一个简单的行李就上路了。
　　这个方法很简便。
　　你能给我想个最简便的方法吗?

见解 jiànjiě　　看法 kànfǎ　　意见 yìjiàn

〈名词〉表示对事物所持有的想法。

(<noun> expressing opinions or views about something.)

"见解"、"看法"、"意见"虽然都可以表示对事物所持有的想法的意思,但是,实际上它们在意义上有着较大的不同,所以在同一场合下很少能够换用。(Although "见解","看法"and "意见"all can express opinions about something, they are considerably different in meaning, so they are seldom exchanged in the same case.)

(一)"见解"与"看法"、"意见"

　1."见解"与"看法"、"意见"最大的区别在于它是经过思考、分析、研究而得出的一种理论上的认识,这种认识一经形成,就具有一定的稳定性。要想否定某种见解,还得需要分析、研究甚至论证。"看法"、"意见"不是这样的,它们是随时有想法,随时就可以说出或写出等,不对也可以随时推翻。因此"见解"的使用,不是随便一种场合都可以的,它一般用于比较郑重的、正式的场合,见解的提出要有一定的严肃性、科学性等。(The greatest difference between "见解" and "看法" or "意见" is that "见解" is a theoretical recognition after careful thinking, analyzing and researching. And while the recognition is formed, it is not easily changed. If "见解" need denying, it needs analyzing, researching and even proving. "看法" and "意见" are not like that. Whenever they appear, they can be spoken out or written down. They can be repudiated if not true. Therefore "见解" is usually used in some solemn and formal occasions. The view put forth should be serious and scientific.)

2. 正是由于上述的不同,"见解"一般不能用于一些很具体的小事上,而应用于带有一定理论性的问题;"看法"、"意见"则可以用于一些很具体的小事。(Because of the differences mentioned above, "见解" generally can not be used for some specific minor things, but for certain theoretical problems. "看法" and "意见" can be used for some specific minor things.)例如:

* 他对大家约定的去吃饭的时间有自己的见解。

* 我同意他的见解,晚上我们在一起聊天儿吧,别去看电影了。

他对污水回用问题,提出了自己的见解。

(He gave his own opinion about the reuse of waste water.)

孙教授在科学报告会上发表了很多新见解。

老师想听听同学们对今年旅游地点的看法/意见。

3. 因为"见解"的形成有思考、分析、研究的过程,不是随随便便提出来的,所以它有可能跟下面一些词发生一定的联系:独到、高明、深刻、精辟等。(Because the forming of "见解" is a process of thinking, analyzing and researching, it may have something to do with the following words: original, wise, profound, brilliant, etc.) 例如：

  他的见解有独到之处。(He has his own unique opinion.)
  他的见解很高明。(His view is very wise.)
  精辟的见解 (a brilliant opinion)
  见解很深刻 (a profound view)

(二) "意见"与"看法"、"见解"

1. "意见"与"看法"、"见解"最大的区别在于"意见"所指的想法是可以而且主要是提供给别人的，而"看法"、"见解"所指的想法主要不是提供给别人的，而是自己所具有的。所以"意见"与许多动词的搭配也是特定的，是"看法"、"见解"不能与之搭配的。例如：提、征求、听取、接受等，"交换"可以用于"意见"和"看法"，但是不能用于"见解"。〔The greatest difference between "意见" and "看法" or "见解" is that "意见" refers to the opinion that can and mainly be offered to others, while "看法" or "见解" refers to one's own idea, therefore, the collocations of "意见" with many verbs are fixed, which can't go with "看法" and "见解". For example: 提 (make), 征求 (ask for or solicit), 听取 (listen to), 接受 (accept), etc. "交换" can be collocated with "意见" and "看法", but not "见解".〕例如：

  提意见　　　　　　征求群众的意见
  听取大家的意见　　我接受你的意见
  * 提看法　　　　　 * 征求群众的看法
  * 听取大家的看法　 * 我接受你的看法
  * 提见解　　　　　 * 征求群众的见解
  * 听取大家的见解　 * 我接受你的见解
  我跟他交换了意见。
  我跟他交换了看法。

＊我跟他交换了见解。

　　2. 因此,"意见"的定语可以有"参考性"、"建设性"这样的定语,"看法"、"见解"不能用这样的定语。(Therefore, "意见" can be modified by "参考性" (for reference), "建设性" (constructive), while "看法" or "见解" can not.) 例如:

　　这只是<u>参考性</u>意见。
　　(This view is only for reference.)
　　他向公司提出了不少<u>建设性</u>意见。
　　(He put forward quite a few instructive suggestions to the company.)
　　＊这只是参考性看法。
　　＊他向公司提出了不少建设性看法。
　　＊这只是参考性见解。
　　＊他向公司提出了不少建设性见解。

　　3. "意见"还可以用于听取意见后,遵照做这种意思的句子里,"看法"、"见解"不能这样用。("意见" can be used in the sentences that express the meaning of doing something according to the opinion. In such sentences, "看法" or "见解" can not.) 例如:

　　他的意见非常正确,照他的意见办。
　　＊他的看法/见解非常正确,照他的看法/见解办。

(三)"看法"、"意见"与"见解"

　　1. "看法"、"意见"在意义上跟"见解"还有一点不同,即"看法"、"意见"还可以表示由于对对方或对某事不满而抱有的想法。"见解"不含有这种不满情绪。(There is another small difference between "看法", "意见" and "见解", that is, both "看法" and "意见" imply ideas which show dissatisfaction with somebody or something. "见解" does not imply such feelings.) 例如:

　　我对你有意见/看法。
　　大家对这个提案意见很大。
　　别生气,有什么看法统统说出来。

(Don't be angry. You can speak out all your opinions.)
* 我对你有见解。
* 大家对这个提案见解很大。
* 别生气,有什么见解统统说出来。

2. 由此,"看法"、"意见"与"见解"有时在相同搭配的前提下,会出现意义上的差别。(As a result, there is sometimes difference in meaning in the same collocation.)例如:

他这个人很有见解。(表示有思想、认识深刻的意思。)

他对领导的决定很有看法/意见。(表示看法、意见中不满的程度很高。)

"看法"、"意见"在表示这种意义时,搭配上也有差别。"意见"可以用"大"来描述,"看法"不能。(When "看法" and "意见" are in this meaning, there is a slight distinction in collocation. "意见" can be modified by "大", while "看法" can not.)例如:

他对你意见很大。
* 他对你看法很大。

(四)"见解"、"看法"、"意见"与量词("见解","看法","意见" and measure words)

"见解"属于一种理性的东西,又有郑重的色彩,所以它一般用"种"这个量词,很少用"个";"看法"口语性较强,比较通俗,多用"个";"意见"也可以用"个",但是提出意见时,常常按条列出,所以"意见"也常常用"条"。"见解"、"看法"不能用"条"。("见解" expresses something rational and implies seriousness, so it is generally modified by "种", seldom by "个"; while "看法" is in spoken language and common and modified by "个"; "意见" can be modified by "个", but when putting forward suggestions, it can be modified by "条". While "见解" or "看法" can not be modified by "条".)例如:

这种见解很有独创性。(This view is quite original.)
这个看法是正确的。
我有个意见,不知道能不能提?

群众给我们提了十条意见,都很尖锐。

(All the ten comments the mass made on us are quite sharp.)

* 这条见解很有独创性。
* 这条看法是正确的。

将 jiāng   将要 jiāngyào   就要 jiùyào

〈副词〉表示动作、行为或某种情况不久就要发生或出现。

(< adverb > indicating action, behavior or some event will happen or occur soon.)

(一)词义色彩有差别:(The difference in the flavour of meaning:)

"将"书面语色彩较重,多用于书面语;"就要"口语色彩较重,多用于口语;"将要"通用于书面语、口语。("将" implies strong written flavour, generally used in written language; "就要" implies strong oral flavour, mostly used in spoken language; "将要" can be used in both written and spoken language.)

(二)"将"表示的不久可长可短;"将要"表示的不久一般不会很长;"就要"则表示在很短的时间内就会发生。(The future that "将" indicates may come soon or after a long time; "将要" indicates the time to come will not be very long after; "就要", whereas, indicates something will take place within a short time.)例如:

不久,你将成为新闻人物。

〔Soon you will become a newsmaker (or a noticeable figure).〕

一个月后,他将毕业回国。

他们将要结婚了。

天将要亮了,一切将从头开始。

假期就要结束了,该做新学期的准备了。

天就要黑了,咱们抓紧时间干吧。

(三)"将"书面语色彩较强,多用于文字简洁的句子里,所以句末很少用"了";"就要"强调短时间内就会发生,一般句子末尾都要加"了";"将要"句后是否加"了",较为自由。("将" implies the flavour of written language strongly, and is often used in brief sentences, so seldom with "了" after it; "就要" emphasizes something will happen soon, and generally with "了" after it; while "将要" can be followed by "了" freely.)例如:

不久,我将走进高等学府,这是我盼望已久的事情。

(Soon I'll enter the institution of higher learning, which I've been long looking forward to.)

新的一年就要开始了!

他将要率考察团赴敦煌考察。

(He will lead a delegation to investigate Dunhuang.)

你听说了吗?刘强的公司将要破产了。

(四)"将"还可以表示接近某个时间的意思;"将要"、"就要"一般不这么用。("将" can also express being close to some moment; "将要" and "就要" can not be used this way.)例如:

天将黄昏,下了班的人们都在匆匆地赶回家去。

(It's getting dark. People off work are hurrying back home.)

他们结婚将有二十年了。

* 天将要/就要黄昏,下了班的人们都在匆匆地赶回家去。

* 他们结婚将要/就要有二十年了。

(五)"将"还可以判断事物未来发展的情况,含有"会"、"一定会"的意思。有时与"必"、"会"连用,肯定的意味更重。"将要"、"就要"一般不这么用。("将" can be also used to assess the situation of development of something, implying "会""一定会". Sometimes it is used with "必" and "会" with a positive tone. "将要" and "就要" can not be used this way.)例如:

理论不与实践相结合,将毫无意义。

(It will be of no significance if the theory is not combined with practice.)

不久的将来,中国必将走在世界的前列。

(Not long after, China will take the lead in the world.)

人类如果不尊重大自然的规律,将会受到大自然的惩罚。

* 理论不与实践相结合,将要毫无意义。

* 不久的将来,中国将要走在世界的前列。

讲 jiǎng   说 shuō   谈 tán

〈动词〉表示用话语来表达意思。

(< verb > express meanings by words.)

(一)"讲"、"说"、"谈"都有用话语来表达的意思,但是,它们在方式上有差别。(All of "讲","说"and"谈"imply expressing meaning by words, but they are different in manner.)

1."讲"在用话语表达内容时,有强调"向他人"的方式,使用时要有一定场合;"说"是就用话语来表达意思的行为的本身;"谈"较多地表示两人及两人以上或双方及双方以上在一起说话的方式。(When "讲"expresses meaning by words, it emphasizes the manner of "to other people" and it is used in certain occasions; while "说"indicates the act of expressing meanings by words; "谈"is more used to indicate way of talking between two persons or parties or more.)例如:

我去跟他讲去。

你把注意事项给大家讲一讲。

上午说得太多了,有点儿累了。

你一个人在这儿自言自语地说什么呢?

为了解决这个问题,我跟他们整整谈了一下午。

你们俩好好地谈一谈吧。

没有"向他人"的方式、不表示两人以上的条件,只表示说的行为或说的内容,不能用"讲"、"谈"。(When only indicating the act or content of saying without concerning the manner of "to other persons" and condition of two persons or more, "讲" and "谈" can not be used.）例如：

你一个人在这儿自言自语地说什么呢？

我说这样不行，你偏不听。

张厂长也在会上讲了话，他说："我们必须在最短的时间内走出经济低谷。"

* 你一个人在这儿自言自语地谈／讲什么呢？
* 我讲／谈这样不行，你偏不听。
* 张厂长也在会上讲了话，他讲／谈："我们必须在最短的时间内走出经济低谷。"

2. 侧重于"向别人描述、叙述事情"多用"讲"，一般不用"谈"。（When emphasizing "describing or narrating to other people", use "讲" but not "谈".）例如：

他跟我讲了那天晚上事情发生时的情景。

他正在那儿讲事情的经过，我们去听听。

"说"可以说"说笑话"、"说谜语"，一般不用于"说故事"，但是"讲"却可以用于"讲笑话"、"讲故事"，不能用于"讲谜语"。这是因为笑话、故事有一定的情节，谜语没有情节。"谈"不能用于以上的情况。〔"说" can be used in "说笑话"（tell a joke），"说谜语"（tell a riddle）, but not in "说故事"（tell a story）, while "讲" can be used as in "讲笑话"（tell a joke），"讲故事"（tell a story）, but not in "讲谜语"（tell a riddle）, because jokes and stories have plots, while riddles do not. "谈" can not be used in the cases above.〕例如：

* 谈笑话　　* 谈故事　　* 谈谜语

3. "谈"除了两人以上的条件外，它跟"讲"还有所不同。"谈"表示的说的行为常常带有一定的目的性。"说"有时也可以这样用。（Besides, the conditions of involving two or more persons mentioned above, "谈" is different from "讲" in some other aspects. "谈" indicates that the behaviour of saying has a certain purpose. "说" can be

325

used this way sometimes.)例如：

这件事我来跟他谈，我想他是会答应的。（为解决某问题而去谈。）

这两天他正在闹情绪，你找他谈一谈吧。（解决闹情绪问题。）

〔He is in low spirit these days. You go to talk with him in order to dispel his low spirits〕

我想跟您谈谈我的打算。（让对方了解打算。）

* 这两天他正在闹情绪，你找他说一说/讲一讲吧。

所以，"谈"可以有"谈恋爱"、"谈朋友"、"谈生意"、"谈心"这样的组合，"讲"和"说"不能这样组合。（Therefore, "谈" can be used as in "谈恋爱"，"谈朋友"，"谈生意"，while "讲" and "说" can not be used in such cases.）

(二) 其他意义的差别：(Difference in other meanings：)

1. "讲"、"说"有"讲解、说明"的意思；"谈"没有。(Both "讲" and "说" imply explaining, while "谈" does not.)例如：

老师，您给我们讲一讲/说一说这个词的用法，好吗？

你能讲讲/说说这句话的含义吗？

2. "谈"有"评论"、"论述"的意思；"讲"很少这样用。〔"谈" implies making comment or arguing; while "讲" is seldom used this way.〕例如：

关于这个问题我来谈谈我的看法。

大家就这个议题充分地谈一谈。

(You can have a comprehensive discussion on this topic.)

请孙教授给我们谈谈字与词的关系问题。

* 大家就这个议题充分地讲一讲。

3. "说"有"批评、责备"的意思；"讲"、"谈"没有这个意思。("说" implies "criticize and blame"; while "讲" and "谈" don't.)例如：

说了你半天，你怎么一点儿也不在意？

(I have talked to you for a long time, but you don't seem to take any notice of what I've said.)

说了他几句,他就受不了了。

老师正在说他呢。

* 讲/谈了你半天,你怎么一点儿也不在意?
* 讲/谈了他几句,他就受不了了。
* 老师正在讲/谈他呢。

4."讲"、"谈"有"商量"的意思,可以直接带宾语。("讲" and "谈"imply "consult or discuss", can be followed by object directly.)例如:

讲条件　　讲价钱　　谈价钱　　谈条件

什么苦他都能吃,从来不讲价钱。

(He can bear whatever hardships, never haggling over the price.)

咱们来谈谈条件吧。

5."讲"还有"讲求"的意思;"说"、"谈"没有这种用法。〔"讲"also implies (pay attention to); while "说"and "谈"can not be used this way.〕例如:

讲卫生 (pay attention to hygiene)

讲文明 (pay attention to civilization)

讲礼貌 (be polite)

讲质量 (stress quality)

讲经济效益 (stress economic benefit)

讲吃穿 (be fastidious about one's food and clothing)

(三) 在功能上,"讲"、"说"、"谈"单用时,在句中主要充当谓语,一般不能单独用来作主语或宾语。但是,当它们跟"的"构成"的字词组"时,在句中可以充当主语、宾语或定语。(In functions, when "讲","说"and "谈"are used respectively, they can function as predicate, but not as subject or object. When they are combined with "的"to form word group of "的", they can be used as subject, object or attribute.）例如：

昨天晚上我们讲/说/谈了很多话。（谓语）

* 他的讲/说/谈对我帮助很大。（主语）

* 我记住了爷爷的讲/说/谈。（宾语）

他认为大家讲的/说的/谈的都不重要。（小句主语）

这是你讲的/说的/谈的，不是我讲的/说的/谈的。（宾语）

我上星期跟你讲的/说的/谈的那件事你忘了吗？（定语）

讲话 jiǎnghuà　　说话 shuōhuà　　谈话 tánhuà

〈动词〉表示用语言表达意思。

(<verb> express by words.)

（一）"讲话"、"说话"、"谈话"都可以表示用语言表达意思。词的构成都是动语素加名语素的支配式形式，因此使用上，都具有支配式离合动词的特点。（"讲话","说话" and "谈话" all mean to express by words. The formation of words is subordination by adding noun morphemes to verb morphemes. Therefore, it possesses the feature of separable verbs.) 即：

1. 后边都不能再带宾语。（Without object followed. ）例如：

* 校长准备讲话大会。

校长准备在大会上讲话。

* 我正在说话他。

我正在跟他说话。

* 他坐在草坪上谈话朋友。

他跟朋友坐在草坪上谈话。

2. 动态助词、表示动作数量的词语须放在"话"前；用趋向动词"起来"时，"话"放在"起来"中间；作为动作补语的时段，也要放在"话"的前面。（The aspect particles and words measuring actions should precede "话"; when the verb of direction "起来" is used,

"话"should be placed between "起来", while the duration of time as complement of the action should also precede "话".) 例如：

讲着话	说着话	谈着话
＊讲话着	＊说话着	＊谈话着
讲过话	说过话	谈过话
＊讲话过	＊说话过	＊谈话过
讲了一次话	说了一次话	谈了一次话
＊讲话了一次	＊说话了一次	＊谈话了一次
讲起话来	说起话来	谈起话来
＊讲话起来	＊说话起来	＊谈话起来
讲了一个钟头的话	说了一会儿话	谈了一晚上话
＊讲话了一个钟头	＊说话了一会儿	＊谈话了一晚上

(二)"讲话"、"说话"、"谈话"意义上有一定差别,所以在许多情况下,不能换用。("讲话", "说话" and "谈话" are slightly distinct in meaning, so in most cases, they are not exchangeable.)

1."讲话"有向他人说的特点,多用于讲演、发言这样的场合;"说话"就是用语言表达意思的行为,没有另外的条件;"谈话"的前提不能是一个人,必须是两个或两个以上的人的行为。("讲话" implies saying to others, frequently used in cases of lectures; "说话" is the act of expressing, without any additional conditions; "谈话" can't take place by one person, it is the behavior of two persons or more.) 例如：

下面请王主任讲话。
他的讲话振奋人心。　（His speech is inspiring.）
＊下面请王主任说话/谈话。
＊他的说话/谈话振奋人心。
你怎么不说话呀?
＊你怎么不谈话呀?
昨天我们几个人谈了一晚上话。
＊昨天我谈了一晚上话。

329

2. "谈话"有时表示的不是几个人随便的说话,而是带有某种目的的说话,这种情况一般不能用"说话"、"讲话"。("谈话" implies talking with some purposes, but not free talks, while "说话" and "讲话"can not be used this way.)例如:

我去跟他谈一次话,尽量把这件事处理好。

(I'll talk with him, and try my best to settle the matter.)

领导正在跟小王谈话,气氛很紧张。

(The leader is talking with Xiao Wang, and the atmosphere is tense.)

我跟他的谈话失败了。

* 我去跟他说/讲一次话,尽量把这件事处理好。
* 领导正在跟小王说/讲话,气氛很紧张。
* 我跟他的说/讲话失败了。

3. "说话"有时可以表示闲聊的意思,"谈话"、"讲话"没有这种意思。("说话"sometimes means free talk, while "谈话" and "讲话" do not.)例如:

闲着没事,来找你说说话。

(Being idle, I came to have a chat with you.)

王奶奶正在跟我妈妈说话呢。

* 闲着没事,来找你谈谈/讲讲话。

教 jiāo 教导 jiàodǎo 指教 zhǐjiào 请教 qǐngjiào

〈动词〉 < verb >

"教"、"教导"、"请教"、"指教"虽然都有传授知识技能等的意思,但是由于传授的事物、对象不同,教与学的关系不同,适用场合不同,所以不能换用。("教","教导","请教"and"指教"all mean passing on knowledge, skill, etc. Since the things being passed on or people who receive these are different, the relation between learning and teaching is different and the occasions for learning and teaching are different as well, the four words can not be used exchangeably.)

(一)"教"与"教导"

1."教"与"教导"传授的事物不同。("教" and "教导" impart different things.)

"教"传授的是知识或技能;"教导"则主要指思想、品德、素质等方面的教育、培养。("教" means to teach knowledge or techniques; while "教导" indicates the education or cultivation of one's thought, morality, character, and so on.)例如:

张先生教我们中国古代文学。

李老师教给我们不少知识。

现代汉语由王老师来教。

小刘,教给我一点儿记单词的方法好吗?

* 张先生教导我们中国古代文学。

* 李老师教导给我们不少知识。

* 现代汉语由王老师来教导。

* 小刘,教导给我一点儿记单词的方法好吗?

孙伯伯多次教导我:好好学习,多学点儿本领,将来干点儿大事情。

在老师的亲切教导下,他又重新振作起来。

(Guided by his teacher, he braced up again.)

* 孙伯伯多次教我:好好学习,多学点儿本领,将来干点儿大事情。

* 在老师的亲切教下,他又重新振作起来。

2."教"与"教导"的宾语有所不同。(The objects are different.)

"教"与"教导"都可以带双宾语,第一个宾语都是表人宾语;第二个宾语不同:"教"带的是事物宾语;"教导"带的是"教导"的具体话语类的宾语,这两种类型的宾语是不能交换使用的。(Both "教" and "教导" can be followed by double objects, among which usually the first objects are those representing people, but the

331

second are different: "教" is followed by the object of things, while "教导" is followed by the object of language related words. The objects of these two types can not be exchanged.)例如:

　　王老师教我们汉语。
　　教他一点儿学习方法。
　　从小妈妈就教导我要做一个诚实的孩子。
　　老师经常教导我们同学之间要互助互爱。
　＊ 王老师教导我们汉语。
　＊ 教导他一点儿学习方法。
　＊ 从小妈妈就教我要做一个诚实的孩子。
　＊ 老师经常教我们同学之间要互助互爱。

"教"与"教导"的表人宾语不能跟"给"组成介词词组放到动词前。(The objects representing people can't combine with "给" to form prepositional phrases and to be used before verbs.)例如:

　＊ 老师给我们教中国歌曲。
　＊ 你给我教汉语,好吗?
　＊ 希望老师给他好好教导教导。
　＊ 妈妈给我教导要自强、自立。

3."教导"有名词用法,"教"没有。("教导" can be used as a noun but "教" can't.)例如:

　　我一定牢记您的谆谆教导,踏踏实实地干一番事业。
　　(I'll surely bear in mind your earnest teachings and be steadfast in my work.)
　　你要听从爷爷的教导。
　＊ 我一定牢记您的谆谆教,踏踏实实地干一番事业。
　＊ 你要听从爷爷的教。

(二)"教"与"请教"

"教"与"请教"主要的区别在于教与被教的关系上。"教"是教者作主语,被教者作宾语;"请教"是被教者作主语,教者作宾语或作介词"向"的宾语。"请教"是被教者求教时表示谦虚、尊敬的用语,所以大多是学生向老师、晚辈向长辈、下级向上级求教的用语。(The essential difference between "教" and "请教" lays on the relation between teaching and being taught. "教" means the one who teaches is the subject and the one being taught is the object. However, the subject of "请教" is the one being taught and the one who teaches is the object or the object of preposition "向". "请教" is a modest and polite term when one asks for advice, mostly when students consult teachers, or the junior consults the senior, or inferiors consults superiors.)例如:

  张文正教我们唱歌呢。
  他不会,你教教他吧。
  你教我做中国菜,怎么样?
  请教您两个问题。
  向您请教来了。
  这道题你还是请教刘先生吧。
  虚心向别人请教。
  * 老师请教我一个问题。
  * 老师,您能请教我用汉语写作文吗?

(三)"教"与"指教"

"教"是真实地把知识、技能传授给别人;"指教"则主要用于客套,用于客气地请人对自己的工作、作品等提出批评或意见。("教" means to pass on knowledge or skills to other people in actuality. "指教" is used when one asks politely others to comment on one's job or works.)例如:

  孙先生,请多指教。
  今后还望老师多多给以指教。
  希望多加指教。

"指教"不带宾语,也不能用于"把"字句。("指教" can't be followed by objects nor used in the sentence of "把".)例如:

  * 请您指教我的作文。

* 您可以指教我工作吗?
* 请您把我的错误指教出来。

进行 jìnxíng　　加以 jiāyǐ
〈动词〉 < verb >

"进行"和"加以"在句子里都是形式上的动词,它们的主要功能都是带双音节的动词宾语,有时可以互换使用。("进行" and "加以" both are verbs in form in sentences. Their principal functions are to be followed by verbal objects of disyllables. They are sometimes exchangeable.)例如:

对这几个问题进行分析、讨论。
对这项工作进行全面的总结。
对这几个问题加以分析、讨论。
对这项工作加以全面的总结。

但是由于它们意义上的不同导致了搭配上的差别,还有形式上的一系列不同,使它们在很多情况下不能换用。(Being different in meaning results in the difference between the two words in collocation. And there is a series of differences in form, in many cases they can't exchange.)

(一) 意义上和搭配上的差别(Difference in meaning and in collocation)

"进行"表示从事某种持续性的活动,"加以"表示对待或处理前面提到的某种人或事物,因此,在与动词宾语的搭配上,出现搭配范围的不同。("进行" indicates being engaged in some continued activities. "加以" means to treat or handle some kind of people or things as mentioned before. Therefore, the range of collocation will be different when "进行" and "加以" are collocated with the verbal objects.)

1."进行"一般要求与持续性动词宾语搭配。("进行" is often used together with objects durative verbs.)例如:

进行讨论　　进行审查　　进行论证

进行表扬　　进行整顿　　进行推广

这一类动词宾语,"加以"大多也能跟它们搭配。(As for these verbal objects, "加以" generally collocates with them as well.)例如:

　　加以讨论　　加以审查　　加以论证
　　加以表扬　　加以整顿　　加以推广

但是,当动词不是表示持续性的行为时,例如:述补结构的动词,是不能跟"进行"搭配的,然而却可以跟"加以"搭配。(But if the verbs are not that of durative actions, such as verb + complement structure, they can't collocate with "进行", but they can do with "加以".)例如:

　　*进行改正　*进行解决　*进行克服
　　*进行纠正　*进行确定　*进行肃清
　　*进行改善　*进行提高　*进行扩大
　　加以改正　　加以解决　　加以克服　　加以纠正
　　加以确定　　加以肃清　　加以改善

2."进行"一般多与一些行为显现的动词搭配,不跟具有对待意义的心理活动的动词搭配;"加以"则可以跟一部分心理活动动词搭配。("进行" usually collocates with verbs which reveal the behaviours but not with verbs of psychological activities with the meaning of handling. "加以" however, can collocate with verbs of some psychological activities.)例如:

　　*进行注意　*进行关注　*进行信任
　　*进行关心　*进行体贴
　　加以注意　　加以关注　　加以信任
　　加以关心　　加以体贴

3."加以"是表示把某种行为加在前面提到的人与事物上,所以某些表示双方配合进行活动的动词,一般不跟"加以"搭配,却可以跟"进行"搭配。同样的道理,某些不及物动词可以跟"进行"搭配,却常常不能跟"加以"搭配。("加以" means to exert an

335

action to somebody or something mentioned before. Therefore some verbs that indicate coordination are seldom used with "加以", but may be together with "进行".)例如：

* 加以谈话   * 加以协作   * 加以配合
* 加以交涉   * 加以谈判   * 加以联欢
* 加以会演

进行谈话   进行协作   进行配合   进行交涉
进行谈判   进行联欢   进行会演   进行活动
进行劳动   进行运动   进行考勤   进行工作
* 加以活动   * 加以劳动   * 加以运动
* 加以考勤   * 加以工作

（二）关于定语、状语等修饰语方面的差别(Differences in modifiers of attributive and adverbial)

1. 定语修饰语的不同。(Attributive modifiers are different.)

名词性定语、动词性定语以及介词词组定语只能作"进行"的动词宾语的修饰语，不能作"加以"的动词宾语的修饰语。(Nominal attributes, verbal attributes and attributes of prepositional phrases can only be modifiers for verbal object of "进行" and can't be that of "加以".)例如：

进行法制建设   进行素质教育   进行技术革新
进行打击刑事犯罪分子的宣传 (to conduct propaganda on taking strong measures against criminals)
进行毕业教育   进行学术研究活动
进行关于爱国主义教育方面的宣传   * 加以法制建设
* 加以素质教育   * 加以技术革新
* 加以打击刑事犯罪分子的宣传   * 加以毕业教育
* 加以学术研究活动
* 加以关于爱国主义教育方面的宣传

2. 状语修饰语的不同。(The adverbial modifiers are different.)

由介词"在"、"向"构成的介词词组一般只能在"进行"句中作状语,不能在"加以"句中作状语。(The prepositional phrases composes of "在" and "向" can only be used as adverbials in the sentence of "进行" and can't be used in the sentence of "加以".)例如:

在这个项目上进行投资(to invest in this project)

在群众中进行调查(to make an investigation in the masses)

在机构内部进行调整(to make an adjustment inside the organization)

向广大顾客进行宣传　　要耐心地向他们进行解释
* 在这个项目上加以投资　　* 在群众中加以调查
* 在机构内部加以调整
* 向广大顾客加以宣传　　* 要耐心地向他们加以解释

(三) 形式上的差别 (Difference in forms)

1."进行"表示的是持续性动作,所以在形式上,有时体和动量的形式;"加以"没有这些形式。("进行" indicates an continuous action. It has aspect and can be measured by classifiers, and "加以" cannot indicate these aspects.)例如:

进行了讨论　　　　进行过宣传
正在进行研究　　　对他已经进行了教育
进行了一回　　　　进行过多次
进行两个多小时了　对这件事要进行一下调查
* 加以了讨论　　　* 加以过宣传
* 正在加以研究　　* 对他已经加以了教育
* 加以了一回　　　* 加以过多次
* 加以两个多小时了　* 对这件事要加以一下调查

2."进行"后面可以有补语形式;"加以"不能带补语。("进行" can be followed by complement and "加以" can't.)例如:

进行到底　　　　进行下去
进行得很顺利　　进行得怎么样
* 加以到底　　　* 加以下去

337

＊加以得很顺利　　　＊加以得怎么样

　3．"进行"可以用肯定、否定并列的形式表示疑问；"加以"不能这样用。（"进行"indicates interrogative mood in the form of positive-and-negative coordination while"加以"doesn't.）例如：

　　进行没进行讨论（进没进行讨论）

　　进没进行处理　　　　进没进行辅导

　　＊加以没加以讨论（加没加以讨论）

　　＊加没加以处理　　＊加没加以辅导

　4．"进行"后边没有其他词语可以结句；"加以"后边没有其他词语不能结句。（The sentence with"进行"can be ended without other composition after"进行"; while there have to be some compositions after"加以"or the sentence can't be ended.）例如：

　　篮球比赛在体育馆进行。

　　讨论怎么进行？

　　辩论还在进行。

　　＊产品的推广要加以。

　　＊对问题补充加以。

（四）"进行"、"加以"使用上共同要注意的问题。（Matters of common concern of"进行"and"加以"in use.）

　1．"进行"、"加以"只能用于正式的、庄重的行为，日常生活中的或非正式的行为不能用"进行"、"加以"。（Both can only be used for formal or solemn acts, but they can not be used for that of daily or informal behaviours.）例如：

　　＊进行打扫　　＊进行说话　　＊进行睡觉

　　＊把碗筷进行洗涮　　　＊对房间进行收拾

　　＊加以打扫　　＊加以说话　　＊加以睡觉

　　＊把碗筷加以洗涮　　　＊对房间加以收拾

　2．"进行"、"加以"连带的动词后不能再带宾语。（The verb used with"进行"or"加以" can not be followed by other objects.）例如：

* 下午进行讨论这个课题
* 我们要进行改革经济体制
* 给学生进行辅导汉语
* 下午加以讨论这个课题
* 我们要加以改革经济体制
* 给学生加以辅导汉语

进行 jìnxíng　　举行 jǔxíng

〈动词〉 < verb >

"进行"、"举行"都有"从事某种活动"的意思,但是"进行"本身的词汇意义很虚,它往往在句中需要构成"进行 + 动词"的方式进行表达;"举行"则除了"进行"的意思外,还有"兴起"的意思。这就决定了它们意义、用法上的差别。〔Both mean "从事某种活动"(being engaged in), but "进行" will not function until it composes the pattern of "进行 + verb", for the meaning of the word itself is void. Besides having the same meaning with "进行", "举行" also means "兴起"(spring up). This determines that they are different either in meaning or in use.〕

(一)"进行"重在活动的持续进行;"举行"常常除活动的进行外,还要涉及兴办者。("进行" emphasizes the continuation of an action. Besides the conduction, it also involves the sponsor of the action.)例如:

隆重的剪彩仪式正在进行。(持续进行。)

(A grand opening ceremony is under way.)

他们为展览会举行了一次隆重的剪彩仪式。(兴办者兴起并进行。)

(They held a grand opening ceremony.)

我们打算跟外商进行一次谈判。(打算谈判。)

我们打算跟外商举行一次谈判。(打算提议并进行谈判。)

(二)"进行"连带的通常是动词性词语,表示某种活动的持续进行;"举行"主要连带名词性词语,有时也可以连带"比赛"、"会谈"、"起义"、"游行"等动词性词语,但表示的只是这样一类的活动。〔"进行" is often used with verbs, indicating the continuation of certain actions. "举行" is often used with nouns, but sometimes with verbal words, such as "比赛" (match), "会谈" (talk), "起义" (uprising), "游行" (parade), are used together with "举行", but just indicating the kinds of activities.〕例如:

  进行讨论　　　进行商谈　　　进行调查
  进行研究　　　进行访问　　　进行斗争
  进行宣传　　　进行攻击　　　进行改革
  进行批评　　　进行实验　　　进行破坏　进行补偿
  举行开学典礼　举行新年晚会
  举行一次读书报告会
  举行一场足球比赛　举行电脑培训学习班
  举行舞会　　　举行一次个人书画展览
  *举行调查　　　*举行研究　　　*举行访问
  *举行斗争　　　*举行破坏　　　*举行补偿
  *举行攻击　　　*举行改革　　　*举行批评
  *进行开学典礼　*进行新年晚会
  *进行一次读书报告会　　　　　　*进行婚礼
  *进行电脑培训学习班　　　　　　*进行舞会
  *进行这次重要的会议

(三)"进行"表示从事持续性的活动,所以它后边可以接表示持续过程情况的补语;"举行"一般不接这类补语。("进行" means to conduct a durative action, so it can be followed by a complement indicating the process of an action, "举行" will not be followed by such complement.)例如:

  进行到哪儿了?——进行到这儿了。

  进行多少了?——进行一半了。

我们一定要把斗争进行到底。
(We must carry the struggle through to the end.)
施工正在进行中。
* 举行到哪儿了？——举行到这儿了。
* 举行多少了？——举行一半了。
* 我们一定要把谈判举行到底。
* 会谈正在举行中。

（四）"进行"、"举行"连带的宾语一般都要求是双音节或双音节以上的词语。(The object of "进行" or "举行" usually is limited to words of disyllable or more.) 例如：

进行谈判	进行斗争	进行调查
进行考验	进行比赛	进行教育
* 进行谈	* 进行斗	* 进行查
* 进行考	* 进行比	* 进行教
举行婚礼	举行会谈	举行会议
举行比赛	举行谈判	举行讲座
* 举行礼	* 举行会	* 举行赛
* 举行谈	* 举行讲	

精神 jīngshén　　精力 jīnglì

〈名词〉 < noun >

"精神"、"精力"都可以表示人的一种内在的心理状态，但是这两个词很少通用，因为它们在意义的侧重点上、用法上等都有较大的差别。(Both indicate the inner psychological state of people. The two words are rarely exchangeable for there is considerable difference in meaning they emphasize and in use.)

（一）意义不同(Differences in meaning)

1. "精神"只指人的内在的心态，包括人的意识、人的思维活动及一般心态等；"精力"不只指这些，而且通常也不侧重于这些，它侧重于"力"，即心力、体力。〔"精神" refers to the inner psy-

chological state of a person, including his consciousness, thinking activity and general mental state. "精神" does not refer to these only, and generally not lay emphasis on these. It emphasizes "力 (strength)", that is mental and physical efforts or physical power.〕例如:

这种公而忘私的精神值得大家学习。
(The selfless spirit is worth learning.)
他虽然得了癌症,但是他的精神状态却很好。
* 这种公而忘私的精力值得大家学习。
* 他虽然得了癌症,但是他的精力状态却很好。
把任务交给他吧,他有精力,承担得了。
我这两天太忙了,没有精力照顾孩子,你帮我照看一下吧。
(I'm too busy these days to have time and energy to take care of my children. Will you please help me?)
* 把任务交给他吧,他有精神,承担得了。
* 我这两天太忙了,没有精神照顾孩子,你帮我照看一下吧。

2. "精神"还可以表示"宗旨"、"主要意义"的意思,所以它的使用不只限于人,还可以指文件、会议、讲话、指示等可以用语言文字表达出来的事物;"精力"没有这种意思,所以它的使用只限于人。〔"精神"also indicates "宗旨" (aim) or "主要意义" (significance), so it can not only be used for people, but also for documents, meetings, speeches, instructions, etc. that can be expressed by spoken and written language. "精力"is limited to people.〕例如:

传达中央会议的精神(relay the spirit of the Central Conference)
要理解文件精神,不要死搬教条(Be sure to understand the essence of the document. Do not copy it mechanically)
学习、体会首长的讲话精神(Study and grasp the essence

of the leader's speech)

大力宣传市委领导的指示精神(to devote one's major efforts to publicize the instruction of the municipal Party Committee)

* 传达中央会议的精力
* 要理解文件精力,不要死搬教条
* 学习、体会首长的讲话精力
* 大力宣传市委领导的指示精力

(二) 用法上的不同(Differences in use)

1. 搭配上(In collocation)

(1)"精神"表示的是人的意识、心理状态等,意义很抽象,所以跟它搭配的词表示它的状态也很抽象,这种抽象的词一般不跟"精力"搭配。("精神" indicates one's consciousness or psychological state. It is abstract. So the words used together with it indicates that its state is also abstract, and this kind of words will not collocate with "精力".)例如:

精神焕发(in high spirits)
精神饱满(full of vigor)
精神抖擞(full of energy)
精神愉快(in a cheerful frame of mind)
精神很好(in good spirits)

* 精力焕发　　* 精力饱满　　* 精力抖擞
* 精力愉快　　* 精力很好

(2)"精力"比"精神"相对具体些,它是可以检测和衡量的,所以它可以用"充沛"、"旺盛"来表示它的多;可以用"过剩"、"有限"来说明它的多与少;可以用"过人"来表示它的强。"精神"不能这样用。〔Compared with "精神","精力" is relatively more specific and it can be tested or measured. So it can be modified by "充沛 (abundant)","旺盛 (vigorous)" to express its large amount, or by "过剩 (surplus)", "有限 (limited)" to express its quantity, or

343

by "过人（surpass）" to express its intensity. "精神"can't indicate these.〕例如：

> 精力充沛　　　　精力旺盛　　　　　精力过人
> 这孩子精力过剩,想办法引导他做点事情。
> 人的精力是有限的。
> * 精神充沛　　　* 精神旺盛　　　　* 精神过人
> * 这孩子精神过剩,想办法引导他做点事情。
> * 人的精神是有限的。

（3）"精力"还可以用"花费"、"浪费"来表示它的使用情况,也可以用"大部分"、"主要"、"全部"、"毕生"来表示它的使用量。"精神"一般不能这样用。〔"精力" is also used together with "花费（spend）", "浪费（waste）" to show the way of using it or together with "大部分（most of）", "主要（main）", "全部（all）" and "毕生（lifetime）", to show the amount it is used. "精神" can't be used this way.〕例如：

> 花费精力　　　　浪费精力　　　　　大部分精力
> 主要精力　　　　全部精力
> 他为科学事业献出了毕生的精力。
> * 他为科学事业献出了毕生的精神。

2."精神"常常用于某种比喻的意义；"精力"一般不这样用。（"精神" is also used in metaphor, but "精力" is not.）例如：

> 精神食粮　　　　精神支柱　　　　　精神负担
> 精神创伤
> * 精力食粮　　　* 精力支柱　　　　* 精力负担
> * 精力创伤

（三）语法功能上的差异（Difference in grammatical function）

"精神"既有名词功能,又有形容词功能；它可以作主语、宾语、定语,也可以作谓语、补语；"精神"作形容词用时,可以接受程度副词的修饰,可以重叠为"精精神神"。"精力"只有名词用法,它不能接受程度副词的修饰,不能作谓语、补语,不能重叠。

344

("精神" functions as a noun as well as an adjective. It can be used as subject, object, attribute and predicate, complement as well. When used as an adjective, it is modified by adverbs of degree and is reduplicated as "精精神神". While "精力" can only be used as a noun and can't be modified by adverbs of degree, and it can't be used as predicate or complement and can't be reduplicated.) 例如：

这种精神值得学习。

我们要发扬这种助人为乐的精神。

他的精神状态不太好。

她总是那么精精神神的。

(She is always full of vitality.)

这小伙子长得很精神。

(The young fellow looks very impressive.)

他比以前更精神了。

(He is more vigorous than before.)

他的精力很旺盛。

你一定要集中精力,把工作做好。

* 她总是那么精精力力的。
* 这小伙子长得很精力。
* 他比以前更精力了。

究竟 jiūjìng   到底 dàodǐ

〈副词〉表示追究和强调事物的本质或特点。

(<adverb> expressing the idea of making a searching enquiry about something or stressing on the nature or characteristic of something.)

(一)"究竟"和"到底"意义很相近,很多情况下可以换用。("究竟" and "到底" are quite close in meaning and they are exchangeable generally.)

1."究竟"和"到底"都可以用于不用"吗"的疑问句中或含有疑问意义的语句中,表示追究的疑问语气。(Both can be used in

345

the interrogative sentence without "吗" or in the sentences implying interrogative meaning, indicating the interrogative mood of investigating.)例如：

你究竟／到底怎么了？你怎么不说话呀？

光天化日之下强抢东西,究竟／到底还有没有王法了？

(Robbing in broad daylight, is there any law at all?)

这种做法究竟／到底可不可行,我也说不好。

她也不知道这样爱下去究竟／到底会是什么结果。

2. "究竟"和"到底"都可以用在陈述句中,用以加强语气,句中多含有评价意义,表示"不管怎么说,还是如此"的意思。多用于"是"字句中。(Both can be used in declarative sentence to stress on the tone. Usually the sentence implies evaluation which means "no matter how..., it is still...". They are mainly used in the sentence of "是".)例如：

究竟／到底是城里的孩子,你看人家多大方呀！

他究竟／到底是个孩子,怎么可能把事情想得那么周全？

(After all, he is a child. How can he be so considerate?)

这里究竟／到底是省城,跟乡下就是不一样。

究竟／到底是春天了,刮这么大的风,还是暖暖的。

(二) "究竟"、"到底"稍有不同。(Slight difference between "究竟" and "到底".)

1. 词义的语体色彩上："究竟"含书面语色彩,多用于书面语；"到底"口语色彩较浓,多用于口语。(In flavour: since "究竟" has the flavour of written language, it is used in written language; while "到底" has strong flavour of spoken language, it is used in colloquial lauguage.)

2. 从意义上说,在表示追究的疑问语气上,二者"追"的角度稍有偏颇："究竟"侧重于事情的原委,即搞清楚是怎么回事；"到底"侧重于深入追问。(In interrogative mood, the investigating angle

of the two words is slightly different. "究竟" emphasizes the cause of a matter, or to make clear what happens; while "到底" mainly means to make a profound inquiry.)

(三) 其他(Others)

"究竟"和"到底"还有意义上、用法上不同的地方。("究竟" and "到底" are also different in meaning and in use.)

1. "到底"还可以表示经过种种变化、曲折最后实现的情况；"究竟"没有这种意思。("到底" indicates that after all the changes or complications something is realized in the end; "究竟" doesn't indicate this.) 例如：

  卫星到底发射成功了。

  你到底来了，我等你等得好苦啊！

  (You've come in the end. I've been waiting for you so painstakingly.)

  他用了三天三夜的时间，到底把设计图拿出来了。

  * 卫星究竟发射成功了。

  * 你究竟来了，我等你等得好苦啊！

  * 他用了三天三夜的时间，究竟把设计图拿出来了。

2. "究竟"还有名词用法，表示"结果"、"原委"的意思，可以作宾语。在结构上，它常常构成"动词+个+究竟"的形式。"到底"不能这样用。〔"究竟" is also used as a noun, indicating (result), (all the details), and to be used as object. In structure, it composes the pattern "verb + 个 + 究竟"。"到底" is not used in this way.〕例如：

  你不是想探个究竟吗？来，我告诉你。

  (You want to find what actually happened. Well, let me tell you the truth.)

  (门外吵吵闹闹的)她推开门，想看个究竟。

  你去把他叫来，我非问出个究竟来不可。

  (Go to get him here. I'll ask him what on earth he has

done.）

* 你不是想探个到底吗？来，我告诉你。
* （门外吵吵闹闹的）她推开门，想看个到底。
* 你去把他叫来，我非问出个到底来不可。

举行 jǔxíng　　举办 jǔbàn

〈动词〉发起、兴办。

(＜verb＞ initiate; set up.)

(一) 词义有差别(Difference in meaning)

"举行"、"举办"都是动词，都有"发起、兴办"的意思，但是意义侧重点分别有所不同。"举行"重在"实行、进行"；"举办"则重在"办理"。〔"举行"and "举办"both are verbs and mean "发起 (initiate)" or "兴办 (set up)", but they emphasize different angles. "举行"stresses on "实行 (practice)", "进行 (conduct)" while "举行"stresses on "办理 (handle)".〕例如：

会议举行得怎么样？（指会议进行的情况。）

会议举办得怎么样？（指举办会议的人或单位办理的情况。）

(二) 搭配上有差别(Difference in collocation)

1. 与"举行"搭配的名词宾语或主语，大多是"集会"、"仪式"等，此外，"举行"还可以带"会谈"、"游行"、"起义"、"比赛"等动词宾语。"举办"则大多带名词性宾语，它的名词性宾语与"举行"也有所不同，它常常可以连带"学习班"、"讲座"、"报告会"、"展览"、"文娱晚会"、"福利事业"等宾语。〔The noun objects or noun-natured subjects which collocate with "举行"are mainly "集会" (rally), "仪式" (ceremony), etc. Besides, "举行"can also be followed by verb objects as "会谈" (talks), "游行" (parade), "起义" (uprising) and "比赛" (match), etc. "举办", in most cases, is followed by noun-natured objects and its noun-natured objects are different from those of "举行"."举办"is generally followed by " 学习班"

(study class), "讲座" (lecture), "报告会" (public report), "展览会" (exhibition), "文娱晚会" (recreational party), "福利事业" (welfare services), etc. as its objects.〕例如:

他们举行了一次盛大的结婚典礼。

每年除夕之夜,中央电视台都要举行盛大的迎春晚会。
(Every lunar New Year's eve, a grand New Year's Eve entertainment will be held on CCTV.)

这次谈判将于明日下午在会议厅举行。

他们决定明日凌晨四点举行起义。

* 这次谈判将于明日下午在会议厅举办。
* 他们决定明日凌晨四点举办起义。

下星期二,图书馆将举办一次软件检索应用讲座。
(Next Tuesday, a lecture on the application of software index searching will be held in the library.)

这次图书展览由十三个单位联合举办。

这种大型的活动,我们已经举办过好几回了,有经验了。

(We have held several such kinds of large-scaled activities, so we are experienced.)

* 这次图书展览由十三个单位联合举行。
* 这种大型的活动,我们已经举行过好几回了,有经验了。

2. "举办"重在"办理",所以通常离不开举办单位或举办者。因此,在一般的记叙或说明句中,主语通常是表示举办单位或举办者的,非描写句的"举办"的宾语通常不能位于主语的位置;宾语位于主语前的话,举办单位或举办者通常用"由"引出或者谓语是表示描写性内容的、主谓词组的句子等。"举行"重在"进行",其主语可以是"举行"的受事,当主语是"举行"的受事时,举办单位或举办者一般不出现,但是却比较强调举行的场所、时间、情况等。〔"举办" emphasizes "办理 (hold)". So it usually in-

cludes a place or a sponsor. So in general narrative or illustrative sentences, subjects are usually the conducting parts or people, and the object of non-illustrative sentence of "举办" can not be placed in the position of subject. If the object is put before subject, the conducting parts or people will be introduced by "由" or its predicates should be descriptive-natured or sentences of subject-predicate phrases. "举行" (emphasizes), "进行" (conduct). When subject is the object of "举行", the conducting parts or people will not appear, but the places, time and situations are strongly emphasized.〕例如：

<u>同学们自己</u>举办的读书报告会很受欢迎。

(The public lecture on reading held by the students themselves is well received.)

新年音乐会<u>由音乐厅</u>举办。

洽谈会举办<u>得很成功</u>。

* 书画展览在展览厅举办。

* 新闻发布会下午两点举办。

书画展览<u>在展览厅</u>举行。

新闻发布会<u>下午两点</u>举行。

觉得 juéde   认为 rènwéi

〈动词〉＜verb＞

"觉得"、"认为"有时都可以表示对人或事物确定某种看法或作出某种判断,因此有时可以换用。但是大多情况下不能换用,这是因为它们在表示同一意义时,仍有意义上的差别,此外它们还有意义上不同的地方,用法上也有不少的差别。("觉得" and "认为" both sometimes indicate to define some opinion or to make some judgement on people or things, so occasionally they are exchangeable, but in most cases they are not exchangeable for there is still difference in meaning even when they are indicating the same thing. Besides, they are also quite different in use.)

(一) 意义上(In meaning)

1."觉得"、"认为"都可以表示对人或事物确定某种看法或作出某种判断,但是"觉得"的意义比较轻,侧重于感觉,"认为"的意义比较重,侧重于理性。(Both indicate to define some opinion or make some judgement on people or things. "觉得" is weaker in meaning, emphasizing one's feeling; while "认为" is stronger in meaning, emphasizing reasoning.)试比较:

你觉得他说的话在理吗?

(Do you think there is any sense in his words?)

我觉得我们该开个会讨论一下这个问题。

你觉得谁做主持人好些?

我认为一个人不能脱离社会而生存。

(I think one cannot live separated from the society.)

他总认为他说的话都是真理。

我认为这是一幅难得的好作品。

以上的例子"觉得"、"认为"可以换用,但是换用后意义的轻重是不同的。有时如果说话人表示的见解、判断确定性或理性很强,就应该用"认为",不要用"觉得"。(In the examples above "觉得" and "认为" are exchangeable, but the meanings they emphasize are different. And if the speaker wants to express his opinion or accurate judgement which is quite definite or rational, he should use "认为" instead of "觉得".)例如:

谁会认为这是事实呢?

孙教授认为这种工艺品的艺术价值高于它的历史价值。

(Professor Sun thought that the artistic value of this handicraft is higher than its historical value.)

但是,有时说话人的看法虽然是非常确定的,但为了表示谦虚、礼貌或者委婉等,用"觉得"可能更合适些。(But even the speaker's opinion is quite definite, in order to appear modest, polite or

351

tactful, it is more proper for him to use "觉得".)

2."觉得"还可以表示通过感官而产生的某种感觉;"认为"不能用于这种情况。("觉得" also indicates some feeling that emerges through sense organs and "认为" can't be used in this case.)例如:

她觉得肚子有点儿不舒服。

我觉得身上很冷。

他觉得心情很舒畅。

从搬到这里以后,她就一直觉得很孤独。

(She always feels lonely since she moved here.)

我觉得很累,一点儿也不想动。

我觉得腿很麻。

* 她认为肚子有点儿不舒服。

* 我认为身上很冷。

* 他认为心情很舒畅。

* 从搬到这里以后,她就一直认为很孤独。

* 我认为很累,一点儿也不想动。

* 我认为腿很麻。

(二)用法上(In use)

1.相同之处(Similarities)

(1)"觉得"、"认为"在句子里都是作带宾语的谓语,在表示确定某种看法或判断的意义时,它们带的宾语大多是由主谓词组充当的,在一定的语境中,可以用动词性、形容词性词语充当,但是不能用名词性词语充当。(In sentence both "觉得" and "认为" are used as predicates taking objects. When indicating to define some opinion or judgement, the objects are mainly subject-predicate phrases. In certain context, words of verb nature or adjective nature can also be used as their objects. But words of noun nature can't.)例如:

他总觉得气氛有点儿不对。

352

(He always feels that there is something fishy about it.)
我觉得她好像有什么心事。
(I feel that she seems to have something on her mind.)
我认为这个办法可行。
老师们都认为他的汉语进步很大。
* 我已经觉得他的变化了。
* 我们觉得中国有意思的风俗。
* 大家都认为这个规律。
* 他认为这本书的价值。

"觉得"在表示感觉器官产生某种感觉的意思时,可以带单个形容词或感受性词。("觉得" can be used with a single adjective or a word expressing feeling, when it expresses the meaning of feeling aroused by sense organs.)例如:

觉得累　　　　　觉得难受　　　　　觉得痛快
觉得热　　　　　觉得闷　　　　　　觉得恶心

(2)"觉得"、"认为"后面都不能接补语,也不能接动态助词。"认为"在极个别的情况下,可以接"过"。("觉得" and "认为" can't be followed by complements nor aspect particles. In fairly rare case "认为" can be followed by "过".)例如:

* 你觉得得很对,她的确有心事。
* 我觉得到他的心跳得很快。
* 对这件事我认为得很清楚。
* 他认为得很快,也很对。
* 我觉得了困,你呢?
* 我正觉得着热。
* 这个屋子你觉得过舒服吗?
* 你认为了这件事好吗?
* 我认为着这样不好。

你错了,我从来也没有这样认为过。

(3)"觉得"、"认为"不能作主语、宾语。("觉得" and "认

为" can not be used as subjects and objects.)例如:
* 来中国后,你的觉得是什么?
* 你的觉得有问题,你应该听听大家的觉得。
* 大家谈谈自己的认为吧。
* 你对这件事的认为不对。

2. 不同之处(Differences)

"觉得"、"认为"由于意义上的差别,在搭配上也稍有不同。"觉得"个人的感觉性比较强,"认为"理性比较强,所以一些表示控制性强的或共通性意义的修饰语一般不能用来修饰"觉得"。(Because of the difference in meaning, "觉得" and "认为" are different in collocation. "觉得" is stronger in feeling. On the contrary, "认为" is stronger in reasoning. Some modifiers that express strong control or common sense cannot modify "觉得".)例如:

公然认为(publicly think)
大胆地认为(daringly think)
消极地认为(think passively)
私自认为(privately think)
固执地认为(stubbornly think)
明确认为(think clearly)
普遍认为   共同认为   一贯认为
* 公然觉得   * 大胆地觉得   * 私自觉得
* 固执地觉得   * 明确觉得   * 消极地觉得
* 普遍觉得   * 共同觉得   * 一贯觉得

K

看 kàn   看见 kànjian

〈动词〉表示视线跟人与物接触。

(< verb > indicating the eyesight cast on people or things.)

"看"和"看见"都可以表示视线跟人与物接触的意思,看起来两个词意思很接近,但是,实际上无论是意义、结构还是用法上都有较大差别,大多数场合中不可以换用。("看" and "看见" both mean the eyesight casting on people or things. The meaning of these two words seems close, but actually either in meaning, in construction or in use, there is large difference and they are not exchangeable on most occasions.)

(一)意义上的差别(Difference in meaning)

"看"表示的视线跟人与物的接触过程,是一种始终相接触的过程,即视线不离开人与物。("看" expresses the state when one's eyes are keeping in touch with an object for a certain period, or when one's line of sight hasn't left its object.)例如:

他坐在沙发上看报。(视线不离开报。)

观众们正在看杂技演员的表演。(视线不离开杂技演员的表演。)

"看见"则不同,它不是视线跟人与物始终相接触的过程,而是一经接触,"看见"的动作就完成了。("看见" differs from "看" in that as soon as one's eyes touch the object, the action of "看见" is finished. One's line of sight doesn't need to fix on the object all the time.)例如:

我看见小王上楼了。(现在视线并没有跟小王接触,而是小王上楼这件事一反映到视觉中,"看见"的动作就结束了。)

因此,"看"的动作自身没有结果;"看见"的动作自身包含了结果。(Therefore, the act of "看" itself has no result, but that of "看见" implies the result.)

(二) 结构上和用法上的差别(Difference in construction and in use)

1. "看"的动作本身没有结果,所以它后面可以接表示结果的补语。"看见"本身包含了结果,所以不能再接表示结果的补语。(The act of "看" itself has no result and it can be followed by the complement of result. Since "看见" itself implies the result, it can't be followed by complement of result.)例如:

我看到大熊猫了。
我看清楚他的长相了。
他看错人了。
报纸看完了。
* 我看见到大熊猫了。
* 我看见清楚他的长相了。
* 他看见错人了。
* 报纸看见完了。

2. "看"是持续性动词,它前面可以用表示正在进行意义的副词"正"、"在"、"正在",后面可以接表示动作持续意义的助词"着"。"看见"是非持续性动词,不能与这些词结合。("看" is a durative verb. Adverbs which indicate progression such as "正","在" and "正在" can be used before "看" and particles which indicate continuance of the action, such as "着", can be used after it. "看见" is a non-durative verb, so it can't be used together with these words.)例如:

他正看你呢。
同学们都在看他表演。
我进屋的时候,他正在看地图。
我看着她消失在夜色中。
(I saw her disappearing in the dark.)
* 他正看见你呢。

356

* 同学们都在看见他表演。
* 我进屋的时候,他正在看见地图。
* 我看见着她消失在夜色中。

3. "看"后面可以接时量补语——动作持续的时段;"看见"不可以。("看" can be followed by complement indicating time-length — the period when an action lasts, and "看见" can't.)例如:

两个孩子看了<u>三四个小时</u>电视。

他看了<u>一假期</u>书。

* 两个孩子看见了三四个小时电视。
* 他看见了一假期书。

4. "看"后面可以接动量补语;"看见"一般不能接动量补语,个别情况下可接,一般用于过去的事情。("看" can be followed by complement of verbal measure. "看见" generally can't be followed by that except in a particular case. It is used for the things happened before.)例如:

我看<u>一下</u>这本词典可以吗?

这部小说我已经看了<u>两遍</u>了。

每人可以看<u>三次</u>。

* 我看见一下这本词典可以吗?
* 这部小说我已经看见了两遍了。
* 每人可以看见三次。

我看见过他打架,看见过两次。

5. "看"可以重叠使用;"看见"不可以。("看" can be reduplicated, but "看见" can't.)例如:

我看看!

看看京剧吧。

* 我看见看见!
* 看见看见京剧吧。

6. "看"是有自主性的动词,可以用于祈使句;"看见"是没有自主性的动词,不能用于祈使句。("看" is an independent verb, which can be used in an imperative sentence. "看见" is not an independent verb and can't be used in an imperative sentence.)例如:

  快来看吧!   看一会儿去吧。
  别看了!   不许看!
  * 快来看见吧!   * 看见一会儿去吧。
  * 别看见了!   * 不许看见!

7. "看"既可以用"不"否定,也可以用"没"否定;"看见"一般情况下用"没"否定。("看" can either be negated by "不" or by "没", "看见" is generally negated by "没".)例如:

  他说他不看电视了。
  那个展览我还没看。
  我没看见彩虹。
  没看见吗?没关系,一会儿再看。
  * 我不看见彩虹。
  * 不看见吗?没关系,一会儿再看。

但是,可以用"看不见"表示不可能出现的结果。(But "看不见" is used to indicate a result which is impossible to appear.)

8. "看"的宾语大多是名词或名词性词语;"看见"也可以是名词性词语,但是"看见"还常常连带小句宾语。(The objects of "看" mostly are nouns and phrases of noun character, "看见" can be words of noun character, but it can also be followed by a short clause as its object.)例如:

  看书 看杂志 看京剧 看风景
  看潺潺的流水(Look at the murmuring stream!)
  看飞机喷洒农药 看见老王了
  看见一位老大娘走了过来
  看见她热情地为顾客服务

(三)"看"还有"探望"、"看望"的意思;"看见"没有这种意思。("看" also means (to visit) or (to go to see), "看见" doesn't have these meanings.)例如：

我们去医院看老李。
星期天,我得去看一位朋友去。
春节,无论如何也得回家看看父母。

(Anyhow, I've got to go home and visit my parents during the Spring Festival.)

* 我们去医院看见老李。
* 星期天,我得去看见一位朋友去。
* 春节,无论如何也得回家看见父母。

考 kǎo   考试 kǎoshì   测验 cèyàn

考、测验〈动词〉< verb >
考试〈名词〉< noun >〈动词〉< verb >

"考"、"考试"、"测验"都可以用于对于学习成绩的考查,但是意义上、用法上有一定差别,所以有时不能换用。("考","考试" and "测验" all can be used for checking the grades of study. Because there is certain difference in meaning as well as in use, sometimes they are not exchangeable.)

(一) 功能不同(Difference in function)

1. "考"只作动词用,不能单独用来作主语或宾语;考试可以用作动词,也可以用作名词,所以,它既可以作谓语,也可以作主语、宾语;"测验"是动词,可以作谓语,也可以作主语和宾语。("考" is a verb. It can not be used as a subject or an object alone. "考试" is either a verb or a noun. So it can be used as either a predicate or a subject, or an object. "测验" is a verb. But it can also be used as either a predicate or a subject, or an object.)例如：

今天考哪一科？——今天考外语。
你想考什么专业？——我想考国际经济。
* 今天的考怎么样？
* 我看了你的考,很好。

359

* 他想参加英语的考吗?
　　我们今天考试了。
　　考试进行得怎么样?
　　你想参加英语考试吗?
　　今天测验体能,大家先活动活动。(谓语)
　　听力测验开始了。(主语)
　　机器出故障了,停止测验。(宾语)
　2."考"和"测验"可以连带宾语,"考试"不可以。("考" or "测验" can be followed by objects, but "考试" cannot.)例如:
　　考外语　　　　考古典文学　　是考老师还是考学生
　　考北京大学　　考什么专业
　　测验技能　　　测验听力　　　测验数学
　　测验长跑　　　测验考生　　　测验智力
　　* 考试外语　　* 考试听力　　* 考试学生
　　* 考试什么专业　　　　　　　* 考试南开大学
(二) 由于意义的差别,词语搭配的范围有所不同(The range of the collocation between words and phrases is different because of their differences in meaning.)

　1.在考查学习成绩方面,"考试"可以用于平日小的考查,也可以用于阶段性的大的正式的考查,例如:期中考试、期末考试等;正式的大的考查,一般不用"测验"。(In aspect of testing the grades, "考试" is used either for the usual quizzes or for the formal periodical examinations, i.e. a mid-term examination or a final examination. As for the formal tests, "测验" is not used.)

　2."考"、"考试"和"测验"在意义上有差别,所以它们连带的宾语不同。"考"还有被考通过考试进入某部门、单位的意思。所以,"考"连带的宾语除了有科目、项目、对象以外,还可以有通过考试进入的部门、单位等;"测验"只有用一定的标准、手段考的意思,所以它不能连带考生想进入的部门、单位等类宾语。(Since there are differences in meaning among "考","考试"and "测验", the objects followed are different. "考" indicates the examinees' admittance to the membership of a department or unit through exams. So the object following can either be a course, an item and an examinee, or be a department or a unit admitted to. "测验" involves only the standard, or the method of a test. So it cannot have a unit as its object.)例如：

科目、项目、对象： 考专业　考外语　考听力　考学生
测验专业　测验外语　测验听力
测验学生
想进入的单位、部门：考清华大学　考中医学院
考三星公司　考中文系
＊ 测验清华大学　＊ 测验三星公司
＊ 测验中文系

3.因为"考"可以用于考生被考的情况,所以"考"后面可以接补充、说明被考考得怎么样的补语;"测验"只是主考对被考的考试,所以不能这样用。"考试"后面不能接补语。(Because "考" can be used in the condition in which examinees are examined, it can be followed by a supplement explaining how the examinee does in the test. "测验" is limited for the examination given by the supervisor, it can't be used in the same way as "考". By the way, there is no complement used after "考试".)例如：

他被考住了。(It put him on the spot.)
我终于考上了。(I passed the entrance examinations at last.)
他这一次考糟了。(He failed in this test.)
我考"糊"了。(I made a bad bungle of the test.)
＊ 他被测验住了。
＊ 我终于测验上了。
＊ 他这一次测验糟了。
＊ 我测验"糊"了。

361

* 他被考试住了。
　　* 我终于考试上了。
　　* 他这一次考试糟了。
　　* 我考试"糊"了。

4. "测验"考查的范围很大,包括知识、技能、性能、心理、意愿等,尤其突出的是它有用仪器检测的意思;"考"、"考试"则主要指考查跟学习有关的知识、技能等。(The range of "测验" is large, including knowledge, technique, performance, psychology, aspiration, and so on. It is specially used when an instrument is used in the test. "考" and "考试" indicate testing the relevant knowledge or capabilities to study.)例如:

　　测验语文　　　专业测验　　　　测验听力
　　写作测验　　　法律知识测验
　　测验体能(physical examination)
　　测验心理(mental examination)
　　测验仪器性能(test the performance of equipment)
　　民意测验(public opinion poll)
　　测验抗菌性(test the function of anti-BIOS's)
　　测验握力(test the power of gripping)
　　考语文　　　　考专业　　　　　考听力
　　考写作　　　　考法律知识　　　语文考试
　　专业考试　　　听力考试　　　　写作考试
　　法律知识考试
　　* 考体能　　　* 考心理　　　* 考民意
　　* 考抗菌性　　* 考握力
　　* 仪器性能考试* 民意考试　　　* 抗菌性考试
　　* 握力考试
　　* 我想考一考你的记忆力。(应改作:我想测验一下你的记忆力。)

(三) 用法上的差异(Difference in use)

1. "考"和"测验"可以重叠使用,"考试"不能重叠使用。("考" or "测验" can be reduplicated, while "考试" cannot.) 例如:

老师要考一考你。
我们来考考他。
现在听一段录音,我要测验测验大家的听力。
* 他的水平怎么样,考试考试就知道了。
* 他想考试考试北京大学。

2. "考"和"测验"后面可以接动量补语,"考试"不能。("考" or "测验" can be followed by a numeral-classifier compound as its complement, but "考试" cannot.) 例如:

考一下没关系。
他考了三次了,都没考上。
我们现在就来测验一下。
测验好几次了,结果都一样。
* 他考试了三次了,都没考上。
* 我们现在就来考试一下。
* 考试好几次了,结果都一样。

口 kǒu   嘴 zuǐ

口、嘴〈名词〉指人或动物进饮食或发音的部位。

口、嘴(< noun > the organ by which human or animals eat or pronounce.)

口〈量词〉 < measure word >

"口"、"嘴"都指人或动物进饮食或发音的部位,但是从字源上看,"口"是指凹进的形,"嘴"是指凸出来的形,因此"嘴"比"口"有明显的部位意义,它们在大多情况下不能互换使用。主要区别在于:(Both "口" and "嘴" refer to the organ by which human or animals eat or pronounce. To study from the etymology, "口" represents the shape of a concaved thing, and "嘴" repre-

363

sents a protruding shape. Therefore,"嘴"has a stronger sense of body part than "口", and in most cases they are not inchangeable. The major differences are：)

(一) 在现代汉语中,"口"大多已经成为构词语素,单用的情况很少。"嘴"却仍然是一个自由语素,可以单用,也可以构词。所以,表示人或动物进饮食的部位的意义时,单用的话,通常用"嘴"。(In modern Chinese,"口"is now mainly used as a language-combining element to form word groups or phrases. It is seldom used alone. "嘴" is still a free language unit, and can either be used alone or form word groups. So when used single to express a part of body through which man or animal takes in food, usually "嘴" is preferred.)例如：

你的嘴怎么了？张开我看看。

你们都闭上嘴吧,这已经够乱的了,别再添乱了。

(Shut up! It's too noisy already. Don't add more mess.)

她上火了,嘴上长了一溜水泡。

(She is suffering from excessive internal heat, with blisters all over her mouth.)

* 你的口怎么了？张开我看看。

* 你们都闭上口吧,这已经够乱的了,别再添乱了。

* 她上火了,口上长了一溜水泡。

(二) 在不是单独使用的情况下,"口"的部位意义常常抽象一些,"嘴"的部位意义相对具体一些。其使用范围和用法有以下不同：(If not used separately, the position meaning of "口" is more abstract, while that of "嘴" is more specific. There are difference in the range of use：)

1. 用"口"构成的词,通常表示用口的方式及其与方式有关的类型,这与部位意义不是直接的具体的联系,所以不用"嘴"。(Words formed with phrases formed with "口" usually express the ways how one's mouth is used or something related to the ways. So "嘴" is

not used in such phrases which have no direct and concrete relationship with the oral part.)例如：

　　口授　口试　口述　口算　口译　口服
　　口令　口供　口角　口语　口信　口腔
　　口琴　口号　口诀　口技　口罩　口水
　　＊嘴试　　＊嘴述　　＊嘴令　　＊嘴供
　　＊嘴语　　＊嘴信　　＊嘴技

2.用"口"构成的词,通常与说话的能力、气势、语音、意思等有关,离具体的部位意义更远,所以也不能用"嘴"。(Phrases formed with "口" are usually related to the ability, manner, sound and meaning of the speaking. It has little to do with any specific parts of one's mouth. So "嘴" still can't be used here.)例如：

　　口才(eloquence)　　　　口齿(enunciation)
　　口气(tone)　　　　　　口音(voice)
　　口若悬河(be eloquent)
　　口风(one's intention or view revealed in what one says)
　　＊嘴才　　＊嘴齿　　＊嘴气　　＊嘴音
　　＊嘴若悬河　　＊嘴风

3.跟"口"的感觉、运气有关的,也具有一定的抽象性,所以一般用"口",不用"嘴"。(Words concerned with feelings or breathing of one's mouth are somewhat abstract. So "口", but not "嘴" is usually used.)例如：

　　口感(the feeling of one's mouth)
　　口味(one's taste)
　　口轻(be fond of food that is not salty)
　　口重(be fond of salty food)
　　口福(the luck to get something very nice to eat)
　　＊嘴感　＊嘴味　＊嘴轻　＊嘴重　＊嘴福

4.表示"嘴"具体怎么样的意义,一般用"嘴"不用"口",这是因为它的部位意义较强。这种词语的结构通常是"嘴+形容性词",意义上借助"嘴"怎么样的描写表示一种形容的意义。(When describing one's mouth,"嘴" is usually used instead of "口",because "嘴" emphasizes the specific part of one's body. Here the pattern is usually "嘴 + adjective" to present a description by using the word "嘴".)例如:

嘴严(able to keep a secret)　嘴松(careless in speech)
嘴直(frank and outspoken)　嘴稳(discreet in speech)
嘴紧(tight lipped)　嘴快(have a loose tongue)
嘴碎(loquacious)　嘴笨(clumsy of speech)
嘴刁(fastidious about one's food)
嘴硬(stubborn and reluctant to admit mistakes or defeats)
* 口严　* 口松　* 口碎　* 口笨
* 口硬　* 口刁　* 口稳

(三)汉语中,一些名词可以临时借用为量词。"口"和"嘴"在临时借用为量词时,有时可以用在相同的词语结构中,例如:"一口饭"、"一嘴饭",但是表示的意思往往是有差别的。"口"表示吃一下的量或通过口的部位动作的量;"嘴"则表示食物等与整个嘴的部位接触或塞满有关的量。(In Chinese, some nouns can be used temporarily as measure words. When "口" and "嘴" are temporarily used as measure words, they can sometimes be used in the same constructions. For example, "一口饭" and "一嘴饭", but there is still some difference in meaning. "口" means the amount that one takes in for one time, or food passes through one's mouth. "嘴" indicates the amount of food or other things that is getting into touch with one's whole mouth, or fills one's mouth.)例如:

一口饭　一口茶　一口酒　一口烟　一口痰
一口菜
咬一口　尝一口　吐一口　吹一口　舔一口
吃一口
灌了一嘴啤酒(pour a mouthful of beer down one's throat)

塞了一嘴面包(fill the mouth with bread)

啃了一嘴泥(get a mouthful of mud)

抽了一嘴的烟味(one's mouth smells of smoke)

烫了一嘴泡(get blisters all over one's mouth through being scalded)

吐出来了一嘴脏话(spout dirty words)

蹭了一嘴油(smear one's mouth with oil)

这菜真好吃,你尝一口试试。

吹蜡烛时,只许吹一口气。

这菜真好吃,你尝一嘴试试。

* 吹蜡烛时,只许吹一嘴气。

慢慢吃,塞那么一嘴,怎么嚼呀?

(Eat slowly. How will you chew with such a mouthful of food?)

你烟抽得太厉害了,抽得一嘴的烟味。

(You smoked too much and smelled of heavy smoke.)

* 慢慢吃,塞那么一口,怎么嚼呀?

* 你烟抽得太厉害了,抽得一口的烟味。

(四)"口"是进饮食的地方,还可以将它引申为通过的地方、凹进的像"口"形的地方及与"人口"有关的量词,这些都远离了部位意义,所以用"口",不用"嘴"。(Besides expressing an opening through which one takes in food, "口" can also indicate a sunken opening or outlet of something or some place, which is shaped like a mouth, or be used as a measure word relating to mouth. All of these have little to do with the position of the mouth, so "口", not "嘴" should be used.)例如:

碗口　井口　出入口　门口　路口　窗口
关口　通道口　胡同口　伤口　把这张纸撕个口儿
人口　户口　家口　三口人
两口钟　一口棺材　五口猪　一口井

* 碗嘴　　* 出入嘴　　* 伤嘴　　* 三嘴人
* 一嘴钟　* 五嘴猪

但是,向外凸出的进出口的部位,可以用"嘴"。(A protruding outlet of something or some place is expressed by "嘴".)例如:

壶嘴　瓶嘴　奶嘴　烟嘴　笼嘴　喷嘴

宽阔 kuānkuò   宽敞 kuānchang
宽广 kuān'guǎng   广大 guǎngdà   广阔 guǎngkuò

〈形容词〉表示面积或空间范围很大。

(< adjective > indicating the range of area or space is broad.)

(一)"宽阔"和"宽敞"

1."宽阔"和"宽敞"都有宽和大的意思,但是语义侧重的角度有所不同。"宽阔"侧重于地面、水面等平面的宽、大、开阔;"宽敞"侧重于建筑物空间的宽、大、没有遮拦。(Both mean being wide and big, but the angles being stressed on are different. "宽阔" emphasizes the broadness, largeness and wideness of a plane, such as a ground and a river. "宽敞" emphasizes the commodiousness, greatness or emptiness of a building.)例如:

宽阔的湖面上飘荡着几只小船。

宽阔的天安门广场中央矗立着人民英雄纪念碑。

宽阔的马路上汽车川流不息。

(Motor vehicles are flowing past in an endless stream along the broad road.)

呼伦贝尔大草原那么宽阔!

(How wide the Hulun Boir Great Prairie is!)

这间屋子真宽敞!

宽敞的一楼大厅中央放着一棵美丽的圣诞树。

这里每家都住着别致的小楼,环抱着小楼的是宽敞而漂亮的院落。

(Every family here lives in a unique building, each surrounded with a spacious and beautiful courtyard.)

2.非建筑物的大的平面的宽、大,一般不用"宽敞"形容;建筑物空间的宽、大,尤其是房间一般不用"宽阔"形容。(When indicating large and wide flatness not of buildings, "宽敞" is not used. While "宽阔"is not generally used for, describing how wide or large the space of the building is, especially not for rooms.)例如:

* 你的房间真宽阔!
* 我们有宽阔的教室和阅览室。
* 宽敞的湖面上飘荡着几只小船。
* 呼伦贝尔大草原那么宽敞!

(二)"宽阔"、"宽广"、"广大"、"广阔"

1."宽阔"、"宽广"、"广大"、"广阔"都有宽、大、开阔的意思,有时可以通用。但是由于它们适用的范围还有一定的差别,所以有时是不能换用的。(All of the four have the meaning of being wide, big and open and sometimes they are exchangeable. But sometimes they are not exchangeable since there is certain difference in the range applicable to them.)

(1)"广大"跟"宽阔"、"宽广"、"广阔"有所不同,"广大"主要用于领土、地域,一般不能用于形容水面、广场、马路等。("广大" is different from "宽阔","宽广"and "广阔";"广大" is mainly used to describe a land or territory, not used to describe the surface of a river, a square, or a street.)例如:

在这个广大的领土之上,有广大的肥田沃土,给我们以衣食之源。

(In this great land, there is a vast fertile farmland to provide us with sources of clothing and food.)

中国领土广大,资源丰富,人口众多。
* 广大的江面上布满了大大小小的船只!
* 广大的天安门广场上人山人海的。
* 这条马路很广大。

(2)"宽阔"、"宽广"、"广阔"都可以用于地面、水面、田野、草原、广场等大的环境。("宽阔","宽广"and"广阔"can all be used for large environment such as ground, surface of water, fields, grasslands and square.)例如:

他骑着快马飞驰在宽阔／宽广／广阔的原野上。

(He rode at full gallop on the broad / vast / wide grassland.)

我站在海岸边,望着宽阔／宽广／广阔的海面上繁忙的船只,感慨万千。

(When I stand by the seashore, looking at the busy ships on the broad / vast / wide sea, all sorts of feelings well up in my mind.)

但是,"宽广"一般多用于原野等大的环境,一般不用于马路等相对小的环境。(But"宽广"is usually used for the big environment as champaign instead of the comparatively narrow environment as streets.)

2."宽阔"、"宽广"、"广大"、"广阔"除了宽、大、开阔的意思外,还有其他意思;大多不能换用。(Besides the meaning of being wide, big and open,"宽阔","宽广","广大"and"广阔"have other meanings, and generally they are not exchangeable.)例如:

(1)"宽阔"、"宽广"可以用于形容人的心胸、视野等。("宽广"and"宽阔"can be used to describe one's mind or eyesight.)例如:

他的心胸很宽阔。

(He is broad-minded.)

视野变得更加宽阔了。

(His field of vision is getting wider.)

他有宽广的胸怀。

他的视野更宽广了。

370

(2)"宽广"还可以形容人的发展道路。("宽广" can also be used to describe people's growth route.)例如:

人生道路还很宽广。
生活道路宽广着呢!

(3)"广大"还可以用于形容人数众多。("广大" can also be used when describing a great many people.)例如:

广大读者　　广大听众　　广大群众　　广大干部
广大足球爱好者

(4)"广阔"可以用于形容背景、前景等。("广阔" can be used to describe a background or foreground.)例如:

把故事的发展放在广阔的时代背景上,这样的小说才会更深刻。

(Put the developing of the story in the broad background of the times, the novel will be more profound.)

前景广阔。

困难 kùnnan　　艰难 jiānnán　　难 nán

困难、艰难、难〈形容词〉表示事情复杂,阻碍多,不容易。

困难、艰难、难 (< adjective > indicating something is complicated, blocked and hard to deal with.)

困难〈名词〉 < noun >

(一)"困难"和"艰难"

1."困难"和"艰难"意义不完全相同。"困难"主要指事情复杂,障碍多,处理起来不容易;"艰难"除了事情复杂,障碍多的意思外,还有要付出很多的辛苦和代价的意思,所以,"艰难"的语义比"困难"重得多。("困难" and "艰难" are not completely the same in meaning. "困难" indicates something complex, obstructive, or not easy to handle. "艰难" indicates something needs to be put in a lot of hard work or be paid a price. The meaning of "艰难" is much stronger than "困难".)例如:

听说他们生活很困难,有条件的话,我们多帮助帮助他们。

凭我们的力量,想打败他们很困难。

(It is very difficult to defeat them only relying on our own power.)

听说他们的日子过得很艰难,我们有可能帮帮他们吗?

队员们奋力拼杀,艰难地拿下了这关键的一局。

(The team members played their best, and arduously won the crucial set.)

2.适用范围不完全相同。"困难"适用范围大,常用。它可以用于生活、条件、处境、工作、学习、举动等等方面;"艰难"适用范围很窄,也不常用。它主要用于生活困苦难过、举止吃力等。(The applicable range of the two words is not quite the same. "困难" is more often and widely used in such as life, condition, situation, work, study and behavior. On the contrary, "艰难" is not so often and widely used. It is mainly used to describe hardness of life, or difficulty of an action, etc.)例如:

家里的生活十分困难。

他在那么困难的条件下,取得了这样好的成绩。

他刚学了几个月的汉语,跟中国人谈话还很困难。

她的腿很疼,每迈一步都十分困难。

那么艰难的日子都过来了,现在的日子倒过不了了。

我眼睁睁地看着老妇人步履艰难地消失在夜色中。

(I watched helplessly the old woman walking with difficulty into the dark.)

* 他刚学了几个月的汉语,跟中国人谈话还很艰难。

* 山区的交通十分艰难。

3.用法不完全相同。"艰难"、"困难"都可以用作谓语、定语,除此之外,"艰难"还常常用作状语,"困难"则很少用作状语。(Being not completely the same in use. "艰难"and "困难" can both be used as predicates and attributes, and besides, "艰难" is also used as an adverbial, while "困难" is rarely used in this way.)例如：

老人虽然行动艰难,精神却很好。

战士们踏上了艰难而漫长的旅途。

(The soldiers set on a long and hard journey.)

他艰难地挥挥手,示意让我走。

她们娘俩相依为命,艰难地度过了十年的光阴。

(Depending on each other for surviving, the mother and her daughter have spent ten years of hard life.)

山太陡了,要爬上去很困难。

我们要想尽一切办法摆脱目前的困难局面。

病人困难地摇了摇头,一句话也没说。

(二)"困难"和"难"

"困难"和"难"无论在意义上还是用法上都有着相当大的差别。(The two words, either in meaning or in use, are considerably different.)

1.意义上："困难"是指事情复杂,障碍多；"难"则主要指不容易,做起来很费事。(In meaning: "困难" refers to things difficult to do, or full of obstacles. "难" means something not easy to do, or to be done with a lot of efforts.)例如：

这条路该修了,一下雨就难走极了。

题出得太难了,学生考得很糟糕。

* 这条路该修了,一下雨就困难走了。

* 题出得太困难了,学生考得很糟糕。

表示生活困难、条件艰苦、举止艰难等,一般都不能用"难"。("难" can not be used to express one's life is hard, condition difficult, or movement difficult.)例如：

* 山区的生活太难了。

* 她们娘俩相依为命,很难地度过了十年的光阴。

* 他很难地挥挥手,示意让我走。

373

2. "难"除了作谓语外,作定语、状语等修饰语时,往往都要受到音节的限制。(Besides being a predicate, "难" is generally restricted by syllables when functioning as an attribute or an adverbial.)

(1)"难"单独作定语、状语时,后面一般不能用"的"或"地",被修饰的词语,也要求是单音节的。(When "难" is used alone as an attribute or adverbial, "的" and "地" can't follow, and even the words or phrases being modified are restricted to monosyllable words.)例如:

定语:这里还有几道难题,留给你了。
　　　这一段的难字难句都解释清楚了。
　＊这里还有几道难问题,留给你了。
状语:难走也要走。
　　　大家都说汉语难学,是吗?
　＊大家都说汉语难学习,是吗?

(2)"难"跟副词组成短语后,作定语的话,可以加"的",也可以修饰双音节词;作状语一般不加"地"。(When "难" makes phrases with adverbs to be used as an attribute, "的" can be placed after it and can also modify disyllabic words. "地" will not be added when it is used as an adverbial.)例如:

定语:这是一道相当难的问题。
　　　那么难的对话他都说出来了。
状语:这件事真难办!
　　　这些东西太难整理了。
　＊这件事真难地办!
　＊这些东西太难地整理了。

(3)"困难"作状语时,一般没有单双音节的限制,通常需要加"地";作定语时,修饰的一般是双音节词,常常也要加"的"。(When "困难" is used as an adverbial, there is no limit of syllables for the words it modifies, and generally "地" has to be added. If "困

难"is used as an attribute, the part it modifies usually is a disyllable and "的"is placed after.)例如：

状语：他困难地说
　　　我困难地挪动着身子
　　＊ 他困难说
　　＊ 我困难挪动着身子
定语：他在那么困难的条件下，取得了这样好的成绩。
　　　我知道办好这件事是一件很困难的事情。

(三)"困难"和"艰难"、"难"在功能上还有一定的差别。(Certain differences in function between "困难" and "艰难", "难".)

"困难"有名词用法，"艰难"和"难"没有名词用法。("困难" can be used as a noun; while "艰难" and "难" can't.)例如：

有什么困难请告诉我，我一定帮助你。
困难没有什么可怕的，只要有勇气、有信心，就一定能够战胜它。

(However great the difficulties, there is nothing to be afraid of. Provided you have enough courage and confidence, you are surely to overcome them.)

刚来这儿的时候，生活上的困难真不少。
＊ 有什么难请告诉我，我一定帮助你。
＊ 难没有什么可怕的，只要有勇气、有信心，就一定能够战胜它。
＊ 刚来这儿的时候，生活上的难真不少。
＊ 有什么艰难请告诉我，我一定帮助你。
＊ 刚来这儿的时候，生活上的艰难真不少。

L

~来/去 lái/qù　　~到 dào

"动词+来/去"和"动词+到("到达"的意义)"所表示的意义是不同的。〔The meanings that "verb + 来/去" and "verb + 到" (with the meaning of arrival) indicate are different.〕

"动词+来/去"：表示动作的方向 —— 表示动作朝着说话人所在方向并向它靠近，或者随动作离开原来的地方

"动词+到"：　表示随动作到达(某处)

(一)"动词+来/去"和"动词+到"在结构上有不同之处。(The patterns of "verb + 来/去" and of "verb + 到" are different in construction.)

1."动词+来/去"可以结句；"动词+到"在表示动作到达(某处)的意思时，不能结句。("verb + 来/去" can put a sentence to a close. When "verb + 到" indicates the meaning of arriving, it doesn't function in this way.) 例如：

几个陌生人朝我们这边走来。

他帮我把行李搬来了。

孩子们朝山顶跑去。

他抓起手榴弹朝敌人投去。

* 他跟我一起回到。

* 我们天黑以前来到。

2."动词+来/去"因为表示的是动作的方向，后面一般不带场所词，可以带其他事物宾语；"动词+到"在表示随动作到达(某处)的意义时，后面要带场所词语，一般不带事物性宾语。(When "verb + 来/去" expresses the direction of the action, it can't be followed by words or phrases of places, but by other objects of things. When "verb + 到" expresses an action reaching some place, it is followed by words indicating places, but is not used together with an object of things.) 例如:

我给你带来一封信。

他怕你闷,给你借来几本小说。

给灾区运去一些救灾物资。

给孩子们送去几个玩具。

* 我给你带到一封信。

* 他怕你闷,给你借到几本小说。

* 给灾区运到一些救灾物资。

* 给孩子们送到几个玩具。

他一直把我送到机场。

我走到村口正好碰见他。

小王九点多才回到宿舍。

我是昨天回到香港的。

* 他一直把我送来机场。

* 我走去村口正好碰见他。

* 小王九点多才回去宿舍。

* 我是昨天回来香港的。

(二)"到"接在动词后作补语时的其他意义。(The other meaning of "到" when used as complement after verbs.)

"到"有时接在动词后作补语,不是表示动作到达(某处)的意思,而只表示得到某一结果或达到某一目的,这时"动+到"可以带事物宾语,也可以结句。("到" sometimes is used after a verb as a complement. It expresses a result or a goal attained, but not an action reaching some place. In this case, "verb + 到" can either be followed by an object of things or finish a sentence.)例如：

  我今天收到一封朋友的来信。

  张先生说他买到那本书了。

  累死我了！好不容易走到了。

  他们已经把货送到了。

了 le   的 de

〈助词〉< particle >

"了"主要有两种用法，一是用在动词或形容词后，表示动作或变化已经完成或实现；一是用在句末或句中停顿的地方，表示变化或出现新情况。"的"也可以用在谓语动词后面表示动作"时"的意义，但是限于过去时间。(There are two essential usages of "了". One is used after verbs or adjectives, indicating the accomplishment of the action or the change. The other is used either at the end of a sentence or in the place when there is a pause in the sentence, indicating changes or new occurrences. "的" is also used after predicative verbs to indicate the act is being taken, but it is restricted to the past time.)

"了"和"的"的主要区别：(Major differences between "了" and "的":)

(一) "了"不限于过去，只要是完成、实现或变化的动作或情况就可以用；"的"却一定限于过去。("了" is not restricted to the past, but used for the fulfilled, realized or changed acts or cases. "的" is strictly restricted to things happened in the past.)例如：

  昨天我去书店买了一本书。(过去完成。)

  明天下了课我去找你。(将来完成。)

  外面下雨了。(已经变化。)

一会儿下雨了的话,你替我把衣服收进来。(将来变化。)

这本书是我昨天去书店买的。(过去。)

你怎么来的?——骑自行车来的。(过去。)

表示将来可能做的事情,不能用"的"表示。("的" can not be used to express a possible future action.)例如:

＊你明天怎么来的?—— ＊骑自行车来的。

(二)用"了"没有强调作用,全句主要在于叙述;用"的"主要在于强调动作的施事者或动作的时间、地点、方式等,全句主要在于说明。(When "了" is used, the sentence is only a narrative, not emphasizing anything. While "的" is used in a sentence, the doer, the time, the place, or the way of the action may be emphasized. The sentence is usually an exposition.)例如:

他下了课去图书馆了。

老王刚刚走了。

上星期,我们参观了 SOS 村。

是小李帮的他。(强调说明施事者。)

这是他上个月给我寄来的。(强调说明时间。)

衣服是在百货大楼买的。(强调说明地点。)

我坐飞机去的香港。(强调说明方式。)

(三)问话人如果询问过去所做动作的施事者、时间、地点、方式等,施事者、时间、地点、方式等便是问话人所要强调的部分,那么,问话人要用动词后加"的"的方式问,答话人也应该用同样的方式回答,不能改用"动+了"的方式回答。(If the subject, the time, the place and the way of the past act are asked, these will be the parts for the speaker to be stressed on , therefore, he will use such pattern as using "的"after verbs and the one who gives the reply has to use the same pattern but he can never use the pattern "verb + 了" to answer instead.)例如:

谁送你的笔?——老师送的。(＊老师送了。)

什么时候回来的?——去年(回来的)。(＊去年回来了。)

在哪儿上的大学?——在北京(上的大学)。(＊在北京上了大学。)

怎么回来的?——坐出租汽车回来的。(＊坐出租汽车回来了。)

(四)在形式上,用"的"的句子,可以用表示强调的"是"跟"的"相配合,构成"是……的"的结构,"是"是否出现在句子里,可以根据表达的需要决定。(In the pattern of "的", the word "是" which is used for emphasis can be used together with "的" to form the pattern "是…的", and whether "是" has to appear in the sentence will be determined by the need of expression.)例如:

(是)大家帮他筹集的路费。

我(是)从前年开始学的汉语。

这是他用毛笔写的。

粒 lì   枚 méi   颗 kē   棵 kē

〈量词〉 <measure word>

(一)"粒"、"枚"、"颗"

"粒"、"枚"、"颗"都可用于形体较小的东西,但是适用范围有差别。(All can be used for small-sized things, but there is difference in their applicable range.)

1. 从形体上说,"粒"和"颗"比较接近,它们都适用于小而圆或小的块状的东西,有时可以换用,有时不能换用,这是因为用"粒"的东西比用"颗"的东西更小。("粒" and "颗" are similar in shape and both are for things small and round or small things in pieces. Sometimes "粒" and "颗" are exchangeable, but sometimes not, for the things "粒" indicates are even smaller than "颗".)例如:

几粒米   一粒种子   一粒盐
几粒砂子   一粒小药丸

一颗子弹　　　一颗牙齿　　　　两颗宝石
　　几颗珍珠　　　无数颗星星

2. "粒"与"颗"除了大小的差别外,有的还有价值的差别。一般来说,属于有价值的东西,还是以用"颗"为常。例如:钻石、宝石、珍珠等,有的颗粒也很小,但是通常用"颗",不用"粒";"心"只能用"颗",不能用"粒"。(Besides the difference in size between "粒" and "颗", there is also difference in value. Generally, when describing something valuable, "颗" is used. For example: sometimes the sizes of diamond, gem, pearls, etc. are very small but "颗" is used instead of "粒"; and "颗" is used to modify "心 (heart)", but never "粒".) 例如:

　　一颗闪闪发光的小钻石 (a small glittering diamond)
　　把一颗颗小珍珠穿起来 (string the small pearls together)
　　一颗不变的心

3. "枚"跟"粒"、"颗"比,除了小以外,在形体上没有特殊的限制,但是在范围上通常多用于佩戴物、饰物或跟文化用品有关的物品。(Compared with "粒" and "颗", "枚" has no special limitation in form, but is usually used to describe wearings, ornaments, or something relating to culture.) 例如:

　　一枚校徽　　　三枚奖章　　　一枚领带夹
　　两枚胸针　　　一枚戒指　　　上千枚邮票

(二) "颗"与"棵"

"颗"与"棵"读音一样,但是用于完全不同的事物。"颗"多用于颗粒状的东西(见上文);"棵"却主要用于植物。〔Pronounced the same way, but they are used for completely different things. "颗" is for things of small and round shape (see the above explanation); while "棵" is mainly used for plants.〕例如:

　　一棵大树　　　几棵草　　　　两棵菊花
　　院子里种了一棵葡萄　　这棵松树真好看

用于植物时,不能用"颗";用于颗粒状的物品时,不能用

"棵"。("颗"can't be used for plants, and "棵", on the other hand, can't be used for things small-and round-shaped.)例如:

* 一颗大树　　　　* 几颗草　　　　* 两颗菊花
* 院子里种了一颗葡萄　　* 这颗松树真好看
* 一棵子弹　　　* 两棵宝石　　　* 几棵珍珠
* 无数棵星星　　　* 一棵不变的心

冷 lěng　　凉 liáng

〈形容词〉表示温度低或感觉温度低。

(< adjective > indicating that the temperature is low or one feels the temperature is low.)

(一)"冷"和"凉"都可以表示温度低或感觉温度低,但是在很多情况下却不能换用,这是因为在语义特征上,它们还有着本质的差别。(Both mean the temperature is low or one feels it is low. In most cases they are not exchangeable for they have essential differences in meaning.)

1."冷"表示的温度低,主要指空气的温度低,人感觉这种温度低,一般不需要靠触摸就可以感觉到。("冷" refers to the coldness of temperature in the air. One can feel it without touching.)例如:

今天真冷。

听说又来了一股冷空气。

他冷得浑身发抖。

(He trembled all over with cold.)

我冷极了。

2."凉"表示的温度低,常常指靠触摸感觉到的温度低。("凉" also indicates the low temperature, but one usually feels the coldness by touching.)例如:

你的手真凉。

地上太凉了,别坐地上。

海水太凉了,不能游泳。

水凉了,可以喝了。

3."凉"有时也可以表示空气温度低,但是它跟"冷"有程度上的差别。"凉"的程度很低,"冷"的程度较高。("凉" sometimes expresses the low temperature of the air, but it is different with "冷" in degree. The degree of coldness of "凉" is lower, while that of "冷" is higher.)例如:

(冬天,摄氏零下20多度)今天真冷啊!(* 今天真凉啊!)

〔In winter, the temperature is under 20 degrees centigrade below zero.) (It is really cold!〕

(夏天,摄氏25度左右)今天有点儿凉。(* 今天有点儿冷。)

〔In summer, the temperature is around 25 degrees centigrade.) It is a bit cool today.〕

他冷得浑身发抖。(* 他凉得浑身发抖)

4.靠触摸或靠触摸的经验而感觉到的温度低,一般用"凉",不用"冷"。(To feel the low temperature by touching or the experience of touching, we usually use "凉" but not "冷".)例如:

* 你的手真冷。

* 地上太冷了,别坐地上。

* 水冷了,可以喝了。

* 饭很冷,不能吃。

你的手很凉(触摸感觉到的),是不是有点儿冷(非触摸感觉到的)?

(二) 因为"冷"有非触摸而感觉到的温度低的特点,所以它还可以形容人的态度不热情。"凉"不能这样用。("冷" is also used to describe people's attitude being not sympathetic; but "凉" can't be used in this way.)例如:

他冷冷地说:"不知道!"

(He said coldly: "I don't know.")

她总是用那种不冷不热的态度对待别人。

(She always treats others in a cold manner.)

这个人冷得像冰块一样。

(The man is icy cold.)

人们都管她叫"冷美人"。

(People all called her "Cold Beauty".)

冷若冰霜(frosty in manner)

冷言冷语(sarcastic comments)

横眉冷对(face others with frowning brows and angry eyes)

冷嘲热讽(freezing irony and burning satire)

冷眼旁观(look on coldly)

* 他凉凉地说:"不知道!"
* 这个人凉得像冰块一样。
* 人们都管她叫"凉美人"。
* 凉若冰霜　　* 凉言凉语　　* 横眉凉对
* 凉嘲热讽　　* 凉眼旁观

里 li　　上 shang

〈方位词〉< word of location >

(一)"里"和"上"都可以接在名词后表示位置,但是它们表示的意义不同。"里"表示周围有一定界限的空间内;"上"则不限定界限,它表示的是物体的表面或顶部表面。("里"and "上" both indicate locations when used after nouns, but their meanings are different. "里" indicates a space within a certain limit. "上" has no such limit, it refers to the surface or the top of an object.)例如:

他站在门里跟我说话。(限定界限。)

门上贴了很多有意思的画儿。(只是表面。)

他住在山里。(有一定界限的空间内,即周围有山环抱。)

他住在山上。(顶部表面。)

用"里"还是用"上",常常受到"里"或"上"前面的动词或名词的意义的制约。(Whether "里" or "上" is used is generally determined by the meaning of the verbs or nouns in the front.)例如:

1. 动词(verb):

攥在手里 　　　　　　　　放在手上
(hold in one's hand) 　　(put on one's hand)
夹在书里 　　　　　　　　摆在书上
(put in between the leaves of a book)(put on the book)
陷到沙发里 　　　　　　　坐在沙发上
(sink into the sofa) 　　(sit on the sofa)
装到信封里 　　　　　　　贴在信封上
(put into an envelop) 　(stick on an envelop)
＊ 陷到沙发上 　　　　　　＊ 装到信封上

要完成"攥"、"夹"、"陷"、"装"这些动作,周围必须带有一定范围的空间 ——"攥",手握的空间;"夹",书、本等作"夹"的动作形成的空间;"陷",进入某物里的空间等。"放"、"摆"、"坐"、"贴"等只要求有相关的场所,不要求一定有周围限定的空间。(The objects of "攥","夹","陷" and "装" must be in something, that is there must be some space around these objects—"攥", to hold something in the hand;"夹", to place something in between, for instance, the pages of a book or a notebook;"陷", to sink into something. However, the objects of "放","摆","坐"and "贴"only need a place to put them on, not necessarily some space around them.)

可见,动词含有一定周围界限的空间意义时,名词后用"里";动词不含有这种周围界限的空间意义时,名词后可以用"上"。(As we can see, "里"is used after nouns when the verb implies some space with boundary around the object. When the verb doesn't have such implication, "上" is used.)例如：

2. 名词(nouns)：

<u>那个孩子</u>坐在地上哭了好一会儿了。

<u>路</u>上一个人也没有。

<u>面子</u>上过不去。

<u>她脸</u>上布满了皱纹。

(Wrinkles spread over her face.)

* 那个孩子坐在地里哭了好一会儿了。
* 路里一个人也没有。
* 面子里过不去。
* 她脸里布满了皱纹。

以上几个例句可见,当名词不含有一定周围界限的空间意义时,后面接"上"不接"里"。(From the above we learn that when a noun does not have the meaning of a limited space, it is followed by "上", not "里".)

水装在瓶子里。

嘴里含着糖。

心里一直想着他。

* 水装在瓶子上。
* 嘴上含着糖。

以上几个例句可见,当名词含有一定周围界限的空间意义时,后面接"里"不接"上。只表示一定界限以内的意思,也可以用"里"。(From the above examples we can see that when a noun implies the meaning of a limited space, it is followed by "里", not "上"。"里" is also used when only indicating something within the boundary.)例如：

菜田里　　　庄稼地里　　　果园里

(二)"名+上"除了表示场所意义以外,还可以表示范围、方面、时间的意义。这时"上"的意义比较虚。"里"不表示这几种意义。("noun + 上" not only means a certain place, but also indicates a sphere, field, or time. Here the meaning of "上" is weak. "里" doesn't indicate these meanings.)例如：

1. 表范围(When indicating the range):

课堂上井然有序。

(The class is in good order.)

世界上有多少动物濒临灭绝。

(How many animals in the world are near extinction!)

报上介绍过那里的情况。

* 课堂里井然有序。

* 世界里有多少动物濒临灭绝。

2. 表方面(When indicating different aspects):

他在语法研究上下了不少工夫。

(He has put a lot of efforts in the study of grammar.)

大家要从思想上认清这一点。

组织上正在想办法解决资金问题。

(The organization is trying to find a solution to the problem of funds.)

实际上,他给了我不少的帮助。

* 他在语法研究里下了不少工夫。

* 大家要从思想里认清这一点。

3. "上"附在表示年龄的词语后表示时间,这种情况不用"里"。("上"is also used after the words of age to indicate time and here "里" can't be used.)例如：

他十四岁上死了父亲。

(His father died when he was 14.)

没想到,七十岁上竟得了个儿子。

(He never expected to have got a son at the age of 70.)

* 他十四岁里死了父亲。

* 没想到,七十岁里竟得了个儿子。

里 li　　中 zhōng　　内 nèi

〈方位词〉 < word of location >

(一)"里"与"中"

1."里"与"中"有时可以通用,一般接在普通名词后表示内部的意思。("里" and "中" sometimes are interchangeable and used after nouns to indicate the meaning of being inside.)例如:

手里/中　　眼里/中　　心里/中
水里/中　　家里/中

但是,用"里"构成的词多用于口语;用"中"构成的词多用于书面语。(But, the words composed of "里" are generally used in oral language and the words composed of "中" are mostly used in written language.)例如:

你手里拿的什么?
他把帽子紧紧地攥在手中。
家里都好吗?
家中一切可好?

2."里"与"中"虽然都表示"里面"、"内部"的意思,但是很多情况下不能通用。一般来说,词义的空间性越强,越倾向于用"里";词义的空间性越弱,抽象性越强,越倾向于用"中"。〔Although "里" and "中" both indicate the meaning of "里面(inside)" or "内部(internal)", they are not interchangeable in most cases. Generally, the more emphasis was laid on space, the more expected to use "里". On the contrary, the less emphasis was laid on space, and more abstract, the more expected to use "中".〕例如:

大厅里　　教室里　　箱子里
肚子里　　杯子里　　嘴里
想像中　记忆中　思想中　胸中　心中

具体来看,有些情况下只用此不用彼。(Specifically, they are used differently in some cases.)例如:

(1)名词表示单位、机关、领导人等,用"里"不用"中"。

("里" is used after a noun expressing a unit, an organization, or leaders. While "中" is not used.)

县里发下来一个通知。
厂里已经对他做了处分的决定。
* 县中发下来一个通知。
* 厂中已经对他做了处分的决定。

(2)空间界限难以确定的,通常用"中"不用"里"。(If the space boundary is hard to decide, usually use "中", not "里".)

空中　　　　途中　　　　一生中
* 空里　　　* 途里　　　* 一生里

具体的时间空间用"里"。("里" is used for particular time and space.)

夜里　　　　半夜里
* 夜中　　　* 半夜中

(3)表示动作进行当中或处于某种状态中的意思,即用在动词、形容词后,用"中"不用"里"。(When expressing an action is going on, or under certain state, or after a verb or adjective, use "中", not "里".)

手术中　　　研究中　　　实验中
进行中　　　休息中　　　调查中
痛苦中　　　焦急中　　　混乱中
甜蜜中　　　幸福中
* 手术里　　* 研究里　　* 实验里
* 进行里　　* 休息里　　* 调查里
* 痛苦里　　* 焦急里　　* 混乱里
* 甜蜜里　　* 幸福里

(4)表示人的空间范围,通常用"中"。(While expressing people's sphere of space, usually use "中".)

朋友中　　　群众中　　　人民中
战士中　　　美人中　　　教师中

389

* 朋友里　　　* 群众里　　　* 人民里
　　* 战士里　　　* 美人里　　　* 教师里

3. "里"接在"这"、"那"、"哪"等词后,表示处所;"中"不可以。(When "里" is used after "这", "那", "哪" etc., it means places; "中" is not.)例如:

　　这里的景色多美呀!
　　银行就在那里。
　　去哪里找这样的好事呀!

(二)"内"与"里"

1. "内"书面语色彩较重;"里"口语色彩较重。("内" is more used in written language; "里" is more used in spoken language.)

2. 表示处所里边的意思时,"内"主要用于单音节名词后;"里"大多用于双音节及双音节以上的名词后。表示某范围里的意思时,通常用"内"。(When expressing the inner part of something, "内" is used after monosyllabic words, while "里" is used after disyllabic or polysyllabic words. When expressing the meaning "within a scope", usually use "内".)例如:

　　校内　厂内　室内　市内　国内　党内　军内
　　* 校里　* 室里　* 国里　* 党里　* 军里
　　学校里　教室里

3. 表示某时间的范围里边,用"内"不用"里"。(When expressing "within a period of time", use "内", not "里".)例如:

　　年内　本周内　近几天内　一小时内
　　* 年里　* 本周里　* 近几天里　* 一小时里

4. 与介词组合时,"内"一般只与"对"、"由"、"向"直接结合,搭配也很受局限。(When used together with prepositions, "内" only combines directly with "对", "由", "向" and their collocation is quite limited.)例如:

　　对内　对外　由内向外　向内(转体一周)

"里"可以接在"从/向/朝/往/由 + 名词"构成的词组后。

("里" is also used after the phrases made up of "从/向/朝/往/由 + nouns".)例如：

从抽屉里　　向怀里　　朝水里　　往杯子里

5."内"还常常用来构成较为固定的成语或用语,这时只能用"内",不能用"里"。("内" can also be used to form fixed phrases or expressions. Here "里" can't replace "内".)例如：

内外有别(treat differently at home and abroad)
内忧外患(domestic trouble and foreign invasion)
色厉内荏(fierce of mien but faint of heart)
请勿入内(Staff Only)
* 里外有别　　* 里忧外患　　* 色厉里荏
* 请勿入里

聊 liáo　　聊天儿 liáotiānr

〈动词〉 <verb> 闲谈(chat)

"聊"、"聊天儿"都是闲谈的意思,但是由于它们的构词方式不同,所以在用法上有一些差别。(Both mean chatting. But there are some differences in meaning since their ways of construction are different.)

(一)"聊天儿"是动宾结构的构词方式,当"聊天儿"作谓语动词时,后面不能再连带宾语；"聊"是单音节、可带宾动词,没有这种限制。("聊天儿" is a verb-object word. When "聊天儿" is used as a verb predicate, it can not be followed by objects. "聊" is a monosyllabic transitive verb, without such restriction.)例如：

* 那天晚上,我们聊天儿了很多小时候的事。
* 他们正聊天儿着工作上的事。
那天晚上,我们聊了很多小时候的事。
他们正聊着工作上的事。

(二)因为"聊天儿"是动宾结构的构词方式,在它的后面接时态助词和补语时,往往形成动和宾分离的形式,因此,这种词又被称作"离合词"。单音动词"聊"没有这个问题,后面直接接时态助词和补语就可以。(Because "聊天儿" is a verb-object pattern, when used before a tense particles, or complements, the verb is usually separated from its object, this kind of words are also called "离合词"(separable words). The monosyllabic verb "聊" can be directly followed by tense particles or complements.)例如:

1. 后接时态助词:(When followed by tense particles:)

他们正在餐厅里聊着天儿。

我们聊了一会儿天儿。

* 他们正在餐厅里聊天儿着。

* 我们聊天儿了一会儿。

他们正在餐厅里聊着。

我们聊了一会儿。

2. 后接补语:(When followed by complements:)

我们聊过两次天儿。

大家聊起天儿来。

同学们兴奋地聊了一晚上天儿。

* 我们聊天儿过两次。

* 大家聊天儿起来。

* 同学们兴奋地聊天儿了一晚上。

我们聊过两次。

大家聊起来。

同学们兴奋地聊了一晚上。

(三)当后接描写动作怎么样的情状补语时,用"聊",不能用"聊天儿"。(When a complement of state expressing how the action is going on is used after, usually "聊" is used, not "聊天儿".)例如:

大家聊得热火朝天的。

(They are having a heated chat.)

你看，他们聊得<u>多投入</u>啊！
(Look! How untiringly they are talking!)
我们聊得饭都忘了吃了。
* 大家聊天儿得热火朝天的。
* 你看，他们聊天儿得多投入啊！
* 我们聊天儿得饭都忘了吃了。

M

满意 mǎnyì　　满足 mǎnzú

〈动词〉感到符合心愿、心满意足。(< verb > feel satisfied.)

"满意"和"满足"都有感到符合心愿、心满意足的意思,但是由于它们在意义上着重点不同,所联系的对象在关系上也有所不同,所以大多场合下不能换用。(Both "满意" and "满足" mean feeling satisfied, but their emphases in meaning are different, and the objects concerned are also different. So they are not exchangeable in most cases.)

(一) 意义着重点不同(Differences in focus)

1. "满意"的意义着重于符合自己的心意;"满足"的意义着重于感到已经足够了,别无所求了。("满意" emphasizes the meaning of meeting one's intention. "满足" emphasizes the meaning of feeling content.)例如:

>她对自己的工作很满意。
>先生,这里的伙食你满意吗?
>有了这样的房子住,他感到很满足了。
>能考上普通的大学我就满足了。

2. "满意"表示的是自己对他人或对某事某一方面的感受;"满足"则主要是自己自身的感受。("满意" expresses the feeling of a person for others or in some fields. "满足" expresses the feeling for oneself.)例如:

>我对这里的服务很满意。(对这里服务的感受。)
>上级领导很满意公司里这一届班子的人选。(对人选的感受。)
>(The higher authorities are pleased with the persons selected for the leading group in the company.)
>虽然工作条件还不是很好,可是我已经很满足了。(自

身的感受。)

她没有要求很多,只要经常陪她说说话,她就很满足了。(自身感受。)

3."满足"还有"使满足"的意思,也就是使要求等得以实现的意思。在结构上,"满足"后面往往要连带着满足的一方或与之有关的要求等(一般是抽象的)。"满意"没有这一意义和用法。["满意" may also mean to make other(s) satisfied, namely to meet the demand of others. In structure, "满足" is often followed by the object whose demand is to be met, or by a demand (often abstract) which is related to the object. "满意" is not used in this sense.] 例如:

他想开车,就让他开吧!满足他一下吧!

(He wants to drive. Well, let him drive. Satisfy him for once.)

我们一定满足你们的要求。

他说他一定满足他妻子的心愿。

我们没有满足你们提出的条件。

* 他想开车,就让他开吧!满意他一下吧!
* 我们一定满意你们的要求。
* 他说他一定满意他妻子的心愿。
* 我们没有满意你们提出的条件。

(二) 搭配的词语不同(Differences in collocation)

跟"满意"搭配的大多是具体的人、事、情况;跟"满足"搭配的大多是抽象的要求、希望等。"要求"、"希望"、"愿望"等不能跟"满意"搭配。(Words collocated with "满意" are mostly specific persons, things, conditions, etc., while those with "满足" are mostly abstract ones such as demands, desires, wishes, etc., which are not used together with "满意".) 例如:

领导对你很满意。

我们都很满意这里的服务。

对儿子的考试成绩,妈妈总是不满意。

他对朋友送来的生日礼物很满意。
满足了大家的要求　　满足了同学们的心愿
满足了消费者的需求(meet the needs of consumers)
满足了孩子们的好奇心
满足了他的求知欲(satisfy his thirst for knowledge)
＊满意了大家的要求　＊满意了同学们的心愿
＊满意了消费者的需求　＊满意了孩子们的好奇心
＊满意了他的求知欲

(三)用法上不同(Differences in usage)

1.跟"满足"的"使满足"和"自身感受"的意义有关,"满足"后面可以接"一下"、"起来"等补语;"满意"不接这样的补语。(Since "满足" may both mean to satisfy others and feel satisfied oneself, it can be followed by complement "一下" or "起来". "满意" cannot.)例如:

你们怎么就不能满足一下他的要求呢?
(Why couldn't you meet his demands?)
成绩刚刚及格,你就满足起来了?
＊你们怎么就不能满意一下他的要求呢?
＊成绩刚刚及格,你就满意起来了?

2."满意"常常用来作状语;"满足"很少作状语。("满意" is usually used as an adverbial; while "满足" is seldom used so.)例如:

父亲看着儿子,满意地点点头。
顾客们非常满意地离开了这里。

3."满足"后面常常可以接由介词"于"构成的介词词组;"满意"基本上不这样用。("满足" is often followed by a prepositional phrase composed of "于". "满意" is not used so.)例如:

满足于现状(be satisfied with the existing state of affairs)
满足于已有的成绩(rest content with one's achievements)
满足于一知半解(be satisfied with the smattering of knowledge)

满足于现有的水平(be content with the present level)
* 满意于现状　　　　* 满意于已有的成绩
* 满意于一知半解　　* 满意于现有的水平

满意 mǎnyì　　　中意 zhòngyì

〈动词〉表示符合心意。(< verb > to be in keeping with one's aspiration.)

(一) 意义上(In meaning)

"满意"、"中意"都有符合心意的意思,"中意"比"满意"多了"中"的意思,即它有"正合(心意)"、"恰好合(心意)"的意思,一般表示的都是由于喜欢而合意的意思。("满意" and "中意" may both mean being in keeping with one's aspiration, but "中意" has the meaning of "中" which means "suit somebody fine" or "just accord with". Generally it expresses the meaning of satisfaction coming from fondness.)例如:

顾客们对这个饭店的服务很满意。
老师对他很满意。
公司经理很满意她的工作。
妈妈对女儿的男朋友十分中意。
这里买不到两个女儿都中意的衣服。

(二) 用法上(In usage)

1."满意"是可以连带宾语的动词;"中意"是动宾结构的构词方式,有离合词的特点,不带宾语,"中"和"意"之间,可以插入其他成分。"满意"不能分离使用。("满意" is a transitive verb; "中意" is a verb-object structure which can be used separately with other words in between and without objects following. "满意" can not be separated.)例如:

大家很满意这里的服务。
领导十分满意你的工作。
* 妈妈十分中意女儿的男朋友。

* 她非常中意朋友们送来的礼物。
　　* 他很中意这辆车。
　　* 他不中意这家宾馆。

跟"中意"相关的人或事物,可以用"对"介引到"中意"前。(People or things related to "中意" can be introduced in front of it in terms of "对" phrases.)例如:

　　她对朋友们送来的礼物非常中意。
　　奶奶对这个媳妇最中意。

感到"中意"的人,也可以放到"中意"之间。"满意"不能这样用。(The persons related to "中意" may be placed between "中意". "满意" can't be used so.)例如:

　　女儿的男朋友十分中妈妈的意。
　　(The daughter's boy-friend is quite to her mother's liking.)
　　这个媳妇最中奶奶的意。
　　(The grandson's wife is most to the grandmother's liking.)
　　* 这里的服务很满大家的意。
　　* 你的工作十分满领导的意。

2."满意"可以作状语;"中意"不能作状语。("满意" can be used as an adverbial. "中意" cannot.)例如:

　　看到孩子懂事了,妈妈满意地笑了。
　　看到大家满意地离去,他也感到很痛快。
　　* 看到朋友们送来的礼物,她中意地笑了。
　　* 看到女儿的男朋友那么好,妈妈中意地点点头。

每 měi　　各 gè

〈代词〉指全体中的个体。(< pronoun > each)

(一) 意义上的差别(Differences in meaning)

"每"和"各"都有指代全体中个体的意思,但是意义的侧重点不同,大多情况下不能换用。"每"着重指以全体中任何一个或任何一组为例;"各"着重同时遍指全体中的每个个体。("每"

and "各" may both mean an individual of the whole, but their emphatic angles in meaning are different, and are not exchangeable in most cases. "每" emphasizes any one or any group of the whole, and attention is directed to the whole. While "各" emphasizes each one, attention is directed to the unit or individual.)例如:

这一周来,每天都下雨。(以"一周"中任何"一天"为例,表示全体如此。)

这孩子真好,各门功课都在90分以上。(遍指一门一门功课,表示全体如此。)

(二)用法上的差别(Differences in usage)

1."各"可以直接跟一般名词结合,构成"各+名"的词组;"每"不能直接跟一般名词结合。("各" can be linked directly with general nouns, composing "各 + n." phrases; "每" can not be linked directly with general nouns.)例如:

各市　　各地　　各部门　　各单位　　各厂
各行业　　各国　　各民族　　各阶层
＊每市　＊每地　＊每部门　＊每单位　＊每厂
＊每国　＊每行业　＊每民族　＊每阶层

2."每"要跟量词或数量词结合,才能用在名词前,即构成"每+(数)量+名"的词组;"各"不能构成"各+数量+名"的词组。〔"每" can be used before a noun only when it is combined with a measure word or numeral classifier compound, forming "每 + measure word (numeral-classifier compound) + n." phrases. "各" cannot form "各 + measure word + n." phrases.〕例如:

每个人　　　每个部门　　　每位教师
每篇论文　　每本词典
每一场球赛　每一个国家　　每一种商品
每一条标准　每一片土地
＊各一场球赛　＊各一个国家　＊各一种商品
＊各一条标准　＊各一片土地

3."各"后面可以跟少量名量词结合,构成"各 + 量 + 名"的词组,一般不跟计量动作的量词结合;"每"都可以。("各" can be followed by some nouns and measure words to form "各 + measure word + n." phrases, but not followed by words measuring acts; while "每" can be followed by such words.)例如:

各类文件　　　各个部门　　　各位教师
各界人士　　　各种标准　　　各条战线
各门功课　　　各种消息　　　各期刊物
各种书籍　　　各项工作
＊各遍录音都费了不少时间。
＊他读课文各遍都有错儿。
＊各次买书都有麻烦。
每遍录音都费了不少时间。
他读课文每遍都有错儿。
每次买书都有麻烦。

4.有些时间名词,可以直接跟数词连用,作用相当于量词,这种作用相当于量词的时间名词,大多不直接跟"各"结合,而可以跟"每"结合。(Some nouns denoting time can be used directly with numerals, functioning as measure words. Most of such nouns can be used directly after "每", but not "各".)例如:

每年　每星期　每天　每夜　每小时　每分钟
＊各年　＊各天　＊各夜　＊各小时　＊各分钟

5.还有些名词,常常被临时借用为量词,这样的词也可以跟"每"直接结合。(Some nouns are sometimes used as measure words. Such nouns can be used directly with "每".)例如:

每家每户　每人　每碗　每车　每瓶　每桌　每笔

(三) 结构上(In structure)

在用"每"的句子中,常常要求用副词"都"与之配合,没有"都"的配合,总括意义的表达显得不够。(In "每" sentences, adverb "都" is usually required to combine with it, without which, the meaning of "wholeness" in the sentence is not expressed sufficiently.)用"各"的句子则较自由。(There is no such requirement when "各" is used.)例如:

她每门功课都那么好。

每人都有不同的要求。

每项工作都需要有人负责。

每一届毕业生都有出类拔萃的人物。

(There are always outstanding figures among every year's graduates.)

各条战线捷报频传。

(News of victory keeps pouring in from every front of endeavour.)

各项工作安排得井井有条。

各个环节都很重要。

各项工作都很有成绩。

401

N

那时 nà shí 这时 zhè shí 当时 dāngshí

这时、那时〈词组〉< word group >
当时〈名词〉< noun >

(一)"那时"和"这时"("那时"and"这时")

"那时"和"这时"都是指示代词"这/那+时"构成的词组,用来指代时间的。"那"是远指,"这"是近指,所以"那时"是指离说话时远的时间,常常指过去的某一时间,也可以指将来的某一时间;"这时"是指离说话时近的时间,常常用来指代说话时或事情发生时的时间。(Both "那时" and "这时" are word groups formed from demonstrative pronouns "这／那" and the word "时", indicating time. "那" refers to a person or thing that is a distance away from you; while "这" refers to a person or thing that is near you. So "那时" refers to the time further away, the time in the past, or in the future; "这时" refers to the time very close to the present, indicating the time when a talk takes place or a thing happens.)

1. 现在回忆过去的事情,只能用"那时",不能用"这时"。(Recalling something happening in the past, only "那时" is used.)例如:

那时我只有八岁,还不懂事。

那时生活很艰难,能读上书是一件很不容易的事情。

(At that time life was hard, and it was not easy to go to school.)

2. 现在说话时的时间,只能用"这时",不能用"那时"。(Saying something at present, only "这时" is used.)例如:

你找小王吗? 他这时可能正在餐厅吃饭呢。

3. 正处于事情发生时的时间里,用"这时"。(Being at the time when something is happening, "这时" is used.)例如:

我什么也不顾了,背着他拼命地朝医院跑去。这时我只有一个念头,一定要救活他。

(Without thinking, I carried him to the hospital with all my might. At that time, I had only one thing in mind: to bring him back to life.)

4."这时"一般不能用于指代尚未发生的事情的时间。("这时" cannot refer to the time at which things are yet to happen.)例如:

* 我这时要看书了,你别打扰我。(改用"现在"。)

* 明天吃午饭这时,我去你房间找你。(改:明天吃午饭的时候,……。)

5."那时"主要用于指过去时间,有时也可以用于将来距离现在说话时远的时间。("那时" is usually used to express the past, but sometimes it can refer to a future time that is far from now.)例如:

毕业以后我会争取去美国的,那时我会去看你的。

(二)"当时"和"那时"、"这时"("当时" and "那时""这时")

"当时"和"那时"、"这时"不同,"当时"只能用于指过去发生某件事情时的时间。它不能用于指"这时"指代的说话时的时间,也不能用于指"那时"指代的将来的时间。(Different from "那时" and "这时","当时" can only be used to express the time in the past when something happened. It cannot be used like "这时" to express a present time, or like "那时" to express a future time.)例如:

这篇论文写于五十年代,当时还没有研究这方面的论文发表。

(The thesis was written during the fifties. At that time there wasn't any paper on this subject published.)

当时妈妈就在我身旁和我一起看榜,看到我考中了,她激动得眼泪都流下来了。

* 我当时要看书了,你别打扰我。

* 毕业以后我会争取去美国的,当时我会去看你的。

403

能 néng　　会 huì
〈能愿动词〉< modal verb >

"能"、"会"都可以表示"有可能"、"有能力"、"善于做某事"等,有时可以通用,但是由于意义侧重角度不完全相同,使用条件也不完全相同,有时不能换用。("能" and "会" can both express the meaning "possibility", "capacity", "adeptness", etc. Sometimes they are interchangeable, but sometimes are not, due to their different focus points and applicable conditions.)

(一)"能"、"会"都可以表示"有可能"的意思,常常用来表示某种估计或推测,可以通用。在非疑问句中用"会"时,表示"有可能"的语气更强,句末常常加"的"表示肯定的语气。("能" and "会" can both express the meaning "possibility", and are often used to indicate estimation or inference, and are exchangeable. It is more emphatic to use "会" in a non-interrogative sentence, usually followed by "的" at the end of the sentence to stress the affirmative mood.)例如:

天上一点儿云也没有,不会/能下雨。

下这么大的雨,他能/会来吗?

──他已经说了要来,能来。

──他已经说了要来,会来的。

这个方案他能/会同意吧?

──能同意。

──会同意的。

(二)表示有能力、有条件做某事时,"能"、"会"有时可以通用,但是各自稍有侧重。表示主观上具备某种技能、客观上具备某种条件,用"能",尤其是只侧重于这种能力时,只能用"能";表示怎样做、掌握某种技能时用"会"。(While expressing "having the ability or condition to do something", "能" and "会" are sometimes interchangeable, but they focus on different parts respectively. When

404

indicating one has a certain kind of technical abilities subjectively, and is provided with certain conditions objectively, "能" is used, especially when focusing on the abilities. When expressing how to do something, or master a skill, "会" is used.)例如：

> 她能用汉语写日记了。
> 最近我很忙,不能参加周末的活动了。
> 我最近没有工作,不能付给你全部房钱,先付一半吧。
> (I have been unemployed recently, so I can't pay you the total rent. I'll pay you half first.)
> 她不怎么会说普通话。
> 你会不会做中国菜？
> * 最近我很忙,不会参加周末的活动了。
> * 我最近没有工作,不会付给你全部房钱,先付一半吧。

（三）表示初次学会某种动作或技能时,用"能"、"会"都可以,但多用"会"。表示某种能力得到恢复时,只能用"能",不能用"会"。(Either "能" or "会" can be used to express beginning to learn an act or a skill, but "会" is more appropriate. Only "能" can be used to express the restoration of certain power.)例如：

> 我儿子刚一岁就能/会走路了。
> 她已经能/会用电脑了。
> 我的牙不疼了,能吃饭了。
> 他清醒过来了,能说话了。
> * 我的牙不疼了,会吃饭了。
> * 他清醒过来了,会说话了。

（四）表示具备了的某种技能,已经达到某种效率、标准,只能用"能",不能用"会"(Only "能" can be used to express certain ability possessed has reached certain effect or standard.)例如：

> 他开汽车每小时能走180公里。
> 她一个小时能打一万字。

* 他开汽车每小时会走180公里。
* 她一个小时会打一万字。

(五)"能"、"会"都可以表示善于做某事,前面都可以用"很"、"最"、"真"等程度副词修饰。但是用"会"时侧重于"技巧",用"能"时侧重于"能力"。(Both "能" and "会" are used to express being good at doing something, and they both can be modified by adverbs of degree, such as "很", "最" and "真". But when "会" is used, it usually refers to "skill"; when "能" is used, it refers to "ability".)例如:

他很能干,总是承担高出别人两到三倍的生产任务。

(He is a man of great ability, always undertaking twice or three times more production tasks than others.)

他很会干,再难的活儿到他这儿也能做出来。

她真能说,一说就是个把小时。

(She is really talkative. Once she speaks, she can speak for more than an hour.)

她真会说,死人也能让她说活了。

(She has such a glib tongue that she can even talk a dead man alive.)

能 néng　　可以 kěyǐ

〈能愿动词〉 < modal verb >

(一)"能"、"可以"都可以表示具备的某种技能,已经达到某种效率、标准;都可以表示"能够"的意思。〔Both "能" and "可以" indicate a certain technique possessed has come up to a certain efficiency or standard, meaning "be able to".〕例如:

他自行车每小时能/可以骑80公里。

他能/可以说出两千以上的成语。

王师傅胳膊上的伤已经好了,能/可以拿东西了。

约翰能/可以用汉语写日记了。

（二）"能"可以表示初次学会某种动作，也可以表示善于做某事；"可以"不能用于这种情况。（"能" may mean learning an act for the first time, or being good at doing something. "可以" does not mean so.）例如：

这孩子才十个月就能走路了。

＊这孩子才十个月就可以走路了。

他很能写，一写就是一个通宵。

（He is really a writer. Once he writes, he usually doesn't stop the whole night.）

＊他很可以写，一写就是一个通宵。

（三）"能"可以表示具有某种客观的可能性，可以表示某种推测、估计，"可以"不行。（"能" may indicate what is possible or likely, and may express an inference or estimation.）例如：

雨下得那么大，他不能来了，别等了。

＊雨下得那么大，他不可以来了，别等了。

天阴得厉害，一会儿一定能下雨。

＊天阴得厉害，一会儿一定可以下雨。

（四）"能"、"可以"都可以表示情理上、环境上"许可"的意思，但肯定形式多用"可以"，否定形式或具有否定意义的句子多用"能"。（Both "能" and "可以" may be used to indicate permission, but the use of "可以" is preferred in an affirmative sentence; while "能" is preferred in a negative sentence or a sentence having negative meanings.）例如：

我能/可以跟他说会儿话吗？

这儿能/可以抽烟吗？

你千万不能把这件事告诉他。

他们正在开会，你不能进去。

我能看着他们有困难不帮助吗？

（五）"可以"还能表示"值得"的意思，"能"没有这一意思。（"可以" may indicate what is worthy of, but "能" may not.）例如：

这件衣服看上去很不错,可以试试。
(The dress looks pretty good. You can try it on.)
他的这个意见很好,可以考虑。
* 这件衣服看上去很不错,能试试。
* 他的这个意见很好,能考虑。

(六) 结构上,"可以"能单独作句中谓语,"能"一般不这样用。(In structure, "可以" can be used as a predicate alone; while "能" is seldom used so.)例如:
这样做也可以。
* 这样做也能。

你 nǐ   您 nín

〈代词〉用来称代对方一个人。(< pronoun > used to address the second person singular.)

"你"、"您"都可以用来称代对方(第二人称),表示单数的意义。但是它们在色彩和用法上却有许多不同。〔Both "你" and "您" are used to address the opposite side (the second person) in singular form, but they are quite different in flavor and usage.〕

(一) 色彩上(In flavor)

"你"用于一般人的称代;"您"带有尊敬色彩,用于称代尊敬的人、长辈、师长、上级等。("你" is used in general sense. "您" is used in a polite way to address a respectable person, an elder, a teacher, or a senior.)例如:
你怎么能跟他开这样的玩笑呢?
(How can you make such fun of him?)
你也跟着去看看吧。
老师,您辛苦了!
您老人家近来身体好吗?
* 老师,你辛苦了!(显得不够尊敬,不得体。)
* 你老人家近来身体好吗?(太随便了,显得不够尊

敬,不合适。)

因为"您"有尊敬色彩,容易产生距离感,所以特别熟悉、特别亲近的人,尤其是朋友之间,用"你"会显得更自然、更亲密。(Since "您" is used in a polite way, it gives one a sense of distance. It is more natural and closer to use "你" to address a person you are quite familiar with, or very close to, especially among friends.)

(二) 用法上(In usage)

1."你"后边可以加"们",变成"你们",表示复数的意义;"您"后边一般不加"们"。"您"表示复数意义时,后边可以加数量表示;"你"一般不用这种方式。("们" can be added after "你" to form "你们", indicating plural. Generally, "们" is not added after "您". When expressing plural sense, numeral-classifier compounds can be added after "您"; "你" cannot be used in this way.)例如:

那一天,你们都说要去,现在真的要去了,你们又都不去了。

你们几个都是好朋友,应该互相帮助才对。

您二位想吃点儿什么?

您几位就别客气了,帮我们出出主意吧。

2."你"后边还可以接"俩",表示"你们两个"的意思;"您"后边一般不能接"俩"或"两个","俩"或"两个"缺少尊敬色彩。"位"是带有尊敬色彩的量词,所以常用"您二位"、"您几位"等。("你" can be followed by "俩", meaning "you two". "您" is rarely followed by "俩" or "两个", because the two words lack the sense of respect. "位" is a measure word expressing respect, so "您二位", "您几位" etc. are usually used.)

3."您"通常只用于明确的、具体的称代对象;"你"不限于这种用法,它还可以用于泛指和不定指。("您" usually is only used to address a definite, specific person ; while "你" has wider usage. It can be used in a general sense, or in an indefinite reference.)例如:

(1)"你"用于泛指任何人。("你" is used to make a general

reference.)
>他这个人就这样,老叫你下不来台。
(He is such a person that he always makes others embarrassed.)
>那种舒适的环境会使你忘掉一切。

(2)"你"用于不定指,常与"我"配合。("你" is used in an indefinite reference, usually in combination with "我".)
>你一言,我一语　你一句,我一句
>你吹我打(You pipe and I drum.)
>你东我西(act or speak separately)
>你来我往(have dealings with each other)
>你看看我,我看看你

4."你"有时还可活用成"你们",表示复数意义。这种用法常常是在"你"后面接单音名词。("你" is sometimes used as "你们", meaning plural. In such a case, "你" is followed by a monosyllabic noun.)例如:
>你班来了几个人?(你班=你们班)
>对于你厂的大力协助,我们表示衷心的感谢!(你厂=你们厂)

暖和 nuǎnhuo　　温暖 wēnnuǎn

〈形容词〉表示温度不冷也不热。(<adjective> indicating the temperature is neither hot nor cold, just warm.)

(一)"暖和"和"温暖"语体色彩稍有不同。("暖和" and "温暖" are slightly different in style and flavor.)

"暖和"和"温暖"都可以用于形容气候不冷也不热,但是比较起来,"暖和"口语色彩重些,"温暖"书面语色彩重些。(Both "暖和" and "温暖" can be used to describe weather neither too hot nor too cold, but "暖和" is relatively more used in spoken language, while "温暖" in written language.)例如:
>今年气候很反常,已经进入12月了,天气还这么暖和。

(The weather is quite unusual this year. It's already December, but the weather is still warm.)

  别看现在是冬季,可是屋里屋外竟温暖如春。

(二)"暖和"和"温暖"使用范围不完全相同。("暖和" and "温暖" are used in different categories.)

1."暖和"主要用以形容天气、环境等;"温暖"主要用以形容气候、阳光。("暖和" is mainly used to describe weather, environment, etc.; "温暖" is mostly used to describe climate, sunlight.)例如:

  天气渐渐地暖和了。
  今天真暖和。
  * 天气渐渐地温暖了。
  * 今天真温暖。
  这间屋子很暖和,在这儿学习很舒服。
  被窝里凉吗?—— 不凉,很暖和。
  * 这间屋子很温暖,在这儿学习很舒服。
  * 被窝里凉吗?—— 不凉,很温暖。
  昆明的气候温暖宜人。
  (The weather in Kunming is warm and pleasant.)
  温暖的阳光照在身上很舒服。

2."温暖"还可以用以比喻组织、集体、家庭等的友爱可亲。"暖和"不可以。("温暖" can also describe the warmth and friendliness of an organization, a collective, or a family. "暖和" cannot.)例如:

  在这样一个温暖的集体中,我感到很愉快。
  他终于回到了祖国温暖的怀抱中。
  (He returned to the warm embrace of his motherland at last.)
  我有一个温暖而幸福的家庭。
  * 在这样一个暖和的集体中,我感到很愉快。
  * 他终于回到祖国暖和的怀抱中。
  * 我有一个暖和而幸福的家庭。

(三) 用法上有所不同(Differences in usage)

1. "温暖"一般不重叠使用;"暖和"可以。"暖和"可以重叠为 AABB 式。("温暖" is not used in a reduplicated way; while "暖和" can be reduplicated as the AABB pattern.)例如:

这件羽绒服暖暖和和的,真舒服!

一家人坐在暖暖和和的热炕头上聊天儿。

(All the family members sit on the warm and cozy *kang* to have a chat.)

* 阳光温温暖暖的,真舒服。

2. "暖和"重叠后可以用作状语;"温暖"不能作状语。("暖和" can be used as an adverbial when reduplicated. "温暖" cannot be used as an adverbial.)例如:

回到家的小刚在妈妈的怀里暖暖和和地睡了一夜。

大家暖暖和和地围坐在火炉旁。

P

怕 pà　　害怕 hàipà　　可怕 kěpà

怕、害怕〈动词〉 < verb >
可怕〈形容词〉 < adjective >

"怕"、"害怕"、"可怕"都有对困难、危险等心中产生恐惧不安的心理状态的意思。("怕", "害怕" and "可怕" all express the feeling of fear caused by the nearness and possibility of difficulties and danger.)例如：

下雨打雷的时候,我很怕。

她很怕数学老师。

你怎么那么怕麻烦？

他的样子很凶,我很害怕。

不能害怕困难。

她害怕走夜路。

他的样子很可怕。

我刚刚做了一个十分可怕的梦。

困难没有什么可怕的。

但是它们在意义上、功能上、用法上还有很大的不同,所以很多情况下不能换用。(But they are quite different in meaning, function and usage. So they are not exchangeable in most cases.)

(一) 意义及某些用法不完全相同 (Differences in meaning and some usages)

1."怕"和"害怕"

(1)"怕"还可以表示"担心"的意思。("怕" may also express the meaning of being anxious.)例如：

她怕迟到了,连饭也没吃就走了。

(She was afraid to be late, so she left without having dinner.)

413

怕妈妈着急,所以打电话来说一声。

怕你不放心,没敢那么晚回来。

(2)"怕"还有承受不住的意思。("怕" can also mean unable to endure.)例如:

你的眼睛怕光,最好戴上一副墨镜。

这种花怕阳光直射,搬到屋里吧。

她现在精神状态很不好,怕刺激,不要告诉她这件事。

(She is quite wretched in spirit, and cannot be provoked. Don't tell her about it.)

(3)"怕"的主语一般情况下是表人主语,可是有时在强调句中,表事宾语被提到主语的位置上时,也可以用"怕",这时候一般不用"害怕"。(The subject of "怕" is usually somebody, but when the object referring to a thing is placed in the position of subject for emphasis, "怕" can also be used. "害怕" is not used in this case.)例如:

天不怕,地不怕。

天大的困难也不怕。

* 天不害怕,地不害怕。

* 天大的困难也不害怕。

2."可怕"与"怕"、"害怕"

"可怕"有使人害怕的意思,所以"可怕"的主语不是施事,而是造成人产生恐惧心理的人或事物。"怕"和"害怕"是指人遇到困难、危险等而产生的心中恐惧不安,所以主语一般是施事。("可怕" means to terrify somebody. So the subject of "可怕" is not the agent of the action, but the person or thing that makes others fear. "怕" and "害怕" indicate the feeling of fearfulness resulted from facing difficulties, dangers, etc. So the subjects are usually the agents.)例如:

刚刚做的那个梦真可怕!

他的样子十分可怕。

没有自信心是一件很可怕的事情。

那是一个风雨交加的可怕的夜晚。
(That was a terrible night with wind and rain.)
* 刚刚做的那个梦真害怕!
* 他的样子十分害怕。
* 没有自信心是一件很害怕的事情。
* 那是一个风雨交加的害怕的夜晚。
* 刚刚做的那个梦真怕!
* 他的样子十分怕。
* 没有自信心是一件很怕的事情。
* 那是一个风雨交加的怕的夜晚。

(二) 功能上的异同(Similarities and differences in function)

1. "怕"、"害怕"是心理动词,可以作带宾谓语;"可怕"是形容词,可以作谓语,但是不能连带宾语。("怕" and "害怕" are psycho-verbs, transitive. "可怕" is an adjective, and can be used as a predicate, but can not take an object.)例如:

我很怕猫。
他总是怕这怕那的。
我怕以后见不到你了。
他怕失去这份工作。
他总是害怕困难。
她害怕走夜路。
我害怕遭人报复。
(I fear to be retaliated.)
女同学都害怕上解剖课。
* 我很可怕猫。
* 他总是可怕这可怕那的。
* 我可怕以后见不到你了。
* 他可怕失去这份工作。
* 他总是可怕困难。
* 她可怕走夜路。

415

* 我可怕遭人报复。
　　* 女同学都可怕上解剖课。

2."怕"、"害怕"、"可怕"都能够接受程度副词的修饰或用程度副词作补语。("怕","害怕" and "可怕" can all be modified by adverbs of degree or have adverbs of degree as their complement.)例如：

　　他最怕他爷爷了。
　　她很怕有人趁机借题发挥。
　　(She feared that somebody might make use of the subject under discussion to put over his own ideas.)
　　事情发生以后,他怕极了。
　　她很害怕这几个人纠缠她。
　　(She feared to be entangled by these few fellows.)
　　我很害怕走夜路。
　　看到黄狗跑了过来,他害怕极了。
　　他凶起来的样子很可怕。
　　(His fierce look is terrific.)
　　最可怕的事情发生了。
　　那里夜里可怕极了。

Q

其他 qítā   其余 qíyú

〈代词〉指示或代指某范围以外的人或事物。

(<pronoun> indicating people or things not already named or implied.)

"其他"、"其余"都可以用来指示或指代某范围以外的人或事物,但是意义不完全相同。"其他"指事物时,可写作"其它"。("其他" and "其余" can both refer to people or things not within a certain scope, but they are slightly different in meaning. When "其他" refers to things, it can be written as "其它".)

(一) 意义上 (In meaning)

1. "其他"是指某范围以外别的人或事物;"其余"则主要有"剩下的"人或事物的意思。句子中没有"剩下的"的意思,只有外加别的、包括别的的意思,不能用"其余"。("其他" refers to people or things beyond a certain scope; while "其余" mainly refers to people or things left over. So "其余" cannot be used if a sentence only has the meaning of "something in addition".) 例如:

我只要这些就够了,其他/其余的你们拿去吧。

这里用不了这么多人,留下十个人,其余的回去吧。

(We don't need so many people here. Ten of you stay. The rest please go home.)

今天的晚会除了小品、魔术以外,还有其他精彩节目。

(Besides short plays and magic, there are other wonderful programs for the evening party.)

他们离开南京后,又去其他地方参观了。

* 今天的晚会除了小品、魔术以外,还有其余精彩节目。

417

* 他们离开南京后,又去其余地方参观了。

2."其他"的范围可以很大,也可以比较小,所指的人或事物可以是确定的,也可以是不确定的;"其余"的范围不会很大,它所指的一般是有明确范围的人或事物,它是指一定范围内的人或事物剩下的部分,所以它代指的人、事物一般是确定的,只是不明说罢了。"其余"的句子前面通常有表示总体或一定数量的词语。(The application sphere of "其他" can be either big or small, and the people or things represented can be either definite or indefinite. "其余" is limited in meaning. It usually refers to people or things within a definite scope. It indicates the remainder of people or things within a certain scope. So the people or things it represents are generally definite, though not stated. There are usually words denoting overall or certain amount in front of "其余" sentences.)例如:

不光东北下了雪,其他地区也下了雪。

* 不光东北下了雪,其余地区也下了雪。(这里的"其余"没有划定范围。)

东北地区不光黑龙江下了雪,其余的地方也下了雪。(这里的"其余"划定了范围——东北地区。)

这里用不了这么多人,留下十个人,其余的回去吧。("这里的这么多人"起了划定范围的作用。)

(二)用法上(In usage)

1."其他"在句子中可以单独作主语、定语、宾语;"其余"一般可以作主语、定语,但是一般不能单独用来作宾语。("其他" can be used alone as a subject, attribute, or object. "其余" is usually used as a subject and attribute, but not as an object independently.)例如:

除了身份证、护照外,其他/其余都是文字材料。(主语)
经他这么一说,其他人再也不好说什么了。(定语)
(After he said this, the rest of the people couldn't say more about it.)

情况那么危急,顾命还来不及呢,谁还能顾及<u>其他</u>呀。(宾语)

(The situation was so desperate that there wasn't even enough time to think about one's life, still less about others.)

看来就这些人了。这样,我先带十五个人进去,半小时后,你带<u>其余</u>十几个人进去。(定语)

* 情况那么危急,顾命还来不及呢,谁还能顾及其余呀。

2."其余"跟数量短语结合后,可以作宾语。(When "其余" combines with numeral-classifier compounds, it can be used as an object.)例如:

我干这五个,你干<u>其余三个</u>。(宾语)

起 qǐ   起来 qǐlái

〈趋向动词〉 < directional verb >

"起"、"起来"都可以表示随动作向上、动作开始并持续、聚拢、集中的动作完成或实现等三种意思。("起" and "起来" both indicate an upward direction of an act, the beginning and continuing of an act, or the completing or realization of a gathering or concentrating act.)例如:

他扶起老人,连声说"对不起"。(随动作向上。)

王先生站起身来,头也不回地走出门去。(随动作向上。)

会场上响起一片雷鸣般的掌声。(动作开始并持续。)

(A thunderous applause broke out in the hall.)

大家热烈地讨论了起来。(动作开始并持续。)

收起你那套鬼把戏吧!(聚拢、集中的动作完成或实现。)

(None of your dirty tricks!)

把这些筷子一把一把捆起来。(聚拢、集中的动作完成

419

或实现。)

但是,"起"、"起来"意义上仍稍有差别,结构上差别较大。(However, "起" and "起来" are slightly different in meaning, and quite different in structure.)

(一) 意义上 (In meaning)

"起来"比"起"表现动作过程、持续过程更强,更加突出动作完成或实现的结果、目的等。(Compared with "起", action expressed with "起来" lasts longer. "起来" more emphasizes the completion, or result of an action or goal.)试比较:

他把包提了起来。

他提起包就走。

他摘下一片树叶吹了起来。

他摘下一片树叶,吹起一支动听的曲子。

把你的钱收起来!

收起你的钱!

(二) 结构上 (In structure)

由于以上意义上的差别,所以形成以下结构上有差别。(Their difference in meaning results in their disparities in structure.)

1."起"主要用于句中或紧凑的连续动作的句中,后边要有宾语,一般不用来结句;"起来"主要用在句子结尾,或非紧凑动作的句中。("起" is mainly used in a sentence in which the continuous actions are well-knit, and it is followed by objects, but rarely ends with "来". "起来" is mainly used at the end of a sentence, or in a sentence without closely-connected actions.)例如:

他抬不起胳膊了。

老大捡起一块石头扔了过去。

同学们昂起头,唱起歌,显得那么有力量。

(Holding up their heads and singing songs, the students looked so full of strength.)

420

市中心建起一座高大而气派的立交桥。

他抬起头来,眼睛注视着前方。

中国人民从此站起来了。

孩子们点起了篝火,然后围着篝火欢快地跳起舞来。

老汉点起烟,慢慢地抽了起来。

她接过钱来,一张一张点了起来。

把大家的意见集中起来。

(Sum up the ideas of all the people.)

* 中国人民从此站起了。

* 老汉点起烟,慢慢抽了起。

* 把大家的意见集中起。

2."起来"还可以表示某种状态开始并持续,表示状态的情况多数是形容词,不涉及宾语,所以在这种情况下,一般用"起来",不用"起"。("起来" can also express the beginning and lasting of a state, which is usually expressed with adjectives, and no object is involved. "起" is not used in such cases.)例如:

看到他,我不由得紧张起来。

(At the sight of him, I can't help being nervous.)

天渐渐地冷了起来。

看到十几年心血的结晶摆在面前,他激动了起来。

(Seeing the fruit of many years' painstaking labour, he was excited.)

* 看到他,我不由得紧张起。

* 天渐渐地冷了起。(或 * 天渐渐地冷起了。)

起 qi　　上 shang

〈趋向动词〉 < directional verb >

(一) "起"、"上"都可以表示随动作向上的方向,但是不能通用,因为它们有不同的条件要求。("起" and "上" both indicate the upward direction of an action, but they are not exchangeable, for they are used under different conditions.)

"起"只表示随动作向上的方向,不涉及向上后的场所,一般事实上也不存在场所问题,动词支配的名词通常是表事物的或表人体部位的。"上"则要求涉及到达点,动词后涉及的名词通常表示场所意义。虽然有时由于对话、语境等原因省掉到达点,但是因为它实际上存在,所以可以意会。("起" only expresses the upward direction of an act. It doesn't involve the place where the act is toward. In fact, there is no place involved in such acts, and the nouns following the verb usually represent things or parts of a human body. "上" involves the place reached by the action. The noun following the verb usually represents a place. Though the place is sometimes omitted in conversations or some language situations, it can be sensed since it is implied.)例如:

　　升起五星红旗　飘起雪花　抬起头　举起胳膊
　　爬上树　登上山顶　走上领奖台　骑上自行车
　　* 飘上雪花　* 抬上头
　　* 登起山顶　* 走起领奖台
　　对话环境:骑上了吗?——骑上了。(指骑上马背等)

(二) "起"、"上"还可以表示动作开始并持续的时态意义,但是稍有差别。("起" and "上" can also indicate the beginning and lasting of an act, but used differently.)

"起"侧重于开始并持续的动作过程;"上"侧重于进入到某种状态或情况之中。所以用"上"的句中常常用"已经"作状语。("起" emphasizes the beginning and continuance of an action. "上" emphasizes entering into a certain condition or being under a certain state. Therefore, the sentence with "上" usually has "已经" as its adverbial.)例如:

会场上响起了热烈的掌声。

她们愉快地唱起了歌。

看,他们已经干上了,咱们也开始吧。

嚯! 已经喝上啦! 来,算上我一个!

(Hey! You are already drinking! Well, count me in.)

起来 qilai   出来 chulai

〈趋向动词〉< directional verb >

"起来"、"出来"的差别主要在于意义的不同。(The difference between "起来" and "出来" mainly lies in their meanings.)

(一)"起来"、"出来"都可以接在动词后表示不同的动作方向。"起来"表示的方向是"向上";"出来"表示的方向是"由里向外,靠近说话人"。("起来" and "出来" can both follow verbs to express different directions of acts. "起来" expresses an upward direction; while "出来" indicates the direction "from inside to outside, approaching the speaker".)例如:

太阳升起来了　站起身来　从床上爬了起来

头发都竖了起来(with one's hair standing on end)

从教室里走出来　拿出一本书来

太阳从云层里钻了出来。(The sun broke through the clouds.)

(二)"起来"、"出来"常常并不表示动作的趋向,而是将其意义引申,表示其他的意义。"起来"常常表示动作开始并继续的意义;"出来"则表示从未显露到显露的意思。("起来" and "出来" do not usually express the directions of acts, but rather extend their meanings to mean other things. "起来" usually indicates the beginning and lasting of an action. While "出来" indicates something changing from invisible to visible.)例如:

干起来了　下起雨来　研究起来　天亮了起来
肚子疼起来
认出他来了(recognize him)
打听出来了(learn about it)
把心里话说出来(give voice to one's innermost feelings)
猜不出来(unable to guess right)

(三)区别"起来"、"出来"的两组用法:(Two kinds of usage to distinguish "起来" from "出来":)

1."想起来"与"想出来"

(1)"想起来"是表示使事物由隐蔽到重现,即原来已经有某事物记忆在脑海里了,后来遗忘了,现在通过回忆,又重新出现了。("想起来" means to make things from hidden to reappearing. Namely, something already existing in the brain has been forgotten, but now reappears through one's recalling.)

(2)"想出来"则表示原先脑海里没有的东西,通过想,使之显现出来,即从无到有。("想出来" means to make things that is new in the mind visible through thinking, that is to grow out of nothing.)例如:

我想起来了,她叫王欣。
张老师的电话号码吗? 对不起,实在想不起来了。
* 我想出来了,她叫王欣。
* 张老师的电话号码吗? 对不起,实在想不出来了。
一定得想出个好主意来。
这是一个孩子想出来的好办法。
你们研究出一个切实可行的方案来。
(You should work out a feasible plan.)
* 一定得想起个好主意来。
* 这是一个孩子想起来的好办法。
* 你们研究起一个切实可行的方案来。

2."看起来"与"看得出来(chūlái)"

(1)"看起来"在句子中作插入语,表示通过一些具体的现象或情况进行推测、估计或评价。("看起来" is used as a parenthesis in a sentence, expressing inference, estimation, or evaluation through concrete phenomena or things.)

(2)"看得出来"在句中作谓语,表示经过观察,发觉或认清人或事物的某种性状、变化等。("看得出来" is used as a predicate in a sentence, expressing the discovery or cognition of the nature and change of somebody or something through observation.)例如:

已经晚了半个多小时了,看起来,他不会来了。

这个菜看起来像是很好吃的样子。

看起来,这件事还挺复杂的。

* 已经晚了半个多小时了,看出来,他不会来了。

* 这个菜看出来像是很好吃的样子。

* 看出来,这件事还挺复杂的。

看得出来,您很富于同情心。

(I can see that you are very sympathetic.)

看得出来,她心里并不痛快。

我看得出来,他听了这句话,震动不小。

(I can see that the words made a great impact on him.)

* 我看起来,他听了这句话,震动不小。

起来 qilai 上来 shanglai

〈趋向动词〉 < directional verb >

(一)"起来"、"上来"都可以表示随动作由低向高的方向,但是不能通用。("起来" and "上来" can both express the direction from low to high, but they are not exchangeable.)

"起来"只表示随动作向上的方向,不涉及向上后的场所,一般事实上也不存在场所问题,动词支配的名词通常是表事物的或表人体部位的;"上来"则要求涉及到达点,动词后涉及的名词通常表示场所意义。虽然有时由于对话、语境等原因省掉到达点,但是因为它实际上存在,所以可以意会。("起来" only indicates an upward direction, not including the place, and in fact, no place is involved since the noun following the verb usually represents a thing, or a part of a human body. "上来" often involves the place reached by the action, so the noun after the verb usually signifies a place. Even if the place is not mentioned, it can be sensed.)例如:

  端起碗来　飞起来了　坐起来　站起身来
  爬上来了(到某处)　跑上楼来　走上主席台来

(二)"上来"还可以表示由远处到近处或靠近的意思;"起来"没有这一用法。("上来" can also mean from the distance to the near place or approaching; while "起来" doesn't mean this.)例如:

  他们追上来了
  敌人包围上来了(The enemy encircled us.)
  跟上来　　把温暖送上门来(bring warmth to the home)
  * 跟起来　　　* 把温暖送起门来

(三)"上来"还可以表示成功的意思(多用于语言活动);"起来"没有这一用法。〔"上来" can also mean being successful (mainly used in language activities). "起来" cannot mean so.〕例如:

  全答上来了。
  我叫不上来他的名字了。
  (I can't call him by his name.)
  * 全答起来了。
  * 我叫不起来他的名字了。

(四)"起来"还可以表示某动作或状态开始并持续的时态意义;"上来"没有这一意义。("起来" can also express the beginning and lasting of an action or state; while "上来" cannot.)例如:

  大家大笑起来　看起电视来　脸红了起来
  生活富裕起来
  * 大家大笑上来　* 看上电视来　* 脸红了上来
  * 生活富裕上来

起来 qilai　　下去 xiaqu
〈趋向动词〉 < directional verb >

(一)"起来"、"下去"都可以接在动词后表示一定的时态意义。"起来"可以表示某动作开始做或某状态开始出现,并有继续下去意思;"下去"则只单纯表示某动作或某状态继续的意义。("起来" and "下去" can be used after verbs to express certain tense. "起来" may mean that an act or a state begins and continues. "下去" only expresses the continuance of an act or a state.)例如:

这个题目很有意思,大家很有兴致地讨论了起来。

(The topic is very interesting. All of us have a hot discussion.)

突然他发现了两只从未见过的小虫,不由得注意了起来。

(Suddenly he found two small insects he had not seen before, and took a notice of them involuntarily.)

孩子说着说着大哭起来。

他又忙起来了。

最近她的心情似乎好起来了。

这个选题很有价值,一定要搞下去,不能半途而废。

(The selected subject is quite worthwhile, and must be carried on. You can't give up halfway.)

你接着说下去。

天再这么热下去,可真有点儿受不了了。

＊你接着说起来。

＊天再这么热起来,可真有点儿受不了了。

(二)"起来"、"下去"接在形容词后时,"起来"多用于具有积极色彩的形容词后;"下去"多用于具有消极色彩的形容词后。(When used after an adjective, "起来" is used after a positive one; while "下去" after a negative one.)例如:

好起来　　亮起来　　坚强起来

427

富裕起来　紧张起来
坏下去　　暗下去　　软弱下去
贫困下去　松懈下去

气 qì　　生气 shēngqì

气、生气〈动词〉表示因不合心意或不满而产生不愉快的心理情绪甚至发怒。

(<verb> expressing unpleasant or angry feeling aroused from dissatisfaction.)

气〈名词〉<noun>

"气"、"生气"看起来意义好像十分接近,但是实际上它们无论在意义上、功能上,还是在用法上都有较大差别,所以在很多情况下都是不能换用的。("气" and "生气" seem close in meaning, but they are actually quite different in meaning, function and usage, so they are not exchangeable in many cases.)

(一) 意义上 (In meaning)

1. "气"在意义上实际有两种:一是表示施事因不合心意或不满而产生不愉快的心理情绪;一是施事采取某种行为使受事生气。("气" may actually express two meanings. One is that the doer feels unpleasant or angry because of being not appealing to his / her mind. The other is that the doer does something to make its object angry.) 例如:

(1) 施事生气。(The doer is angry.)

听了王山的这些事,他是又气又恨。

主任气得脸都青了。

(The director got red in the face with rage.)

母亲气坏了。

我气这孩子一点儿也不争气。

(I was angry with the child for his being disappointing.)

428

(2) 使受事生气。〔(The doer) makes the recipient angry.〕
　　我偏要气气他不可。
　　(I was deliberately trying to annoy him.)
　　我什么时候气过爷爷了。
　　听说小李把厂长气病了。
　　真气人!

2."生气"则只有施事因不合心意或不满而产生不愉快的心理情绪的意思。("生气" only expresses the unpleasant feeling of the doer because of anger or dissatisfaction.)例如：
　　奶奶生气了。
　　她为孩子被欺负的事生气。
　　(你)别生气了!
　　我生了他好几天气。

3."生气"不能表示使受事生气的意思。("生气" cannot express the meaning of making the object angry.)例如：
　　* 我偏要生气生气他不可。
　　* 我什么时候生气过爷爷了。
　　* 听说小李把厂长生气病了。
　　* 真生气人!

(二)"生气"不能用作名词;"气"可以用作名词。("生气" cannot be used as a noun; while "气" can.)例如：
　　* 等她的生气消了,再跟她好好谈谈。
　　* 怎么? 你的生气还这么大?
　　等她的气消了,再跟她好好谈谈。
　　(You get to talk with her again after she cools down.)
　　怎么? 你的气还这么大?

(三)用法上 (In usage)
　　1."气"不能接受程度副词的修饰;"生气"可以接受程度副词的修饰。("气" cannot be modified by adverbs of degree; while "生气" can.)例如：

* 看到孩子那么淘气,妈妈很气。
* 听了小张被打的事,大家十分气。

看到孩子那么淘气,妈妈很生气。
听了小张被打的事,大家十分生气。

2."气"可以连带宾语;"生气"是动宾式构词方式,一般不连带宾语,尤其是名词性宾语。("气" can be used with an object; while "生气" is a "verb + object" structure, and cannot take other objects, especially noun objects.)例如:

我气这孩子一点儿也不争气。
他不气别的,就气你说话不算数。
(He is angry at nothing but your going back on your words.)
我偏要气气他。
我什么时候气过奶奶了。
别气老师了。
真气人!
* 他不生气别的,就生气你说话不算数。
* 我偏要生气生气他。
* 我什么时候生气过奶奶了。
* 别生气老师了。
* 真生气人!

3."气"后面可以带描写性补语;"生气"后面不能带。("气" can be followed by a descriptive complement; while "生气" cannot.) 例如:

气极了　　气得直发抖(tremble with rage)
气得不得了(be very angry)　气死了(be enraged)
气疯了(be mad with rage)
气病了　　气跑了　　气哭了
* 生气极了　　* 生气得直发抖
* 生气得不得了　* 生气死了
* 生气疯了　　* 生气病了

＊生气跑了　　　＊生气哭了

4. "气"可以用于"把"字句、"被"字句;"生气"不可以。("气" can be used in the "把" sentence, or the "被" sentence; while "生气" cannot.)例如:

　　把我气死了。
　　把他气得一句话也说不出来。
　　＊把我生气死了。
　　＊把他生气得一句话也说不出来。
　　被他气坏了。
　　被孩子气得不知道怎么办才好。
　　〔(He was so) angry with the child that he didn't know what to do with him.〕
　　＊被他生气坏了。
　　＊被孩子生气得不知道怎么办才好。

5. "气"可以重叠使用;"生气"不能重叠使用。("气" can be reduplicated; while "生气" can't.)例如:

　　气气这个坏家伙
　　＊生气生气这个坏家伙

6. "生气"有"生"和"气"分离使用的方式,插在"生"和"气"之间的一般是宾语、时态助词、数量补语、趋向补语等。("生气" can be used in a way that "生" and "气" are separated, with an object, aspect particles, numeral-classifier complement or directional complement in between.)例如:

　　我生过他一次气　生了半天气　生这么大气
　　生起气来　　　　生够了气　　生不得气

千万 qiānwàn　　万万 wànwàn

〈副词〉 <adverb>

"千万"、"万万"都可以表示说话人对听话人的劝告、请求、叮咛。用在祈使句中,作状语,含有"一定"的意思。但是,两词

431

在语气上、使用上有一定差别,大多不能换用。〔"千万" and "万万" are used as adverbials in imperative sentences to express advice, request, or urge of the speaker to the listener, meaning "(be sure)". They are different in mood and usage, and not exchangeable.〕

(一)"万万"的语气比"千万"更重。〔"万万" is more emphatic than "千万" in tone.〕例如:

千万不可粗心大意。
(Do be careful!)
千万不能失信于民。
(Be sure not to break your promise to the people.)
万万不可粗心大意。
万万不能失信于民。

(二)"万万"只能用于否定句中,而且通常只与"不可"、"不能"、"不要"连用。"千万"不受此限,它既可用于否定句,也可用于肯定句。"千万"通常与"要"或否定词"别"、"不"连用。("万万" is only used in negative sentences, usually connected with "不可", "不能" or "不要". "千万" is not restricted by this. It can be used either in negative or positive sentences. "千万" is usually used with "要" or the negative "别" or "不".)例如:

实验已经到了关键时刻,万万不可掉以轻心。
(The experiment is in the crucial moment. We must not take it lightly under any circumstances.)
她知道了这件事,一定会受不了,万万不要告诉她。
千万别忘了我告诉你的事。
过马路时,千万要小心呀!
* 你万万要保重身体呀!(不是否定句。)
* 那儿太危险,你万万不去。(改:"不能去"。)
* 文件太多了,千万/万万看不完。(不是祈使句。)

(三)"万万"还可以用于陈述句中表示事情非常出人意外的语气,通常与"没有料到"、"想不到"、"没想到"连用。"千万"没有这种意思,"千万"只能用于祈使句。("万万" can also be used in a declarative sentence, expressing something beyond expectation, usually connected with "没有料到","想不到", or "没想到"."千万" is only used in imperative sentences.)

万万料想不到,那么本分的人竟会做出这等事来。
(It never occurred to me that such a well-behaved person would go so far as to do such a thing.)
万万没想到,他这么早就离开了我们。
* 千万料想不到,那么本分的人竟会做出这等事来。
* 千万没想到,他这么早就离开了我们。
走之前,千万别忘了切断电源。
千万记住妈妈的嘱咐。

前 qián   前面 qiánmian
〈方位词〉 < noun of locality >

(一)"前"、"前面"都可以表示空间、位置或次序靠前的部分。("前" and "前面" can both signify the front part of a space, a place, or a sequence.)例如:

教学楼前/ 前面有一大片草坪。
老师站在讲台前/ 前面。
前几排先走,后边的稍等一下。
前面的已经检查完了,后面的可以进来了。

但是,它们在意义上稍有差别,比较起来"前面"比"前"所指的靠前的部分显得更具体些。在用法上它们还有一些差别,所以常常不能换用。(However, they are slightly different in meaning. Compared with "前", the front part expressed by "前面" is more specific. They are also used differently, and usually not exchangeable.)

主要的差别在于:"前"单用不自由,"前面"单用自由。(Their main differences are: "前" can not used alone, while "前面" can.)

1. 单用的时候,"前"通常要跟"后"呼应使用。"前面"没有这种限制。(While used alone, "前" is usually used in concert with "后"."前面" has no such restriction.)例如:

前怕狼,后怕虎(to fear wolves ahead and tigers behind - to be full of fears)

前不着村,后不着店(to reach neither a village ahead nor a restaurant behind-to be stranded in the midway)

正好,前十后十我居中(There are ten ahead and ten behind. I'm just in the middle.)

* 前有一个人,我们去问问他吧。
* 前有一家银行。
* 前排了十几个人。

前面有一个人,我们去问问他吧。

前面有一家银行。

前面排了十几个人。

2. 组成词组用:"前"与单音节词或双音节结合较自由;"前面"多与双音节词结合。(While used in word groups, "前" is combined freely with either monosyllables or disyllabic words. "前面" is usually combined with disyllabic words.)例如:

门前　窗前　碑前　桌前　楼前　床前

讲台前　大楼前　座位前　写字台前

讲台前面　大楼前面　座位前面

写字台前面　停车场前面　广告牌前面

* 门前面　* 窗前面　* 碑前面　* 桌前面

3. "前"常常可以放在名词性词语前面,表示处所;"前面"基本不这样用。("前" is usually placed before substantial words, expressing places. "前面" is rarely used in this way.)例如:

前厅　前院　前窗　前门　前楼

* 前面厅　* 前面院　* 前面窗

* 前面门　* 前面楼

(二)"前"在与数量及其他词语组合后,可以表示时间。"前面"没有这种用法。(When used with numeral-classifier compounds or other words,"前" can signify time, but "前面" can't.)例如:

前半夜　前半学期　前几天　前三年　前些时候
一年前　几天前　一周前　春节前　饭前
开学前　演出前　临出发前
＊前面半夜　＊前面半学期　＊前面几天
＊前面三年　＊前面一些时候
＊一年前面　＊几天前面　＊一周前面
＊春节前面　＊饭前面　＊开学前面
＊演出前面　＊临出发前面

前 qián　　以前 yǐqián

〈方位词〉表示比某时间早的时间。(< noun of locality > expressing the time earlier than a certain time.)

"前"、"以前"都可以表示比现在或某时间早的时间。(Both "前" and "以前" can express the time earlier than the present or a certain time.)例如:

天黑前我就能回家。
晚上九点前一定要完成任务。
解放以前,这里是一片荒地。
放假以前要把论文写完。

但是,"前"、"以前"在用法上还有一定的差别。(But there are some differences in their usage.)

(一)"前"可以表示比某时早的某一时间,也可以表示靠前的某一段时间;"以前"只能表示比某时早的某一时间,不能表示靠前的某一段时间。("前" may indicate the time that is earlier than a certain time, or the earlier part of a certain period of time; "以前" only expresses the time earlier than a certain time, but not the earlier part of a certain period of time.)例如:

435

1.比现在早的某一时间:(a certain time earlier than the present:)

饭前　春节前　五点前　出发前
睡觉前　毕业前
吃饭以前　春节以前　五点以前
出发以前　睡觉以前　毕业以前

2.靠前的某一段时间:(the earlier part of a certain period of time:)

前半学期上课,后半学期社会实践。
我来天津三十年了,前二十年一直住在乡下。
考试一共才两个小时,前一个小时我几乎没做什么题。
* 以前半学期上课,以后半学期社会实践。
* 我来天津三十年了,以前二十年一直住在乡下。
* 考试一共才两个小时,以前一个小时我几乎没做什么题。

3."前"表示时间还可以用"前+数量"的方式;"以前"不能这样用。("前" can also express time in the "前 + numeral-classifier compound" pattern."以前" can't.)例如:

前半夜　前不久　前几天　前几年　前些时候
* 以前半夜　* 以前不久　* 以前几天
* 以前几年　* 以前些时候

(二)"前"可以跟单音节词组合,也可以跟双音节词组合;"以前"一般只跟双音节词组合。("前" can be used together with either monosyllabic or disyllabic words; while "以前" is only used with disyllabic words.)例如:

饭前　课前　事前　年前　走前　睡前　生前
* 饭以前　* 课以前　* 事以前
* 年以前　* 睡以前　* 生以前
上课前　临走前　清明前　下班前
不久前　几年前　天亮前

上课以前　临走以前　清明以前　下班以前
　　　不久以前　几年以前　天亮以前
(三)"以前"表示时间时可以单用;"前"表示时间时不能单用。("以前" can be used alone while expressing time."前" can't.)例如:
　　　以前,我从来没有来过这里。
　　　他以前有过一个女朋友。
　　　以前的事我还记得。
　　　以前是以前,现在是现在。
　　* 前,我从来没有来过这里。
　　* 他前有过一个女朋友。
　　* 前的事我还记得。
　　* 前是前,现在是现在。

亲切 qīnqiè　　亲热 qīnrè

〈形容词〉表示亲密、热情而关心的意思。(< adjective > indicating being close, enthusiastic and concerned.)

"亲切"和"亲热"意思很接近,但是有时不能换用,它们在意义的着重点上和适用的范围上还有一定差别。("亲切" and "亲热" are very close in meaning, but not always exchangeable. Their emphasis in meaning and their application spheres are different.)

(一) 意义着重点有所不同 (Differences in emphatic meaning)

"亲切"着重于"切",即侧重在态度上,有态度热情、诚恳、关切的意思;"亲热"着重于"热",侧重于表现出来的热情而亲密的动作。(In the word "亲切", attention is paid to "切". It emphasizes one's attitude or manner, meaning warmhearted, amiable, or solicitous. In the word "亲热", attention is paid to "热". It emphasizes the presentation of the warm and intimate action.)例如:

　　　老首长亲切地嘱咐我不要辜负同志们的期望。
　　　(The old leading cadre exhorted me kindly to live up to the

expectations of the comrades.)

没想到,中国的老师那么亲切、热情。

大娘亲热地拉着我的手问这问那。(The aunt grasped my hand and made warmhearted inquiries.)

她亲亲热热地喊了一声:"老李!"

(二)适用范围有一定差别(Differences in application)

1."亲切"一般用于形容人的态度或表现态度的有关方面:表情、目光、语气、语调、声音等。("亲切" is usually used to describe one's attitude or manner, or something like that, such as expression, look, mood, tone and sound.)例如:

别看他是那么大的官儿,可是待我们这些小人物却是那么亲切。

(Though he is such a high official, he treats us nonentities so kindly.)

看到老师那亲切的目光,我身上感到热乎乎的。

临行前,妈妈那亲切的声音还在我耳边回荡。

"亲热"一般较多地用于形容表现出来的热情而亲密的动作:拉、拥抱、招手、招呼、说、喊、询问等。("亲热" is usually more used to describe the warm and intimate action, such as drawing, embracing, waving, greeting, addressing, shouting and inquiring.)例如:

他们亲热地拥抱在一起。

师生们亲热地交谈着。

乡亲们亲热地招呼着我们这些城里的孩子们。

2."亲切"因为着重于态度,所以只能用于人,不能用于动物;"亲热"着重于动作,所以既可以用于人,也可以用于动物。("亲切" emphasizes attitude, so it is only used to describe people, not animals. "亲热" emphasizes action, and it can be used to describe either people or animals.)例如:

* 两只小动物亲切地滚打在一起。

＊ 几只猴子亲切地互相捉着虱子。

两只小动物亲热地滚打在一起。

几只猴子亲热地互相捉着虱子。

3."亲切"一般没有重叠用法;"亲热"可以重叠使用。(Generally,"亲切"is not used in an reduplicated way; while "亲热" can be reduplicated.)例如:

小两口儿亲亲热热地偎倚在一起。

(The young couple lean close to each other affectionately.)

乡亲们围着子弟兵亲亲热热地问长问短。

(The villagers gathered round their own army men, asking all sorts of questions affectionately.)

＊ 小两口儿亲亲切切地偎倚在一起。

＊ 乡亲们围着子弟兵亲亲切切地问长问短。

亲自 qīnzì   亲身 qīnshēn

〈副词〉表示由自己(去做某事)。[< adverb > indicating (to do something) by oneself.]

(一) 意义着重点不同 (Difference in focus of meaning)

"亲自"强调某事由自己直接去做,含有不由别人去做的意思;"亲身"则强调由本人自身从事,投身进去的意思。("亲自" emphasizes something is done by oneself, not done or helped by others; while "亲身" emphasizes personal experience, namely, throwing oneself into something.)例如:

我想亲自把毕业证书交到他手里。

临走的那天,妈妈带着病,亲自下厨房为我做菜。

(The day I left home, Mother made dinner for me herself in spite of her illness.)

孩子的书法不要到外面学了,由他爷爷亲自教他好了。

这是他亲身经历的事,怎么会忘呢?

我们亲身领略了长江三峡的美丽风光。

439

(We get some idea personally of how beautiful the sights of the Three Gorges of Yangtze River are.)

(二) 使用范围不同 (Differences in application)

"亲自"使用频率较高,而且能较广泛地跟许多动词组合;"亲身"使用频率较低,只能与"经历"、"感受"、"体验"等少数较为抽象的动词组合。"经历"等抽象的动词一般不能接受"亲自"的修饰;具体的动作性的动词也不能跟"亲身"组合。("亲自" is more frequently used, and can be combined more widely with many verbs. "亲身" is less used, and can only be combined with a few abstract verbs such as "经历","感受","体验". Generally, abstract verbs like "经历" cannot be modified by "亲自". Yet specific motional verbs can not be used with "亲身".)例如:

我想亲自教他弹钢琴。

这件事还是由你亲自告诉他好。

让他亲身体验一下才好。

你亲身感受一下那种气氛,就不会这么说了。

* 这是他亲自经历的事,怎么会忘呢?

* 让青年朋友们亲自投入到火热的斗争中去,接受锻炼和考验。

* 我想亲身把毕业证书交到他手里。

* 临走的那天,妈妈带着病,亲身下厨房为我做菜。

* 由爷爷亲身教孩子书法。

全 quán   都 dōu

〈副词〉表示总括。(< adverb > meaning totally.)

(一)"全"、"都"的相同之处:(Similarities of "全" and "都":)

1."全"、"都"在表示总括整个范围时,可以通用。"全"、"都"还可以连用成——"全都",有强调的意思。(While indicating the whole scope, "全" and "都" are interchangeable. "全"

and "都" can be combined together as "全都", used for emphasis.)例如：

> 县里的干部全/都去乡下搞秋收了。
> 这些照片全/都是你的。
> 你们怎么全都不说话？／这里的人我全都不认识。

2.否定词"不"或"没"放在"全"或"都"的前与后,表示的意思不同。(Different locations of the negative word "不" or "没" in front or after "全" or "都" can cause differences in their meanings.)例如：

> 这些礼物他全/都不要。(否定总括的全部礼物)
> 这些礼物他不全/都要。(否定总括中的部分礼物)
> 这三部外国影片我全/都没看。(否定总括的全部影片)
> 这三部外国影片我没全/都看。(否定总括中的部分影片)

(二)"全"、"都"在意义上和结构上还有差别：(other differences of "全" and "都" in meaning and structure：)

1."全"侧重指所总括的范围内无一例外,有"全部"、"完全"的意思。"都"则侧重总括范围内的每一个。所以,表示"全部"、"完全"的意思时,要用"全"。("全" means whole, entire, or total, without exception. "都" emphasizes each one of the whole. Thus, "全" is used to express the meaning "wholly" or "completely".)例如：

> 这时,天全黑了,路上一个行人也没有。
> 我能找到失散多年的兄弟,全靠他帮忙。
> (Thanks to his help, I could find my brother, whom I had no news of for years.)
> 这条鲫鱼全变红了。
> ＊这时,天都黑了,路上一个行人也没有。
> ＊这条鲫鱼都变红了。

441

2."都"侧重表示总括范围内的每一个,所以它总括的人或事物一般不能是单数,应该是复数。尤其句中总括的内容是由表示任指意义(任意的一个)的词语来担当时,要用"都"。("都" emphasizes every one of the whole, so the people or things it includes should be plural, not singular. "都" is used particularly when the content of the total is expressed by the word signifying any one of the whole.)例如:

　　＊ 这次见到她,我觉得她都变了,不再是三年前的苏苏了。

　　这次见到她,我觉得她全变了,不再是三年前的苏苏了。
(When I met her this time, I found that she had changed completely, no longer Susu three years ago.)

　　谁都不同意他的这个建议。

　　＊ 谁全不同意他的这个建议。

　　每个周末我们都到这里举行一个小型晚会。

　　＊ 每个周末我们全到这里举行一个小型晚会。

3.作为副词,"都"还有表示强调的"甚至"的意思,"全"没有这种意思。(As an adverb, "都" can also express the emphatic meaning "even", but "全" can't.)例如:

　　整个卷子,她连一个字都没错。
(She didn't make a single mistake on the whole examination paper.)

　　连我的好朋友都不支持我。

　　＊ 整个卷子,她连一个字全没错。

　　＊ 连我的好朋友全不支持我。

全 quán　　全部 quánbù　　所有 suǒyǒu

全、全部、所有〈形容词〉表示整个、无一例外。(< adjective > indicating whole, complete, without exception.)

全、全部〈副词〉表示总括。(< adverb > indicating entirely,

totally or completely.)

(一)"全"、"全部"、"所有"是形容词,在句中都可以作定语。("全","全部" and "所有" are adjectives, and can be used as attributes in sentences.)

1."全"与"全部"

(1)"全"、"全部"一般不能通用,它们所表示的"整个"的含义有差别。"全"通常指一个事物的"整个";"全部"通常指各个部分的总和。(Generally, "全" and "全部" are not exchangeable. Their meaning of "wholeness" is different. "全" usually refers to the whole part of a substance. "全部" usually refers to the summation of the individual parts.)例如:

全书共五百多万字。
全村三百多口人,都被敌人赶到村口的广场上。
* 全部书共五百多万字。
* 全部村三百多口人,都被敌人赶到村口的广场上。
全部费用由公司支付。
我们把全部资金都投到这个项目上了。
(We have put all the funds into the project.)
* 全费用由公司支付。
* 我们把全资金都投到这个项目上了。

(2)"全"、"全部"所修饰的对象有所不同。"全"用于某个有一定范围、空间、面积、长度等的具体事物;"全部"用于某些抽象事物或具有集合意义的事物。(The targets modified by "全" or "全部" are different. "全" is used to modify something concrete and with certain scope, space, area, or length. "全部" is used to modify something abstract or collective.)例如:

全书 全公司 全楼 全车厢 全村
全世界 全长 全程
* 全部书 * 全部公司 * 全部世界 * 全部长
全部才华(all the talents)

443

全部心血(all one's energy)
全部精力(all one's efforts)
全部财富(all one's wealth)
全部收入　全部资料　全部零件　全部车辆
＊全才华　＊全心血　＊全财富　＊全资料

(3)"全"作定语不用"的";"全部"作定语可以用"的",但是通常不用。(While used as attributes, "全" is not followed by "的"; "全部" may have "的" after it, but usually "的" is not used.)例如:

全中国人民都投入到四化建设之中。

＊全的中国人民都投入到四化建设之中。

她把全部(的)心血都倾注到教育事业中。

(She threw all her energy into the educational undertakings.)

这是有关敦煌的全部(的)资料。

(4)功能不完全相同。"全"作为形容词,可以作定语,也可以作谓语和补语;"全部"是非谓形容词,只能作定语,不能作谓语和补语。(Their functions are different. As an adjective, "全" can be used as an attribute, a predicate or a complement. "全部" is a non-predicative adjective, and is only used as an attribute, but not as a predicate or a complement.)例如:

这家商店不大,商品却挺全。

我要的零件都配全了吗?

(Is every spare part I need fitted?)

＊这家商店不大,商品却挺全部。

＊我要的零件都配全部了吗?

2."所有"与"全"、"全部"

(1)"所有"跟"全部"一样,也是非谓形容词,只能作定语,只是作定语时通常要用"的"。(Like "全部", "所有" is also a non-predicative adjective, and can only be used as an attribute, usually with "的" after it.)

(2)"所有"跟"全"不同,它所概括的人或事物一定是复数的;它跟"全部"不完全相同,它的使用范围要比"全部"大得多。它可以用来概括某范围内存在的或具有的全部人或事物,而"全部"不能用来概括人。对于没有集合意义的一般事物来说,通常选用"所有"来修饰。("所有" is different from "全" in that the persons or things it modifies must have plural meaning. Not quite the same as "全部", its application is much wider. It can be used to state succinctly all the people or things within a certain scope; while "全部" cannot be used to generalize people. "所有" is usually preferred while modifying general things which have no collective meaning.)例如:

> 公司里所有的职员都有这个要求。
>
> 我把所有的脏衣服都洗了。
>
> 他把所有的知识和才华都献给了科学事业。
>
> (He devoted all his knowledge and talent to the scientific undertakings.)
>
> * 公司里全部职员都有这个要求。(表示人员总和时,不要用"全部",最好用"全体")

(二)"全"、"全部"还有副词用法,在句中作状语,表示总括。("全" and "全部" can also be adverbs, used as adverbial in a sentence, meaning totally.)

1."全"、"全部"大多可以通用。("全" and "全部" are exchangeable in most cases.)例如:

> 人全/全部都在这儿,有什么话您就说吧。
>
> 所有的问题全/全部解决了。
>
> 他把所有的晚报全/全部买了去。
>
> 这部书介绍的全/全部都是三十年代的事情。

2.意义上稍有差别。"全部"比"全"语义稍重,对"无一例外"有所强调。(Their meanings are slightly different. "全部" is more emphatic than "全", stressing on "without exception")例如:

445

这里的书我那儿全部都有。
理想终于全部实现了。
把这里的垃圾全部清理出去。

3.由于音节个数的影响,用"不"、"没"否定时,通常用"全"。〔Restricted by the numbers of the syllables, when used with the negative word "不" or "没", "全" is more appropriate (than "全部").〕例如:

机器没全大修,只修了一部分。
不知为什么,三班的同学没全来。
今天的事不全是他的错,我也有责任。
(Today's matter is not entirely his fault. I should also be blamed.)

全 quán　　完全 wánquán

〈副词〉表示整个、全部,无一例外。(< adverb > indicating wholly, all, without exception.)

(一)"全"、"完全"大多可以通用。("全" and "完全" are exchangeable in most cases.)例如:

大树把阳光全/完全遮住了。
你的意见我全/完全同意。
今天的事全/完全是你的不对。

但是"全"、"完全"能够通用时,意义上和色彩上仍有细微差别。意义上,"完全"表示的程度更深,更加强调无一例外;色彩上,"完全"通用于口语和书面语,"全"则多用于口语。(Though exchangeable, they are slightly different in meaning and flavor. In meaning, the degree of "完全" is higher, with more emphasis on "without exception". In flavor, "完全" is both used in spoken and written languages, but "全" is more used in spoken language.)例如:

老师的嘱托你全忘了。
老师的嘱托你完全忘记了。(程度深而书面语色彩强。)

刘先生的讲演太精彩了,把同学们全吸引住了。

刘先生的讲演太精彩了,把同学们完全吸引住了。(程度深而书面语色彩强。)

(Mr. Liu's lecture is so interesting that the students are entirely fascinated by it.)

(二)"全"、"完全"有时意义侧重点不完全相同。("全" and "完全" do not emphasize on the same point in meaning.)

1."全"有时只侧重表示"全部",概括一定数量的人、事物。所概括的人或事物通常有具体数量的表示,句中通常使用具有具体动作意义的动词。("全" only emphasizes "wholly", summarizing a certain amount of people or things which are usually expressed with concrete numbers. The verb used in the sentence usually represents a specific action.)例如:

他怎么能不醉呢? 一瓶白酒全叫他喝了。

他把所有的书全卖了。

* 他怎么能不醉呢? 一瓶白酒完全叫他喝了。

* 他把所有的书完全卖了。

2."完全"有时只侧重表示程度,所指事物一般没有数量的表示,且多为抽象事物,句中谓语多为形容词或抽象意义的动词。("完全" sometimes only emphasizes the degree of something. No numbers are involved in the modified object, which is usually an abstract thing. The predicate in the sentence is usually an adjective or a verb of abstract meaning.)例如:

他为什么会这样想,我完全不明白。

这件事跟我预计的完全相同。

她完全不能控制自己的感情,眼泪泉涌般地流了出来。

(She absolutely lost control of her feelings, and tears welled up in her eyes.)

* 他为什么会这样想,我全不明白。

447

* 这件事跟我预计的全相同。
* 她全不能控制自己的感情,眼泪泉涌般地流了出来。

3. "全"和"都"常常连用,有强调意味;"完全"自身就有强调意味,所以一般不跟"都"连用。("全" and "都" are often used together, expressing emphatic meaning. "完全" itself alone is emphatic, so it is not used with "都".)例如:

在座的代表我全都认识。
孩子们的身体全都很健康。
* 他为什么会这样想,我完全都不明白。
* 这件事跟我预计的完全都相同。

全体 quántǐ   全部 quánbù   整个(儿) zhěnggè(r)

〈形容词〉表示各个部分的总和。(<adjective> indicating summation of individual parts.)

(一) 意义及使用范围不同 (Differences in meaning and application)

"全体"主要用来指人员的总和,一般不用于事物;"全部"则主要用于事物,一般是指多个事物的总和。所指之物可以是具体的,也可以是抽象的。"整个"只用于指事物,它指一个完整而具体的事物的各个部分的总和。("全体" is mainly used to express summation of people, not things. "全部" is mainly used to modify things, meaning the summation of many things, which may be concrete or abstract. "整个" is only used in things, meaning a complete and specific total of individual parts.)例如:

全体人员马上到门前集合!
我代表全体将士向大家问好!
全体同学都在病房外等待着,希望见到他们尊敬的老师。
(All the students were waiting outside the ward, hoping to see their respectable teacher.)
这间屋子里的东西就是我的全部家当。

这篇文章代表了他的全部观点。

整个假期我一天也没有休息。

整个苹果都红了。

1.用于指人员总和时,最好不要用"全部",更不能用"整个"。(While indicating the summation of people, it is better not to use "全部", and never use "整个".)例如:

* 全部人员马上到门前集合!
* 全部同学都在病房外等待着,希望见到他们尊敬的老师。
* 我代表整个将士向大家问好!

他把全部精力都倾注到科学事业上。

(He threw all his energy into the scientific undertakings.)

今年的全部收入可望突破三百万。

2."整个"只用于指事物,所指事物一般是一个完整而具体的事物,"整个"指这个事物各个部分的总和。("整个" is only used to indicate things, usually a complete and specific thing. "整个" indicates the summation of the individual parts of the whole thing.)例如:

整个下午,我都在图书馆看书。

整个会场鸦雀无声。

(In the whole assembly hall silence reigns.)

他被打得很厉害,整个脑袋没有一块好地方。

3.用于指一个完整而具体的事物的各个部分的总和时,不要用"全部"。("全部" is not used to express the summation of individual parts of a complete and specific thing.)例如:

* 全部下午,我都在图书馆看书。
* 全部会场鸦雀无声。
* 他被打得很厉害,全部脑袋没有一块好地方。

(二) 功能不同(Differences in function)

1."全体"在句中主要用作定语。("全体" is usually used as

an attribute in a sentence.)例如：

全体运动员都到齐了。

全体同学一条心，一定能成功！

2."全部"、"整个"除作定语外，还可以作为副词用于动词前作状语，尤其是"全部"，常常用作状语。"全体"不能用作状语。(Besides being used as an attribute, "全部" and "整个" can also be used as an adverbial in front of verbs, especially "全部", which is usually used as an adverbial. "全体" cannot be used as an adverbial.)例如：

今天学的单词我全部记下来了。

问题已经全部解决了。

我们这个农场终于全部实现了现代化。

我把这辆自行车整个翻修了一遍。

(I have the bicycle repaired completely.)

虽然这件大衣只是弄脏了前襟，但是最好整个地洗一下。

(Though the coat is only dirty in the front part, it's better to get the whole coat washed.)

* 问题已经全体解决了。

* 我把这辆自行车全体翻修了一遍。

群 qún　　帮 bāng　　伙 huǒ　　批 pī

〈量词〉用于由两个以上的个体组成的集体或事物。

(< measure word > indicating two or more things, or a group composed of two or more individuals.)

"群"、"帮"、"伙"、"批"虽然都可以表示由两个以上的个体组成的集体或事物，但是由于意义和用法还有许多不同，所以常常不能换用。(Though "群", "帮", "伙" and "批" are used to express a group, or two or more things, there are many differences in their meanings and usages. So they are not often exchangeable.)

(一) 用于集体或事物时,范围有所不同。(They are used in different categories when expressing groups or plural things.)

1. "群"、"帮"、"伙"、"批"都可以用于由两个以上的人组成的集体;"群"和"批"除了用于人以外,还可以用于事物;"帮"和"伙"却只能用于人。("群","帮","伙" and "批" can all be used to indicate a group composed of two or more people or things. "群" and "批" can be used to describe both people and things. While "帮" and "伙" are only used to describe people.)例如:

(1) 用于人(Used to describe people):

一群人围在那儿看什么?

外面来了一帮人,不知干什么的。

这伙流氓终于被逮住了。

又毕业了一批学生。

(2) 用于事物(Used to describe things):

那群小岛上还住着不少人家呢。

昨天又进了一批货。

* 那帮小岛上还住着不少人家呢。

* 昨天又进了一伙货。

2. "群"和"批"虽然都可以用于事物,但是范围完全不同。"群"一般只能用于"岛";"批"则可以用于货物。(Though both are used to describe things, "群" and "批" are used in different categories. Generally, "群" is only used to modify "岛"(islands); while "批" may be used to modify goods.)例如:

三门峡两岸石壁陡峭,中间一群石岛也是悬崖绝壁。

(It's precipitous on both sides of the Sanmen Gorges, and the stone islands in the middle are also full of sheer precipices and overhanging rocks.)

远处一群小岛密密麻麻的。

仓库昨天来了一批货,让我们最晚明天提走。

图书馆里最近新购进了一批图书。

＊ 远处一批小岛密密麻麻。
　　＊ 图书馆里最近新购进了一群图书。
　3."群"还可以用于有生命的动物,无论天上飞的、地上跑的、水里游的都可以用"群";"批"则只能从批次的角度用于货物。("群" can also be used to describe living creatures, either in the sky, or on the ground, or in the water."批" can only be used to describe goods in terms of batches.)例如:
　　一群大雁拍着有力的翅膀,向南飞去了。
　　山坡上,一群羊安详地吃着草。
　　一群鱼朝垂进水中的鱼饵冲去。
　　第一批羊已经运到了,第二批羊一周以后可以运到。
　　＊ 山坡上,一批羊安详地吃着草。
　"批"用于货物时,主要带有批次的意义。所以它通常与货物的进出有关。句中动词也常用位移性动词。例如:"到"、"来"、"进"、"送来/去"、"运来/去"、"奔"等。(When used to describe goods, "批" usually means batches. It is usually concerned with the import and export of goods, and verbs of displacement are usually used in the sentences, such as "到", "来", "进", "送来／去", "运来／去", "奔".)例如:
　　前几天进了一批货,过两天还要来一批。
　　一批批救援物资被送往灾区。
(二)"群"、"帮"、"伙"用于人时,意义也有所不同。(When "群", "帮" and "伙" are used to describe people, their meanings are not quite the same.)
　1."群"、"帮"、"伙"都可以用于人群,但是,"群"一般指不突出有什么目的而聚集的人群;"帮"、"伙"则常常指有一定目的组成的人群。("群", "帮" and "伙" can all be used to indicate a crowd, but "群" generally is used to indicate a crowd that is not gathered for a specific purpose. "帮" and "伙" are usually used to refer to a gang of people gathering for a specific purpose.)例如:

前边可能发生交通事故了,一群人围在那里看。

一群孩子围坐在爷爷身旁,听爷爷讲故事。

一帮人在楼下吵着讨债,不肯走,您去看看吧。(以讨债为目的组成的人群。)

(A gang of people are noisily demanding the payment of debts downstairs, and won't leave. Would you go and have a look?)

我们旁边又来了一帮卖水果的。(以卖水果为目的组成的人群。)

一伙人拦在路上,不许他们走。(以某目的组成的人群。)

一伙歹徒朝山里逃去了。(以为非作歹为目的组成的人群。)

2. "群"是中性词,没有褒贬色彩;"帮"、"伙"可以用于中性,也可以用于贬义(即用于不好的人),尤其是"伙"。("群" is a neutral word, neither commendatory nor derogatory. "帮" and "伙" can either be used in neutral terms or in derogatory terms, especially "伙".)例如:

一帮流氓　一帮强盗　一帮恶棍
一伙流氓　一伙强盗　一伙恶棍
一伙歹徒　一伙匪徒　一伙敌人

"帮"可以说"一帮客人"、"一帮同学"等,"伙"一般不用于这样的情况。"伙"用于中性词时,一般用于"人"或什么样的人。除此之外主要用于贬义。〔"帮" may be used in "一帮客人"(a group of guests), "一帮同学"(a group of schoolmates), etc. "伙" is not used in this sense. While used as a neutral word, "伙" is usually used to modify "人"(people) or a kind of people. Otherwise it is mainly used in derogatory sense.〕例如:

一伙人　一伙卖菜的　一伙打工的

此外,"帮"还有批次的意义。(In addition, "帮" also has

453

the meaning of batches)例如:

今天来了好几帮客人,刚走了一帮又来了一帮。

3."批"用于人时,也同样带有批次的意义,通常与进出有关,有动态意义。与"群"、"帮"、"伙"不同。(Different from "群","帮" and "伙", when used to modify people,"批" also has the meaning of batches, usually related to the act of coming and going, with dynamic sense.)例如:

我们学校今年毕业了一批博士研究生。

大陆来了一批有文化的人,提高了华人群体的文化素质。

(A group of cultured people coming from the mainland enhanced the cultural quality of the Chinese colony.)

＊我们学校今年毕业了一群/帮/伙博士研究生。

＊大陆来了一群/帮/伙有文化的人,提高了华人群体的文化素质。

(三)用法上也有差别(Differences in usage)

1."群"、"帮"、"伙"、"批"形式上都可以构成重叠方式。("群","帮","伙" and "批" can all be used in a reduplicated way.)例如:

一群一群 一群群 一帮一帮 一帮帮
一伙一伙 一伙伙 一批一批 一批批

也都可以构成指量词组。(And they can also constitute demonstrative measure word group.)例如:

这/那群 这/那帮 这/那伙 这/那批

2."群"、"帮"、"伙"、"批"这种表示集合量的量词,一般在数词和量词中间可以加上形容词"大"或"小"。但是,习惯上可以加"大"还是可以加"小",却有所不同。(Generally, adjectives "大" or "小" may be added between numerals and the collective words "群","帮","伙" and "批". But whether "大" or "小" is added is determined by the common usage.)例如:

(1)"群"通常可以加"大",而不加"小"。(Usually "大", not "小" is added before "群".)

　　一大群工人

　　* 一小群工人

(2)"帮"通常可以加"大",也可以加"小",但"小"用得少。(Either "大" or "小" may be added to "帮", but "小" is less used.)

　　来了一大帮学生 / 来了一小帮农民

(3)"伙"则通常可以加"小",而不加"大"。"小"也用得很少。(Generally, "小", not "大" is added to "伙". But even "小" is seldom used.)

　　一小伙歹徒朝西南流窜了。

　　* 一大伙歹徒

(4)"批"通常可以加"大",也可以加"小",但"小"用得少。(Either "大" or "小" may be added to "批", yet "小" is less used.)

　　购进了一大批新书　　只进了一小批货

R

然而 rán'ér　　反而 fǎn'ér

然而〈连词〉 < conjunction >
反而〈副词〉 < adverb >

(一) 功能不同 (Differences in function)

"然而"是连词,"反而"是副词,所以,"然而"可以用于主语前,"反而"不能用于主语前,只能用于谓语前。("然而" is a conjunction, while "反而" is an adverb. So "然而" may be placed before a subject, but "反而" may only be placed before a predicate.) 例如:

虽然失败了很多次,然而他并不灰心。

(Though having failed many times, he didn't lose heart.)

这次考试失败后,他不但没有灰心,反而更加努力了。

(Though failed in the exam, he didn't lose heart, but worked harder instead.)

年岁大了,身体反而更好了。

* 考试失败了,反而他更努力了。

* 年岁大了,反而身体更好了。

(二) 意义、用法不同 (Differences in meaning and usage)

"然而"只具有转折的意义和作用,常常与"虽然"呼应使用;"反而"除转折作用外,还有表示出乎意料、违反常情的意思。此外,"反而"还可以表示向相反的方向推进一步的意思,因此,它常常与"不但不/没"、"不仅不/ 没"呼应使用。("然而" is only used as a transition, often in concert with "虽然"."反而" not only is used as a transition, but also expresses the meaning of exceeding one's expectation or going against the common sense. Furthermore, it also means to develop to the opposite direction, so it is often used in concert with "不但不 / 没" or "不仅不 / 没".)例如:

虽然这里此时并不是春天,然而又有哪儿的春天比得上这里?

(Though it is not spring here, is there any spring elsewhere compared favourably with this place?)

虽然现在医学非常发达,然而对某些疑难病症仍然束手无策。

(Though medical science is very developed now, there are still some difficult and complicated cases remained unsolved.)

你太客气了,反而显得见外了。

(Please don't stand on ceremony, or I'll feel I'm being treated as a stranger.)

下了一阵雨,天气不仅没有凉下来,反而更加闷热了。

(A spatter of rain didn't make the weather cool. On the contrary, it was even muggier.)

这些活动不但不会影响学习,反而还会促进学习。

* 虽然现在医学非常发达,反而对某些疑难病症仍然束手无策。

* 你太客气了,然而显得见外了。

* 这些活动不但不会影响学习,然而还会促进学习。

热情 rèqíng　　热烈 rèliè

〈形容词〉 < adjective >

"热情"、"热烈"都具有"有热情"的意思,但是意义的着重点不同,适用的范围也有较大差别。(Both "热情" and "热烈" may mean enthusiastic, but their emphases in meaning are different, and their application is also quite different.)

(一) 意义及适用范围上 (In meaning and application)

1. "热情"主要是形容人有热烈的感情,所以它较多地用于形容有热烈感情的人,或表现人具有热烈感情的言行举止等。("热情" is used to describe a person's warm feeling. So it is usually

used to describe a man with enthusiasm, or one's enthusiastic behavior.)例如:

  主人很热情　接待我们的张经理十分热情
  中国朋友对我们非常热情
  热情的服务员　热情的读者　热情的观众
  热情的人们
  热情称赞这些白衣使者(enthusiastically praise these medical workers)
  热情讴歌我们伟大的祖国(enthusiastically eulogize our great country)
  热情地慰问了敬老院的老人们(convey warm greetings to the old people in the old folks' home)
  热情地招待了我们　热情地拉着他们的手
  热情地邀请他们来做客
  他们表现得十分热情　她的信写得无比热情

2."热烈"也可以形容人具有热烈感情的举止,但是情绪比"热情"要高涨,此外它还含有兴奋的、激动的情绪,所以多适用于充满了热烈感情的场面的环境。("热烈" can also be used to describe one's enthusiastic behavior, but the morale is higher than "热情". It also involves the feeling of excitement, so it is usually used in a situation that is full of warm feelings and enthusiasm.)例如:

  会场的气氛非常热烈　大家的发言十分热烈
  如此热烈的场面我第一次看到
  同学们讨论得十分热烈　大家争论得热烈极了
  联欢会进行得很热烈
  热烈的掌声　热烈的欢迎场面　热烈的情绪
  热烈的气氛
  热烈拥护　热烈支持　热烈祝贺　热烈欢迎
  热烈拥抱　热烈赞美

(二) 具体搭配上 (In specific collocations)

1.主语是人的,或中心语是人的,可以与"热情"组合,不能跟"热烈"组合。(If the subject or the central word is a person, it can go together with "热情", but not with "热烈".)例如:

* 主人很热烈 * 接待我们的张经理十分热烈
* 中国朋友对我们非常热烈
* 热烈的服务员 * 热烈的读者 * 热烈的人们
* 热烈的乡亲们

2.表示以某种态度对待的行为,一般不用"热烈"。(Generally "热烈" is not used to express an act to approach with certain attitude.)例如:

* 热烈地款待了我们 * 热烈地拉着他们的手
* 热烈地邀请他们来做客

3."场面"、"气氛"等一般不能跟"热情"组合。(Words like "场面(scene)" and "气氛(atmosphere)" are generally not used together with "热情".)例如:

* 会场的气氛非常热情
* 如此热情的场面我第一次看到 * 热情的气氛

4.讨论、争论等具有激动情绪的活动,一般不用"热情"描写。(Generally "热情" is not used to describe exciting activities such as discussions and disputes.)例如:

* 同学们讨论得十分热情。 * 大家争论得热情极了。

S

身体 shēntǐ　　身材 shēncái
身子 shēnzi　　个子 gèzi

〈名词〉 < noun >

"身体"、"身材"和"身子"、"个子"有时都可以指人的身躯。(They can all be used to indicate one's body.)例如：

他的身体条件很好，可以做舞蹈演员。

突然她的身体失去了平衡，从平衡木上掉了下来。

(Suddenly she lost her balance, and fell off from the balance beam.)

他身材很高大，眼睛也很有神。

他身材真好。

把身子挺直了，别那么无精打采的。

(Straighten up! Don't be so listless.)

你把身子蜷起来干什么？

(Why are you curling up?)

他的个子是我们班最高的一个。

个子高矮不是关键，关键在于有没有精神。

(It's not one's height, but one's spirit that really counts.)

但是它们有时所指范围各有侧重。(But sometimes they refer to different parts in particular.)

(一)"身体"主要是指人或动物生理组织的整体，不光指外形，还包括生理组织内部怎么样。("身体" refers to the body of a man or an animal, not only the outward shape, but also the inner physiological organizations.)例如：

他最近身体很不好，医生建议他住院治疗一段时间。

生命在于运动，经常锻炼身体，身体才会健康。

因此它在词语搭配上常常有：(So it is usually used in such

collocations:)
>   身体素质　　　身体健康　　　身体不舒服
>   身体恢复得很不错(recover very well from one's illness)

"身子"有时也可以指身体怎么样,只是口语色彩很浓。("身子" is sometimes used to indicate how one's health is. It is of strong flavor of the spoken language.)例如:

> 你怎么了?身子不舒服吗?

"身子"有时还专指妇女怀孕。("身子" sometimes refers in particular to women's pregnancies.)例如:

> 她已经有身子了,你多照顾她点儿。
> 听说她已经有五个月的身子了,怎么一点儿也看不出来。
> (It's said that she is five months' pregnant. However, she doesn't look like that at all.)

"身子"口语色彩重,只通用于口语,所以不能说"身子素质"、"身子健康"。("身子" is more used in spoken language, so it is not appropriate to say "身子素质" or "身子健康".)

"身材"、"个子"没有生理组织内部怎么样的意思,不能用于这一方面。("身材" and "个子" have nothing to do with one's inner physiological organizations, so they are not used in the same way as "身体".)例如:

> * 他最近身材很不好,医生建议他住院治疗一段时间。
> * 生命在于运动,经常锻炼身材,身材才会健康。
> * 身材素质　* 身材健康　* 身材不舒服
> * 身材恢复得很不错

(二)"身材"主要表示人身体的外形,侧重于表示人的高矮和胖瘦。只能用于人,一般不用于动物。("身材" emphasizes one's physical stature. It is only used to describe human, not animals.)

1.表示女性身材很好的,通常用"苗条"表示。("苗条" is usually used to describe a woman beautifully built.)例如:

她身材很苗条,样子也挺俊俏。
(She is slender and looks pretty.)
这姑娘,身材多苗条啊!

2. 表示男性身材很好的通常用"魁梧"、"高大"等表示。("魁梧","高大", etc. are often used to describe a man of good stature.)例如:

他是一个身材高大的男人。
他魁梧高大,眉宇不凡。
(He is big and tall, having an imposing appearance.)

3. 经常用以描写身材的还有以下词语。(The following are some other words usually used to describe a person's stature.)

(1)好的身材的描写(description of good figure):
身材匀称(to be of proportional build) 身材很好
身材修长(have a slender figure) 身材秀美

(2)不好的身材的描写(description of poor figure):
身材矮小 身材矮胖(short and fat stature)
身材肥胖 身材瘦小

(3)一般状态的身材的描写(description of average figure):
身材一般 身材细长 中等身材

4. 只表示人身体外观高矮胖瘦情况的,一般不要用"身体"。(Generally "身体" is not used to describe only the outward condition of one's body.)例如:

* 她身体很苗条,样子也挺俊俏。
* 这姑娘身体多苗条啊!
* 他是一个中等身体的男人。

(三)"个子"对于人来说主要侧重于身体外形的长短,对于动物来说,主要指长短或大小。一般用"高"、"矮"或"大"、"小"来描写。〔"个子" stresses on the height as far as man is concerned. As for an animal, the word refers to its length or size. Generally, "高"(tall), "矮"(short), "大"(big), or "小"(small) are used to describe

"个子"。]例如：

> 我第一次看到个子这么高的人。
> 个子矮的在前头,个子高的在后头。
> 这个小象才一岁,个子就那么大了。

时代 shídài　　年代 niándài

〈名词〉表示一段时间。(< noun > Indicating a period of time.)

(一)"时代"专指具有历史发展特征的某一段时间,而且时间较长。"年代"则指某几年内,或指年月、岁月,多用于不太长的一段时间。("时代" refers in particular to a period of time with the feature of historical development, a relatively long period of time. "年代" refers to a shorter period of time, perhaps within several years, or refers to years of time.)例如：

> 封建时代(feudal times)
> 文艺复兴时代(the Renaissance)
> 信息时代(the information epoch)
> 新时代(the new era)
> 战争年代(during the years of war)
> 在我厂经济困难的年代里(during the years when our factory was in economic difficulty)
> 最艰苦的年代(the most difficult years)
> * 封建年代　　　* 文艺复兴年代
> * 信息年代　　　* 新年代
> * 战争时代　　　* 在我厂经济困难的时代里
> * 最艰苦的时代

(二)"年代"还可表示每一世纪中从"……0"到"……9"的 10 年,称为"~年代"。例如:1980~1989 是 20 世纪 80 年代。"时代"没有这一意义。("年代" can also indicate a decade in a century, written as "~年代". For example: 1980~1989 is called the eighth decade in the 20th century. But "时代" cannot be used in this sense.)例如：

19 世纪 20 年代　　20 世纪 90 年代
他是 30 年代的作家。
50 年代初期的事我还记得清清楚楚。
(I still clearly remember the things in the early fifties.)
* 30 时代　　* 50 时代

(三)"时代"还可以用于生理或受教育过程的某发展阶段。"年代"没有这种用法。("时代" can also refer to a stage of physiological development or educational process. "年代" cannot be used in this sense.)例如：

儿童时代　　　青年时代
中学时代　　　大学时代
* 儿童年代　　* 青年年代
* 中学年代　　* 大学年代

(四)"时代"可以用来比喻前进着的历史潮流,也可以用于比拟。"年代"没有这种用法。("时代" can be used as a metaphor for the advancing historical trend, or to draw a parallel between two things. "年代" cannot be used in this sense.) 例如：

时代的洪流(the powerful current of the times)
时代的巨轮 (the wheel of the times)
* 年代的洪流　　* 年代的巨轮
时代在召唤(The time is calling.)
时代赋予我们历史的重任(The time entrusts us with the important historical task.)
* 年代在召唤　　* 年代赋予我们历史的重任

时代 shídài　　时期 shíqī

〈名词〉表示一段时间。(< noun > indicating a period of time.)

464

(一)"时代"、"时期"都可以用来表示一段较长的时间,但是范围不完全相同。"时代"多用来指以政治、经济、文化等状况为依据而划分的一个阶段,或指个人生命中、受教育过程的某一阶段;"时期"则指具有某具体特征的一段时间。"时期"前可以有政治、经济等方面特征的修饰语,也可以有非政治、经济等断代意义的修饰语,以具体的修饰语表示这一段时间的具体特征。(Both "时代" and "时期" can express a long period of time, but somewhat different in category. "时代" is more used to indicate a period differentiated according to political, economical and cultural situations, or a period in one's life or one's educational process. "时期" indicates a period of time with specific features. The word "时期" may have modifiers describing the political or economical features of the period, or modifiers of division of historical periods in front of it, namely to use specific modifiers to describe the specific features of such periods.)例如:

  石器时代(the Stone Age)
  封建时代(the feudal age)
  明清时代(the times of Ming and Qing dynasties)
  信息时代 儿童时代 少女时代
  青年时代 黄金时代 学生时代
  政治、经济鼎盛的时期 三年困难时期
  经济蓬勃发展时期   和平时期

"时期"也可以表示以人的生命过程或经历为具体特征的一段时间。("时期" can also indicate a period of time with specific features of a person's life experience.)例如:

  孩童时期 中年时期 老年时期
  长身体时期 自我调整时期 发展时期

(二)"时代"只指较长的一段时间;"时期"则可长可短,可以用于不太长的一段时间。("时代" only refers to a long period of time; while the time indicated by "时期" may be long or short, or

middle-lengthed.)例如:
前几年,我还做了一个时期的妇女工作。
秋收起义时期,我还参加了这里的农民运动。
(In the period of the Autumn Harvest Uprising, I also took part in the peasant movement here.)
* 前几年,我还做了一个时代的妇女工作。
* 秋收起义时代,我还参加了这里的农民运动。

(三)"时代"作为大的特定的历史阶段,可以提出要求,赋予使命,"时期"没有这一用法。"时代"可以单用;"时期"一般不单用,通常需要与表示具体特征的修饰语组合后才能用。("时代", as a specific long historical period, may set a demand, or entrust a task; while "时期" is not used so. "时代" can be used alone, but "时期" is usually used together with modifiers indicating the specific features.)例如:

时代向我们提出更高的要求。
(The times set a still higher demand on us.)
时代赋予我们历史重任。
(The age entrusts us with the important historical task.)
要不断学习,以赶上时代的要求。
(Keep study to keep abreast of the times.)
时代不同了,男女都一样。
* 时期向我们提出更高的要求。
* 时期赋予我们历史重任。
* 要不断学习,以赶上时期的要求。
* 时期不同了,男女都一样。
这一时期的锻炼很有效果。
我们终于从困难时期走过来了。
* 时期的锻炼很有效果。
* 我们终于从时期走过来了。

时候 shíhou   时 shí

〈名词〉表示时间里的某一点或有起止点的某一段时间。
(<noun> indicating an appointed time or a period of time having definite beginning and ending points.)

(一) "时候"、"时"都可以表示时间里的某一点或有起止点的某一段时间。(Both "时候" and "时" can indicate an appointed time, or a period of time having definite beginning and ending points.)

1. 表示时间里的某一点时间。(Indicating a point in time.)

到时候了,该说说了。

(It's time to say something.)

现在什么时候了?

吃饭时,一定叫我。

见到他时,我激动得不知说什么才好。

(At the sight of him, I was so excited that I didn't know what to say.)

2. 表示有起止的某一段时间。(Indicating a period of time having definite beginning and ending points.)

在家乡的时候,我还小,不太懂得这些事情。

我在美国读书的时候认识他的。

上小学时,我就读过这几部名著。

(二) "时候"、"时"用法上的不同之处。(The differences of "时候" and "时" in their usage.)

1. "时"有书面语色彩,多用于书面语;"时候"则通用于口语和书面语。"时候"可以单独用作主语、宾语,也可以构成"……的时候"、"在/当……的时候"的格式作状语;"时"不能单用,多构成"……时"、"在/当……时"的格式作状语。("时" has literary flavor and is more used in written language; "时候" is used both in spoken and written language. "时候" can be used as a subject or object by itself, or forms structures like "…的时候", "在／当…时候" to serve as adverbials. "时" cannot be used alone, but usually forms "…时",

467

"在／当…时" to serve as adverbials.)

时候到了,组织队伍出发!

你真勤快,简直没有闲着的时候。

(You are really diligent and keep yourself busy all the time.)

上大学的时候,他们就恋爱了。

刚来的时候,我谁也不认识。

下班时,我在门前等你。

考试时,不要交头接耳。

(Don't whisper to each other while taking examinations.)

她好像很喜欢细雨,每当细雨蒙蒙时,总能看到她的身影。

(She seems to like fine rain. Every time it drizzles, you can see her figure.)

2. "时候"构成"……时候"或"在/当……时候"时,"时候"前必须用"的",但是与"这"、"那"、"古"等少数单音节修饰语结合时不能用"的";"时"构成"……时"、"在/当……时"时,"时"前都不能用"的"。(When "时候" forms structure "…时候" or "在/当…时候", it should have "的" in front of it, but when it is combined with some monosyllabic words such as "这", "那", "古", no "的" is used before it. When "时" forms the structure "…时" or "在/当…时", it should not have "的" in front of it.)例如:

古代的时候人们就会制作这种茶。

* 古代时候人们就会制作这种茶。

刚来的时候,我谁也不认识。

走的时候你招呼我一声。

* 刚来时候,我谁也不认识。

* 走时候你招呼我一声。

* 她好像很喜欢细雨,每当细雨蒙蒙时候,总能看到她的身影。

468

古时候人们就会制作这种茶。
　　那时候生活有多难啊!
　　* 古的时候人们就会制作这种茶。
　　* 那的时候生活有多难啊!
　　初到中国时,幸亏有你帮助我。
　　上课时要注意听讲。
　　* 初到中国的时,幸亏有你帮助我。
　　* 上课的时要注意听讲。
　　* 她好像很喜欢细雨,每当细雨蒙蒙的时,总能看到她的身影。

时候 shíhou　　时间 shíjiān　　时刻 shíkè

〈名词〉表示某一点或某一段时间。(< noun > Indicating a moment or a period of time.)

(一)"时候"与"时间"

1. 表示某一点时间。(Indicating a moment of time.)

(1)"时候"、"时间"有时可以通用,所不同的是"时候"有较浓的口语色彩。("时候" and "时间" are sometimes interchangeable, only that "时候" has stronger spoken language flavor.)例如:
　　时候/时间不早了,我该走了。
　　现在什么时候/时间了?

(2)当所指的是已经确定了的时间时,要用"时间"。(When the time indicated is definite, "时间" is used.)例如:
　　不要忘了集合的时间和地点。
　　把开会的时间通知下去。
　　我利用这个时间说几句话。
　　* 不要忘了集合的时候和地点。
　　* 把开会的时候通知下去。
　　* 我利用这个时候说几句话。

(3)有具体特征的时间用"时候",前面通常有表示具体特征

469

的修饰语。("时候" is used to indicate a specific time, usually with modifiers indicating the specific features in front of it.)例如：

乐曲奏起的时候(when the music is played)
眼睛瞥向她的时候(when the eyes shot a glance at her)
天蒙蒙亮的时候(at daybreak)
* 乐曲奏起的时间　　　* 眼睛瞥向她的时间
* 天蒙蒙亮的时间

2. 表示某一段时间。(Indicating a period of time.)

"时候"所指的时段长度界限模糊，其前通常有表示该时段具体特征的修饰语；"时间"所指的时段长度界限明确，其前后通常有表示具体钟点或日期的时间。(The length of time indicated by "时候" is not definite, usually with modifiers expressing the specific features of the period in front of the time. The length of time indicated by "时间" is definite, usually with modifiers expressing a specific time or date in front of or after it.)例如：

放假的时候　　　秋收的时候
忙的时候　　　　那时候
整整一天的时间，你干什么了。
下午三点到五点为体育活动时间。
他只用了一个小时的时间。
给我五分钟的时间就够了。
* 忙的时间，你不要来找我。
* 那时间我们都还小。
* 这张卷子他只用了一个小时的时候就做完了。
* 给我五分钟的时候就够了。

3. 结构上的差异：(Difference in structure:)

(1) 其前有表示时间特征的词语、时间名词或表示时点的时间时，用"时候"；有表示时段的时间时用"时间"。(When there are words indicating the features of time, nouns denoting time, or time indicating the minute or hour in front, "时候" is used. When there is

a time phrase indicating a period of time, "时间" is used.) 例如:

<u>开学</u>的时候　　　　<u>傍晚</u>的时候
<u>月圆</u>的时候　　　　<u>三点</u>的时候
<u>两个小时</u>的时间　　<u>一个假期</u>的时间
<u>整整一夜</u>的时间　　<u>那么长</u>的时间

* 月圆的时间,我们常去海边散步。

* 他们用了一个月的时候,去农村搞调查。

(2)"时间"可以接受专用数量词的修饰;"时候"不能。("时间" can be modified by specific numeral-classifier compounds, but "时候" can't.)

一段时间

* 一段时候

4."时间"还可表示空闲时间的意思,"时候"没有这种意思。("时间" can also indicate a spare time, but "时候" can't.)

有时间的话,咱们坐下来聊聊。

(If you have time, come to sit down and have a chat with me.)

我有的是时间,可以帮帮你。

* 有时候的话,咱们坐下来聊聊。

* 我有的是时候,可以帮帮你。

(二)"时刻"与"时候"、"时间"

1."时刻"表示某一特定的、短暂的时间。"时候"、"时间"不能用于这种时候。"时刻"特定的时间意义,要求它前面一定要有修饰限制语。(Unlike "时候" and "时间", "时刻" indicates a particular, temporary time. The specific meaning of "时刻" requires modifiers in front of it.) 例如:

在<u>这千钧一发的关键</u>时刻,他站了出来。

(At this critical moment he stood out.)

这是<u>她渴望已久的幸福</u>时刻。

在他<u>生命的最后</u>时刻,他想到的还是人民的利益。

471

<u>五星红旗升起的那一时刻</u>,她激动得流下了热泪。

在<u>火车就要被惊马颠覆的危急</u>时刻,欧阳海冲上去推开了战马。

(At the critical moment when the train was going to be overturned by the startled horse, Ouyang Hai rushed forward and pushed the war-horse aside.)

* 在这千钧一发的关键时候/时间,他站了出来。

* 这是她渴望已久的幸福时候/时间。

2."时刻"不能接受数量词语的修饰。("时刻" cannot be modified by numeral-classifier compounds.)

* 一段时刻　　* 十二点时刻　　* 两分钟时刻

时机 shíjī　　机会 jīhuì

〈名词〉指恰好的或有利的时候。(<noun> indicating just the right time or opportune time.)

"时机"和"机会"都有恰好的或有利的时候的意思,但是意义的着重点不同,搭配上也有所不同。(Both "时机" and "机会" may indicate at the right or opportune time, but have different emphases in meaning, and have different collocations.)

(一) 意义上 (In meaning)

"时机"着重于时间上的某种有利的客观条件;"机会"则指时间本身,它是指恰到好处的某一个时候。("时机" emphasizes some favorable conditions of a moment. "机会" refers to the moment itself, namely just the right moment.)例如:

不失时机地抓好春播春种工作。

(Seize the opportune moment to start spring sowing and ploughing.)

谈判的时机还不成熟。

(The time for negotiation is not yet ripe.)

起义的时机已经来到了。

我有一个去南方开会的机会。

找机会我们好好谈一谈。

我想趁这个机会说两句话。

(I want to avail myself of the opportunity to say a few words.)

(二) 搭配上 (In collocation)

1. 因为"时机"侧重于时间上的客观条件,所以搭配上常常有:(Since "时机" emphasizes the objective conditions of the time, it usually has such collocations as:)

时机成熟(The time is ripe)

不失时机(lose no time)

把握时机(seize the opportunity)

掌握时机(grasp the opportunity)

错过时机(miss the chance)

等待时机(wait for an opportunity)

正是时机(at the right moment)

有利的时机　大好时机　合适的时机

2. "机会"是一个恰到好处的时候,有偶然性和不易得到的特点,所以搭配上常常有:("机会" means just the right moment, characterized by fortuity and rarity, so it usually has such collocations as:)

难得的机会　好机会　偶然的机会

合适的机会　不少机会

得到机会　抓住机会　看准机会

找机会　　碰机会

提供机会　放弃机会

(1) 有些只属于条件方面的搭配词,就不适合跟"机会"搭配。(Some collocations only indicating conditions are not suitable to go together with "机会".) 例如:

＊不失机会地抓好春播春种工作。

473

* 谈判的机会还不成熟。

* 起义的机会已经来到了。

(2)有些常与"机会"搭配的词也不适合用于"时机"。(Some commonly used collocations of "机会" are not fit for "时机".)例如：

* 我有一个去南方开会的时机。

* 找时机我们好好谈一谈。

* 我想趁这个时机说两句话。

* 他放弃了这次出国深造的时机。

3. "机会"还可以跟介词"趁"搭配，组成"趁……机会"的词组，也可以说"趁机"；"时机"一般没有这种用法。("机会" can also be used with the preposition "趁", forming "趁…机会" or "趁机". Generally "时机" cannot be used so.)例如：

趁来中国旅游的机会，学一点儿汉语。

趁这个机会帮帮他。

* 趁来中国旅游的时机，学一点儿汉语。

* 趁这个时机帮帮他。

4. "机会"常与量词"个"、"次"、"种"等组成"数+量+名"或"指示代词+量+名"词组；"时机"大多场合不与量词组合，个别时候可与"个"组合。("机会" is usually used with measure words "个"，"次"，"种", etc., forming phrases like "numeral + classifier + noun" or "demonstrative pronoun + classifier + noun". "时机" cannot be used with such measure words in most cases. It may occasionally be combined with "个".)例如：

一次去学习的机会　　这个机会很难得

这种机会并不多

* 一次去学习的时机　* 这种时机并不多

一个很有利的时机

事 shì　　事情 shìqing　　事件 shìjiàn　　事故 shìgù

〈名词〉指人类生活中的活动或社会现象。(<noun> indicating activities in human life or social phenomena.)

(一) "事"与"事情"

"事"与"事情"都指人类生活中普通的活动或社会现象,意义很接近,但是用法有较大差别。(Both "事" and "事情" indicate ordinary activities in human life, or social phenomena, very close in meaning, but quite different in usage.)

1. 意义上 (In meaning)

"事"的意义范围比"事情"大。(The meaning of "事" is wider than that of "事情".)

(1) "事"可以表示职业、工作的意思;"事情"一般不表示这种意思。("事" may indicate occupation or work, but "事情" generally does not have this sense.) 例如:

退了休,在家里闲着没事做,怪没意思的。

(After retiring, I stayed at home with nothing to do and felt rather bored.)

让老板在公司里给你安排个事做做吧。

(2) "事"还可以表示意外的灾祸的意思;"事情"不表示这种意思。("事" may indicate accident. "事情" cannot.) 例如:

听说老张的儿子在工厂里出事了。

天黑路滑,开车要小心,千万别出事!

(It's dark, and the road is slippery. Be careful when driving. Be sure not to have an accident.)

你放心吧! 他已经没事了。

* 听说老张的儿子在工厂里出事情了。

* 天黑路滑,开车要小心,千万别出事情!

* 你放心吧! 他已经没事情了。

2. 语体色彩上 (In flavor)

"事"带有较强的口语色彩;"事情"则多用于书面语。("事"

475

has a strong spoken language flavor, while "事情" is more used in written language.)例如:

有什么事说一声,大家都会帮助你的。

事情来得太突然了,我们一点儿心理准备也没有。

(It happened too unexpectedly. We haven't got least prepared psychologically.)

3.结构上(In structure)

(1) 有单音修饰限制语时,一般用"事",很少用"事情"。(When monosyllabic restrictive words are used as modifiers, generally "事", not "事情" is used.)例如:

大事小事你都管,你管得了吗?

* 大事情小事情你都管,你管得了吗?

好事他也做了,坏事他也做了。

* 好事情他也做了,坏事情他也做了。

我有点儿私事要办,下午请半天假可以吗?

* 我有点儿私事情要办,下午请半天假可以吗?

这事我做不了主,你得找主任说去。

* 这事情我做不了主,你得找主任说去。

(2) 用"有"或"没(有)"作谓语时,宾语一般要用"事",不用"事情"。〔When "有" or "没(有)" is used as a predicate, the object is usually "事", not "事情".〕例如:

你下午有事吗?——没事啊。

* 你下午有事情吗?——没事情啊。

没事去一边去,别在这儿捣乱!

(Stay away from here if you have nothing to do. Don't disturb us here.)

* 没事情去一边去,别在这儿捣乱!

(3) 组成成语等时,要用"事",不用"事情"。(Use "事", not "事情", to form idioms.)例如:

实事求是(seek truth from facts.)

476

万事如意(Everything turns out as one wishes.)
平安无事(All is well.)
万事俱备,只欠东风(Everything is ready, and all that we need is east wind——All is ready except what is crucial.)

(4) 单独用来作句子成分时,用"事情",一般不用"事"。(When used alone as a sentence component, "事情" is used.)例如:

请你把事情的经过详细地谈一谈。
事情总归要一件一件地做。
事情好像并不像你说的那么简单。
(Things don't seem so simple as you've said.)
你去了解一下事情的全部经过。
* 请你把事的经过详细地谈一谈。
* 事好像并不像你说的那么简单。
* 你去了解一下事的全部经过。

(二) "事情"、"事件"、"事故"

"事情"是就一般的、普通的生活中的活动或社会现象而言的;"事件"、"事故"则是指生活中特别的活动或社会现象而言的。("事情" refers to general or common happenings in life or social phenomena. "事件" and "事故" refer to particular happenings in life or social phenomena.)

"事件"通常指已经发生的历史上或社会上不寻常、不普通的大的事情。("事件" usually refers to unusual or uncommon big events having happened in history or in society.)例如:

政治事件 历史事件 重大事件
水门事件 核泄漏事件 卢沟桥事件

"事故"则特指在生产、工作、交通中等发生的意外的灾祸。("事故" usually refers to unexpected accidents or disasters that happen in production, at work, or in traffic.)例如:

据说,这场火灾事故是由一个烟头引起的。
他进入工地时,没戴安全帽,才发生了这次恶性事故。

酒后开车容易发生交通事故。

"事故"通常有人为的因素,自然灾害一般不用"事故"。例如:洪水、地震、台风、冰雹等,虽然是灾祸,但是不能用"事故"。不能说洪水事故、地震事故、台风事故、冰雹事故等,因为它们是大自然中的自然现象,没有人为的因素,这些现象要称为"灾害"。〔"事故" usually involves man-made factors. It cannot be used to describe natural disasters. For example, though flood, earthquake, typhoon, and hailstones are disasters, we cannot use "事故" to express them. We cannot say "flood accident", "earthquake accident", "typhoon accident" or "hailstone accident", because they are all natural phenomena in the nature, without man-made factors. Those phenomena are called "灾害(disasters)".〕

送 sòng　　送行 sòngxíng　　送别 sòngbié

〈动词〉 <verb>

"送"、"送行"、"送别"都可以表示到启程的地方,与人告别,看人离开的意思。("送","送行" and "送别" can all indicate coming to the place where somebody is going to start a journey, bidding farewell to him and watching him leave.)例如:

明天早上,我去火车站送你们。

刚才我去火车站为朋友送行了。

我含着泪,一一送别了我的朋友。

但是除少数作定语的情况外,一般不能换用。(But except being used as attributes, which is not often, they are generally not exchangeable.)主要差别有:

(一)意义范围不同 (Differences in meaning)

1."送"除了表示到启程的地方,与人告别,看人离开的意思外,还可以表示陪着离去的人一起走的意思;"送行"、"送别"没有这种意思。(Besides expressing the above meaning, "送" also indicates accompanying the person who is going to leave for some place.

"送行" and "送别" do not express this sense.)例如:
>外面太黑了,让老李送送你。
>我把他一直送到车站才回来。
>今天我有事儿,你送孩子去幼儿园吧。
>* 外面太黑了,让老李送行/送别你。
>* 我把他一直送行/送别到车站才回来。
>* 今天我有事儿,你送行/送别孩子去幼儿园吧。

2."送行"除了表示到启程的地方,与人告别,看人离开的意思外,还可以表示"饯行"的意思,即并不是到启程的地方,而是在某处为送行而设酒席请吃饭;"送"、"送别"没有这种意思。(Besides expressing the above meaning, "送行" also indicates "give a farewell dinner", namely, not going to the place where someone is going to set off, but giving a farewell dinner elsewhere. "送" and "送别" do not have this sense.)例如:
>今天晚上,在餐厅举行宴会,为离开天津的同学送行。
>周末去我那儿聚聚吧,就算是为小刘赴美送行了。
>(Let's get together in my home during the weekend to give a send-off party for Xiao Liu's going to America.)
>* 今天晚上,在餐厅举行宴会,为离开天津的同学送/送别。
>* 周末去我那儿聚聚吧,就算是为小刘赴美送/送别了。

3."送别"只表示到启程的地方,与人告别,看人离开的意思。("送别" only means to be at the place where someone is going to leave, bid farewell, and see him off.)例如:
>我送别了所有的同学,才返回了学校。
>送别朋友后,我立刻安下心来,开始工作。

(二) 结构形式不同 (Differences in structure)

1."送"后边一般要带上宾语——被送人,基本格式一般有两种:("送" is usually followed by an object—the person(s) being sent off. The basic patterns are:)

(1)"送+宾语"("送 + object")

  来,我送送你。

  她害怕,谁去送她一下。

(2)"送+宾语+动词+要去的场所"("送 + object + verb + the place to go")

  奶奶天天送小孙子上学。

  路不熟没关系,我送你去车站。

2."送行"后边不能带宾语。它的基本格式通常是:("送行" is not followed by any object. Its basic pattern is:)

"为+被送人+送行"("为 + the person(s) being sent off + 送行")

  不管我有多忙,一定抽时间为你送行。

  (No matter how busy I am, I'll surely manage to find time to see you off.)

  这么多人来为我送行,我真高兴啊!

  * 不管我有多忙,一定抽时间送行你。

  * 这么多人来送行我,我真高兴啊!

3."送别"后边可以带宾语,但是它一般用于完成时,常用的格式为:("送别" can be followed by objects, but it is usually used in perfect tense. Its basic pattern is:)

"送别+(了)+宾语"("送别 + (了) + object")

  送别了朋友,她一个人难过了好半天。

  (She has been sad for a long time after she sent her friends off.)

  送别父母以后,他满怀信心地踏上了征程。

4."送别"不能构成"送+宾语+动词+要去的场所"这种格式。("送别" cannot form "送 + object + verb + the place to go" pattern.)例如:

  * 他送别朋友去车站。

480

* 他们送别几个日本同学回国。

5."送"后边还可以接补语;"送行"、"送别"后边不可以。("送" can also be followed by a complement; "送行" and "送别" cannot.)例如:

妈妈送了我<u>好长一段路</u>。

启程那天,乡亲们为我送行,他们送了<u>一程又一程</u>。

(The day I started on my journey, the villagers sent me off. They accompanied me league after league before parting.)

下星期我出差,送<u>不了</u>你了。

他把孩子送<u>过了</u>马路。

* 妈妈送行/送别了我好长一段路。

* 启程那天,乡亲们为我送行,他们送行/送别了一程又一程。

* 下星期我出差,送行/送别不了你了。

(三) 文体色彩不同 (Difference in style)

比较起来,"送"口语色彩较重;"送别"书面语色彩较重。(Compared with "送", which is stronger in spoken language flavor, "送别" is more used in written language.)

随便 suíbiàn   顺便 shùnbiàn

随便〈形容词〉 < adjective >

顺便〈副词〉 < adverb >

(一)"随便"、"顺便"在意义上差别较大。(They are quite different in meaning.)

"随便"主要指对于范围、数量等不加以限制或者怎么方便怎么做,不多加考虑。总之它的意义的核心就是"比较自由",做什么、涉及哪些方面、采取什么方式、有多少数量等等是自由的,目的性或制约性是不强的。"顺便"的意义核心是"不是专门的",它是指在专做某事的时候,乘做这件事的方便去做另一件事。("随便" means not to be restricted in range or in number, or to do what one likes without much consideration. In general, its principle meaning is "free", what to do, in what aspect(s), in what way, how many (much), etc. are all decided carelessly, or depend on oneself, without much purpose or restriction. The basic meaning of "顺便" is "not specially". It means to do some other thing in passing while specially doing something.)例如：

"随便"：

咱们随便谈谈。〔谈什么没有限制（without restriction as what to talk）。〕

我只是随便转转,不一定买东西。〔想去哪儿或想看什么没有目标,不加限制（without definite purpose as where to go or what to see）。〕

随便吃,别客气。〔想吃什么或吃多少没有限制（without restriction as what to eat or how much one eats.）。〕

这些书我们班的学生也想要,随便分给我们几本行吗？〔数量上不加限制（not explicit in number）。〕

说什么、做什么不能那么随随便便的。〔怎么方便怎么做,不多加考虑（to do as one likes without much consideration）。〕

"顺便"：

出来办事,路过这里,顺便进来看看你。〔乘办事路过此地的方便（at one's convenience when one is passing by the place）。〕

你去邮局顺便替我发一封信好吗？〔乘去邮局办事的方便（at one's convenience of doing something in the post-office）。〕

你去见他,顺便代我向他问好。〔乘见他的方便（at your convenience of seeing him）。〕

你去买报的时候,顺便看一看这一期的《读者》来没来。〔乘买报的方便（at your convenience of buying newspapers）。〕

(二) 用法上的差异：(Difference in usage.)

1."随便"可以构成 AABB 的重叠式，"顺便"不可以。("随便" can form the AABB reduplicated pattern, but "顺便" cannot.)

  他说话总是随随便便的。
  你看他那随随便便的样子，真让人受不了。
  (Look at his slipshod manner. It's really unbearable.)

2."随便"可以接受程度副词的修饰，"顺便"不可以。("随便" can be modified by adverbs of degree, but "顺便" cannot.)

  这孩子太随便了，太缺少教养了。
  (The child is too careless. He really lacks cultivation.)
  他到我这儿来特别随便。
  * 他到我这儿来特别顺便。
  * 我去邮局很顺便给你发信。

3."随便"可以作谓语，"顺便"只能作状语，不能作谓语。("随便" can be used as a predicate. "顺便" can only be used as an adverbial.)例如：

  他这个人不拘小节，很随便的。
  (He is very careless, never bothering about trifles.)
  去他那儿随便一些，不要那么拘谨。
  (Make yourself at home while going to his place. Don't be so reserved.)
  没有什么麻烦的，我只是顺便来看看你。
  你们去西安办事的时候，顺便去看看兵马俑吧。
  * 没有什么麻烦的，我来看你很顺便。
  * 我们已经到了西安，去看看兵马俑很顺便的。

T

谈 tán   谈话 tánhuà   交谈 jiāotán

〈动词〉表示两个或多个人在一起说话。

(< verb > talk in pairs or groups.)

(一) 意义上 (In meaning)

"谈"、"谈话"、"交谈"都可以表示两个或多个人在一起说话,它们表示的说话,有时也可以不突出什么目的性,但是大多数场合则带有较强的目的性。("谈","谈话" and "交谈" can all express the meaning "talking in pairs or in groups". Sometimes the talk may not focus on anything special, but in most cases the talk focuses on a special topic.)例如:

不突出目的性 (not focus on anything special):

他们一边走,一边谈,不知不觉已经到了中午了。

我们谈话谈得正高兴,忽然一个人闯了进来。

(We were just at the height of our conversation when suddenly a man rushed in.)

他们正用英语愉快地交谈着。

目的性较强 (focus on a special topic):

我想跟领导谈谈这件事。

由我去跟老张谈吧。

主任要找小王谈话。

我们的谈话不能泄露出去。

(Our conversation cannot be revealed.)

关于项目的合作问题,他们正在交谈。

双方交谈了一个多小时了。

(二) 用法上 (In usage)

1. 相同之处:(Similarities:)

"谈"、"谈话"、"交谈"都可以表示两个或多个人在一起说话

484

的意思,所以它们往往要求动作者具有复数意义,尤其是"谈话"、"交谈"动作者只能是复数意义。通常有两种方式,一是句子的主语具有复数意义;一是主语加"跟"等介词词组,表示动作是两个或两个以上的人的动作。("谈","谈话" and "交谈" can all mean talk in pairs or in groups, and the doers are usually in plural forms, especially "谈话" and "交谈", the actors of which can only be plural ones. They are usually used in two patterns. One is that the subject is plural in meaning, the other is that the subject is followed by a prepositional phrase with "跟(with)", implying that the action involves two or more persons.)例如:

大家正在谈这起交通事故。

老孙正跟小王谈工作呢。

大家围坐在一起谈起话来。

厂长正在跟工人们谈话。

我们双方已经交谈五次了。

你们交谈得怎么样?

* 他谈起话来。
* 厂长正在谈话。
* 我已经交谈五次了。
* 你交谈得怎么样?

2. 不同之处:(Differences:)

(1)"谈"可以连带宾语,"交谈"、"谈话"不能连带宾语。"交谈"意义侧重于"交",即两个人或双方交互(谈)的方式;"谈话"则是动宾式构词方式,后面不能再带表人或表事宾语。("谈" can be followed by objects; "交谈" and "谈话" can't. The meaning of "交谈" lies in "交", the way in which the two people or two sides talk. "谈话" is a "verb + object" formation, not followed by any other person or thing as its object.)例如:

你们不要再在我面前谈张力了。

他们正在谈工作,别去打搅他们。

＊我们交谈一下张力吧。
　　＊他们正在交谈工作，别去打搅他们。
　　＊我们谈话一下张力吧。
　　＊他们正在谈话工作，别去打搅他们。

(2)"谈"、"交谈"后面可以直接接数量、情状等补语或"过"、"着"等时态助词；"谈话"不可以。"谈话"接这类补语或助词时，往往采取"谈"和"话"分离的方式，即把补语或助词放在"谈"和"话"之间。("谈" and "交谈" can be directly followed by a complement of numeral-classifier compounds or conditional words, or aspect particles, such as "过", "着", etc.; "谈话" can't be used so. When "谈话" is followed by complements or particles, "谈" and "话" are usually separated, namely, the complements or particles are put between "谈" and "话".)例如：

　　谈了<u>一晚上</u>　　　交谈了<u>一晚上</u>

　　＊谈话了一晚上

　　谈了<u>一晚上</u>话

　　我们谈过　　　　同学们正谈着

　　我们交谈过　　　他们亲切地交谈着

　　＊我们谈话过　　　＊同学们正谈话着

　　我们谈过话　　　他们正谈着话呢

(三) 其他 (Others)

1."谈"在意义上还可以表示评论、论述的意思，这时它的主语可以是单数。"交谈"、"谈话"没有这个意思。("谈" can also mean to discuss or comment. Its subject may be singular. "交谈" and "谈话" don't mean so.)例如：

　　我们请<u>李董事</u>谈谈公司目前经济发展的状况。

　　(We would like Director Li to talk about the present economic development of the company.)

486

大家就这个议题谈谈自己的看法吧。
(You may give your viewpoint on this topic.)
* 我们请李董事谈话公司目前经济发展的状况。
* 大家就这个议题谈话自己的看法。
* 我们请李董事交谈公司目前经济发展的状况。
* 大家就这个议题交谈自己的看法。

2."谈"还有"商谈"的意思,可以用于"谈价钱"、"谈条件"等;"交谈"、"谈话"没有这种意思和用法。〔"谈" can also mean negotiating, and can be used in "谈价钱"(haggle over the price),"谈条件"(negotiate the terms), etc. "交谈" and "谈话" don't have such a meaning and usage.〕

特意 tèyì　　专门 zhuānmén

特意〈副词〉 < adverb >
专门〈形容词〉 < adjective >

(一)"特意"和"专门"在意义上有相同的意思,都可以表示专为某事的意思,都可以用在谓语动词前作状语。但是,它们在意义的侧重点上稍有偏颇。"特意"着重于特别的,有强调的意味;"专门"着重于"专",表示集中在某一方面。("特意" and "专门" are similar in meaning, both indicating to do something specially and can both be placed before predicates as adverbials. But they have different emphases in meaning. "特意" means in particular, used for emphasis. "专门" focuses on "专", meaning concentrating on a certain aspect.)例如:

我特意来这里看你。
这件衣服是他特意买来给你做生日礼物的。
我专门为取这份材料来的。
他为了给您祝寿专门赶到这里。
(He came specially to congratulate you on your birthday.)

(二)"特意"和"专门"还有不同的意思。"专门"有专从事某一特定专业或门类的意思,"特意"一般不能用于这种情况。("特意" and "专门" have other different meanings. "专门" may mean specializing in a particular field or major. "特意" is seldom used in such a sense.)例如:
>他是专门从事计算机研究的专家。
>(He is an expert in computer research.)
>我是专门研究儿童心理学的。
>这次会我们专门研讨了汉字教学问题。
>* 他是特意从事计算机研究的专家。
>* 我是特意研究儿童心理学的。
>* 这次会我们特意研讨了汉字教学问题。

(三)功能上的差别(Difference in function)

"特意"只有副词用法,只能用在谓语动词前作状语;"专门"属于非谓形容词,它可以用在动词前作状语,但更多的是用在名词性词语前作定语。"特意"没有定语用法。("特意" is only used as an adverbial before the predicate. "专门" is a non-predicative adjective. It can be used in front of a predicate as an adverbial, but more often it is used before nouns as an attribute. "特意" cannot be used as an attribute.)例如:
>他是个不可多得的专门人才。
>(He is a rare person with professional skills.)
>这是培养医护人员的专门学校。
>这家文化用品的专门商店刚刚开业。
>关于这个问题,可以查看这里有关的专门规定。
>(With regard to this problem, you can refer to the relevant special rules here.)
>* 他是个不可多得的特意人才。
>* 这是培养医护人员的特意学校。
>* 这家文化用品的特意商店刚刚开业。
>* 关于这个问题,可以查看这里有关的特意规定。

天天 tiāntiān　　每天 měitiān
〈名词〉 < noun >

(一) 意义不完全相同：(They are not quite the same in meaning:)

"天天"只表示"逐一"的意思，是"一天 + 一天 + 一天……"的意思；"每天"则重在"每一"，即总体的天数中的任何一天。("天天" only indicates one day after another, namely "one day + one day + one day...". "每天" emphasizes "every", namely, any day of all the days.) 例如：

好好学习，天天向上。

＊好好学习，每天向上。

其中的"天天"含有"一天比一天"的意思，所以不能换用"每天"。(In this sentence, "天天" involves the meaning "each day is (better) than the previous day", so it cannot be replaced by "每天".)

她每天/天天都是六点起床。

这个句子用"每天"、"天天"都可以，意思上稍有差别。用"每天"表示许多天中，其中的任何一天都是如此；用"天天"表示所有的天中，无一例外的都是这样。(Here "每天" and "天天" are both acceptable, but slightly different in meaning. "每天" implies every day is the same as the other day. "天天" implies there is no exception.)

(二) 功能用法不同：(Differences in function:)

"天天"只用作状语，修饰动词、形容词，如果修饰名词的话，一般只限于时间名词，与之共同构成时间状语；"每天"既可以用作状语，修饰动词、形容词，又可以用作定语，修饰名词性词语。("天天" only serves as an adverbial, modifying verbs or adjectives. If ever modifying nouns, it only modifies nouns denoting time, together with which, it serves as an adverbial of time. "每天" can either be used as an adverbial, modifying verbs or adjectives, or as an attribute to modify nouns.) 例如：

这个星期天天下雨。(状语)
最近工作太忙,不能天天回家了。(状语)
天天晚上看电视可不行。(天天晚上 —— 状语)
她每天都得去幼儿园接孩子。(状语)
每天的日程都安排得很满。(定语)
(The programme for each day is fully arranged.)
这是他每天病情的记录。(定语)
* 天天的日程都安排得很满。(定语)
* 这是他天天病情的记录。(定语)

听 tīng　　听见 tīngjiàn

〈动词〉表示用耳朵接受信息。

(<verb> perceive with the ears.)

(一)"听"、"听见"都可以表示用耳朵接受信息,所不同的是,"听见"比"听"多了得到了所听信息的含义。(Both "听" and "听见" may mean to get information through the ears. The only difference is that "听见" also implies being able to get the meaning of what one has heard.)例如:

他正在听音乐。
我在听她说话呢。
这一部分听得怎么样?
我听见他的声音了。
你没听见妈妈在喊你吗?
我没听见歌声。

正因为这种意义上的差别,使得它们在使用上有一系列的不同。(Therefore, there are some differences in their usage.)

1."听"是持续性动词,"听见"是非持续性动词,所以"听"前面可以接受"正"、"在"、"正在"等副词的修饰,后面可以接助词"着",可以接持续的时段;"听见"不能这样用。("听" is a durative verb; while "听见" is not. So "听" can be modified by adverbs such as "正", "在", "正在", and followed by the particle "着", or a period of time. "听见" is not used so.)例如：

同学们正在听重要新闻。

＊ 同学们正在听见重要新闻。

听着老师和蔼可亲的话语,我心里感到无限温暖。

(Hearing the teacher's kind words, I felt immeasurably warm.)

＊ 听见着老师和蔼可亲的话语,我心里感到无限温暖。

你已经听了<u>两个多小时</u>音乐了。

＊ 你已经听见了两个多小时音乐了。

2. "听"可以用在表示请求、命令等的祈使句中；"听见"不能用于祈使句中。("听" can be used in an imperative sentence expressing requests or demands; "听见" is not used in imperative sentences.)例如：

妈妈快来听电话!

你耐心地听听他的要求吧!

都已经十二点了,别听了!

＊ 妈妈快来听见电话!

＊ 你耐心地听见他的要求吧!

＊ 都已经十二点了,别听见了!

3. "听见"的"见"已经表示了"听"的结果,所以"听见"后面不再接表示结果、情态类的补语；"听"可以。("见" in "听见" suggests the result of "听", so the verb "听见" is not followed by words expressing a result, or complement expressing moods; but "听" can.)例如：

＊ 你听见清楚了没有?

＊ 他听见得怎么样?

＊ 大家听见得十分认真。

你听<u>清楚</u>了没有?

491

他听得怎么样？

大家听得十分认真。

4."听见"只能用"没(有)"否定，不能用"不"否定；"听"用"没(有)"和"不"都能否定。("听见" can only be negated with "没有", not with "不". "听" can be negated either with "没有" or "不".)例如：

你说的话我一点儿也没听见。

他边走边听音乐,没听见喇叭声,差点儿撞了车。

(Listening to music while walking, he didn't hear the whistling of vehicles, and almost rushed into a car.)

* 你说的话我一点儿也不听见。

* 他边走边听音乐,不听见喇叭声,差点儿撞了车。

我下午不听录音了。

今天晚上没听新闻。

5."听见"中间加进"不"，构成"听不见"的形式时，跟在"听见"前加否定词否定"听见"的意义不同,它表示的是不能或不可能得到所听的信息的意义；"听不见"的肯定形式是"听得见"。(Adding "不" between "听见" to form "听不见" phrase is different from adding negative words before "听见" in meaning. The former indicates that it is impossible to get the meaning of what is heard. The affirmative form of "听不见" is "听得见".)例如：

A：他讲的话你听得见吗？（表示"能听见吗？"的意思。）

B：听不见。（表示"不能听见"的意思。）

6."听"可以重叠使用；"听见"不能重叠使用。("听" can be reduplicated. "听见" can't.)例如：

你听听他都说了些什么？

我们听听歌曲吧！

* 你听见听见他都说了些什么？

* 我们听见听见歌曲吧！

(二)"听"还有"听从"的意思;"听见"没有这个意思。("听" can also mean to agree to a suggestion, request, etc.; but "听见" doesn't mean so.)例如:

我劝了他好半天,他就是不听。

(I talked to him for a long time, but he just wouldn't listen.)

别人说什么他都听,没有一点儿自己的主见。

(He accepted whatever others said without any definite views of his own.)

你听他的准没错。

(You can be sure to listen to him.)

我听你的。

(I do your bidding.)

* 我劝了他好半天,他就是不听见。

* 别人说什么他都听见,没有一点儿自己的主见。

* 你听见他的准没错。

* 我听见你的。

通过 tōngguò   经过 jīngguò

〈介词〉以某人、某事或某活动为媒介,达到某种目的。

(< preposition > meaning to attain some goal through somebody, something or activities.)

〈动词〉经由某处所。(< verb > pass by some place.)

(一)"通过"和"经过"都可以用作介词,表示以某人、某事或某活动为媒介,达到某种目的的意思,意义极为接近。稍有侧重在于,"通过"的意义更虚一些,主要用以引进作为媒介的人、事、方式、手段等;"经过"少含一定的实在意义,还有"经历……"的意思,因此它引进的通常是某个过程。(Both "通过" and "经过" can be used as prepositions, indicating to attain a goal through somebody, something or some activity, very similar in meaning. The only ence is that the meaning of "通过" is more functional, mainly used to introduce a person, a thing, a method or means which is used as an intermediary. "经过" includes more or less practical meaning, also indicating "experiencing...". So what it introduces is usually a process.)例如:

通过大家的帮助,他的认识提高了不少。

通过这次讨论,大家取得了较为一致的意见。

(After discussion, unanimity was achieved.)

经过这场激烈的比赛,中国女排终于再次夺得冠军。

(After the grueling match, the women's volleyball team of China carried off the first prize again.)

经过一个假期的钻研努力,他终于完成了这篇有一定分量的论文。

(After a whole vocation's endeavour, he finally completed this significant thesis.)

(二)作为动词,"通过"、"经过"在经由某地的意义上也比较接近,但是有时不能换用,这是因为"通过"只有"穿过"的意思,即从一端或一侧到另一端或另一侧的意思;"经过"则既有"通过"的意思,又有"路过"的意思。(As verbs, "通过" and "经过" both mean passing some place, but they are not always exchangeable for the reason that "通过" only means "pass through", namely, to pass from this end or side to that end or side. "经过" can either mean "pass through" or "pass by".)例如:

火车通过了长江大桥。

十个小时的时间,火车通过了三十多个隧道。

战士们终于顺利地通过了敌人的封锁线。

(The soldiers finally managed to run through the enemy blockade.)

我去邮电局时从银行门前经过。

下班打你家门前经过时,我去看看你。

(After work, I'll go to see you while passing your home.)

我几乎每天都经过百货大楼,但是很少有时间进去。

表示"路过"的意思,一般不能用"通过"。(When expressing "passing by", "通过" is generally not used.)例如:

* 坐火车通过上海时,我会去看你的。

* 我几乎每天都通过百货大楼,但是很少有时间进去。

(三) 动词用法的其他意义上的差别。(Other differences as verbs.)

1."经过"常常可以表示时间上延续的意思,用法上,动词后接有表示时段意义的词语。这种场合一般不能用"通过"。("经过" is usually followed by words expressing a period of time to indicate the lasting of the time and "经过" cannot be used in this case.)例如:

经过五天五夜的时间,他才恢复神志。

(After five days and nights, he finally regained consciousness.)

经过十年的时间,我才懂得了这个道理。

* 通过五天五夜的时间,他才恢复神志。

* 通过十年的时间,我才懂得了这个道理。

2.表示议案等经过法定人数的同意而成立的意思,用"通过",不用"经过"。(When expressing bills, motions, etc. are adopted by means of quorum agreement, usually "通过", not "经过" is used.)例如:

这项议案已经通过半年多了。

我的论文答辩顺利地通过了。

* 这项议案已经经过半年多了。

* 我的论文答辩顺利地经过了。

495

W

往 wǎng 向 xiàng 朝 cháo
〈介词〉 < preposition >

(一)"往"、"向"、"朝"都可以构成介宾词组表示动作行为的方向,作状语时,大多可以换用。("往","向" and "朝" can all form preposition-object phrases to indicate the directions of acts. When used as adverbials, they are interchangeable in most cases.)例如:

战士们迅速地往/向/朝村外跑去。
那架飞机往/向/朝东边飞去了。
载满旅客的列车往/向/朝北京飞驰而去。

其不同之处:(Differences:)

1."往"、"向"构成介宾词组表示动作行为的方向时还可以用作补语;"朝"不可以。(Besides indicating the directions of acts, "往" and "向" phrases can also be used as complements; but "朝" can't.)例如:

这条小路通往/向山顶。
大客船开往/向东京。
* 这条小路通朝山顶。
* 大客船开朝东京。

2."往"、"向"构成的介宾词组用于动词后表示的方向意义有差别。"往"构成介宾词组只表示具体的方向,它表示"向……方向去"的意思;"向"构成的介宾词组只表示单纯的方向性,它除了表示具体的方向外,还可以表示抽象意义的方向性。("往" and "向" phrases are not quite the same in meaning when expressing directions. "往" phrases only indicate the concrete directions, meaning "(to go) toward …". "向" phrases only express pure directions, not only concrete, but abstract directions as well.)例如:

飞机飞往/向广州。

走向成功　　走向胜利　　走向光明

走向前方　　走向未来

＊走往成功　＊走往胜利　＊走往光明

＊走往前方　＊走往未来

(二)"向"、"朝"构成的介宾词组还可以表示动作的对象,"往"构成的介宾词组则只表示方向,不表示对象。("向" and "朝" phrases also indicate the target of an act. "往" phrases only indicate the direction, not the target.)例如:

他向/朝我使了一个眼色。

他站在甲板上,向/朝送他的人们挥手告别。

(He was standing on the deck, waving good-bye to the people who came to see him off.)

＊他往我使了一个眼色。

＊他站在甲板上,往送他的人们挥手告别。

(三)"向"、"朝"构成表示动作对象的介宾词组时,对动词的选择有所不同。"朝"构成的介宾词组通常只用在跟人体动作有关的动词前;"向"构成的介宾词组既可以用在跟人体动作有关的动词前,也可以用在其他动词前。(When "向" and "朝" form preposition-object phrases to indicate the target of an act, they require different kinds of verbs to go together with. "朝" phrases are usually used before verbs relating to human actions. "向" phrases can either be used before such verbs or before other verbs.)例如:

他向/朝我瞪了一眼。

女歌手又一次向/朝观众们深深鞠了一躬。

(The woman singer made another deep bow to the audience.)

外宾们向演员们赠送了花篮,表示他们真诚的谢意。

(The foreign guests presented a basket of flowers to the performers, expressing their sincere gratitude.)

我们要敢于向困难作斗争。

孩子们表示一定要向英雄学习,做品学兼优的好学生。

(The children stated that they are determined to learn from the heroes and become the students of good character and scholarship.)

服务员向我介绍了这里的情况。

* 外宾们朝演员们赠送了花篮,表示他们真诚的谢意。

* 我们要敢于朝困难作斗争。

* 孩子们表示一定要朝英雄学习,做品学兼优的好学生。

* 服务员朝我介绍了这里的情况。

为 wèi   为了 wèile   因为 yīnwèi

为、为了、因为〈介词〉< preposition >

因为〈连词〉< conjunction >

(一)"为"与"为了"

1. "为"、"为了"都可以用来表示动作、行为的目的、动机,有时可以通用。("为" and "为了" can both indicate the purpose or motive of an act or a behavior, sometimes are exchangeable.)例如:

为/为了实现四个现代化贡献自己的力量。

我为/为了学好汉语想了不少办法。

但是有时在结构上有差别。(But sometimes they are different in structure.)

(1)"为了"构成的介宾词组,通常对动作、行为的目的、动机有强调作用,所以常常用于主语前;"为"构成的介宾词组一般出现在谓语动词前。(Preposition-object phrases formed by "为了" usually emphasizes the purpose or motive of an act or a behavior, so they are often placed before subjects. "为" phrases usually appears before the predicate.)例如:

为了培养下一代,她费尽了心血。

498

(She extended all her energies for the training of the younger generation.)

为了适应经济发展,企业必须要进行体制改革。

(To suit the economic development, enterprises must carry out their system reform.)

为了你,我也要完成这项研究。

英语角为同学们练习口语创造了条件。

他为科学事业献出了自己宝贵的生命。

(2)"为"可以构成"为……起见"的固定格式;"为了"不能。("为" can form the fixed pattern "为…起见"; "为了" can't.)例如:

为慎重起见,大家再仔细检查检查。

(For the sake of cautiousness, please check up carefully again.)

为方便顾客起见,从即日起,我店开始实行上门售货服务。

(In order to make things convenient for the customers, our store begins to deliver goods to the doorstep from now on.)

(3)"为"、"为了"都可以跟"而"搭配使用,但是意义有差别。"为……而"通常用来表示一种顺接的目的关系;"为了……而"通常用来表示一种逆接的目的关系,"而"的前后带有意义相反的词语。(Both "为" and "为了" can be used with "而", but they are different in meaning. "为…而" expresses an objective relationship in sequence; while "为了…而" expresses an objective relationship in contrary sequence, and words before and after "而" are contrary in meaning.)例如:

为人民而死,虽死犹荣。

(To die for the people, he will be honoured though dead.)

运动员们为五星红旗的升起而激动得热泪盈眶。

499

(The athletes' eyes were filled with tears with excitement at the sight of the uprising of the Five-Starred Red Flag.)

为实现世界和平而努力奋斗。

(Exert ourselves in the struggle for the realization of the world peace.)

为了自己而损害他人利益,太不道德了!

(It's not ethical to infringe upon the interests of others to benefit oneself.)

为了绝大多数人的明天,而牺牲自己的今天。

(Sacrifice one's today for the tomorrow of the vast majority.)

2."为"构成的介宾词组还可以表示动作行为的原因;"为了"不可以。("为" phrases can also express the cause of an act or a behavior. "为了" can't.)例如:

大家都为他安全返回高兴得不得了。

母亲为你不争气不知流了多少泪。

(Your mother has shed countless tears for your being disappointing.)

* 大家都为了他安全返回高兴得不得了。

* 母亲为了你不争气不知流了多少泪。

3."为"构成的介宾词组还可以表示动作行为的对象,有"给"、"替"的意思。"为了"没有这一意义。〔"为" phrases also indicate the target of an act or a behavior, meaning "for (somebody / something)", or "on behalf of (somebody or something)". "为了" does not have this sense.〕例如:

我们都要树立为人民服务的思想。

他为妈妈买了一件贵重的生日礼物。

大家不要为我担心,我的身体还可以。

* 我们都要树立为了人民服务的思想。

* 他为了妈妈买了一件贵重的生日礼物。

* 大家不要为了我担心,我的身体还可以。

(二)"为"、"为了"与"因为"

1."为"和"因为"

(1)"为"和"因为"都可以用作介词,构成介宾词组后表示动作行为的某种原因,有时还可以通用。("为" and "因为" can both form preposition-object phrases to indicate the cause of an act or a behavior, sometimes they are interchangeable.)例如:

大家不要为/因为一点儿小事就闹意见。

母亲为/因为你不争气不知流了多少泪。

但是即使在可通用的情况下,意义也稍有差别。用"因为"比用"为"更加强调原因,此外"为"还可以表示动作目的、对象等,所以它们有时不能互换使用。(Even if they are interchangeable, they are slightly different in meaning."因为" is more emphatic on the cause than"为". And"为" also expresses the purpose or target of an act, so they are sometimes not exchangeable.)例如:

他因为书法而出了名。

* 他为书法而出了名。

她当时的英勇无畏都是因为你。

(Her heroic deeds at the time was all for you.)

因为他,我们才相识。

(Owing to him, we are able to get acquainted.)

* 她当时的英勇无畏都是为你。

* 为他,我们才相识。

(2)"因为"还可以构成"因为……关系/缘故"等格式;"为"不能。("因为" can also form "因为…关系／缘故 (for the reason that…)" pattern. "为" can't.)例如:

因为天气关系,我们出发的时间向后推迟了一天。

因为她一向喜欢孩子的缘故,她十分热爱自己的工作。

* 为天气关系,我们出发的时间向后推迟了一天。

* 为她一向喜欢孩子的缘故,她十分热爱自己的工作。

(3)"为"只用作介词,"因为"除介词外,主要用作连词。作连词用时,它的功用是连接因果关系的复句。("为" is only used as a preposition. "因为" is used not only as a preposition, but mainly as a conjunction to connect complex sentences of causality.)例如:

因为自己资格老,就不把别人放在眼里。

(Because of his seniority, he doesn't take others into account.)

因为她热情、大方、乐于助人,所以大家都很喜欢她。

2."为了"和"因为"

"为了"只用作介词,构成的介宾词组只表示动作的目的、动机,不表示原因;"因为"无论作介词用,还是作连词用,都只用来表示原因,所以两个词不能通用。("为了" is only used as a preposition. The preposition-object phrases formed by "为了" only indicate the purpose or motive of an act or a behavior, not the cause. "因为", either used as a preposition or conjunction, only indicates the cause. So they are not exchangeable.)例如:

为了不让妈妈伤心,她一直没有把离婚的事告诉妈妈。

(In order not to make Mother sad, she didn't tell her about her divorce.)

为了这项实验,他三天三夜没休息。

因为你,我才来的。

因为劳累过度,他终于病倒了。

(Because of excessive hard work, he was laid up at last.)

* 为了劳累过度,他终于病倒了。

因为西湖景色很美,所以每年来这儿旅游的人很多。

* 为了西湖景色很美,所以每年来这儿旅游的人很多。

未必 wèibì　　不必 búbì

〈副词〉< adverb >

"未必"的"未"和"不必"的"不"虽然都有否定的意义,但是当它们分别组成"未必"和"不必"时,两词的意思却完全不同。
(The words "未" in "未必" and "不" in "不必" are both negative in meaning, but when they form word groups "未必" and "不必" respectively, the meaning of the two word groups are quite different.)

(一) 意义上 (In meaning)

"未必"表示的是"不一定"的意思,是一种委婉否定的方式。"不必"则是真实的否定,它是对"需要"、"必要"的否定,表示不需要或者没有必要的意思。("未必" means uncertain — a mild negation. "不必" is a true negation to "需要" or "必要", meaning needn't or unnecessary.)例如:

他未必肯听你的。(不一定听你的 —— 有不听的可能。)

我想张先生未必不想去。(不一定不想去 —— 有可能想去。)

你不必来了。(不需要来。)

你不必去看他。(不需要你去看。)

(二) 使用上 (In usage)

1. "未必"和"不必"构成的句式不同。"未必"后面既可以接肯定式又可以接否定式,但是表达的意思截然相反,后面接肯定式表示否定,后面接否定式表示肯定。("未必" and "不必" constitute different sentence patterns. "未必" can be followed by either affirmative or negative words, but expressing contrary meanings, the former negative, and the latter affirmative.)例如:

小李未必了解这件事的全部经过。(可能不了解。)

(Xiao Li doesn't necessarily know the whole process from the beginning to the end.)

我觉得她未必不愿意留在中国。(可能愿意。)

(I think she may not be necessarily unwilling to stay in China.)

"不必"后面只能接肯定式,表示的只能是否定。("不必" is

only followed by affirmative words, and expresses the negative meaning only.)例如：

> 不必悲观,只要你肯努力,前途总是光明的。
>
> (There is no need to be pessimistic. The future will always be bright, provided you are willing to work hard.)
>
> 同学之间应该互相谅解,不必为一些鸡毛蒜皮的小事斤斤计较。
>
> (Mutual understanding should be reached among you fellow students. It's unnecessary to argue about trivial matters.)

2. "未必"、"不必"在一定的语言环境中可以省略后面的动词或形容词,单独用来回答问题,但是结构方式有所不同。因为用"未必"的句子带有不定的意味,所以句末常常接不定语气词"吧"或者只用"未必";用"不必"的句子因常含有变化意义,所以句末常常接"了"。(The verb or adjective after "未必" or "不必" can be omitted under certain language situations, and they can be used singly in answering questions, but their sentence structures are somewhat different. The sentence with "未必" involves the meaning of uncertainty, so it usually ends with "吧", or just "未必" itself. The sentence with "不必" usually implies the meaning of change, so it often ends with "了".)例如：

> 他一定愿意跟你一起去旅游。—— 未必吧!
>
> 你的病越来越重了,找个医生看看吧! —— 不必了。

问 wèn　　打听 dǎting

〈动词〉 <verb>

(一) "问"、"打听"意义不同。("问" and "打听" are different in meaning.)

"问"是指有不知道、不明白的事情请人解答。("问" means to call for an answer to, or request information about something one doesn't know.)例如：

504

  他问我："你知道这个字怎么读吗？"
  一个客户问我们什么时候进货。
  我想问老师一个问题。

"打听"则是一种探问的行为，通过这个行为，了解有关的情况。（"打听" means the act of inquiring, through which one can get information about something.）例如：

  我想打听一个人，他叫王怡。
  你先去打听一下路，问清楚了再走。

（二）"问"、"打听"用法不同。（They are different in usage.）

1. "问"通常要和具体的内容相联系，所以"问"后面常常连带具体要问的内容。（"问" is usually connected with specific content, so it is often followed by words denoting the specific content that one wants to know.）例如：

  他问你<u>这样做行不行</u>。
  我想问问你<u>这道题怎么做</u>。

"打听"通常单独用，一般不跟具体要问的内容相联系，但是当构成重叠式或后加"一下"的形式后，则可以询问要了解的具体内容。（"打听" is usually used alone, not connected with specific content. When it is reduplicated, or is followed by "一下", it can go together with the words denoting specific content.）例如：

  我想打听一个人。
  谁去打听路？
  他总在打听你的情况。
  你去打听打听<u>前面怎么回事</u>。
  我去打听一下<u>去百货大楼怎么走</u>。
  ＊你去打听前面怎么回事。
  ＊我去打听去百货大楼怎么走。

2. 适应范围："问"的宾语常常是"问题"、"情况"、"事"等；"打听"的宾语常常是"消息"、"下落"、"底细"、"情况"、"事"等。〔Their usage: the objects of "问" are usually "问题"

(questions),"情况"(conditions),"事"(things),etc.;while those of "打听" are usually "消息"(information),"下落"(whereabouts), "底细"(exact details),"情况"(conditions),"事"(things),etc.]
例如:

>老师,我问您一个问题,可以吗?
>我想问你一件事,希望你实话实说。
>(I have something to ask you. I hope you'll tell me the truth.)
>* 老师,我打听一个问题,可以吗?
>他到处打听你的消息。
>先打听一下他的下落,然后再决定怎么办。
>* 他到处问你的消息。
>* 先问一下他的下落,然后再决定怎么办。

3."问"可以带两个宾语,一个是表人的,一个是表事的;"打听"则不可以。"打听"的对象如果是人时,一般要用介词"向"、"跟"引出,构成介宾词组,在句子里作状语。("问" can be followed by double objects, one denoting person(s), the other denoting thing(s). "打听" cannot be used so. If the object of "打听" is a person, it is usually introduced by "向" or "跟", forming preposition-object phrases, used as an adverbial in the sentence.)例如:

>我问你一件事。(你 —— 表人;事 —— 表事。)
>他问我几点了。(我 —— 表人;几点了 —— 表事。)
>* 我打听你一件事。
>* 他打听我几点了。
>上次他来的时候,还跟我打听过你的消息呢。(跟我打听。)
>(Last time he came, he had asked me about you.)
>玛丽正向行人打听路呢。(向行人打听。)

问 wèn   询问 xúnwèn   质问 zhìwèn
疑问 yíwèn   提问 tíwèn

问、询问、质问、提问〈动词〉< verb >

疑问〈名词〉< noun >

(一)"问"、"询问"、"质问"

"问"、"询问"、"质问"都可以用作动词,表示"有不知道、不明白的事情请人解答"的意思,但是意义、色彩和用法上都有所不同。("问","询问" and "质问" can all be used as verbs, meaning "to call for an answer to what one does not know or is not clear about", but they are somewhat different in meaning, flavor and usage.)

1.色彩和意义上 (In meaning and flavor)

(1)"问"有口语色彩,多适用于口语,使用频率很高。("问" is more used in spoken language and is very frequently used.) 例如:

他问你他可不可以去。

关于这件事,你可以去问问小李。

(2)"询问"具有一定的书面语色彩,多适用于书面语。"询问"的动作含有一定的"关切"的意味,因此它多用于领导问群众、上级问下级、长辈问晚辈等,也可以用于同辈或同事之间等。此外"询问"有时还含有用问的方式进行了解、打听的意思。("询问" is more used in written language. "询问" involves the meaning of concern, so it is mostly used when a leader inquires about the mass, the senior asks about the junior, the elder about the young. It is also used in the same generations or among colleagues. Furthermore, "询问" sometimes involves the meaning of finding out or inquiring about (something) through the method of asking.)例如:

老校长询问了我们的学习情况后,满意地点点头。

老同学们互相询问着,激动得不得了。

他还询问了其他一些有关细则。

(He also inquired about other relevant detailed rules and regulations.)

(3)"质问"在动作方式上有特定的要求,它是以一定的事实

507

为根据而问的动作方式,语气多强硬、尖锐甚至含有不满或斥责。("质问" has special demand on the form of actions. It means to question based on certain facts. The tone is usually strong and sharp, implying discontentment or reprimand.)例如:

众人高声质问:"你凭什么欺负人?"

(Everybody asked loudly: "Why do you bully others?")

你这样质问我,我可受不了。

(I can't stand to be questioned by you like that.)

* 关于这件事,你可以去询问小李。
* 老校长质问了我们的学习情况后,满意地点点头。
* 众人高声询问:"你凭什么欺负人?"

2. 用法上 (In usage)

(1)"质问"还可以用作状语,表示一种动作的方式。("质问" can also be used as an adverbial to indicate the way of an act.)例如:

他质问地看着班长,把班长弄得满脸通红。

(He looked at the monitor questioningly, making him blush scarlet.)

(2)"质问"还可以作"提出"的宾语,"询问"和"问"一般不这样用。〔"质问" can serve as the object of "提出"(raise); "询问" and "问" usually can not.〕例如:

对科员们这样不公平,科员们当然会提出质问。

* 对科员们这样不公平,科员们当然会提出询问/问。

(3)"询问"一般不能只带一个表人的宾语,还应该带有其他成分;"问"、"质问"则可以。(The object of "询问" is not just person(s) alone, but together with other elements as well; "问" and "质问" can be use without this restriction.)例如:

他仔细地询问了<u>工人们对厂里的意见</u>。

* 他仔细地询问工人们。
* 老校长询问我们。

508

这件事我不太了解,你去问他吧。

他当众质问我,太不像话了!

(It's really outrageous that he questioned me in public.)

(二)"提问"与"问"、"询问"、"质问"

1."提问"与"问"、"询问"、"质问"不同,"提问"是提出问题问,要求对方给予回答,而且"提问"大多用于老师对学生、上级对下级等。(Different from the other three, "提问" is to ask a question, and then require an answer to the question. It is mainly used when a teacher asks the students, or the senior asks the junior, etc.)例如:

老师:下面我提问,同学们回答。

这个问题好像有人提问过。

2."提问"除可以带表人的宾语外,表事的宾语一般只限于"问题"类,不能连带所问具体内容的宾语。〔The objects of "提问" are usually persons, or the limited sort like "问题(questions)", no object of specific content is acceptable.〕例如:

这个问题辅导员提问过我。

他多次提问过我这个问题。

* 他提问这本书的作者。

* 我提问公司里的情况。

(三)"疑问"与"提问"、"问"、"询问"、"质问"

"提问"、"问"、"询问"、"质问"都可以用作动词,"疑问"则只能用作名词。它表示怀疑的问题或不能确定、不能解释的问题。因为是名词,在句子里主要作主语、宾语,不能作连带宾语的谓语。("提问","问","询问" and "质问" are all used as verbs; while "疑问" is only used as a noun. It means something questionable or uncertain, or not to be explained. As a noun, it is mainly used as a subject, or object, but not as a predicate.)例如:

她心中的疑问到现在也没解开。

(She has not found a clue to her doubt yet.)

你对这个问题还有什么疑问吗？
毫无疑问，一定有人捣鬼。
(It is doubtless that someone is doing mischief.)
* 你疑问这件事吗？
* 我疑问这个问题。
* 老师疑问张文为什么不来上课。

X

希望 xīwàng　　愿望 yuànwàng

希望〈名词〉〈动词〉 < noun > < verb >
愿望〈名词〉 < noun >

(一)"希望"、"愿望"都用作名词时,意义不同。(While both used as nouns, "希望" and "愿望" are different in meaning.)

1."希望"主要是对有关的客观事物或他人等而言的。(When "希望" is used, the action is toward objective things or people.)

(1) 表示实现某种愿望的可能性。常作动词"有"、"没有"的宾语。〔("希望") indicates the possibility of realizing some wishes, and is often used as the object of the verb "有" or "没有"。〕例如:

他自己感觉题答得不错,看来考上大学有希望了。(对考上大学来说)

(He felt good himself about the examinations. He seemed full of hope to be admitted to a university.)

我们有成功的希望了!(对成功来说)

只要大家齐心协力,争夺冠军不是没有希望的。(对争夺冠军来说)

(It isn't at all hopeless to win championship, provided we all make concerted efforts.)

她还有生还的希望,我们要全力抢救。(对生还来说)

希望落空了,她从此陷入苦闷之中。(对某事来说)

(Unable to attain her hope, she sank into deep depression.)

表示"实现某种愿望的可能性"的意思时不能用"愿望"。("愿望" is not used to indicate "the possibility of realizing some wishes".)例如:

511

* 只要大家齐心协力,争夺冠军不是没有愿望的。

(2) 表示希望所寄托的对象。("希望" refers to the target that hope is placed on.)例如:

现在,儿子是她惟一的希望。

青少年是祖国的未来,祖国的希望。

(The youth is the future and the hope of the country.)

我们的希望就落在你的身上了。

表示"希望所寄托的对象"的意思时,不能用"愿望"。("愿望" is not used to indicate "the object that hope is placed on".)例如:

* 青少年是祖国的未来,祖国的愿望。
* 我们的愿望就落在你的身上了。

2."愿望"主要用于表示将来实现某种目的的主观心愿。("愿望" is used to express the subjective desire, namely one wishes to attain some goals in the future.)例如:

她虽然有回到亲人怀抱的愿望,但是很难实现。

(Though she wishes to return to the embrace of her dear ones, her desire is hard to come true.)

主观愿望代替不了客观现实。

(Subjective desire cannot replace the objective reality.)

他多年的愿望终于实现了。

(His years-long wish has at last come true.)

光有良好的愿望是不够的,还必须付出辛勤的劳动。

(It's not enough to have only good wishes. One must put in actual work.)

表示"将来实现某种目的的主观心愿"的意思时不能用"希望"。("希望" is not used to express "the subjective desire to attain some goal in the future".)例如:

* 他多年的希望终于实现了。
* 主观希望代替不了客观现实。

(二)"希望"还可以用作动词,"愿望"则只能用作名词,所以它们有不同的功能和用法。("希望" can be used as a verb. "愿望" is only used as a noun. So they are different in function and usage.)

1."希望"可以接受副词的修饰;"愿望"不可以。("希望" can be modified by adverbs. "愿望" cannot.)例如:

我很希望去中国的愿望早日实现。

我的确希望这是事实。

来中国是她多年来的愿望。

愿望一定会实现。

* 来中国是她很愿望的事情。

* 我的确愿望这是事实。

2."希望"是动词,可以作带宾谓语,常带非名词性宾语;"愿望"是名词,不能带宾语。(As a verb, "希望" can be used as a predicate, often followed by objects not of noun character. "愿望" is a noun, without any object after it.)例如:

她希望你谅解她。

我们希望得到你们的帮助。

她对孩子没有更多的要求,只希望他将来能够自食其力。

(She has no higher demand on her child than wishing him to be able to support himself by his own labour in the future.)

* 我们愿望得到你们的帮助。

* 我们愿望加强两国人民的友谊。

下来 xiàlái   下去 xiàqù

〈趋向动词〉 < directional verb >

(一)"下来"、"下去"都可以用在动词后表示动作趋向,但方向不同。"下来"表示向下并靠近说话人;"下去"表示向下并离开说话人。(Both "下来" and "下去" can be used after verbs, but indicate different directions of the actions. "下来" means the direction of an

513

action is getting downward and towards the speaker. "下去" means the direction of an action is getting downward and away from the speaker.)例如：

小溪是从山腰流下来的。(说话人在山下。)

泉水从这儿流下去,汇入河中。(说话人在高处的泉水处。)

(The spring water flows down from here and joins the river.)

他走上台来,接过鲜花,……又慢慢走下台去。(说话人在台上。)

(二)"下来"、"下去"都可以用在动词后表示动作继续,但是"下来"主要表示从过去继续到现在;"下去"主要表示从现在往后继续。(Both "下来" and "下去" can be used after verbs to indicate the continuation of the action. "下来" means an action lasting from the past till now. "下去" means to start and continue from now on.)例如：

她终于坚持下来了。(从以前开始坚持,到现在完成。)

你一定要坚持下去,不能半途而废。(继续往后坚持。)

(You must persist in it. Don't give up halfway.)

这个宝贝是祖上传下来的。(从祖上传到现在。)

把光荣传统一代一代传下去。(继续传给后代。)

因为"下去"表示从现在往后继续的意义,所以动词前常常可以使用"接着"、"再"、"又"一类词。"下来"表示从过去延续到现在的意思,所以一般不跟这些词结合。(As "下去" indicates an act continues, there are always such words as "接着", "再", "又", etc. in front of the verb. "下来" indicates an act lasting from the past till now, so it is not used together with such words.)例如：

他看了我一眼,又接着说了下去。

你再这样干下去,身体就会垮掉。

(If you go on doing it like that, you'll be worn down.)

* 他看了我一眼,又接着说了下来。
* 你再这样干下来,身体就会垮掉。

想 xiǎng　　要 yào

〈动词〉表示做某事的意志或愿望。(< verb > indicating the will or desire to do something.)

"想"和"要"都可以表示做某事的意志或愿望,但是几乎不能换用,这是因为它们在意义上和用法上都有差别。(Both "想" and "要" indicate the will or desire to do something, but they are hardly exchangeable due to their differences in meaning and usage.)

(一) 意义上 (In meaning)

"想"主要着重于一种愿望,是一种愿望或者打算。"要"则着重于做某事的意志,是一种意志上的要求。("想" emphasizes one's desire, hope or plan. "要" emphasizes one's will or determination to do something.) 例如:

我想去美国留学。(一个愿望。)
我要去美国留学。(一种意志上的要求。)

再比较几组:

儿子想搞自然科学方面的研究。
他们很想为老百姓做一点儿实事儿。

(They wish very much to do some actual work for the common people.)

我想在经济上帮帮他。
女儿想跟妈妈一起住。
儿子要搞自然科学方面的研究。
他们要为老百姓做一点儿实事儿。
我要在经济上帮帮他。
女儿要跟妈妈一起住。

(二) 用法上 (In usage)

1."想"前面可以接受程度副词的修饰,表示愿望强烈;"要"

不能这样用。("想" can be modified by adverbs of degree to indicate a strong desire; while "要" cannot.)例如：

我很想满足你的要求，可是我不能违反规定。

(I really want to satisfy your demands, but I can't violate the rules.)

他很想到这儿来看你。

她很想在母亲身边多陪陪母亲，可惜没有那么多的时间。

* 我很要满足你的要求，可是我不能违反规定。
* 他很要到这儿来看你。
* 她很要在母亲身边多陪陪母亲，可惜没有那么多的时间。

2. "要"表示的是一种意志上的要求，它前面可以接受"非"、"偏"、"一定"等副词的修饰，表示坚定的意志或不变的决心。"想"一般不能这样用。("要" indicates the will to do something, so it may be modified by adverbs such as "非"，"偏"，"一定" to indicate the strong will or firm determination.)例如：

我非要找他们评评理去。

(I really must go and have it out with them.)

她偏要送我礼物以示感谢不可。

(She insisted on sending me a gift to express her gratitude.)

我一定要去北京看你。

* 我非想找他们评评理去。
* 她偏想送我礼物以示感谢不可。
* 我一定想去北京看你。

(三)"要"、"想"被否定后意义上和使用上的变化和差异。(The differences and changes in meaning and usage when "要" and "想" are negated.)

1. 当"要"是肯定的意义时，它可以表示意志上的要求；但是当表示没有做某事的意愿要求时，却不能用"不要"，而应该用"不想"。(When "要" is used in an affirmative sentence, it may

516

indicate the will to do something. When expressing not willing to do something, we can only use "不想", not "不要".)例如：

　　我要参加 HSK 汉语水平考试。(肯定)
　　＊ 我不要参加 HSK 汉语水平考试。
　　我不想参加 HSK 汉语水平考试。(否定)
　　＊ 他不要去青岛旅游。
　　＊ 这儿不方便,我不要住在这里。
　　＊ 我不要给他去电话。
　　＊ 谁不要住得宽敞些？
　　他不想去青岛旅游。
　　这儿不方便,我不想住在这里。
　　我不想给他去电话。
　　谁不想住得宽敞些？

　　2. 当"要"前面接受否定副词"不"时,表示的是对他人的限制,而不是自身的愿望要求。这时,"不要"只用于祈使意义的句子里。(When "要" is followed by the negative adverb "不", it expresses the restriction on others, not a wish or demand of oneself. In this case, "不要" is only used in imperative sentences.)例如：

　　你不要一个人去那么偏远的地方旅游。
　　不要看这些不健康的录像。
　　(Don't watch these unhealthy videos.)
　　不要为我担心,我一切都很好。

(四)"想"和"要"在句法结构上的共同特点。(The similarities of "想" and "要" in syntactic structure.)

　　1."想"和"要"后边都应该接谓词性成分,不能接名词性成分。(Both "想" and "要" should be followed by predicative words, not nominal components.)例如：

　　我想去,但是我没去。
　　我想尽力帮助他。
　　我想带他们去北京看看。

　　　　我要给他打电话。
　　　　他要跟我学汉语。
　　　　他要帮助那些穷人。
　　　* 我想北京旅游。(改:"想去"。)
　　　* 我想这本词典。(改:"想买"。)
　　　* 他想汽车去。(改:"想坐"。)
　　　* 他要幼儿园的参观。(改:"要参观幼儿园"。)
　　　* 我要名牌大学。(改:"要上"。)

　2.在"把"字句中,"想"、"要"要用在"把"字词组前。(In sentences where "把" is involved, "想" or "要" must be placed before "把" phrases.)例如:
　　　　我想把书还给他。
　　　　她想把屋子好好打扫一下。
　　　* 我把书想还给他。
　　　* 她把屋子想好好打扫一下。
　　　　假期里,我要把论文写完。
　　　　我一定要把这件事处理好。
　　　* 假期里,我把论文要写完。
　　　* 我一定把这件事要处理好。

　3.在连动句和兼语句中,"想"和"要"要用于第一个谓语动词前。(In a sentence containing two or more verbs, or several acts going together, "想" or "要" is placed before the first verb.)例如:
　　　　他想去百货大楼买东西。
　　　　我一定要去上海看你们。
　　　* 他去百货大楼想买东西。
　　　* 我一定去上海要看你们。
　　　　我想让他把这个好消息亲口告诉你。
　　　(I want him to tell you the good news himself.)
　　　　我要叫他在众人面前出丑。

(I want him to make an exhibition of himself.)
* 我让他把这个好消息想亲口告诉你。
* 我叫他在众人面前要出丑。

像 xiàng   好像 hǎoxiàng

〈动词〉< verb >
〈副词〉< adverb >

"像"、"好像"都可以表示十分相似的意思,但是在意义上、用法上还有很多不同,所以大多情况下不能互换使用。("像" and "好像" may both mean very similar. But there are also some differences in their meanings and usage, so they are not usually exchangeable.)

(一)关于用作动词的意义和用法(Their meanings and usage as verbs)

1.意义上(In meaning)

"像"表示在形象上相同或有某些相同点,这种相同是一种具体形象的相同。"好像"不能用于这种具体形象的相同,它一般用于比拟某种情景或事物。("像" expresses the likeness in appearance. Such likeness is specific and vivid. "好像" can't be used to describe such concrete likeness. It is used to draw a parallel between things.)例如:

你不像本地人。
小王长得有点儿像日本人。
她长得很像她妈妈。
* 你不好像本地人。
* 小王长得有点儿好像日本人。
* 她长得好像她妈妈。
灯火星星点点,好像空中闪闪烁烁的星星。

(Lights glimmered all over the place, as if the glittering stars in the sky.)

这里有一眼望不到边的麦田,金黄色的麦子被风一吹,好像翻滚的海浪。

(On the boundless stretch of wheat field, golden wheat is blown by the wind, just like seething waves.)

他们谈得很投入,好像多年不见的老朋友。

(They talked very congenially, just like old friends who hadn't met for years.)

2. 用法上 (In usage)

(1)"像"前可以接受程度副词或有程度意义的词语的修饰,"像"后面也可以带补语;"好像"不可以。("像" can be modified by adverbs or other words of degree, and also be followed with a complement. "好像" cannot.) 例如:

你长得很像你父亲。

(You take after your father.)

你装得真像。

(You really looked the part you were acting.)

他演女人演得不太像。

(He acted a woman, but didn't look the part.)

娘俩的相貌像得惊人。

(The mother and daughter are very much alike.)

你们俩的声音像极了。

* 你长得很好像你父亲。

* 娘俩的相貌好像得惊人。

* 你们俩的声音好像极了。

(2)"像"一般情况下带宾语,但是也可以不带宾语;"好像"必须带宾语。("像" may or may not be followed by objects. "好像" must be followed by objects.) 例如:

他思考问题的样子很像一个作家。

她们俩很亲密,好像有血缘关系的亲姐妹。

他演得一点儿也不像。

你画得真像。

他演女人演得不太像。

* 他演得一点儿也不好像。
* 你画得真好像。
* 他演女人演得不太好像。
* 他们谈得很投入,好像多年不见。
* 灯火星星点点,空中闪闪烁烁的星星好像。

(二) 关于用作副词的意义和用法（Their meanings and usage as adverbs）

"好像"可以表示推测、判断或感觉不十分确定的意思,有"仿佛"、"似乎"、"大概"的意思。"像"跟"好像"意义、用法很接近,只是它判断、感觉不确定的意味少一些,它主要是"仿佛"、"似乎"的意思,即状态上十分接近,所以后面常跟"似的"、"一样"等词语配合。〔"好像" can express inference, judgement, or the feeling of uncertainty, meaning "仿佛"(seem), "似乎""as if", or "大概"(general). "像" is very similar in meaning and usage with "好像", only that it is weaker in the meaning of uncertainty while expressing inference or judgment. It mainly means "seem", "as if", namely very similar in state, and is often followed by words like "似的","一样".〕例如:

屋子里好像一个人也没有。

孩子的头挺热的,好像有点儿发烧。

天闷得厉害,好像要下雨。

你好像不太高兴,怎么回事?

这菜看上去好像不太好吃,实际上还真不错。

她突然感觉眼睛看东西模模糊糊的,像蒙上了一层白雾(似的)。

老人像疼自己的儿子一样疼我。

他像丢了魂似的坐在那里。

小时 xiǎoshí   钟头 zhōngtóu

〈名词〉表示时间的单位。(< noun > time unit.)

(一) 相同之处 (Similarities)

作名词用时,"小时"、"钟头"可以通用,只是"钟头"口语色彩较浓一些。(When used as nouns, "小时" and "钟头" are interchangeable, only "钟头" is more used in spoken language.)例如:

桃花堤并不远,骑自行车用不了一个小时/钟头就到了。

这车修起来挺麻烦,估计几个小时/钟头修不完。

(It will take a lot of efforts to repair this car. Maybe it can't be finished within hours.)

现在人太多,你一个小时/钟头以后再来吧。

(二) 不同之处 (Differences)

"小时"既可以用作名词,又可以用作量词;"钟头"只用作名词,不能用作量词。因此,它们在结构上不完全相同。作名词用时,应该构成"数+量+名词"的格式;作量词用时,可以构成"数+量"的格式。所以,"小时"既可以用作"某个小时",也可以用作"某小时";"钟头"则只能用作"某个钟头"。("小时" can be used either as a noun or classifier. "钟头" is only used as a noun, not as a classifier. So they are not quite the same in structure. When used as a noun, "小时" forms "numeral + classifier + noun" pattern; while as a classifier, it forms "numeral + classifier" pattern. So "小时" can be used as "某个小时", or "某小时". "钟头" can only be used as "某个钟头".)例如:

李大夫在手术台上连续做了二十四个小时/钟头的手术。

李大夫在手术台上连续做了二十四小时的手术。

* 李大夫在手术台上连续做了二十四钟头的手术。

时间一小时一小时地过去了,他还是处在昏迷中。

* 时间一钟头一钟头地过去了,他还是处在昏迷中。

现在人太多,你一小时以后再来吧。

* 现在人太多,你一钟头以后再来吧。

信心 xìnxīn　　决心 juéxīn

信心〈名词〉< noun >
决心〈名词〉〈动词〉< verb >

(一)"信心"、"决心"都可以用作名词,但是词义不同。(Both "信心" and "决心" can be used as nouns, but they are different in meaning.)

1."信心"表示一种相信自己的愿望或预料一定能够实现的心理,因此它侧重于强调某一有价值的结果;"决心"表示一种坚定不移的意志,因此它侧重于强调某一动作行为。("信心" expresses a firm belief about one's wishes or expectations being realized. It emphasizes a worthwhile result. "决心" expresses a strong will, emphasizing a certain action.)例如:

他有信心学好汉语。(相信自己有"学好"这一结果。)
他有学汉语的决心。(可以不必强调"学好"这一结果。)
＊ 他有学汉语的信心。(表达不十分明确,应该有相信实现的目标。)
我有帮助他的决心。
小张有排一夜队买球票的决心。

上面两句都表示"有做什么事情的意志",强调某一动作行为。如果用"信心",就显得不那么合适。例如:

＊ 我有帮助他的信心。
＊ 小张有排一夜队买球票的信心。

这两句都缺少实现自己所期望的结果的内容。如果改成下面的句子就好些。

我有帮助他提高汉语水平的信心。
小张有买到球票的信心。

2.在不表示具体做什么事而只是表示对某事的态度的句子中,一般不能用"决心",而用"信心"。(While expressing not doing something specifically, but indicating the attitude towards something,

"信心", not "决心", is usually used.)例如：

他对未来有信心。

＊他对未来有决心。

3.表示决计做某事不能用"信心",而要用"决心"。(While expressing the determination to do something, "决心", not "信心", should be used.)例如：

我决心已定,一定要接受这项艰巨的任务。

(I have made my mind to accept the difficult assignment.)

＊我信心已定,一定要接受这项艰巨的任务。

(二) 功能用法不同 (Differences in function and usage)

"信心"只有名词用法,单独作句子成分时,通常作句子的主语、宾语。"决心"除了名词用法外,还有动词用法,它可以作句子的谓语。("信心" is only used as a noun. When used alone, it usually serves as a subject or object. "决心" is used either as a noun or as a verb. It can serve as a predicate in a sentence.)例如：

我决心实现自己的理想。

我决心跟他结为好朋友。

我决心这样做下去。

＊我信心实现自己的理想。

＊我信心跟他结为好朋友。

＊我信心这样做下去。

＊我信心学好汉语。

(三) 组合搭配不同 (Differences in collocation)

"信心"因为是表示相信自己的愿望或预料一定能够实现的心理,因此,它常常跟"建立"、"失掉"、"增强"、"增添"、"充满"、"满怀"、"百倍"、"足"等词组合搭配;"决心"是一种意志,所以它常与"下"、"坚定"、"动摇"、"抱定"等词组合搭配。〔"信心" expresses a firm belief about one's wishes or expectations being realized, so it is usually combined with such words as "建立"(build),"失掉"(lose),"增强"(strengthen),"增添"(gain),"充满"(be brimming with),"满怀"(be imbued with),"百倍"(a hundredfold),"足"(full),;"决心" expresses the strong will, and often goes together with such words as "下"(make),"坚定"(strengthen),"动摇"(shake),"抱定"(hold).]例如:

你对自己的将来要建立信心。
她对实现自己的理想信心十足。
(She is quite confident of realizing her ideal.)
他对公司的前景充满信心。
她信心百倍地迎接挑战。
(She accepted the challenge with full confidence.)
* 你对自己的将来要建立决心。
* 她对实现自己的理想决心十足。
* 他对公司的前景充满决心。
* 她决心百倍地迎接挑战。
他下决心实现自己的理想。
大家都抱定了吃苦的决心。
(All of us are determined to bear hardship.)
他决心已定,谁也动摇不了他的决心。
* 他下信心实现自己的理想。
* 大家都抱定了吃苦的信心。
* 他信心已定,谁也动摇不了他的信心。

兴趣 xìngqù　　乐趣 lèqù　　爱好 àihào

兴趣、乐趣〈名词〉< noun >
爱好〈名词〉〈动词〉< noun >　< verb >

(一)"兴趣"与"乐趣"

1. 意义不同 (Differences in meaning)

"兴趣"主要表示对事物、对人喜好的态度、情绪,这种态度、情绪主要来自事物、人对感受者的吸引;"乐趣"主要表示参加某种活动后自身产生的快乐的感觉,有"产生了乐在其中的感觉"

的意味。因此,用"兴趣"时,应该是很抽象的或没有具体活动行为的情况;用"乐趣"时,则应该有具体的活动行为的情况。("兴趣" mainly expresses one's attitude or manner to somebody or something which has an attraction for the person affected. "乐趣" mainly expresses one's happy feeling after taking part in some activities, meaning "find pleasure in something." So "兴趣" is used in the situation that is abstract and in which no concrete activity is involved. "乐趣" is used in the situation where the concrete activity is involved.) 例如:

我对中国的风土人情很感兴趣,所以选了这门课。

(I am very interested in the local conditions and customs of China, so I take it as a selected course.)

我的兴趣不在这里,我的兴趣在果树嫁接上。

闲下来,我最大的乐趣就是一个人静静地欣赏音乐。

(In my spare time, my greatest pleasure is to appreciate music alone.)

他们尽情地享受着日光浴的乐趣。

(They enjoyed the pleasure of sun-bath as much as they can.)

"乐趣"由于是某种活动而使人产生的快乐的感觉,所以它只能用于事物;"兴趣"是人对事物、对人的喜好情绪,所以可用于事物,也可用于人。(As "乐趣" means the happy feeling aroused from certain activities, it is only used to describe things. "兴趣" means one's fondness for somebody or something, so it can be used to describe people or things.) 例如:

剪纸已成为她生活中不可多得的乐趣。

(Paper-cut has become one of her rare joys.)

他对研究昆虫有浓厚的兴趣。

(He took a great interest in studying insects.)

听说首长对你很感兴趣,可能让你给他作勤务兵。

(It's said that the senior officer takes a great interest in you, and may ask you to be his odd-job man.)

2.结构形式不同(Differences in structure)

"兴趣"常常与"有/没有"、"感/不感"构成较为固定的格式,在"有/没有"、"感/不感"的对象前加"对"构成介词词组放到动词前作状语,"有"、"感"前还常常加上程度副词表示喜好的程度;"乐趣"不能构成这种形式。("兴趣" is often combined with "有／没有" or "感／不感" to form fixed patterns, with "对" in front of the target of "有／没有" or "感／不感" to form prepositional phrases to be placed before the verb as adverbials. Adverbs of degree are often added in front of "有" or "感", indicating the degree of fondness. "乐趣" cannot form such patterns.)例如:

听说他对你的那个提议很有兴趣,可能会跟你具体谈谈。

大家对这个话题十分感兴趣,谈得非常热烈。

他对下棋一点儿也不感兴趣。

对生活持乐观态度的人才能享受到生活中的乐趣。

(Only those who have an optimistic attitude in life are able to enjoy the pleasure of life.)

* 对生活持乐观态度的人才能对生活很感乐趣。

* 我对一个人静静地欣赏音乐很有乐趣。

(二)"兴趣"与"爱好"

1."兴趣"与"爱好"都可以用作名词,但是意义和用法有所不同。("兴趣" and "爱好" can both be used as nouns, but they are different in meaning and usage.)

(1)一般的喜好之情可以称之为"兴趣";"爱好"则不行,它必须是对事物具有浓厚的兴趣才行。(General fondness can be said as "兴趣", but not "爱好", which means great interest for something.)例如:

各人有各人的兴趣和爱好,不能强求一律。

(Each one has his own interest and hobbies. No rigid uniformity should be sought.)

人们怀着极大的兴趣参观了这次展览。

你怎么对什么都感兴趣?

她的爱好十分广泛。

集邮是他四大收集爱好之一。

(2)"爱好"只能用于事物,不能用于人;"兴趣"可用于事物,也可用于人。("爱好" is only used to describe things not people; while "兴趣" can be used to describe both people and things.)例如:

* 李妈妈从心里爱好小华。

* 他对你爱好。

他好像对你特别感兴趣。

老首长对你很感兴趣,想让你给他当通讯员。

(3)"兴趣"常常可以构成"有兴趣"、"感兴趣"这样的结构形式;"爱好"不能构成这种结构形式。("兴趣" usually forms patterns as "有兴趣","感兴趣";"爱好" cannot form such patterns.)例如:

他说他对这个选题有一定的兴趣。

在所有的外语学习中,约翰对学习汉语最感兴趣。

* 人们对这次展览很有爱好。

* 约翰对学习汉语最感爱好。

2.功能不同:(Differences in function:)

(1)"兴趣"只用作名词;"爱好"除名词外,还用作动词,表示对事物有浓厚的兴趣并积极投入。"爱好"可以作谓语,前边可以直接接受副词的修饰,后边可以带宾语、补语。("兴趣" is only used as a noun. "爱好" can be either used as a noun or verb, meaning to be greatly interested in something and take an active part in it. "爱好" can be used as a predicate, modified by adverbs, or followed by objects or complements.)例如:

他从小就住在海边,十分爱好游泳。

这里的外国留学生都特别爱好中国的书法和绘画。

他现在年龄大了就是了,其实年轻的时候是十分爱好<u>体育活动</u>的。

(He is old now. While he was young he took great interest in sports.)

他对什么都爱好,爱好了半天,一无所长。

(He is interested in everything, but has no special skill for anything.)

(2)由于"兴趣"只作名词用,所以它不具有"爱好"前可以直接接受副词,后边可以带宾语、补语的功能。("兴趣" is only used as a noun, so it cannot be modified directly by adverbs, or followed by objects or complements.)例如:

* 我对中国的历史、文化十分兴趣。

* 在北京,我最兴趣长城。

* 他对什么都兴趣,兴趣了半天,一无所长。

兴趣 xìngqù   兴致 xìngzhì

〈名词〉表示喜好的情绪。(< noun > indicating the feeling of fondness.)

"兴趣"主要表示对事物、对人喜好的态度、情绪,这种态度、情绪主要来自事物、人对感受者的吸引;"兴致"则主要表示保持着一种兴奋的情绪去做所喜好的活动,做的时候情绪高、兴头足。("兴趣" mainly expresses one's attitude or manner to somebody or something that has an attraction to the person affected. "兴致" means to happily carry on activities one is interested in. It mainly expresses one's high morale and keen interest.)所以它们的区别在于:(The following are their differences:)

(一) 涉及的对象有所不同 (Differences in the objects involved)

"兴趣"可以用于人,也可以用于事物;"兴致"只可用于事物,而且是具体的活动或行为。(The object(s) of "兴趣" can be people or things; "兴致" can only be used to describe things, especially the concrete activities or behavior.)例如:

虽然只见了一面,可是他对你很感兴趣。

以前他对网球、羽毛球很感兴趣,最近他又对高尔夫球感起兴趣来。

(He was interested in playing tennis and badminton before and now he also begins to take interest in playing golf.)

今天大家游园的兴致很高。

(Today all of us are in a high mood to enjoy visiting the park.)

我对这些没有兴致。

* 虽然只见了一面,可是他对你很有兴致。

(二) 句法功能有所不同 (Differences in syntactic function)

"兴致"除作主语、宾语外,还可以构成词组作状语和补语;"兴趣"一般情况下不用作状语、补语。("兴致" can be used as an adverbial and complement while forming word groups, as well as a subject and object. "兴趣" generally is not used as an adverbial or complement.)例如:

虽然面前到处是美丽动人的景象,可是她只是毫无兴致地瞥了它们一眼,就低下头去想心事了。

(Though the scenery everywhere in sight is so beautiful, she just shot a glance at it without any zest, and hung her head to think about something.)

大家饶有兴致地观看这一老一少的表演。

(All the people watched the performance of the old and the young with zest.)

孩子们玩得很有兴致。

* 大家兴趣地观看这一老一少的表演。

* 孩子们玩得很有兴趣。

(三) 词语搭配上有很大不同 (Differences in collocation)

"兴趣"常与"广泛"、"浓厚"、"强烈"等形容词搭配,常受"感"、"怀着"、"产生"、"引起"等动词的支配。但是它一般不跟"好"、"坏"、"高"、"低"等形容词组合;"兴致"常与"好"、"坏"、"高"、"低"等形容词组合,还能构成成语"兴致勃勃"、"兴致索然"、"饶有兴致"等。〔"兴趣" often goes together with adjectives like "广泛(wide)", "浓厚(deep)", "强烈(strong)", or is usually governed by such verbs as "感(feel)", "怀着(cherish)", "产生(bring about)", "引起(arouse)", but it is not used together with adjectives as "好(good)", "坏(bad)", "高(high)", "低(low)". "兴致" is often combined with adjectives as "好(good)", "坏(bad)", "高(high)", "低(low)", and also form phrases such as "兴致勃勃(full of zest)", "兴致索然(uninterested)", "饶有兴致(with keen interest)".〕例如:

他对什么都感兴趣。

* 他对什么都感兴致。

他对这项实验产生了浓厚的兴趣。

* 他对这项实验产生了浓厚的兴致。

大家游园的兴致很高。

* 大家游园的兴趣很高。

孩子们兴致勃勃地放着焰火。

(The children set off fireworks with keen interest.)

* 孩子们兴趣勃勃地放着焰火。

(四) 语体色彩上稍有不同 (Slight differences in style and flavor)

"兴趣"通用于口语、书面语;"兴致"多用于书面语。("兴趣" is both used in spoken and written languages. "兴致" is more used in written language.)

兴趣 xìngqù   有趣(儿)yǒuqù(r)

兴趣〈名词〉< noun >
有趣(儿)〈形容词〉< adjective >

(一) 意义不同 (Differences in meaning)

"兴趣"主要表示感受者主观上对事物、对人产生的喜好之情;"有趣(儿)"则指人、事物本身使感受者引起的好奇心或喜爱之情。〔"兴趣" expresses the fond feeling one feels for somebody or something. "有趣(儿)", on the contrary, refers to somebody or something that arouses the curiosity or concern of others.〕例如:

同学们怀着极大的兴趣观看着杂技团的表演。
(The students watched the performance of the acrobatic troupe with great interest.)

他说他对你很感兴趣,哪天过来跟你聊聊。
(He said he was interested in you and wanted to come and have a chat with you some day.)

这个小猫真有趣儿,真逗人!
小刘真有趣儿,就是不说话也会把你逗乐。
(Xiao Liu is so funny that he can amuse us even without saying a word.)

(二) 词性和功用不同 (Differences in syntactical function)

"兴趣"是名词,"有趣(儿)"是形容词,不同的词性,有不同的功用。〔"兴趣" is a noun. "有趣(儿)" is an adjective. So they have different functions.〕

1. "有趣(儿)"可接受副词的修饰;"兴趣"不可以。("有趣(儿)" can be modified by adverbs. but "兴趣" can't.)例如:

很有趣	十分有趣	不太有趣
真有趣	一定有趣	的确有趣
*很兴趣	*十分兴趣	*不太兴趣
*真兴趣	*一定兴趣	*的确兴趣

2. "有趣"在句中主要作谓语、定语、补语,作宾语是有条件

的;"兴趣"在句中主要作主语、宾语,不能作谓语、补语。("有趣" is mainly used as a predicate, attribute, complement, or object under certain conditions. "兴趣" is mainly used as a subject or object, but not as a predicate or complement.)例如:

听说那部电影很有趣,我们也去看看吧。(谓语)
爷爷讲了一个十分有趣的故事。(定语)
今天的生日过得真有趣。(补语)
我觉得那里的习俗很有趣。(小句作"觉得"的宾语)
他的兴趣不在这里,他的兴趣在研究计算机上。(主语)
我对邮票很感兴趣,所以搜集了很多邮票。(宾语)
* 听说那部电影很兴趣,我们也去看看吧。
* 爷爷讲了一个十分兴趣的故事。
* 今天的生日过得真兴趣。
* 我对邮票很感有趣,所以搜集了很多邮票。

3.使用"有趣"时还需要注意:"有趣"是形容词,可以作谓语,但是不能直接陈述人,不能带宾语或涉及事物。(Notice that "有趣" is an adjective, and can be used as a predicate, but can not be used directly after persons, or followed by objects, nor can it relate to things.)例如:

* 我有趣中国的历史和文化。
* 他说他有趣这项活动。
* 他们对那里的风俗有趣。
* 他说他对这项活动有趣。

Y

沿着 yánzhe　　　顺着 shùnzhe

〈介词〉引进动作所经过的路线。(< preposition > introducing the route an action goes along.)

"沿着"、"顺着"跟名词构成的介词词组都可以表示动作所经过的路线,在句中作状语。〔"沿着" and "顺着" can be combined with nouns to form prepositional phrases, meaning (an action going) along a route, used as an adverbial.〕例如:

沿着/顺着这条小路一直走就到了。

沿着/顺着墙边画了一条粗粗的黑线。

沿着/顺着操场边跑了三圈。

但是这两个词在意义上、词语搭配上,还有一定差别,有时不能换用。(But there are some differences between these two words, and they are not always exchangeable.)

(一)"沿着"引进的路线往往是可以实际经过的路,所以与"沿着"搭配的名词一般都具有场所意义。(The part introduced by "沿着" is usually the actual route one may go along, the nouns combined with "沿着" usually suggest places.)例如:

沿着马路　　沿着大街　　沿着小道　　沿着墙边
沿着池边　沿着河边　沿着铁路

而且,"沿着"引进的路,一般要有清楚的实际的边界,使之成为可经过的线路或可遵循的线路。(The route introduced by "沿着" usually has a clear and actual boundary, making it a passable line.)例如:

靠池边水浅,沿着池边游,就不会发生危险。

沿着这条公路一直走,不要拐弯儿,就可以找到那家公司。

沿着田埂望去,似乎看不到尽头。

(Looking along the ridge, you seem unable to see the end of it.)

(二)"顺着"引进的路线则不完全强调有清楚的实际的边界,与"顺着"搭配的名词也不一定具有场所意义。(The part introduced by "顺着" does not necessarily have clear and actual bounds, and the nouns combined with "顺着" may not suggest places.)例如:

  顺着头发　　顺着裤腿　　顺着脸颊
  顺着山坡　　顺着水流　　顺着这个方向

这是因为"顺着"构成的介词词组所表达的主要意思是"按照……方向"、"按照……路线"等,所以与之搭配的词可以是一般事物的名词,而且这些名词也不一定要有清楚的实际的边界。(The reason is that the prepositional phrases formed with "顺着" mainly express the meaning "in the direction of...", "following the route of", so the words collocated with it may be nouns denoting general things unnecessarily having clear and actual bounds.)例如:

  敌人追上来了,没有退路了,咱们顺着山坡滚下去吧!

(The enemy is catching up with us, and we have no way to retreat. Let's roll down along the hillside.)

  汗水顺着头发滴滴嗒嗒往下落。
  他吓坏了,管不住的尿顺着裤管儿一个劲儿地往下流。

(He was so frightened that he couldn't refrain his urine from flowing along his trouser legs.)

  顺着水流的方向望去,看不到河的尽头。
  ＊敌人追上来了,没有退路了,咱们沿着山坡滚下去吧!
  ＊汗水沿着头发滴滴嗒嗒往下落。
  ＊他吓坏了,管不住的尿沿着裤管儿一个劲儿地往下流。
  ＊沿着水流的方向望去,看不到河的尽头。

一般来说,用"沿着"的地方,可以换用"顺着",用"顺着"的地方,不一定都能换用"沿着"。那种不强调实际边界、不强调规定路线的一般事物名词,一般不能接在"沿着"后面。(Generally speaking, "沿着" can be replaced by, but seldom substitute for "顺着". General nouns not emphasizing actual bounds or fixed route cannot be used after "沿着".)

(三)"顺着"还可以引进抽象的事物,有"按照……"、"遵照……"的意思;"沿着"不能这样用。("顺着" can also introduce abstract things, meaning "according to…", "in accordance with…". "沿着" cannot be used so.)例如:

顺着这条线索摸下去,一定会查个水落石出。

(Track it down by following the clue, and you'll surely get to the bottom of it.)

咱们就顺着他的话题往下说,怎么样?

你就别再坚持了,还是顺着她的意思把屋子布置布置吧。

(You'd better not hold your own and arrange the room according to her idea.)

* 沿着这条线索摸下去,一定会查个水落石出。

* 咱们就沿着他的话题往下说,怎么样?

* 你就别再坚持了,还是沿着她的意思把屋子布置布置吧。

要不 yàobu　　不然 bùrán

〈连词〉用于连接表示假设或者选择关系的句子。(< conjunction > used to connect sentences of assumptive or alternative relations.)

(一) 相同之处 (Similarities)

1."要不"、"不然"都可以用来连接假设关系的句子,表示"如果不这样"的意思,全句表示如果提到的情况跟上文相反,就会产生什么样的后果。("要不" and "不然" can both be used to connect sentences of assumptive or alternative relations, meaning "if

536

not". The sentence means that if the condition mentioned is opposite to the above, certain kind of result will be produced.)例如:

这件事,你应该跟他解释清楚,要不/不然他会误会的。

(You should explain to him about this matter, or else he will misunderstand it.)

幸亏戴了安全帽,要不/不然命可能都保不住了。

(Luckily I was wearing a safety helmet, otherwise I would have even lost my life.)

2."要不"、"不然"都可以连接选择关系的句子,用来对上文做假定性否定,然后在下文做出另一选择,表示"如果不这样,那就……"的意思,后一分句常用"就"呼应。(Both "要不" and "不然" can link up sentences of alternative relation to supposedly negate the previous clause, and then give another choice in the following clause, meaning "if not ... or else ...", usually with "就" in the second clause to work in concert.)例如:

他可能去图书馆了,要不/不然就是去资料室了。

我肚子疼,不能参加比赛了。让小王代我吧,要不/不然让小李代我也行。

3."要不"、"不然"后面都可以接"……的话",用以加强假设语气。("要不" and "不然" can be followed by "…的话" to emphasize the tone of the assumption.)例如:

咱们找小孙聊聊天儿去,要不的话,出去散散步也行。

她一定没接到信,要不的话就是没在家,不然,不会不给你来信的。

(She must have not got the letter, or she might not be at home, otherwise she would have written to you.)

他一定是被什么重要的事情耽搁了,不然的话不会迟到的。

他怎么没来开会?——也许是去北京还没回来吧,不然的话就是有什么事耽搁了。

537

(二) 不同之处 (Differences)

1. 色彩和语气有一定差别 (Some differences in flavor and tone.)

"要不"含口语色彩;"不然"具有书面语色彩。"不然"否定意味更重,更果断,所以语气较重;"要不"跟"不然"比稍显婉转。("要不" is used in spoken language, while "不然" in written language. The negative meaning of "不然" is stronger and firmer, so it is more emphatic. "要不" is relatively milder than "不然".)

2. 表示选择关系时,结构上稍有差别 (Slight differences in structure while expressing alternative relations.)

表示选择关系时,"不然"前还可以用"再"、"要",构成"再不然"、"要不然"的格式;"要不"不能这样用。("不然" can have "再","要" in front, forming the patterns "再不然" or "要不然"。"要不" can not be used so.)例如:

他可能去办公室了,要不然就是回家去了。

他这样说,只能说明他不懂得这个起码的道理,再不然该怎样解释呢?

(His saying only indicates that he didn't know this rudimentary principle, or what else could explain it?)

* 他这样说,只能说明他不懂得这个起码的道理,再要不该怎样解释呢?

此外,"不然"除连词用法外,还可以表示"不是这样"的意思,只作谓语。"要不"没有这种用法。(Besides being used as a conjunction, "不然" can also mean "being not so", and is only used as a predicate. "要不" cannot be used so.)例如:

大家都以为我能喝酒,其实不然。

老周是个很实在的人,小李就不然了,显得有些虚伪。

(Lao Zhou is an honest man; while Xiao Li is not so. He seems somewhat hypocritical.)

* 大家都以为我能喝酒,其实要不。

* 老周是个很实在的人,小李就要不了,显得有些虚伪。

要不是 yàobushi　　要不然 yàoburán

"要不是"和"要不然"都是可以起到关联作用的词语,它们通常用于假设关系的复句中,表示假设性的否定,下文再说出否定后将会出现的情况。(Both "要不是" and "要不然" are words functioning as relatives, often used in complex sentences to express supposed negation, and then give the situation which will occur in the following clause after the negation.)

"要不是"、"要不然"意义和用法都不同,不能通用。(They are different in meaning and usage, not interchangeable.)

(一) 意义上 (In meaning)

"要不是"表示的是"如果不是"的意思,有假设性否定判断的意义。所以它通常用于句首,后面直接跟上否定判断的内容;"要不然"表示的是"如果不是这样"的意思,它本身就可以构成一个假定的条件,所以通常独自成句,下文再接表示结果的句子。("要不是" means "if not", expressing supposedly negative judgment. It is usually used at the beginning of a sentence, followed directly by the content it judges negatively. "要不然" means "if it is not so". It can constitute a hypothetical condition itself. So it usually makes a clause alone, and then is followed by a clause expressing the conclusion.)例如:

要不是他帮助我,我简直不知道该怎么办好。

(If it were not for his help, I simply didn't know what to do.)

要不是你告诉了我,我还一直蒙在鼓里呢。

(If you hadn't told me, I might have been kept in the dark up till now.)

要不是你这个专家亲自来看一下,非出大问题不可。

(If the expert yourself hadn't come to check it up, some-

539

thing terrible might have happened.)

准是塞车了,要不然,他们早该到了。

幸亏出门时又加了一件衣服,要不然,一定会感冒的。

写文章一定要详略得当,要不然,中心思想就不清楚。

(Details and sketches must be arranged properly in writing an article. Otherwise, the main idea will be unclear.)

(二) 用法上 (In usage)

"要不然"本身就是一个假定的条件,可以独自成句,后面不能再接表示假定条件的内容。"要不然" itself is a hypothetical condition, and can make a sentence alone, without any other hypothetical substance after it.)例如:

* 要不然你告诉了我,我还一直蒙在鼓里呢。

* 要不然你这个专家亲自来看一下,非出大问题不可。

"要不是"不是一个完整的结构,不能独立构成假定条件。 ("要不是" is not a complete structure, so it cannot form a hypothetical condition alone.)例如:

* 准是塞车了,要不是,他们早该到了。

* 幸亏出门时又加了一件衣服,要不是,一定会感冒的。

此外,"要不然"还可以用于选择关系的复句中,表示在两者中选择一项,相当于"要不"。通常已表示出说话人的选择意向,即前项,但是如果前项不行,选择后项也行。〔"要不然" can also be used in a complex sentence denoting alternative relations, meaning to choose one between two. It is the same as "要不(or)". Usually the speaker's choice is implied, namely he prefers the former item. But if it is not available, the speaker may choose the latter instead.〕例如:

这事恐怕您出头才办得了,要不然,您给写封信或者打个电话招呼一声也行。

(I'm afraid you have to come forward to deal with it yourself, or you may write a letter or make a phone call to notify them.)

咱们走着去得了，要不然就骑自行车，反正不坐汽车。

要么 yàome　　或者 huòzhě

〈连词〉表示选择关系，在两项或更多的选择项中选择一项。
(< conjunction > expressing alternative relations, meaning to choose one from the two or more items.)

(一)"要么"、"或者"在句中都可以只用一次，也可以用两次或两次以上，用两次的话，构成"要么……要么……"、"或者……或者……"的格式，表示非此即彼的意思。("要么" or "或者" may be used once, twice or more times in a sentence. When they are used twice in a sentence, they may form the patterns "要么…要么…" or "或者…或者…", meaning "either this or that".)例如：

你最好去跟他谈谈，要么我去也行。

今天周末，咱们去哪儿玩玩吧，或者去麦当劳吃点儿什么，你说呢？

要么他来，要么我去，你看怎么办好？

对于困难或者你压倒它，或者它吓倒你，二者必居其一。

(Either you overcome the difficulty, or you are frightened by it. There is no other alternative.)

(二)"要么"、"或者"在用法上有一定差别。"要么"只能连接句子，不能连接词；"或者"既可以连接句子也可以连接词。(There are some differences in their usage. "要么" can only be used to link sentences, not words. "或者" can link sentences as well as words.)例如：

要么/或者克服困难搞下去，要么/或者现在就停下来，没有别的路可走了。

(We shall either surmount difficulties and carry it on or stop right now. There is no other way out.)

要么/或者你去，要么/或者我去，要么/或者他去，去一个人就行。

早饭前,我喜欢翻翻报纸或者杂志什么的。

* 早饭前,我喜欢翻翻报纸要么杂志什么的。

你或者他陪老张去一趟就行了。

* 你要么他陪老张去一趟就行了。

(三)"要么"、"或者"在色彩和语气上也稍有差别。"要么"含一定的口语色彩,商量的意味也显得更重些,所以在表示商量的选择句中选用"要么"会显得更合适些。"或者"在这两方面没有明显的特点,甚至在有的商量意味很重的句子中,用"或者"会显得不合适。("要么" and "或者" are slightly different in coloring and tone. "要么" is used somewhat more orally, the meaning of consulting is stronger. So it's more suitable to use "要么" in a sentence involving consultation. "或者" is not special in these two aspects, rather it is not appropriate to use "或者" in sentences strongly implying consultation.)例如:

你不想去找他? 要么我去?

* 你不想去找他? 或者我去?

小张病了,今天的郊游他可能去不了了,要么咱们改个日子?

* 小张病了,今天的郊游他可能去不了了,或者咱们改个日子?

要是 yàoshi 如果 rúguǒ 假如 jiǎrú 倘若 tǎngruò

〈连词〉< conjunction >

用于假设关系复句的偏句中,引出假设性的前提、条件或情况,后面正句常用"就"、"那么"、"则"等词呼应,推断出相应的结论、结果或提出问题。(They are used in the assumptive clauses of complex sentences, introducing hypothetical prerequisites, conditions or situations. In the main clauses, "就", "那么", "则", etc. are usually used to infer corresponding conclusions, results, or to raise questions.)

(一)"要是"、"如果"、"假如"、"倘若"虽然在复句中都是表示假设关系的连词,但是用法上稍有差别,它们的差别主要在词语的色彩上。(Though "要是", "如果", "假如" and "倘若" are all conjunctions expressing hypothetical relations in complex sentences, they are slightly different in usage, and quite different in coloring.)

"要是"有很浓的口语色彩,只能用于口语中。("要是" has a strong oral language flavor, so it is only used in spoken language.)例如:

要是你不答应,我今天就不走了。

要是那孩子不听话,你就好好地管教管教他。

"如果"则通用于口语和书面语中,所以使用的频率也最高。("如果" can be both used in spoken and written languages, and are also most frequently used.)例如:

你先回去吧! 如果有什么新情况,我会通知你的。

如果你们不把基层的情况了解清楚,你们怎么制定方针、政策呢?

(If you had not found out about the situations in the grass-roots units, how could you formulate general and specific policies.)

"假如"有较浓的书面语色彩,多用于书面语。("假如" has a strong literary language flavor, so it is more used in written language.)例如:

假如我把这个意见强加给他,他也会同意的,但是我不想这样做。

(If I forced my views on him, he might have agreed, but I wouldn't do so.)

假如这个项目没被批准,我自己也要搞下去。

"倘若"跟前三个词比,不仅有很强的书面语色彩,而且还有较浓的文言意味。因此,它不仅只能用在书面语中,而且对句子的文言色彩还有所要求。此外它表达的语气也比其他词重。

543

(Compared with the former three words, "倘若" is not only of more literary, but also of more classical flavor. So it is only used in written language, and it also has special demands in the classical style of the sentence. Moreover, the tone it expresses is stronger than that of the other three words.) 例如:

倘若你能从错误中吸取教训,以鉴将来,那就是一个很大的收获。

(If you could draw a lesson from your mistake and take warning from it in the future, you would be duly rewarded.)

倘若有时间,请务必出席会议。

(二) 为加强假设语气,表示假设条件的分句,常常还用"……的话"相配合,尤其是口语色彩较强的"要是"句和通用于口语和书面语的"如果"句。(To emphasize the hypothetical meaning, "…的话" is usually used to correspond in the hypothetical clauses, especially in strongly oral-flavored clauses introduced by "要是" or "如果".) 例如:

要是找不到钥匙的话,就糟啦。

(It would be terrible if I couldn't find the key.)

如果你感到不舒服的话,就回去休息吧!

如果没有这次中国之行的话,我是不可能说出这么好的汉语的。

也 yě   都 dōu

〈副词〉表示强调语气,有"甚至"的意思。

(<adverb> used for emphasis, meaning "even".)

(一)"也"、"都"在表示"甚至"的意思时,有时可以通用。(When "也" and "都" express the meaning "even", they are sometimes exchangeable.) 例如:

车间里一个人也/都没有。

昨天晚上他想了一夜,一点儿觉也/都没睡。

连他也／都不相信我。
他什么也／都不会做。
无论什么人也／都得按照法律办事。
(Everyone must act according to the laws.)
这么大的事他连想也／都不想。

但是,"也"、"都"所强调的内容还是稍有差别的。"也"的基本意义主要是表示"类同",表示强调时,依然侧重于对类同的强调。(But there are some differences in the substances they emphasize. The primary meaning of "也" is "to be of a kind". When used emphatically, it also emphasizes the same kind.)例如:
不光你挨批评了,我也挨批评了。(强调"我"跟"你"一样)
他人品很好,工作也很出色。(强调"工作"跟"人品"一样)
连他也不相信我。(这句话是以"他"为例,"他"是最相信我的人,用"也"强调"他"跟别人一样不相信"我",说明没有人相信我。〔Take "他(he)" as an example. "He" is the person who trusts me most. Use "也" to emphasize that "he", just like others, didn't believe me. That indicates no one believed me.〕

"都"的基本意义主要是表示总括,表示强调时,依然侧重于对总括的强调。(The basic meaning of "都" is "inclusive". When used emphatically, it still emphasizes "inclusion".)例如:
所有的汽车都开出来了。(总括了所有的汽车。)
每个人的脸上都露出了笑容。(总括所有的人。)
连他都不相信我。(这句话是以"他"为例,"他"是最相信我的人,用"都"强调不相信"我"的人甚至包括"他",说明没有人相信我。〔Take "他"(he) as an example. "He" is the person who trusts me most. Use "都" to emphasize that those who didn't believe me even included "him". That indicates no one believed me.〕

(二)"也"、"都"通用的句子主要有两种:(Sentence patterns in which both "也" and "都" can be used:)

1. "连……也/都……"句式,即隐含"连"字的强调句。(The pattern "连…也／都…", or emphatic sentences implying the meaning of the word "连".)

2. "谁/什么/怎么/哪儿等……也/都……"句式,即句中有表示任指疑问代词的句子,或隐含任指的句子。(The pattern "谁(who)／什么(what)/怎么(how)／哪儿(where), etc. …也／都…", or sentences containing or implying any indefinite interrogative pronouns.)

在第二种句式中,通常否定式多用"也",肯定式多用"都";"谁"、"什么"可用"也"、"都",其他表任指的疑问代词句多用"都"。〔In the second pattern, "也" is usually used in the negative sentences, while "都" in affirmative ones. Both "也" and "都" can be used in sentences containing interrogative pronouns "谁(who)" and "什么(what)". Otherwise "都" is usually used.〕例如:

他什么也不知道。
谁也说服不了他。
(No one can persuade him.)
我怎么解释他也听不懂。
你来对付他吧,怎么说都行。
(You go to deal with him. You may say whatever you like.)
什么时候去都可以。
任何困难我们都能克服。

也 yě 又 yòu

〈副词〉 < adverb >

"也"和"又"这两个副词,意义完全不同,不能互换使用。(These two adverbs are quite different in meaning, never interchangeable.)

(一)"也"主要表示相同;"又"主要表示重复或累积。("也" mainly refers to similarity. "又" indicates repetition or accumulation.)
例如:

546

我也是北京大学的学生。(在说话的场合中,一定有北京大学的学生,"我"与他相同。)

你们去医院看张先生吗? 我也去。("我"与"你们""去"的动作相同。)

社会实践也是学习,而且是更重要的学习。("社会实践"与"课堂学习"相同。)

你又来了。(已经来过,再次来。)

真糟糕! 又找错了。(找错过一回,再次找错。)

我又看了两遍,还是没看明白。(在这之前已经看过,现在再重复两次。)

由以上例句可见,"也"主要表示并列实体共有的特性,也就是不同实体的相似性,因此它的主语一般是不同的;"又"表示的是同一实体有关特性的积累或重现,因此它的主语一般是相同的。("也" mainly expresses the common feature of two parallel substances, or the similarity of different things. So its subject is usually not the same with the former part of the sentence. "又" indicates the repetition or accumulation of some features of the same substance. So its subject is usually the same with the former part of the sentence.)再看两例:

小王感冒了,小李也感冒了。(小王、小李不同的人;主语不同;共有特性:感冒)

小王不是前些日子感冒过吗? 怎么又感冒了? (同一个人:小王;主语相同;重现感冒)

(二)"也"还可以构成"也……也……"方式,"又"也可以构成"又……又……"方式,都可以表示两种动作或状态同时存在。但是用法有所不同,常常不能换用。("也" can form the pattern "也…也…", and "又" forms the pattern "又…又…". Both indicate that two acts or states exist simultaneously. But they are different in usage and seldom exchangeable.)

1."又……又……"既可以连接动词,也可以连接形容词,而且使用起来比较自由:可以连接单音节词,也可以连接多音节词语;可以连接两项,也可以连接多项;可以单用,也可以作句子成分。但是所连接的词语意义上应该是同类或相近的;结构上也应该是基本相同的。"也……也……"一般不能连接形容词,只能连接动词,使用起来也有一定限制,常常需要跟其他成分配合。("又…又…" can link verbs as well as adjectives, and is used rather freely. It may either join monosyllabic words or join multi-syllabic words, either two items or several items, and is either used alone or as a sentence component. But the words it connects must be the same kind or similar in meaning and structure. "也…也…" generally is not used to link adjectives. It can only link verbs, and is limited in usage. It is usually used in combination with other components.)例如:

新建的立交桥又高又大又气派。
这里的商品又好又便宜。
八达岭长城又雄伟又壮观。
* 新建的立交桥也高也大也气派。
* 这里的商品也好也便宜。
* 八达岭长城也雄伟也壮观。
大家又唱又跳,高兴了整整一个晚上。
我们又学汉语,又学英语,又在课堂中学习,又在社会中学习,收获可大了。
* 大家也唱也跳,高兴了整整一个晚上。
* 我们也学汉语,也学英语,也在课堂中学习,也在社会中学习,收获可大了。
他虽然也说也笑,可总像有什么心事似的。

(Though also chatting and laughing, he seemed to have something on his mind.)

他尽管也住上高级住宅了,也有了自己的汽车了,可是心里还是觉得空空的。

（Though he lived in a high-level residence, and had a car of his own, he still felt empty in the mind.）

2. 一般来说, AB 两分句主语相同时, 一般用"又……又……"连接; AB 两分句主语不同时, 一般用"也……也……"连接。在 AB 两分句主语不同时, "也……也……"有时也可以连接形容词, 但是一般是有条件的, 通常 AB 两分句使用相同的形容词。(Generally speaking, if the subjects of clause A and clause B are the same, use "又…又…" to link them. If the subjects of clause A and clause B are different, usually use "也…也…" to link them. When the subjects of clause A and clause B are different, "也…也…" sometimes can be used to link adjectives, but usually under the conditions that the two clauses use the same adjective.) 例如：

屋里又闷又热, 叫人喘不过气来。(主语: 屋里; 谓语: 形容词)

（The room is stuffy and hot, almost making one out of breath.）

他又会写诗, 又会作画, 本事大着呢！(主语: 他; 谓语: 动词)

儿子也睡了, 妻子也睡了, 只有他还在灯下工作。(主语: 儿子、妻子; 谓语: 动词)

屋里也热, 外头也热, 真不知道躲到哪里才好。(主语: 屋里、外头; 谓语: 相同的形容词)

（It's hot both inside and outside the room. I really don't know where to hide myself.）

一边……一边……　　yìbiān……yìbiān……
又……又……　　　　yòu……yòu……

（一）意义上有差别 (Differences in meaning)

"一边……一边……"跟"又……又……"都可以表示两个动

549

作或情况的发生或进行,但是时间意义不同。"一边……一边……"表示两个动作在同一时间里进行;"又……又……"则表示两个动作或情况累积在一起,可以在不同的时间里,也可以在同一时间里,但是说话人并不强调同一时间,只在说明累积做了两个动作或事情。(Both "一边…一边…" and "又…又…" can express two actions or things occurring, but different in time. "一边…一边…" indicates the two actions happen at the same time. "又…又…" indicates the two actions or things pile up, maybe at the same time, or at different times. The speaker doesn't emphasize doing something at the same time, but only explains two actions or things have been done altogether.)例如:

她一边倒茶,一边招呼客人坐下。("倒"和"招呼"同时进行)

他一边走着,一边想着自己的发言稿。("走着"和"想着"同时进行)

王芳又背课文,又写作业,忙了一晚上。("背"和"写"不是同时发生)

看到我们来了,她又是倒茶,又是递糖果,热情极了。("倒"和"递"不是同时发生)

你到我这儿来,又哭又闹的,干什么?("哭"、"闹"可能同时出现,但不强调同时)

表示不同时间里做的事情或者事实上不可能同时做的事情,可以用"又……又……",但不能用"一边……一边……"。(When expressing things not done or not able to be done at the same time, "又…又…" can be used, but "一边…一边…" cannot.)例如:

他又参观工厂,又参观农村,搜集了很多第一手材料。

(He visited factories as well as countrysides, and collected a lot of first-hand materials.)

* 他一边参观工厂,一边参观农村,搜集了很多第一手材料。

他又踢足球,又打网球,玩得很痛快。

＊他一边踢足球,一边打网球,玩得很痛快。

"一边……一边……"表示同时的时间,有时还可以是某一相对大的时间空间,在这一时间空间里同时做两种事情。〔"一边… 一边… " indicates (things done) at the same time, sometimes may be a relatively large time-length, during which one does two things simultaneously.〕例如:

<u>在美国时</u>,他一边学习,一边打工,很不容易。

<u>在那里</u>,李大夫一边为病人看病,一边研究病因形成的条件。

(Dr. Li studied the condition that caused the illness while he treated patients there.)

这两个句子也可以用"又……又……"表示,但是强调的角度不同。(The above two sentences can also be expressed with "又…又…", but the emphatic parts are different.)例如:

在美国时,他又学习,又打工,很不容易。

在那里,李大夫又为病人看病,又研究病因形成的条件。

"一边……一边……"强调同步进行;"又……又……"则不一定同步进行,它主要表示累积做了哪几件事。("一边…一边…" emphasizes that the two actions occur simultaneously, but "又…又…" does not necessarily stress on this. It only expresses several things having been done altogether.)

(二)搭配的词语有很大不同(Differences in collocation)

1."一边……一边……"只连接动词不连接形容词;"又……又……"既可以连接动词,又可以连接形容词。("一边…一边…" only connects verbs, not adjectives. "又…又…" can connect either verbs or adjectives.)例如:

我总是一边吃饭,一边看电视。

她一边收拾着屋子,一边哼着小曲。

551

这种鞋又轻便,又便宜,真好。

校园里又干净,又整齐。

* 这种鞋一边轻便,一边便宜,真好。
* 校园里一边干净,一边整齐。
* 她们一边说着、唱着,一边很愉快。

2."一边……一边……"只连接有具体动作、行为的动词或结构,不连接抽象意义的动词或结构。也不连接"是"、"有"、"当"等一类没有具体动作的动词。"又……又……"不受动词或结构具体意义与抽象意义的限制。("一边… 一边…" connects only verbs of concrete action or behavior or structures, not abstract ones. It does not link verbs without concrete actions, such as "是","有" and "当"."又…又…" has no restriction about concrete or abstract verbs or structures.)例如:

这种活动真好,又锻炼了身体,又增进了友谊。

(This activity is really good. It both helps to build up physical strength and helps to promote friendship.)

他又当队长,又当队员。

这是一代又有知识、又有文化、又有思想的年青人。

* 这种活动真好,一边锻炼了身体,一边增进了友谊。
* 他一边当队长,一边当队员。
* 这是一代一边有知识、一边有文化、一边有思想的年青人。
* 他们一边进行比赛,一边加强友谊。

3."一边……一边……"不能连接表示能愿意义或心理活动的动词;"又……又……"可以。("一边…一边…" cannot connect verbs denoting wills or psychological activities, but "又…又…" can.)例如:

他又会写诗,又会写小说,本事大着呢!

你又要去这儿,又要去那儿,有那么多时间吗?

妈妈又欢喜,又难过,脸上又是泪,又是笑。

(Mother is both happy and sad, with both tears and smile on her face.)

* 他一边会写诗,一边会写小说,本事大着呢!
* 你一边要去这儿,一边要去那儿,有那么多时间吗?
* 妈妈一边欢喜,一边难过,脸上一边是泪,一边是笑。

一般 yìbān　　普通 pǔtōng

〈形容词〉表示不是特殊的,跟大多数的情况一样。

(< adjective > not special, just like most cases.)

"一般"和"普通"都可以表示不是特殊的,跟大多数的情况一样的意思,意义很接近,有时可以通用,但是意义的着重点稍有不同,有时不能通用,主要是意义和用法的差别。(Both "一般" and "普通" can mean "not special", "just like most cases"; they are very similar in meaning, and sometimes exchangeable. Their stresses are put on different parts, so they are sometimes not interchangeable.)

(一) 意义上的差别 (Differences in meaning)

1. "一般"表示的是跟大多数情况一样,主要侧重于不是特别好,也不是特别差,居于中间状态的。("一般" means neither very good nor very bad, just ordinary or average.)例如:

　　一般人物　　一般教师　　一般干部　　一般工人
　　一般社员　　一般党员　　一般人
　　一般的商店　一般的工厂　一般的学校　一般的电影院
　　一般的医院

表现人的相貌、身材的:

　　相貌一般(average-looking)　　长相一般
　　个子一般(of average height)　身材一般

表现抽象事物的:

　　见解一般(mediocre idea)

553

学问一般(average learning)
能力一般(mediocre abilities)
水平一般(ordinary level)
境遇一般(common circumstances)
感情一般(ordinary feeling)
关系一般(general relationship)
这次考试我的成绩很一般。(不好也不坏)
* 这次考试我的成绩很普通。
价钱一般。(不算高,也不算低)
* 价钱普通。
这个人可不一般。(有特殊的本事)
(This fellow is not so simple.)
* 这个人可不普通。

2."普通"主要侧重于以相当的数量为基础的,居于普遍状态的,不是特殊的。〔"普通"stresses that (something is) based on large quantity, in a general state, or not special.〕例如:

普通教育(指接受人数最多的、最普遍的教育——在中国包括小学和中学三年这两个阶段)
普通朋友(指不是特殊的朋友,即不是男朋友、女朋友、关系密切的朋友等)
普通劳动者　普通战士　普通一兵　普通人
普通人物　　普通教师　普通干部　普通工人
普通社员　　普通党员
普通的商店　普通的工厂　　普通的学校
普通的电影院　　普通的医院

3.表示通常的、具有相当的规律性的行为,要用"一般",不用"普通"。(When expressing some common or fairly regular actions, we use"一般", not"普通".)例如:

吃完饭,我们一般都到外面散散步。
他一般下半夜才睡觉。

星期六一般没有课。

一篇五百字的作文,他一般用一个小时就能写完。

我一般不到外面饭店吃饭。

* 吃完饭,我们普通都到外面散散步。
* 他普通下半夜才睡觉。
* 星期六普通没有课。

(二) 用法上的差别 (Differences in usage)

1. "一般"、"普通"都可以用作谓语,但是结构有所不同。"一般"可以单独作谓语,也可以与其他词语组合后作谓语,"普通"一般不能单独作谓语,通常需要跟其他词语组合后作谓语。(Both "一般" and "普通" can serve as a predicate, but in different patterns. "一般" can be used as a predicate independently, or in combination with other words. "普通" cannot be used as a predicate alone, but usually used together with other words to serve as a predicate.) 例如:

他在我们班里一般。

他的水平一般吧。

价钱嘛,一般吧。

他的手艺太一般了。

这套家具太普通了。

这种款式很普通。

* 价钱嘛,普通吧。
* 这套家具普通。
* 这种款式普通。

2. "一般"在句子里可以修饰动词,可以作状语和补语;"普通"不能。("一般" can modify verbs, serving as an adverbial or complement; while "普通" cannot.) 例如:

一般地说,这种可能性的确不大。

(Generally speaking, such possibility is indeed rather little.)

＊普通地说,这种可能性的确不大。

我一般不太在意别人说闲话。

他晚上一般都学习。

＊我普通不太在意别人说闲话。

＊他晚上普通都学习。

文章写得很一般。

演得很一般。

＊文章写得很普通。

＊演得很普通。

3. "普通"可以重叠为"AABB"式;"一般"不能。("普通" can be reduplicated as AABB pattern; but "一般" cannot.)例如:

我只是个普普通通的小人物。

(I am only an ordinary cipher.)

这是一家普普通通的小饭店。

＊我只是个一一般般的小人物。

＊这是一家一一般般的小饭店。

4. "一般"还常常有一些习惯性的组合。"普通"一般不这样组合。("一般" can form set phrases;"普通" seldom can.)例如:

一般化　一般见识　在一般情况下　一般地说

＊普通化　＊普通见识　＊在普通情况下

＊普通地说

一点儿 yìdiǎnr　　有点儿 yǒudiǎnr

一点儿〈数量词组〉〈副词〉 < numeral-classifier compound > < adverb >

有点儿〈副词〉 < adverb >

"一点儿"和"有点儿"虽然都有"点儿"的意思,但是词义和用法几乎完全不同,所以不能通用。(Though both "一点儿" and "有点儿" mean "a little / few", they are quite different in meaning and usage. So they are not interchangeable.)

(一)"一点儿"是数词"一"加量词"点儿"构成的数量词组,可以用于修饰限制人或事物,表示少而不定的数量;"有点儿"是副词,表示"稍微"的意思,不能用以修饰限制人或事物。("一点儿" is formed by the numeral "一" and the measure word "点儿", and can be used to modify or confine people or things, indicating a small and uncertain number. "有点儿" is an adverb, meaning "somewhat", not used to modify or confine people or things.)例如:

买一点儿水果　做一点儿吃的　学一点儿外语
干一点儿实事
＊买有点儿水果　＊做有点儿吃的　＊学有点儿外语
＊干有点儿实事

注意:"我还有点儿积蓄。"或者"锅里有点儿饭。"这样的句子"有点儿"不是副词,是动词"有"加量词"点儿","点儿"限制的还是名词性词语。〔Notice: In sentences "我还有点儿积蓄 (I still have some savings.)", "锅里有点儿饭 (There is still some rice in the pot.)", "有点儿" is not an adverb, but the verb "有" plus the measure word "点儿", and "点儿" modifies the nouns.〕

(二)"一点儿"和"有点儿"都可以跟形容词或心理活动动词发生联系,表示程度不高的意思,但是用法完全不同。(Both "一点儿" and "有点儿" can be used with adjectives or verbs denoting psychological activities, meaning in a low degree. They are used in different ways.)

1.在句中的位置完全不同。"一点儿"只能用于形容词后("一点儿"的"一"可以略掉);"有点儿"要用在形容词前。基本结构是:〔Their places in sentences are different. "一点儿" is only used after adjectives ("一" in "一点儿" can be omitted.); "有点儿" must be placed before adjectives. Their basic structures are:〕

形容词+(一)点儿〔an adjective + (一)点儿〕
有点儿+形容词(有点儿 + an adjective)

例如:
你来得早了(一)点儿。
这件衣服贵了(一)点儿。
人多了(一)点儿。
这间屋子小了(一)点儿。
* 你来得一点儿早。
* 这件衣服一点儿贵。
* 人一点儿多。
* 这间屋子一点儿小。
* 这么晚了,他还不回来,我心里一点儿不安。
你来得有点儿早了。
这件衣服有点儿贵。
人有点儿多。
这间屋子有点儿小。
这么晚了,他还不回来,我心里有点儿不安。
(It's so late. He hasn't come back yet. I feel a little worried.)
* 你来得早了有点儿。
* 这件衣服贵了有点儿。
* 人多了有点儿。
* 这间屋子小了有点儿。

2.在表示比较的"比"字句中,表示程度不高时,只能用"一点儿",不能用"有点儿"。(In comparative sentences composed of "比", when expressing being low in degree, only use "一点儿", not "有点儿".)例如:
他比你胖一点儿。
这间屋子比那间大一点儿。
这本教材比那本难一点儿。

558

＊他比你胖有点儿。
　　＊这间屋子比那间大有点儿。
　　＊这本教材比那本难有点儿。
　　＊他比你有点儿胖。
　　＊这间屋子比那间有点儿大。
　　＊这本教材比那本有点儿难。

3."有点儿"对于形容词或动词的色彩有选择。"有点儿"多用于不如意的事情,所以多选择带有消极意义或贬义的形容词、动词;"一点儿"没有这种限制。("有点儿" has special choices of adjectives or verbs about their colorings. "有点儿" is usually used for something not after one's own heart. It is always used with adjectives or verbs that have negative or derogatory meanings. "一点儿" is not limited to this.)例如：

　　有点儿笨　　有点儿难　　有点儿糊涂
　　有点儿吃力　有点儿难受　有点儿紧张
　　＊有点儿聪明　＊有点儿清楚　＊有点儿舒服
　　＊有点儿轻松　＊有点儿高兴
　　这个学生笨了(一)点儿。
　　这里还算舒服(一)点儿。
　　别紧张,轻松(一)点儿。
　　找两个聪明(一)点儿的学生。
　　照相的时候高兴(一)点儿。

　　同样,如果构成"有点儿 + 不 + 形容词／动词"的形式的话,即形容词或动词前有否定词的话,形容词或动词就应该多是积极意义或褒义的。(Similarly, when forming the pattern "有点儿 + no (not) + an adjective／verb", namely there are negative words in front of the adjectives or verbs, these adjectives or verbs should have positive or commendatory meanings.)例如：

　　有点儿不痛快　有点儿不舒服　有点儿不高兴
　　有点儿不懂事　有点儿不讲道理

(三)"一点儿"和"有点儿"都有副词用法,但是意义和使用的语言环境完全不同。"一点儿"只能用于"不"、"没(有)"等否定词前,表示完全否定,常与副词"也"或"都"配合;"有点儿"可以用于否定词前,也可以用于非否定句,它表示的只是"稍微"的意思。(Both "一点儿" and "有点儿" can be used as adverbs, but they are different in meaning and are used in different context. "一点儿" often combined with the adverb "也" or "都" is only used before the negative "不" or "没有", indicating denying completely. "有点儿" can be used either before negative or in non-negative sentences. It only means "a little".) 例如:

他一点儿也不知道这件事。

第一次上讲台,她居然一点儿也不紧张。

(To our surprise, she wasn't nervous at all the first time she mounted the platform.)

那个老乡说的话我一点儿都没听懂。

* 他有点儿也不知道这件事。
* 第一次上讲台,她居然有点儿也不紧张。
* 那个老乡说的话我有点儿都没听懂。

这孩子有点儿不知深浅。

(The child has little sense of propriety.)

她好像有点儿不高兴了。

不知为什么,我总有点儿担心。

他有点儿生气了。

一点儿 yìdiǎnr　　一会儿 yíhuìr

一点儿〈数量词组〉 < numeral-classifier compound >

一会儿〈名词〉 < noun >

(一)"一点儿"是数量词组,可以用来修饰限制人或事物,表示少而不定的数量;"一会儿"是时间名词,表示很短的时间的意思,它一般跟动作发生关系,表示动作持续的时间或两个动作间隔的时间等。("一点儿" is a numeral-classifier compound, and can be used to modify or confine people or things, indicating a small and uncertain number. "一会儿" is a noun denoting time, indicating in a very short time. "一会儿" is only related to actions, expressing the continuation of an act, or the interval between two acts.)例如：

现在还有时间,写一点儿作业吧。
我去买一点儿吃的吧。
帮妈妈做一点儿事吧。
收拾一点儿东西走吧。

以上例句中的"一点儿"都是跟后面的名词发生直接联系的：一点儿作业、一点儿吃的、一点儿事、一点儿东西。"一点儿"表示这些事物的数量少。(In the above sentences, "一点儿" is directly related to the nouns after it："一点儿作业","一点儿吃的"…."一点儿" means only a few / little of these things.)

有些类似的句子也可以用"一会儿"。(Sometimes "一会儿" can also be used in the similar sentences.)例如：

现在还有时间,写一会儿作业吧。
咱们看一会儿电视吧。
我们谈一会儿话吧。

但是,这些例句中的"一会儿"并不是跟事物发生关系,而是跟动作发生关系：写一会儿、看一会儿、谈一会儿。它们表示动作持续或将持续的时间很短。〔But in the above sentences, "一会儿" is not related to the things following it, but rather to the actions. "写一会儿"(write for some time) "看一会儿"(watch for some time), "谈一会儿"(talk for a little while)all indicating the action has lasted or will last for a very short time.〕

因此,只有表示人或事物少而不定的数量意义时,才能用"一点儿"；表示跟动作有关的时间,只能用"一会儿"。(So "一点儿" is only used to express a small and uncertain amount of people or things. "一会儿" is only used to express the time related to an act.)

当动作并没有支配名词性宾语时,或所支配的宾语不可能用"一点儿"计量时,不能用"一点儿"。如果表示的是时间很短的意思,可以用"一会儿"。(When an action doesn't govern a noun object, or the object governed by the action can't be measured with "一点儿", we do not use "一点儿". When expressing in a very short time, "一会儿" can be used.)例如:

* 太累了,休息一点儿再走吧。
* 让孩子们去玩一点儿吧!
* 你们先走吧,我等他一点儿。
* 她心情不好,你陪她一点儿。

太累了,休息一会儿再走吧。

让孩子们去玩一会儿吧!

你们先走吧,我等他一会儿。

她心情不好,你陪她一会儿。

注意:"还有一点儿时间"这句话是把"时间"作为事物来计量的;"睡(一)点儿觉吧!"也是把"觉"当作事物看待的,因此可以用"一点儿"。"睡一会儿觉吧"也可以说,这里的"一会儿"是表示"睡"将持续的时间。〔Notice: In the sentence "还有一点儿时间"(There is still a little time left.),"时间"(time) is considered as a thing, and in "睡(一)点儿觉吧"(Have a little sleep.),"觉"(sleep) is also regarded as a thing. So they can be modified by "一点儿". We can also say "睡一会儿觉吧"(Sleep for a while). Here, "一会儿" indicates the time the act "睡觉"(sleep) lasts.〕

(二)"(一)点儿"有时可以直接跟形容词、动词发生联系,表示程度不高的意思,这时要注意跟表示短时间的"一会儿"区分清楚。〔"(一)点儿" sometimes can be directly connected with adjectives or verbs, meaning not high in degree. But we must pay attention to the difference between it and "一会儿".〕例如:

下午我有点儿事,晚<u>(一)点儿</u>到。

你提前<u>(一)点儿</u>走,没事儿!

"一点儿"在这里表示程度不高,没有时段意义。("一点儿" here indicates not high in degree, not suggesting time.)

明天早来一会儿,我找你有点儿事儿。

晚走一会儿没关系。

"一会儿"在这里表示时间很短,它表示的是与基准时间比相差的时段的意义。("一会儿" here means in a very short time. It indicates the time differing from the base time.)

一定 yídìng　　　肯定 kěndìng

〈副词〉表示必然、确定无疑。(<adverb> "一定" or "肯定" means inevitable or incontestable.)

(一)在表示必然、确定无疑的意思时,"一定"、"肯定"意思基本一样,只是"肯定"表示"确定无疑"的意味更重。(When expressing the meaning "inevitably" or "incontestably", "一定" and "肯定" are almost the same. Only the tone of "肯定" is stronger.)例如:

他从来不缺席,今天没到,一定/肯定有什么原因。

上午的电话一定/肯定是刘伟他们打来的。

他一定/肯定遇到了不少麻烦,不然不会那么沮丧。

(He must have come across a lot of trouble, or he wouldn't have been so depressed.)

这件事他一定/肯定不知道。

我要是知道这件事,一定/肯定会帮助他的。

对已然的事实进行确定,表示毫无疑问的语气时,多用"肯定",动词后常用"过"、"了"。(When defining a fact already being so, and expressing incontestable tone, we usually use "肯定". The verbs are usually followed by "过" or "了".)例如:

这个人我肯定在哪儿见过,只是一时想不起来了。

(I'm sure I have seen this person somewhere, but I simply can't recollect at this moment.)

这间屋子肯定有人住过。

　　　　他今天肯定病了,不然不会不来的。
(二)"一定"还可以表示"坚决"的语气,"肯定"不用于表示这种语气,尤其不能用于祈使句中。("一定" can also express the resolute tone. "肯定" can't express this meaning, especially can't be used in an imperative sentence.)例如:
　　　　这项工程这个月内一定要完成。
　　　　我们一定不辜负师长们的殷切期望。
　　　　(We will certainly live up to the ardent expectations of the teachers.)
　　　　这件事关系重大,一定不能传出去。
　　　　(It's of great significance. Be sure not to spread it out.)
　　　　过马路时一定要注意安全!
　　　　他一定要参加这项活动,怎么办?
　　　　* 这件事关系重大,肯定不能传出去。
　　　　* 他肯定要参加这项活动,怎么办?
　　　　* 过马路时肯定要注意安全!
　　　　* 你肯定记住我的话!

一会儿 yíhuìr　　　不一会儿 bù yíhuìr

　　"一会儿"、"不一会儿"都可以表示短时间的意义,意义和用法上有一定差别,大多不能换用。(Both "一会儿" and "不一会儿" can mean in a short time, but they are different in meaning and usage, thus not exchangeable.)
(一)"一会儿"和"不一会儿"都可以表示时间很短,但是"不一会儿"比"一会儿"表示的时间更短,说话人用"不一会儿"也是为强调时间很短,强调不需要多少时间。("一会儿" and "不一会儿" can both mean a short time, but the time indicated by "不一会儿" is even shorter than "一会儿". So, to use "不一会儿" is to emphasize that the time involved is very short or not much time is needed.)试比较:

1. 表示经历了的很短的时间。(Indicating after a short time.)

一会儿,她就把饭做好了。

不一会儿,她就把饭做好了。

她一会儿就把屋子收拾好了。

她不一会儿就把屋子收拾好了。

我们边走边聊,一会儿就到家了。

我们边走边聊,不一会儿就到家了。

2. 表示在很短的时间之内。(Indicating within a short time.)

别着急,一会儿他就回来了。

稍等一下,妈妈不一会儿就会回来的。

(二) 表示经历从现在往后的一段短时间,不能用"不一会儿",可以用"一会儿"。(When expressing going through a short period of time from now till later, we can not use "不一会儿". But "一会儿" may be used.)例如:

一会儿,我们上街去。

一会儿,你帮我修修自行车。

* 不一会儿,我们上街去。

* 不一会儿,你帮我修修自行车。

再过一会儿,我们就要启程了。

(After a while, we shall set out.)

* 再过不一会儿,我们就要启程了。

(三) "一会儿"还可以表示并没有强调一段短时间的意义,有时甚至表示不算短的一段时间;"不一会儿"只有强调时间短的意义,不能表示不算短的时间的意思。("一会儿" can also express a period not necessarily short, or even a rather long period. "不一会儿" only emphasizes the briefness of the time.)例如:

他睡了多长时间了?—— 睡了<u>一会儿</u>了。(一段时间)

他出去有<u>一会儿</u>了,怎么还不回来?(不算短的一段时间)

(He is out for quite a while. Why hasn't he come back yet?)

565

他睡了多长时间了？—— ＊ 睡了<u>不一会儿</u>了。

＊ 他出去有<u>不一会儿</u>了,怎么还不回来?

他才睡了不一会儿,别叫醒他。(强调时间很短)

(四)"一会儿"还可以构成"一会儿……一会儿……"的格式表示动作或情况不断地变化;"不一会儿"没有这种用法。("一会儿" can form the pattern "一会儿…一会儿…" to indicate the constantly changing actions or conditions. "不一会儿" is not used so.)例如:

他一会儿听音乐,一会儿看电视,不知道做什么才能排除掉烦恼。

(He is now listening to music, now watching TV, not knowing how to divert himself from worry.)

雨一会儿大,一会儿小,下了整整两天两夜。

＊ 他不一会儿听音乐,不一会儿看电视,不知道做什么才能排除掉烦恼。

＊ 雨不一会儿大,不一会儿小,下了整整两天两夜。

一起 yìqǐ　　一齐 yìqí

〈副词〉表示行动一致。(< adverb > meaning acting together.)

"一起"和"一齐"表示行动一致的着重点是不同的。("一起" and "一齐" emphasize different parts when used to express the meaning "acting together".)

(一)"一起"着重于在空间上合在一处或在同一地点发生的事情。("一起" emphasizes being together in space, or things happening in the same place.)例如:

小刘和老师一起走了。

明天我把信和照片一起寄给您。

我们俩是老同事了,一起工作了二十几年了。

雨带着雪,雪夹着雨,一起从天而降。

(Rain accompanied by snow falls down from the sky.)

表示空间上合在一处的意思,不能用"一齐"。(When expressing being together in space, we can not use "一齐".)例如:

* 小刘和老师一齐走了。
* 我们俩是老同事了,一齐工作了二十几年了。
* 雨带着雪,雪夹着雨,一齐从天而降。

(二)"一齐"则着重于时间上的同时发生。因此用"一齐"的句子,句中的动词都是具体动作的动词。("一齐" emphasizes happening simultaneously. So in sentences where "一齐" is used, the verbs are all those that express specific acts.)例如:

大家听我的口令,一齐迈步。

歌声一落,全场一齐鼓起掌来。

行李和人一齐到达。

他刚走到教室门口,学生们便一齐起立放开喉咙喊道:"老师好!"

(He has just reached the door of the classroom when the students stand up and shout loudly in unison: "Good morning, teacher!")

听到敲门声,两个孩子一齐奔过去开门。

表示强调在一个时间起点开始的或同时发生的意思,不能用"一起"。["一起" cannot be used to emphasize (acts) beginning at a certain time or happening simultaneously.]例如:

* 大家听我的口令,一起迈步。
* 歌声一落,全场一起鼓起掌来。

一向 yíxiàng   一直 yìzhí

〈副词〉< adverb >

"一向"、"一直"都可以表示从来如此的意思,但是两词意义上、用法上都有较大差别,一般不可换用。(Both "一向" and "一直" can indicate being always the same from the beginning up to now, but the two words are quite different in meaning and usage. Generally they are not interchangeable.)

(一) 意义的着重点不同 (Different emphases in meaning)

"一向"主要着重于保持不变,即指动作行为或情况从过去到现在都很稳定,不改变;"一直"主要着重于连续性,不间断,指在某段时间内不间断地(做某事)。("一向" stresses the consistence of an action. Namely an action or state is always stable from past till now, without any change. "一直" stresses the continuation of an action. That is to do something continuously without stop during a period of time.)例如:

他一向铁面无私,违背原则的事决不做。

(He has been impartial and incorruptible all along, never doing anything violating the principles.)

我们一向主张和平,反对战争。

这里的商贸一向很发达。

她的服务态度一向很好。

五年来,他一直在攻读研究生,现在已经读了两年博士了。

三天三夜了,他一直在实验室里观察实验进展情况。

(He has been observing the progress of the experiment in the laboratory for three days and nights on end.)

放假以来,他一直在写论文。

工作一直很忙,没有时间去看你,请谅解。

由以上例句可以看到:

1.用"一向"的句子多用于表现品质、性质、态度等,因为这些都是一些稳定因素,所以句中谓语多是形容词或意义抽象的动词;用"一直"的句子可以用具体的动作性动词。("一向" is usually used to describe one's character, nature, manner, etc., which are all stable factors. So the predicates in these sentences are mostly adjectives or verbs of abstract meanings. While "一直" can be used with verbs indicating concrete actions.)

2. 在用"一直"的句子中,常常可以看到起止的时间,这是不间断(做某事)的时间范围。这种时间范围往往可长可短;用"一向"的句子一般不需要划定时间范围。(In a sentence with "一直", there is usually a beginning and ending time which is the time-length of a continuous action. Such time-length can either be long or short. In sentences where "一向" is used, there are usually no time limits.)

(1)既有起止时间,又是具体动作性动词谓语的句子,一般不能用"一向"。(Generally "一向" is not used in sentences indicating the beginning and end of a period of time and with predicates of specific action.)例如:

* <u>五年来</u>,他一向在攻读研究生,现在已经读了两年博士了。

* <u>三天三夜了</u>,他一向在实验室里观察实验进展情况。

* <u>放假以来</u>,他一向在写论文。

(2)谓语是抽象意义的,又没有起止时间的句子,有时可以用"一直",只是跟用"一向"的着重点不同,用"一直"着重于连续性,而不是稳定不变的意义。(If the predicate is of abstract meaning, and there is no specific time limit, sometimes "一直" can be used, but it is different from "一向" in terms of the focus of emphasis. "一直" stresses on the continuity of an action, not the stability.)例如:

这里的商贸一直很发达。

她的服务态度一直很好。

(二)用法上的异同(Differences and similarities in usage)

1."一向"、"一直"都有副词用法,都可以用作状语。(Both "一向" and "一直" can be used as adverbs and serve as an adverbial.)例如:

他一向艰苦朴素。

这里的人一向热情好客。

我一向说话算数。

整整一个晚上,他一直坐在电视机前。

我一直都在为这件事烦恼。

(I have been always bothered by this.)

2."一向"表示的稳定不变也许可以到永远,但是句中如果有表示现在以后的时间意义,尤其表示在时间上继续到什么时候或继续下去的意思,就不能用"一向"了;"一直"既可以用于现在以前的时间,也可以用于现在以后的时间。("一向" means being always the same. If there are words indicating the future time in the sentence, especially indicating an act lasts till some time or will continue, "一向" cannot be used. "一直" can be used to express a period before or after the present.)例如:

他一向遵守诺言。(从来都这样,可能永远是这样。)

(He has consistently kept his words.)

你应该把这项研究一直搞下去。("下去"有继续到将来的意义。)

(You should keep doing the research.)

* 你应该把这项研究一向搞下去。

明天晚上六点,我在公园门口等你,六点见不到你,我也会一直等下去的。(将来时间)

* 明天晚上六点,我在公园门口等你,六点见不到你,我也会一向等下去的。

已经 yǐjīng　　曾经 céngjīng

〈副词〉 < adverb >

"已经"、"曾经"都是表示时间意义的副词,而且主要都用于表示现在以前的时间,但是它们表示的时间意义完全不同,用法上差别也很大,不能互换使用。("已经" and "曾经" are both adverbs denoting time, and mainly used to express a period before the present time. There are great differences in their meanings and usage, so they are not exchangeable.)

(一) 意义上 (In meaning)

1."已经"主要表示事情的完成;"曾经"主要表示经历或有过某种行为、某种事情。("已经" usually means the completion of something. "曾经" usually means having experienced something.)例如：

  这部电影我已经看了。(这件事做完了)
  这部电影我曾经看过。(有过这件事)

2."已经"表示的过去的时间可能离说话时有很远的距离,但是也可能很近,就在不久前甚至就在说话前;"曾经"则一定离说话时有一定的距离,不可能离说话时很近,更不可能就在说话前的时间里。("已经" indicates that the past time involved may be far from now or close to the present time, not long before or just before the talk. While "曾经" indicates the past time involved has certain distance from now, not close to the present time, nor during the talk.)例如：

  1949年解放的时候,我已经参加工作了。(距离说话时很远)
  (刚停下笔说:)我已经写完了,你呢? (就在说话前)
  1949年解放的时候,我曾经参加过工作。(距离说话时很远)
  * (刚停下笔说:)我曾经写完了,你呢?
  * 他刚才曾经帮过我。

3."曾经"表示的动作行为或情况一定是早已结束的;"已经"表示的动作行为或情况可以是结束了的,也可以是还在继续的,"已经"表示的是其中完成或实行的那一部分。(The action or state modified by "曾经" must have been finished long ago. The action or state modified by "已经" may have been finished, or may be still going on. What "已经" expresses is the part that has already been completed.)例如：

  他们曾经是睡过同一个热炕头的战友。(现在早已不

睡一个热炕头了）

(They were once comrades-in-arms, sleeping on the same warm *kang*.)

我曾经在那儿住了二十年。(现在肯定没住在那儿)

有关电路的设计图纸已经出来了。(设计结束了)

(The circuit diagram has been designed.)

考试已经进行一个多小时了。(考试没结束,还在继续着)

＊考试曾经进行一个多小时了。

苹果已经红了一半了。(苹果还将继续红)

＊苹果曾经红了一半了。

4."已经"可以表示经历了多少时间或到了什么时刻、什么阶段等;"曾经"没有这个意思。("已经" may indicate having experienced for some time, or having reached certain time or stage; while "曾经" cannot be used so.)例如:

我在这儿已经住了三十年了。

她已经十八岁了。

现在已经十二点了。

现在,实验已经到了关键的时刻了。

＊她曾经十八岁了。

＊现在曾经十二点了。

＊现在,实验曾经到了关键的时刻了。

5."已经"还可以表示即将完成而现在还没有完成的事情,句中多与"快"、"要"、"差不多"等词配合;"曾经"不能这样用。("已经" can also indicate something nearly finished but not finished yet. It is usually collocated with "快","要","差不多", etc.; "曾经" is not used so.)例如:

天已经快要亮了。

他已经要出发了,你快点儿吧!

差不多已经五点了。

* 天曾经快要亮了。
* 他曾经要出发了,你快点儿吧!
* 差不多曾经五点了。

(二) 用法上 (In usage)

1. "已经"后面多与助词"了"配合,也可以跟助词"过"配合;"曾经"后面多与"过"配合,也可以跟"了"配合。("已经" is usually used together with the particle "了", sometimes with "过"; "曾经" usually with "过", sometimes with "了".)

衣服我已经买来了。
信已经发走了。
那张报他已经看过。
在我遇到麻烦的时候,他曾经帮过我。
他曾经去过美国。
为这事我曾经费了不少的时间。

"已经"、"曾经"大多数情况下都需要"了"或"过"配合才能完成句子,极少数的情况下不用是有条件的。如:该句只是一个分句,处于全句的句中停顿、书面语色彩很强、动词后有表示完成意义的补语、谓语动词是"是"类的动词等。(In most cases, "已经" or "曾经" must be used together with "了" or "过" to complete a sentence, only with a few exceptions, such as when the sentence is only a clause which comes to a pause in the middle of a complete sentence, or the sentence is of strong literary flavor, or there is a complement denoting completion, or the predicate is such verbs as "是".)例如:

* 那张报他已经看。
* 我在这里已经住三十年。
* 他曾经去美国。
* 他曾经帮我。

信已经发走,追不回来了。
他们已经成为好朋友,就别再说三道四的了。

(They have already become close friends. Don't make irresponsible remarks about them.)

我曾经记起那段时间的往事,可是后来统统都给忘了。

(I once recalled the past events during that time, but later I forgot all about it.)

他们曾经是很要好的朋友。

但是"已经"、"曾经"如果用来修饰限制形容词或心理活动动词时,后面的"了"或"过"一般是不可缺的。(When "已经" and "曾经" are used to modify restrictive adjectives or verbs denoting psychological activities, "了" or "过" after them is generally indispensable.)例如:

树叶已经黄了。

他的病已经好了。

我已经伤心过,不想再伤心了。

* 树叶已经黄。

* 他的病已经好。

* 我已经伤心,不想再伤心了。

去年他俩曾经好过一些日子,可是不知怎么后来又完了。

虽说他是一个很坚强的男子汉,可是也曾经悲观过。

(Though he is a strong-willed man, he once felt disheartened.)

* 去年他俩曾经好一些日子,可是不知怎么后来又完了。

* 虽说他是一个很坚强的男子汉,可是也曾经悲观。

2."已经"既可以修饰肯定式,也可以修饰否定式;"曾经"只能修饰肯定式,不能修饰否定式。("已经" can either modify affirmative sentences or negative ones. "曾经" can only be used in affirmative sentences.)例如:

肯定:他已经去了。

人已经走了。

商店已经关门了。

否定：他已经不看了。
　　　商店已经不营业了。
　　　天已经不热了。
肯定：他曾经在这里干过。
　　　我曾经学过英语，后来又改学日语了。
否定：＊他没曾经在这里干过。
　　　＊我没曾经学过英语。
　　　＊他不曾经吃过中国菜。

表示"曾经"的否定意义，可以直接用"没(有) + 动词 + 过"的形式。〔In negative sentences expressing the meaning of "曾经", the pattern "没(有) + verb + 过" can be used.〕例如：

　　他没在这里干过。
　　我没学过英语。
　　他没吃过中国菜。
　　他没有得罪过我。

3."已经"可以直接修饰数量词或时间名词；"曾经"不可以。("已经" can directly modify numeral-classifier compounds or time nouns. "曾经" can't.)例如：

　　已经三十年了。
　　已经上千册书了。
　　已经五点了。
　　已经夏至了。
　＊曾经三十年了。
　＊曾经上千册书了。
　＊曾经五点了。
　＊曾经夏至了。

以后 yǐhòu　　后来 hòulái　　然后 ránhòu

以后、后来〈名词〉< noun >
然后〈连词〉< conjunction >

575

(一)"以后"与"后来"

1. "以后"、"后来"都可以单独使用或用在词组中表示时间。("以后" and "后来" can both be used independently or in phrases to express time.)例如：

> 以后,我们有机会再聚一次。
>
> 后来,他们再也没有见过面。
>
> 毕业以后,我一直在这个研究所里工作。
>
> 后来的情况我确实不太了解。

(1)从时间上说,"以后"是跟"以前"相对的,"后来"是跟"起初"、"原先"、"开始"相对的。"以后"的"以"具有划界的意义,是指某动作或情况后的时间,单用时,是以当时或现在来划界,即从当时或现在开始往后;要么就得接在作为时间划界的词语后,如:"下课以后"、"起床以后"等。〔In terms of time, "以后" is the opposite of "以前"; "后来" is the opposite of "起初", "原先" or "开始". "以" in "以后" has the meaning of delimitation. "以后" refers to a period after an act or a state. When used alone, "以后" delimits time from the present, namely from that time or the present to the future. Otherwise it has to be placed after words of delimitation, for example "下课以后 (after class)", "起床以后 (after getting up)", etc.〕例如：

> 以前让你在这儿吃了不少苦头,以后不会再让你吃苦头了。
>
> (You suffered a lot here in the past. I won't let you bear any hardships from now on.)
>
> 放心吧,以后,我一定刻苦努力。
>
> 从此以后,我要把全部精力都投入到这项研究中。
>
> (From now on, I'll put all my energies into the research work.)
>
> 春节以后我们要到农村搞社会调查。
>
> 吃完饭以后,我到你那儿去一趟。

(2)"后来"的"来"表示的是持续时间,是指到说话时为止的时间或到某时为止的时间。"以后"的时间起点很清楚,"后来"的时间起点模糊,没有一个清楚的起点,它所指的后一件事跟前一件事在时间上是有一段距离的,所以它不可能直接用在某动作或时间词语后表示时间。("来" in "后来" indicates durative time. "后来" refers to the time till the moment of speaking, or till a certain time. The beginning time of "以后" is clear, but that of "后来" is somewhat vague. There is some distance between the times when the former and the latter events take place, so "后来" cannot be used immediately after a verb or time phrase to express time.)例如:

* 下课后来   * 起床后来   * 毕业后来

* 春节后来

原先她就住在这儿,后来不知搬到哪儿去了。("住在这里"离"搬走"有一段时间。)

开始我做得很糟糕,后来在师傅的指导下才逐渐好起来。(At first I did it badly. Later, under the guidance of the master worker, I began to do better.)

她们几个人先后结了婚,后来像商量好了似的,又先后离了婚。(从"结了婚"到"离了婚"有一段时间的距离。)

(They got married one after another, but got divorced successively later on as if arranged.)

* 以前让你在这儿吃了不少苦头,后来不会再让你吃苦头了。

* 从此后来,我要把全部精力都投入到这项研究中。

2."以后"表示的是某动作或情况后的时间,因此叙述的事情不限于过去、现在或将来;"后来"则不同,它只限于叙述过去的事情,不能用于叙述现在或将来的事情。("以后" indicates the time after a certain act or state, so what it describes is not limited to the past, present or future. "后来" is different. It is only used to describe something happening in the past, but not present or future

577

things.)例如:

参加工作以后,我再也没有见过他。(过去)
以后,你别来找我了。(从现在开始到将来)
你记着,出差回来以后一定去医院好好检查检查。

(将来)

* 后来,你别来找我了。
* 你记着,出差回来后来一定去医院好好检查检查。
原先他和我都在这个公司干,后来不知去了哪里。

(过去)

听说,她后来又嫁给一个商人了。(过去)

(二)"然后"与"后来"

"然后"、"后来"都可以用在复句中,但是意义不同。"然后"是连词,主要功能是在句与句中起连接作用。它常跟"先"、"首先"配用,表示两个动作或两个事件的先后顺序,"然后"表示后一个动作或事情。"后来"则不同,它是时间名词,主要用来表示时间。"然后"因为表示的是动作的先后顺序,所以它所表示的两个动作或事件是接连发生的;"后来"所表示的时间具有到某时间为止的持续意义,所以前后两个动作应该具有相隔一段时间的意义。(Both "然后" and "后来" can be used in complex sentences, but they are different in meaning. "然后" is a conjunction whose major function is to join sentences. It is usually used together with "先" or "首先", indicating the sequence of the two acts or events, and "然后" refers to the latter. "后来" is different. It's a noun expressing time. Since "然后" expresses the sequence of acts, the two acts or events it indicates happen one after another. "后来" expresses a period lasting till a certain time, so it suggests that there are intervals between the two acts.)例如:

大家先谈谈情况,然后我们再具体分析分析。
首先由代表们汇报情况,然后大会主席作总结发言。

(First, the delegates report the situations, then the chairman of the conference makes a summary.)

起初他们以为人人都得查,后来才知道只查几个人。

(At first, they thought everyone should be examined. Later they knew that only a few people needed to be examined.)

开始她还给我来过几封信,后来就一点儿音信也没有了。

(At first she had wrote me a few letters, but later I have never heard anything from her.)

* 王欣给丽丽三十块钱,告诉她是学校发给的救济金,然后丽丽才知道,这钱是王欣自己的。

* 然后的事我一点儿都不知道。

* 写文章时,先构思,列出提纲,后来再写。

(改:然后再写)

"后来"只跟过去时间相联系;"然后"既可用于过去,也可用于将来。("后来" is only related to a past time; "然后" can either be used in the past time or the future time.)例如:

过去:三年前她去了美国,后来情况怎么样,我一点儿也不了解。

听说后来她跟张力结了婚,日子过得还挺好。

过去:她先收拾好屋子,然后坐下来静静地写作业,一切做得井井有条。

将来:来,我们先来谈谈情况,然后再分析分析。

* 来,我们先来谈谈情况,后来再分析分析。

以前 yǐqián 从前 cóngqián

〈名词〉 < noun >

"以前"、"从前"都可以表示早于现在的时间或过去的时候,都可以单用或作名词性成分的修饰语。(Both "以前" and "从前" can express a period earlier than the present time or a past time, and both can be used independently or as modifiers of nominal components.)例如:

以前/从前我不认识他。

以前/从前这里没有人家,只是一片荒草地。

再不要想以前／从前那些不愉快的事情了。

但是"以前"、"从前"表示的时间意义还有差别,用法上也有很大的不同。(However "以前" and "从前" are somewhat different in meaning and usage while used to express time.)

(一) 意义上 (In meaning)

1. "从前"表示的时间是指往过去追溯距离现在较久的时间;而"以前"则不同,"以"具有划界的作用,它可以指现在或某时间前的时间。因此,"以前"可以表示过去较久的时间,也可以表示刚才动作前的时间。("从前" indicates the time in the past far from now. While "以前" is different. "以" has the function of delimitation. "以前" refers to the time before present or before a certain time. So "以前" may indicate the time long ago, or just before the act.)例如:

从前,我在这个学校里读过书。(距离现在较久的时间)

以前,这里连一所中学都没有,就不用说大学了。(过去较久的时间)

(In the past, there was not even a middle school here, not to mention universities.)

上课以前,他来找过你。(动作可能刚做完不久)

2. "以前"既可以表示过去的时间,也可以表示将来的时间;"从前"只能表示过去的时间,不能表示将来的时间。("以前" can express a past time, or a future time; while "从前" can only express a past time.)例如:

晚饭以前,你到我这儿来一下。(现在还没吃晚饭)

天黑以前,一定要把这项工程全部结束。(现在天没黑)

* 晚饭从前,你到我这儿来一下。

* 天黑从前,一定要把这项工程全部结束。

(二) 用法上 (In usage)

"以前"是方位词,有两种使用方式,一是可以单独作句子成分,表示时间;一是不单独使用,接在其他词语后,跟其他词语一起组成方位词组,表示时间。"从前"只是时间名词,可以单独作句子成分,不能跟其他词语组成作中心语的表示时间意义的词组。("以前" is a noun of locality, and has two kinds of usage, one is to be a sentence component independently, indicating time, the other is to follow other words to form phrases of locality, also indicating time. "从前" is only a time word. It can be used alone as an element of a sentence, but not used with other words to form phrases of locality.)例如:

以前,这里只是一片荒地。
以前的苦日子不应该忘记。(单独作句子成分)
在一千多年以前的唐代,中国的陶瓷工艺就已经很发达了。("数量+以前"的方位词组)
(In the Tang Dynasty more than a thousand years ago, the ceramic technology of China was already quite advanced.)
下课以前,大家把作业交上来。("动宾词组+以前"的方位词组)
春节以前,一定要结束工程。("名词+以前"的方位词组)
从前,我们家的日子过得很苦。
她从前当过老师。(单独作句子成分)
* 在一千多年从前的唐代,中国的陶瓷工艺就已经很发达了。
* 下课从前,大家把作业交上来。
* 解放从前这里还只是个小镇子。
* 春节从前,一定要结束工程。

以来 yǐlái　　后来 hòulái　　从来 cónglái

以来、后来〈名词〉 < noun >

从来〈副词〉< adverb >

"以来"、"后来"、"从来"都可以表示从过去到现在的意思。("以来","后来" and "从来" can all indicate a period of time from the past till now.)例如：

复习考试以来,她每天都睡得很晚。

改革开放以来,这里发生了巨大的变化。

(After the reform and opening to the outside world, great changes have taken place here.)

刚出国的时候,他还来过两封信,后来就一点儿音信也没有了。

(When he just went abroad, he had written us several letters. But later on we have not heard from him any more.)

他从小就喜欢游泳,后来果然成了一名游泳健将。

无论遇到什么困难,他从来不叫苦。

(No matter what difficulties he meets, he never complains of hardship.)

我从来没吃过这么好吃的东西。

但是,"以来"、"后来"、"从来"功能上、意义上、搭配上都有一定的差别。(There are some differences in their meanings, functions and collocations.)

(一) 功能上和意义上 (In function and meaning)

1."以来"不能单用,只能用在有时间意义的词语后,与之构成词组,表示从过去某时直到说话时为止的一段时间;"后来"、"从来"不能这样用。("以来" cannot be used alone, but only after words denoting time to form phrases, expressing a period from some time in the past till the time when the talk occurs. "后来" and "从来" cannot be used this way.)例如：

自古以来,我就没听说过这样的事。

(I've never heard about this from ancient times.)

长期以来,他们一直在努力寻找病因。

解放以来	三年以来	入秋以来
长期以来	自古以来	
*解放后来	*三年后来	*入秋后来
*长期后来	*自古后来	
*解放从来	*三年从来	*入秋从来
*长期从来	*自古从来	

2."后来"是名词,它可以单独出现在主语前,也可以作修饰名词性成分的定语。"以来"、"从来"不能这样用。("后来" is a noun, it can be placed before the subject independently, or serve as an attribute to modify noun components. "以来" and "从来" are not used so.)例如:

单用:

三年前看到过他一次,后来我也不知道他去哪儿了。

修饰名词性成分:

后来的情况　　后来的想法

*三年前看到过他一次,以来我也不知道他去哪儿了。

*三年前看到过他一次,从来我也不知道他去哪儿了。

*以来的情况　　*以来的想法

*从来的情况　　*从来的想法

3."后来"表示的时间意义除有从过去到现在的意义外,还可以表示过去某时间之后的时间。"以来"、"从来"没有这一意义。("后来" indicates the time from past till now, as well as the time after a certain time in the past. "以来" and "后来" do not have this sense.)例如:

我早先在家里种地,后来参了军,五年前才来到这里。

(I did farming in my early years at home, and joined the army later on. I came here only five years ago.)

4."从来"是副词,它不能修饰名词,只能出现在动词、形容词等谓语前,不能出现在主语前。("从来" is an adverb. It cannot modify nouns, or appear before the subject, but can only be placed before predicative verbs or adjectives.)例如：

　　＊从来的习惯　　＊从来的主张　　＊从来的道理
　　他从来不迟到、不早退。
　　＊从来他不迟到、不早退。

"从来"不能修饰单个动词或形容词,它所修饰的应该是一个谓词性词组,即谓语性词语前后一般有其他附加成分。("从来" cannot modify single verbs or adjectives. What it modifies should be a predicate phrase, namely a predicate together with other attached elements.)例如：

　　＊她脸上从来笑。
　　＊他从来诚实。
　　她从来不对别人说起自己的身世。
　　(She never tells others about her life experience.)

5. "从来"所表示的从过去到现在主要是强调"一向"、"一贯"、"历来如此"的意思。"以来"、"后来"没有这种意思。(When "从来" indicates a period from the past till now, it mainly stresses on "all the time", or "always". "以来" and "后来" don't mean so.)例如：

　　他从来都十分自信。
　　这孩子打小就诚实,从来不说谎。
　　(The child is honest from very young, never telling lies.)

(二)搭配上(In collocation)

1. "以来"常与"从"、"自"、"自从"等词语呼应。("以来" is often used in combination with "从","自","自从", etc.)例如：

　　这本书自出版以来,已经是第十次印刷了。
　　自从开展"做学校主人"的活动以来,学校的面貌发生了很大变化。
　　(Since the launching of the movement "To be the masters of the school", the school has taken on a new look.)

2. "后来"常与"原先"、"起先"、"早先"、"先"、"开始"等词语呼应,或者前面有过去某一时间里发生的某种情况的句子。("后来" is usually used in combination with "原先","起先","早先","先","开始", etc., or follows a sentence in which a past time is involved.)例如:

原先拿起笔来画画,只是作为一种消遣,后来就不同了,完全把它当做一件重要的大事来做。

(At first I took painting just as a divertissement, but I changed later and took it as an important thing.)

那年大伯领我见过他一面,后来再也没见到他。

3."从来"强调一贯性,所以常与"都"搭配,尤其是肯定句。("从来" emphasizes consistency, so it is always used together with "都", especially in affirmative sentences.)例如:

他从来都是这么虚伪。

(He is always so hypocritical.)

她对同事从来都是那么热情。

4."从来"多用于否定句,常与"也"搭配,表示绝对否定的语气。("从来" is mostly used in negative sentences, often in combination with "也", implying absolute negation.)例如:

他非常要强,从来也不让别人说一句不是。

(He is very eager to excel, never allowing others to blame him.)

我从来没见过昙花,这是第一次。

(It's the first time I saw a broad-leaved epiphyllum. I've never seen it before.)

5."从来"还常与"就"搭配,表示强调的语气。("从来" is also often used together with "就", expressing emphasis.)例如:

在这个问题上,从来就存在着两种思想的斗争。

(The conflict between the two thoughts on this problem always exists.)

以为 yǐwéi   认为 rènwéi

〈动词〉表示对人或事物的看法、态度或判断。

(< verb > expressing opinions, attitude or judgement about other people or things.)

"以为"、"认为"都表示对人或事物的看法、态度或判断,但是大多不能换用,这主要是它们的意义有所不同,因此所使用的语言环境不完全一样。(Both "以为" and "认为" express one's opinions, attitude or judgement towards other people or things, but in most cases they are not exchangeable due to the differences in their meanings. Thus they are used in different language situations.)

(一) 意义上的不同 (Differences in meaning)

1. "以为"表示的看法强调主观性,即个人的认识、见解,个人的推想等,因此语气不十分肯定;"认为"表示的看法、判断通常是在分析、理解、认识的基础上得出的,因此,"认为"作出的判断,语气较为肯定。("以为" emphasizes subjectivity, or personal cognition, view, guess, etc., so the tone is not quite certain. "认为" means to give one's view based on analysis, understanding and knowledge. So the tone is relatively definite.) 例如:

我以为这样做多少有些压制民主了。

(I think such doing somewhat stifles democracy.)

我以为,人的机遇当然是很重要的,但是人的真实能力恐怕更重要一些吧。

(I think that one's opportunity is certainly important, but one's real ability may be even more important.)

我们一向认为,人是不能脱离社会而生存的。

马克思主义认为,只有人们的社会实践才是检验真理的惟一标准。

(According to Marxism, the only criterion for judging truth is people's social practice.)

我们认为抓教育是一件大事。

因此,"认为"既可用于重大事情,也可用于一般事情;"以为"则多用于一般事情。"认为"的主语可以是个人或某些人,也可以是集团、组织、会议、政党、国家等;"以为"的主语一般多用于个人或某些人。(Therefore, "认为" can be used either for great events or common things. "以为" is mostly used for ordinary occurrences. The subject of "认为" can be one person or several persons, or a group, an organization, a conference, a party, a country, etc. The subject of "以为" is usually a person or some persons.)例如:

我认为他不会支持你的。
大家都认为你做代表比较合适。
这部作品被学会认为是一部佳作。
(This work is considered as a fine piece of writing by the learned society.)
马克思主义认为,只有人们的社会实践才是检验真理的唯一标准。
我们国家历来认为:每个国家都有自己的主权,任何一个国家都不能干涉别国的内政。
(Our country has invariably insisted that each country has its own sovereign rights, and no country can interfere in other's internal affairs.)
我还以为你不喜欢这本书呢。
大家都以为你不来了呢。
* 这部作品被学会以为是一部佳作。
* 马克思主义以为,只有人们的社会实践才是检验真理的唯一标准。
* 我们国家历来以为:每个国家都有自己的主权,任何一个国家都不能干涉别的国家的内政。

2."以为"还可以表示判断、猜测是主观的、片面的、不符合实际的。"认为"一般不太用于这种语言环境。("以为" may also mean that the judgement or inference is subjective, lopsided, or unrealistic. "认为" is seldom used in such language situations.)例如:

我还以为他早到了呢,……(现在他可能还没到——估计得不对)

他以为活儿不多,两天就会干完的,要我看,五天也干不完。(他的估计不符合实际)

别人都以为我们俩的关系很好,实际不是那么回事。(别人的判断主观、片面)

(All the people thought that we were on very intimate terms with each other, but that isn't the case.)

* 我还认为他早到了呢,……
* 他认为活儿不多,两天就会干完的,要我看,五天也干不完。

(二) 句子的意义关系及结构搭配(The relationship in meaning and the structural arrangement of the sentences)

由于"以为"多用于由主观、片面的估计、分析而出现不符合实际的甚至错误的推断的情况,所以用"以为"的句子,前后两分句多为对立的或矛盾的意义关系:前一分句用"以为"表示不符合实际的甚至错误的推断,后一分句指出相反、相对的真实情况;在结构上,也有许多较常用的相关联的搭配格式来表示这种对立的、矛盾的意义关系。(Since "以为" is mostly used in situations where a subjective and lopsided judgement or analysis does not conform to the reality, or is even false, in the sentence where "以为" is used, the meanings of the two clauses are usually antithetical or contradictory: the first clause uses "以为" to introduce an unrealistic or false inference, while the second clause gives the antithetical or contradictory real situation. In structure, there are a lot of commonly-used interrelated collocating patterns to express such antithetical or contradictory relations.)例如:

我满以为这样做对他会有帮助的,没想到反而害了他。
(I had counted it helpful to him by doing so. I didn't expect

to have done harm to him.)

我们本以为接到通知她会高兴得跳起来,谁知她竟如此冷静。

(We had thought that she would have jumped with joy when receiving the notice. We didn't expect her to be so calm.)

他们以为我懂日语,其实我一句日语也不会说。

原本以为能帮帮他,没料到竟给他添了麻烦。

我还以为你会生气呢,没想到你这么高兴。

你以为我会帮他? 错了,这种违背原则的事我才不会做呢!

因为有这种意义关系和相关联的词语的前后呼应,"认为"一般都不能用在这种关系句中。(Because of such relationship and collocations, "认为" is generally not used in such complex sentences.)例如:

　　＊我满认为这样做对他会有帮助的,没想到反而害了他。
　　＊我们本认为接到通知她会高兴得跳起来,谁知她竟如此冷静。
　　＊他们认为我懂日语,其实我一句日语也不会说。
　　＊原本认为能帮帮他,没料到竟给他添了麻烦。
　　＊我还认为你会生气呢,没想到你这么高兴。

有时,用"以为"的句子常常只用一个单句的形式完成,但是不等于没有第二个分句的意思,实际上第二个分句的意思已经靠语言环境揭示出来了。因此,在语言环境清楚的情况下,可以不必说出第二个分句。(Sometimes the sentence with "以为" has only one single clause, but the meaning of the second clause is implied through language situations. Thus, when the language situation is clear, it may not be necessary to give the second clause.)例如:

　　我以为你不想去了呢。("你"现在一定是要去)
　　我们以为领导会反对我们的行动呢。("领导"一定是支持的态度)

意见 yìjiàn　　成见 chéngjiàn

〈名词〉表示对人或事的看法或想法。

(< noun > indicating one's view or idea about other people or things.)

"意见"、"成见"都可以表示对人或事的一种看法或想法,但是它们所指的看法在意义上有出入,两词在色彩上、用法上也有差别,一般不能互换使用。(Both "意见" and "成见" can express the views or ideas about other people or things, but the views indicated by the two words are different in significance, and there are also some differences in their flavor and usage, so they are generally not interchangeable.)

(一) 意义上 (In meaning)

1. "意见"的看法或想法是可以发表或者提供给别人的;"成见"则是个人内心的、非发表或非提供的看法或想法。("意见": view or idea that can be published or given to others. "成见": idea or view from one's heart, not published or given to others.)例如:

无论什么意见都可以发表。

关于个别干部的工作作风问题,群众还有一些意见,想跟有关领导反映反映。

(The masses have some complaints about a few cadres' style of work and want to report to the relevant leading cadre.)

这是我对住房改革的几点意见,提出来供你们参考。

(These are my few opinions about the housing reformation. I would like to put them forward for your reference.)

大家有意见尽管提。

* 无论什么成见都可以发表。

* 关于个别干部的工作作风问题,群众还有一些成见,想跟有关领导反映反映。

* 这是我对住房改革的几点成见,提出来供你们参考。

* 大家有成见尽管提。

2."意见"可以是积极的 —— 为做好某事提出看法,也可以是消极的 —— 认为不对而产生的不满意的想法,无论积极的还是消极的,都是可以随时产生或改变的;"成见"则不同,它不但只是消极的,而且是积聚而成的、固定不变的。("意见" can be positive — giving one's idea in order to do something well; or negative — producing a discontented thought toward something regarded wrong. Whether positive or negative, the view or idea may emerge or change at any time. "成见" is not the same. It is not only passive, but accumulated and fixed.)例如:

你的这个意见不错,我相信领导会采纳的。

(Your suggestion is quite good. I believe the leader will accept it.)

大家发表了不少建设性的意见。

* 你的这个成见不错,我相信领导会采纳的。
* 大家发表了不少建设性的成见。

这个旅馆服务很差,顾客们很有意见。

你不能一视同仁,我对你有意见。

(You are not treating everyone equally without discrimination. I have some complaints about you.)

以上是我的几点意见,若有不合理之处,还可以修正。

他好像对你有成见。

不知为什么,他对老李的成见很深。

他对我有成见已是由来已久的了。

(His prejudice about me is of long standing.)

(二) 感情色彩不同 (Differences in emotional coloring)

"意见"没有褒贬色彩;"成见"的看法带有固执性,所以含有贬义。("意见" doesn't involve complimentary or derogatory sense. "成见" means stubborn opinion, so it is used in derogatory sense.)

(三) 用法不同 (Differences in usage)

1.搭配上有差别。(Differences in collocation.)

因为意义上的差别,"意见"和"成见"在跟谓语和修饰语的搭配上有很大不同。(Because of their differences in meaning, "意见" and "成见" are quite different in their collocations with predicates and modifiers.)

(1) 常与"意见"搭配的谓语有:(Predicates that usually go together with "意见":)

<u>提</u>意见　<u>提出</u>意见　<u>交换</u>意见　<u>征求</u>意见
<u>转达</u>意见　　有什么意见都可以<u>发表</u>
<u>把意见反映上去</u>　<u>广泛听取</u>群众的意见
<u>大家的意见被采纳了</u>　<u>虚心接受</u>大家的意见

(2) 常与"成见"搭配的谓语有:(Predicates that usually go together with "成见":)

<u>有</u>成见　<u>存有</u>成见　<u>抱有</u>成见　<u>怀有</u>成见
<u>形成</u>成见　　成见<u>消除了</u>　　成见<u>很深</u>

(3) 常用来修饰"意见"的修饰语有:(Words often used to modify "意见":)

<u>朋友</u>的意见　<u>群众</u>的意见　<u>个人</u>的意见　<u>大家</u>的意见
<u>双方</u>的意见　<u>口头</u>意见　　<u>书面</u>意见　　<u>具体</u>意见
<u>重要</u>意见　　<u>诚恳</u>的意见　<u>合理</u>的意见　<u>建设性</u>的意见
<u>参考性</u>意见

(4) 常用来修饰"成见"的修饰语有:(Words often used to modify "成见":)

<u>个人</u>成见(personal prejudice)
<u>派别之间</u>的成见(prejudice between factions)
<u>不应有</u>的成见(undeserved prejudice)
<u>很深</u>的成见(deep prejudice)
<u>积下</u>的成见(accumulated prejudice)
<u>固有</u>的成见(intrinsic prejudice)

2. 跟"意见"可以搭配的量词有:"种"、"条"、"个"、"点"或不定量词"一点儿";"成见"很少跟量词搭配,如果搭配的话,一般

只能跟"种"和"一点儿"搭配。(Measure words that usually go together with "意见" are: "种","条","个","点" or indefinite classifier "一点儿". "成见" is seldom used together with classifiers, if there are any, they are usually "种" and "一点儿".)例如:

归纳一下,一共有三种意见。
(To sum up, there are altogether three kinds of opinions.)
大家提出十条建设性意见。
(We put forward ten suggestions altogether.)
这个意见很好。
我来谈几点意见。
他对你们有一点儿意见。
消除这种狭隘的成见。
(Eliminate such narrow prejudice.)
他可能对你有一点儿成见。

永远 yǒngyuǎn   永久 yǒngjiǔ

永远〈副词〉 < adverb >
永久〈形容词〉 < adjective >

"永远"和"永久"都可以表示时间长久的意思。但是由于两词词性不同,所以在功能用法上有很大的差别。(Both "永远" and "永久" mean permanent, but as they are different in part of speech, their function and usage are quite different.)

(一)"永远"、"永久"的相同用法 (Similarities in their usage)

1."永远"是副词,不能接受程度副词的修饰,不能作谓语;"永久"属于非谓形容词,也不能接受程度副词的修饰,不能作谓语。("永远" is an adverb, can't be modified by adverbs of degree, nor used as a predicate. "永久" is a non-predicative adjective, not used as a predicate either. It is also not modified by adverbs of degree.)例如:

＊ 我们将很永远地友好下去。

* 他们对我的关怀,我非常永远地记在心里。
* 我相信我们的关系一定永远。
* 两国的友谊将永远。
* 我们将很永久地友好下去。
* 他们对我的关怀,我非常永久地记在心里。
* 我相信我们的关系一定永久。
* 两国的友谊将永久。

2."永远"和"永久"在句中都主要用来作状语。("永远" and "永久" are mainly used as an adverbial in sentences.)例如:

她们将永远年轻。

我们将会永远友好。

我们永远是朋友。

我们的友谊永远长存。

(Our friendship lives for ever.)

不能让他永久享有这种特权。

(Do not let him enjoy the prestige for ever.)

这种作风应该永久保持下去。

他们将永久地分开了。

(二)"永远"、"永久"的不同用法 (Differences in their usage)

"永远"是副词,只能作修饰谓词性词语的状语,不能作直接修饰名词性成分的定语;"永久"是形容词,可以作定语。("永远" is an adverb, only used as an adverbial to modify predicates, and not used as an attribute to modify noun components. "永久" is an adjective, and can be used as an attribute.)例如:

* 永远的纪念　* 永远的思念　* 永远的住处
* 永远的痛苦　* 永远的伤痛

永久的纪念　　永久的思念　　永久的住处

永久的痛苦　　永久的伤痛

由 yóu   由于 yóuyú

由、由于〈介词〉< preposition >
由于〈连词〉< conjunction >

"由"、"由于"意义上、结构上、用法上有很大不同,所以一般不能换用。("由" and "由于" are quite different in meaning, structure and usage, so they are hardly exchangeable.)

(一)意义上的不同(Differences in meaning)

1."由"可以表示动作的起点,可以用来引进施动者、动作方式、组成成分等。"由于"不能表示这种意义。("由" can indicate the beginning of an action, used to introduce the doer, the way of the action, or the components. "由于" cannot.)例如:

大家由东向西"一"字排开。
(Everyone stands in a line from east to west.)
这次春游活动由工会组织。
水的分子由两个氢原子和一个氧原子组成。
* 大家由于东向西"一"字排开。
* 这次春游活动由于工会组织。
* 水的分子由于两个氢原子和一个氧原子组成。

2."由"和"由于"都可以表示原因,但是大多情况下并不通用。"由"表示的原因主要是"由来"的意思;"由于"表示的原因主要是形成动作某一结果的条件。(Both "由" and "由于" can form prepositional phrases to express causes, but they are not interchangeable in most cases. "由" indicates a cause mainly coming from "an origin". The cause indicated by "由于" is mainly the conditions of something that leads to a result.)例如:

由感冒引起发烧。
(a fever resulted from cold.)
琥珀是由远古时代的松胶变成的。
(Amber is formed by pine glue from ancient times.)
* 琥珀是由于远古时代的松胶变成的。

由于你,我们才相识、恋爱并结婚。

(Owing to you, we are able to be acquainted with each other, fall in love, and get married.)

由于劳动,语言才得以形成。

(Language came into being as a result of labour.)

他由于自己的过失而感到难过。

(He felt sorry for his own fault.)

* 由你,我们才相识、恋爱并结婚。

* 他由自己的过失而感到难过。

(二) 结构方式不同 (Differences in structure)

1. "由"构成的介词词组一般出现在谓语动词前;"由于"构成的介词词组既可以出现在谓语动词前,也可以出现在主语前。(Prepositional phrases formed by "由" usually occur before the predicative verbs. While "由于" phrases can either occur before predicative verbs, or before subjects.) 例如:

大会代表由民主协商,选举产生。

(The deputies of the conference are elected after democratic consultation.)

由工人中选出五名代表,参加谈判。

* 由民主协商大会代表选举产生。

他由于自己的刻苦努力而获得成功。

由于彼此互不迁就的缘故,我和她分开了好长时间。

(Because we couldn't accommodate ourselves to each other, I parted with her long ago.)

由于工作关系,我在这儿又呆了一年多。

"由"还可以构成"由此"的固定用法;"由于"不可以。("由" can also form the fixed pattern "由此"; while "由于" cannot.)

由此我想到,人真是一种不可思议的动物。

(I think therefrom that man is really an inconceivable animal.)

* 由于此我想到,人真是一种不可思议的动物。

2. "由于"因为表示的是一种结果的条件,所以句中常用"才"、"也"、"就"等词配合。(Since "由于" expresses the condition(s) of a result, it is usually used in combination with words like "才", "也", "就", etc.)例如:

由于老师的耐心帮助,我才有今天的进步。

由于条件的不同,最后的结果也不相同。

(三)功能不同(Differences in function)

"由"只有介词功能,只能构成介词词组出现在谓语动词前;"由于"除了介词功能外,还有连词功能,即除可以构成介词词组说明动作结果的条件外,还可以连接复句,构成复句中表示原因的分句。("由" only functions as a preposition and constitutes prepositional phrases to occur before predicative verbs. "由于" functions as a preposition as well as a conjunction. That is to say, besides forming prepositional phrases to express the condition of the result of an action, it can also connect complex sentences, leading the clause of causality.)例如:

介词:由他负责这项工作。

介词:由于长年的劳累,她的身体早早地就垮了。

(Due to many years' overworking, she had long been worn down.)

连词:由于生产管理不严,生产秩序才会这么混乱。

(Because of the slack management, the order of the production is so confused.)

由于提出的问题正是大家所关心的问题,所以讨论起来十分热烈、深入。

(Because the problem raised is just the one of interest to all, the discussion on it is very lively and thorough.)

友好 yǒuhǎo   友爱 yǒu'ài   友谊 yǒuyì

友好、友爱〈形容词〉 <adjective>

友谊〈名词〉< noun >

"友好"、"友爱"、"友谊"都有关系亲近和睦的意思,但是由于意义上的出入,适用对象的不同、功能用法上的差别,使得它们在很多情况下不能换用。("友好","友爱"and"友谊"can all mean being close and harmonious in relationship. But they are not interchangeable in most cases due to some discrepancies in their meanings and differences in their applicable objects and in their functions.)

(一)"友好"和"友爱"

1."友好"和"友爱"词义很接近,词义的着重点稍有出入。"友好"较侧重于相互关系上亲近,也可以表示态度上的亲近。但是,只表示相互关系如何的通常不用"友爱"。("友好"and"友爱"are very close in meaning, but their emphatic points are slightly different."友好"emphasizes closeness in relationship or manner. But when only describing the relations,"友爱"is generally not used.)例如:

友好邻邦(friendly nations)
友好相处(get along with each other friendly)
关系友好(friendly relations)
友好的桥梁(the bridge of friendship)
友好的使者(an emissary of friendship)
友好往来(exchange of friendly visits)
友好访问(friendly visit)
* 友爱邻邦   * 关系友爱   * 友爱的桥梁
* 友爱的使者   * 友爱往来   * 友爱访问

"友爱"较侧重于相互对待上的亲近。("友爱"emphasizes treating each other friendly.)例如:

友爱的态度   团结友爱
这是一个十分友爱的集体。
她用友爱温暖了我的心。(She warmed my heart with friendly affection.)

2. "友好"和"友爱"主要差别在于适用对象上的不同。"友好"较多地适用于地区与地区、民族与民族、国家与国家之间,也可以适用于人与人之间、组织与组织之间。只表示地区、民族、国家之间的亲近关系的,一般不用"友爱"。(The main differences between "友好" and "友爱" are that their applicable objects are different. "友好" is more applicable to the relations among areas, nations, countries, as well as persons, organizations, etc. When only expressing the intimate relations among areas, nations or countries, "友爱" is seldom used.)例如:

> 中国的天津和日本的神户是友好城市。
>
> 为增进两个民族友好合作而努力。
>
> 两国关系十分友好。
>
> 那里的老乡们对我们十分友好。
>
> 你对他们太不友好了。
>
> * 中国的天津和日本的神户是友爱城市。
>
> * 为增进两个民族友爱合作而努力。
>
> * 两国关系十分友爱。

"友爱"较多地适用于集体内、组织内成员间相互对待的亲近,也可以用于人与人相互间的亲近。("友爱" is more applicable to relations among members within a unit, an organization, etc.)例如:

> 同学之间应该友爱。
>
> 建立一个团结友爱的集体。
>
> (to build a collective of fraternal unity)
>
> 我们连队战士之间非常友爱。

(二)"友好"和"友谊"

1."友好"和"友谊"词义不同。"友好"表示亲近和睦;"友谊"表示朋友间的交情。因此与"友好"和"友谊"搭配的词语有很大的不同。("友好" and "友谊" are different in meaning. "友好" means friendly and harmonious. "友谊" indicates the friendship among friends. Thus the words collocated with "友好" and "友谊" are quite different.)例如:

友好的关系(friendly relations)
友好的言辞(friendly words)
友好的态度(friendly manner)
友好的气氛(friendly atmosphere)
友好的姿态(friendly attitude)
友好的主人(friendly host)
继续友好　恢复友好　破坏友好　保持友好
友谊的赞歌(a paean of friendship)
友谊的象征(a symbol of friendship)
友谊的诗篇(poems of friendship)
友谊的结晶(a crystallization of friendship)
友谊的基础(the foundation of friendship)
建立友谊(build ties of friendship)
增长了友谊(promote friendship)
发展友谊(develop friendship)
充满了友谊(brimming with friendship)
珍惜友谊(treasure the friendship)
注重友谊(attach importance to friendship)

2."友好"和"友谊"主要差别在于功能用法上。(The major differences of "友好" and "友谊" are in their functions and usage.)

(1)"友好"是形容词,可以接受程度副词的修饰,可以在句中作谓语,也可以带补语;"友谊"是名词,不能接受程度副词的修饰,不能直接作谓语,更不可能带补语。("友好" is an adjective, and can be modified by adverbs of degree, can be used as a predicate, and can have complement attached. "友谊" is a noun. It cannot be modified by adverbs of degree, nor can it be used directly as a predicate or have a complement attached.)例如:

他们对我们非常友好。

两国关系十分友好。
　　＊他们对我们非常友谊。
　　＊两国关系十分友谊。
　　两队关系友好极了。
　　他们对我们友好得不得了。
　　＊两队关系友谊极了。
　　＊他们对我们友谊得不得了。

(2)"友好"常常用来作状语或修饰动词;"友谊"不能作状语,也几乎不修饰动词。("友好" usually serves as an adverbial to modify verbs. "友谊" cannot serve as an adverbial, and rarely modify verbs.)例如:
　　两国的代表们正在友好地交谈着。
　　接待站的同志非常友好地接待了他。
　　当地的老百姓非常友好地把外宾们迎到家里。

　　(The local civilians very friendly welcomed the foreign guests to their homes.)
　　＊两国的代表们正在友谊地交谈着。
　　＊接待站的同志非常友谊地接待了他。
　　＊当地的老百姓非常友谊地把外宾们迎到家里。

有名 yǒumíng　　著名 zhùmíng　　闻名 wénmíng

有名、著名〈形容词〉＜adjective＞
闻名〈动词〉＜verb＞
"有名"、"著名"、"闻名"都有名气很大的意思,但是它们在意义的着重点上、用法上有所不同。("有名","著名" and "闻名" all mean being quite well-known, but there are some differences in their emphasis of meanings and in their usags.)
(一)意义的着重点不同(Differences in emphases of meanings)
　　"有名"强调有了名气,"著名"强调名字突出、显著,"著名"

601

的词义要比"有名"重。"闻名"则主要强调名字传得很广,很多地方、很多人都听说过这个名字。("有名" emphasizes that one enjoys some reputation. "著名" emphasizes that one's name is distinguished or outstanding. "著名" is more emphatic than "有名". "闻名" mainly emphasizes that one's name is widespread, well-known in many places and by many people.)例如:

李白的诗很有名。

大连是个很有名的城市。

黄山是非常有名的山。

李白是中国唐代著名的诗人。

这是我国著名的风景区。

著名的长江三峡引来了无数中外游客。

(The famous Three Gorges of Yangtze River attract innumerable guests from both China and abroad.)

中国的长城闻名世界。

(The Great Wall in China is well-known in the world.)

他的名字闻名于海外。

两万五千里长征是举世闻名的壮举。

(二) 用法上的异同 (Differences and similarities in usage)

1. "有名"、"著名"是形容词,"闻名"是动词,都可以用作谓语。("有名" and "著名" are adjectives. "闻名" is a verb. They can all serve as predicate.)例如:

苏州园林非常有名。

他的幽默很有名。

日本的富士苹果非常著名。

景德镇瓷器很著名。

景德镇瓷器闻名中外。

中国的长城举世闻名。

2. "有名"、"著名"都是形容词,都可以接受程度副词的修饰;"闻名"是动词,不能接受程度副词的修饰。("有名" and "著名" are adjectives and can be modified by adverbs of degree;"闻名" is a verb and cannot be modified by adverbs of degree.)例如：

这是一幅特别有名的作品。

他是非常有名的登山运动员。

中国古代最著名的时期是唐代。

他是世界上最著名的科学家了。

* 苏州园林非常闻名。

* 他是非常闻名的登山运动员。

* 他是世界上最闻名的科学家。

3."有名"、"著名"、"闻名"都可以用作定语,但是"有名"用作定语时,通常不能没有"的";"著名"可以有"的",也可以没有"的";"闻名"单独不能作定语,通常组成词组加"的"后才能作定语。("有名","著名" and "闻名" can all be used as attributive, but when "有名" serves as attribute, it is seldom used without "的". "著名" can be used with "的" or without "的"."闻名" is not used alone as an attribute. It usually forms phrases and together with "的" to serve as an attribute.)例如：

有名的大桥　　有名的歌曲　　有名的公园
有名的诗人　　有名的牌子
* 有名大桥　　* 有名歌曲　　* 有名公园
* 有名诗人　　* 有名牌子
著名的画家　　著名的科学家　著名的理论
著名的实验　　著名的名胜
著名画家　　　著名科学家　　著名理论
著名定律

著名佛教圣地五台山每年吸引无数游客。

(The famous sacred place of Buddhism Wutai Mountain attracts innumerable guests every year.)

著名语言学家赵元任教授于 1982 年 2 月 25 日因病在美国逝世。

(On February 25, 1982, the famous linguist Prof. Zhao Yuanren passed away in America because of illness.)

闻名世界的埃菲尔铁塔(world-famous Eiffel Tower)
举世闻名的工程(a project of world renown)
闻名全国的茶叶产地(nation-famous tea-producing area)
远近闻名的气功师(a master of qigong known far and wide)

* 闻名世界埃菲尔铁塔　　* 举世闻名工程
* 闻名全国茶叶产地　　　* 远近闻名气功师
* 闻名的埃菲尔铁塔　　　* 闻名的工程
* 闻名的茶叶产地　　　　* 闻名的气功师

4. "有名"有时可以作补语;"著名"、"闻名"不能作补语。("有名" sometimes serves as a complement. "著名" and "闻名" cannot.)例如:

她唱得很有名。
他在这一带富裕得有名。
(He is famous for his wealth in this area.)
他老实得都有名了。

* 她诗写得很著名。
* 他在这一带富裕得著名。
* 他老实得都著名。
* 她唱得很闻名。
* 他在这一带富裕得闻名。
* 他老实得都闻名了。

5. "闻名"从意义上说是名字传得很远的意思,所以它的前后一定要有地方、处所意义的词或词组。"闻名"后面还可以接用"于"构成的表示处所意义的补语或不用"于"的处所意义的补语。"有名"、"著名"不能接这样的补语。(The meaning of "闻名" is that one's name is known far and wide, so it must be used with words or phrases indicating place or location. "闻名" can also be followed by a complement of location formed with "于" or without

"于"."有名" and "著名" cannot be followed by such complements.) 例如：

那就是天津闻名的蝶式立交桥。
故宫是闻名世界的古代宫殿。
(The Summer Palace is a world-famous ancient palace.)
他的武功远近闻名。
他的中医术闻名于海内外。
(His art of healing in traditional Chinese medicine is well-known throughout the country and abroad.)
桂林山水闻名于世。
(The mountains and waters of Guiling are the finest under heaven.)
他的山水画闻名于全国。
(His landscape painting is well-known throughout the country.)
* 他的中医术有名于海内外。
* 桂林山水有名于世。
* 他的山水画有名中外。
* 他的中医术著名于海内外。
* 桂林山水著名于世。
* 他的山水画著名中外。

又 yòu　　再 zài　　还 hái

〈副词〉 < adverb >

"又"、"再"、"还"都是表示频率或重复意义的副词。它们都可以表示动作重复发生或继续的意义，但是角度有所不同。("又"，"再" and "还" are all adverbs indicating repetition and frequency. They may all indicate an act repeatedly occurs or continues, but emphasize different parts.)

(一)"又"与"再"

1. 意义上：(In meaning：)

在表示动作重复发生或继续进行时,"又"表示客观性,即用以表示说话人陈述自己或别人的动作、状态已经或将要重复、继续的情况,多用于已完成或者新情况已出现,也可用于新情况即将出现;"再"表示主观性,即用以表示说话人自己重复或继续某动作的打算、愿望或者要求、命令听话人重复或继续某动作等,多用于未完成。(When expressing an act repeatedly occurs or continues, "又" expresses objectivity. It is used when the speaker states that the action or state of himself or others has been or will be repeated or continued. It's usually used to express something finished, or something new emerging. "再" expresses subjectivity. It is used to describe the speaker's desire or plan to repeat or continue some action himself, or the speaker's demands on the listener to repeat or continue some action. It's usually used to express something unfinished.)例如:

他又写了一遍。(客观 —— 陈述,已重复。)
我再写一遍。(主观 —— 打算,待重复。)
下星期又要考试了。(客观 —— 陈述,将重复。)
我又坐了一会儿。(客观 —— 陈述,已继续。)
你再坐一会儿吧。(主观 —— 请求,待继续。)

2. 用法上:(In usage:)

(1) "再"可以用于祈使句、假设句;"又"一般不可以。("再" can be used in imperative sentences or assumptive sentences; "又" cannot.)例如:

这件事很麻烦,你再帮帮我吧。(祈使句)
* 这件事很麻烦,你又帮帮我吧。
你要是再这么不讲理,我就不客气了。(假设句)
(If you go on being so unreasonable, I won't be so easy on you.)
* 你要是又这么不讲理,我就不客气了。

(2) 在能愿动词句中,"再"只能用在能愿动词后;"又"只能用在能愿动词前。(In sentences containing modal verbs, "再" is

only used after the modal verbs; while "又" is only placed before them.)例如：

你能再帮帮他吗？

你应该再检查一遍。

* 你再能帮帮他吗？

* 你再应该检查一遍。

他又能说话了。

他又要学游泳了。

* 他能又说话了。

* 他要又学游泳了。

3.关于"又"、"再"后面接否定词的意义：(The meaning of "又" and "再" after being followed by negative words：)

"又"、"再"后面都可以接否定词"不"、"没"，但是意义完全不同。"又不"或"又没"表示没有再次出现重复或继续。"再不"表示不再继续或重复；"再没"表示从发生后持续到说话前的某一时或说话时没有出现继续或重复。("又"and "再"can be followed by the negative words "不"and "没", but their meanings are different. "又不"or "又没"indicates not repeating or continuing again; "再不"means no longer repeating or continuing; "再没"indicates an act not repeating or continuing during the time from its occurring till before or at the time of speaking.)例如：

你怎么又不说话了？

我又没给你借书，真对不起。

(I am so sorry that I forgot to borrow books for you again.)

那个鬼地方，我再(也)不去了。

(I won't go to that damnable place again.)

从那以后，她再(也)没见到丈夫的面。

(After that she has never seen her husband again.)

(二)"再"与"还"

1.意义上：(In meaning：)

607

(1)在表示动作重复和连续时,"再"主要用于说话人、听话人说话时临时形成某种新意愿、新打算时;"还"主要用于说话人或别人在说话前已有某种意愿、打算时。(While indicating the repetition and continuance of an act, "再" is used when the speaker or listener has some new idea or plan in the process of speaking. "还" is used when the speaker or others has/have already had some idea or plan before speaking.)例如:

A:实在对不起,明天还得让您跑一趟。

B:——没关系,明天我再来一趟。(临时决定。)

——没关系,正好明天我还来这儿办事。(原来就有打算。)

A:你还借什么吗?

B:——我再借两本杂志看看吧。(临时决定。)

——我还想借两本书。(原来就有打算。)

不要急于答复,考虑考虑再说。(临时决定。)

(Don't be anxious to answer. Think it over first.)

他们还想跟工人们一起劳动劳动。(原来就有计划。)

(2)"再"、"还"还可以侧重强调"持续不变"的意义,这时它们的区别主要在持续时间上:"再"强调继续向后持续到某时,常含假设意味;"还"强调从过去某时到现在。("再" and "还" can also emphasize the meaning of continuity. Their difference in this sense lies in the time they last. "再" emphasizes that an action continues and lasts till some time, usually signifying supposition. "还" emphasizes (lasting) from some time in the past till now.)例如:

你再不说,我就不理你了。(强调"不说"继续保持不变向后到某时点,含假设意味。)

(If you still don't say it, I'll not pay attention to you any more.)

你怎么还看哪,都十二点了。(强调"看"从过去某时持续不变到现在。)

(How come you are still watching! It's already 12 o'clock.)

2.用法上:(In usage:)

(1)"再"可以用于祈使句;"还"一般不用于祈使句。("再" can be used in imperative sentences; while "还" seldom can.)

咱们再玩一会吧!

您再陪我说一会儿话吧。

* 咱们还玩一会吧。
* 您还陪我说一会儿话吧。

(2)"还"可以用在能愿动词前;"再"一般不能用在能愿动词前。("还" can also be used before a modal verb, but "再" seldom can.)例如:

你还能帮帮我吗?

我还要看一次这部电影。

* 你再能帮帮我吗?
* 我再要看一次这部电影。

3."还"和"再"配合使用:("再" and "还" are used together:)

"还"和"再"有时相互配合,同时出现在一个句子中,构成"还+能愿动词+再……"的形式,更加强调动作行为的继续或重复。(Sometimes "再" and "还" appear in a sentence together, forming the pattern "还 + a modal verb + 再", stressing the repetition or continuation of the action.)例如:

北京真好,我还想再去一次。

我还想再看一会儿,你们等我一会儿好吗?

原来 yuánlái　　　本来 běnlái

〈形容词〉< adjective >

〈副词〉< adverb >

"原来"、"本来"都有形容词和副词两种功能,有的意义很接近,有的意义相差很大。("原来" and "本来" can both function as

609

adjectives and adverbs, sometimes they are very close in meaning, but sometimes quite different.)

(一)"原来"、"本来"相近的意义(Similarities in meaning)

1."原来"、"本来"都可以表示起初的、原先的意思,常常可以换用。("原来"and"本来"can both signify original, or former, and they are often exchangeable.)例如:

> 这本词典原来/本来是旧的,现在怎么又变成新的了。
> 我原来/本来学医,后来改学法律了。
> 他俩原来/本来不是一个学校的。

2.在表示这种相近的意义上,"原来"是形容词的用法,"本来"是副词的用法。所以,在使用上"原来"可以修饰名词性词语做定语,"本来"只能修饰动词、形容词作状语。(In expressing such similar meanings, "原来" serves as an adjective, "本来" an adverb. So "原来" can be used as an attribute to modify noun components, "本来" as an adverbial to modify verbs or adjectives.)例如:

> 她是我原来的女朋友。
> 原来的房子比这所好多了。
> 孩子长得太快了,原来的衣服大部分都不能穿了。
> (The child grows too fast. Most of his former clothes are too small to wear.)
> * 她是我本来的女朋友。
> * 本来的房子比这所好多了。
> * 孩子长得太快了,本来的衣服大部分都不能穿了。

(二)"原来"、"本来"不同的意义(Differences in meaning)

1."原来"可以表示"没有改变的"的意思;"本来"不表示这种意思。("原来"can mean "unchanged"."本来"doesn't mean so.)例如:

> 领导决定按照原来的图纸制作。
> 赵州桥虽然经历了1300多年的风吹雨打,但是原来的雄姿却依然不减。

610

(Though having undergone 1300 years' wind and rain, the original magnificent view of Zhaozhou Bridge remains unchanged.)

* 领导决定按照本来的图纸制作。
* 赵州桥虽然经历了1300多年的风吹雨打,但是本来的雄姿却依然不减。

2."本来"还可以表示"本有的"意思,"原来"没有这种意思。("本来"can also mean "originally having","原来"doesn't mean so.)例如:

这件衣服本来的颜色是灰色的,可是现在几乎看不出来了。

(The original colour of this dress was grey, but now it's hard to recognize it.)

他终于露出了本来的面目。

(He finally revealed his true face.)

* 这件衣服原来的颜色是灰色的,可是现在几乎看不出来了。
* 他终于露出了原来的面目。

3."原来"还可以表示发现了真实情况,含有对从前的情况有所认识或恍然醒悟的意思;"本来"没有这种意思。("原来"can also mean having found the truth, implying having some knowledge about previous situations, or suddenly realizing what has happened. "本来" does not mean so.)例如:

从来不言不语的小刘原来也有这样的心计。

(So taciturn a person as Xiao Liu also has such calculation.)

原来你还没睡呀!
原来他出国了,怪不得有日子没看到他了。

(So he has gone abroad. No wonder I haven't seen him for some time.)

原来是你呀!我还以为是谁呢。
* 从来不言不语的小刘本来也有这样的心计。
* 本来你还没睡呀!
* 本来他出国了,怪不得有日子没看到他了。
* 本来是你呀!我还以为是谁呢。

4."本来"还可以表示"按道理就该这样做"的意思,句末常与表示理应如此的语气助词"嘛"连用;"原来"没有这种意思。("本来" can also mean "something should have been done this way", usually with the modal particle "嘛" which signifies "should have been so" at the end of the sentence;"原来" does not have this sense.)例如:

你本来就应该赔礼道歉嘛!
(Of course you should apologize.)
学生本来就该搞好学习嘛!
本来嘛,你都答应去了,现在又变了,人家当然会有想法了。
* 你原来就应该赔礼道歉嘛!
* 学生原来就该搞好学习嘛!
* 原来嘛,你都答应去了,现在又变了,人家当然会有想法了。

原来 yuánlái　　起初 qǐchū

原来〈副词〉〈形容词〉 < adverb > < adjective >
起初〈名词〉 < noun >

(一)"原来"和"起初"都可以表示起先的、先前的意思,都含有现在或后来不是那个样子了的意思,但是意义的着重点稍有不同。"原来"强调起先具有的、原先的;"起初"则着重于最初的、开始的时候。(Both "原来" and "起初" may mean in the beginning, previously, implying "not like that now or any more". But they have different emphases. "原来" stresses previously having, original;"起初" emphasizes at first, at the beginning.)例如:

612

他原来／起初打算学文,后来受几个好朋友的影响,又改学理工了。

她原来只有40多公斤重,不知怎么搞的,一下子胖成现在这个样子了。

(At first she only weighed 40 kg., then all of a sudden she got so fat.)

原来她胆子可小啦,没想到她竟能锻炼成现在这个样子。

(She was really timid at first. Who knows she has tempered herself like this today.)

起初妈妈不同意我离开她,经过几次说服,才点了头。

(At first Mother didn't allow me to leave her. After talking to her several times, she finally agreed.)

起初他一句汉语也不会说,这才十个月左右的时间,你看他说得多流利呀!

(At first he couldn't say a single word in Chinese. Only after ten months or so, you see, how frequently he has spoken it.)

(二)"原来"除了具有副词功能,可以修饰谓语以外,还有形容词的功能,它还可以作定语,修饰名词性词语。"起初"是时间名词,它主要的功能是作状语,一般不用来修饰名词性词语。("原来" can function as an adjective to be used as an attribute to modify nouns in addition to being an adverb to modify predicates. "起初" is a time noun, mainly functioning as an adverbial, seldom used to modify noun components.)例如:

他原来的样子我现在已经记不清了。

你原来的那些"雄心壮志"怎么现在一个都没有了。

(How come you have not any of your original lofty aspirations and great ideals!)

村东头原来的那片荒地已经变成果园了。

他原来的名字叫张欣。

＊他起初的样子我现在已经记不清了。

* 你起初的那些"雄心壮志"怎么现在一个都没有了。
* 村东头起初的那片荒地已经变成果园了。
* 他起初的名字叫张欣。

愿意 yuànyì　　情愿 qíngyuàn

〈动词〉 < adverb >

"愿意"、"情愿"意义上有一定差别,使用的语言环境有所不同。(There are some differences in their meanings and in the language situations in which they are used.)

(一) 意义上的差别 (Differences in meaning)

1. "愿意"主要表示认为符合自己的心愿而同意去做;"情愿"主要表示甘心乐意地去做。("愿意" mainly means that one agrees to do something because he/she thinks it in keeping with his or her aspirations. "情愿" mainly means to be willing to do something.)
例如:

　　她愿意走着去,就让她走着去吧。
　　我们非常愿意参加这次义务劳动。
　　我喜欢他,他让我做什么我都情愿去做。
　　他们俩要结为夫妻,是他们两相情愿的事,我们不要干涉。

　　(They wanted to get married by mutual consent. We shouldn't interfere.)

　　她情愿用自己的生命换回儿子的生命。

2. "愿意"是完全符合心愿而同意做的事,没有丝毫的勉强,完全是出于内心的要求;"情愿"有时还含有"宁愿"的意思,即所做的事是甘愿做的,但是并不一定是符合心愿或出于内心要求的,而是为了实现某种条件所甘愿作出的牺牲。表示这种意义时,不要用"愿意"。("愿意" means to do something because it is in keeping with one's aspiration, and to do it without any reluctance. "情愿" sometimes means "宁愿(would rather)", that is what one is ready

to do is not necessarily in keeping with one's aspirations or on a voluntary basis, but is willing to sacrifice in order to attain some goals. We do not use "愿意" to express this sense.)例如：

他要是能帮我们村富起来，我情愿嫁给他。(不是相中而嫁，是为条件而嫁)

(If he can help our village to become rich, I would rather marry him.)

为了儿子回来能找到她，她情愿住在这低矮潮湿的小屋里。(为儿子而吃苦)

(She'd rather live in this low and damp shed in order that her son could come back and find her.)

他要是不答应我，我情愿去死。(为不能满足某种条件而死)

* 他要是不答应我，我愿意去死。

(二) 用法上的异同 (Differences and similarities in usage)

1. "愿意"可以接受程度副词的修饰；"情愿"一般不接受。("愿意" can be modified by adverbs of degree. "情愿" cannot.)例如：

我很愿意帮助你。

大家都非常愿意这样做。

* 为了儿子回来能找到她，她非常情愿住在这低矮潮湿的小屋里。

2. "愿意"、"情愿"后面应该接非名词性词语，不能直接接名词性词语。("愿意" and "情愿" cannot be immediately followed by nominal words.)例如：

* 大家都选他，我也愿意他。
* 他愿意商店，我愿意公园，服从谁好呢？

大家都选他，我也愿意选他。

他愿意逛商店，我愿意逛公园，服从谁好呢？

* 虽然父母都反对我嫁给他，可是我情愿他。
* 我情愿自行车，也不坐汽车。

虽然父母都反对我嫁给他,可是我情愿嫁给他。
我情愿骑自行车,也不坐汽车。

愿意 yuànyì　　希望 xīwàng
〈动词〉 < verb >

"愿意"、"希望"词义上有差别,用法上也有所不同。(There are some differences in their meanings and usage.)

(一)"愿意"、"希望"意义上的差别 (Differences in meaning)

"愿意"表示认为符合自己的心愿而同意去做;"希望"则表示心里想着达到某种目的或出现某种情况。因此两词不能换用。("愿意" means one is willing to do something because it is in keeping with his / her aspirations. "希望" means one wishes to attain some goals or wishes something to happen. So the two words are not exchangeable.)例如:

我愿意参加这次活动。
("参加这次活动"符合自己的心愿,因此同意或要求做)
我希望参加这次活动。
("参加这次活动"是心里想要达到的那个目的)
你放心吧,同学们都愿意帮助你克服困难,度过难关。
嫁闺女也不能光由娘说了算,还得看闺女愿意不愿意呀。

(To marry the daughter is not only decided by the mother, it also depends on the daughter's own will.)

不管愿意不愿意都得去。

＊ 嫁闺女也不能光由娘说了算,还得看闺女希望不希望呀。

＊ 不管希望不希望都得去。

我们都希望我们的祖国繁荣富强。

(We all wish our country to be rich, strong and prosperous.)

我们大家都希望你能夺得冠军。

我希望以后有机会去你们国家看你。

大家都希望你幸福快乐。

＊我们都愿意我们的祖国繁荣富强。

＊我们大家都愿意你能夺得冠军。

＊我愿意以后有机会去你们国家看你。

＊大家都愿意你幸福快乐。

(二) 用法上的相同之处 (Similarities in usage)

1."愿意"、"希望"都可以接受程度副词的修饰。("愿意" and "希望" can both be modified by adverbs of degree.)例如：

他很愿意帮助你。

我非常愿意参加你的婚礼。

他非常希望到中国学习汉语。

说心里话,我很希望得到他的理解。

2."愿意"、"希望"后面所连带的应该是非名词性成分,不能直接连带名词性成分。("愿意" and "希望" cannot be directly followed by noun components.)例如：

＊他愿意这个活动。

＊我们都愿意新年联欢会。

＊我们都愿意篮球的比赛。

他愿意搞这个活动。

我们都愿意参加新年联欢会。

我们都愿意看篮球比赛,不愿意看排球比赛。

＊他希望这个活动。

＊我们都希望新年联欢会。

＊我们都希望篮球的比赛,不希望排球比赛。

他希望搞这个活动。

我们都希望参加新年联欢会。

我们都希望看篮球比赛,不希望看排球比赛。

617

越……越…… yuè……yuè……
越来越…… yuè lái yuè……

"越……越……"和"越来越……"是由副词"越"组成的两种格式,都可以表示程度随某种原因的影响而加深的意思,但是意义上和用法上有所不同。("越…越…" and "越来越…" are two patterns composed of the adverb "越". Both of them may mean the degree increases for some reasons, but there are some differences in their meanings and usage.)

(一) 意义不完全相同 (Slightly different in meaning)

"越……越……"表示在程度上 B 随 A 的增加而增加,句子总是涉及前后两项;"越来越……"则表示程度随时间的推移而增减,句中只涉及一项。("越…越…" means B increases as A does in degree. The sentence always includes two parts. "越来越…" means something increases in degree as time passes. It only involves one part of a sentence.)例如:

风越刮越大。(风 —— 刮;风 —— 大。)

文章越啰嗦越不能说明问题。(文章——啰嗦;文章——不能说明问题。)

(The more wordy the article is, the less likely it elucidates problems.)

风越来越大了。(风 —— 大)

经济的发展越来越好了。(经济 —— 好)

(二) 用法上有很大差别 (Quite different in usage)

1."越……越……"的 AB 两项可以有一个主语,也可以有两个主语;"越来越……"则只能有一个主语。(The items A and B in the pattern "越…越…" may share one subject, or have separated subjects. The pattern "越来越…" involves only one subject.)例如:

雨越下越大。(主语:雨)

把电视的声音弄小点儿,声音越大,我们越听不清楚。

(主语:声音、我们)

大家越是劝,她越是哭。(主语:大家、她)

他在学习上越来越努力了。(主语:他)

天越来越凉爽了。(主语:天)

2.组合方式上:(In ways of combination:)

(1)"越……越……"一般组成"(越+动／形)+(越+动／形)"的形式。("越…越…" usually forms the pattern "(越 + v.／adj.) + (越 + v.／adj.)".)例如:

他的乒乓球越打越猛。(越+动　越+形)

情况越紧急,越保持冷静。(越+形　越+动词组)

(The more critical the situation is, the more necessary it is to keep calm.)

大家越听越觉得有意思。(越+动　越+动)

(2)前后两项主语不同的时候,还可以组成"(越+形)+(越+形)"的形式。(If the subject of A is different from that of B, the pattern "(越 + adj.) + (越 + adj.)" can be formed.)例如:

夏至这天,北半球昼长夜短,纬度越高,白昼越长。

(On the Summer Solstice, the day is long and the night is short in the Northern Hemisphere. The higher the latitude is, the longer the day is.)

(3)"越来越……"只能组成"越来越+形／心理动词"的形式。("越来越…" can only form the pattern "越来越 + adj.／psyche-verb".)例如:

商品的价格越来越贵了。

人们的生活水平越来越高了。

妈妈越来越担心了。

儿子越来越喜欢弹钢琴了。

(4)"越来越……"一般不能组成"越来越+一般动词"的形

619

式。("越来越…" seldom forms the pattern "越来越 + general verb".)例如：

* 风越来越刮大了。
* 大家越来越跑步了。
* 玛丽越来越学习了。
* 雨越来越下。

3."越来越……"强调随时间的推移而增减,句子表示的变化意义较突出,所以句末常常加助词"了";"越……越……"强调的是程度的增加,所以句末一般不加"了"。〔"越来越…" emphasizes (something) increases or decreases with the passing of time. Changes of meaning are obviously shown in the sentence. Thus such sentences are usually ended with the particle "了"。"越…越…" stresses the increase of degree, so there is usually no "了" at the end of the sentence.〕例如：

他的精力越来越充沛了。
(He is more and more vigorous.)
问题的讨论越来越深入了。
(The discussion of the problem is getting more and more thorough.)
他越来越不理解我了。
(He is more and more unable to understand me.)
这个人我越看越面熟。
(The more I look at the man, the more familiar he looks.)
知识只会越积累越多。
(Knowledge grows with accumulation.)
要我看,你越不服气越糟糕。
(As I see it, the more unconvinced you are, the worse it will be.)

Z

在 zài 到 dào 于 yú

在、于〈介词〉介绍出动作的时间、场所等。
(<preposition> introducing the time or place of an act.)

到〈介词〉介绍出随动作到达的某时间、场所等。
(<preposition> introducing when and where an act arrives.)〔也有将这种用法讲作动词的。(Such usage is also regarded as a verb.)〕

"在"、"到"、"于"都跟动作的时间、场所等有关系,但是由于它们的意义不完全相同、词义色彩也不同、还有搭配习惯上的差别,所以大多不能换用。("在", "到" and "于" are all related to the time or places of acts, but there are some differences in their meanings, coloring and collocations, so they are not interchangeable in most cases.)

(一)"在"和"到"

1."在"跟表示时间的词语组成介词词组介绍出动作发生的某个时间。一般来说,用"在"引出的时间,是一种静态的时间,也就是说,它跟前后的其他时间没有联系,即使有某种联系,说话人的目的也不在于突出这种联系。"在"构成的介词词组在句子里,一般作状语或补语,作补语的时候,谓语动词一般都不是动作性很强的动词。("在" is used to form prepositional phrases with the words indicating time to introduce a certain time at which an act occurs. Generally speaking, the time introduced by "在" is a kind of static time, that is to say, it has nothing to do with other time before or after, and even if there is any relation, the speaker doesn't mean to emphasize the relation. The prepositional phrase made up of "在" generally functions as an adverbial or complement in the sentences. While it functions as a complement, generally the predicative verbs are not the verbs of strong action character.)例如:

我们在校庆日那天,举行了一次大型音乐会。

小李在采访结束以前不会离开这里的。

他生在夏天。

我们把参观活动安排在明天下午。

2."到"跟表示时间的词语组成的介词词组表示随动作到达或继续到某个时间的意思。它所表示的时间是一种动态的时间,即现在的时间一定是前面某一时间延续过来的。说话人用"到+时间"时强调的是这种动态的延续的时间意义。"到+时间"用在动词谓语前,表示到达某时间的意思;用在动词谓语后表示继续到某时间的意思。"到+时间"用在动词后时,前面的动词一般都是动作性较强的动词。("到" forms phrases with the words indicating time with the meaning of reaching or continuing till a certain time. The time it indicates is that of dynamic state, namely the present time is sure to continue from a certain time before. The speaker uses "到 + time" to emphasize the meaning of this dynamic and continuous time. The structure "到 + time" is used in front of the verbal predicates with the meaning of reaching a certain time and with the meaning of going on till a certain time when used after the verbal predicates. When this structure is used after verbs, the verbs in front are generally those of strong action character.)例如:

到昨天,我才接到他的来信。(本该早接到,可是事实上一直延续到昨天。)

我到现在才明白他为什么会说出那种话来。(以前听过那种话,不知道它真正的意思;延续了很长时间,到了现在才明白。)

他们一直干到下午两点才干完。(从某时间开始,延续到两点。)

房子照这个速度装修,恐怕得装修到下个月。(从某时间开始,继续向后延续。)

(If the house is fit up at such speed, the project won't be

finished until next month.)

(1)静态的"在+时间"与动态的"到+时间"是不能换用的。(Static "在 + time" and dynamic "到 + time" are not interchangeable.)例如：

* 我们到校庆日那天,举行了一次大型音乐会。
* 他生到夏天。
* 在昨天,我才接到他的来信。
* 我在现在才明白他为什么会说出那种话来。
* 他们一直干在下午两点才干完。
* 房子照这个速度装修,恐怕得装修在下个月。

(2)一个句子在个别情况下,可能"在"与"到"都可以用,但是意思不同。(Under specific conditions, either "在" or "到" can be used in a sentence, but they express different meanings.)例如：

我们把参观活动安排 在 明天下午。(可能本来就是这样安排的。)

我们把参观活动安排 到 明天下午。(原来可能有某种安排,由于某原因不能实施改到明天下午。)

3."在"跟表示场所的词语组成介词词组介绍出动作发生的某个场所。"在+场所"在句子里可以用在动词前作状语,也可以用在动词后作补语。"在+场所"表示的是人或事物所存在的场所,跟"到+场所"比,具有相对静态的意义。"到+场所"用在动词后,表示随动作到达某场所的意思,所以具有动态或相对动态的意义。("在" forms prepositional phrases with the words indicating places to introduce certain place that action occurs. "在 + a place" in a sentence can be used either as an adverbial before the verb, or as a complement after the verb. The structure "在 + a place" indicates places where people or things are, and compared with the structure "到 + a place", it has the meaning of being comparatively static. The

623

structure "到 + a place" is used after verbs, indicating the meaning of arriving at a certain place with the action, therefore it is of the dynamic or comparatively dynamic meaning.)例如：

同学们都在阅览室里看书。
汽车在马路上飞驰。
爸爸坐在沙发上看报纸。
圣诞树摆在大厅的正中央。
他走到我身边停了下来。
把车开到前面的停车场那儿。

(1) "在 + 场所"与"到 + 场所"不能换用，虽然有时可以出现在同一种类型的句子中，但是表达的意义不同。("在 + a place" and "到 + a place" can't be interchanged. Though they may sometimes occur in the same sort of sentences, they express different meanings.)例如：

* 汽车到马路上飞驰。
* 他走在我身边停了下来。
* 把车开在前面的停车场那儿。

他在这儿卖东西。（本来就在这儿。）

他到这儿卖东西。（本来不在这儿，从别处移动到这儿的。）

你怎么又躺在床上看书了？（本来就在床上，说话人可能表示不该躺在床上看书。）

你怎么又躺到床上看书了？（刚才不在床上，从别处移到床上的。）

(2) 一般来说，具有移动意义的动词，后边大多接"到 + 场所"，不接"在 + 场所"。(Generally speaking, the verbs of movable meaning are followed mostly by the structure "到 + a place", but not by "在 + a place".)例如：

把车开到马路上／跑到操场上／搬到前边／移到左边／冲到外面／匆忙赶到这儿

＊把车开在马路上／＊跑在操场上／＊搬在前边／＊移在左边／＊冲在外面／＊匆忙赶在这儿

4."到"还可以表示动作或性质、状态达到某种程度，是一种动态的意义，所以"在"不能用在这种场合。(The word "到" also indicates a certain degree that action or character and state reach. It is of dynamic meaning, so the word "在" can't be used on such occasion.)例如：

孩子已经烧到四十度了。

事情发展到不可收拾的地步。(The matter has got out of control.)

他的汉语水平降到初级三级了。

价钱已经高到顶点了，不会再高了。

(The price has been forced up to its summit and it could no longer be higher.)

人多到连插脚的地方都没有。

(There are so many people that there is not even room for standing.)

＊孩子已经烧在四十度了。

＊事情发展在不可收拾的地步。

＊他的汉语水平降在初级三级了。

＊价钱已经高在顶点了，不会再高了。

＊人多在连插脚的地方都没有。

(二)"在"与"于"

1."在"和"于"都可以为动作引进时间、处所、方位等，意义一样，但是由于"于"是文言虚词，跟"在"有明显的语体色彩上的差别和构句格式上的差别，有一些较为固定的搭配词，所以在使用范围上，跟"在"有很大的差别。(Both "在" and "于" can introduce the time, place, locality, etc., similar in meaning; but the word "于" is a function word in classical style of writing, and it differs distinctly in the style and in the sentence structure from the word "在"."于" is used fairly fixed with some other collocations, so it differs greatly from "在" in the way of use.)例如：

(1)"于+时间"可以作状语,跟"在+时间"的差别主要在色彩上。"于+时间"有文言色彩,主要用于书面语。"在+时间"通用于口语、书面语。("于 + time" can be used as an adverbial, different from "在 + time" in coloring. "于 + time" is of classical Chinese flavor and is mainly used in the written language. And "在 + time" is generally used in both the spoken language and the written language.)试比较：

晚会于下午五点准时开始。
他将于下半年回国。
货物于明天中午一定运到。
晚会在下午五点准时开始。
他将在下半年回国。
货物在明天中午一定运到。

"于+场所"用在动词前作状语的情况很少。"在+场所"作状语的情况比较常用。("在 + a place" is often used as an adverbial, but "于 + a place" is rarely used before verbs as an adverbial.)例如：

科学报告会在会议厅举行。
我们在这儿坐一会儿,好吗?
＊ 科学报告会于会议厅举行。
＊ 我们于这儿坐一会儿,好吗?

(2)"于+场所"一般用在动词后作补语,大多跟单音动词配合。搭配有一定的固定性,所以多数情况下不宜用"在+场所"替换。("于 + a place" is generally used as a complement after verbs and more often collocates with monosyllable verbs. Its collocation is fairly fixed, so it is not appropriate to substitute it for "在 + a place" so often.)例如：

常用的动词有:生、死、位、出、产、用、源、毕业等等。例如:

生于北京／位于中部／产于广东／源于青海／毕业于清华大学

这里除了"生／死于北京"可以说成"生／死在北京"外,其他的一般都不能用"在"。

2."于"还可以为动作或状态引出方向、方面、对象、原因等,"在"一般不能用在这些方面。("于" can also introduce the direction, aspect, target, or cause of an act or a state. Generally "在" can't be used so.)例如：

天气趋于暖和(The weather is tending towards warmth.)

献身于事业(devote oneself to the cause)

从事于自然科学的研究(be engaged in the study of the natural science)

忙于写论文(be busy at writing the thesis)

天才出于勤奋(Talent is born of diligence.)

苦于没有办法(to suffer from lacking of methods)

乐于助人(to take delight in helping others.)

形势有利于我们(The situation is favorable to us.)

无济于事(of no avail)

＊天气趋在暖和／＊献身在事业／＊从事在自然科学的研究／＊忙在写论文／＊天才出在勤奋

＊苦在没有办法／＊乐在助人／＊形势有利在我们／＊无济在事

在……上 zài……shàng　　在……中 zài……zhōng
在……下 zài……xià

〈介词词组〉< prepositional phrases >

(一)介词"在"与"……上"、"……中"、"……下"等方位词组构成介词词组,表示某空间、范围、方面、条件等,但是由于后面的方位词不同,所以意义和用法也不相同。(Preposition "在" is used to form prepositional phrases with phrase of locality as "…上",

627

"…中" and "…下", indicating a certain space, range, aspect and condition, etc., but for the reason that the nouns of locality after are different, the meaning and usage are different as well.)

1."在……上":主要表示方面、空间范围、条件等。(mainly indicates aspects, space, conditions, etc.)例如:

他在搜集邮票上,下了不少工夫。

(He has put in a lot of effort in stamp collecting.)

科学技术是一种在历史上起推动作用的革命力量。

(Scientific technology is a revolutionary force which has been playing a motive role in history.)

在大量实验的基础上,他又作了理论上的总结。

(On the basis of doing hosts of experiments, he also made the theoretical summation.)

2."在……中":主要表示环境里、范围里等。(mainly means in an environment, range, etc.)例如:

青年人要在艰苦中奋斗,在奋斗中创业,在创业中成长。

(Young people have to strive in difficult conditions and make progress in striving and to grow through making progress.)

他在研究生物工程工作中取得了可喜的成绩。

3."在……下":主要表示前提条件 (mainly indicates premise conditions.)

在大家的帮助下,他很快就适应了这里的生活。

这些作品是在老作家的指导下创作出来的。

(These works are produced under the guidance of the senior writers.)

4.要注意的是:"在……上"、"在……下"都可以表示"条件",但是它们使用的环境不同。"在……上"所表示的条件不是前提条件,它有一定的工作基础,然后进一步向高发展。(Notice that "在…上" and "在…下" can both express "conditions", but they are used in different language situations. The condition that "在

628

…上" indicates is not the premise condition. It has a certain working basis and will develop further.)例如：

我们要在发展生产的基础上,不断改善人民的生活水平。(前—低;后—高)

(We must improve people's living standard uninterruptedly on the basis of developing production.)

* 我们要在发展生产的基础下,不断改善人民的生活水平。

5."在 ……下"所表示的条件是前提条件,无论肯定的或否定的,都是一种条件。在表示肯定意义的条件中,由于有了这一条件才会出现某种情况,所以形成这一条件的因素通常是高的。(The condition "在…下" indicates is the premise condition, and there will be one condition no matter it is positive or negative. When "在…下" indicates the positive meaning, certain situation may come into being because of this condition, therefore the factor of forming this condition is generally important.)例如：

在李老师的启发下,大家终于弄明白了这道难题。(前—高;后—低)

在社会主义制度下,实行的是按劳分配的分配原则。(前—高;后—低)

(The rules of distribution according to work is carried out under the socialist system.)

* 在李老师的启发上,大家终于弄明白了这道难题。

(二)由"在"构成介词词组表示某空间、范围、方面、条件等时,后面一定要有"上"、"中"、"下"等相应的方位词配合,没有是错的。(Besides, when the prepositional phrases made up of "在" indicates some space, range, aspect and condition, etc., there must be nouns of locality "上", "中", "下" and so on to coordinate after, and it is incorrect without those nouns of locality.)例如：

这件事一定要在思想上引起注意。

在众多的朋友中,我们俩最要好。

(Among so many friends, we are the closest.)

他在没有任何先进设备的条件下,自己克服困难取得实验的成功。

* 这件事一定要在思想引起注意。

* 在众多朋友,我们俩最要好。

* 他在没有任何先进设备的条件,自己克服困难取得实验的成功。

再三 zàisān　　反复 fǎnfù　　屡次 lǚcì

〈副词〉表示一次又一次或多次。(< adverb > indicating time and again, many times.)

"再三"、"反复"和"屡次"都可以用在谓语动词前表示一次又一次或多次的意思,但是由于它们意义侧重的角度有所不同、使用范围有所不同、结构上也有一定的差别,所以多数情况下不能换用。("再三","反复"and"屡次"can all be placed before predicative verbs to indicate time and again, or many times, but they have different emphatic angles, applicable ranges and structural arrangements. Therefore, they are not interchangeable in most cases.)

(一) 意义侧重的角度不同 (Differences in emphatic angles)

1."再三"跟"反复"和"屡次"比,有强调意味,即它强调"不止一次地",因此用"再三"作状语的句子,大多有在不止一次的动作的作用下而产生的某种效果——有效的或无效的。(Compared with "反复" and "屡次", "再三" is of emphasizing meaning, namely it stresses "more than once". So the sentences with "再三" as an adverbial mostly show the results — might be effective or invalid results which are affected by the act more than once.)例如:

妈妈再三挽留,他才勉强同意留下来吃饭。

(After Mother repeatedly urged him to stay, he reluctantly agreed to stay for the meal.)

我再三解释，他就是不听。

大家再三地安慰她，她还是担心得不得了。

在他的再三劝导下，我才想通了。

(After his repeated persuasion I become convinced.)

2."反复"不只是有次数多的意思，它还有"重复"的意义，即它的次数多常常指同一类动作的多次出现。没有"再三"的强调意味。("反复" not only means "many times", but means "repeatedly" as well. It generally refers to the repeated happening of the same kind acts, but has no emphasizing meaning of "再三".)例如：

有关部门反复向工人们进行安全教育。

他反复琢磨这句话的意思。

(He turned the meaning of this statement over and over again in his mind.)

3."屡次"只是次数多的意思，没有"再三"的强调意味，也没有"反复"的"重复"意义。("屡次" only means high frequency, without emphasizing meaning of "再三", or the meaning of "repeatedly" indicated by "反复".)例如：

为此，他屡次遭到领导的批评。

他在射击中屡次创造新记录。

(He has made new records in shooting competitions time and again.)

(二) 使用范围有所不同 (Differences in applicable ranges)

1."再三"多用于具体动作，具体动作还多限于语言类的动作。("再三" is used to indicate the specific acts and the specific acts are mostly limited to those of the language category.)例如：

再三向他道谢 / 再三警告他 / 再三要求参加这项活动 / 再三提醒他注意

2."反复"一般也多用于具体动作，但是不限于语言类。("反复" is also used to indicate the specific acts which are not limited

631

to those of the language category.)例如：

  反复商量／反复做／反复看／反复检查／反复研究／反复听

 3."屡次"大多是指整个事情的多次出现,所指的事情多是比较抽象的、笼统的。("屡次" most often refers to the frequent happening of the whole matter and the things it refers are mostly comparatively abstract and sweeping.)例如：

  屡次犯错误(frequently make mistakes)
  屡次建立功勋 (to perform immortal feats time and again)
  屡次失败 (to be defeated time and again)
  屡次被查处 (to be investigated and dealt with over and over again)
  屡次遭审查 (to be examined over and over again)

(三) 使用方式上的不同 (Differences in ways of application)

 1."反复"因为主要有"重复"的意思,而不只是次数的意义,所以动词后可以接"次"、"遍"等表示动作数量的词语；"再三"、"屡次"只是表示次数的意思,所以动词后不能再接表示动作数量的词语。(As "再三" mainly means "repeatedly", not simply the frequency, the verbs can be followed by words "次", "遍", etc. denoting the numbers of the acts. "反复" and "屡次" only express frequency, so the verbs cannot be followed by words denoting the numbers of the acts.)例如：

  反复商量了好几次／反复计算了好几遍／反复研究多次／反复做三次

  ＊再三挽留多次／＊再三道谢好几次／＊再三嘱咐好几遍

  ＊屡次犯多次错误／＊屡次建立好几次功勋／＊屡次失败三次

 2."再三"、"反复"后面可以加"地",突出一遍又一遍或反反复复的方式；"屡次"只是数量,不表示方式,所以不能接"地"。

("再三" and "反复" can be followed by "地", stressing the ways in which the act is done again and again or done repeatedly. "屡次" is only the number, not indicating the ways, so it can't be followed by "地".)例如：

我再三地提醒他／他再三地解释道／领导再三地强调安全

反复地琢磨／反复地计算／反复地看、反复地听

＊屡次地失败／＊屡次地被查处／＊屡次地遭审查

3. "再三"除了可以用在动词前作状语外,还可以用在动词后作补语;"反复"、"屡次"没有这种用法。(Besides serving as an adverbial before verbs, "再三" can also be used as a complement after verbs. Whereas "反复" and "屡次" can't be used like this.)例如：

我叮嘱再三,他还是出了问题。

(He still got into the trouble even though I exhorted him again and again.)

思之再三,还是决定放弃。

(I finally decided to give up after thinking it over again and again.)

＊研究反复,才作出决定。

＊计算反复,总算算对了。

＊犯屡次错误／＊遭到屡次批评／＊建立屡次功勋

4. 为了强调多次,"再三"还可以跟"再四"合用,构成一种固定的使用格式;"反复"也可以用 AABB 的重叠式;"屡次"没有这些方式。(In order to emphasize the repetition, "再三" also can be used together with "再四" to form a fixed pattern; and "反复" can be used in the AABB structure, but "屡次" doesn't have these patterns.)例如：

再三再四地说明,可是他就是不听。

(He would just refuse to listen though it was explained over and over again.)

633

再三再四地想,也想不明白。

反反复复地问了好几遍。

法制教育必须反反复复地进行。

* 你怎么屡屡次次地犯错误?

咱 zán　　咱们 zánmen

〈代词〉< pronoun >

"咱"、"咱们"有时都可以称代说话人、听话人双方,这时可以通用。(Sometimes both "咱" and "咱们" can indicate both the speaker and the listener(s), and are exchangeable.)例如:

咱/咱们就别去了,叫小张去问问有什么事儿,回来告诉咱/咱们一声不就行了。

有时不能通用,区别在于:(But sometimes they are not exchangeable due to the following differences:)

"咱"有时只称代说话者一人;"咱们"则称代包括自己在内的若干人。("咱" sometimes only represents the speaker himself. "咱们" represents a certain number of people including the speaker himself.)例如:

有什么好事你别一个人享受,也让咱分享一下。("咱"如果只是说话人自己,只能用"咱",不能用"咱们"。)

咱们也上台表演一个节目吧。("咱们"一定代替若干人,如果只是一个人,不能用"咱们"。)

咱们 zánmen　　我们 wǒmen

〈代词〉表示包括自己在内的若干人。

(< pronoun > indicating a number of people including oneself.)

"我们"、"咱们"都可以表示包括自己在内的若干人,所以有时可以通用。(Both "咱们" and "我们" can indicate a number of people including oneself, so they are sometimes interchangeable.)例如:

我们/咱们开个会,研究研究这个方案。

634

正好我也要去商店,我们/咱们一起走吧。

区别在于(Their differences):

(一) 语体色彩不同 (Different in style and coloring)

"咱们"一般只用于口语;"我们"通用于口语和书面语。("咱们" is usually used in spoken language; while "我们" is commonly used in spoken and written languages.)

(二) 词义范围不同 (Different in the range of meaning)

当说话人强调说话人、听话人某一方时"我们"、"咱们"通常不能通用。这是因为"我们"有时只称代说话人一方;而"咱们"有时可以称代说话人和听话人双方。("咱们" and "我们" are generally not interchangeable when the speaker emphasizes the single side of either the speaker or the listener. The reason is that "我们" sometimes only represents the speaker's side, but "咱们" sometimes can represent both speaker and listener.)例如:

晚会上,几个人向另外几个人告辞说:"你们继续玩吧,我们先走了。"(此时,"我们"不能用"咱们",在这里"我们"只称代说话人一方。)

另几个人说:"着什么急呀,咱们好不容易凑到一起,再玩一会吧。"(此时,"咱们"可以换成"我们","咱们"称代了说话人、听话人双方。)

暂时 zànshí　　临时 línshí

〈副词〉< adverb >

〈形容词〉< adjective >

(一) "暂时"、"临时"都有副词用法,用在动词前,表示某种时间的意义。(Both "暂时" and "临时" can function as adverbs and be used before verbs to indicate time.)

1."暂时"和"临时"有时都可以表示"短时间内"的意思,表示这种意思时,基本上可以换用,但是意义有偏差。"临时"所修饰的动作一般都不是正式的或最终决定的事情,"暂时"没有这

635

个意思。(Sometimes "暂时" and "临时" can both express the meaning "within a short period". In this sense, the two words are generally interchangeable, with only a little deviation. Usually the acts modified by "临时" is not a regular or settled thing.)试比较:

你暂时先在这儿住几天,等找到房子,再搬出去。
你临时在这儿住几天,等找到房子,再搬出去。
这台录音机我只是暂时用一用,明天就还给你。
这台录音机我只是临时用一用,明天就还给你。

但是,当只有"短时间内"的意思时,不能用"临时",只能用"暂时"。(While indicating the meaning of "within a short period", "临时" can't be used but "暂时" works.)例如:

这件事请你暂时不要告诉他。
关于我的病情,请大夫暂时向我的家人保密。
(As for my illness, I would ask the doctor to keep secret temporarily to my family.)

* 这件事请你临时不要告诉他。
* 关于我的病情,请大夫临时向我的家人保密。

2. "临时"主要表示"临到事情发生的时候"的意思,只有这种意思时,也不能跟"暂时"换用。("临时" mainly indicates "at the time when something happens". In this sense, it is not interchangeable with "暂时" either.)例如:

我临时接到通知赶来的,没做发言的准备,请原谅。
(I dashed my way off at the time when the notice arrived, so please excuse me for not preparing for the speech.)

家里出了事,我只好临时决定回国,什么时候回来不好说。

* 我暂时接到通知赶来的,没做发言的准备,请原谅。

(二) "暂时"、"临时"都有形容词用法,在句中主要作定语,也可以用在"是……的"结构中。"暂时"表示"短时间的"意思;"临时"表示"短期的"、"非正式的"意思。(Both "暂时" and "临时"

can function as adjectives and be used as attributes or in the "是…的" pattern. "暂时" means "within a short period"; "临时" means "temporary", "irregular".) 例如:

这只是一种暂时的现象,想想办法,会克服的。

要有信心,困难只是暂时的嘛。

情况很紧急,赶快成立一个临时的领导班子,解决一下这个问题。

(The situation is quite urgent. A temporary leading group must be set up quickly to solve this problem.)

这个政府机构只是临时的。

* 要有信心,困难只是临时的嘛。

* 情况很紧急,赶快成立暂时领导班子,解决一下这个问题。

怎么 zěnme　　为什么 wèi shénme

"怎么"是疑问代词,"为什么"是"为"加疑问代词"什么"构成的。它们有时意义用法完全不同,但有时又有相近或有联系的地方。("怎么" is an interrogative pronoun. "为什么" is formed from "为" and the interrogative pronoun "什么". They are sometimes quite different in meaning and usage, but sometimes similar and associated.)

(一)"怎么"和"为什么"不同的地方:(Differences between "怎么" and "为什么":)

1. "怎么"可以询问方式、方法;"为什么"不可以。("怎么" can inquire about ways or manners; "为什么" can't.) 例如:

你怎么来的,走着来的,还是坐车来的?

怎么做? 你教教我。

* 你为什么来的,走着来的,还是坐车来的?

* 为什么做? 你教教我。

2. "怎么"可以询问或虚指情状、性质、程度,"为什么"不可以。("怎么" can inquire about or indicate conditions, nature, degree; "为什么" can't.)例如：

> 她怎么了？好像有些不舒服。
> 这到底是怎么一回事？
> 外面怎么好,也不如自己家好。
> (No matter how wonderful the outside world is, it is no better than one's own home.)
> 她今天不怎么高兴,别惹她了。
> (Don't bother her since she is not happy today.)
> * 她为什么了？好像有些不舒服。
> * 这到底是为什么一回事？
> * 外面为什么好,也不如自己家好。
> * 她今天不为什么高兴,别惹她了。

3."为什么"可以询问目的,"怎么"不可以。("为什么" can inquire about purpose; "怎么" can't.)例如：

> 你爷爷为什么来中国？是为了回忆过去吗？
> 你为什么学医,难道忘了你的追求了吗？
> * 你爷爷怎么来中国？是为了回忆过去吗？
> * 你怎么学医,难道忘了你的追求了吗？

4."为什么"可以构成"是 + 为什么"的结构,即"为什么"作"是"的宾语;"怎么"不可以。("为什么" can form the "是 + 为什么" structure, namely, "为什么" is the object of "是". "怎么" can't.)例如：

> 这到底是为什么？命运为什么对我这样不公正？
> 你们这样动怒究竟是为什么？
> * 这到底是怎么？命运为什么对我这样不公正？
> * 你们这样动怒究竟是怎么？

(二)"怎么"和"为什么"相近或有联系的地方：(Similarities or associations of "怎么" and "为什么":)

"怎么"和"为什么"的相同之处是都可以问原因,但不完全相同,有时不能互换使用。(The similarity of "怎么" and "为什么" is that they both can inquire about causes, but there are still some differences, so they are sometimes not interchangeable.)

1. 结构上虽然可以互换,但是意义侧重点有所不同。(Though interchangeable in construction, they emphasize different points.)

(1)"怎么"侧重于诧异、不理解,"为什么"侧重于询问。("怎么" emphasizes surprise or being beyond one's comprehension and "为什么" emphasizes inquiry.)例如:

小王怎么没来?他亲口告诉我一定来的。(因为说一定来,所以对于没来感到诧异。)

小王没来吗?谁知道他为什么没来?(不知道原因,想知道原因。)

这么好的电影你怎么不看呢?(感到奇怪、不理解。)

电影那么好,你为什么不看呢?(主要想知道原因。)

(2)"怎么"一般为新信息,"为什么"一般为已知信息。("怎么" generally indicates new information and "为什么" indicates the known information.)例如:

你怎么连这个字都不会写?(刚知道的。)

玻璃怎么碎了?(刚发现的。)

为什么不让他学会自己生活?(已经知道他不会自己生活。)

你知道他为什么半年来一点儿消息也没有吗?(没有消息是很久以来的事。)

(Do you know why he hasn't given any information for this half year ?)

(3)"怎么"有时含有"不该"的意思,所以带有轻微指责的意味;"为什么"也可以表示不满的意味,用"为什么"主要用以追究质问,语气显得重。("怎么" sometimes implies the meaning of "shouldn't", with the meaning of slight criticism; "为什么" can

639

also indicate dissatisfaction, but mainly it is used to enquire and question with a serious tone.)例如:

你怎么不早告诉我呢?(说话人认为不该晚告诉我。)
他们怎么不帮帮李娜呢?(说话人认为不该不帮。)
她病了,你为什么不在家里照顾她?(不满,追究质问。)
你为什么不说实话?(不满,追究质问。)

2. 虽然都是询问原因,但是不能互换使用。(Though both used to inquire about causes, they cannot be used interchangably.)

(1) 用"怎么"构成的反问句,句中常常可以加上能愿动词"能"、"会"等,不能与"为什么"互换。(In rhetorical questions formed with "怎么", modal verbs "能" and "会" are usually added in the sentences, and "怎么" cannot be exchanged with "为什么".)例如:

你怎么能不知道呢? 我明明告诉过你呀。
(How couldn't you know this? I did tell you this before.)
电视怎么会坏呢? 我们刚刚还看过呢。
* 你为什么能不知道呢? 我明明告诉过你呀。
* 电视为什么会坏呢? 我们刚刚还看过呢。

(2) 只表示诧异,不表示询问时,只能用"怎么",不能用"为什么"。"怎么"一般用在句首。(When indicating only surprise but not inquiry, only "怎么" can be used. "怎么" is usually placed at the beginning of a sentence.)例如:

怎么!他敢欺负你?(What! How dare he bully you?)
怎么,钥匙没了?
* 为什么!他敢欺负你?
* 为什么,钥匙没了?

(3) 只表示询问,不表示诧异时,只能用"为什么",不能用"怎么"。(When indicating only inquiry but not surprise, only "为什么" can be used.)例如:

640

谁知道她为什么哭?
哪位同学能说说,海水为什么有涨有落?
* 谁知道她怎么哭?
* 哪位同学能说说,海水怎么有涨有落?

怎么 zěnme　怎样 zěnyàng　怎么样 zěnmeyàng

〈疑问代词〉 < interrogative pronoun >

"怎么"、"怎样"、"怎么样"在意义和用法上有时大体相同,可以互换使用,也都可以活用为非疑问的方式,但是有时意义和用法却又完全不同。("怎么","怎样"and"怎么样"are roughly the same in meaning and usage, are interchangeable, and can all be flexibly used in non-interrogative ways. But there are some differences in their meanings and usage.)

(一)"怎么"、"怎样"、"怎么样"在意义上或用法上大体相同之处。(Similarities in their meaning and usage.)

1."怎么"、"怎样"、"怎么样"在表示疑问时,在句子里都能作询问方式的状语,基本上可以互换使用。(When"怎么","怎样"and"怎么样"are used to express query, they all can be used as an adverbial of inquiry in the sentences, usually exchangeable.)例如:

你是怎么/怎样/怎么样说服她的?
我们怎么/怎样/怎么样向他们提出这个要求好?
外面下了那么大的雨,他们是怎么/怎样/怎么样去的?

2."怎么"、"怎样"、"怎么样"在句子里都可以活用为非疑问的方式。(They can all be used flexibly in non-interrogative ways.)

(1)"怎么"、"怎样"、"怎么样"都可以用来表示不定指,句中都可以用"无论"、"不管"、"都"、"也"配合使用,表示所说的范围之内没有例外。有时可以互换使用。("怎么","怎样"and"怎么样" can all be used to express indefinite reference, and can be collocated with"无论","不管","都"or"也", indicating there is no exception in the stated area. They are sometimes interchangeable.)例如:

641

不管条件怎么/怎样/怎么样差,他都决心把这件事做到底。
(No matter under what condition / how the condition is / how poor the condition is, he is determined to do the thing to the end.)

无论怎么/怎样/怎么样忙,她都坚持来我家给奶奶看病。
不管他怎么/怎样/怎么样打我,我都不会说的。

(2)"怎么"、"怎样"、"怎么样"都可以用在"A(动)就A(动)"的格式里,表示不定指。["怎么","怎样"and "怎么样" can all be used in the "A (verb) 就 A (verb)" pattern, indicating indefinite reference.]例如:

我不管,你想怎么说就怎么说吧。
(You can just say anything you want to say, I don't care.)
这没有什么难的,你们怎样想的就怎样说好了。
(It is nothing difficult, just say what's on your mind.)
你想怎么样就怎么样,我们不干涉你。
(You may do anything you like, we won't interfere you.)

(3)"怎么"、"怎样"、"怎么样"都可以用来代替不知道的或不必、不便说出来的方式、状况、性质等。("怎么","怎样" and "怎么样" can all be used to represent the manner, state, or nature that is not known or is unnecessary or inconvenient to be spoken out.)例如:

你对我帮助这么大,我不知道怎么/怎样/怎么样感谢你才好。
听说他最近病得不轻,我想去看看他到底怎么样了。
她把那个人怎样帮助她的事向大家述说了一遍。

(二)"怎么"、"怎样"、"怎么样"在意义上或用法上的不同之处。(Differences in their meaning and usage)

1."怎么"、"怎样"、"怎么样"在表示疑问时意义上或用法上的差别。(The differences of "怎么", "怎样" and "怎么样" in expressing query.)

(1)"怎么"作状语时可以询问原因;"怎样"、"怎么样"没有这种用法。(When "怎么" is used as an adverbial, it can ask about the causes; "怎样" and "怎么样" are not used so.)例如:

这么重要的会,他怎么没参加呢?

你怎么也跟他一样地来教训我?

你是那样大度的一个人,怎么倒在这件小事上斤斤计较起来了?

(Since you are such a generous person, how could you haggle over every ounce at such small matter?)

* 这么重要的会,他怎样/怎么样没参加呢?

* 你怎样/怎么样也跟他一样地来教训我?

* 你是那样大度的一个人,怎样/怎么样倒在这件小事上斤斤计较起来了?

(2)"怎样"、"怎么样"可以单独作谓语问情况,后边没有"了"、"啦"等词可以成立,"怎么"不行,它后边必须加上"了"、"啦"等词,才能作谓语询问情况。("怎样" and "怎么样" can be used independently as predicates to ask about the situation. They may work without "了" or "啦" after them; but "怎么" can't, it can only be used as a predicate to inquire information when it is followed by "了" or "啦", etc.)例如:

你怎样/怎么样? 最近忙吗?

他老人家近来怎样/怎么样? 身体还好吗?

* 你怎么? 最近忙吗?

* 他老人家近来怎么? 身体还好吗?

此外,"怎么"加上"了"、"啦"后跟"怎样"、"怎么样"所问的内容也不同。(What is asked with "怎么" after being followed by "了" or "啦" is different from what is asked with "怎样" or "怎么样".)例如:

你怎么啦? (不知道"你"有什么情况而问。)

你快来看,电脑怎么啦? (不知道电脑出了什么问题而问。)

"怎么"加上"了"、"啦"后,是在新情况出现后,问话人不知道情况怎么回事的情况下发问的;"怎样"、"怎么样"却不同,它是在已经知道某种情况的情况下,为了了解其进一步的发展情况而发问的。(When "怎么" is followed by "了" or "啦", it is used after the new situation comes into being, when the speaker knows nothing about the situation; "怎么" and "怎么样" are different. They are used when a certain situation is known but further information is required.)例如:

老刘的病最近怎样/怎么样啦?(已知老刘生病的事。)
(How about Lao Liu's illness these days? / How is Lao Liu's illness these days?)

工程进展得怎样/怎么样了?(已知某项工程在进行。)

(3)"怎样"、"怎么样"还可以作宾语问意愿、看法,作补语一般问情况,"怎么"没有这样的用法。("怎样" and "怎么样" can serve as objects to ask about one's wishes, or views; or as complements to ask about the situations. "怎么" is not used so.)例如:

你想怎样/怎么样?(问意愿。)
他们打算怎样/怎么样?(问意愿。)
你认为怎样/怎么样?(问看法。)
论文写得怎样/怎么样啦?(问情况。)
* 他们打算怎么?
* 你认为怎么?
* 论文写得怎么?

但是有时"怎样"、"怎么样"、"怎么"都可以作宾语问情况,后边都要加上"了"、"啦",但是所问内容不同。(Sometimes "怎么", "怎样" and "怎么样" can all be used as objects to ask about conditions after being followed by "了" or "啦", but the contents asked are different.)例如:

你以为怎样/怎么样啦?(问某种已知的情况的进展情况。)

你觉得怎样/怎么样啦?(问某种已发生的情况的进展情况。)

你以为怎么啦?(问不知道的情况。)

你觉得怎么啦?(问刚发生的情况。)

(4)"怎样"、"怎么样"、"怎么"也都可以作定语询问性质,但是用法上有差别。"怎样"可以直接作定语,名词前没有数量词也可以;"怎么样"作定语时,"怎么样"的前或后通常要有数量词;"怎么"作定语时,"怎么"的后边必须要有数量词。("怎么"、"怎样" and "怎么样" can all serve as attributes to ask about the nature of something, but are different in usage. "怎样" can be used directly as an attribute, and it may work without a numeral-classifier compound in front of the noun being modified by it. When "怎么样" is used as an attribute, it usually takes numeral-classifier compound before or after it. When "怎么" is used as an attribute, it must be followed by a numeral-classifier compound.)例如:

面对这种情况,我们到底应该采取怎样的行动?大家说说看。

(Facing such situation, everyone may give his own opinion as to what exact action we should take.)

那是<u>一个</u>怎样的年代?你能给我们讲讲吗?

(What age was that? Could you tell me?)

他到底是<u>一个</u>怎么样的人?你能给我们描述一下吗?

(What kind of person indeed is he? Can you describe a bit for us?)

这到底是怎么<u>回事</u>呀?

* 面对这种情况,我们到底应该采取怎么的行动?大家说说看。

* 他到底是一个怎么的人?你能给我们描述一下吗?

* 这到底是怎么事呀?

2."怎么"、"怎样"、"怎么样"在活用为表示非疑问的方式

645

时,意义上和用法上的差别。(When "怎么", "怎样" and "怎么样" are used in non-interrogative ways, they are different in meaning and usage.)

(1)"怎么"可以用于否定,构成"不+怎么"的方式,表示一定的程度;"怎样"有时也可以这么用,但是很少;"怎么样"没有这种用法。("怎么" can be used in negative sentences, forming the "不 + 怎么" pattern to express a certain degree. "怎样" is seldom, and "怎么样" never used so.)例如:

今年冬天不怎么冷。

他已经十五岁了,个子长得不怎么高。

我以前不怎么了解他,最近在一起工作才了解了一点儿。

(I didn't know much about him before and I do know a little since we work together these days.)

家里出了这么大的事,他好像也不怎样着急。

(He seems not so worried though such incident happened in his family.)

* 今年冬天不怎么样冷。

* 我以前不怎么样了解他,最近在一起工作才了解了一点儿。

* 家里出了这么大的事,他好像也不怎么样着急。

(2)"怎么"在句中单独使用,可以表示出乎意料、惊讶的意思。"怎样"、"怎么样"没有这种用法。(When "怎么" is used alone in the sentence, it indicates exceeding one's expectations or astonishment. "怎样" and "怎么样" are not use no.)例如:

怎么?! 又烧起来啦? 不是说他的病已经完全稳定下来了吗?

怎么?! 他没来? 他明明告诉我他一定来的呀。

(3)"怎样"还可以用在陈述句中强调程度,用在感叹句中表示强烈的感情;"怎么样"很少这样用;"怎么"没有这种用法。("怎样" can also be used in the declarative sentence to stress the degree and in the exclamatory sentence to indicate strong emotion. "怎么样" is seldom, and "怎么" never used so.)例如：

宋先生执教三十多年来,为教育事业做出了怎样大的贡献,是大家有目共睹的。

(It is there for all to see that Mr. Song has made such great dedication to the course of education since starting teaching 30 years ago.)

从这里可以看出他们对战士是怎样地热爱了。

这是怎样的一种精神啊!

这是一个怎样激动人心的场面啊!

(What an exciting scene it is !)

* 宋先生执教三十多年来,为教育事业做出了怎么大的贡献,是大家有目共睹的。

* 从这里可以看出他们对战士是怎么地热爱了。

* 这是怎么的一种精神啊!

* 这是一个怎么激动人心的场面啊!

怎么样 zěnmeyàng　　什么样 shénmeyàng

"怎么样"是疑问代词,"什么样"是疑问代词"什么"加"样"构成的。这两个词语有时可以出现在相同结构的句子中,但是表示的意义有出入;多数情况下,它们的意义、用法完全不同,不能出现在相同结构的句子中。("怎么样" is an interrogative pronoun. "什么样" is the interrogative pronoun "什么" plus "样". These two sometimes can be used in sentences of the same grammatical structures, but expressing different meanings. In most cases, they are quite different in meaning and usage, and can not appear in sentences of the same grammatical structure.)

(一)"怎么样"、"什么样"可以出现在相同结构的句子中,但是表达的意义有出入。一般来说,"怎么样"侧重内部性状,"什么样"侧重外部特征、具体类别等。(When "怎么样" and "什么样"

647

occur in sentences of the same structure, they express different meanings. Generally speaking, "怎么样" emphasizes the internal character and state, while "什么样" emphasizes the external character and the specific classification, etc.)例如：

1. 作定语修饰名词时（When used as an attribute to modify nouns）

(1)询问性质,回答应该说明是忠诚、老实、认真、狡猾、奸诈等等。(To inquire about the character. The responses should explain whether (he) is honest, faithful, earnest or cunning, crafty, etc.)例如：

他究竟是一个怎么样的人,你了解吗？

(Exactly what kind of person he is, do you know?)

(2)询问类别,回答应该说明是好人、坏人等或者是干什么的等等。(To inquire about the specific classification. The response should explain whether (he) is a good man or a bad man, or what does he do, etc.)例如：

他究竟是一个什么样的人？(Exactly what kind of person is he?)

(3)询问外貌特征,回答应该是长得什么样、穿什么衣服等等。(To inquire about the external features, the responses should explain how he looks or what he wears.)

询问外貌特征一般不用"怎么样"。("怎么样" is seldom used to inquire about the external features.)例如：

来的那个人是个什么样的人,你能描绘描绘吗？

(4)只表示具体类别时,一般只能用"什么样"。(When just indicating the specific category, generally only "什么样" is used.)例如：

他什么样的苦没吃过,什么样的罪没受过？

(What hardships didn't he bear and endure ?)

＊他怎么样的苦没吃过,怎么样的罪没受过？

2.作谓语、补语时 (When used as a predicate or complement)

(1)询问性状,回答应该是好看、漂亮、新颖、别致、不太好、难看等。(To inquire about the shape and properties. The answers should be good-looking, beautiful, novel, unique, average, ugly, and the like.)例如:

我新买的这件衣服怎么样?

她长得怎么样?

(2)询问外部具体特征,回答应该是黑色的、长裙式的晚礼服等等;高高的个子、大 大的眼睛、苗条的身材或者小眼睛、瓜子脸等等。(To inquire about the specific external features. The answers should be a black evening dress in long-skirt style and the like; or a tall person, big eyes, a slim figure, or small eyes, an oval face, etc.)例如:

你新买的那件衣服什么样?

她长得什么样?

(二)"怎么样"、"什么样"完全不同的用法:(Different usage of "怎么样" and "什么样":)

1."怎么样"可以用在动词前表示动作方式,"什么样"不可以。("怎么样" can be used before verbs indicating the way of acts, while "什么样" can't.)例如:

你告诉我怎么样说,好吗?

怎么样下笔才是正确的?

大家想一想,我们怎么样帮助他他才肯接受。

* 你告诉我什么样说,好吗?

* 什么样下笔才是正确的?

* 大家想一想,我们什么样帮助他他才肯接受。

2."怎么样"可以作谓语表示状况;"什么样"不能用于这种情况。("怎么样" can be used as predicate indicating state; while "什么样" cannot be used in this case.)例如:

今天天气怎么样?

他的病怎么样了?

* 今天天气什么样?

* 他的病什么样了?

3."怎么样"可以作"觉得"、"感觉"、"认为"、"以为"、"打算"等动词的宾语,也可以单独成句提出问题,"什么样"不可以。["怎么样" can serve as the objects of "觉得"(feel).,"感觉"(perceive),"认为"(think),"以为"(consider),"打算"(plan), etc., or be used alone to raise questions. While "什么样" cannot.]例如:

你觉得这个计划怎么样?

今后你打算怎么样?

怎么样?身体好一点儿了吗?

* 你觉得这个计划什么样? / * 今后你打算什么样?

* 什么样?身体好一点儿了吗?

4."什么样"有时可以构成"动词+成+什么样"的结构,表示虚指具体的样子,"怎么样"不能作这样的成分。("什么样" can sometimes form the "verb + 成 + 什么样" pattern, indicating the specific looking, while "怎么样" cannot.)例如:

你都病成什么样了,还勉强自己干?

(How could you force yourself to do this since you have been so seriously ill?)

她都打扮成什么样了,你还不管管她?

(What has she made herself up like? Why don't you subject her to discipline?)

* 你都病成怎么样了,还勉强自己干?

* 她都打扮成怎么样了,你还不管管她?

5."怎么样"可以代替动词、形容词作谓语,表示动作或性质。"什么样"没有这种用法。("怎么样" can serve as a predicate in place of the verbs or adjectives to indicate actions or character. "什么样" cannot be used so.)例如:

他这样蛮横,你也不能怎么样他。(不能处置他。)
(He is so rude and unreasonable, but you can't do much to him.)

他怎么样你了?(他对你做了什么?)
(What did he do to you?)

这里的条件怎么样? —— 不怎么样。(不太好、并不好。)

* 他这样蛮横,你也不能什么样他。
* 他什么样你了?
* 这里的条件什么样? —— 不什么样。

这么 / 那么 zhème/nàme 太 tài

这么 / 那么〈指示代词〉< demonstrative pronoun >
太〈程度副词〉< adverb of degree >

"这么"/"那么"和"太"都可以表示较高或很高的程度,但是意义和用法差别较大,一般的情况下不能互换使用。("这么 / 那么" and "太" can both express a relatively high or very high degree, but they are different in meaning and usage, and not interchangeable in general cases.)

(一) 意义上的差别 (Differences in meaning)

1. "这么"/"那么"是指示代词,它跟表示程度的"太"比,带有指示性,因此它指示的程度一般是非常具体的,是可看到、可感知的或可比况的等等。"太"没有这种用法。("这么"/"那么" is a demonstrative pronoun. Compared with "太" which indicates degree, it has the character of demonstration, and the degree it demonstrates is generally fairly specific, visible, sensible or comparable, etc. "太" does not have such usage.)例如:

(1) 与其他事物比较,"这么"/"那么"指示比较的程度。构成:"有/像……+ 这么/那么 + 形/动"。("这么 / 那么" demonstrates the degree of something compared with other things. The pattern is "有/像 …+ 这么/那么 + adj. / v.".)例如:

651

门前的小树有碗口那么粗了。

(The small tree in front of the gate has grown that thick like bowl size.)

女儿已经有我这么高了。

事情可不像你想像的那么容易。

(The matter is not as easy as you imagined.)

我就像他那么不讲理吗?

* 门前的小树有碗口太粗了。
* 女儿已经有我太高了。
* 事情可不像你想像的太容易。
* 我就像他太不讲理吗?

(2) 用手势比况、指示。(To indicate comparison with gestures.)例如:

我买了一个这么大(做手势)的西瓜。

他做的风筝真好,飞得那么高(用手指示)。

(The kite he made is excellent and it flies that high.)

* 我买了一个太大(做手势)的西瓜。
* 他做的风筝真好,飞得太高(用手指示)。

(3) 没有事物、手势比况,但是可以看到、感受到等,此时,"这么/那么"指示的程度比较虚,含夸张意味。(Though without things or gestures to make the contrast, yet the comparison can be seen or sensed. In this sense, the degree demonstrated with "这么/那么" is not specific, implying exaggeration.)例如:

这里这么热闹呀(看到、感受到。)

衣服这么贵呀(看到或听到价钱。)

你怎么这么忙啊?(看到或听说。)

人这么多呀!(看到。)

你这么不讲理呀!(看到、感受到。)

(How could you be so impervious to reason ?)

2."太"没有上述意思,所以不能用在上述语言环境中。

"太"表示的程度高,有主观色彩,它或者表示程度过头(多用于不如意的事情),或者表示程度高(主要用于赞叹),尤其用于赞叹时,主观感情色彩、主观评价性很强。"太"表示的程度高不带有指示性。["太" doesn't have the above meanings. Thus it can't be used in the above situations. The degree that "太" indicates is high and of subjective flavour. It indicates the overdone degree (mainly indicating unsatisfactory things), or indicates high degree (mainly for high praise), especially in high praise, it is fairly strong in the emotional flavour and subjective appraising character. The degree that "太" indicates is not demonstrative.]例如:

时间可以延长,但不能延得太长。
这次考试,我们班的成绩太差了。
你太不讲理了。
妈妈太宠爱她了。(Mother spoils her too much.)
你太不爱惜自己的身体了。
他也太过分了。(He's gone too far.)
* 这次考试,我们班的成绩这么差了。
* 你这么不讲理了。
* 妈妈那么宠爱她了。

景色太美了!
他们的表演太精彩了!
你们对我们照顾得真是太周到了(You've taken care of us so thoughtfully.),我们太感谢你们了!
她这么快就康复了,真是太让人高兴了!
* 景色这么美了!
* 他们的表演那么精彩了!
* 她这么快就康复了,真是那么让人高兴了!

(二)用法上的异同 (Similarities and differences in usage)

1. "这么/那么"和"太"表示程度高的意思时,都不能直接用在名词性成分前。(When "这么/那么" and "太" indicate high

degree, they can't be used directly before the compositions of the noun character.)例如：

* 这么天气,真让人受不了。
* 今天商店里怎么这么人?
* 你那么心情,他也不理解你。
* 老师那么道理,他也不听。
* 这么的房间你还不满意,你到底想要什么样的房间?
* 这次去旅游,我有太教训。
* 实验中出了太问题。
* 我希望你太朋友。

2."这么/那么+形"常常作名词性成分的修饰语,构成"这么/那么+形+的+名"的格式;"太"的这种用法很少。(The "这么/那么 + adj." pattern is usually used as a modifier of noun components, forming the "这么/那么 + adj. + 的 + n." structure. "太" is seldom used so.)例如：

这么漂亮的风景

那么尴尬的场面(that awkward occasion)

这么重的行李

那么难的题

那么大的房间

* 太漂亮的风景
* 太尴尬的场面
* 我拿了一个太重的行李
* 他给我出了一道太难的题
* 我住了一间太大的房间

3."太+形/动"主要作句子的谓语或补语。("太 + adj./v." is mainly used as a predicate or complement.)例如：

风景太漂亮了

场面太尴尬了

行李太重了

题出得太难了

房间布置得太美了

4. "这么 / 那么 + 形"("形"一般是单音节的,具有积极意义的)前面受到副词"只"、"就"、"才"限制时,"这么 / 那么"有强调的作用,此时积极意义的形容词相当于跟它相对的消极意义的形容词的意思。常用的形容词有"大"、"多"、"高"、"长"、"宽"等。〔When "这么 / 那么 + adj." (the adjective is usually monosyllabic, and of positive meaning) is restricted by adverbs "只", "就" and "才", "这么 / 那么" is used emphatically, and the positive adjective means the same as its opposing adjectives of passive meaning. The commonly used adjectives are "大" (big), "多" (many), "高" (high), "长" (long), "宽" (wide), etc.〕例如:

钱就这么多了。(All the money is here.)(只有这么少的钱的意思)

那个孩子才这么高。(That kid is just this tall.)(那个孩子不高,挺矮的)

就这么大的地方啊!(The place is just this big?)(地方很小)

"太"没有这种用法。

* 钱就太多了。

* 那个孩子才太高。

* 就太大的地方啊!

5. "这么 / 那么"还常常构成"怎么 + 这么 / 那么 + 形 / 动"的格式,虽然有疑问词"怎么",但是常常主要不是为了问,而是表示一种很高或较高的程度;"太"没有这种用法。("这么/那么" also usually forms the "怎么 + 这么/那么 + adj. / v." pattern. Though the interrogative word "怎么" is involved, generally it is not mainly used to ask, but indicates a very high or higher degree. "太" is not used so.)例如:

这里的交通怎么这么不方便?

(How could the transportation here be so inconvenient?)

他怎么那么厉害?

今天怎么这么热啊?

你怎么那么忙啊?我想找你都找不到。

(How could you be so busy? I can't find you when I do want to.)

* 这里的交通怎么太不方便?
* 他怎么太厉害?
* 今天怎么太热啊?
* 你怎么太忙啊?我想找你都找不到。

6."这么/那么"还可以跟活用以后表示不确定数目的"几"、"两"和不定量词"点儿"组合,表示数目很少的意思。("这么/那么" can also be used together with the indefinite numbers "几" or "两" and the indefinite measure word "点儿" after to indicate a small sum.)例如:

就来了这么几个人。

他才说了那么两句。

这么点儿吃的哪儿能够?(How could so little food be enough for eating?)

"这么/那么"跟不定量词"些"组合,表示数目多的意思。("这么/那么" is used together with the indefinite measure word "些" to indicate a large sum.)例如:

这么些人哪!

那么些作业,什么时候才能做完?

"太"没有这种用法。("太" doesn't have such usage.)例如:

* 就来了太几个人。
* 他才说了太两句。
* 太点儿吃的哪儿能够?
* 太些作业,什么时候才能做完?

7.用"这么/那么"表示程度构成的句子跟用"太"表示程度

构成的句子,句末的语气助词是不同的。"这么/那么"句末接语气助词的话,一般是"啊"(没有情况变化的意义时);"太"句末接语气助词的话,一般是"了"或者"啦"。(The particles at the end of the sentences formed with "这么 / 那么" indicating degree are different from those at the end of the sentences formed with "太" indicating degree. If a particle is added to the end of "这么/那么" sentence, it generally is "啊" (while no sense of change is involved.) If a particle is added to the end of "太" sentence, it generally is "了" or "啦".)

例如:

天津骑自行车的人这么多啊!

那么费事儿啊! 那么费事儿就算了。

这里的物价那么高啊!

* 这道题那么难了。

* 那么费事儿了! 那么费事儿就算了。

天气太好了!

这道题也太难啦!

这里的服务太周到了!

你太不讲理啦!

* 天气太好啊!

* 这道题也太难啊!

* 这里的服务太周到啊!

* 你太不讲理啊!

真 zhēn　　太 tài　　很 hěn　　更 gèng

〈副词〉表示程度高。(< adverb > indicating high degree.)

"真"、"太"、"很"、"更"都有表示性状程度深的意义,但是大多不能通用。区别在于:("真","太","很" and "更" all indicate in the highest possible degree, but they are hardly interchangeable. Their differences are as follows:)

（一）意义和用法不同（Differences in meaning and usage）

1. "真"所表示的程度深,主要在于"确认"方面,所以含有"的确"、"确实"的意思。另外"真"带有一定的感情色彩,只是客观的叙述,不能用"真"。(The degree that "真" indicates is strong, mainly in the aspect of confirmation, so it implies being real and true. Besides, "真" is of certain emotional flavour, and if it is the objective narration, "真" can't be used.)例如：

他们精神真叫人感动啊！

这部电影揭示的社会问题真深刻呀。

(This movie is really subtle in revealing the social problems.)

我真喜欢这些孩子。

* 孩子们真高兴地玩着。

* 这里是一个真美丽的地方。

2. "太"表示的程度非常高,带有主观评价性,所以也不能用于客观叙述。(The degree that "太" indicates is very high and is of the character of subjective appraisal, so it can't be used in the objective narration.)有两种意义：

（1）表示程度过头,多用于不理想、不如意的事情。(Indicating overdone degree, mainly used for things not ideal and not as one wishes.)例如：

这里人太多了。

车开得太快了,太危险了。

屋子太乱了,快收拾一下吧。

给孩子太多的关心,不利于培养孩子的自立。

(Paying too much attention to the children is unfavourable for fostering their ability to be independent.)

* 晚上吃完饭以后,我觉得肚子太难受。(改成:很难受)

* 乡亲们准备了太多新鲜水果,盛情地招待我们。

(改成:很多)

(2) 表示程度非常高,多用于赞叹。(Indicating a fairly high degree, mainly in high praise.) 例如:

这本小说太吸引人了!
这儿的景色太美了!
晚会的节目太精彩了!
* 我昨天看了一部太精彩的小说。

3. "很"表示程度非常高,侧重于客观叙述。("很" indicates a fairly high degree and emphasizes the objective narration.) 例如:

他们的生活很幸福。
孩子们玩得很开心。
这是一件很有纪念意义的礼物。
他们说着、笑着,一直到很晚。
在中国,我跟中国人谈话的机会很多。
* 这是一件真有纪念意义的礼物。
* 他们说着、笑着,一直到太晚。
* 在中国,我跟中国人谈话的机会太多。

4. "更"所表示的程度在于"加深",所以它跟"很"、"太"、"真"最大的不同是用于比较,表示比原有的程度或情况进了一步,没有比较不能用"更"。(The degree that "更" indicates is "deepening", and its greatest difference from "真", "太" and "很" is that it can be used in comparison, indicating a step further than its former degree or situation. "更" is not used without comparison.) 例如:

我爱这里的山水,更爱这里的人民。
他比以前更懂事了。
他现在更需要我们大家的帮助。(He is much more in need of our help now.)
* 这个地方的商品比别处很/太便宜。
* 她比我真喜欢看电影。
* 我喜欢这里的物品,太喜欢这里重感情的人们。

(二) 结构上的某些不同点 (Some differences in structure)

1."真+形容词"在句中可以作谓语和补语,不能作定语;"太"、"很"、"更"可以作定语。("真 + adjective" can be a predicate or complement in the sentences, but can't be an attributive. "太","很" and "更" can be attributives.)例如:

　　长城真雄伟啊!
　　校园修整得真漂亮啊!
　* 中国的女人是真幸福的女人啊!
　* 我跟别的留学生进行了真有意思的交流。
　　太多的死记硬背只能培养孩子机械的、被动的学习习惯。

(Too much mechanical memorizing will only foster children to get used to the mechanical and passive study habits.)

　　很多外国人来这儿参观访问。
　　我们要生产出更多、更好的优质产品。

2."更"可以用在比较句中形容词或动词前表示程度加深,"真"、"太"、"很"不可以。("更" can be used before adjectives or verbs in comparative sentences to indicate higher in degree. "真","太" and "很" can't.)例如:

　　今天比昨天更冷了。
　　他比过去更注重实际了。(He pays much more attention to the reality than before.)
　　她比以前更不愿意说话了。
　* 他比过去真注重实际了。
　* 今天比昨天太冷了。
　* 她比以前很不愿意说话了。

3."很"可以单独用作补语,"真"、"太"、"更"不可以。("很" can be used alone as a complement. "真","太" and "更" can't.)例如:

　　好得很/清楚得很/喜欢得很/激动得很

660

* 好得真/ * 清楚得太/ * 喜欢得更/ * 激动得太

　　4."太"表示赞叹时,句末要用"了"、"啦"等助词表示语气;"更"在修饰谓语形容词或动词时表示原来就有一定的程度,现在又进一步,因有程度的变化,句尾常带"了";用"真"、"很"作谓语修饰语的句子,句末不能加"了"。(When "太" indicates high praise, there should be "了", "啦", etc. at the end of the sentence to express the mood. When "更" modifies predicative adjectives or verbs, it indicates a certain degree was reached, and now the degree is higher, and as the degree changes, there is usually "了" at the end of the sentences. "了" can't be added at the end of the sentences with "真", "很" as the predicative modifiers.) 例如:

　　这里的景色太迷人了! (The scenery here is really enchanting!)

　　你太好啦!

　　他学习更努力、更刻苦了。

　　我更喜欢这个地方了。

　　这里的景色很/真迷人。

　　* 这里的景色很/真迷人了。

　　他学习很/真努力、很/真刻苦。

　　* 他学习很/真努力、很/真刻苦了。

　　* 他最近工作很/真忙了。

整洁 zhěngjié　　整齐 zhěngqí

　　<形容词> <adjective>

　　"整洁"、"整齐"都有有条理、不乱的意思,但是意义上、用法上还有差别。(Both "整洁" and "整齐" mean in an orderly way; not in a mess. But there are still some differences in their meanings and usage.)

(一) 意义上有差别 (Differences in meaning)

　　"整洁"除了"有条理、不乱"的意思外,还有"清洁"的意思,

661

所以它只能用于描写既有条理,又清洁的事物。(Besides indicating "in an orderly way, tidy", "整洁" also means "clean". It can only be used to describe orderly and clean things.)例如:

她衣着整洁大方,言谈也十分得体。

(Her dressing is tasteful and neat and her speech is appropriate.)

你的屋子整洁得让我无法落脚了。

(Your room is too tidy to get me to stop over.)

环境漂亮整洁,工作、学习、生活才有情趣。

(Only if the environment is beautiful and neat, could work, study and living be charming.)

妹妹虽小,可是房间却收拾得很整洁。

(Younger sister is very young, but she tidies her room up very neatly.)

"整齐"词义重在"齐",没有"清洁"的意思。它的"齐"的范围很大,包括:有条理、有秩序、有规则、大小长短差不多、水平接近等等。它只用于描写或只侧重描写表示"齐"的意思的事物。(The meaning of "整齐" emphasizes "orderliness", but not "cleanness". Its concept of orderliness is vast, including proper arrangement, being in sequence, regulating, being about the same length and shortness and being near the same level, etc. It is only used to describe or only emphasize the things of orderliness.)例如:

桌子排列得很整齐。

他穿戴得整整齐齐的。(只从有条理、平整、不乱的角度说)

买票的人虽然很多,但是队伍却排得很整齐。

战士们步伐整齐,歌声嘹亮。

模特队的姑娘们个子十分整齐。

(The girls in the model team are well balanced in height.)

水平整齐才有利于教学。

(Regular level is favourable for teaching.)

(1)只有"齐",而没有"洁"的时候,不能用"整洁"。(When there is only "order", not "cleanness", "整洁" is not used.)例如:

  * 战士们整洁地喊道:"一定完成任务!"
  * 书柜里的书排列得十分整洁。

(2)有"清洁"的意思时,用"整齐"也不合适。(It is not appropriate to use "整齐" when the meaning of "cleanness" is implied.)例如:

  * 你的屋子整齐得让我无法落脚了。
  * 教室打扫得整齐极了。

(二)用法上的差别(Differences in usage)

1."整齐"可以重叠为AABB式,"整洁"不可以。("整齐" can be reduplicated as AABB pattern, while "整洁" cannot.)例如:

  孩子们都穿得整整齐齐的。
  小树一行一行整整齐齐的。
  * 孩子们都穿得整整洁洁的。
  * 房间收拾得整整洁洁的。

2."整齐"可以作动作的状语,描写动作的方式、状态等,"整洁"不可以。("整齐" can be the adverbial of acts, describing the ways or state of the acts, while "整洁" cannot.)例如:

  几幅字画整齐地挂在墙上。
  她把要带的衣服、用品整整齐齐地摆放在箱子里。
  (She put orderly in the suitcase all the clothes and necessities that she was going to take with.)
  战士们整齐地喊道:"一定完成任务!"
  (Soldiers shouted like through one throat: "We are sure to complete the mission!")
  * 书和杂志在桌子上整洁地摆放着。

正 zhèng   在 zài   正在 zhèngzài

〈副词〉表示动作在进行中或状态在持续中。(<adverb>

indicating an act is going on, or a state remains.)

"正"、"在"、"正在"都可以表示动作在进行中或状态在持续中,但是在意义和用法上还有一定差别。("正","在"and"正在"can all mean an act going on or a state lasting, but there are some differences in their meanings and usage.)

(一) 意义上 (In meaning)

"正"侧重强调动作、状态进行、持续于此刻的时间;"在"侧重强调进行、持续中的状态;"正在"是"正"和"在"意义的综合,既强调进行、持续在此刻的时间,又强调进行、持续着的状态。("正" emphasizes the exact time at which the action or the state is going on or continues; "在" emphasizes the state going on or continuing; "正在" is the synthetic meaning of "正" and "在". It either stresses the exact time which is going on or continuing, or the state which is going on or continuing.)例如:

曹太太正沉醉在优美的旋律之中。

(Mrs Cao is intoxicated in the graceful melody.)

她正难受呢,别去烦她了。

张伟在写信,王克在读小说。

大家都在为你着急,你却不紧不慢的。

李先生正在做实验,不要去打搅他。

我回来的时候,她正在伤心落泪呢。

(She was weeping sadly when I came back.)

(二) 用法上 (In usage)

1."正"后边一般不用动词的单纯形式,常常构成"正+动+着…/呢/着呢"的形式,或者动词后接趋向动词等。"在"和"正在"不受这种限制。(The simple form of verbs isn't generally used after "正". "正" often forms the "正 + verb + 着…/ 呢 / 着呢" pattern, or the verbs are followed by directional verbs. "在" and "正在" have no such restrictions.)例如:

他正吃呢。

我正听着呢。

他正向我走来。

大夫们正忙着抢救病人呢。

我在看/他在学习/他正在申请/王师傅正在搬运

＊ 那部电视剧我们正看。

关于项目问题老李讲了吗？—— ＊ 他正讲。

2."在"侧重状态，所以可以同"一直"、"总"、"还"等表示长时的副词或"又"等表示频率的副词结合，动词前也可以有表示长时时段的词语。"正"、"正在"不可以。("在" emphasizes the state so it can be used together with "一直（all along）", "总（always）", "还（still）" etc. indicating long time or "又", etc. indicating frequency before verbs. There may also be words indicating a long period of time before the verbs.)例如：

我一直在研究这个课题。

他总在思考那个问题。

到现在，他还在忙着收拾行李。

你又在想家了？

整整一个晚上，她都在哭。(She was weeping the whole night.)

整整三十个年头，她一直在等你。

(She has been waiting for you for fully 30 years.)

＊ 几年来，他一直正打听着你的消息。(改：在打听你的消息。)

＊ 我总正在考虑那个问题。(改：总在考虑那个问题。)

＊ 整整三十个年头，她一直正在等你。(改：在等你。)

665

正好 zhènghǎo　　正巧 zhèngqiǎo　　凑巧 còuqiǎo

〈副词〉 < adverb >
〈形容词〉 < adjective >

"正好"、"正巧"、"凑巧"都有正是时候、巧合的意思,有时可以换用,但是它们在意义上有一定差别,在用法上也有很大不同,有时不能换用。("正好","正巧"and"凑巧"all mean just the time, coincident, and sometimes they are interchangeable. But there are still some differences in their meanings, and they are quite different in usage. Thus they are sometimes not interchangeable.)

(一) 意义上的异同 (Similarities and differences in meaning)

1. "正好"、"正巧"、"凑巧"在表示正是时候、很巧合的意思时,常常可以换用。(When "正好","正巧"and"凑巧"indicate just the right time, coincidentally, they are often interchangeable.) 例如:

我气冲冲地冲出门外,正好/正巧/凑巧跟他撞了个满怀。

(I furiously rushed out of the room and was just bumping into him / happened to bump into him / luckily bumped into him.)

房屋倒塌时,正好/正巧/凑巧屋里没有人。

但是,意义的侧重点稍有不同。"正好"侧重的是"正是时候;"正巧"和"凑巧"侧重在"巧"上。"正巧"侧重"正得巧";"凑巧"侧重赶得巧。(But their focuses in meaning are slightly different. "正好" emphasizes "it is just the time","正巧"and "凑巧" emphasize coincidence。"正巧" emphasizes "just coincidentally","凑巧" emphasizes "happen to".)

2. "正好"还有正合适的意思,通常指时间不早不晚或不长不短、位置不前不后、体积不大不小、数量不多不少、程度不高不低等。("正好" can also mean "just right", usually referring to the time neither too early nor too late, or neither too long nor too short; a

place neither too front nor too back; a volume neither too big nor too small; an amount neither too large nor too small; a degree neither too high nor too low, etc.)例如：

下个星期就放假了,正好我们一起去海滨度假。

用这个速度读完这篇稿子,正好二十分钟。

剩下这块地方正好放一个小床头柜。

(The space left is just enough to put a small bedside cupboard.)

一棍子打出,球正好掉进球洞。

这本教材不难,你们用正好。

(This teaching material is not difficult and is just right for your level.)

3."正好"表示"正合适"的意思,也适用于某些抽象的动词。(The meaning of "just right" expressed by "正好" is also applicable to some abstract verbs.)例如：

这场舌战正好显示了我的口才。

(This heated dispute just shows my eloquence.)

他不敢面对事实,正好说明他心虚。

4.当说话人侧重"正合适"的意义时,不能用"正巧"、"凑巧",只能用"正好"。用于抽象的动词时,也只能用"正好"。(When the speaker emphasizes the meaning "just right", it is only right to use "正好", not "正巧" or "凑巧". When describing abstract verbs, also only "正好" is used.)例如：

* 下个星期就放假了,凑巧我们一起去海滨度假。

* 这本教材不难,你们用正巧。

* 这场舌战正巧显示了我的口才。

* 他不敢面对事实,凑巧说明他心虚。

(二) 用法上的差别 (Differences in usage)

1."凑巧"可以接受程度副词,构成"很凑巧"、"真凑巧"或"很不凑巧"、"真不凑巧"等词组;"正好"、"正巧"没有这种用法。

667

〔"凑巧" can be used together with adverbs of degree to form "很凑巧 (very luckily)", "真凑巧 (really luckily)" or "很不凑巧 (unfortunately)", "真不凑巧 (really unfortunately)", etc. "正好" and "正巧" cannot be used so.〕例如:

你来得真不凑巧,他刚刚离开这儿。

(What bad luck for your coming! He has left just now.)

很凑巧,中秋节和国庆节赶在同一天里。

* 你来得真不正好,他刚刚离开这儿。
* 很正好,中秋节和国庆节赶在同一天里。
* 你来得真不正巧,他刚刚离开这儿。
* 很正巧,中秋节和国庆节赶在同一天里。

2. "正好"、"正巧"、"凑巧"在句子里都可以作状语。("正好","正巧" and "凑巧" can all serve as adverbial in sentences.)例如:

我去玛丽的房间,正好把她的票捎给她。

(I am going to Mary's room and will just bring her the ticket.)

他打来电话的时候,正巧我刚进门。

下班后,我想去看看小王,刚走到车站,凑巧碰见了他。

3. "正好"可以单用作谓语;"正巧"一般不能这样用;"凑巧"作谓语时,一般须构成带状谓语或带补谓语。"凑巧"可以带程度补语,"正好"、"正巧"不能带补语。("正好" can be used alone as a predicate. "正巧" is generally not used so. When "凑巧" is used as a predicate, it must form the predicate with adverbial or predicate with complement. "凑巧" can be used together with complements of degree. "正好" and "正巧" cannot have complements attached.)例如:

你来得不早也不晚,正好。

* 你来得不早也不晚,正巧。

很不凑巧,他刚走了。

不凑巧得很,他出差去了。(It is bad luck that he is away on business.)

＊很不正好,他刚走了。
　　＊正好得很,他出差去了。
　　＊很不正巧,他刚走了。
　　＊正巧得很,他出差去了。

4."正好"、"正巧"不能作定语,"凑巧"有时可以作定语。("正好" and "正巧" cannot serve as attributives,"凑巧" sometimes can be used as an attributive.)例如:

　　中秋节和国庆节赶在一起了,这是一件很凑巧的事。
　　一件件不凑巧的事怎么都让我遇上了?
　　(How could I just meet with one after another unfortunate things?)
　　＊中秋节和国庆节赶在一起了,这是一件很正好/ 正巧的事。
　　＊一件件不正好/ 正巧的事怎么都让我遇上了?

知道 zhīdào　　　了解 liǎojiě

〈动词〉＜verb＞

"知道"和"了解"在意义上和用法上都有较大差别,大多情况下不能换用。("知道" and "了解" are quite different in meanings and usage, and not interchangeable in most cases.)

(一)意义上 (In meaning)

1.对人或事只是通过看见、听说、接触等而得知的,都可以用"知道"表示,但是不能用"了解"表示。"了解"所表示的"知道",一定是全面的、深入的、详细的、清楚的。(The people or things known by seeing, hearing or touching can be indicated by "知道", but can't be indicated by "了解". "知道 (knowledge)" indicated by "了解" is sure to be overall, deep forward, detailed and clear.)例如:

　　我知道你说的那个人,昨天我见过他一面。
　　下午东马路发生的那起车祸大家都知道了,因为只是

669

听说,详细情况都不了解。

(Everyone has heard about the traffic accident in Dongmalu this afternoon, but the detail of it is unknown since we just heard about it.)

你说的那个问题我知道,上次开会还有人提过呢。

我们只是听说王教授很有成就,对于他的为人一点儿也不了解,你们可以介绍一下吗?

(We just heard that Professor Wang is very successful, but we know nothing about his behavior. Will you just give us a brief introduction?)

他虽说不是这儿的人,但是对这里的情况却了解得十分清楚。

* 我虽然跟他住在一间屋子里,却不太知道他。
* 我想更多地知道中国,你能告诉我有关中国的事情吗?
* 我还不知道他更多的方面。

2. 表示对某事有认识或懂得,用"知道";不是表示知道得多而全面等,不用"了解"。("知道" is used to indicate knowing or understanding something, and "了解" is not used when indicating knowing not much or partly.)例如:

我知道你心里不痛快。

(I know you feel unhappy in your mind.)

老师知道这件事是小王的不是。

(The teacher knows Xiao Wang is wrong in this matter.)

大家都知道目前公司很困难。

这个道理谁不知道。

大家都十分了解公司目前的情况。

我们不十分了解他。

3. 表示懂得该做什么事,用"知道"表示;不能用"了解"。(When indicating knowing what to do, "知道" is used, but not "了解".)例如:

670

孩子这么小,就知道孝敬父母了。

(Such a little kid has already known to give presents to the parents.)

你应该知道这样做是违反规定的。

* 孩子这么小,就了解孝敬父母了。
* 你应该了解这样做是违反规定的。

4.表示掌握问题的答案时("知道"的宾语一般是含有疑问词的词组),用"知道"表示,不能用"了解"。〔When indicating knowing the answers to the questions (the objects of "知道" are generally phrases with interrogative words), "知道" is used; but "了解" can't be used so.〕例如:

这句话我不知道用汉语怎样说。

我知道他什么时候走。

我不知道怎样才能帮助他们。

* 这句话我不了解用汉语怎样说。
* 我了解他什么时候走。
* 我不了解怎样才能帮助他们。

5."了解"还可以表示"打听"、"调查"的意思;"知道"没有这种意思。("了解" can also indicate the meaning of "asking about" or "investigation"; "知道" does not have this sense.)例如:

我们想向您了解一下老张的情况。

中央领导下来了解一下普及义务教育的情况。

(The leaders of the Central Committee come to find out how the compulsory education is popularized.)

* 我们想向您知道一下老张的情况。
* 中央领导下来知道一下普及义务教育的情况。

(二) 用法上 (In usage)

1."知道"只能用"不"否定,不能用"没(没有)"否定;"了解"用"不"、"没(没有)"都可以否定。〔"知道" can only be negated with "不", not "没(没有)". "了解" can be negated either with

"不"or"没(没有)".]例如：

　　师傅不知道那件事。
　　我不知道你不愿意。
　　我不知道他们厂有哪些产品。
　　* 师傅没知道那件事。
　　* 我没有知道你不愿意。
　　* 我没知道他们厂有哪些产品。
　　不了解情况就不要乱发言。
　　(Don't speak arbitrarily if you don't know it.)
　　领导没有了解生产情况，只是了解了一下设备情况。

2."了解"可以重叠使用,构成"了解了解"的形式;"知道"一般不能重叠使用,个别情况下使用是有条件的。如:表示使动意义时,可以重叠用。("了解" can be reduplicated to form "了解了解"; "知道" cannot be reduplicated except under certain conditions, such as indicating the meaning of causing to do or to be.)例如：

　　你们应该了解了解农村儿童的失学情况。
　　下车间了解了解生产情况。
　　你应该好好了解了解他和他的家庭，再做是否结婚的决定。
　　* 你知道知道那件事吧。
　　* 我想知道知道这学期的课程安排。

使动意义：让他知道知道我的厉害。／让他知道知道这学期的课程安排也好。

(The causative meaning: Just let him know my true colours. / It is all right just let him know the arrangement of the courses of this semester.)

3."了解"可以接受程度副词的修饰;"知道"一般不能这样用。("了解" can be modified by adverbs of degree; "知道" usually can not.)例如：

　　我很了解他的为人。

我们非常了解你的用意。
他的底细我们不很了解。
* 我很知道你的意思。
* 他很知道我的秘密。
* 我们不很知道那里现在的情况。

4. "知道"表示的对事物的得知具有永久性,即无论通过什么方式、手段,一经得知某事,就意味着永远地知道了。所以它一般不表示经历和进行的意义,它后面一般不接"过",前面一般不接"正在"这样的词,它也不能作"进行"的宾语。"了解"的动作通常意味着多次地询问、调查、访问等,所以它可以表经历和进行,可以跟"过"或"正在"这样的词结合,也可以作"进行"的宾语。(The knowledge of things that "知道" indicates is of permanence, namely no matter by what ways or means, once something is known, it means it is forever being known. Therefore it doesn't generally indicate the meaning of experiencing and being in progress, there isn't "过" following and there aren't words like "正在" in front, and it can't be the object of "进行". The act of "了解" generally means inquiring, investigating or visiting time and again, so it may involve experience and being in progress and can be used together with "过" or "正在" and it can be the object of "进行" as well.)例如:

* 我们知道过那件事的原因。
* 他们正在知道事情的来龙去脉。
* 马上派人对那里的旱情进行调查、知道、分析。
我们了解过那件事,事情的经过并不像你说的那样。
他们正在了解事情的来龙去脉。
(They are finding out the cause and effect of the matter.)
马上派人对那里的旱情进行调查、了解、分析。

5. "了解"后面可以接表示动作数量的词语;"知道"一般不能接。个别情况下接是有条件的。如:表示使动意义时,可以接。("了解" can be followed by words denoting the amount of the

673

acts;"知道" usually can't, except under certain conditions, such as indicating the meaning of causing to do or to be.)例如：

了解一下资金调用情况。

我们三人分头了解了一番，却没有了解到什么情况。

(We three did investigation separately but haven't found out anything.)

* 知道一下他们的情况怎么样了。

* 我们知道了一番他们的计划。

也应该让他们知道一下群众的反映。（使动意义）

6."知道"一般情况下不用表示方式、状态的形容词、副词作状语修饰语；"了解"可以。(Generally "知道" is not modified by the adjectives and adverbs indicating ways and state as adverbials; while "了解" does not have this restriction.)例如：

我想仔细地了解一下小王的情况。

深入地了解一下那里的情况

张经理想亲自去了解一下。

这件事需要好好了解了解。

深入下去，可以随时了解情况。

* 我想仔细地知道一下小王的情况。

* 深入地知道那里的情况。

* 张经理想亲自去知道一下。

* 这件事需要好好知道知道。

* 深入下去，可以随时知道情况。

7."知道"后面连带的宾语可以是名词性词语，也可以是非名词性词语；"了解"连带的宾语主要是名词性的，个别情况下可以带主谓词组，但是一般情况下不能带动宾词组。(The objects of "知道" can be of noun character or not. The objects of "了解" mainly are of noun character, and in isolated cases subjective phrases can be used after "了解", but generally verb-object word groups can't follow.)例如：

674

他不知道那件事。
你做事总是不知道深浅。
我知道错了。
这孩子这么小就知道讲卫生。
我知道应该多关照她,可是一忙起来就顾不上了。
(I do know it is reasonable to take much care of her, but I can't attend to her when I am busy.)
你知道他们去哪儿了吗?
我了解王大爷。
他并不了解事情发生的原因。
主任下来了解产品质量下降的原因。
你去了解一下,假期他们有什么安排。
* 这孩子这么小就了解讲卫生。
* 我了解应该多关照她。
* 我了解群众有反映。
* 主任了解产品质量下降了。

8. "知道"是非自主性动词,一般不能用于祈使句中;"了解"是自主性动词可以用于祈使句中。("知道" is a non-independent verb and generally can't be used in imperative sentences. "了解" is an independent verb and can be used in imperative sentences.)例如:

* 你去知道一下这学期的课,好吗?
* 别知道那件事,知道那件事对你不好。
* 你帮我知道一下他们的想法,好吗?
你去了解一下这学期的课,好吗?
别了解那件事,了解那件事对你不好。
你帮我了解一下他们的想法,好吗?

只好 zhǐhǎo　　只有 zhǐyǒu

只好〈副词〉< adverb >
只有〈副词〉〈连词〉< adverb > < conjunction >

（一）功能不同：(Differences in function:)

"只有"有连词的功能、用法，"只好"没有这一功能用法。"只有"作连词用时，通常用在前一分句，表示唯一的条件，后一分句往往用副词"才"呼应。("只有" has the function and usage of conjunction, while "只好" doesn't. When "只有" functions as a conjunction, it is usually used in the first clause, indicating the only condition, usually in combination with the adverb "才" in the latter clause.)例如：

只有深入实际，才能真正了解情况。

只有你去请他，他才肯给面子。

(Only when you go to request of him could he show due respect.)

只有热爱工作的人，才会热爱生活。

只有在紧急情况下，才能动用这个闸。

* 只好深入实际，才能真正了解情况。
* 只好你去请他，他才肯给面子。
* 只好热爱工作的人，才会热爱生活。
* 只好在紧急情况下，才能动用这个闸。

（二）"只好"、"只有"都有副词功能，意义很接近，但是仍有细微差别；用法上也有一定差别。(Both "只好" and "只有" can function as adverbs, very close in meaning, but with slight differences, and there are also some differences in their usage.)

1. 意义上 (In meaning)

"只好"带有较强的主观色彩，突出说话人对某种选择不是出于主观愿望，虽然做了某种选择，但是出于无奈，所以选择得极为勉强；"只有"可以表现主观出于无奈的选择，但是它常常还可以用于客观的、理智的、非此不可的唯一选择，不一定有主观不情愿的意味。("只好" is of fairly strong subjective flavour, emphasizing that the speaker's some choice making is not out of the subjective desire. Although a certain choice is made, the speaker has no alternative, the choice is made exceedingly grudgingly; "只有" can indicate subjectively having no alternative, but it can also be used for the objective, sensible and inevitably the only choice. It is unnecessarily with the meaning of the subjective reluctance.)例如：

资金不足,只好放弃这个项目了。(主观无奈。)

(Lacking of funds, the project is forced to be given up.)

再不卖地,公司只有倒闭了(客观的),没有办法,他只好忍痛卖了那块地。(主观无奈。)

(The company would be forced to close if the land was not sold. There was no other way out, so he reluctantly sold that piece of land.)

电话打不通,我只好亲自走一趟了。(无奈的选择。)

电话打不通,我只有亲自走一趟了。(惟一的选择。)

救灾如救火,我们只有冒风险提高水位了。(客观的惟一的选择。)

2. 用法上 (In usage)

"只有"一般用于动词或动词性词语前;"只好"既可以用于动词性词语前,也可以用于形容性词语前。("只有" is generally used before verbs or words of verb character. "只好" can be used either before words of verb character or before words of adjective character.)例如：

明天有大雨,运动会只有向后推迟了。

明天有大雨,运动会只好向后推迟一天。

时间不够了,我们只好快一点儿了。

买不到新鲜菜了,只好简单一点儿,大家将就一下吧。

只要 zhǐyào　　只有 zhǐyǒu　　除非 chúfēi

〈连词〉表示条件关系。(< conjunction > indicating condition.)

(一) 意义和用法不同。(Differences in meaning and usage.)

"只要"表示的是充足条件,只要具备这一条件就可以产生相应的结果。但是这一条件不是唯一的,它跟相应的结果之间是多条件的联系,即别的条件也可能产生这一结果;"只有"则不同,它所连接的条件是唯一的、必备的,即除了这一条件,任何其他条件都不能产生这一结果;"除非"所连接的条件跟"只有"一样,也是唯一的,不同的是,它是从反面强调这一条件的不可缺少。在强调条件的必要性上,"除非"比"只有"程度更深,语气更重。("只要" indicates full condition and so long as there is such condition provided the corresponding result will be produced. But the condition is not the sole one. Its relationship with its corresponding result is that of many conditions, namely the same result can be produced from other conditions; "只有" is different. The condition it connects is the only and necessary one, namely besides this, any other conditions can not produce such result. The condition that "除非" connects is the same with that of "只有", it is the only condition. The difference is that it emphasizes from the opposite side that the condition can't be lacked. When emphasizing the necessity of conditions, "除非" is stronger than "只有" in degree and in mood.)例如:

只要工夫深,铁杵磨成针。

(If you work at it hard enough, you can grind an iron into a needle.)

你只要有信心、有恒心,就会取得成功。

只要多听、多说,就能学好汉语。

* 只有工夫深,铁杵磨成针。

* 只有多听、多说,就能学好汉语。

只有深入实际,才能真正地了解情况。

你只有亲自体会一下,才会理解我说的话的意思。

(Only when you experience by yourself, could you understand what I mean.)

这样重大的事情,除非得到领导的同意,否则他是不会做的。

若要人不知,除非己莫为。

(If you don't want others to know about it, don't do it.)

(二)相呼应的关联词语不同,结构形式不同。(Differences in corresponding connected words and in structure.)

1."只要"通常跟"就"、"便"等词配合使用。"只有"往往跟"才"配合使用。"除非"可以跟"才"配合,也可以构成"除非……,不……"的句式。"只有"不能构成"只有……,不……"的句式。("只要" is usually used together with "就", "便", etc. "只有" is often used with "才". "除非" can be used with "才", or form the "除非…, 不…" sentence pattern. "只有" cannot form the "只有…, 不…" pattern.)例如:

只要你愿意,他就会来帮助你的。

* 只要你愿意,他才会来帮助你的。

只有不畏劳苦,努力攀登,才有希望达到光辉的顶点。

(As long as you don't fear to do hard work and clamber diligently, it is hopeful for you to reach the apex of brilliance.)

* 只有不畏劳苦,努力攀登,就有希望达到光辉的顶点。

除非你答应,他才会来见你。

除非你去,否则他不会去。

* 只有你去,否则他不会去。

2."除非"还可以构成"除非是……"的句式,"只有"不能;"除非"可以用在后一分句,表示排除或惟一条件,"只有"一般不这样用。("除非" can also form the "除非是…" pattern, but "只有" can't. "除非" can be used in the latter clause of a sentence, indicating exclusion or the only condition. "只有" is generally not used so.)例如:

很少见到这样尖锐明亮的眼睛,除非是在白洋淀。

(Except in Baiyangdian, it is rare to see so sharp and bright eyes.)

679

* 很少见到这样尖锐明亮的眼睛,只有是在白洋淀。
他从不迟到,除非发生特殊情况。
* 他从不迟到,只有发生特殊情况。

只是 zhǐshì 不过 búguò 可是 kěshì 但是 dànshì 然而 rán'ér

〈连词〉表示转折关系。(<conjunction> indicating transition.)

(一) 转折轻重不同 (Different in the degree of transition)

这几个词虽然都含有转折意味,但是转折的轻重有所不同。比较起来,"只是"、"不过"只带有很轻微的转折意味,"只是"的转折意味比"不过"更轻些;"可是"、"但是"、"然而"的转折意味较重,尤其"然而",转折意味最重。这三个词比较起来,"可是"的转折意味稍轻些。(Though they all signify transition, they express different degrees in transition. Comparatively, "只是" and "不过" are of light transitive meaning, and the transitive meaning of "只是" is even lighter than "不过"; The transitive meaning of "可是", "但是" and "然而" is stronger, and "然而" is the strongest. Among these three words, that of "可是" is relatively lighter.)

(二) 语体色彩不同 (Different in style and coloring)

"只是"、"可是"多用于口语;"不过"、"但是"通用于口语和书面语;"然而"含有文言意味,主要用于书面语。("只是" and "可是" are mostly used in spoken language, "不过" and "但是" are commonly used in spoken and written languages. "然而" is of literary flavor, and mainly used in written language.)

(三) 意义有所不同 (Slightly different in meaning)

1. "只是"所表示的转折通常只是对前面的部分进行补充、修正或者解释,"不过"有时也有补充或修正的作用。(The transition expressed by "只是" is usually supplement, revision or explanation to the former part. "不过" sometimes has the function of supplement or revision.)

他的出发点是好的,只是有点儿急躁。

(His starting point is good but is a bit impatient.)

我早想来你这儿看看,只是没有时间。

张先生很欣赏你的才干,不过他还是希望你在下面多锻炼锻炼。

(Mr. Zhang appreciates your ability very much, but he also hopes that you will get more exercises at the lower levels.)

2. "可是"、"但是"、"然而"则主要表示上下文互相排斥的、相对或相反的意思,所以句子的重心主要在后。("可是","但是" and "然而" mainly express the meaning of repelling, contrary or opposing between the two parts of a sentence, and the focus of the sentence lies in the latter part.)例如:

这菜看上去不怎么样,可是吃起来却挺不错。

(The dish doesn't look nice but is delicious while being tasted.)

她的声音虽然不大,但是却很坚决。

试验多次被迫停止,然而他们并不灰心。

3. 只是表示某种补充、解释,不能用"可是"、"但是"、"然而";表示相反、相对的意义,不能用"只是"。(When only indicating supplement or explanation, "可是", "但是" and "然而" can't be used; while indicating contrary or opposite meanings, "只是" is not used.)例如:

* 有时两人互相讽刺、互相攻击,但是这不是真的。(改用"只是"。)

* 这件衣服虽然很漂亮,只是我不喜欢。(改用"但是"。)

(四) 词语搭配不同 (Different in collocation)

1. 用"只是"、"不过"表示转折的句子大多语气轻微、委婉,所以通常前一分句不与"虽然"连用,后一分句不与"却"连用。(The tone of the sentences in which transition is expressed by "只是"or"不过"is usually light and mild. They are usually not used together with"虽然"in the first clause, or with"却"in the latter clause.)例如:

我其实很想去看看那个展览,只是太忙。

他的脾气一向很大,不过现在好多了。

(He had always been bad-tempered but he has changed a lot these days.)

* 虽然对各种意见都要听,不过听了要作分析。
(改用"可是"。)

* 他各方面都很好,只是身体却不大好。
(改用"然而"或"但是"。)

2. 用"可是"、"但是"表示转折的句子大多转折意味较重,所以前一分句常与"虽然"、后一分句常与"却"、"还"等副词配用。"然而"一词文言意味较重,虽然转折意味很重,但是一般较少跟"虽然"配用。(The sentences in which transition is expressed with"可是"or"但是"are of strong transitive meaning, so the first clause usually has"虽然", the latter clause has"却"or"还"to collocate with"可是"or"但是"。"然而"is of strong literary flavor. Though of strong turning meaning, it is seldom used together with"虽然".)例如:

他虽然很忙,可是还是抽出时间来医院看你。

实验虽然被迫停止,但是他并没有停止研究。

虽然两只眼睛停在书上,但是他的心思却并不在那里。

(Although he fixed his eyes on the book, his mind is absent.)

条件确实很差,然而没有一个人被它吓倒。

(The condition is really poor but nobody is frightened by this.)

中 zhōng   中间 zhōngjiān

〈方位词〉 < noun of locality >

(一)"中"与"中间"都可以表示周围界限以内,但是基本上不能互换使用。主要有以下区别:(Both "中" and "中间" can indicate within the surrounding boundary, but generally they are not interchangeable. Their main differences are:)

1. 意义上有差别。(Differences in meaning.)

(1)"中"表示的周围界限以内,一般没有具体位置的点;"中间"一般指有具体位置的点。("中" indicates within the bounds. Generally there is no specific point of the position. "中间" generally refers to the point of the specific position.)例如:

心中　脑海中　家中　书本中　信中　人群中

"信中"是以"信"作为周围界限,其中没有再具体的位置的点。

屋子中间　池子中间　人群中间　绳子中间

"屋子中间"是指屋子内的某一点,通常指与周围等距离的那个位置。

(2)"中间"表示具体位置的点,可以有两种。一是表示"与两端等距离的位置或在两端距离之内的某位置";一是表示与周围等距离的位置或在周围界限之内的某位置。(The point of the specific position indicated by "中间" includes two kinds. One indicates the position of the two equal-distanced ends or certain location within the two ends, the other indicates the position of equal distance with the surroundings or a certain position within the surroundings.)例如:

第一排中间的那位就是我们的老院长。

五米的绳子,在中间等距离地截两次。

(The five-metered rope was cut twice at the equal distance in the middle.)

爷爷坐在中间,孩子们围坐在四周。

盘子中间有几道划痕。

683

2. 结构上有差别。(Differences in structure.)

"中"一般不能单用,常常要构成"名+中"的词组,与"在"、"向"等介词组合时,常常要构成"介+名+中"的词组;"中间"则可以单用,与"在"、"向"等介词组合时,可以直接用在介词后,即可以构成"介+中间"的形式。("中" generally cannot be used alone, but often forms the "n. + 中" phrases. When used with prepositions "在", "向", etc., it often forms the "prep. + n. + 中" phrases. "中间" can be used alone. When it is used with prepositions "在", "向", etc., it can directly follow these prepositions to form the "prep. + 中间" pattern.)例如:

她沉醉<u>在</u>迷人的音乐<u>中</u>。

(She was intoxicated in the graceful sound of music.)

他把纪念章紧紧地攥<u>在手中</u>。

(He clasped the souvenir badge tightly in his hand.)

<u>黑暗中</u>只能听到轻轻的叹息声,看不到人。

(In the darkness, it was invisible and the light sighs were the only things to be heard.)

* 她沉醉在迷人的音乐中间。
* 黑暗中间只能听到轻轻的叹息声,看不到人。

人们坐在四周,<u>中间</u>留出好大一块空地来。

这趟火车直达北京,<u>中间</u>一站也不停。

紧张地干了一上午,<u>中间</u>只休息了十分钟。

(We intensely worked for the whole morning during which there was only a ten-minute break.)

* 人们坐在四周,中留出好大一块空地来。
* 这趟火车直达北京,中一站也不停。

两个大灯笼挂在<u>中间</u>,两侧是许许多多的小灯笼。

* 两个大灯笼挂在中,两侧是许许多多的小灯笼。

(二)"中"常常用来指一定范围以内,范围的界限是虚的或看不到的;"中间"则通常用于具体可见的界限以内,一般不用来表示虚指的范围。("中" usually indicates within a certain scope, and the bounds of the scope are usually imaginary or abstract, unseen. "中间" is commonly used to indicate within specific and visible bounds, seldom used to indicate abstract ones.) 例如:

在这两项中,选择一项。
我们的生活中到处充满着阳光。
(There is sunshine everywhere in our life.)
在所有的意见中,这一条是最值得我们考虑的。
桌子中间放着一个好大的盘子,里面的菜好看极了。
* 我们的生活中间到处充满着阳光。
* 在所有的意见中间,这一条是最值得我们考虑的。

中间 zhōngjiān　　当中 dāngzhōng　　之间 zhījiān

〈方位词〉表示处在人或事物中,或者两端及某范围之内。

(< noun of locality > indicating among many people or things, or within two ends or a certain scope.)

(一)"中间"与"当中"

1. 表示与两端等距离的位置或两端距离之内的意义时,尤其是具体的位置时,多用"中间"。(When indicating a position of equal distance to the two ends or within the two ends, especially a specific position, "中间" is mainly used.) 例如:

中间的那位就是我们的老师。
大的放在中间,小的放到两边。
找一根中间粗、两头细的木棍来。
把这块布从中间裁开。
旅游安排在最后不太好,安排在中间比较好。
(It is not good to have the tour arranged in the end. It is better to have it arranged in the middle.)

2. 表示与周围等距离的位置或在一定的范围之内,"中间"、"当中"可以通用,但是通常具体的位置用"中间"或"当中"表示,抽象的范围多用"当中"表示。(When indicating the position is equal-distanced with the surroundings or within a certain scope, "中间" and "当中" are exchangeable, but while indicating the generally specific position, "中间" or "当中" is used and "当中" refers to the abstract range.)例如:

(1)具体位置(specific position):

水池中间/当中有一个大型音乐喷泉。

老人坐在当中/中间,周围是他的十六个子孙。

学生们把老师围在中间/当中。

(2)抽象的、非具体的范围(abstract, not specific range):

今天参赛的马拉松运动员当中,年龄最大的76岁,最小的仅仅14岁。

工人当中,这种乐于助人的人很多。

在所有的古典小说当中,她最喜欢的是《红楼梦》。

从这些病句当中,我发现了一个共同的错误。

(I've found a common mistake in these problem sentences.)

3."中间"还可以表示不偏向哪一端的意思,只作修饰性构词成分或定语,其作用类似非谓形容词。"当中"没有这种用法。("中间" can also mean not partial to either side, only serving as an attribute and functioning as non-predicative adjectives. "当中" is not used so.)例如:

中间人(middleman)

中间派(middle-of-the-roader)

中间状态(intermediate state)

中间势力(intermediate forces)

* 当中人　* 当中派　* 当中状态　* 当中势力

(二)"中间"与"之间"

"中间"与"之间"在意义上有不同的偏重,结构上有不同的制约条件。("中间" and "之间" have different emphases in meaning, and have different restrictive conditions in structure.)

1. "之间"自己不能单独作句子成分,它前边必须有修饰性成分,构成"~之间"的词组;"中间"自己单独作句子成分不受限制。("~之间" cannot be used as an independent sentence component. It must have qualificatory components in front, forming "~之间" word groups. "中间" can serve as sentence components independently, without any qualification.)例如:

两座大楼之间/中间是一片绿色的草坪。

左边是图书馆,右边是中心教学楼,中间是一个巨型雕塑。

＊左边是图书馆,右边是中心教学楼,之间是一个巨型雕塑。

中间休息的时候,我跟你说件事。

(I will talk to you when we have a break in the middle.)

＊之间休息的时候,我跟你说件事。

你坐中间,让两个孩子站在两边。

＊你坐之间,让两个孩子站在两边。

2. "之间"前边的修饰语必须是具有一定相互关系的复数意义的词语或者是具有相互关系的两个点、两个项目的词组。"中间"一般不表示相互关系,而表示具体位置,表示具体位置时,不受单复数的限制。(The modifier before "之间" must be the words of certain mutual relation and of the plural meaning or be the phrases of the two mutual related points or items. "中间" generally does not express mutual relations. It indicates specific positions. The modifiers before "中间" may not necessarily be plural words.)例如:

朋友之间要实实在在的,不要虚伪。

(The relationship between friends should be honest but not hypocritical.)

同志之间互相帮助是应该的。

(To help one another among comrades is what ought to be done.)

我希望人与人之间多一些真诚、多一些爱。

(I do hope there will be more sincerity and love among people.)

人与动物之间有着非常密切的关系。

(Between man and animal there is a fairly close relationship.)

* 朋友中间要实实在在,不要虚伪。
* 同志中间互相帮助是应该的。
* 我希望人与人中间多一些真诚、多一些爱。
* 人与动物中间有着非常密切的关系。

大厅中间摆了一棵很大的龟背竹。

从人群中间传出一声尖利的喊叫。

* 大厅之间摆了一棵很大的龟背竹。
* 从人群之间传出一声尖利的喊叫。

3. "之间"还可以用来表示两个点内的具体时间,"中间"一般不用来表示两个点内的具体时间。("之间" can be used to indicate the specific time between two points; "中间" generally not.) 例如:

中午11点到12点之间,将发生日全食现象。

下半年的社会实践可能安排在9月至10月之间。

下面的表达方式不可取:

* 中午11点到12点中间,将发生日全食现象。
* 下半年的社会实践可能安排在9月至10月中间。

只有一个点的时间,不能用"之间"。("之间" cannot be used to indicate time with only one point.) 例如:

* 三点之间,我去找你。
* 今年暑假之间,我去南方旅游了。

应改为:

三点左右,我去找你。

今年暑假期间,我去南方旅游了。

4."之间"还可以与动词、副词构成表示时间短暂的特定意义的词组;"中间"没有这种用法。(Together with verbs and adverbs,"之间" can also form phrases indicating the definite meaning of a short time."中间" is not used so.)例如:

说话之间(just during talking)
转眼之间(in the twinkling of an eye)
突然之间(with abruptness)
忽然之间(all of a sudden)
* 说话中间　* 转眼中间　* 突然中间　* 忽然中间

中间 zhōngjiān　中央 zhōngyāng　中心 zhōngxīn

〈名词〉表示和周围上下左右距离相等的位置。

(<noun> indicating the position which is of equal distance from the top to the bottom or the left to the right.)

"中间"、"中央"、"中心"都可以表示和周围上下左右距离相等的位置。("中间","中央" and "中心" all mean in the middle.)例如:

广场中间/中央/中心有一个大型的雕塑群。

在桌子的中间/中央/中心刻着一颗红色的标志。

但是它们在多数情况下不能互换使用,这是因为它们的意义和使用范围还有所不同。(But they are not interchangeable in most cases due to some differences in their meanings and applicable ranges.)

(一)"中间"和"中央"

1."中间"和"中央"在表示和周围上下左右距离相等的位置时,意义大体相同,但是使用范围有所不同。"中间"既可以用于具体的、视线可以感觉得到的地方,也可以用于非具体的、视线感觉不到的地方;"中央"则一般只用于具体的、视线可以感觉得到的地方。(When indicating being at equal distance from all directions,"中间" and "中央" almost have the same meaning, but

689

are different in applicable ranges. "中间" can either be used for the places which are specific and within the eye-sight or for the places unspecific and beyond the eye-sight; "中央" is generally used for the places specific and within the eye-sight.)例如:

站在队伍中间/中央讲话的那个人就是我们的团长。
书签夹在书中间。
* 书签夹在书中央。
用了一个多月的时间才解决了这件事,这中间发生了不少麻烦事。

(It took more than one month to settle the matter for a lot of troubles occurred during that period.)

* 用了一个多月的时间才解决了这件事,这中央发生了不少麻烦事。

2."中央"的位置是相对具体而确定的,一般就是指居中的那个位置;"中间"除了可以表示和周围距离相等的位置的意思外,它还可以表示与两端等距离的位置,还可以表示某范围内,"中央"不能表示这样的意思。(The position indicated by "中央" is relatively specific and definite, usually referring to the position in the middle. "中间" can also indicate the position being of equal distance with the two ends, or being within a certain range, in addition to indicating the position being at equal distance with all directions.)例如:

书柜中间有一块宽板,可以临时伏在上面写字。
* 书柜中央有一块宽板,可以临时伏在上面写字。
她在朋友中间有一定的威信。
* 她在朋友中央有一定的威信。
那部电影长达八个多小时,中间休息过三次。
* 那部电影长达八个多小时,中央休息过三次。

(二)"中央"、"中心"与"中间"

1."中央"、"中心"都可以表示相对具体而确定的位置,即居中的位置。但是"中央"只能表示具体而确定的位置;"中心"则既可以表示具体而确定的位置,也可以表示感受不到的事物的位置。("中央" and "中心" can both indicate relatively specific and definite position, the position in the middle. But "中央" only indicates such position; while "中心" can either indicate such position, or indicate the position of something that cannot be felt.)例如:

从受灾中心的情况看来,灾害的程度很严重。

(Judging from the information provided by the centre of the disaster area, the losses caused by the disaster are serious.)

* 从受灾中央的情况看来,灾害的程度很严重。

2."中心"与"中间"都可以表示抽象的位置,但是它们通用的范围有所不同。"中心"可以表示在某一方面占重要地位的城市或地区,也可以指事物的主要部分。"中间"不能用于这两个方面,在表示抽象的位置意义上,它只能表示在周围的界限之内。(Both "中间" and "中心" can indicate abstract position, but they are used in different categories. "中心" can indicate a city or district which occupies an important position in some aspects, or refers to the major part of something. "中间" can't be used in this two senses. While expressing the abstract meaning, it only refers to the position within surrounding bound.)例如:

北京是中国的政治、经济、文化中心。

* 北京是中国的政治、经济、文化中间。

当前的中心工作是抓好经济建设。

* 当前的中间工作是抓好经济建设。

代表中间,他是最年轻的一个了。

* 代表中心,他是最年轻的一个了。

他一个人在国外呆了五年,这中间的酸甜苦辣只有他自己心里最清楚。

(He has lived abroad for 5 years alone and he is the only person clear-minded about the joys and sorrows in his life during the period.)

＊他一个人在国外呆了五年,这中心的酸甜苦辣只有他自己心里最清楚。

3.因为"中央"含有居于中心的地方的意思,所以它被用来特指国家政权或政治团体的最高领导机构。(Since "中央" implies being in the center, it is usually used to refer particularly to the highest leading administration of the government or political organizations of a country.)例如:

党中央　团中央　中央人民政府

终于 zhōngyú　　到底 dàodǐ　　毕竟 bìjìng

〈副词〉表示经过较长时间的过程最后出现某结果。

(< adverb > indicating a certain result comes out in the end after a long process.)

(一)"终于"、"到底"、"毕竟"虽然都有经过较长时间的过程最后出现某结果的意思,但是可以换用的时候不是很多,这是因为这几个词有不同的语言前提。(Though "终于", "到底" and "毕竟" all mean a result appearing in the end after a long process, they are seldom exchangeable due to the differences in their language prerequisites.)

1."终于"主要侧重于所期望的事情经过的时间久、很难或不容易才如愿实现。表示这种意义很少用"到底",不能用"毕竟"。("终于" mainly emphasizes the hopes expected are fulfilled as wished after a long time, with many difficulties or with uneasiness. "到底" is seldom used to express this meaning, and "毕竟" is never used in this sense.)例如:

经过三个多月的努力,机器的安装终于成功了。

我终于考上大学了!

2.表示某事的结果如预料的那样经过一段时间后发生了,用"终于"、"到底"都可以。但是不能用"毕竟"。(When

indicating the result of something occurs as expected after a period of time, "终于" and "到底" can both be used. "毕竟" cannot be used in this sense.)例如:

她哽咽了好半天,终于放声哭了起来。

(She had choked with sobs for a long time before she finally burst into tears.)

经不起继母折磨的桂花终于／到底离家出走了。

(Having been no longer able to endure her step-mother's torment Guihua finally / in the end ran away from her home.)

火灾终于／到底发生了,而且发生得那么突然、那么惨。

3."到底"还常常表示所担心的事、所不期望发生的事经过一段时间发生了,这种时候大多不用"终于",更不能用"毕竟"。("到底" usually indicates the worried and unexpected things happen after a period of time. "终于" is seldom, and "毕竟" never used in this sense.)例如:

他到底把那件事说出去了。(事先可能多次告诫、嘱咐不要说出去。)

你到底把花瓶打碎了。(事先可能多次提醒不要打碎了。)

*他毕竟把那件事说出去了。

*你毕竟把花瓶打碎了。

4."毕竟"表示某事情到最后还是发生了,一般多用在让步转折关系的句子里。它表示某种期望或不期望的事情尽管很困难、尽管采取了措施、尽管有种种理由,但是还是发生了,强调的点在于"事实上如此"。这种时候大多不用"到底"、"终于"。("毕竟" indicates something finally happens, usually used in sentences of concessive and transitive relations. It indicates some expected or unexpected things finally happen, though there are many difficulties, or measures have been taken, or there are many reasons. The emphasis lies in "this is how things are". "终于" and "到底" are seldom used in this sense.)例如：

虽然费了不少时间,碰了不少钉子,但是他毕竟成功了。

(Although having spent a lot of time and met with rebuffs, he became successful after all.)

你们光说采取了措施没有用,火灾毕竟已经发生了。

(It is useless just to say that you'd taken measures, for the conflagration did occur after all.)

尽管冬天那么漫长、寒冷,但是它毕竟已经过去了,你还担心什么?

(The winter was that long and cold, but after all it has already passed. Then what else would you worry about?)

(二)"到底"、"毕竟"还可以表示对事物本质、特点、状态等的确认和强调,有不管怎么说,究竟如此的意思。"终于"没有这个意思。("到底" and "毕竟" can also indicate the confirmation and emphasis of the nature, character and state of the things, with the meaning of "no matter what to be said, it is the same". "终于" is not used in this sense.)例如：

他到底／毕竟是个孩子,你怎么能这样要求他?

(How can you require him in this way? In the end / after all he is only a child.)

职业棋手到底／毕竟跟业余棋手不同。

(The professional chess players are different from the amateurs in the end / after all.)

他的话再怎么说得不合适,他毕竟是老师,你不能这么没有礼貌。

(After all he is a teacher though what he said is not appropriate. You should not be so impolite.)

* 他终于是个孩子,你怎么能这样要求他?

* 职业棋手终于跟业余棋手不同。

"到底"、"毕竟"还常常构成这种格式:"A 到底 / 毕竟是 A"。("到底" and "毕竟" also form such pattern:"A 到底 / 毕竟是 A".)例如:

专家到底 / 毕竟是专家,就是与众不同。

(In the end / after all the experts are worthy of the name and really out of the ordinary.)

年轻人到底 / 毕竟是年轻人,学东西就是快。

(The young people in the end / after all are worthy of the name as they master knowledge so quickly.)

(三)"到底"还可以表示追究的语气,用于疑问句或有疑问意义的语句里;"终于"、"毕竟"没有这种意义和用法。("到底" can also indicate the mood of investigating, used in interrogative sentences or sentences of interrogative meanings. "终于" and "毕竟" have no such meaning and usage.)例如:

你们这些人当中到底谁是负责的?

到底谁是谁非,我们找个地方评评理去。

(We have to find a place to judge in the end who is right and who is wrong.)

* 你们这些人当中终于谁是负责的?

* 毕竟谁是谁非,我们找个地方评评理去。

(四)在使用上,"终于"、"到底"、"毕竟"都可以用在主语后动词前作状语;"终于"有时可以单独用在句首,后边用逗号断开;"到底"、"毕竟"没有这种用法。(In usage, "终于","到底" and "毕竟" can all be used after the subjects and before the verbs to serve as adverbials. Sometimes "终于" can be used at the beginning of a sentence alone, punctuated by a comma. "到底" and "毕竟" can't be used so.)例如:

<u>终于</u>,他取得了惊人的成功。

他<u>终于</u>取得了惊人的成功。

他<u>到底</u>取得了惊人的成功。

他**毕竟**取得了惊人的成功。

* 到底,他取得了惊人的成功。

* 毕竟,他取得了惊人的成功。

重 zhòng　　重量 zhòngliàng　　分量 fènliàng

〈名词〉表示物体由于地心引力作用而具有的重力的大小。

(< noun > indicating the weight of an object because of the terrestrial gravity.)

重〈形容词〉表示事物重量大的、比重大的或程度深的等。

(< adjective > indicating an object heavy in weight, large in proportion or high in degree.)

"重"、"重量"、"分量"都可以表示物体由于地心引力作用而具有的重力的大小,但是由于使用范围上、用法上、功能上有所不同,所以大多不能换用。("重","重量"and"分量"can all indicate the weight of a substance because of the gravity, but they are different in application, in usage and in function, so they are not interchangeable in most cases.)

(一) 使用范围上的差别(Differences in application)

1."重"可以用于体育活动之一——"举重"上,在这种专门术语中,不能用"举重量"、"举分量"的说法。举重活动中,按照重量的级别,分作不同的等级,这时只能用"重量",不能用"重"或"分量"。("重" can be used in one of the sports —"weight-lifting". For this special term, there are no such sayings as "举重量" or "举分量". In weight-lifting, different grades are divided according to the ranks of weight, and here only "重量" is used but "重" and "分量" aren't.)例如:

举重

* 举重量　　* 举分量

重量级

* 重级　　* 分量级

696

2."重量"表示一定的轻重,多用于较重较大的实物;"分量"含有数量多少的意味,多用于较小较轻的实物。("重量" emphasizes a certain weight and is mainly used for the heavier and larger material objects; while "分量" implies the meaning of the amount and is mainly used for the smaller and lighter material objects.)例如:

大象的重量有几吨,小象的重量也有一吨左右。

这一小箱书的重量跟那件大行李差不多。

＊ 大象的分量有几吨,小象的分量也有一吨左右。

我们这个菜市场在分量上保管没有问题。

(Our vegetable market surely hasn't found any problem in its measuring.)

这点儿肉够分量吗?

(Have you given the piece of meat full measure?)

＊ 我们这个菜市场在重量上保管没有问题。

＊ 这点儿肉够重量吗?

3."分量"还可以用于指说的话或写的文章内容重要或有深度、有水平等;"重量"不能表示这种意思。("分量" is also used for the words mentioned or the articles which are important or profound and of higher standard. "重量" does not have this sense.)例如:

老师的这番话说得很有分量。

(The words that the teacher said is of great weight.)

这篇论文分量很重,值得推荐。

(This thesis is of great weight and is worth recommending.)

＊ 老师的这番话说得很有重量。

＊ 这篇论文重量很重,值得推荐。

(二) 用法上的差别 (Differences in usage)

1."重"一般用作"数量+重"或"多(疑问词)+重"的形式;"重量"、"分量"不能用于这种形式。("重" is usually used in the

697

patterns "numeral + 重" or "多(how) + 重";"重量" and "分量" are not.)例如:

>这个西瓜恐怕有<u>十几斤重</u>。
>你的身体有<u>多重</u>?
>小姐,我要一条大约<u>二斤重</u>的鱼。
>* 这个西瓜恐怕有十几斤重量/分量。
>* 你的身体有多重量/分量?
>* 小姐,我要一条大约二斤重量/分量的鱼。

2."分量"常跟"足"、"够"等词搭配,"重量"一般不跟它们搭配。〔"分量" is usually collocated with "足"(full), "够"(enough), etc.; but "重量" is usually not.〕例如:

>这些菜好像分量不足。(These vegetables seem inadequate in weight.)
>你看看我买的饭分量够不够?
>(Will you have a look at the weight of the rice I've brought to see whether it is enough?)
>* 这些菜好像重量不足。
>* 你看看我买的饭重量够不够?

(三) 功能上的差别 (Differences in function)

"重"除了名词用法外,还有形容词用法,表示"重量大"、"分量重"、"程度深"等意义,可以接受程度副词的修饰;"重量"、"分量"没有形容词的功能,不能接受程度副词的修饰。(Besides being used as a noun, "重" can also be used as an adjective, meaning "heavy in weight", "full in measurement", "great in degree", etc., and can be modified by adverbs of degree. "重量" and "分量" cannot function as adjectives or be modified by adverbs of degree.)例如:

>这个提包怎么那么重啊?
>这孩子说话的分量还挺重。
>你的话说得太重了,她肯定接受不了。
>* 这个提包怎么那么重量/分量啊?

* 你的话说得太分量了,她肯定接受不了。
* 这个箱子太重量/分量了,我实在搬不动了。

重点 zhòngdiǎn　　要点 yàodiǎn

重点、要点〈名词〉< noun >
重点〈形容词〉< adjective >

(一)"重点"、"要点"作名词用时,都有重要的或主要的部分的意思,但是在意义上、使用范围上和用法上有一定差别。(While "重点" and "要点" are used as nouns, they both mean the important or major part, but there are some differences in their meanings, application spheres and usage.)

1. 意义上 (In meaning)

"重点"的意义是由"杠杆中承受重量的一点"引申而来的意思,因此"重点"一般指在一定范围内(同类事物中或某一整体中)的某一重要或主要的部分;"要点"则可能具有多个点,在某一范围内所有的重要或主要的内容。(The meaning of "重点" is extended from "the part of a lever that bears weight", so it generally refers to the important or major part within a certain range (among the same kind or of a whole); "要点" may include several points, all the important or major content within a certain range.)例如:

这句话是这篇文章的重点。

我们这个方案的重点部分就在这里。

(The main part of our project is just here.)

* 这句话是这篇文章的要点。
* 我们这个方案的要点部分就在这里。

我们来理解一下,看看这篇文章有哪些要点。

(Let's take a long look to find out what are the main points in this article.)

话虽然说得很多,要点其实只有三点。

* 我们来理解一下,看看这篇文章有哪些重点。

* 话虽然说得很多,重点其实只有三点。

2. 使用范围上 (In application range)

"重点"使用范围大,人、物、工作、文章等都可以用;"要点"使用范围很小,一般只用来指话、文章、战略等的主要内容。(The range that "重点" is used in is large. It can be used in people, in things, in work, in articles, etc. The range that "要点" is used in is limited, and generally it only refers to the main content of the words, articles and strategy, etc.) 例如:

他是我们的重点人选。

游艇比赛是我们这次活动的重点项目。

这是我们的科研重点。

这一时期的重点工作是搞好经济建设。

他的发言重点突出,号召力强。

(The focal points of his speech is prominent and is of strong appealing power.)

你把文章的要点归纳一下。

我来讲解一下这一部分的要点。

谈话的要点是什么?

我们来研究一下今后工作的战略要点。

(Let's discuss the strategic key points of our work in the days to come.)

* 他是我们的要点人选。
* 游艇比赛是我们这次活动的要点项目。
* 这一时期的要点工作是搞好经济建设。

3. 用法上 (In usage)

"重点"在句子里除了可以作主语、宾语以外,还可以用作描写性定语;"要点"在句子里主要作主语和宾语,一般不用作描写性定语,可用作限定性定语。("重点" can be used as subjects, objects, as well as descriptive attributive. "要点" is mainly used as subjects and objects in sentences and is not generally used as a descriptive attributive, but can be used as a restrictive attribute.)例如：

我们今后五年的科研重点是污水处理问题。
你难道忘了我们的工作重点了？
重点项目　重点工作　重点业务　重点地区
重点学校　重点参考书　重点对象
复习要点已经跟同学们说过了。
把要点记一下。
他的讲话我只记住了一个要点。
　＊要点讲话　＊要点内容　＊要点发言
　＊要点文件　＊要点策略
要点的说明　要点的解释　要点的归纳

(二)"重点"还有形容词用法，表示"有重点地"的意思，在句子里主要作状语；"要点"没有这种意义和用法。("重点" can also be used as an adjective, meaning "with focus on", mainly serving as an adverbial in a sentence. "要点" does not have this meaning and usage.)例如：

重点汇报一下大家的思想情绪。
(Focus the report on everyone's mood of thinking.)
我想重点说明两个问题。
对于那些有头脑、有才干、肯于奉献的年轻人要重点培养。
　(As for those bright-minded, competent and dedicated young men, focal training is needed.)
这一时期要重点发展实用学科。
　＊要点汇报一下大家的思想情绪。
　＊我想要点说明两个问题。

重要 zhòngyào　　重点 zhòngdiǎn

重要、重点〈形容词〉< adjective >
重点〈名词〉< noun >

(一)"重要"、"重点"都可以作形容词用，但是意义和功能都有

701

差别。意义上,"重要"表示的是"具有重大意义、作用和影响的"意思;"重点"表示的是"有重点地"的意思。功能上,"重要"是一般形容词,"重点"是非谓形容词。具体有以下差别:(Both "重要" and "重点" can be used as adjectives, but are different in meaning and function. In meaning, "重要" indicates the meaning of great significance, influence and effect in sense, "重点" indicates "emphatically". In function, "重要" is a general adjective and "重点" is a non-predicative adjective. Their specific differences):

1."重要"在句子里可以作谓语或补语;"重点"不可以。("重要" can be used as a predicate or complement in a sentence, but "重点" can't.)例如:

这个问题很重要。

这个前提特别重要。

时局的发展使得统战工作变得越来越重要了。

(The development of the current political situation makes the united front work more and more important.)

* 这个问题很重点。

* 这个前提特别重点。

* 时局的发展使得统战工作变得越来越重点了。

2."重要"可以构成"重要不重要"式;"重点"不能。("重要" can form the pattern "重要不重要", but "重点" can't.)例如:

今天的会重要不重要?

不管会重要不重要都得来。

* 今天的会重点不重点?

* 不管会重点不重点都得来。

3."重点"可以作状语,"重要"不能作状语。("重点" can be used as an adverbial, but "重要" can't.)例如:

把这几个问题重点说明一下。

重点培养年轻干部。

重点研究一下房改问题。

＊把这几个问题重要说明一下。
　　＊重要培养年轻干部。
　　＊重要研究一下房改问题。

4."重要"可以接受程度副词修饰、补充；"重点"不可以。("重要" can be modified or complemented by adverbs of degree, but "重点" can't.)例如：

　　很重要　非常重要　特别重要　更重要
　　＊很重点　＊非常重点　＊特别重点　＊更重点
　　比它重要得多　这个文件重要得很
　　＊比它重点得多　＊这个文件重点得很

(二)"重点"还有名词的意义和功能；"重要"没有这种意义和功能。("重点" is also of the sense and function of nouns; "重要" isn't.)

1."重点"作名词用时，表示的是同类事物中或整体中重要或主要的部分的意思。它在句子里可以单独作主语、宾语，还能接受数量词语的修饰。"重要"不可以。(While "重点" is used as a noun, it refers to the important or major part of the same kind or the whole. It can serve as a subject or object independently, and be modified by numeral-classifier compounds, but "重要" can't.)例如：

　　下一步的工作重点是打击伪劣产品问题。

　　(The next working focus is to crack down on the faked products.)

　　把经济建设作为今后工作的重点。
　　我认为这里只有一个重点。
　　＊下一步的工作重要是打击伪劣产品问题。
　　＊把经济建设作为今后工作的重要。
　　＊我认为这里只有一个重要。

2."重要"可以作"觉得"、"认为"、"以为"等可带谓词性宾语的动词的宾语；"重点"具有非谓性，所以没有这种功能。("重要" can be objects of "觉得", "认为" and "以为", etc. that can be

703

followed by predicative objects; while "重点" is of the non-predicative character, it hasn't this function.)例如：

大家都认为这个问题很重要。

我觉得这句话并不重要。

只是他以为重要，实际并不重要。

(Only he takes it seriously, it is not important in fact.)

* 大家都认为这个问题很重点。
* 我觉得这句话并不重点。
* 只是他以为重点，实际并不重点。

重要 zhòngyào　　主要 zhǔyào

〈形容词〉 < adjective >

(一)"重要"和"主要"意义上有差别：("重要" and "主要" are different in meaning:)

"重要"是指自身具有重大影响、作用的；"主要"则指在有关事物中起决定作用的、地位在先的，所以跟"主要"相对的词是"次要"，"重要"跟"次要"不是相对的关系。〔"重要" indicates that the thing itself or the person himself is of great effect and influence, while "主要" indicates the person or thing which plays a decisive role and leads an advanced position in the related affairs. Thus the opposite of "主要" is "次要(secondary or minor)", but "重要" is of no opposite relation with "次要".〕例如：

不可小看他，他可是个重要人物。(有举足轻重作用的人物。)

(You can't look down upon him. He is an important figure.)

这是我们完成这项工作的重要环节。(有关键作用的环节。)

他是这部电视连续剧的主要人物。(在这部电视剧中起决定作用的、地位在先的人物。)

(He is the main character in this TV series.)

他的主要作品有四部。(在他所有的作品中起决定作用的、地位在先的作品。)

(二) 功能用法上的差别：(Differences in function and usage:)

"重要"和"主要"虽然都是形容词，但是不属于同一类的形容词，"重要"是一般形容词，"主要"是非谓形容词。所以它们有以下不同：(Though "重要" and "主要" are both adjectives, they are not of the same category. "重要" is a general adjective, while "主要" is a non-predicative adjective. Their differences are:)

1."重要"在句子里可以作谓语或补语；"主要"不可以。("重要" can be used as a predicate or complement in sentences; "主要" can't.)例如：

这项工作很重要。

这个前提相当重要。

时局的发展使得统战工作变得越来越重要了。

* 这项工作很主要。
* 这个前提相当主要。
* 时局的发展使得统战工作变得越来越主要了。

2."主要"可以作状语，"重要"一般不能作状语。("主要" can be used as an adverbial, "重要" generally not.)例如：

主要讲以下几个问题。

主要培养培养年轻人。

主要研究一下体制改革问题。

* 重要讲以下几个问题。
* 重要培养培养年轻人。
* 重要研究一下体制改革问题。

3."重要"可以接受程度副词修饰、补充；"主要"不可以。("重要" can be modified or complemented by adverbs of degree; "主要" can't.)例如：

705

很重要　非常重要　特别重要　更重要

* 很主要　* 非常主要　* 特别主要　* 更主要

比它重要得多　　这个补充重要得很

* 比它主要得多　* 这个补充主要得很

4."重要"可以构成"重要不重要"式;"主要"不能。〔"重要" can form the pattern "重要不重要(important or not)"; "主要" can't.〕例如:

今天的讲座重要不重要?

无论文件重要不重要都全文传达,太浪费时间了。

(It is just a waste of time to transmit the document in full no matter it is important or not.)

* 今天的讲座主要不主要?

* 无论文件主要不主要都全文传达,太浪费时间了。

逐渐 zhújiàn　　逐步 zhúbù

〈副词〉 < adverb >

"逐渐"、"逐步"都可以表示程度或数量随时间缓慢地增加或减少,事物的变化较缓慢。但是意义和用法还有一定差别。(Both "逐渐" and "逐步" can indicate the degree or number gradually increases or decreases as time passes. The change is rather slow, but there are some differences in their meanings and usage.)

(一) 意义上 (In meaning)

1."逐渐"的变化是一种连续的、有序的、渐变的过程,没有明显的阶段性,常常用来表示事物自身自然而然的变化;"逐步"表示的变化则有明显的阶段性,是一步一步的变化,而且常常用来表示人有意识的动作。(The change of "逐渐" is a continuous, orderly and ever-changing process, with no obvious character of stage and it is usually used to indicate natural changes of the thing itself; the change "逐步" indicates is of the obvious character of stage, it is a step-by-step change and is usually used to indicate the conscious acts of people.)例如：

我们之间的感情在逐渐加深。

草逐渐地绿了起来，一片一片的。

我逐渐地懂得人生存的价值。

(I've gradually got to know the value of man's existence.)

天上的星星逐渐地退了下去。

搞好建设,逐步提高人民群众的物质生活水平。

在老师们的热情帮助下,同学们的汉语交际能力在逐步提高。

把计划逐步落实下去。

我们要想尽一切办法,逐步改善老百姓的住房。

(We must try every means to improve common people's housing progressively.)

2.一般来说,表示有意识、有步骤的变化不用"逐渐"。(Generally speaking, "逐渐" is not used to indicate the conscious and progressive change.)例如：

* 搞好建设,逐渐提高人民群众的物质生活水平。

* 把计划逐渐落实下去。

* 我们要想尽一切办法,逐渐改善老百姓的住房。

3.没有明显的阶段性的变化,是一种自然而然的缓慢的变化,一般不能用"逐步"。("逐步" is generally not used to indicate the natural and slow changes without obvious character of stages.)例如：

广场上的人逐渐多了起来。

天色逐渐暗了下去。

他的怒气逐渐消失了。

(Gradually his anger died away.)

* 广场上的人逐步多了起来。

* 天色逐步暗了下去。

* 他的怒气逐步消失了。

707

(二) 用法上 (In usage)

"逐步"用来修饰有意识、有步骤、有阶段性变化的动作,因此只是表示性质状态的形容词一般不能被"逐步"修饰;"逐渐"则可以。("逐步" is used to modify actions which are conscious, step by step and with the change of stage character, so the adjectives indicating character and stage only can't be modified by "逐步", but can be modified by "逐渐".)例如:

* 树上的苹果逐步红了。
* 夜深了,街上逐步地冷清了。
* 天气逐步地暖和了。

树上的苹果逐渐红了。

夜深了,街上逐渐地冷清了。

(It was deep night and it gradually became desolated in the street.)

天气逐渐地暖和了。

自己 zìjǐ 本人 běnrén 本身 běnshēn

〈代词〉 < pronoun >

"自己"、"本人"、"本身"都可以代指前面出现过的人称、名词等所指的说话人、当事人,但是,由于它们的代指范围和功能有很大的不同,所以大多不能换用。("自己","本人" and "本身" all indicate the personal pronoun or noun mentioned formerly, which represents the speaker or the person(s) concerned. But they are quite different in their representative references and functions, hardly exchangeable.)

(一) 指代范围不同 (Differences in their representative references)

1."自己"可以代指前文已经出现过的人、事物,也可以泛指人与事物。("自己" can representatively refer to people and things that appeared formerly and refer to people and things in general as well.)例如:

我好不容易上了大学,不会放松自己的。(特指"我"。)

自己的事情自己做。(泛指所有的人。)

"本人"、"本身"则只能用于特指,不能用于泛指。("本人" and "本身" are only used for the definite indication but not for the general indication.)例如:

参赛者必须提交本人2寸近照两张。("本人"指"参赛者"。)

本人不慎将钱包丢失,请拾到者……("本人"指说话人。)

(I myself carelessly lost my wallet, and just appeal to the person who has picked it up…)

人类本身就是社会最大的财富。("本身"指"人类"。)

(Human himself is the greatest wealth to the society.)

科学本身是没有国界的。("本身"指"科学"。)

2. "自己"既可以代人,也可以代事物,但通常是代具体的人、事物。〔"自己" can refer to people or things, but usually refers to specific person(s) or thing(s).〕例如:

急也没有用,他只好自己安慰自己。(代人。)

有些事情你不去理它,它也会自己了结。(代事物。)

(For some things, though you pay no attention to them, they will settle themselves.)

"本人"则只可代人,不可代事物。("本人" can only refer to person, not things.)例如:

究竟是什么病,连他本人也不知道。

"签字"一栏只能由申请者本人填写。

(The column of "signature" can only be filled in by the applicant himself.)

"本身"可以代人,也可以代事物,并以代事物为多;它所指代的人与事物必须在上文出现过;它可以指代抽象事物。"自

709

己"一般不指代抽象事物。("本身" can either refer to people or things, but mostly used to represent things. The people or things it represents should have appeared formerly. It can also refer to abstract things. "自己" is seldom used to refer to abstract things.)例如:

他们正以本身的经历和感受打动孩子们。(代人。)

(They are using their own experiences and feelings to make the children moved.)

地球本身也在不停地转动。(代物。)

这个想法本身是没有错的。(代抽象事物。)

(This idea itself is not wrong.)

* 这个想法自己是没有错的。

(二) 功能不同 (Differences in function)

1. "本人"表示说话人自己、"自己"表示泛指自身时,可以独立地作主语;"本身"只有指代前文已出现的人与事物时才可以独立地作主语。(When "本人" refers to the speaker himself, and "自己" generally refers to oneself, they can be used as subjects independently. "本身" may be used as a subject independently only when it refers to the person(s) or thing(s) previously mentioned.)例如:

本人貌虽不扬,但很有才华。

(I myself don't have the appearance out of the ordinary but I am a person of literary talent.)

自己有了缺点,就要敢于做自我批评。

他身为著名的艺术家,能如此平易近人,本身就难能可贵。

(Being a famous artist, he is so amiable and easy of approach and this itself is difficult of attainment.)

* 本身有很多缺点,请大家多多包涵。

* 本身有了缺点,就要敢于做自我批评。

2. "本人"、"本身"可以与某成分构成同位关系用来强调宾语,可是"本人"只能用以强调表人宾语,"本身"只能用以强调表物宾语。"自己"与某成分构成同位关系后不能用来强调宾语。("本人" and "本身" can form appositive relations with some composition to emphasize the objects. "本人" can only be used to emphasize the objects representing people, while "本身" is only used to emphasize the objects representing things. When "自己" forms an appositive relation with some composition, it can't be used to emphasize the objects.)例如：

我很想见见<u>当事者本人</u>。

他说他这次去文化部,有幸见到了<u>部长本人</u>。

我们要进行语法分析,就不能只研究符号的组成材料,必须进一步研究<u>符号本身</u>。

(Since we are going to make grammar analysis, we can't merely study the component materials of the symbols, but must make further study on the symbols themselves.)

* 我很想见见当事者自己。

* 他说他这次去文化部,有幸见到了部长自己。

* 我们要进行语法分析,就不能只研究符号的组成材料,必须进一步研究符号本人。

3."自己"、"本人"、"本身"都可以与主语构成同位关系用以强调主语。但是"本身"强调表人主语时,只跟表存在意义的"有"、"存在"等动词搭配,宾语必须是抽象名词。("自己","本人" and "本身" can all form appositive relations with the subjects to emphasize them. But when "本人" emphasizes the subject denoting persons, it only cooperates with the verbs indicating the meaning of existing, such as "有" and "存在", and the objects must be abstract nouns.)例如：

张老师得了癌症,可<u>他本人</u>并不知道。

张老师得了癌症,可<u>他自己</u>并不知道。

* 张老师得了癌症,可他本身并不知道。

<u>他本身</u>有许多长处,值得我们学习。

* 他本身有许多朋友。
* 我本身有不少这方面的工具书。

4."自己"、"本人"、"本身"都可以用以强调定语,但是"自己"、"本人"只能用以强调表人定语,"本身"可以强调表人定语,也可以强调表事物定语。"本身"与被强调的定语构成同位关系后,只能修饰抽象名词,不能修饰具体名词。("自己","本人" and "本身" can all be used to emphasize the attributive, but "自己" and "本人" only emphasize the attributive representing people. "本身" can emphasize either the attributive representing people or the attributive representing things. When "本身" forms an appositive relation with the stressed attributive, it can only modify the abstract nouns but not the specific nouns.)例如:

这是我自己的全部语法参考资料。

这件事,他本人的看法你了解过吗?

他本身的这些缺点并不影响他接受这个项目。

(The shortcomings of himself will not affect him accepting this project.)

这件事本身的意义在于,它向人们敲响了保护环境的警钟。

(The significance of the matter itself is to sound the alarm of protecting the environment.)

他引用的这段话选自他自己以前的论文。

* 他引用的这段话选自他本身以前的论文。
* 这是我本身的全部语法参考资料。

5."自己"还可以用于谓语动词前,表示动作的方式,即表示"不用别人帮助,独自地或自动地进行某种动作或处于某种状态"。"本人"、"本身"没有这一用法。("自己" can be used before predicative verbs, indicating the way of the acts, namely, "independently or automatically doing something or being in a state without the help of others". "本人" and "本身" can't be used so.)例如:

全自动洗衣机可以自己入水、自己漂洗、自己甩干并停机。

(The overall automatic washing machine can do the water pouring, the rinsing, the drying itself as well as stopping the operation.)

灯怎么自己亮了?

* 全自动洗衣机可以本身入水、本身漂洗、本身甩干并停机。

* 灯怎么本人亮了?

自己 zìjǐ   自我 zìwǒ

〈代词〉 < pronoun >

"自己"、"自我"意义和用法不同。("自己" and "自我" are different in meaning and usage.)

(一)"自己"可以作主语,"自我"不能作主语。("自己" can be used as subject, "自我" can't.)例如:

自己要学会照顾自己。

* 自我要学会照顾自我。

(二)"自己"、"自我"都可以作宾语,但意义不同。"自己"是指"自身","自我"是指一种抽象的意识。("自己" and "自我" can both be used as objects, but different in meaning. "自己" refers to "自身(oneself)", and "自我" refers to an abstract concept.)例如:

嘲弄历史的人最终是嘲弄了自己。

(The one who mocks history will be mocked by himself in the end.)

年轻人总希望多一些自我。

不能再过多地强调自我了。

(We should no longer emphasize ourselves excessively.)

* 嘲弄历史的人最终是嘲弄了自我。

* 年轻人总希望多一些自己。

713

（三）"自己"、"自我"都可以作定语,但意义不同。"自己"是指"自身","自我"是指"自己对自己的",即含有以"我"为对象的意思,它所修饰的中心词都是含有感觉、意念或抽象意义的具有动作性的词。("自己" and "自我" can both be used as attributive, but different in meaning. "自己" refers to "oneself", "自我" indicates "to oneself", implying "I" am the object. The central words modified by "自我" are the words implying feelings, thought or those of abstract sense and with the character of action.)例如:

  他终于实现了自己的理想。
  自己的事情自己做。
  他的自我意识太强了。
  他说他自我感觉不错。
  * 他终于实现了自我的理想。
  * 他的自己意识太强了。

（四）"自己"、"自我"都可以作状语,但意义和组句结构都有不同。"自己"表示的只是动作的方式,即表示"不用别人帮助,独自地或自动地进行某种动作或处于某种状态"。"自我"除表示动作方式以外,还表示动作对象,即表示这个动作由自己发出,同时又以自己为对象。因此,"自我"所修饰的谓语动词后,不可能再带宾语。此外,"自我"所修饰的动词,必须是双音节动词,一般是具有言语意义或抽象意义的动词。("自己" and "自我" can both be used as adverbial, but different in meaning and sentence structure. "自己" refers to the way of the acts, namely "independently or automatically doing something or being in a state without the help of others". "自我" can indicate the way as well as the target of an act, namely, the act is done by and for oneself. Therefore, after the predicative verbs modified by "自我", there can't be objects. Moreover, verbs modified by "自我" must be disyllabic ones, usually those related to language or of abstract meanings.)例如:

  我喜欢自己静静地坐在河边。

今天中午我自己做饭。
气球自己飞走了。
下面请大家自我介绍一下。
他总是自我欣赏。
(He always does self-admiration.)
* 我喜欢自我静静地坐在河边。
* 今天中午我自我做饭。
* 他总是自我欣赏海边的夜景。

总(是) zǒng(shì)   一直 yìzhí

〈副词〉 < adverb >

(一)"总(是)"、"一直"都可以表示持续不变的意思,但是它们在表示这个意思时的前提条件是不同的。(Both "总(是)" and "一直" may mean always, but there are different premises while the two words are used to express this meaning.)

"总(是)"的前提条件是"多次",每次所表现出来的情况、状态不变;"一直"的前提条件不是多次,而是"一"。它指某一动作、情况一经出现,便在某段时间内持续不变,有时它可以表示事情的整个过程持续不变,不管在这个过程中,有多少次动作,它都把整个过程看做"一"。(The premise of "总是" is "on many occasions", and the condition and state appearing each time will not change; while the premise condition of "一直" is not on many occasions, but is "one". It indicates that once a certain action or condition occurs, it will remain unchanged within a certain period of time. Sometimes it indicates that the whole process of something remains unchanged. No matter how many acts have taken place during the process, the whole process is regarded as "one".)例如:

他怎么总往这边看?(往这边看的动作一次次发生。)
他怎么一直盯着你看?(从眼睛看到你后,没有再离开你。)

晚饭前他总是做功课。(每天都这样。)

晚饭前他一直在做功课。(从下午的某时间开始做功课后,到晚饭前再没有改变。)

病人总不退烧。(指尽管采取了各种治疗措施,但是都没有改变病人发烧的情况。)

病人一直不退烧。(指从病人开始发烧到说话时,病人的发烧持续不变。)

他晚上总是只睡4、5个小时的觉。(每天晚上都这样。)

自从接受这个工程以后,他晚上一直只睡4、5个小时的觉。(从接受工程开始到说话时看做一个过程,在这个过程中,他一直持续晚上睡4、5个小时觉的情况。)

(二)语句的条件限制有具体表现时,注意区分"总(是)"、"一直"的选用。(When the restrictive conditions of the sentence are expressed specifically, pay attention to the difference in choosing "总(是)" or "一直".)

1.在一定的语句条件的限制下,只可能有多次的意思时,一般只能用"总(是)",不能用"一直"。(Under certain linguistic restrictions, generally only "总(是)", not "一直", is used to express only the meaning "on many occasions".)例如:

他总是提起你。("起"表示一次动作的开始,所以只能用"总是"表示多次的意思。)

＊他一直提起你。

他总在这个时候来电话。("这个时候"在一天里只会有一次,这说明前提条件一定是在不同的"日子"里,因此有多次的意思。)

＊他一直在这个时候来电话。

每次给他读书的时候,他总要提出好多稀奇古怪的问题。("每次"本身是不止一次的意思。)

(Every time someone reads a book to him, he always

asks many strange questions.)

* 每次给他读书的时候,他一直要提出好多稀奇古怪的问题。

2. 在限定为一次性动作的句子中,动词谓语后有表示持续的时段或终止的时间、到达的场所、位置等词语时,只能用"一直",不能用"总是"。(In a sentence with an action taking place once and with words after the predicate verb indicating the duration of time or the ending time, the place or the position reached, only "一直" can be used but "总是" can not.)例如:

晚会一直持续了三个多小时。

大雨一直下了五天五夜。

战斗一直进行了十几个小时。

那天晚上,我们一直谈到深夜。

那天大爷一直把我们送到山下。

温度将会一直降到零下十度。

* 晚会总是持续了三个多小时。

* 大雨总下了五天五夜。

* 战斗总是进行了十几个小时。

* 那天晚上,我们总谈到深夜。

* 那天,大爷总是把我们送到山下。

* 温度将会总降到零下十度。

(三)"总(是)"、"一直"还有其他完全不相同的意义。(Other different meanings of "总(是)" and "一直".)

1."总(是)"可以用于表示对数量、时间、情况的估计或推测,常与"大概"、"恐怕"、"看样子"等词配合,估计、推测中含"至少"、"起码"等较为肯定的意思和语气,估计、推测的情况多是数量大的或肯定的,否定式还常用"总不至于"、"总不会"等,表示估计不会出现某种不如意的或不可想象的不好的情况,句末常用表推测的语气词"吧";"一直"不能用于这种情况。〔"总(是)" can be used to indicate the estimation or inference about the quantity, time, conditions, etc., usually together with "大概(generally)", "恐怕(be afraid)", "看样子(seem)", etc. The relatively affirmative meaning and tone such as "至少(at least)", "起码(rudimentary)", etc. can be implied in the estimation or inference, and what is estimated or inferred is usually in large numbers or affirmative. In the negative sentences, "总不至于", "总不会", etc. are usually used, indicating that according to one's estimation there is not going to be any undesired or unimagined bad situation appearing, usually with the particle "吧" indicating the inference at the end of the sentence. "一直" is not used in such case.〕例如:

广场上的人黑压压的,看样子总有上万人。

(The square is packed with a dense mass of people. It looks there will be more than ten thousand people in all.)

这个西瓜真不小,恐怕总有十七、八斤。

他从来不迟到,今天迟到了,总是有原因的吧。

你已经通知他们接站了,总不至于没有人接吧。

(Since you have already informed them of going to meet them at the station, it is not likely that nobody does this.)

你们是多年的好朋友了,你还常常帮助他,如今你遇到了麻烦,他总不会看着不管吧。

(Since you are good friends for years and you help him very often, right now you're in trouble, it is not likely that he will sit by and watch.)

2. "总(是)"还可以表示"不管怎么样,最后必然如此"的意思,这种意思有时隐含在句子里,有时"总(是)"的前一分句直接用无条件的分句表示;"一直"不能用于这种情况。〔the "总(是)" can also mean "anyway, sooner or later". Such meaning is sometimes implied in the sentence. Sometimes the former clause of the "总(是)" sentence is an unconditional clause. "一直" is not used in such situations.〕例如:

正义总是要战胜邪恶的。

不怕一万,就怕万一,防总比不防好一些。

(We are not afraid of making overall preparation but eventualities. Anyway, it is better to be on guard than not.)

无论我有多忙,总会去接你的。

不管有多难,这件事总还是要做的。

* 正义一直是要战胜邪恶的。

* 不怕一万,就怕万一,防一直比不防好一些。

* 无论我有多忙,一直会去接你的。

* 不管有多难,这件事一直还是要做的。

3. "一直"可以表示顺着一个方向不变的意思,"总(是)"没有这种意思。["一直" can mean toward one direction without any change. "总(是)" doesn't mean so.]例如:

一直往前走,过了第二个十字路口就到了。

顺着这条小路一直往西走,就能到海边。

从车窗一直向远处望去,看到的都是黄灿灿的滚滚麦浪。

* 总往前走,过了第二个十字路口就到了。

* 从车窗总向远处望去,看到的都是黄灿灿的滚滚麦浪。

4. "一直"还可以表示对范围的强调,为了划定范围,"一直"的前后常有由"从"和"到"构成的介词词组。"总(是)"没有这种用法。["一直" can also express emphasis on the range. To delimit the bounds, "从(from)" and "到(to)" prepositional phrases are usually used before and after "一直"."总(是)" is not used so.]例如:

全村从大人一直到孩子都来为他送行。

(The whole village from adults to children all came to see him off.)

从穿衣、吃饭一直到上厕所用手纸,没有她不操心的。

(From dressing, serving meals to the toilet paper, there is not anything that she does not worry about.)

最 zuì　　更 gèng　　极 jí

〈副词〉表示程度很高。(< adverb > indicating very high in degree.)

(一)"最"与"更"

"最"与"更"都可以用于比较,但是有以下不同:(Both "最" and "更" can be used in comparison, but there are some differences:)

1."最"所用于的比较,是一种不具有比较标记的暗比,即没有表示比较的"比"字,也不能用于有比较标记的"比"字句;"更"则可以用于具有比较标记的"比"字句。(The comparison with "最" is a hidden comparison, i.e. without using the comparative mark, nor is the word "最" used in sentences with the comparative mark "比". "更" can be used in sentences with comparative marks.) 例如:

故宫是我国现存的最完整的古代宫殿建筑群。

(The Forbidden City is the most intact ancient palace complex group existing in our country.)

他最有资格说这种话。

我最讨厌你的优柔寡断。

他比以前更有信心了。

跟别的干部们相比,他更注意表率作用。

(Compared with other cadres, he pays more attention to playing a model role.)

* 他汉语说得比我最流利。

* 这趟车比78次最晚。

2."最"所用于的比较是与众相比,表示所有的人、事物的性状都不及它;"更"所用于的比较则是两种情况、两个方面等的比较。(The comparison "最" is used in is to compare with all the others, indicating that all the shapes and properties of other people or things are inferior to it. "更" is used in the comparison of two things or aspects, etc.)例如:

我最喜欢足球运动,最不喜欢棋类活动。(所比较的范围是在所有的体育活动中。)

她是最受顾客欢迎的售货员。(在所有的售货员中比较。)

(She is the shop-assistant who is most popular to the customers.)

表示这种意义的比较,不能用"更"。

* 我更喜欢足球运动,更不喜欢棋类活动。
* 她是更受顾客欢迎的售货员。

有了孩子以后,她更懂得了做母亲的不易。(与没有孩子时比。)

(After having a kid of her own, she knows better the hardships of being mother.)

今天不是周末,怎么商店里的人显得更多了。(与周末比。)

* 有了孩子以后,她最懂得了作母亲的不易。
* 今天不是周末,怎么商店里的人显得最多了。

3. 表示程度高的侧重点不同:"最"表示的程度是极点,即没有比它更高的;"更"表示的程度不在于是否为极点,只在于在原有一定程度的基础上加深一步、进一步。(The emphatic points in degree that the two words indicate are different. The degree "最" indicates is the extreme, namely there is nothing higher than it; while the degree "更" indicates doesn't lie in whether it is the extreme but in the further step forward from its original certain degree.)例如:

入夏以来,今天最热了。(其他日子都没有今天热。)

在这些教材中,这一本是最难的。(别的都没有它难。)

这样一修改,这本教材显得更难了。(以前就难,现在难的程度又加深一步。)

在这里住了一段时间以后,我更不愿意离开这里了。(以前就不愿意离开这里,现在又进一步。)

(二)"最"与"极"、"更"

"最"与"极"都可以表示程度很高,没有比它更高的程度。其区别在于:("最" and "极" can both indicate very high in degree, there is nothing higher than them. Their differences are:)

1. 侧重角度不同 (Different in emphatic points)

"最"含有比较,是指在同类事物中,它的性状超过其他;"极"没有比较意味,只表示程度达到顶点。("最" implies comparison, indicating its state and conditions exceed all others of the same kind. "极" has no meaning of comparison but only indicates the degree has reached the top.)例如:

她是我们班最活跃的人物了。

在最近播放的电视剧中,这部电视剧最受欢迎。

他是个极认真的人。

这是一部极受欢迎的电视剧。

2. 功能不同 (Different in function)

(1)"最"、"更"只能作状语,不能单独作补语;"极"可以单独作补语。("最" and "更" are only used as adverbials, not as complements alone. "极" can serve as a complement alone.)例如:

我最喜欢看晚报。

我极喜欢看晚报。

今天的晚报好极了。

* 今天的晚报好最了。

* 八月十五的月亮圆更了。

(2)"最"还可以与部分单音形容词连用,表示说话人对状况的程度作最大限度的估计、限制等;"极"、"更"没有此种用法。("最" can also be used together with some monosyllable adjectives, indicating that the speakers make the fullest estimation to and restriction on the degree of the state. "极" and "更" cannot be used so.)例如:

这个箱子最多三十公斤重。

722

晚上最晚十二点睡觉,不能再晚了。
这儿最低气温可达四十摄氏度。
* 这个箱子极多三十公斤重。
* 晚上极晚十二点睡觉,不能再晚了。
* 这儿更低气温可达四十摄氏度。

左右 zuǒyòu　　前后 qiánhòu　　上下 shàngxià

〈方位词〉表示数量的约数。(< nouns of locality > indicating the approximate number.)

(一)"左右"、"前后"、"上下"都可以用于表示数量的约数,但是使用的范围有所不同。("左右","前后" and "上下" can all indicate the approximate numbers, but are different in application spheres.)

1."左右"、"前后"都可以用于表示时间的概数,"上下"一般不用来表示时间。("左右" and "前后" both can be used to indicate the approximate numbers of time, and "上下" isn't generally used to indicate time.)例如:

五点左右　一个小时左右　三十分钟左右
两点前后　五月前后　春节前后
* 五点上下　* 一个小时上下　* 两点上下
* 春节上下

"左右"、"前后"虽然都可以用于表示时间的概数,但是使用范围也有差别。一般来说,"左右"既可以表示时点,又可以表示时段,"前后"则只能表示时点;"左右"表示时点时,只能用于数量词后,不能用于名词、动词后,"前后"则既可以用于数量词后,也能用于名词、动词后。(Though both "左右" and "前后" can be used to indicate the approximate time, there are some differences in their ranges of application. Generally speaking, "左右" can indicate either point of time or period of time, "前后" can only indicate point of time; when "左右" is used to indicate point of time, it can only be

723

used after the numerals but not after nouns or verbs, but "前后" may be used either after numerals or after nouns or verbs.)例如：

时点　：十点左右　十点前后
时段　：三个小时左右　＊三个小时前后
数量词：六个月左右　五月前后／五点前后
名词　：＊春节左右／＊秋分左右　春节前后／秋分前后
动词　：＊毕业左右／＊天亮左右　毕业前后／天亮前后

(二) "左右"除了可以表示时间的约数以外,还可以表示年龄、距离、重量等的约数;"前后"不能表示除时间以外的约数;"上下"多用于表示年龄的约数,重量等约数有时也用,但用得很少。("左右" can also indicate the approximate numbers of age, distance, weight, etc., in addition to indicating time. "前后" cannot be used to indicate the approximate numbers other than time. "上下" is more used to express the approximate numbers of age, sometimes used in the approximate numbers of weight.)例如：

五十岁左右　　　　　　长三米左右
身高一米八零左右　　　亩产千斤左右
＊五十岁前后　　　　　＊长三米前后
＊身高一米八零前后　　＊亩产千斤前后
五十岁上下　　　　　　＊长三米上下
身高一米八零上下　　　亩产千斤上下

(三) "前后"还可以用于时间词语的前面,不表示约数,而表示从开始到结束或到说话时为止总计所用的时间(时段——从开始到结束的一段时间),也可以用重叠式表示。"左右"没有这种意义和用法。["前后" can also be used before time words, not indicating the approximate numbers, but indicating the time spent from the beginning to the end, or till the time of the speaking (time length — a period of time from the beginning to the end), such usage can also be expressed with the overlapped pattern. "左右" is not of such meaning and usage.]例如：

前后二十几个小时的时间,他一直在紧张地观察着、记录着。

前前后后五十几年,他一直奋斗在这片黄土地上。

＊左右二十几个小时的时间,他一直在紧张地观察着、记录着。

＊左左右右五十几年,他一直奋斗在这片黄土地上。

"前后"表示这种意思时,还常常单独用在动词前,动词后面加上总计的时段。(While "前后" is used in this sense, it is usually used alone before a verb, and the verb is followed by the overall period of time.)例如:

前后进行了五个多小时的时间。

前后花费了三个多月的时间。

做 zuò　　干 gàn　　搞 gǎo

〈动词〉 < verb >

"做"、"干"、"搞"都有从事某种事业、工作、活动的意思,但是词义侧重角度、搭配习惯及词语组合上还有很大差异。("做","干" and "搞" all signify being engaged in a cause, job, activity, etc., but their emphasis in meaning, habitual collocation and word combinations are quite different.)

(一)词义侧重的角度不同,因此相关联的事物也不同。(Differences in emphatic points result in the disparities in things concerned.)

1."做"主要指具有操作性的制作动作,跟它相关的事物一般都是非常具体的可操作的事物。("做" mainly refers to the manufacturing acts of operating character and the things concerning with it are generally all those fairly specific, operational things.)例如:

做饭　——　煮、炒等

做作业　——　写等

做针线　——　缝制等

725

做试验 —— 测量、检验、操作、记录等
做手术 —— 开刀、缝合等
做玩具 —— 制造等

"干"和"搞"不能用于这种一般的、非常具体的、与具体相关事物相联系的操作性的动作。("干" and "搞" cannot be used is such general, specific, or operational acts connected with specific corresponding substances.)例如：

* 干饭　　* 干作业　　* 干针线　　* 干试验
* 干手术　* 干玩具
* 搞饭　　* 搞作业　　* 搞针线　　* 搞书架
* 搞手术　* 搞玩具

"干"可以表示操作性的动作，但是一般不与具体的事物相联系，"干"本身的动作是笼统的，能跟它相关联的事物往往也是笼统的。("干" can refer to operational acts, but generally not connected with specific things. The act "干" itself is general, so usually the things connected with it are also general.)例如：

你在干什么呢？—— 做家具。

他正在干活，出不来。

多干一点儿好事。

2. "做"有时也可以用于非操作性的一般动作，一般连带表示工作、事情一类的宾语。"干"和"搞"大多不能用于这种情况。("做" sometimes can be used for the general acts of the non-operating character and it is generally followed by the objects indicating work or things. "干" and "搞" cannot be used so in most cases.)例如：

多做一点儿群众的思想工作　做<u>学术报告</u>
做点儿实事儿　做学问　做生意　做<u>事</u>
* 多干一点儿群众的思想工作
* 干生意　* 干学术报告
* 多搞一点儿群众的思想工作
* 搞学术报告　* 搞点儿实事儿

"事情"是一种笼统事物的名词,有一定的抽象性。它一般可以直接跟"做"结合。〔"事情(thing)" is a general noun, of certain abstract character. It usually connects with "做" directly.〕例如:

　　做事情应该讲求认真。

　　做事情要多动脑子。

　　多做一些有利于人民的事情。

"干"有时可以支配笼统的事物,但是"干"和"事情"往往不能直接结合,需要一定的限制语才能结合。"搞"一般不能跟"事情"结合。〔"干" sometimes can govern general things, but generally not directly connect with "事情(thing)". It must be used together with certain restrictive words. "搞" generally is not connected with "事情(things)".〕例如:

　　* 干事情应该讲求认真。

　　* 干事情要多动脑子。

　　干这种事情需要勇气。

　　多干一些有利于人民的事情。

　　领导应该多干一些实事。

　　* 搞事情应该讲求认真。

　　* 搞事情要多动脑子。

　　* 领导应该多搞一些实事。

3. "干"所表示的动作常常跟出力地做、很有劲头儿地做有关,一般不直接连带所做的具体事物。(The action of "干" often indicates exerting oneself or working vigorously, generally is not followed by the specific things being done.)例如:

　　加油干哪!　　拼命地干　　苦干、实干加巧干

　　干得满头大汗　　干得很起劲儿

4. "搞"主要用于用一定智力、一番规划和一定方式作的动作,它支配的事物往往带有一定的抽象意义或"类"的概括意义。"干"和"做"往往不用于这种情况,个别可结合的,在意义的侧重点上仍有差异。("搞" is mainly used for the acts done by certain

intelligence, with a lot of plans and in certain patterns. The things it budgets usually have certain abstract sense or the summarizing meaning of "type". "干" and "搞" are seldom used in such case, if ever used so, the emphatic points are different.)例如：

搞革命　搞卫生　搞副业　搞设计
搞科研　搞实验　搞技术革新
搞了一个方案　搞好精神文明建设
搞建设需要吃苦精神　把国民经济搞上去
把站台服务搞好
＊干设计　＊干科研　＊干技术革新
＊干好精神文明建设　＊干建设需
要吃苦精神　＊把国民经济干上去
＊做设计　＊做科研　＊做技术革新
＊做好精神文明建设　＊做建设需
要吃苦精神　＊把国民经济做上去

(1)"搞"的意义中含有用心智的因素,所以它可以带下面的宾语;"干"和"做"一般不能。(The meaning of "搞" involves intelligence, so it can be followed by the following objects. "干" and "做" cannot.)例如：

搞阴谋诡计（go in for intrigues and conspiracy）
搞手段（use artifices）
搞手腕（play tricks）
搞花样（play tricks）
搞鬼（be up to some mischief）
＊干阴谋诡计　＊干手段　＊干手腕
＊干花样　　　＊干鬼
＊做阴谋诡计　＊做手段　＊做手腕
＊做花样　　　＊做鬼

(2)"搞"有时也可以支配一些非常具体的事物,但是"搞"的动作一般带有突出的采用一定手段、方式获取的意义。"干"和

"做"没有这种意思。("搞" sometimes can budget some fairly specific things, but the act of "搞" generally indicates the meaning of obviously adopting certain means or method to obtain. "干" and "做" do not have this sense.)例如:

我搞来了一点儿水,让重病号每人先喝一点儿吧。

他搞到那份文件了。

(He has got hold of that document.)

我来设法搞球票。

(I will manage to get the ticket for the ball game.)

* 我干来了一点儿水,~。
* 他干到那份文件了。
* 我来设法干球票。
* 我做来了一点儿水,~。
* 他做到那份文件了。

"我来设法做球票。"和"我来设法搞球票。"意思完全不同,"做"是制作的意思,"搞"是设法得到的意思。("我来设法做球票"and "我来设法搞球票" are quite different in meaning. "做" means to make. "搞" means to manage to get.)

(3)"搞"有时可以代替很多动词,可以根据不同的宾语,理解它所表示的动词的意义。("搞" sometimes can represent many verbs, and the meanings of the verbs it represents are decided by the objects following it.)例如:

要凭自己的本事,不要总想搞关系。("拉"的意思。)

我想搞一个改革的方案。("设计"的意思。)

大家都在搞卫生,你在这儿干什么?("打扫"的意思。)

领导不能带头搞不正之风。("树立"的意思。)

我准备搞文学创作。("从事"的意思。)

5."干"和"搞"还可以表示从事某一类别的职业或某一方面的工作的意思,"干"一般指具体的,"搞"一般指抽象的。("干" and "搞" can also indicate being engaged in certain kind of occupation or work. "干" is used in the specific kinds, and "搞" in the abstract ones.)例如：

我不想干车床,我想干木匠。
你去干乘务员倒挺合适的。
他搞美术,我搞文学。
他是搞科研出身的。
搞业务他很有一套。
* 他干美术,我干文学。
* 他是干科研出身的。

"做"表示这方面的意思时,一般表示的是"当"、"担任"的意思,它连带的宾语一般跟人有关。表示这种意思时,不能用"搞"。(When "做" indicates such meaning, it generally means "to be" or "holding the post of". The objects following it generally relate to people. "搞" is not used to express such meaning.)例如：

做客　做官儿　做代表　做人民的勤务员
欲做先生,得先做学生。
你来做董事长吧。
谁都不愿意做这个厂的厂长。
* 搞客　* 搞官儿　* 搞代表
* 你来搞董事长。
* 谁都不愿意搞这个厂的厂长。
* 干客　* 干官儿　* 干代表　* 干人民的勤务员
* 欲干先生,得先干学生。

6. "做"还可以表示与人结成的某种关系或家庭的庆祝、纪念活动。"干"和"搞"都没有这种意思。("做" also indicates certain relations made with people or celebrations or commemorative activities of families. "干" and "搞" do not have this meaning.)例如：

我们做个朋友吧。
咱们做亲家吧。
我想给他们做干儿子。

做生日　做寿　做满月
* 我们干／搞个朋友吧
* 咱们干／搞亲家吧
* 我想给他们干／搞干儿子
* 干／搞生日　* 干／搞寿　* 干／搞满月

（二）词语组合上（In collocation）

1. 状语上（In the combination with adverbials）

由"干"的意义所决定，"干"可以用描写有干劲儿的形容词作状语，尤其是不加"地"的用法和单音节形容词。"做"、"搞"大多不这样用。（Due to its meaning, "干" can have adjectives describing full of vigour as its adverbial, especially those without "地" or the monosyllabic adjectives. "做" and "搞" cannot be used so.）例如：

大干　苦干　实干　拼命干　加油干　埋头苦干
* 苦做　* 实做　* 加油做　* 埋头苦做
* 苦搞　* 实搞　* 加油搞　* 埋头苦搞

有时"搞"也可以用"大"修饰。（Sometimes "搞" can also be modified by "大".）例如：

大搞爱国卫生运动　　　大搞精神文明建设

"做"只有"大做文章"可以用，这是因为这里的"做文章"有它特定的意义，不是普通的写文章，而是指抓住一件事发议论或在上面打主意的意思。（Only in "大做文章", "大"can modify "做". Here, "做文章" is not the original sense "write articles", but has its special meanings. It means to seize upon a matter and talk about or make an issue of it.）

2. 补语上（In the combination with complements）

（1）"搞"有时可以借助一些词语表示由于处理得不好，而使事情出现不好的局面，使人的头脑出现不清楚的状态；"干"和"做"则常常受到一定的限制。（Sometimes with the help of some words, "搞" indicates the situation which is not well handled and worse situation is brought about, or the state by which people become unclear-minded. "干" and "做" are often restricted in such usage.)例如：

  让他把事情搞糟了(It is him that made the matter worse.)
  把试验搞砸了(to make the experiment failed)
  搞出乱子了(to have created a disturbance)
  搞出麻烦了(to have caused trouble)
  你把我搞糊涂了。
  搞得他莫名其妙的。
  * 让他把事情干糟了。
  * 让他把事情做糟了。
  * 干得他莫名其妙的。
  * 做得他莫名其妙的。

（2）"搞"可以表示通过动作获取的意思，因此它可以与含"获取"义的补语组合；"干"和"做"不能用于这种场合。〔"搞" may mean to get by means of actions. Thus it can be combined with complements implying "获取(get)"; "干" and "做" cannot be used in such case.〕例如：

  搞到开门的钥匙了 我搞到吃的了
  搞来一部分资料
  * 干到开门的钥匙了 * 我干到吃的了
  * 干来一部分资料
  * 做到开门的钥匙了 * 我做到吃的了
  * 做来一部分资料

做 zuò 造 zào 制造 zhìzào
〈动词〉 < verb >

（一）"做"和"造"、"制造"都有通过人工将原材料变成某种物品的意思，但是它们在制作方式上有很大的不同。"做"主要侧重于手工的加工制作；"造"、"制造"则主要指用机械或大型、复杂的工具加工制作,因此它们在搭配对象上也有很大不同。("做","造" and "制造" may all mean to make something from material by manual work, but they are quite different in the ways of making. "做" mainly emphasizes manufacturing by hand; "造" and "制造" mainly indicate manufacturing by machines or large-scaled, complicated tools. So they are quite different in their collocations either.)

1. "做"可以带食物类的名词宾语;"造"、"制造"不能带。("做" can be followed by objects denoting food; "造" and "制造" cannot.)例如:

做饭　做饺子　做好吃的　做食品
做蛋糕　做汤　做冰淇淋
* 造饭　* 造饺子　* 造好吃的　* 造食品
* 制造蛋糕　* 制造汤　* 制造冰淇淋

2. "做"可以带穿戴类及日常用品类的名词宾语;"造"、"制造"不能带。("做" can also be followed by objects denoting apparel or daily necessities; "造" and "制造" cannot.)例如:

做衣服　做裤子　做鞋　做帽子　做手套
做书包　做窗帘　做床罩　做台布
* 造衣服　* 造裤子　* 制造鞋
* 制造帽子　* 制造手套
* 造书包　* 造窗帘　* 制造床罩　* 制造台布

3. "做"可以带手工艺品类、玩具类或小型手工制作的东西。"造"、"制造"不能带。("做" can be followed by objects denoting handicrafts, toys or small hand-made things. "造" and "制造" can't.)例如:

做泥人　做花瓶　做壁毯　做瓷瓶　做竹器
做玩具　做茶具　做花盆
* 造泥人　* 造花瓶　* 造壁毯　* 制造瓷瓶
* 制造玩具　* 制造茶具

733

4."做"可以带家具、小用具等名词宾语;"造"、"制造"大多不能带。("做" can be followed by objects denoting furniture, small utensils, etc.; "造" and "制造" usually not.)例如:

做衣柜　做桌子　做沙发　做书架
做毛笔　做刷子　做拖布
＊造衣柜　＊造桌子　＊制造沙发
＊造毛笔　＊制造刷子　＊制造拖布

5."造"、"制造"的东西从形式上来说,一般是大型的或复杂的;从原料上来说,大多跟金属、土木等有关。(Speaking in form, things for "造" and "制造" are of huge shapes or complicated; as far as the raw materials are concerned, they mostly concern metals and buildings, etc.)例如:

造船　造纸　造军舰　造机器
造大炮　造房子　造大桥
制造飞机　制造火箭　制造工具
制造轮船　制造武器　制造拖拉机

当这些东西不是玩具或模型时,一般不用"做"跟它们配合。(When these things are not of toy or model types, "做" generally is not used to cooperate with them.)

＊做船　＊做军舰　＊做机器
＊做大炮　＊做房子　＊做大桥
＊做飞机　＊做火箭　＊做轮船
＊做武器　＊做拖拉机

(二)"做"、"造"、"制造"在其他意思上还有差别。(The differences of "做","造" and "制造" in expressing other meanings.)

1."做"可以用于从事学习或工作的活动;"造"、"制造"一般不能。("做" can be used in activities involving study or work; "造" and "制造" generally not.)例如:

做作业　做练习　做功课　做文章
做论文　做计划

＊造作业　＊造练习　＊造功课
　　＊制造文章　＊制造论文　＊制造计划

但是,有一点需要注意,习惯上说"造句",而不说"做句"。(Notice: Customarily, we say "造句 (make sentences)", not "做句".)

2. "造"和"制造"可以用于声势大的或虚假的跟话语有关的活动;"做"一般不能这样用。("造" and "制造" can be used in powerful and dynamic or false activities related to languages; "做" is generally not used so.)例如:

　　造舆论 (spread public opinions)
　　造谣 (start rumours)
　　制造谣言 (create rumours)
　　制造借口 (find excuses)
　　＊做舆论　＊做谣　＊做谣言　＊做借口

3. "制造"还可以用于人为地造成某种不好的气氛、局面或事件等;"做"和"造"一般不能用于这种场合。("制造" can also be used for creating some unpleasant atmosphere, situation or incident, etc. purposefully; while "做" and "造" can't generally be used for these occasions.)例如:

　　制造紧张空气　制造混乱　制造纠纷
　　制造矛盾　制造事端　制造恐怖
　　制造分裂　制造障碍
　　＊做紧张空气　＊做混乱　＊做纠纷　＊做矛盾
　　＊造事端　＊造恐怖　＊造分裂　＊造障碍

(三)"做"、"造"、"制造"在色彩及结构搭配上的不同。(The differences of "做", "造" and "制造" in coloring and collocation.)

1. "做"的口语色彩很强,使用也很普遍;"造"通用于口语和书面语;"制造"则多用于书面语。("做" is of strong spoken language flavor, and is very commonly used; "造" is commonly used in spoken and written languages; "制造" is more used in the written lan-

guage.)

2."做"、"造"在结构的搭配上一般不受单音节词和双音节词的限制;"制造"则受到严格限制,一般来说,它只能与双音节词组合,不能与单音节词组合。("做" and "造" generally are not limited to monosyllabic and disyllabic words in collocation. "制造" is strictly restricted. Generally speaking, it only collaborates with disyllabic words, not monosyllabic ones.)例如:

做饭 做事 做船 做汤 做工
做衣服 做食品 做竹器 做玩具
造船 造谣 造福 造林 造纸
造句 造舆论 造房子 造机器 造大炮
＊制造船 ＊制造谣 ＊制造福 ＊制造林
＊制造纸 ＊制造句
制造轮船 制造谣言
制造机器 制造工具 制造舆论 制造事端

座 zuò　　家 jiā　　所 suǒ

〈量词〉< classifier >

"座"、"家"、"所"都是量词,所计量的物大多跟一定的建筑物有关,但是它们对计量对象的选择却有很大不同。("座", "家" and "所" are all measure words. The things measured by them are usually related to buildings, but the measuring objects they choose are quite different.)

(一)"座"对计量对象的选择主要侧重于外观,从外观上看,高大的、固定的物体一般可以用"座"计量。(The measuring targets "座" chooses mainly emphasize the appearance. By appearance, the tall and fixed objects can generally be measured by "座".)例如:

一座大山 那座立交桥 一座高大的塑像
一座古老的城市 座座铁塔
路口并排矗立着两座近百米高的大楼。

紫禁城是一座气势宏伟而又精美完整的古代宫殿。

不是侧重于建筑物外观如何的,而只是反映建筑物里具体单位经营管理情况的,不能用"座"。(When it reflects the business management of the specific units in the building and doesn't emphasize the appearance of the building, "座" can't be used.)例如:

* 这座饭店的菜做得很好吃。
* 那座宾馆的服务是一流的。
* 张老板苦心经营这座公司二十年。
* 这座展览馆正在展览明清两代著名画家的作品。

(二)"家"对计量对象的选择主要侧重于性质,具有企业、事业、经营部门这种性质的单位或者是人家都可以用"家"计量。(The measuring targets of "家" are determined by their nature. Units with the nature of enterprise, institution and managing department or household can all be measured by "家".)例如:

这家工厂是一家国营企业。

这家公司经营装饰业务。

那家出版社出了不少新书。

一家商店　一家饭店　两家医院

一家银行　几家人家

侧重于表现建筑物外观如何的,不能用"家"。(When emphasizing the appearance of the buildings, "家" can't be used.)例如:

* 那家立交桥　* 一家高大的塑像
* 一家人民英雄纪念碑
* 那家大楼很漂亮
* 这家电视塔有四、五百米高。

(三)"所"对计量对象的选择有两个角度,一是从外观上,用于不是以高大为特点或者不是以突出高大为特点的房屋建筑物;一是从性质上,用于学校、医院等文化事业性质的单位。(The measuring targets "所" chooses are from two aspects. One is from its appearance, "所" is used for houses and buildings which don't take height as the character or take height as the prominent character; another is from its nature, "所" is used for these cultural institutions as schools, hospitals, etc.)例如：

　　这儿有几所房子。
　　山里有一所房子。
　　这所房子是谁的？
　　这是一所很有名的学校。
　　那所医院骨科很有名。
　　这所幼儿园条件不错。

以高大为特点的建筑物，一般不能用"所"。(A tall building is generally not modified by "所".)例如：

　　＊一所所高大的楼房整齐地排列着。
　　＊那所摩天大厦真气派。

不是学校、医院、幼儿园这样的文化事业性质的单位，不能用"所"。(The units not belonging to cultural institutions as schools, hospitals, kindergartens, etc. are not modified by "所".)例如：

　　＊这附近有好几所商店。
　　＊那所宾馆服务很好。
　　＊这所书店来了不少新书。

词目音序索引
Pinyin Index

以汉语拼音字母次序为序。先以词目第一个字的第一个字母为序,然后分别以第二、第三、第四个字母为序;词目第一个字读音相同者以声调的阴平、阳平、上声、去声、轻声为序。

A

啊	1
矮	150
爱好	525
安静	10
按	14
按照	14

B

吧	1
把	18
把	21
把	22
白	23
白白	23
办法	209
帮	25
帮	450
帮忙	25
帮助	25
被	18
被	29
被	31
本来	609
本人	708
本身	708
比较	183
毕竟	692
~边	36
便利	208
遍	101
别的	38
别的	42
别人	42
别人	44
冰冷	47
冰凉	47
不	50
不比	53
不必	502
不过	680
不然	536
不如	56
不同	58
不一会儿	564
不一样	58
不再	61

C

才	64
才	249
参观	66
测验	359
曾经	570
差	288
差(一)点儿	69

739

差不多 …… 69	凑巧 …… 666	到处 …… 99
差点儿 …… 295	村庄 …… 112	到达 …… 132
产生 …… 198	村子 …… 112	到达 …… 133
常常 …… 74		到底 …… 345
常常 …… 79	**D**	到底 …… 692
朝 …… 162	达 …… 133	的 …… 142
朝 …… 496	达到 …… 132	的 …… 378
朝（着）…… 82	打 …… 104	地 …… 142
成见 …… 590	打听 …… 504	得 …… 142
迟 …… 85	大概 …… 115	等 …… 144
迟到 …… 85	大概 …… 118	等 …… 147
持续 …… 313	大家 …… 44	等待 …… 144
充分 …… 87	大量 …… 119	等等 …… 147
充满 …… 91	大批 …… 119	等候 …… 144
充沛 …… 87	大体 …… 115	低 …… 150
充实 …… 91	大约 …… 115	的确 …… 154
充足 …… 87	耽搁 …… 122	地 …… 155
出来 …… 423	耽误 …… 122	地点 …… 155
初 …… 93	但是 …… 680	地方 …… 155
除 …… 97	当 …… 124	地区 …… 155
除非 …… 677	当 …… 127	第二 …… 193
除了 …… 97	当初 …… 93	点儿 …… 159
处处 …… 99	当时 …… 124	点子 …… 202
次 …… 101	当时 …… 402	都 …… 64
匆忙 …… 302	当中 …… 685	都 …… 440
从 …… 104	倒 …… 138	都 …… 544
从 …… 108	倒（倒是）…… 139	短 …… 186
从来 …… 109	到 …… 133	短促 …… 186
从来 …… 581	到 …… 621	短暂 …… 186
从前 …… 579	~到 …… 376	对 …… 162

对 ……………… 165	房间 …………… 213	刚 ……………… 249
对 ……………… 171	房屋 …………… 213	刚 ……………… 250
对 ……………… 174	房子 …………… 213	刚才 …………… 250
对 ……………… 176	访问 ……………… 66	刚刚 …………… 250
对/对于…来说	费 ……………… 285	搞 ……………… 725
……………… 165	分量 …………… 696	告诉 …………… 256
对(对于)…来说	吩咐 …………… 217	个个 …………… 259
……………… 168	丰富 …………… 219	个子 …………… 460
对比 …………… 181	风景 …………… 222	各 ……………… 398
对比 …………… 183	富有 …………… 219	各个 …………… 259
对于 …………… 165	富裕 …………… 219	各自 …………… 259
对于 …………… 179		给 ……………… 171
对照 …………… 181	**G**	给 ……………… 305
顿时 …………… 188	改 ……………… 224	给以 …………… 305
	改变 …………… 224	根 ……………… 262
E	改变 …………… 227	根据 …………… 265
二 ……………… 193	改进 …………… 227	跟 ……………… 171
	改善 …………… 227	更 ……………… 269
F	干 ……………… 725	更 ……………… 273
发明 …………… 201	赶紧 …………… 247	更 ……………… 657
发生 …………… 198	赶快 …………… 247	更 ……………… 720
发现 …………… 201	赶忙 …………… 247	更加 …………… 273
法子 …………… 202	赶忙 …………… 303	更加 …………… 274
反而 …………… 456	感到 …………… 237	关怀 …………… 276
反复 …………… 630	感动 …………… 230	关切 …………… 276
反响 …………… 204	感动 …………… 234	关心 …………… 276
反应 …………… 204	感激 …………… 230	关于 …………… 179
反映 …………… 204	感觉 …………… 239	关照 …………… 276
方便 …………… 208	感受 …………… 239	广大 …………… 368
方法 …………… 209	感谢 …………… 242	广阔 …………… 368

741

H

害怕	413
好	176
好像	519
很	657
后来	575
后来	581
忽而	282
忽然	282
花	285
花费	285
坏	288
还	269
还	605
还是	293
会	291
会	404
会见	291
伙	450
或者	293
或者	541

J

几乎	295
几乎	297
机会	472
激动	234
极	720
急	299
急忙	302
急忙	303
给予	305
记	307
记得	310
记忆	307
记住	310
继续	313
加以	334
家	736
假如	542
艰难	371
简便	315
简单	315
简易	315
简直	297
见	291
见解	317
见面	291
将	21
将	322
将要	322
讲	324
讲话	328
交谈	484
叫	29
教	330
教导	330
进行	334
进行	339
经过	493
精力	341
精神	341
景象	222
究竟	345
就	64
就要	322
举办	348
举行	339
举行	348
据	265
决心	523
觉得	237
觉得	350

K

开始	93
看	66
看	355
看法	317
看见	355
考	359
考试	359
棵	380
颗	380
可怕	413
可是	139
可是	680
可以	406
肯定	563

恐怕	118	满意	394	普通	553
口	363	满意	397	**Q**	
宽敞	368	满足	394		
宽广	368	没(有)	50	其他	417
宽阔	368	没有	53	其他的	38
困难	371	没有	56	其余	417
		枚	380	起	419
L		每	398	起	422
~来/去	376	每天	489	起初	612
乐趣	525			起来	419
了	378	**N**		起来	423
冷	382	拿	22	起来	425
里	384	那时	402	起来	427
里	388	难	371	气	428
历来	109	内	388	千万	431
粒	380	能	404	前	433
俩	193	能	406	前	435
连忙	303	呢	1	前后	723
凉	382	你	408	前面	433
两	193	年代	463	浅	150
聊	391	您	408	亲切	437
聊天儿	391	宁静	10	亲热	437
了解	669	农村	112	亲身	439
临时	635	暖和	410	亲自	439
另外的	38			情景	222
楼房	213	**P**		情愿	614
屡次	630	怕	413	请教	330
		~旁	36	全	440
M		批	450	全	442
吗	1	平静	10	全	446

743

全部	442	时	467	谈	324
全部	448	时代	463	谈	484
全体	448	时代	464	谈话	328
却	138	时候	467	谈话	484
确实	154	时候	469	倘若	542
群	450	时机	472	趟	101
		时间	469	特意	487
R		时刻	469	提问	506
然而	456	时期	464	天天	489
然而	680	事	475	条	262
然后	575	事故	475	听	490
让	29	事件	475	听见	490
热烈	457	事情	475	通常	74
热情	457	是	176	通过	493
人家	44	双	174	通知	256
认为	350	顺便	481	突然	282
认为	586	顺着	534		
如果	542	说	256	**W**	
		说	324	完全	446
S		说话	328	万万	431
上	384	送	478	往	496
上	422	送别	478	往往	79
上来	425	送行	478	为	498
上下	723	随便	481	为了	498
身材	460	所	736	为什么	637
身体	460	所有	442	未必	502
身子	460			温暖	410
生气	428	**T**		闻名	601
什么的	147	太	651	问	504
什么样	647	太	657	问	506

744

我们	634	要	515	以来	581
屋子	213	要不	536	以前	435
X		要不然	539	以前	579
		要不是	539	以为	586
希望	511	要点	699	意见	315
希望	616	要么	541	意见	590
下来	513	要是	542	因为	498
下去	427	也	544	永久	593
下去	513	也	546	永远	593
乡村	112	也许	118	由	31
想	515	一般	553	由	104
向	162	一边…一边…		由	595
向	496		549	由于	595
向来	108	一点儿	556	友爱	597
像	519	一点儿	560	友好	597
小时	522	一定	563	友谊	597
些	159	一会儿	560	有点儿	556
谢	242	一会儿	564	有名	601
谢谢	242	一齐	566	有趣(儿)	532
信心	523	一起	566	又	546
行	176	一时	188	又	605
兴趣	525	一向	567	又…又…	549
兴趣	529	一直	567	于	621
兴趣	532	一直	715	原来	609
兴致	529	依	14	原来	612
询问	506	依据	265	愿望	511
Y		依照	14	愿意	614
		疑问	506	愿意	616
沿(着)	82	已经	570	越发	274
沿着	534	以后	575	越…越…	618

745

越来越………… 618	这时 ………… 402	钟头 ………… 522
Z	真 …………… 657	中意 ………… 397
	整个(儿) …… 448	重 …………… 696
再 …………… 605	整洁 ………… 661	重点 ………… 699
再不 ………… 61	整齐 ………… 661	重点 ………… 701
再三 ………… 630	正 …………… 663	重量 ………… 696
再也不 ……… 61	正好 ………… 666	重要 ………… 701
在 …………… 127	正巧 ………… 666	重要 ………… 704
在 …………… 621	正在 ………… 663	逐步 ………… 706
在 …………… 663	之间 ………… 685	逐渐 ………… 706
在…看来 …… 168	支 …………… 262	主要 ………… 704
在…上 ……… 627	知道 ………… 669	嘱咐 ………… 217
在…下 ……… 627	只好 ………… 675	著名 ………… 601
在…中 ……… 627	只是 ………… 680	专门 ………… 487
咱 …………… 634	只要 ………… 677	着急 ………… 299
咱们 ………… 630	只有 ………… 675	自 …………… 104
咱们 ………… 634	只有 ………… 677	自 …………… 108
暂时 ………… 188	指教 ………… 330	自从 ………… 108
暂时 ………… 635	至于 ………… 179	自己 ………… 708
造 …………… 732	制造 ………… 732	自己 ………… 713
怎么 ………… 637	质问 ………… 506	自我 ………… 713
怎么 ………… 641	中 …………… 388	总(是) ……… 715
怎么样 ……… 641	中 …………… 683	嘴 …………… 363
怎么样 ……… 647	中间 ………… 683	最 …………… 720
怎样 ………… 641	中间 ………… 685	左右 ………… 723
照 …………… 14	中间 ………… 689	座 …………… 736
这么／那么	中心 ………… 689	做 …………… 725
…………… 651	中央 ………… 689	做 …………… 732
	终于 ………… 692	

746

词目笔画索引
Stroke Index

以词目第一个字笔画多少为序,笔画少的在前,笔画多的在后;笔画相同的根据字的起笔,按以下顺序:一(横) 丨(竖) 丿(撇) 丶(点) ㇕(折)。

一画

一边……一边……	549
一向	567
一会儿	560
一会儿	564
一齐	566
一时	188
一直	567
一直	715
一定	563
一点儿	556
一点儿	560
一起	566
……一般	553

二画

二	193
人家	44
几乎	295
几乎	297
了	378
了解	669
又	546
又	605
又…又…	549

三画

干	725
于	621
才	64
才	249
下去	427
下去	513
下来	513
大约	115
大批	119
大家	44
大量	119
大概	115
大概	118
大体	115
万万	431
上	384
上	422
上下	723
上来	425
小时	522
口	363
千万	431
个个	259
个子	460
广大	368
广阔	368
之间	685
已经	570
也	544
也	546
也许	118
乡村	112

747

四画

丰富	219
开始	93
天天	489
专门	487
支	262
不	50
不一会儿	564
不一样	58
不比	53
不必	502
不过	680
不再	61
不同	58
不如	56
不然	536
太	651
太	657
历来	109
友好	597
友爱	597
友谊	597
比较	183
中	388
中	683
中心	689
中央	689
中间	683
中间	685
中间	689
中意	397
内	388
见	291
见面	291
见解	317
气	428
什么的	147
什么样	647
反而	456
反应	204
反映	204
反响	204
反复	630
从	104
从	108
从来	109
从来	581
从前	579
分量	696
风景	222
方法	209
方便	208
为	498
为了	498
为什么	637
认为	350
认为	586
办法	209
以为	586
以后	575
以来	581
以前	435
以前	579
双	174

五画

未必	502
打	104
打听	504
正	663
正好	666
正巧	666
正在	663
本人	708
本来	609
本身	708
可以	406
可怕	413
可是	139
可是	680
左右	723
平静	10
宁静	10
由	31
由	104
由	595
由于	595
只有	675
只有	677

748

只好 ……… 675	对/对于…来说 ……… 165	有名 ……… 601
只要 ……… 677		有点儿 ……… 556
只是 ……… 680	对(对于)…来说 ……… 168	有趣(儿) ……… 532
叫 ……… 29		达 ……… 133
另外(的) ……… 38	对于 ……… 165	达到 ……… 132
生气 ……… 428	对于 ……… 179	成见 ……… 590
白 ……… 23	对比 ……… 181	毕竟 ……… 692
白白 ……… 23	对比 ……… 183	至于 ……… 179
乐趣 ……… 525	对照 ……… 181	当 ……… 124
匆忙 ……… 302	**六画**	当 ……… 127
处处 ……… 99		当中 ……… 685
主要 ……… 704	考 ……… 359	当时 ……… 124
让 ……… 29	考试 ……… 359	当时 ……… 402
记 ……… 307	地 ……… 142	当初 ……… 93
记忆 ……… 307	地 ……… 155	因为 ……… 498
记住 ……… 310	地区 ……… 155	吗 ……… 1
记得 ……… 310	地方 ……… 155	刚 ……… 249
永久 ……… 593	地点 ……… 155	刚 ……… 250
永远 ……… 593	机会 ……… 472	刚才 ……… 250
出来 ……… 423	再 ……… 605	刚刚 ……… 250
加以 ……… 334	再三 ……… 630	年代 ……… 463
~边 ……… 36	再也不 ……… 61	伙 ……… 450
发生 ……… 198	再不 ……… 61	自 ……… 104
发现 ……… 201	在 ……… 127	自 ……… 108
发明 ……… 201	在 ……… 621	自己 ……… 708
对 ……… 162	在 ……… 663	自己 ……… 713
对 ……… 165	在…下 ……… 627	自从 ……… 108
对 ……… 171	在…上 ……… 627	自我 ……… 713
对 ……… 174	在…中 ……… 627	向 ……… 162
对 ……… 176	在…看来 ……… 168	向 ……… 496

749

向来	109	关切	276	村庄	112
后来	575	关心	276	极	720
后来	581	关怀	276	更	273
行	171	关照	276	更	257
全	440	兴致	529	更	269
全	442	兴趣	525	更	720
全	446	兴趣	529	更加	273
全体	448	兴趣	532	更加	274
全部	442	安静	10	两	193
全部	448	讲	324	还	605
会	291	讲话	328	还	269
会	404	农村	112	还是	293
会见	291	访问	66	~来/去	376
各	398	那时	402	连忙	303
各个	259	如果	542	时	467
各自	259	好	176	时代	463
冰冷	47	好像	519	时代	464
冰凉	47			时机	472
交谈	484	七画		时间	469
次	101	进行	334	时刻	469
产生	198	进行	339	时候	467
决心	523	坏	288	时候	469
充分	87	批	450	时期	464
充足	87	把	18	里	384
充沛	87	把	21	里	388
充实	91	把	22	困难	371
充满	91	却	138	听	490
问	504	花	285	听见	490
问	506	花费	285	吩咐	217
关于	179	村子	112	吧	1

别人	42	改进	227	依据	265
别人	44	改变	224	依照	14
别的	38	改变	227	的	142
别的	42	改善	227	的	378
告诉	256			的确	154
我们	634	**八画**		质问	506
每	398	其他	417	往	496
每天	489	其他的	38	往往	79
但是	680	其余	417	所	736
低	150	枚	380	所有	442
你	408	或者	293	忽而	282
身子	460	或者	541	忽然	282
身材	460	事	475	浅	150
身体	460	事件	475	法子	202
希望	511	事故	475	沿(着)	82
希望	616	事情	475	沿着	534
条	262	到	621	怕	413
冷	382	到	133	房子	213
这么/那么	651	~到	376	房间	213
这时	402	到处	99	房屋	213
没(有)	50	到达	132	询问	506
没有	53	到达	133	参观	66
没有	56	到底	345	艰难	371
完全	446	到底	692	终于	692
究竟	345	肯定	563	经过	493
初	93	些	159		
迟	85	呢	1	**九画**	
迟到	85	制造	732	帮	450
改	224	知道	669	帮	25
		依	14	帮忙	25

751

帮助 …… 25	重要 …… 701	前 …… 435
持续 …… 313	重要 …… 704	前后 …… 723
指教 …… 330	重点 …… 699	前面 …… 433
按 …… 14	重点 …… 701	总(是) …… 715
按照 …… 14	重量 …… 696	测验 …… 359
要 …… 515	便利 …… 208	举办 …… 348
要么 …… 541	俩 …… 193	举行 …… 339
要不 …… 536	顺便 …… 481	举行 …… 348
要不是 …… 539	顺着 …… 534	觉得 …… 237
要不然 …… 539	信心 …… 523	觉得 …… 350
要点 …… 699	很 …… 657	突然 …… 282
要是 …… 542	急 …… 299	说 …… 256
点儿 …… 159	急忙 …… 302	说 …… 324
点子 …… 202	急忙 …… 303	说话 …… 328
临时 …… 188	将 …… 21	屋子 …… 213
是 …… 176	将 …… 322	费 …… 285
咱 …… 634	将要 …… 322	除 …… 97
咱们 …… 634	亲切 …… 437	除了 …… 97
咱们 …… 634	亲自 …… 439	除非 …… 677
钟头 …… 522	亲身 …… 439	给 …… 171
看 …… 66	亲热 …… 437	给 …… 305
看 …… 355	闻名 …… 601	给以 …… 305
看见 …… 355	差 …… 288	给予 …… 305
看法 …… 317	差(一)点儿 … 69	
怎么 …… 637	差不多 …… 69	十画
怎么 …… 641	差点儿 …… 295	赶忙 …… 247
怎么样 …… 641	送 …… 478	赶忙 …… 303
怎么样 …… 647	送行 …… 478	赶快 …… 247
怎样 …… 641	送别 …… 478	赶紧 …… 247
重 …… 696	前 …… 433	起 …… 419

起 …… 422	座 …… 736	著名 …… 601
起来 …… 419	凉 …… 382	常常 …… 74
起来 …… 423	~旁 …… 36	常常 …… 79
起来 …… 425	害怕 …… 413	第二 …… 193
起来 …… 427	宽广 …… 368	做 …… 725
起初 …… 612	宽敞 …… 368	做 …… 732
都 …… 64	宽阔 …… 368	您 …… 408
都 …… 440	家 …… 736	假如 …… 542
都 …… 544	请教 …… 330	得 …… 142
恐怕 …… 118	被 …… 18	凑巧 …… 666
热烈 …… 457	被 …… 29	着急 …… 299
热情 …… 457	被 …… 31	粒 …… 380
耽误 …… 122	谈 …… 324	情景 …… 222
耽搁 …… 122	谈 …… 484	情愿 …… 616
真 …… 657	谈话 …… 328	随便 …… 481
根 …… 262	谈话 …… 484	**十二画**
根据 …… 265	能 …… 404	
原来 …… 609	能 …… 406	越发 …… 274
原来 …… 612	通过 …… 493	越…越… …… 618
逐步 …… 706	通知 …… 256	越来越… …… 618
逐渐 …… 706	通常 …… 74	提问 …… 506
顿时 …… 188	难 …… 371	朝 …… 162
啊 …… 1	继续 …… 313	朝 …… 496
特意 …… 487	教 …… 330	朝(着) …… 82
造 …… 732	教导 …… 330	棵 …… 380
倒 …… 138	**十一画**	确实 …… 154
倒(倒是) …… 139		暂时 …… 188
倘若 …… 542	据 …… 265	暂时 …… 635
拿 …… 22	聊 …… 391	最 …… 720
爱好 …… 525	聊天儿 …… 391	景象 …… 222

短	186	想	515	满意	397
短促	186	楼房	213	群	450
短暂	186	感动	230		
等	144	感动	234	**十四画**	
等	147	感到	237	愿望	511
等待	144	感受	239	愿意	614
等候	144	感觉	239	愿意	616
等等	147	感谢	242	颗	380
然而	456	感激	230	疑问	506
然而	680	暖和	410	精力	341
然后	575	照	14	精神	341
就	64	跟	171		
就要	322	矮	150	**十五画**	
普通	553	简直	297	趟	101
曾经	570	简易	315	嘱咐	217
温暖	410	简单	315		
富有	219	简便	315	**十六画**	
富裕	219	像	519	整个(儿)	448
遍	101	意见	317	整齐	661
谢	242	意见	590	整洁	661
谢谢	242	满足	394	嘴	363
屡次	630	满意	394	激动	234

十三画

搞 ……………… 725

754

主要参考文献
Main References

汉语大词典编辑委员会			
汉语大词典编纂处	汉语大词典	汉语大词典出版社	1997年4月
辞海编辑委员会	辞海(缩印本)	上海辞书出版社	1980年8月
中国社会科学院语言研究所词典编辑室	现代汉语词典	商务印书馆	1995年5月
吕叔湘主编	现代汉语八百词	商务印书馆	1980年
冯志纯 周行健主编	新编汉语多功能词典	国际文化出版公司	1989年
刘叔新主编	现代汉语同义词词典	天津人民出版社	1987年10月
李忆民主编	现代汉语常用词用法词典	北京语言学院出版社	1995年8月
北京大学中文系1955、1957级语言班编	现代汉语虚词例释	商务印书馆	1986年
曲阜师范大学本书编写组	现代汉语常用虚词词典	浙江教育出版社	1995年3月
张寿康 林杏光主编	现代汉语实词搭配词典	商务印书馆	1992年
林杏光等主编	现代汉语动词大词典	北京语言学院出版社	1994年11月
王砚农 焦庞	汉语常用动词搭配词典	外语教学与研究出版社	1984年12月
李临定	现代汉语句型	商务印书馆	1986年
	现代汉语动词	中国社会科学出版社	1990年
马庆株	汉语动词和动词性结构	北京语言学院出版社	1992年10月
宋玉柱	语法论稿	北京语言学院出版社	1995年1月
刘月华等	实用现代汉语语法	外语教学与研究出版社	1983年4月
李英哲等	实用汉语参考语法	北京语言学院出版社	1990年6月
房玉清	实用汉语语法	北京语言学院出版社	1992年1月
王松茂等	汉语代词例解	书目文献出版社	1983年
卢福波	对外汉语教学实用语法	北京语言学院出版社	1996年6月
景士俊	现代汉语虚词	内蒙古人民出版社	1980年
杨从洁	"怎么""怎样""怎么样"		

	用法的分析和比较	语文战线	1982年第2期
史锡尧	"口"、"嘴"语义语用分析	汉语学习	1994年第1期
	副词"才"与"都"、"就"语义的对立和配合	世界汉语教学	1991年第2期
蒋琪 金立鑫	"再"与"还"重复义的比较研究	中国语文	1997年第3期
邢福义	方位结构"x里"和"x中"	世界汉语教学	1996年第4期
周小兵	"进行""加以"句型比较	汉语学习	1987年第6期
刘月华	从"天天"和"每天"所想到的	语言教学与研究	1979年第2期
王还	"只有……才""只要……就"	语言教学与研究	1989年第3期
陈小荷	主观量问题初探 ——兼谈副词"就""才""都"	世界汉语教学	1994年第4期
李绍林	"房子"和"屋子"的区别	语言教学与研究	1989年第3期

王还汉语词典（汉英双解）
Wang Huan's Chinese Dictionary [with English Translation]

即将推出

王还 主编
开本：大32　页数：1800

[适用对象]　以汉语为外语或第二语言学习的成年人；
　　　　　　对外汉语教师

　　本词典是一部为外国人编写的汉语学习词典，由中国对外汉语教学开创者、北京语言大学教授王还先生主编，历经十余年编修打磨。

学汉语用例词典
A Learner's Chinese Dictionary: Illustrations of the Usages

刘川平 主编
开本：大32　页数：1660
定价：98.00　出版日期：2005年11月
ISBN 7-5619-1460-1/H·05074

[适用对象]　具有中级汉语水平的学汉语的外国人；
　　　　　　对外汉语教师

　　本词典汇集大连外国语学院对外汉语教学的第一线教师，历时八载编写而成。收词10000余条，每条除提供简明的释义外，还配有大量的词语运用实例，实用性强。

汉语近义词典（汉英双解）
A Dictionary of Chinese Synonyms [with English Translation]

王还 主编
开本：大32　页数：540
定价：48.00　出版日期：2005年6月
ISBN 7-5619-1413-X/H·05024

[适用对象]　具有初级以上汉语水平的学汉语的外国人；
　　　　　　对外汉语教师

　　本词典从《汉语水平词汇与汉字等级大纲》中选出420组使用时易混淆的近义词，从词义、搭配、用法等方面作了细致的描写和辨析，并举了大量例句。辨析和例句都有意义恰切的英文翻译。

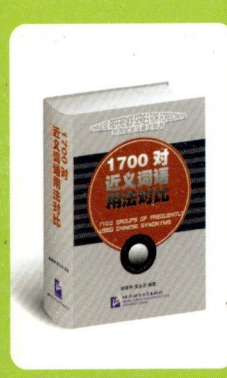

1700对近义词语用法对比
1700 Groups of Frequently Used Chinese Synonyms

杨寄洲 贾永芬 编著

开本：大32　页数：1718
定价：108.00　出版日期：2005年7月
ISBN 978-7-5619-1265-2/H·03091

[适用对象]　已经学习了汉语基本语法，掌握1500个以上汉语常用词语的学汉语的外国人；对外汉语教师

　　本词典是《汉语教程》作者杨寄洲集几十年教学经验、研究心得编写的一部实用近义词工具书。本书不求深层的学术性，力求教和学的有效性，解决学习中的问题和教学中的疑难。

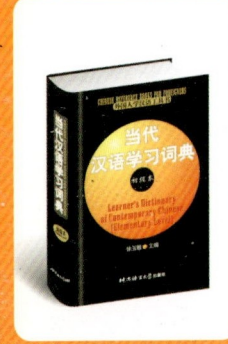

当代汉语学习词典（初级本）
Learner's Dictionary of Contemporary Chinese [Elementary Level]

徐玉敏　主编

开本：大32　页数：1183
定价：79.00　出版日期：2005年3月
ISBN 7-5619-1210-2/H·03041

[适用对象]　具有初级汉语水平的学汉语的外国人；对外汉语教师

　　本词典通过最常用的词语和最简单的示例帮助汉语初学者理解词义、掌握语法。本词典不重书面解惑，重在口语生成，是一部初级外向型单语词典。

实用字素词典（汉英本）
A Practical Dictionary of Chinese in Graphic Components
[Chinese-English Edition]

北京语言大学《实用字素词典》编写组

开本：大32　页数：830
定价：55.00　出版日期：2003年10月
ISBN 7-5619-0882-2/H·0068

[适用对象]　不懂汉语或初学汉语的外国人；以汉语为第二语言的少数民族学习者

　　本词典采用独特方便的汉字"字素"查字法，使初学者在不了解汉字读音，不熟悉偏旁的情况下，也能检索到3000多汉语常用字和16000个常用和实用词条。